# PHILOSOPHY & ETHCS

042008
190 COH
PHILOSOPHY
ETHICS
DEFINITIONS
DICTIONARY
CLLC

the essentials of...

# PHILOSOPHY & ETHICS

Martin Cohen

# Hodder Arnold

A MEMBER OF THE HODDER HEADLINE GROUP

First published in Great Britain in 2006 by Hodder Education, a member of the Hodder Headline Group, 338 Euston Road, London NW1 3BH

**www.hoddereducation.com**

Distributed in the United States of America by Oxford University Press Inc.
198 Madison Avenue, New York, NY 10016

Hodder Headline's policy is to use papers that are natural, renewable and recyclable products and made from wood grown in sustainable forests. The logging and manufacturing processes are expected to conform to the environmental regulations of the country of origin.

The advice and information in this book are believed to be true and accurate at the date of going to press, but neither the authors nor the publisher can accept any legal responsibility or liability for any errors or omissions.

*British Library Cataloguing in Publication Data*
A catalogue record for this book is available from the British Library

*Library of Congress Cataloging-in-Publication Data*
A catalog record for this book is available from the Library of Congress

ISBN-10 0 340 90028 8
ISBN-13 978 0 340 90028 4

1 2 3 4 5 6 7 8 9 10

Typeset in 8/10pt New Baskerville by Dorchester Typesetting Group Ltd
Printed and bound in Spain

What do you think about this book? Or any other Hodder Education title?
Please send your comments to the feedback section on www.hoddereducation.com

# Contents

# Introduction

## Dictionaries, democracy and the internet

Categorising their subject through dictionaries and encyclopaedias has always exerted a strange spell on philosophers. Aristotle started in the *Metaphysics*, and Avicenna continued with the *Compendium Philosophiae* (circa 1327), but Diderot and Voltaire made it *really* fashionable with their *Encylopédie et Dictionnaire Philosophique* in the late eighteenth century. Contemporary philosophers regularly come forth with new works, each seeking to be *at least* as authoritative and scholarly as Aristotle. But then philosophers claim a special place in the shared enterprise of knowledge. They see their subject as not only the keystone of the arch, but (metaphors notwithstanding) the foundations as well.

Traditionally, philosophy dictionaries (like others) are produced in two stages. The first is the editor chatting with a few chums in the senior common room or (if ambitious) over coffee at a conference. From such contacts arise an 'editorial board' who produce a list of 'experts' in various areas. Such an approach has its place, of course, but it has more than slight tendency towards entrenching the conventional view, of reinforcing the status quo. Opportunities for the dissemination and discussion of new ideas and new interpretations are lost. Hence, the recent crop of philosophy dictionaries covers the work of obscure male Oxford and Harvard professors rather better than they do of women in philosophy over the millennia, let alone the myriad world perspectives. These have just disappeared, not so much by malice, but (worse) by method.

Yet with the internet, it is possible not only very cheaply and quickly to reach colleagues, but to reach far beyond them. Academic hierarchies and geographical borders disappear. Now, an editor such as myself is able to write simultaneously to hundreds of conventional and unconventional philosophers alike and allow *them* to decide if they are interested in making a case for their approach to a topic. So in this *encylopédie*, from professors and amateurs alike we have articles on Confucian philosophers from China, on *Vedanta* from India, on African philosophers from America (we must not fall victim to reverse discrimination!). It is, I like to think, the first dictionary of philosophy for the new century (one hesitates to say 'millennium'). But there are innovations here:

■ A more global perspective.

For too long Europeans have disparaged other philosophical traditions and denied the global nature of ideas . We still see today the weasel word 'Western' used before philosophy, when what is going on is the arbitrary exclusion of great swathes of the subject on little more than cultural or even colour prejudice. Why has the philosophy world refused to allow Chinese, Indian and African philosophy to be discussed on the same level as anglophone philosophy? We would not tolerate an 'Encyclopaedia of White People's Philosophy', so let us not cling to the myth that there is a 'Western' tradition that can be kept apart from the rest of history.

■ An emphasis on being interesting.

I don't know who philosophy reference works are written for, but it certainly is not the general reader. Why otherwise are they full of obscurities, logical notation, Greek script, the names and research interests of Ivy League and Oxbridge professors? Why is one piece of subject-specific jargon, that the reader earnestly looks up, 'explained' with terms even more obscure, so that, for example, 'consciousness' might become 'the epiphenomenalist study of volitions'. Here, and it has been a hard task, we have all tried to write the entries so that they are accessible to the general reader, any thinking person – not merely the fellow philosopher in the famous 'ivory tower'. And better than that, the contributors themselves are not drawn merely from the narrow ranks of philosophy, but from the richer pastures of the world's 'thinkers' whatever their profession. For the third innovation in our work is:

■ It is democratic.

At this point, you could still filter such enquiries by ranking people by post or title – or by email domain! – but it would seem perverse to do so. Why not consider what they are willing to contribute on its own merits? And the implications of that shift are profound, particularly if you allow this great unknown audience to actively influence the original plan. So the original selection of entries for this encyclopaedia, largely based on existing standards and judgements, has been amended to include longer entries on some figures such as Proclus, or Durkheim, and less on those such as Wittgenstein and Heidegger (the two figures in philosophy who dominate conventional publishing, as well as dictionaries). We include essays on 'imperialism' and 'vegetarianism' as well as on 'love' and 'Zionism'.

Some will sniff at this, but in the internet age, the production of knowledge has become more active, more democratic, and the days of narrow circles of academics assessing each other's merits and controlling the dissemination of knowledge are numbered. But they, as much as (if not more than) everyone else, will surely be the beneficiaries of that.

*Martin Cohen*
*Normandie, 2006*

# How to use the book

This is a book of 'two halves', as the saying goes, usually of football games. In this case, the first half is the five hundred or so short entries, and the 'essentials' paragraphs at the start of the longer entries, which make the work into a quick reference, a kind of 'dictionary of philosophy and ethics'. The second half, though, is the one hundred plus essays on key topics, which make the work both more philosophical, and more informative. This is the 'encyclopaedia' half.

Entries are arranged under 'common sense' headings so that if the reader thinks of a topic, it is to be hoped that it will be directly included there. But this is only a short 'encyclopaedia' and the number of headings is limited. There is more information than the headings suggest. 'Hot links' to other entries are indicated with **GREEN CAPITAL LETTERS**.

Second, 'further reading' is offered, but not comprehensively, by any means. It would distract and confuse, as well as being of debatable practical use. The compromise adopted is to offer as advice on further reading key historic texts, only where (for whatever reason) these have not been indicated in the entries. Where we felt a relatively recent book will be of use to the reader, these are also indicated.

Third, and most importantly – who wrote what? The bulk of the shorter entries are written by the editors, using secondary sources. In this sense, we must thank the hard work of preceding dictionary and encyclopaedia editors and contributors, who we must assume have indeed been sure to construct the edifice of knowledge on sound foundations. A smaller proportion of the shorter entries, although 'unsigned', were written by the team of contributors. All the signed essays are of course written by those who have signed them, albeit in close consultation over style and scope with the editors. The 'essentials' paragraphs preceding the essays, however, are not the responsibility of the essayists, but only the views of the editors.

# Biographies

## The Editor

**Martin Cohen** is a philosophy lecturer, with a PhD in Philosophy of Education, and now a full-time writer, whose popular and accessible introductions to philosophy have been translated into many foreign languages – except alas the language of Voltaire, near whose chateau he now lives. (Albeit in a former cowshed, not in a chateau.) His books include *101 Philosophy Problems, 101 Ethical Dilemmas, Political Philosophy from Plato to Mao* and *Wittgenstein's Beetle and other Classic Thought Experiments.* He is currently working on a series of 'philosophical tales', drawing on some of the interesting titbits thrown up in the process of a project such as this (!), as well as a vigorously polemical political work constructed around the theme of unlikely holidays. A pedagogical commitment to stripping out the windy and overblown, and identifying instead the central core of interest, has contributed to a reputation, as one publisher enthusiastically put it, as the 'enfant terrible' of philosophy.

## Associate Editor

As well as writing a number of key essays for this volume, including ones on Indian philosophy and vegetarianism, **Colin Kirk** has helped edit and compile other entries. The innovative and revealing 'philosophical maps' are typical of his contributions. His personal philosophical heroes include the saintly Aquinas and Augustine, not so much for what they say, as for the determined way they set about saying it. He now runs a philosophically inspired vegetarian bed and breakfast in Normandy, France.

## The team of contributors

**Elena Alessiato** studied Philosophy at the University of Turin and, with an Erasmus scholarship, spent one year (2001–02) at Heidelberg (Germany), Karl Jaspers' university. Her degree thesis was on 'The Origins of the Political Thought of Karl Jaspers'. At the moment she is working on her PhD dissertation in Political Philosophy at the University of Turin.

**Brenda Almond** is Emeritus Professor of Moral and Social Philosophy at the University of Hull in England. She is the author of a number of books including *Exploring Ethics: A Traveller's Tale* and *The Philosophical Quest.* In her latest book, *The Fragmenting Family*, she challenges a familiar credo of received opinions that constitute the new 'personal life' credo of our times, in particular the idea that 'family' can mean whatever anyone wants it to mean.

**Andrea Boggio** is currently working at the Institute of Bioethics at the University of Geneva. He completed his doctoral degree in socio-legal studies at Stanford and his interests range from science, ethics and policy, to dispute resolution, human rights and globalisation.

**Gideon Calder** teaches ethics and social theory at the University of Wales, Newport. His interests have included the philosophy of Richard Rorty (about which he has written two books), whether there is anything wrong with the selling of live bodily organs, and various issues in between.

**John Caruana** is Assistant Professor of Philosophy at Ryerson University in Toronto, Canada. His publications include articles on Adorno, Freud and Levinas, on the last of whom he is currently writing a book.

**Anna Cohen** is a Child and Adolescent Psychotherapist at Maudsley Hospital in London. Before qualifying as a psychotherapist, she studied social anthropology at the London School of Economics, where she obtained a PhD dealing with the anti-psychiatry movement in Italy.

**Andrew Fagan** is a moral philosopher and Director of the MA Theory and Practice of Human Rights at the University of Essex, UK. He is editor of *Making Sense of Dying and Death* (2004) and co-editor of *Human Rights and Capitalism* (2005). He has written journal articles on the philosophical basis of human rights, the relationship between religion and democracy in human rights and the application of the autonomy principle in medical ethics.

**Ted Falconar**, after working as an Officer of Gurkhas, a tea planter, and managing director of a company, entered a quest for meaning in life. He spent 8 years in India and visited there 15 times, seeking the highest wisdom: Realisation. He found it in Count Alfred Korzybski's *Science and Sanity*.

**Benjamin Franks** is Lecturer in Social and Political Philosophy at the University of Glasgow's Crichton Campus in Dumfries. He is the author of *Rebel Alliances: The means and ends of contemporary anarchisms* (2006), published by AK Press.

**Tony Greenstein** is the author of a number of pamphlets on the history of Zionism, helped found Palestine Solidarity Campaign and was a contributing editor to *Return*. He holds a Masters degree from the University of London in British Imperial History. Tony works as a welfare rights and legal adviser to Brighton and Hove TUC Unemployed Workers Centre.

**Wendy C. Hamblet** is a Canadian philosopher at Adelphi University, New York. Her research focuses upon the problems of peaceful engagement within and among human communities, especially for communities that have suffered histories of radical victimisation. She has published two books on violence: *The Sacred Monstrous: A Reflection on Violence in Human Communities* (Lexington Press, 2005); *Savage Constructions: A Theory of Rebounding Violence in Africa* (Rodopi, forthcoming) She is also an alumnus of the Center for Advanced Holocaust Studies and affiliated with the International Association of Genocide Scholars and Concerned Philosophers for Peace.

**Fred Holman** became addicted to the subject after reading Russell's *Problems of Philosophy*. He sudied philosophy under Sir Alfred Ayer at University College London, and thereafter remained devoted as an amateur, as a member of the Society for Applied Philosophy and the Philosophical Society of England, of which he is Treasurer. The twin abilities to clarify, through analysis, vague or complex ideas and, through logic, to detect and expose invalid arguments – things philosophy par excellence develops – were of great value in his job as an inspector of taxes. It is not unknown for some solicitors and accountants to describe their clients' tax affairs somewhat vaguely and to produce involved but specious arguments to try to show there is no tax liability.

**Dylan Kerrigan,** born (of a Trinidadian mother and Scottish father) and bred in London, lives somewhere between Port of Spain and his hometown. He is a regular contributor to *Carlos, Caribbean Beat* and *The Caribbean Review of Books.*

**Mary Lenzi** teaches Philosophy at the University of Wisconsin-Platteville after taking her PhD at the University of Pennsylvania. She enjoys teaching, composing poetry and writing on issues in the history of philosophy, theoretical and applied ethics, psychology, feminism and peace studies.

**Yuli Liu** is a senior lecturer in the Department of Philosophy, the Party School of the Central Committee of the Communist Party of China, Beijing. For her PhD at the University of Hull in the UK she undertook a comparison of Aristotelian and Confucian approaches to ethics. Her books include *The Unity of Rule and Virtue: a critique of a supposed parallel between Confucian ethics and virtue ethics* (2004); *Conceptions of Virtue: East and West* (co-edited with Kim-chong Chong, 2005); and *Mencius: the Second Sage of Confucianism* (in Chinese, co-authored with T. Zhang, 1996).

**Matthew Del Nevo** has published on education and Jewish philosophy. He conducts research on philosophy in schools and is a founder of Sydney's Philosophy cafe. He lectures within Sydney College of Divinity.

**Rajgopal Nidamboor** is a Mumbai-based writer of articles, critiques and essays, on a host of subjects, including philosophy. His books include *Cricket Boulevard*, a coffee-table book on some of the game's greatest players, and *People Who Influenced the World Over the Past 100 Years*, co-authored with Peter Murray. Nidamboor calls himself an 'irrepressible idealist'. What he likes best is spending quality time with his family and close friends, and in reading, writing, listening to music and meditation.

**Chris J. Onof** is Associate Research Fellow in Philosophy at Birkbeck College, London. He is also Senior Lecturer at the Faculty of Engineering, Imperial College London. His main philosophical interests are the philosophy of Kant, the problem of consciousness and existential phenomenology.

**Andrew Porter** teaches English, History and Ethics at Dublin School, an independent college-preparatory school in Dublin, New Hampshire, USA. He writes about all aspects of philosophy. He is currently interested in natural 'wholes' and how they indicate certain optimal directions for human life. He lives at the base of Mount Monadnock with his poet wife.

**Travis Rieder** received his BA in Philosophy from Hanover College, in Hanover, Indiana, USA, and his interest in philosophical romanticism first peaked while writing his undergraduate thesis, which he titled, 'A "Romantic" Look at Ethics: Recovering from a History of Rationalism'. Travis plans to pursue a doctorate in philosophy, and eventually to return to a small, liberal arts setting to teach.

**Constantine Sandis** is an Associate Lecturer in Philosophy at the Open University, a tutor in Philosophy at the University of Bath, and a visiting teacher for the Royal Institute of Philosophy. His research interests include the philosophy of action and topics within ethics, and his philosophical interest in animals began five years ago, while teaching a course on values and virtues.

**Hugo Santander** is a Colombian-born writer and film maker naturalised in France. Having produced and directed several short films, he was appointed Assistant Professor of Screenwriting and Creative Writing at the Catholic University of Portugal. In 2000 he moved to England, where he lectured on Theatre and Spanish in the north of England, as well as on American Media at the American University of Central Asia in Kyrgyzstan. He has written several philosophical and literary essays and a novel: *Nuevas Tardes en Manhattan* (Manhattan New Soirées).

**John Sellars** is currently a Junior Research Fellow at Wolfson College, Oxford. He works mainly in ancient philosophy and is also interested in its later reception. He has taught ancient philosophy at the University of Warwick and King's College London. His first book, entitled *The Art of Living* (Ashgate, 2003), explores Stoic ideas about the nature and function of philosophy. He has recently edited a translation of Justus Lipsius' sixteenth-century Neo-Stoic text *De Constantia* (Bristol Phoenix Press, 2005). He is currently completing a short introduction to Stoicism (for Acumen).

**Zura Shiolasvili** is a Georgian philosopher. Most of his life has been devoted to researching the Christian idea of nature. His basic interest embodies the true face of art in the science of soul. Some of his ideas are reflected in the magazine *Philosophical Writings*, the *New York Review* and the journal *The Philosopher* – for which he is Aesthetics editor. He is currently preparing a book on 'The Art of the Aphorism'.

**Daniel Silvermintz** is Assistant Professor of Humanities at the University of Houston-Clear Lake. His areas of scholarship include Homeric Kingship, Ancient Philosophy and the History of Political Economy.

**Dean D'Souza** graduated from the Peace Studies department at the University of Bradford in 2000 and is now director of the Black Ice Corporation. He is currently researching 'Ancient Cultures and Civilisations', 'Myths and Cosmology', and writing a thesis on 'Eliminativism in the Philosophy of Mind'.

**John H. Spencer** is researching for a PhD in Philosophy at the University of Liverpool under the supervision of Stephen Clark. He believes that a modern understanding of Proclus' philosophy can explain the underlying unity of scientific and spiritual knowledge by clarifying their shared metaphysical presuppositions. He would particularly like to add his thanks to Stephen Clark, Pierre Grimes, Tim Addey and David Leech for their helpful comments on the draft entry on Proclus.

**Zenon Stavrinides** was born in Cyprus, studied at the Universities of London, Cambridge and Leeds, and conducted research at the University of St Andrews. For many years he taught Philosophy in various academic institutions in the UK, including the Open University and the Universities of Leeds, Bradford and Manchester. He is currently Deputy Editor of the journal *The Philosopher*.

**Stephen Thornton** is Lecturer in Philosophy at Mary Immaculate College, University of Limerick, Ireland, and editor of *Minerva – An Internet Journal of Philosophy*. His primary research focus is on philosophy of language, science and religion, and he has published on both Wittgenstein and Popper.

**Adrian Viens** is a postgraduate student in philosophy at Oxford University. His research interests are moral philosophy, legal philosophy, and applied ethics (especially medical ethics).

**Lisa Wang** is Professor and Dean at Qingdao University, People's Republic of China. A distinguished 'Confusion Scholar' as she puts it, she is an enthusiastic advocate of educational reform and renewal in China. She has a PhD in Education from the University of Exeter in the UK and is an editor for the UK journal, *The Philosopher.*

**Brad Weslake** is a PhD candidate at the Centre for Time, Department of Philosophy, University of Sydney. His research focuses on the temporal asymmetry of causation, and his interest in time and causation stems from a broader interest in the relation between everyday experience and the scientific view of the world.

**Stephen de Wijze** teaches political philosophy at the University of Manchester. He is presently writing a book on the problem of 'dirty hands', which investigates, among other things, the problem of choosing in the face of intractable moral conflict, especially in the political domain.

## The artist and the Chinese line drawings

**Hui Wan,** the artist who created the images of the philosophers in this book, is a young fashion designer for a company in Qingdao on the east coast of China. Though trained as a professional Western artist, her first love is for the Chinese 'fine line' drawing. Very much influenced by both Western and Chinese philosophical thought, the creative work in the line drawings of the philosophers for this book has clearly benefited and drawn on her appreciation and understanding of philosophy.

The origin of Chinese painting can be traced back to as early as 6000 years ago (for example, with the clay fish design characteristic of 'Yangshao culture'). Even during its primitive period, 'line' drawing was very much aware from an aesthetic perspective. With a history of development now covering several thousand years, line drawing, as a traditional method, has been greatly enriched with various styles and multiple functions. It has become both a powerful expression and a powerfully expressive form of Chinese art.

The natural flow of lines easily demonstrates delicate emotions and meanings. The beauty of the Chinese line drawing is shown through the shapes of lines, for example, the straight horizontal lines indicate 'calmness', whereas vertical lines represent 'elegance' and 'solemnity', and twisted lines indicate 'conflict' or 'excitement', while curved lines represent 'gentleness' and 'a graceful quality'. On one hand, thick lines symbolise plumpness and maturity, while on the other, thin lines symbolise slimness and stylishness.

The lines are even more subtle when it comes to drawing a person. Sometimes the line may look broken, but actually it is not. Norman Brason, a well-known American art philosopher, once commented that 'while the traditional Western drawing is result-oriented, the Chinese drawing is process-oriented'. All the meaning is embedded in the whole process of the drawing. Every single line, no matter how casual it may look, records the inspiration and skill of the artist and has a clear message which cannot be repeated nor edited. They are genuine with no intention of being added as mere decoration. Thus, this particular Chinese style of art expresses, as he remarks, the highest level of art.

From a philosophical point of view, this very unique art of Chinese line drawing brings to our mind some deep reflection, peace, simplicity and human values which have long been lost in the hurried, fast-paced society we have created today.

## THE ABSOLUTE

From the Latin *absolutus*, meaning whole or complete, as in 'absolute nonsense'. In philosophy, however, its use is slightly more rarified, as in the 'idealist' writings of the eighteenth-century epic poet Friedrich SCHELLING and his schoolmate and fellow German, HEGEL. Schelling used it to signify the unity of knower with that which is known, while for Hegel it was synonymous with the final triumph of abstract logic. This he predicted as a (somewhat implausible) consequence of the evolution of human society.

## ABSTRACTION

Abstraction is the process by which we arrive at general words to describe specific things. To say 'Socrates is a man' is problematic, not because of anything about Socrates but because of what the 'abstract' term 'man' may or may not signify. The point was explored in some technicality by the logician Gottlob FREGE, who decided settling it was part of the greater task of understanding the way LANGUAGE works, but long before that it had been debated by the ancients. The problem about abstract objects, on the other hand, is that they may not really exist.

## THE ACADEMY

The Academy was a garden open to the public, six stadia outside the walls of Athens, throughout the 'golden age' of Greek philosophy. PLATO's dialogues and, to a lesser extent, ARISTOTLE's writings have conveyed to later generations an impression of what went on there that if it is perhaps misleading is none the less influential. 'Academe' is used by Shakespeare in *Love's Labour's Lost* as something of a literary conceit.

Plato founded 'the Academy' around 387 BCE and taught there, together with other philosophers, in a garden by the side of the river Cephissus. The name seems to have come from its being part of an estate said to have belonged to Academus. The inspiration behind the Academy, however, was the school established by PYTHAGORAS at Croton. When Plato died, leadership of the Academy was passed to his nephew Speusippus, who was later followed by SCEPTICS such as Arcesilaus and Carneades. With the fall of Athens in CE 88, all the original buildings were destroyed.

## ADORNO, THEODOR WIESENGRUND (1903–69)

A 'musicologist' and SOCIAL SCIENTIST with MARXIST pretensions, Adorno was responsible for the creation of the CRITICAL THEORY phenomenon, which spread from its base at the Institute for Social Research in Frankfurt, Germany across much of the world, affecting not just philosophy departments but English and sociology too. Modifying MARX's theories, Adorno said that the two terrors of modern life – injustice and NIHILISM – stem from the ENLIGHTENMENT elevation of abstract reason over SUBJECTIVITY and sensuality. Instead, Adorno tries to recreate the 'dynamic links' between the MIND and its objects.

## *ADVAITA* PHILOSOPHY

See Sankara.

## AESTHETICS, ART AND BEAUTY

The hallmarks of BEAUTY, from classical times, were held to be harmony, proportion and unity. The term 'aesthetic' is derived from the Greek word for perception, and originally applied to things that are perceived by the senses as opposed to being objects of thought. The narrower and more recent meaning of the term in the philosophy of art is that it involves the *criticism* of taste and the *appreciation* of the beautiful.

And beauty was linked by the ancient Greeks to goodness. The phrase *kalos kai agathos* (beautiful and good) was the standard description of the Homeric heroes. PLATO also linked beauty to TRUTH, generating the historic, philosophical trilogy: truth, beauty and goodness. But what *is* beauty's relation to truth and VIRTUE? Some have suggested that beauty has its own value, independent of morality or truth, others that it offers a unique path to higher truths and morality. But is it only what is beautiful that can do this, and not what is merely ordinary or even ugly?

In his *Enquiry Concerning Beauty, Order, Harmony, Design* (1725), Francis HUTCHESON (1694–1746) argued that recognising an object as beautiful was a matter of distinguishing its special aesthetic qualities from factual or empirical ones. The beauty of an object was essentially a matter of its capacity to affect an observer in some particular way. But different kinds of arts (genres) produce different responses: comedy from tragedy, exotic art from music, and so on. That suggests that a person's emotional or aesthetic response will depend not only on the object itself, but on what *aspect* of it the observer is looking at or focusing on. But SCHOPENHAUER argued that there was such a distinctive EXPERIENCE since viewing a beautiful object requires 'distancing' ourselves – that is, forgetting our will and our individuality. We lose ourselves in pure contemplation, becoming a mirror of the object contemplated; or indeed, even identical with it. Like Plato, Schopenhauer believed that in art we see the universal in the particular: 'In such contemplation the particular thing becomes at once the *Idea* of its species, and the perceiving individual becomes *pure subject of knowledge.*'

KANT discussed beauty and taste in his influential *Critique of Judgement* (1790), saying there that beauty depends on appearance and within that on form and design. In visual art, he said, it is not the colours but the pattern that the colours make; in music, the relation between the sounds, not timbre or pitch that matter. The English art critic John Ruskin (1819–1900) distinguished *aesthesis* – a kind of 'animal consciousness of the pleasantness' of the object – from *theoria* – the sense that beauty has a spiritual core.

Such accounts of art were influential in the nineteenth century, but the twentieth brought a greater concern with matter over form and a challenge to the idea of art and beauty as *moral* concepts. What *kind* of judgement is it to say that something is beautiful? Is it like having a taste for apple pie, or disliking witnessing cruelty or violence – or is it a judgement of a different kind altogether? That a judgement of this sort has a special character is suggested by the fact that the special name 'aesthetic judgement' is reserved for it.

The question remains, though: Are aesthetic judgements true or false, or are they SUBJECTIVE – a matter of personal taste? Kant said that, unlike moral judgements, which are universal imperatives based on REASON, aesthetic judgements *are* judgements of taste, and not based on principles. Nevertheless, he said, aesthetic judgements have 'subjective universality and necessity'.

That is to say, they are not just an expression of personal likes or dislikes; it is reasonable to expect that other people will agree with them. David HUME saw judgements of beauty in a way not so different from this, arising from sentiment, but still deserving, on the whole, of universal acceptance. In *Of the Standard of Taste* (1757) Hume wrote: 'It appears then, that, amidst all the variety and caprice of taste, there are certain general principles of approbation or blame, whose influence a careful eye may trace in all operations of the mind.'

---

**ON AESTHETICS**

'To feel beauty is a better thing than to understand how we come to feel it.' (G. Santayana, 1896, *The Sense of Beauty*, 11)

' . . . each thing has its own characteristic beauty, not only everything organic which expresses itself in the unity of an individual being, but also everything inorganic and formless, and even every manufactured article.' (A. Schopenhauer, 1819, *The World as Will and Idea*)

'You should use the things of this world as rungs in a ladder. You start by loving one attractive body and step up to two; from there to the beauty of people's activities, from there to the beauty of intellectual endeavours and from there you ascend to that final intellectual endeavour which is no more and no less than the study of that beauty, so that you finally recognise true beauty.' (The 'Wise Woman', Diotoma, explaining beauty to Socrates in Plato's *Symposium* dialogue)

Contributor: Brenda Almond

---

# AFRICAN PHILOSOPHY

## Essentials of African philosophy

The earliest African philosophy was that shared across African social groups, passed down from elders to the young of each new generation, transmitted and preserved in verbal genealogical records. It consisted of shared mythologies, wise sayings, the memories of the elderly, traditional proverbs, stories, and the living religions and socio-political structures of the African peoples. Because of the lack of written records to formalise these philosophical traditions and because of the lack of specific authors to whom the original ideas could be attributed, the first Europeans to enter Africa interpreted this lack as an absence of philosophical activity on the part of Africans.

The first African philosophers were responding to a deep anxiety, the felt absence of logical Western-style philosophy, but also against neo-colonialism. African philosophy arose to serve the EXISTENTIAL needs of the African peoples, whose very right to free existence, to self-government, and to valorisation for their inclusion in the 'human' world and for their positive contribution to human 'civilisation' had been placed in question in the colonial, prejudicial, reality postulates that emerged to justify colonial oppressions.

## AFRICAN PHILOSOPHY AND COLONIALISM

Ethnocentric European philosophers, such as Lucien Lévy-Bruhl, ascribed this lack of (Western-style) philosophy to the supposedly unevolved 'primitive mentality' of the 'pre-logical' African mind. When African philosophers following the Western tradition finally arose in the closing decades of the twentieth century, they too suffered from and reasserted this Western prejudice. Kwasi Wiredu, author of *Philosophy and an African Culture* (1980), holds that traditional African philosophy only begins where the bald dogmatic assertions of traditional belief meet with the activity of Western-style philosophical reflection and argumentation to form true philosophy – the fruit of a reasoning and logical process.

However, just as the long centuries of colonial slaughter and abuse obliterated the bodies, the political alliances and the sacred territorial holdings of African peoples, colonialism also obliterated their histories, their cultural traditions and their prolonged and deep intellectual customs and practices.

Contributor: WCH

## African philosophy, negritude and healing the scars of colonialism

Ancient Greek philosophers saw themselves responding to a divine calling to be 'physicians of the soul'. Yet philosophy can be rallied by the unscrupulous to wound as quickly as to heal. This was never truer than with modern European philosophy. Since René DESCARTES asserted in his *Discourse on Method* the limitless possibilities of the human mind to probe the secrets of the universe by dissecting and reducing each thing to 'clear and distinct ideas', ENLIGHTENMENT philosophy provided formidable justifications for, and found amplification in, the slaughters and exploitations of the European IMPERIALISTIC era.

Under the reigning conviction that 'history is progress' and the concomitant prejudice that some human CULTURES have historically advanced beyond others, Europeans, across every discipline, agreed that Europe was the centre of the intellectual universe and the cultural gem of god's creative project.

The Eurocentrism of the philosopher and the scientist went hand in hand with projects for and exploiting the bodies of non-Europeans. In the 'glory centuries' of the various European empires, the 'civilised' nations launched themselves upon small bands of self-sufficient tribal peoples around the globe. In the name of moral and industrial progress, enlightenment and the expansion of knowledge, as much as in the name of king and god, 50 million or so tribal peoples were forced to surrender great swathes of the globe to the Europeans.

African philosophy always remained active in the lived wisdoms of the African peoples, passed through genealogies, wise sayings, religious beliefs and socio-political traditions from across the African continent and throughout the African diaspora. African philosophy proper, at first fashioned after the Western-style argumentative tradition, finally arose phoenix-like from the smouldering ashes of the colonial ruin, and has demonstrated the healing power for which it was known in the ancient world. In the evolving forms that post-colonial African philosophy has assumed since its inception in the 1930s, African philosophy has been responding to what Tsenay Serequeberhan calls the anxiety of an 'African humanity [that] does not find itself at home.'

The path that African philosophy has taken since the 1930s confirms not only the richness of African cultural tradition and the profundity of African philosophical talent, but the multifold effects of colonial violence. The first wave of African philosophy, ETHNO-PHILOSOPHY, occurring between the 1930s and the 1960s, we might call the substantialist stage, because this early period describes a substantialising moment, a HUSSERLIAN 'back to the things themselves', as first European, then African, thinkers sought to redeem the denigrated cultures and histories of African societies by a return to a 'glorious black past' through (often over-essentialised and nostalgic) re-evaluations of African social beliefs and practices which were then translated into philosophical nomenclature.

This phase composes a redemptive apology for African belief and thought systems in the face of their overwhelming historical denigration. We see attempts to escape Western categories of thought – and evidence of their continuing hegemony. We see challenges to historical interpretations and the articulation of more 'authentic' formulations of African self and community. To this end, early African philosophers sought to deconstruct colonial representations of the Africans and to replace the

---

### FORCE VITALE

Human beings, *muntu*, occupy the centre of this field of invisible realities, because the vital force is supreme in humans. To be wise, among the Bantu, is to know the forces and their effects, to be capable of explaining events in terms of the *force vitale*, that is, capable of giving metaphysical explanations for the physical events that occur. Specialists in the form of diviners and magicians held sway in their communities for having precisely this capability. Since the universe is the outward manifestation of an inner dynamism of forces, names acquire a special significance for the Bantu, both as signs of inner strength and as the expression of connections with the forces of others, including the dead ancestors. The contemporary writer, D.A. Masolo confirms: 'By acquiring a name, every person becomes a link in the chain of forces linking the dead and the living genealogies'.

Ultimately, however, it could be argued that Tempels' sympathetic reading of the Bantu belief system was duplicitous. While insisting upon its inclusion in the body of true 'philosophy' and carefully articulating a systematic ontological vision that governed everyday beliefs and behaviours, ritual practices and ethical understandings in Bantu societies, Tempels concludes that Christian beliefs and scientific knowledge form the paradigm of rationality, while traditional African religious belief systems and magical explanations of life are the 'paradigm of irrationality' and ignorance.

Contributor: WCH

---

latter denigrating images with positive substantialised expressions of self. These new, 'refound' self-images were articulated either as continuous with the dominating philosophical order (and thus fittingly 'civilised' in already acceptable ways), or in polar opposition to a demonised (and thus rejected while still existentially dominating) radical other, the evil white colonist. These new self-descriptions also included sketches of the unique brands of SOCIALISM peculiar to Africa, revalorising African culture by positing its focus as communal, to be positively compared to European EGOISMS celebrating autonomy and individuality.

Ironically though, many of the first new 'African philosophers' were neither Africans nor philosophers, but Europeans living among the Africans, mostly theologians and anthropologists, attempting to articulate what they recognised as an identifiable world view among Africans that could be said to be 'philosophical' in some sense. The most important of these early thinkers was Father Placide Frans Tempels, a white Franciscan missionary, who studied and recorded the behaviour patterns and the language of the Shabu Baluba of Zaire, among whom he lived and served as a mission priest for years. Tempels' project was to write for colonials, and especially for missionaries, to demonstrate to Europeans that African systems of thought and belief exhibited a systematicity and a defining LOGIC of their own that might qualify their inclusion in the world's true 'philosophies'. In his primary work, *La Philosophie Bantoue* (1944–48), Tempels unfolded the philosophical underpinnings of the everyday beliefs and practices of the Bantu peoples. He demonstrated that their world view had a definite ONTOLOGICAL structure, envisioning the universe as a vast field of vital forces or life forces which he termed *force vitale*.

Ethno-philosophy composed a kind of defensive 'apology' for African thought systems. This first stage of African philosophy composes a 'self-empowerment stage' for African thought traditions through nostalgic reclamation of their histories, yet, in so far as those reclamations are over-essentialised and static descriptions of dynamic groups, they tend to repeat Eurocentric prejudices and to reassert the European logical categories that served in colonial abuse. Ethno-philosophy maintained a foundational assumption consistent with the Hegelian notion of the universality of being; it maintained the notion of an inherent coherence to the natural (and human) order that allowed differing thought systems to be expressed and understood in universalist terms, according to some fundamental unifying logical principle. In effect, then, African ethno-philosophy remained faithful to the assumption of a natural order to things (people, events and history) that had served to legitimise historical abuse. Moreover, early African philosophies, composing merely descriptive accounts of lived philosophies of tribal life, rather than idealised ABSTRACTIONS of metaphysical formations, failed to answer challenges about rigorous form and methodology, leaving earliest thought traditions as 'pre-logical' (by Western logical terms) and more recent African intellectuals defensive of their philosophical prowess.

Later African ethno-philosophers attempted to break free of this universalising feature by employing a logic that was more pluralistic in its assumptions and approach. Melville Herskovits, an anthropologist who was a pioneer of African Studies in the United States, argued for a 'cultural relativism' born of a 'respect for differences' and an 'affirmation of the values of each culture', whereby philosophy becomes more generous in its categories and seeks to 'understand and harmonise goals'. Though this second phase of ethno-philosophy was more generous in its approach, perhaps because of its anthropological roots, perhaps because undertaken by non-Africans, the African societies, no matter how philosophically expounded and positively extolled, remained as an exotic specimen under the scientist's microscope, rather than a viable subject of philosophical discourse and participant in philosophical dialogue. Alexis Kagame and John S. Mbiti remained some of the few Africans to engage in the ethno-philosophical debate during this earliest stage of African philosophy.

Almost simultaneous with ethno-philosophy emerged another universalising voice in the 'negritude movement' that sought the formulation of an 'African identity' characterised by common fundamental cultural features. Launched during the 1930s in the Latin Quarter of Paris by young black students from Africa and the Caribbean, NEGRITUDE drew its inspiration from the African American 'Harlem Renaissance' and writers like W.E.B. Du Bois, Langston Highes, Claude McKay, Sterling Hayden, Countee Cullen, Paul Vesey and James Weldon Johnson. The Negritude debate served well during the crucial era of independence struggles against colonial rule and in the early life of the new independent states. Writers such as Léopold SENGHOR and Aimée CÉSAIRE struggled to overcome the latent Eurocentrism of the founders of African philosophy, but, in so far as they continued to employ colonial categories to measure the worth of African thought systems, it was difficult for the African mentality to come out ahead in calibrations of rationality and systematicity.

Late in his life, Senghor came to recognise his philosophical generation's inherited ethnocentrism and attributed it to the instruction they had received in the 'white man's schools', public or private, in the colonies. Consequent to this new philosophical awakening, Senghor attempted to turn the Eurocentric discourse inside out with his theory of the civilisational complementarity of races, but his essentialist renderings on the basis of racial difference, figuring the 'Negro [as] the man of Nature' (albeit loving, feeling, sensual, living off the soil in the immediacy of sound, smell, rhythms and forms) against the European with his 'discursive reason', once again reasserted the idea of abiding essentialised 'natural kinds' of human beings that Europeans had applied to Africans to justify their oppression.

No matter how copacetic a mix the complementary races might make in the grand scheme of cosmic being, ultimately, it remained difficult to distinguish the *Africanité* of a Senghor from the racism of a LÉVY-BRUHL. Africans may be no less 'human' for their immersion in a state of NATURE, but, according to Senghor's own final accounting, the 'proper characteristic of Man is to snatch himself from the earth'. On Senghor's own terms, then, Africans are not endowed with the 'proper' characteristics of real human beings.

The NATIONALISTIC poet, Aimée Césaire, served an important phase of African self-discovery and identity reclamation, but his was an equally unfortunate platform for establishing an Africanist position that was to persevere beyond early independence struggles. His *Discourse on Colonialism* (1955) focused on the problem of recovering lost African histories. The fundamental difficulty for African philosophy, by Césaire's calculation, was facing the problematic of the new kinds of SUBJECTIVITIES that colonial denigrations had constructed –

ahistorical beings. The charge that the native Africans were 'primitives' had robbed Africans of their 'humanity' precisely because human beings have memories, genealogies – histories. Human beings take up their destinies and throw themselves toward their futures. They act. The downtrodden apolitical masses were reduced to beasts of burden. The fundamental concern of post-colonial Africans must be to retake the initiative and enter the DIALECTIC of history by taking up the counter-violence that their prior negation (as historical subjects) evoked.

The second wave of African philosophy was equally reactive in nature. This period we might name the 'self-critical' stage because it composes a challenge against the approach and methodology of the various strains of ethno-philosophy. It was recognised by African thinkers of the 1970s and 1980s as insufficient, both to the task of philosophy per se and to the needs of post-colonial Africans, that African philosophy confine itself to definitions of how, and to what extent, African traditions exhibited those features of 'civilisation' denied them in colonial discourse. It was agreed that African civilisation in general could prove itself more convincingly by its particular philosophy extending itself beyond the mere task of locating vague philosophical components in traditional African cultures.

Since a huge feature of colonial myth had been its challenge to the 'African mentality' as 'pre-logical' and incapable of abstract thought or systematic shrewdness, African philosophers had to step outside colonial categories and extend beyond reactionary discourses of identity, as well as nostalgic and purified discourses of traditional life, and produce a bona fide philosophy of culture that was capable of self-critique. African philosophers needed to develop peculiarly African standards that could be called upon to evaluate African belief systems and customs.

This phase of African philosophy was Socratic in a sense in seeking to reconceptualise its mission as an active critical engagement with the biases of its own thought, seeking to reflect upon and, where necessary, to transcend the logical paradoxes embedded in African world views and systems of thought. Thinkers raised such questions as the relation between race and culture, the appropriate role of intellectuals in new African nations, the implications of global forces

in the production of African culture, the effects of the contest between indigenous and global EPISTEMOLOGIES on African modes of production of knowledge and definitions of 'development'. They asked: What is true development in the African context, how is it to be pursued and measured, and what are its costs? And this phase was characterised by its virulent critique of colonial descriptive categories.

Others, such as P.O. Bodunrin, Kwasi Wiredu and Odera Oruka, advocated a universalist approach. For them, African philosophy had to oppose itself to traditional beliefs, behaviours and folklore and rise above particularities peculiar to African socio-political contexts to the level of 'universal' discussion. A second wave, represented by the work of Paulin Hountondji, Eboussi Boulaga and the MARXIST IDEALISTS, Marcien Towa and Amilcar Cabral, favoured a dialectical approach to the new philosophy.

African philosophy, argues Hountondji, needs to carve out its own intellectual space within the global discourse. Philosophy, he asserts, is 'a perpetual movement, a chain of responses from one individual philosopher to another across the ages'. African 'texts' need to be taken up and

## EXISTENTIALISM AND AFRICAN PHILOSOPHY TODAY

Kwasi Wiredu's *Cultural Universals and Particulars*, Paulin Hountondji's *African Philosophy: Myth and Reality*, V.Y. Mudimbe's *The Invention of Africa, The Idea of Africa*, K. Anthony Appiah's *In My Father's House: Africa in the Philosophy of Culture* and, with Amy Gutmann, *Color Conscious: The Political Morality of Race*, as well as the above-mentioned D.A. Masolo's *African Philosophy in Search of Identity*, head the impressive parade of African literature which seeks to move away not only from ethno-philosophy's repetitions of colonial categories, but also from reactionary discourses struggling against colonial hegemony. These authors are carving out new philosophical territory that is uniquely African, unquestionably 'philosophical' (beyond self-defensive claims of same) and yet deeply in touch with the thoughts and beliefs of African peoples now, in their dynamic shifting contextualised realities.

Contributor: WCH

Algorithm    7

criticised to usher their inclusion into the history of philosophical dialogue. In order for this to occur, four criteria must be met. African philosophy must be written, not oral, in its form; it must become 'scientific' (that is, give up its metaphysical, moral and religious questions as illegitimate for philosophical reflection); it must be produced by thinkers who are of African geographic and ethnic origin; and it must be purely dialectical in its form.

With the 1990s, we find African thinkers freeing themselves from self-defensive or critical obsession with their cultural and philosophical pasts, and their work takes on a new focus that is self-determinative. This phase of African philosophy we might name the 'existential' stage, since problems of freedom, responsibility and the role of the INDIVIDUAL in the post-colonial nation have come to the foreground of philosophical discourse.

In the last years of the 1990s there was evidence of a growing philosophical refinement, a new subtlety, in African philosophy. Criticism still played a crucial role in the politics of knowledge, but a new appreciation has emerged for the complexity of structural modes and epistemological foundations of, and TELEOLOGICAL motivations driving, knowledge-production systems and governing cultural creation and transformation.

African philosophers have been calling for explanations of reality and analysis of ideas, beliefs and cultural practices that bring the social realities of their people to sophisticated levels of conceptual awareness, while remaining true to the everyday experiences of African life. These thinkers still work against the hegemony of conceptual structures that repeat colonial domination, but, significantly, they seek to maintain the intimate link with African people's everyday thought, closing the divide that splits academia from the social realities at large, a split that characterises and plagues philosophy throughout the Western world.

African philosophers of the twenty-first century seek to reclaim both the theory and praxis of the past. Extending themselves beyond essentialist descriptions of their people, beyond polar categories of self-identity, beyond the merely negative phase of resentful critique of demonic forces troubling their past, they have reached a phase of self-determination where they are able to achieve very practical effects in healing the wounds of a violent history. There is every reason to credit African philosophy with fulfilling philosophy's ancient calling, because in stark contrast to Western philosophy's hermetic isolation in the ivory tower of academia, African philosophy's integral connections with the realities of African life mean that scholarly discourse maintains the possibility of proving itself truly 'healing'.

Contributor: Wendy Hamblet

## AGNOSTICISM

Agnosticism is used today to describe people who neither believe nor disbelieve in GOD, maintaining instead only that they do not know. Strictly speaking, however, to be an agnostic you need to go a bit further, and maintain that it is impossible for anyone to know. The word comes from the Greek *gnostikos*, that which is suitable for knowing, with the prefix 'a' for not.

KANT attempted to map out systematically the areas of human knowledge that could and could not be known, but since the triumph of scientism, such 'metaphysical' debates have been frowned upon, and the existence of God is about the only question on which agnosticism is allowed.

SEE ALSO

Atheism

## AKRASIA

From the Greek, *akrasia* means 'lack of self-control'. In an ETHICAL sense, it is the tendency to act in a way that, in at least one sense, one knows is not right. In his dialogue, 'Protagoras', SOCRATES argues that it is impossible for someone who really knows that doing something is wrong to still do it.

## ALGORITHM

An algorithm is a sequence of steps set out with the aim of solving a problem. It is a way of addressing questions sharing a similar character in a systematic manner. The term is used in computing to describe the essential first step in programming, that is the intuitive understanding of both the nature of a problem and its solution. Because the steps of an algorithm are all simple, in a sense they do not require great INTELLIGENCE. Alas, attempts to break down philosophical problems similarly into simple steps have fallen short of the hopes of such as PASCAL and LEIBNIZ.

## ALIENATION

Alienation, from the Latin *alienus*, meaning 'strange', became a popular term in the discussion of social theory and criticism, used as a blanket term for a variety of social evils with PSYCHOLOGICAL effects. People are said to be alienated from one another or from their governments, and even from their own BELIEFS and VALUES. In his *Phenomenology of Spirit* (1807), HEGEL says the *Geist* or spirit of the universe becomes alienated from its logical essence by becoming part of the physical world. In 1844, MARX adapted this to produce the more powerful notion of workers being alienated from their own labour by CAPITALISM.

## ALTHUSSER, LOUIS PIERRE (1918–90)

Althusser, born in Algiers, became a MARXIST philosopher, who taught at the *École Normale Supérieure*. He was most influential during the late 1960s and the 1970s when his ideas were taken up enthusiastically by political scientists and sociologists in France and abroad.

Althusser was a STRUCTURALIST, taking an extreme position on MARX's theory of economic determinism. He thought that economic relations were the underlying structure which determined everything in society. INDIVIDUALS have no free will but are in some way the superficial embodiments of economic relationships. Similarly, ideas, history and political structures have no actual significant content. Althusser's views have sunk somewhat into obscurity in recent decades, partly as a result of the personal tragedy of his own life, which ended in pervasive mental illness.

## Further reading

Althusser, L.P. (1969) *For Marx* (Penguin)

## ALTRUISM

From the Latin, *alter* (other), meaning a benevolent concern for others. The term seems to have been first used by Auguste COMTE in the early nineteenth century.

## ANALYSIS, PHILOSOPHICAL

### Essentials of philosophical analysis

During the first quarter of the twentieth century, some of the most eminent practitioners of such philosophy, such as Bertrand RUSSELL, his sometime student Ludwig WITTGENSTEIN, Gottlob FREGE and G.E. MOORE, reacted against the METAPHYSICAL preoccupations of the previous century. The result was to reactivate the empiricist tradition in British philosophy, but to add to it the element of analysis and an interest in LANGUAGE.

The movement had its heyday in the inter-war period, centred in the traditionally conservative academic centres of Britain and the United States. Its stated aim was to promote the breaking down or 'analysis' of statements into a form in which they were considered to be more philosophically rigorous. None of its practitioners were minded to trace their approach back, but they all shared a similarity of approach to LEIBNIZ, with his search for a way of computing the answers to philosophical questions, and indeed, the ancient Greeks, with their attempts to treat philosophy as a kind of linguistic geometry.

By the end of the Second World War, philosophers had moved on slightly and Wittgenstein drolly parodied his own position on the nature of language as over-simplistic. Gilbert RYLE disputed the idea that the so-called simple ATOMIC propositions philosophers sought in language could reflect 'facts', when reality itself is not composed of bits like this. According to such as Willard QUINE, the attempt was doomed from the start as language has no defining structure.

### Philosophy in the Petri dish

Of course, philosophy has always sought to 'analyse' claims and often the method adopted has been to 'translate' them into several simpler, smaller ones. PLATO in *The Republic* seeks to analyse the meaning of justice in terms of harmony in an ideal state; LOCKE, BERKELEY and HUME seek to analyse the meaning of 'physical object' in terms of ideas in the mind.

So, 'analytic philosophy' was really more a new name than a new idea, and a new way of phrasing very old debates. Leaving aside the name of the movement itself, its practitioners frequently used terms from chemistry, such as 'atomic' and 'molecular', suggesting an analogy with chemical analysis, where chemists analyse or break down ordinary, everyday substances into their basic constituents, atoms and molecules. What, in fact, Russell and others conceived themselves as doing was attempting to analyse ordinary, everyday propositions, that is statements of fact, into logically equivalent but far more basic 'atomic' propositions. They had a metaphysical purpose in so doing. They had a view of reality as consisting of simple, basic entities with simple attributes. They thought that their atomic propositions illustrated and helped us to understand that reality; that they would more easily be seen to be true or false than ordinary propositions and so provide a sound basis for claims to knowledge. As they saw it, the vague, clumsy, imprecise, insufficiently discriminating, descriptive propositions of ordinary speech hid true reality from us and made claims to knowledge dubious. The logical atomists, as these analytical philosophers were also known, were agreed about the subject-predicate form of atomic propositions, but not about the kinds of basic entities in reality that were capable of being their subjects. Sense data were popular candidates for that role.

As the twentieth century progressed, a new and different purpose seized those engaged in analytical philosophy. Ostensibly rejecting metaphysics, they could not conceive of themselves as translating ordinary propositions into metaphysically superior ones, the better to picture ultimate reality. Instead, they conceived the purpose of their analytical procedures as being to produce PROPOSITIONS, logically equivalent to ordinary, descriptive propositions, which better served the purposes of SCIENCE, whose methods involved basing its conclusions (laws) on the evidence of human observation and EXPERIENCE. In spite of ostensibly rejecting all metaphysics, they adopted what many thought to be a metaphysical position that only empirical statements, including scientific ones, and TAUTOLOGICAL statements were meaningful: all others, including ETHICAL, theological and AESTHETIC statements, lacking a 'truth value', were, strictly speaking, 'non-sense'.

Whatever the purposes of philosophical analysis, its possibility depended on reducing ordinary propositions to more basic propositions, such that for each ordinary proposition there was a set of basic propositions that was logically equivalent to the original, ordinary, everyday proposition. Reductive analysis proved problematic, for example, statements about physical objects could not be reduced logically to statements about sense data.

Reduction having failed to live up to expectations, the next trend in analytic philosophy (and

that name began to disappear) was to rephrase traditional philosophical problems into supposedly more precise language. In so doing, as Wittgenstein famously claimed, they aimed not to solve what they regarded as unreal problems, but to dissolve them and remove the puzzlement.

Contributor: Fred Holman

## ANARCHISM

PROUDHON said, 'I destroy and I build up', while Bakunin urged us to 'put our trust in the eternal spirit which destroys and annihilates only because it is the unsearchable and eternally creative source of all life'.

Anarchists despise DEMOCRACY as enslavement by the majority – voting is the act of betrayal, both symbolically and practically. 'Universal suffrage is the counter-revolution', declared Proudhon in one of his less catchy rallying cries. ('Property is theft' was perhaps the most famous, adopted by MARXISM, but 'God is evil' had its followers too.) As William GODWIN put it, more powerfully, 'There is but one power to which I can yield a heartfelt obedience, the decision of my own understanding, the dictate of my own conscience.'

The word 'anarchy' comes from the Greek *anarkhos*, without a ruler: cynics cite a headless chicken running around aimlessly. At its heart is the rejection of all authority. If anarchism is constructive in intention, it must still always start with a destructive phase, and hence may be crushed before it can proceed beyond that stage. Nonetheless, anarchistic ideas have always pervaded the lower echelons of managed societies with elitist hierarchies, effectively all societies.

Popular revolts (from that of the slaves led by Spartacus against the Roman Republic 73–71 BCE to the Solidarity movement started in the Lenin Shipyards, Gdansk in 1981) often draw on anarchistic motivations, even if their leaders are far from being anarchists themselves. But they all face organised suppression. And although anarchism was compatible with COMMUNISM during the destructive phase that displaced the previous regimes, once construction was required the anarchists were marginalised.

Anarchism – like BUDDHISM – preaches the virtue of surviving on only just enough. Its leaders were from the aristocracy and the churches,

## SOCIAL AND LIFESTYLE ANARCHISM

'Anarchism' is a highly contentious term, which has been used to describe a range of political movements and disparate range of political ideas, including Tolstoyan pacifists, militant terrorists, hyper-capitalists, punk entrepreneurs and primitivists as well as anarchist communists, situationists and revolutionary syndicalists. Indeed, it is probably better to speak of 'anarchisms'.

The distinction made by the contemporary sociologist Murray Bookchin between lifestyle anarchists and social anarchists, although perhaps flawed, is still useful.

Lifestyle (also known as liberal or individualist) anarchism, borrows from the liberal enlightenment tradition and regards the abstract ego as central. Not unlike Kantian ethics, this form of anarchism holds that there should be no limits placed on rational individuals from pursuing their own interests so long as they do not coerce others. However, an important difference from Kant is that impersonal universal reason imposes constraints, unheard of in anarchist thought and lifestyles.

Criticisms of such individualist politics are that it does little to eradicate oppressive power; so long as the individualist is free it does not matter if others remain exploited. Others have pointed to the inherently hierarchical nature of such egoism. The individualist's 'self' is at the top, as their perceptions are the ultimate source of knowledge, with all other egos having the same, lesser value. Thus it also ignores the inequalities of power that mould us and against which we define ourselves. As such, there appears little to separate this form of individualism from free-market libertarianism.

Social anarchism (or 'class struggle') can be identified through four criteria, which are used by many contemporary anarchist groups. The first is a complete rejection of capitalism and the market economy, as a form of hierarchical relationship; second, an egalitarian concern for the interests and freedoms of others, recognising that individuals' identities are not fixed but based on social forces. The third is that anarchists reject state power and all other intermediary forces. The final criterion is that, for anarchists, methods have to prefigure the ends. It is this prefigurative feature that sets class struggle anarchism apart from many other socialist movements. James Guillaume, a colleague of Michael Bakunin, considered prefiguration the defining distinction between anarchism and orthodox Marxism. 'How could one want an equalitarian and free society to issue from authoritarian organisation? It is impossible.' The methods involved have to embody the goals, and the appropriate agent performing the act is fundamental to the classification and assessment of that act.

While the broad themes of anarchism have existed in many epochs, anarchist movements have developed in response to modern capitalism. Their fortunes have fluctuated enormously since the middle of the nineteenth century when Pierre Proudhon became the first to use the term in a non-pejorative sense: from the high points of the early twentieth-century anarchist federations, to the low points when Leninism had hegemony among the revolutionary milieu. Although anarchism never completely died out, its reappearances have been sporadic and short-lived, notably in the student protests of 1968. However, since the decline of the state-socialist model, following the collapse of the Berlin Wall, anarchism has had a greater impact, both in radical environmental campaigns and among sections of the anti-capitalist, 'anti-globalisation' movement.

Contributor: Benjamin Franks

not from the industrial or political classes, and it only became a mass movement among the very poorest peasants of Andalusia and Ukraine: among even middling peasants it had little appeal. The anarchist not only despises the wealthy – the anarchist despises wealth itself. Much of its literature arose from the English Revolution of the mid-seventeenth century, which saw the King of England beheaded and the anarchistic Levellers ruthlessly killed by Oliver Cromwell.

Celebrated anarchist works include William Godwin's 'Political Justice', one among the wide range of pamphlets, essays and poems of the English ROMANTIC movement. Similar publications across central Europe led to the widespread turmoil of 1848, the year of revolutions, none of which survived for long.

Libertarians assert the 'freedom of the will', and often trace their origins to John Locke and the notion of fundamental 'rights'. Robert Nozick (1938–2002) argues, for example, in *Anarchy State and Utopia* (1974) that the interests of the individual and the 'majority' (as the State seeks to present itself as representing) are opposed and that actions should be judged instead on a 'case-by-case' basis for their uncontroversial beneficence.

Contributor: MC

## Further reading

Bakunin, M. (1973) *Selected Writings*

Woodcock, G. (1962) *Anarchism*

## ANATHEMA

That is, views, ideas or opinions (or the person holding them) that cannot be tolerated. In a regulated society, this is because they are considered to threaten its foundations. The word derives from papal bulls (called after the 'bulla' or seal attached), which were the documents in which the Roman Curia condemned to everlasting damnation anyone holding heretical views. The documents stated the views condemned and concluded by cursing those who held the views... *anathema sit.*

## ANGLO-AMERICAN PHILOSOPHY

See Analysis.

## *ANGST*

*Angst* is a German word for a special kind of fear. The **EXISTENTIALISTS** introduced it to describe the sickening feeling produced when someone becomes aware of being finite in a universe that is infinite, of a sense of dropping into a bottomless void.

## ANIMALS

### Essentials of animals

From the Genesis story of the Bible, to the analytic arguments of Donald Davidson in the twentieth century, Western thought has allotted non-human animals a relatively low status, both cognitively and ethically. Some philosophers, most notably **DESCARTES**, have even insisted that animals are mere machines that are incapable of sensation and **PERCEPTION**, let alone **BELIEF** and **EMOTION**. Most, however, are happy to allow that animals feel pain, though they stop short of attributing any kind of rationality to them, on the ground that they do not have **LANGUAGE**. This has potential **ETHICAL** consequences, for according to many popular Kantian systems of ethics, if a being is to be of moral concern, it is *necessary* for it to possess rationality. Against this view, **UTILITARIANS** such as Jeremy **BENTHAM** and Peter Singer have argued that sentience is *sufficient* to render animals worthy of moral consideration. This has led to the movement of animal liberation, whose aim is to defend the interests of animals. Some of its proponents go so far as to talk of animal **RIGHTS** (for example, the right to a peaceful life), yet on the whole the West continues to believe that some animals are more equal than others, with exception occasionally being made in cases of extreme cruelty to animals (such as fox hunting). In the East, by contrast, the principle of non-injury to *all* living creatures (*ahimsa*) has long been widespread among many religions and philosophies, such as **BUDDHISM**, **HINDUISM** and **JAINISM**.

### Duty and the beast: animals in ethics and the philosophy of the mind

**ARISTOTLE** (384–322 BCE) argued that what distinguishes animals from plants is sense-perception, and what distinguishes humans from other animals is **REASON**. This intuitive picture seems more or less right, but it leaves many questions unanswered. Do animals have language? Do they have beliefs, desires and emotions? Can they make choices? Do we have any moral **DUTIES** towards them? Aristotle believed that their lack of rationality entitled us to use them for our own purposes.

Although one of Aristotle's own pupils (Theophrastus) and many modern-day Aristotelian philosophers (such as Rosalind Hursthouse) stray on this point, this view was to set the standard for Western philosophy over most of the next 2000 years.

According to René Descartes (1596–1650), animals are non-conscious automata which only differ from man-made machines, such as clocks, in their degree of complexity, and in the fact that warm blood runs through their bodies, keeping them alive. This view was the result of his (dualistic) division of the world into two kinds of substance: mind and matter. Human bodies, he believed, were made of matter and functioned according to Newtonian mechanics. Human minds, by contrast, were made of an entirely different substance, and their primary function was not movement, but thought. Since Descartes did not believe that animals could think, he did not attribute minds to them. Given his additional belief that it is the human mind (and not the human body) that is conscious, it would *seem* that Descartes cannot allow animals *any* ability that requires consciousness, such as perception, sensation, recognition, INTEN-TION, emotion, attention, imagination, and so on. This may well be true of shrimps and worms, but to maintain that, say, monkeys cannot feel pain is nothing short of absurd. Indeed, in February 1649, a year before he died, Descartes wrote to Henry More: 'to animals...I do not even deny sensation, in so far as it depends upon a bodily organ'. So we might best read Descartes as suggesting that animals have sensations but no judgements about them; it remains unclear, however, how Descartes can consistently say this, unless he is working with far narrower notions of mind and consciousness than critics have supposed.

Another 'rationalist' thinker, Baruch (Benedict) de SPINOZA (1632–73) allowed that animals are sentient, but claimed that their lack of rationality prohibited them from qualifying as members of our moral community. This view is not dissimilar from that of the materialist Thomas HOBBES (1588–1679), whose bleak view of HUMAN NATURE (we are all brutish and power-seeking) led him to believe that morality is *constructed* only when human beings of roughly equal strength and intelligence enter into agreements or social contracts with each other, and whose moral rules help ensure their mutual security, and the better life which follows. If animals lack rationality (as Hobbes and Spinoza believed) they cannot enter into any mutual agreements with us (or indeed each other), and consequently remain in a state of WAR with both humans and themselves. Hobbes' metaphorical talk of war may seem extreme when conceiving of the typical relation between a pet-owner and her pet (though it rather neatly describes my own relationship with a dog I once had), nevertheless it is true that most (if not all) animals are amoral, that is to say, incapable of acting either morally

or immorally. This entails that they are not moral subjects, but it does not follow from this that they cannot be objects of moral consideration.

Immanuel KANT (1724–1804) also maintained that the suffering of animals does not matter because *mere* animals are not rational beings and therefore cannot be considered as ends in themselves. Be that as it may, Kant does allow that cruelty to animals is often wrong, but only because he believes that repeated cruelty will give rise to cruel habits and dispositions that may well affect our behaviour towards each other.

Recent debate has centred on the views of contractualists, such as T.M. Scanlon, who consider the possibility that humans can act as trustees of animals, representing them whenever a new moral contract is called for. Scanlon's own view is that pain, whether that of rational creatures or non-rational ones – is something we have prima facie reason to prevent, and stronger reason not to cause. Both suggestions are promising, but nothing has been said about why humans who are motivated to find general regulative principles of behaviour could not reasonably reject the proposal to enter such contracts with animals (by proxy), and consequently also the claim that they have any (contract-based) reasons not to cause animals pain.

The so-called empiricist philosophers, such as John LOCKE (1632–1704) and David HUME (1711–76), found it easier to endow animals with not only perception and sensation, but also *some* degree of rationality, maintaining that there was no great gulf between humans and animals, a belief they shared with Chinese neo-Confucian philosophers such as Chu Hsi (1130–1200), as well as Native American peoples. Hume writes that only the most stupid and ignorant do not recognise thought and reason in animals. Despite this philosophical LIBERALISM (not to mention their political one), both Locke and Hume condoned the killing of animals, because they were not said to have a *high* degree of reason and, more importantly, although mutual benefit rationally prevented humans from harming each other, there were no benefits to be gained from our not harming animals. This argument bears many similarities to that of Hobbes and Spinoza. For example, although Locke believed that the laws of any given society are entered into by public consent, he argues that these agreements are only made to enable the weak to defend their rights and duties, which are literally given to them by GOD.

Indeed, Locke's view regarding animals ultimately stems from the Christian view (defended by AUGUSTINE and much later by AQUINAS) that God placed animals on earth for human use. However, it is worth noting here that the RSPCA was formed by an Anglican clergyman in 1824, and almost all its first supporters were Christians, and that Christian theologians (such as Andrew Linzey) have recently made a strong case in favour of rights for animals, with whose welfare God is said to have entrusted us.

Hume's belief that reason alone cannot tell us what we ought to do, but only inform us of which actions would best fulfil our PASSIONS, and his further claim that these desires lead us to develop an artificial system of rules based on CONVENTIONS which aim to propagate our overall well-being, is more amenable to a Hobbesian reading. However, Hume also believed, contra Hobbes, that we have a natural disposition to sympathise with others, and to receive by communication their inclinations and sentiments, especially when these are useful or agreeable to us.

All of the above views seem motivated by a kind of *rule-consequentialism* which maintains that laws ought to be implemented whenever following them would advance the overall benefits to members of any given society. However, the arguments of utilitarians such as Jeremy Bentham (1748–32) and John Stuart MILL (1806–73), which simply count as a benefit or a GOOD, the presence of pleasure and absence of pain, have had an enormous influence on our thinking about animals, since the approach dispenses with any connection between being rational and being the object of moral concern. Even so, Bentham did not hesitate to add that a full-grown horse or dog is beyond comparison a more rational, more conversible animal than an infant of a day, or a week, or even a month, old. This was not because he took rationality and language to play an important moral role, but, on the contrary, because he wanted to show that our moral intuitions may be contaminated by unrelated factors revealing despicable motives. (By way of illustration, Bentham notes with approval that the French do not see skin colour as a reason to abandon someone to torment.) Likewise, modern-day utilitarians such as Peter Singer

(1946–) argue that anybody who favours the well-being of, say, a baby with a serious mental illness over that of an advanced animal like an ape or even a pig is guilty of speciesism, a frame of mind analogous to RACISM and sexism. Some have accused Singer of attempting to provide a utilitarian justification of infanticide, but perhaps the point of the argument is not that infanticide is as harmless as eating a steak, but rather that eating meat is equally morally repugnant. The comparison also reminds us that even if suffering is all that matters, levels of cognition remain relevant to moral debate.

Recent research on the question of whether or not animals possess the power of cognition has done much to combat the view that animals have no thoughts at all. BEHAVIOURAL scientists, such as Marc Bekoff, have advanced evidence in support of animal displays of consciousness, cognition, MEMORY, intelligence, passion, emotion, devotion, jealousy, playfulness, anger, and more. More radically, in a recent article in *The Times*, a journalist declared that scientists have shown that cows bear grudges and nurture friendships. The assessment of such claims, however, requires a conceptual investigation which no amount of scientific research (or indeed the existence of talking lions) could possibly settle.

Contributor: Constantine Sandis

## DO ANIMALS HAVE BELIEFS?

According to Donald Davidson (1917–2003), animals do not have any thoughts, beliefs or intentions. His reasoning is that a creature cannot be properly said to believe (think, intend, etc.) anything unless it has a full-blown language. John McDowell (1942–) goes even further, adding that animals have no inner experience and consequently cannot be said to have a fully-fledged subjectivity, but only proto-subjective perceptual sensitivity to the environment.

What underlies these puzzling claims is the conceptualist view that it is a necessary condition of a creature having some belief or experience that it possess a full mastery of the concepts which we would use to describe it. In so doing, however, they are relying on *technical* definitions of these terms which do not exhaust the multifarious ways in which we *ordinarily* use them.

Fox hunting with dogs is now illegal in England and Wales. However, it is still legal for hunters to flush out foxes, as long as they shoot them rather than set their hounds on them. What the law primarily objects to would therefore appear to be the intensity and duration of the pain which certain methods of killing may cause the hunted animal in question. This raises the question: Is it acceptable to kill animals in a painless fashion?

According to Aristotle's pupil Theophrastus, what is wrong with killing animals is the very fact that in doing so we are robbing them of life. Yet we rightly do not feel the same way about each and every plant. What Theophrastus (who was no fruitarian) had in mind, no doubt, was that we were robbing them of a sentient life. On this view, it is the fact that animals have consciousness that gives us reason not to kill them, no matter how painless the procedure may be. This is certainly the way we think about human life. Can one argue differently about animals without being a speciesist?

One does not need to be utilitarian in order to accept the validity of the speciesism argument. Indeed, the very term was first introduced by animal activist and philosopher Tom Regan (1938–), who argues against utilitarianism and, inspired by Gandhi, in favour of the deontological view that animals have rights (based on their inherent value) that we have a duty to respect no matter what the consequences. There has been much talk as to whether it even makes sense to talk of animals having moral or legal rights. Strictly speaking, having a right implies the ability to make a justifiable claim, which animals lack (moreover, as Roger Scruton has argued, if animals can have legal rights it must also make sense to ascribe legal duties to them!). However, this is neither here nor there, since we can make a claim on their behalf. No matter what our moral theory, these considerations urge us to review our thoughts concerning commercial agriculture, animal experimentation, zoo keeping, the management of wildlife and the use of animals in travel, entertainment, clothing and sport.

# Further reading

Hursthouse, R. (2000) *Ethics, Humans, and Other Animals* (London: Routledge)

Singer, P. (2001) *Animal Liberation*, 2nd edition (New York: Eco Press Books)

Taylor, A. (1999) *Magpies, Monkeys, and Morals* (Ontario: Broadview Press)

# ANSELM, SAINT THOMAS (1033–1109)

Anselm was an eleventh-century Italian Benedictine monk, who became an Abbot at Bec in Normandy and, finally, Archbishop of Canterbury in England. He was a philosopher–theologian in the Augustinian tradition, credited with the first 'ontological' (from the Latin for the study of 'being') theory of the existence of GOD. This stated that God, being the greatest possible object of thought, cannot lack existence, otherwise He would not be the greatest. There are several other, perhaps more persuasive expressions of the ONTOLOGICAL ARGUMENT, but that is enough here.

He was summoned to Canterbury to succeed Lanfranc as Archbishop in 1093 and died there in 1109. In between, he had been critical of the English kings William II and Henry I, to the extent of being exiled by both. Italian Christendom took God's existence for granted, saying God was manifested to the senses throughout creation. It is possible Anselm was shocked to find the Norman dukes and kings were openly pagan. For whatever reason, Anselm sought necessary reasons for religious beliefs.

Anselm's inspiration came from AUGUSTINE's *De Trinitate*. His aim was to create a philosophy of natural religion and a rational foundation for the love of God he sought from his monks. As a writer, Anselm was a consummate rhetorician, who intended to achieve this remodelling of his readers by rekindling and then developing their rational love of God.

# ANTINOMIES

From the Greek *nomos* for law, with the prefix 'anti', indicating 'the opposite of'. KANT produces a set of arguments with contrary conclusions called the 'antinomies' in his *Critique of Pure Reason* (1781). These purport to show, for example, that the world must have had a beginning and cannot have had a beginning, or that the universe must be all made of one underlying substance or cannot be made up of just one substance.

## APEIRON

From the ancient Greek term *apeiria*, Doric for *peiras*, denoting want of skill, lack of experience, without trial or acquaintance with (a thing). It is privative of *peira* (trial, attempt, essay), connected to the verb *peirein* (to pierce through, cleave). The term is noted for its use by pre-Socratic philosopher Anaximander of Miletus in Asia Minor (610–546 BCE) to signify the underlying principle of unity binding the 'many' beings of empirical experience into the 'one' of cosmos or world. Anaximander employs the term *apeiron* to highlight the fact that the force or principle of cosmic order is unknowable by human minds, beyond the scope of human rationality or empirical experience. The sole existing fragment of Anaximander's book (DK 12B1) may be rendered:

Whence things have their rise, thence also occurs their destruction, as is meet. For they render justice upon one another – the accountability for the crime – in accordance with the dictate of Time.

The passage lends itself to broad interpretative possibility, but, as Martin HEIDEGGER points out in his essay on Anaximander in *Early Greek Thinking* (1946), there exists an unmistakable ethical undercurrent to the fragment, suggesting that the very coming to be and the passing away of mortal things serves a fundamental JUSTICE inherent in the universe.

## APODEICTIC

An impressive-looking word used, particularly by logicians, to indicate a statement that is either necessarily true or necessarily false.

## APORIA

From the ancient Greek term, *poros*, denoting a way or means of accomplishing, a resource or device. SOCRATES reports, in PLATO's dialogue, the *Symposium*, or Drinking Party, that the father of Eros, god of love, is Poros, the god of Resource or Plenty. *Aporia* are apparently insoluble problems: ARISTOTLE says philosophical inquiry should start from them, and offers some 15 puzzles in his *Metaphysics*.

*Poros* also denotes a means of passing a river, a ford or ferry, passageway or strait, through its connection to *peira* (to ferry over or through, to convey). The term has been employed since ancient times to express the essentially ethical character of PHILOSOPHY and the necessity of maintaining the humility of 'unknowing' (philosophers having no way through to true wisdom, which is possessed by the gods alone). Socrates embodies and articulates this 'unknowing' in his ironic claim to 'human wisdom'. He will admit to being wise, only in so far as he knows that he knows nothing.

## APPEARANCE

Philosophers have long been concerned about the misleading nature of 'appearance'. PLATO uses many examples of how the senses can be deceived, including for instance, the case of a straw in a glass, while examples such as the so-called Müller-Lyer figure (let alone Escher's much more sophisticated perspective tricks) provide harmless amusement.

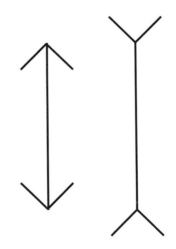

The Müller-Lyer figure: the vertical lines are exactly the same length, but appear to be different lengths because of the 'arrowheads' at either end

One question raised is whether reality is what we think we see or what we think we ought to see.

## APPLIED PHILOSOPHY

### Essentials of applied philosophy

Applied philosophy is marked out from PHILOSOPHY in general by its focus on matters of practical concern. It is often identified with applied **ETHICS**, but although this forms a large part of the area of applied philosophy, the broader term includes discussion of philosophical problems, some metaphysical, some epistemological, in fields such as law, education or art, that are not strictly or uniquely ethical. Applied ethics also includes the area of professional ethics; it examines the ethical dilemmas and challenges met with by workers in health care, business and other areas where specific ethical issues such as confidentiality and truth-telling may arise.

## The proper preoccupations of philosophy

Philosophy is often regarded as the most abstract of studies, so the term 'applied philosophy' needs some explanation. It represents the claim that it is possible to build bridges between theory and practice and, in particular, that philosophy is not only an internal movement in philosophy, but that it can and should play a role in public debate. However, this should not be seen as a bid to claim expertise on the part of philosophers, but rather as a reassertion of the traditional conception of the philosopher, not as an expert, but as an honest and open seeker after **TRUTH**. This search involves accepting the possibility of rational argument about **NORMATIVE** directions. It does not mean, though, maintaining a posture of uninvolved neutrality. As philosophy, indeed, it involves a prior commitment to the values of rationality, impartiality and **EQUALITY** of respect for **INDIVIDUALS**, and these provide the foundation for the moral **VALUES** and range of **RIGHTS** that are fundamental to applied ethics. Applied philosophy, then, is part of a whole view of the human condition and takes a broad view of ethical decision-making. It can therefore accept as part of its task the identification and discussion of values capable of securing widespread acceptance in the contemporary world. For philosophy has traditionally been concerned not only with abstract reflection, but also with questions about how we should live and how we should conduct our social life and political affairs.

Today's applied philosophy, then, marks a return to what have always been proper preoccupations of philosophers. Some of these preoccupations are old and could be said to have a perennial interest – intimate relationships and family life, for example, or global issues of peace and **WAR**. Others are the product of new technologies, revolutions in communication, new

weapons of indiscriminate destruction and an unprecedented increase in the impact of humans on their environment and support systems. Applied philosophy, and especially applied ethics, yields scope and space for discussion of these issues of public policy. To all these debates it can bring clarity, openness, critical analysis and respect for careful evaluation of **ARGUMENTS**. At the same time, it represents a shift from the view that philosophy can only analyse and clarify problems and is not able to take on the task of seeking answers to them.

Applied philosophy differs in style and approach from some mainstream philosophy in other ways, too. It gives greater attention to context and to the detailed texture of complex situations and it is also more holistic in approach – that is to say, it is much more ready to include the insights of **PSYCHOLOGY**, sociology and other relevant areas of knowledge in its deliberations, and to allow the facts it finds there to influence its conclusions. Its method of reasoning could be compared to that of a designer who starts with a blueprint, but has to adapt it to the materials to hand and to the situations in which it is required.

The origins and background of applied philosophy go back to the first of the early Greek philosophers. **THALES** (*c.* 585 BCE) could well qualify as the first applied philosopher. Having been scorned for his speculative and impractical interests – he was so preoccupied with studying the stars that he fell down a well! – he decided, very successfully, to go into business and use those observations to make a fortune, thus demonstrating that philosophical abstraction had its uses, and even a potential cash value.

Later schools of philosophy in ancient times – Pythagoreans, Epicureans, **STOICS** – offered their followers principles for living and guidance on lifestyle. **SOCRATES** (469–399 BCE), too, while he avoided preaching any dogma, did offer in his own approach to life (and also to **DEATH**) an example of a way of living appropriate to the pursuit of philosophy.

**PLATO** (*c.* 430–347 BCE), the chronicler of Socrates' discussions, described his own blueprint for the good society in his dialogue, *The Republic*, which covered not only political arrangements, but also the way social life should be organised. He set out there his ideals for education, for sexual relations and reproduction, for art, literature and censorship.

In the modern period, too, many philosophers have applied their philosophical insights to practical issues. St Thomas AQUINAS (1225–74) treated such topics as marriage and the family in his *Summa Theologica*. John LOCKE (1632–1704) wrote on TOLERATION and also on EDUCATION; his political theory also provided the philosophical underpinning of the American Declaration of Independence. The principle of human dignity formulated by Immanuel KANT (1724–1804) is central to most modern conventions of HUMAN RIGHTS, and Kant also treated the subject of SUICIDE, and the question of whether it is ever right to tell a lie from benevolent motives – questions which continue to be important for MEDICAL ETHICS. UTILITARIANS like Jeremy BENTHAM (1748–1832) and John Stuart MILL (1806–73) have a continued, if not always acknowledged, influence on public policy, while Karl MARX's (1818–83) political philosophy has played a dramatic role in the shaping of the modern world.

Applied philosophy, then, is not a new subject. Nevertheless, it suffered a period of neglect as the pendulum in philosophy swung from the speculative METAPHYSICS of the nineteenth century to the materialistic scientism of the twentieth.

A number of factors contributed to the return to applied ethics, dating from approximately the mid-twentieth century. Perhaps the most important of these was the development of new kinds of medical technology, particularly those involving new methods of reproduction and those affecting the end of life; another has been controversy about war and international relations. The publication of Peter Singer's *Animal Liberation* (1975) prompted increased academic debate about the relationship between humans and the ANIMAL world, and at the same time there was a dawning public awareness of environmental threats on a global scale. Finally, interest in business and corporate ethics has grown, in reaction to scandals of public and business life. For all these reasons, then, and many others, applied philosophy has today entered a new, more self-conscious and better-defined phase of development.

Contributor: Brenda Almond

# A PRIORI AND A POSTERIORI

Latin for the 'earlier' and the 'later'. Philosophers since KANT have used the terms to differentiate between two kinds of KNOWLEDGE, that which comes 'prior' to looking at the world (prior to experience) and that which can only come after looking. For Kant, there is some knowledge – of spatial relationships, of TIME, of cause and effect – that is 'prior' and only thanks to this can we then make anything out with our senses. Unfortunately, some would say that, on the contrary, our notions of space, time and cause and effect arise from our sense experiences. For many, but not all, philosophers, the claims of LOGIC are said to be a priori, but the apparently fairly logical claims of MATHEMATICS are considered less clear: Kant called them 'synthetic a priori', meaning they are independent of the world but we still make them up.

# AQUINAS, SAINT THOMAS (1225–74)

## The essential Aquinas

Thomas, as he is generally known, was born, in Castello Roccasecca, Aquino, close to Monte Cassino, and died at Fossanuova en route to the Council of Lyons. Aquinas replaced neo-Platonic ideas with ARISTOTLE's in Christian theology, in the process developing Aristotelian METAPHYSICS, LOGIC and ETHICS.

The Latin vocabulary he used for them still underpins much of European philosophy and culture. The Church continues to hold its 'Doctor Angelicus' in the highest regard. His *Summa Theologica* is the bedrock of Catholic teaching, while for non-Catholic philosophers, his mammoth compilation, *Summa contra Gentiles*, concerning the principles of natural religion, is the key text.

Dante awarded St Thomas a pinnacle in paradise, a little higher than Aristotle, and called him a flame of heavenly wisdom. Certainly, the influence of Thomas, and his promotion of

Aristotle, on all aspects of Western civilisation is profound. However, Bertrand RUSSELL considered his work to be flawed, saying his conclusions were determined by Christian dogma rather than the disinterested detachment of SOCRATES or PLATO.

## Faith and reason in harmony

Thomas was born into the landowning elite and chose the religious life against vicious family opposition. He was a student at the Benedictine monastery at Monte Cassino and at Naples University before joining the Dominican Order in 1244, less than 30 years after its foundation. However, his family were opposed to his plan. His brothers kidnapped him and held him prisoner in Castello Roccasecca, where they tried, unsuccessfully, to arouse him sexually. Thomas, unlike the young St AUGUSTINE, cherished purity. After a year, Thomas finally escaped and went to study Aristotelian philosophy at Cologne, renowned because of the teaching of a fellow Dominican, Albert Graf von Bollstadt, later known as Albertus Magnus, who was canonised and named Doctor Universalis in 1931 by Pius XI. Albertus Magnus is regarded as the father of SCHOLASTICISM, the union of Christian theology and Aristotelian philosophy. He laid the foundations for the work of Aquinas, his star pupil.

Thomas moved to the School of Paris in 1252 and taught there until 1258, when in obedience to the Pope he moved back to Italy and taught at Amagni, Orvieto, Rome and finally at Viterbo, from where he was summoned to the Council of Lyons. Both his great works were written in Italy: *Summa contra Gentiles* between 1259 and 1264; *Summa Theologica* between 1266 and 1273. Although unfit and grossly overweight, the result of an enforced sedentary existence, he insisted on his vow of poverty and set off for Lyons on foot. He died on the journey in 1274 and was canonised in 1323.

By the time of Albertus Magnus, enough translations from Arabic were available for Siger of Brabant to be causing chaos in the School of Paris. According to Siger, Aristotle had taught that the world was eternally in existence and eternally self-sustaining. There was no need for a GOD. All mankind shared but one intellect. There was no question of IMMORTALITY of the individual. Corruptions of these kinds were called Averroisms, from Averroës, the Latin name for the great Muslim philosopher Abu'l

Walid Ibn Rushd of Cordoba, whose teaching was being corrupted in translation as much as was Aristotle's.

None of Aristotle's works are, or were then, extant. They had survived in Greek as copies of notes and texts of a succession of students. Many had been translated into Arabic and Hebrew and used to provide a philosophical basis for Islam by Ibn Rushd, FARABI and Ibn Sina, and for Judaism by Rabbi Moses ben Maimon, usually known by his Latin name MAIMONIDES. Albertus Magnus was fluent in Arabic and Hebrew and able not only to translate Aristotle's works from these sources, but also to convey the profound exposition and development of his thinking in Islamic and Hebrew tradition.

In addition, Aquinas benefited from translations directly from the Greek produced for him by his fellow Dominican, William of Moerbeck. By these means Aquinas furnished himself with Latin translations of all the available texts of Aristotle and proceeded to standardise a vocabulary that achieved internal consistency. This was in keeping with Aristotle's principle demands for agreed definitions of words and statements of problems. Indeed, Aquinas achieved a greater internal consistency than Aristotle ever had and defended some of Aristotle's conclusions with a subtlety they did not merit.

Aquinas made common ground with St Augustine and Plato to achieve the fundamental principle of his teaching, namely that faith and REASON cannot contradict each other because God is the source of both. Aquinas held with Aristotle that *nihil est in intellectu quod prius non fuerit in sensu* (roughly, nothing is known to the mind that was not first known by the senses), for which reason the existence of God is known to man because God can be sensed in all things. Here he far exceeded Aristotle's notion of God as disinterested architect.

To expound on this he produced his five proofs of the existence of God, which are a set of metaphysical statements that depend on sensing God in all things. If nowadays PERCEPTION is recognised to be an unreliable tool, neither Aristotle nor Aquinas would have had any truck with such doubts. It is sometimes difficult for the modern mind to think back into the certainty of the mindset of MEDIEVAL PHILOSOPHY, although metaphysical, logical, scientific and mathematical method are utterly dependent on it. Aquinas treated ethics, as Aristotle had done, by reference to purpose and its fulfilment.

However, whereas Aristotle's model seeks to achieve the egocentric development of the individual, Aquinas's model seeks to achieve supernatural enjoyment of God. Aquinas appears to vacillate between a legalistic model and a MYSTICAL one. This may have been because he was undergoing a spiritual awakening, which overtook his rigorously logical thinking towards the end of his short life. Tolerance is incompatible with divinely inspired truth expressed in terms of Aristotelian logic. For Saint Thomas and his followers, such as the Dominican monks of the Inquisition, the saints in heaven do look down with pleasure on the eternal sufferings of the damned in hell, not least because they denied the self-evident and perverted others.

Contributor: Colin Kirk

## Further reading

*Summa contra Gentiles* (roughly: A Summary of Christian Doctrine Directed Against Non-Believers)

## ARENDT, HANNAH, (1906–75)

Arendt fled Nazi Germany in 1933, where her influences philosophically had been Karl JASPERS, Edmund HUSSERL and Martin HEIDEGGER, travelling first to France and then to the United States. *The Origins of Totalitarianism* (1951) attempts to link IMPERIALISM, RACISM and the 'lust for power' (as praised by NIETZSCHE). Later books included *The Human*

*Condition* (1958), which examines MODERNITY in the light of modern working patterns and borrows its title from André Malraux; *On Revolution* (1963) and *On Violence* (1970). Her diagnosis of society's ills is partly centred on what she thinks is a regrettable invasion of the 'public' sphere, with its duties to protect the weak, by private interests and private profit which recognise no such duties. Her remedy centres on a revitalisation of democratic life through small-scale representative forums such as PLATO condemned in ancient Athens for sentencing SOCRATES to death.

SEE ALSO

Heidegger

## Further reading

Arendt, H. (1958) *The Human Condition*

## ARETE

*Arete* is an ancient Greek term denoting excellence, goodness, exceptionality of any kind but especially of manly virtues (valour, prowess, courage in battle). It relates to the verb *aretao* – (to be fit or proper, to thrive or prosper). In accord with the ancient Greek aristocratic, militaristic world view, the moral sense of virtuous character connects with *areiksis* (help, succour against a thing) and Ares (the god of war and slaughter, strife and pestilence). The old, aristocratic families of ancient Greece traced their lineages back to gods and heroes. Their family names were made and their individual reputations rendered timeless through acts of valour in war, but they also prized themselves for a noble-mindedness and a generous liberality that sought to provide succour to the weak and the helpless.

The virtues of *arete* are decidedly militaristic, evident from Homeric times and a consistent theme maintained throughout the classical period; indeed, even to this day. Thus, even SOCRATES boasts of his courage in battle (rather than of his private contemplations) when he wants to prove his goodness to the Athenians in *Apology*.

## ARGUMENTS AND ARGUMENT TYPES

In common parlance, an argument is a quarrel or acrimonious dispute, but even so, there is much in everyday argumentation that can be expressed philosophically. Most disagreements centre upon a fact or claim, and the argument proceeds by working backwards, as it were, by offering reasons why the statement is either true or false, depending on the point of view of the speaker. In philosophy, arguments are typically presented as a series of statements which are themselves either true or false (generally called PROPOSITIONS), coupled with a conclusion. The philosopher then judges whether the statements 'entail' or logically necessitate the conclusion. This depends not only on the truth of the propositions themselves, but on the structure of the argument. Favourite evergreen examples include the argument to show that Socrates is mortal. This runs:

> Socrates is a man (first proposition).
> All men are mortal (second proposition).
> 'Therefore' (that is the all-important 'conclusion marker') Socrates is mortal.

Philosophers examine the 'structure' of arguments such as this and decide whether they are 'sound' or not. A sound argument is 'truth preserving', that is, if the assumptions made are all true, so will the conclusion be. ARISTOTLE called such arguments syllogisms, and started the fascination with the structure of arguments by trying to identify and classify all the various types.

## BIGGLES USES LOGIC

In one of Captain W.E. Johns' famous storybooks, the heroic fighter ace, Biggles, uses cool logic to explain his indifference to risk:

'When you are flying, everything is all right or it is not all right. If it is all right there is no need to worry. If it is not all right one of two things will happen. Either you will crash or you will not crash. If you do not crash there is no need to worry. If you do crash one of two things is certain. Either you will be injured or you will not be injured. If you are not injured there is no need to worry. If you are injured one of two things is certain. Either you will recover or you will not recover. If you recover there is no need to worry. If you don't recover you can't worry.'

From W.E. Johns, *Spitfire Parade* (1941)

SEE ALSO

Aristotle, Fallacies

# ARISTOTLE (384–322 BCE)

## The essential Aristotle

Aristotle was born just in time to know PLATO, and worked on every subject under the sun with alarming taxonomical zeal. Substantial amounts of his labours have survived and been very influential historically, but he actually wrote even more than this, including some apparently very lively dialogues in the manner of his illustrious predecessor. None of these have survived, leaving only a dry pseudoscientific collection of notes and theories. Despite, or perhaps because of this, throughout the Middle Ages, no other thinker had as great an influence as Aristotle, and he merited in the thirteenth century alone some five separate papal bans.

## Erratic observations

Neither Aristotle nor the other Greek philosophers made any distinction between scientific and philosophical investigations. Aristotle was particularly interested in observing nature and his biology was much admired by DARWIN, among others. Aristotle influenced subsequent studies by his view that organisms had a function, were striving towards some purposeful end, and that NATURE is not haphazard. If plant shoots are observed to bend towards the light they are 'seeking the light'. The function of mankind is, he suggests, to reason, as this is what people are better at than any other member of the animal kingdom – 'Man is a rational animal'. This approach is in contrast to that of today's biologist or scientist who tries to explain things by reference to 'mechanisms' (as if they explain anything).

Aristotle marks the watershed in Greek philosophy, born 15 years after the execution of SOCRATES in 399 BCE, studying at the ACADEMY in Athens under Plato until 347 BCE. Although he had hoped to become Plato's successor, in fact Aristotle's approach was out of favour with the mathematicians of the time, and Plato's nephew, Speussippus took over instead. After this, Aristotle left Greece for Asia Minor, where for the next five years he concentrated on developing his philosophy and biology. He then returned to Macedonia to be tutor to the future Alexander the Great, which might have been an opportunity for him to inculcate his political views, but if he did try to do so, there is little evidence of him influencing his pupil, and indeed Aristotle seems to have been largely oblivious to the social and geopolitical changes that were already making his *Politics* largely irrelevant.

For even while Aristotle was teaching about the *polis* in the Lyceum, Alexander was already planning an empire in which he would rule the whole of Greece and Persia, in the process producing a new society in which both Greeks and barbarians would become, as Plutarch later put it, 'one flock on a common pasture' feeding under one law. In fact, for almost two millennia the area was to see no city states, but instead a succession of empires. The rule of Macedonia, of Rome and of Charlemagne came and went, with Aristotle not even so much as a footnote. Yet for much of this time, Aristotle was widely studied in the Islamic world, where he was hailed as 'the wise man' and his texts were carefully preserved. In the Middle Ages his ideas were 'rediscovered' by St Thomas AQUINAS and, especially given the effective marriage of the Catholic Church with the State, became highly influential.

Aristotle's greatest achievement is generally supposed to have been his LAWS OF THOUGHT, part of his attempt to put everyday language on a logical footing. Like many contemporary philosophers he regarded logic as providing the key to philosophical progress. The traditional 'laws of thought' are that:

- whatever is, is (the law of identity);
- nothing can both be and not be (the law of non-contradiction); and
- everything must either be or not be (the law of excluded middle).

Aristotle's *Prior Analytics* is the first attempt to create a system of formal deductive LOGIC, while the *Posterior Analytics* attempts to use this to systematise scientific knowledge. In fact, about a quarter of Aristotle's writing seems to have been concerned with categorising nature, in particular animals. He describes the nature of SPACE and TIME, and the different forms that the SOUL takes in different creatures. His views on morality are set out in the *Nicomachean* and the *Eudaemian Ethics*. The *Nicomachean Ethics* is one of the most influential books of moral philosophy, including accounts of what the Greeks considered to be the great virtues, and Aristotle's great-souled man, who speaks with a deep voice and level utterance, and who is not unduly modest either, as well as reminding us wisely that 'without friends, no one would choose to live, though he had all other goods'. The main idea in Aristotle's ETHICS is that the proper end of mankind is the pursuit of *EUDAIMONIA*, which is Greek for a very particular kind of 'happiness'. *Eudaimonia* has three aspects: as well as mere pleasure, there is political honour and the rewards of contemplation; quintessentially, of course, as philosophy.

Other doctrines often attributed to Aristotle, notably the merit of fulfilling your 'function', of cultivating the 'virtues' (see 'virtue ethics') and of the 'golden mean' between two undesirable extremes, are, of course, all much older. Indeed, Plato puts the ideas forward much more cogently.

Nonetheless, one important difference between Aristotle and Plato is there in the *Nicomachean Ethics,* where Aristotle starts with a survey of popular opinions on the subject of 'right and wrong', to find out how the terms are used, in the manner of a social anthropologist. Plato makes very clear his contempt for such an approach. Thomas HOBBES said that it was this method that had led Aristotle astray, as by seeking to ground ethics in the 'appetites of men', he had chosen a measure by which (for Hobbes) correctly there *is* no law and no distinction between right and wrong. In fact, in passing, it should be noted that Hobbes considered Aristotle a great fool, protesting repeatedly the 'folly' of 'the Ancients'. And certainly, Aristotle has his fair share of foolish views, such as the influential but false doctrine that bodies fall to earth at speeds relative to their mass, or the uninfluential but foolish claim that women had fewer teeth than men.

For Thomas Hobbes, writing in the middle of the seventeenth century in England, political concerns were naturally focused by the English Civil War. Aristotle was similarly concerned at the fractious nature of the Greek city states in his time, the fourth century BCE. The states were small, but that did not stop them continually splitting into factions that fought among themselves. A whole book of Aristotle's political theory is devoted to this problem. And Aristotle shared Plato's aversion to tyranny, warning that under such government, all citizens would be constantly on view, and a secret police, 'like the female spies employed at Syracuse, or the eavesdroppers sent by the tyrant Hiero to all social gatherings', would be employed to sow fear and distrust. For these are the essential and characteristic hallmarks of tyrants.

Aristotle sees the origin of the STATE differently from Plato, stating explicitly that 'a State is not a sharing of a locality for the purpose of preventing mutual harm and promoting trade'. True to his being a keen biologist first, a metaphysician second, he believed the State should be understood as an organism with a purpose, in this case, to promote happiness, or *eudaimonia*. Of course, this is only a particular type of happiness, quintessentially that of philosophical contemplation, that the Greeks – or at least the philosophers! – valued most. But in this basic assumption, Aristotle's theory of human society is actually fundamentally different from Socrates' and Plato's.

For Aristotle, society is a means to ensure that the social nature of people – in forming families, in forming friendships and equally in trying to rule and control others – is channelled away from the negative attributes of human beings (greed and cruelty) towards the positive aspects (love of truth and knowledge) – those of what he classed misleadingly as 'the rational animal'. Misleading, because, after all, any animal is rational to the extent that it takes decisions to obtain food or to preserve its life. (The Chinese sages instead defined humans as 'moral animals'.) Certainly, rationality pursued as a philosophical venture remained only available to an aristocratic leisured few.

In other ways, too, Aristotle's *Politics* strikes a discordant note. He defined the state as a collection of a certain size of citizens participating in the judicial and political processes of the city. But the term 'citizens' was not to include many inhabitants of the city. He did not include slaves, nor (unlike Plato) women, nor yet those who worked for a living. 'For some men', Aristotle wrote, 'belong by nature to others' and so should properly be either slaves or chattels.

For Aristotle, LIBERTY is fundamental for citizens – but it is a peculiar kind of liberty even for these privileged members of society. The State reserves the right to ensure efficient use of property, for its own advantage, and Aristotle agrees with Plato, that the production of children should be controlled to ensure the new citizens have 'the best physique'. (In Plato, it is put more generally so as to 'improve on nature'.) And, again like Plato, naturally, they will have to be educated in the manner determined by the state. 'Public matters should be publicly managed; and we should not think that each of the citizens belongs to himself, but that they all belong to the State.' Aristotle even produces a long list of ways in which the lives of citizens should be controlled. For the State is like the father in a well-regulated household: the children, (the citizens) 'start with a natural affection and disposition to obey.'

Contributor: Martin Cohen

## ARITHMETIC

Arithmetic is the study of natural NUMBERS, 1, 2, 3, and so on. Although quite what a number is remains suitably mysterious (is it an ABSTRACTION or a thing?), statements like 2+2=4 have often been fallen back on gratefully by philosophers looking for examples of something that is indubitable and certain. Euclid based his mathematical demonstrations on 'truths' that he offered as 'self-evident', but as philosophers know that such truths are often anything but reliable guides, the nineteenth and twentieth centuries saw considerable effort go into establishing a LOGICAL base for arithmetic. Recognition of the BARBER PARADOX (also known as Russell's paradox) caused the collapse of that project, while the philosophical question continues to dog arithmetic: just how certain are its foundations?

## ARTIFICIAL INTELLIGENCE

In the sixties, Joseph Weizenbaum, a researcher in artificial intelligence at the Massachusetts Institute of Technology, developed a number of programs that accepted natural LANGUAGE from a user typing on a typewriter, and responded with what appeared to be natural language via a printer. The most celebrated of these was 'Eliza', a program that was modelled on psychotherapy. Eliza generally returned whatever people typed in in a slightly different order, perhaps having picked out a keyword. Simple though the program was, it became very popular. Psychiatrists adopted it as the basis for actual therapy sessions. Users became attached to and dependent on 'Eliza', and computer pundits cited it as an example of how COMPUTERS could learn to 'talk'.

After this experience, Weizenbaum decided that computers should not be allowed to give responses that appear 'human'. 'What I had not realised is that extremely short exposure to a relatively simple computer program could induce powerful delusional thinking in quite normal people', he noted sadly. This warning, which is more about human PSYCHOLOGY than anything else, nonetheless has had little effect.

Weizenbaum recounted the case in a 1964 paper, 'Against the Imperialism of Instrumental Reason'. The purely random responses of 'Yeses' and 'Noes', to a fully aware patient, Weizenbaum says, are interpreted as deep thought, reflecting the aura that computers have for many. Weizenbaum hoped to demonstrate that computers could appear to talk without understanding the content of what they were saying, a debate carried on from Alan Turing's Second World War challenge to researchers. Alan Turing suggested that when we are unable to tell the difference, after prolonged questioning, between whether we are talking to a machine or to a human being, we ought to consider the machine to have INTELLIGENCE.

The original so-called 'Turing test', where computers are in one room, people in another, and a third group of human testers are in another, is regularly carried out today. The testers can communicate with the other people and the computers only by typing questions in on keyboards. Since, after a period of thinking up questions and discussing points of view, the testers are now unable to tell the computer from the human, we should, on the face of it, concede that the computer has 'intelligence', but this notion of machine intelligence is what Weizenbaum finds less comfortable to allow. Weizenbaum distinguishes between 'moral' and 'instrumental' reasoning. Computers, he warns, represent the victory of instrumental reasoning over moral reasoning.

This victory is reflected by the habit, (noted by the educationalist and psychologist Jerome Bruner) of people to increasingly compare themselves to information-processing machines. Thus, comparisons are increasingly made with computers for the workings of the mind, for instance suggesting that the mind has ALGORITHMS which it is following. A UK government poster in the early 1980s depicted a human being as a 2,048,000 kilobyte memory. (That's only two megabytes, but at the time it sounded a lot!)

And anthropomorphism is endemic to discussions about computers. Much of this comes from the industry's jargon. Computers are said to be 'smart' machines with 'memories', who 'talk' to each other in 'languages' and develop 'artificial intelligence'. This kind of language was dominant throughout the 1980s, among computer professionals as well as the general public.

Attempts to develop the thinking machine originally followed a 'top-down' approach, using complex programmed rules, largely as a result of the influence of Marvin Minsky and Seymour Papert. Their influence in the late sixties, ridiculing the attempts to 'model' biological systems to make the computer mimic the physical and biological architecture of the brain, together with the actual hardware available, resulted in artificial intelligence (AI) attempting the emulation of the characteristics of human reasoning.

Artificial intelligence soon abandoned the tidy, rules-based approach for a more irrational, organic one. 'Neural networks' became much more fashionable, with their advocates making enormous claims for them. A neural network is a series of 'simple processing elements' based on memory chips, connected together and to various 'inputs' and 'outputs'. Information is fed into these inputs and the resultant activity is monitored. The relationships between the parts are 'tweaked' until certain inputs always produce a desired output. In this way, the neural network is said to 'learn'.

The first commercial neural network, built by Igor Aleksander and others in London, was successfully employed in picking out defective components on production lines and distinguishing between bank notes in banks. Rules-based artificial intelligence systems have, by contrast, been very poor at recognising shapes and patterns.

It seems that computers may now be intelligent after all, but Marvin Minsky has claimed instead that the element computers lack now is

'COMMON SENSE'. In this respect he is following the proposal of the cybernetics researcher W. Ross Ashby in the 1960s, who said that artificial intelligence systems must be able to cope with *variety* in the area they were designed for. Or, put another way, computers are good at thinking precisely, but only humans are good at thinking fuzzily.

Contributor: Martin Cohen

SEE ALSO

The 'Chinese Room'

---

### COMPUTERS AS MEDIA CELEBRITIES

The researcher William Stahl conducted a survey in the mid-1990s of the representation of computers by US current affairs magazines.

*Newsweek*'s cover boldly proclaimed 'Machines That Think' (30 June 1980). *Time* described computer toys as 'clever new playmates' and 'as teachers they can form bonds of a sort – friendships? – with their pupils' (10 December 1979, 68). One computer 'pays imaginative court to details' (*Time*, 31 January 1983, 65), whereas others are 'expert assistants' (*Time*, 2 September 1985, 43). The machines are endowed with emotions. The article on computer toys had them pondering, cheerful, and 'becomes impatient within a couple of minutes when its opponent is thinking' (10 December 1979, 71). Teaching programs were said to be 'very patient and non-judgmental' as well as polite (*Time*, 21 September 1981, 60).

(Stahl, 1995)

Indeed, *Time* added, 'the most successful machines have a built-in emotional component, something that connects the tools in the computer with the whims of its user' (24 October 1988, 76). In these human–machine relationships, the machine was frequently portrayed as the active partner. Computers were spoken of in the active voice, as if they had volition.

---

## ASS, BURIDAN'S

Buridan's ass is the hypothetical donkey placed equidistant from two identically tasty bales of hay. Lacking any rational criterion to make a decision, the unfortunate animal was unable to choose between them and eventually starved.

## ASTROLOGY

Astrology was as much part of philosophy as LOGIC or ETHICS is today, a crucial part of educated people's intellectual apparatus. Ancient Rome relied heavily on its court astrologers for warnings of natural or political disasters, exercising an influence that Tacitus denounces in his *History* as 'a deceitful attempt to run the affairs of State'. The stars and planets were understood to be part of the same great system that human beings struggled along in, and understanding their movements, it was felt, could shed light on human affairs too – without there necessarily being a simple causal connection, as anti-astrologers today like to allude derisively.

The heyday of astrology was from about 1300 to 1700 in Europe, where the study guided medicine, farming, chemistry, navigation, warfare and indeed all areas of life. Even the Pope asked astrologers for advice. Alas, over the last three to four hundred years, astrology has fallen out of favour with philosophers, with little remaining but the superficial popular and psychological forms. But even Isaac NEWTON was brought up in a world where astrology ranked as one of the great studies of mankind. Medieval universities taught it as one of the core subjects, and it was part of a sophisticated system of medical knowledge, involving the different parts of the body and different herbs.

Astrology's origins are lost in antiquity, but it probably started in Mesopotamia (modern Iraq), then was transmitted via Babylon to the Greeks, and to the East. As astrologers needed to examine the heavens for 'signs' such as shooting stars that might portend cultural events – usually calamities – a Babylonian sect called the Chaldeans built ziggurats. These were pyramids with the edges not smooth but stepped, to better examine the heavens. It is thought that it is they who first speculated that there might be a link between the heavenly bodies and the human ones so far below. In fact, the Greeks developed the methods of personal horoscopes, although it is the Roman names that have survived.

The Magi were said to have known of the coming of a Messiah by consulting the heavens, and recognising there was a particular celestial pattern predicted in the sixth century BCE by

Zoroaster. Although the Christian Church allowed the heavenly sign of the 'star of Bethlehem', and although many churches contain astrological symbols in their masonry, stained-glass windows and paintings, officially, astrology is frowned upon (even in 2005, the newly elected Pope cited belief in astrology as one of the 'evils' he would be working to root out), and in 333 the Emperor Constantine forbade the study in Europe in the name of Christianity. After this, astrology flourished in India, China and Tibet instead.

The next low point in the subject's fortunes comes with the critique of Giovanni Pico della Mirandola in 1493–94, centred on the 'problem', pointed out by AUGUSTINE and others, of twins, who share many more details in their charts than can be allowed, given what can be their totally different personalities. This 'problem' is trotted out regularly, as is the supposed 'problem' that the planets are not in the same positions as they used to be, with relation to the constellations. As recently as 1975, 186 self-styled 'leading scientists' produced a new collection of such 'Objections to astrology'; this group later amusingly debunked by Paul FEYERABEND, the contemporary American philosopher.

The traditional Ptolemaic understanding of the workings of astrology, described in the *Tetrabiblios*, some 200 years BCE, sets out all the knowledge of the astrologers and provides details of how to create personal horoscopes. For PTOLEMY, the system involved questions of TIME, objectivity and, above all, symbolism. And while astrology does not seem to match modern notions of SCIENCE, it does seem to offer an incredibly rich and subtle array of cultural, AESTHETIC and psychological insights. The descriptions of astrological types are all ambiguous, containing within each sign opposite tendencies. Capricorn, for example, is correctly a mythical creature, with a fish's tail, not the farmyard goat at all. The goat half gives people born under the sign the characteristics of being steady, hard-working and materialistic, while the fish's tail makes them dreamy, imaginative and spiritual. Capricorn comes at the beginning and the end of the zodiac, so it is a specially ambiguous sign, but all the signs contain the same PARADOXES. They cannot be understood by 'linear' thinkers at all, and so the subject could easily be dismissed. But then, Pico, we learn, was advised helpfully by astrologers in the sixteenth century that he would die before the 33rd year

of his life, due to Mars and the direction of his ascendant. This unfortunate feature did indeed turn out to be fatal in Pico's 32nd year.

As has been pointed out, the story, if true, is still not really within the potential scope of astrological judgement.

## ATHEISM

Atheism (from the Greek *theos* for GOD and the prefix 'a' for not) is the conviction that there are no gods, not even one. Much philosophical energy has gone into presenting and then refuting arguments for the existence of at least one God, and this has at least had the benefit of honing the skills of intellectuals, but there is also the danger in finally identifying the negative case, that not only their ETHICAL systems, but their whole METAPHYSICS, begin to fall apart too. What ARISTOTLE called 'the Prime Mover' still seems to have a role, even if it is not clear that this bears any resemblance to conventional notions of God.

## ATOMISM

The Greek word *atomos* means literally 'uncuttable' and atoms are historically precisely that, the smallest possible part, beyond which one cannot go. Unfortunately, nowadays we use the term to describe entities that can indeed be divided, and subdivided. Atomism as a philosophical doctrine starts with LEUCIPPUS and DEMOCRITUS, in the fifth century BCE, who supposed the universe to consist of an infinite number of these little particles moving in the void. They were attempting to combat the earlier notion, associated with the likes of PARMENIDES, that the universe was all one.

## SAINT AUGUSTINE OF HIPPO (354–430)

### The essential Augustine

Augustine was born and died in North Africa, then part of the Roman Empire. He taught philosophy in Rome and Milan where he converted to Christianity in 387. He returned to North Africa to spearhead the assault on the MANICHEAN religion and the Donatist and Pelagian heresies. He was consecrated bishop of Hippo in 395.

As a student in Carthage he had been influenced by Manicheanism, which has an explanation of the problem of EVIL, a lifelong concern of his. For Manichists, GOOD and evil

the Middle East and North Africa, the latter an area much favoured by the Roman elite. Augustine was born in 354 CE at Tagaste, in the Roman Province of Numidia (modern-day Algeria). His father was a pagan. His mother was a Christian, who told her son of a miraculous experience she had concerning him. Her attempts to make a Christian of Augustine when he was young met with some success, but he was too keen to explore a world brimming with interesting ideas to make any commitment.

He read the great Latin poets: he enjoyed Virgil, Horace and Juvenal, but took particular delight in the poetry of Catullus and Ovid, with their revelry in the arts of love. He received his formal education in Carthage, in the neighbouring Roman province of Africa (now Tunisia), the nearest celebrated seat of learning. Here, in this city of Phoenician origin, were myriad influences, not only Roman and Semitic ones, but also the Persian doctrines of the third-century prophet Mani, the prophet of light. Mani had produced a universal creed from the common ground in the teachings of Zarathrustra, GAUTAMA and Jesus, which was popular at the time in the Middle East, North Africa and Southern Italy.

are two opposing forces, and human SOULS are the battleground. Augustine did not like the idea that GOD was not omnipotent, and his solution instead was to abolish evil, declaring it merely the appearance of things that had become less and less good, although in some sense everything was as God intended still. Although this sounds reassuring, as his *Confessions* make clear, human beings are actually born evil, and only through God's grace (which cannot of course be demanded) can they be saved.

Augustine was remarkable in Christianising classical Greek and Roman philosophical thinking, particularly of the NEO-PLATONISTS, who spoke of 'God' as being like a light that touches everything, raises it to a higher reality. As Augustine puts it, 'in filling all things, you [God] fill them all with the whole of yourself' (Book I). Other subjects covered included self-examination, motivation, LANGUAGE, DREAMS, SCEPTICISM, TIME, theories of 'just war' and history. The *Confessions*, one of the most influential autobiographies ever, is intended to remodel the reader, while *The City of God* debates many philosophical issues.

Augustine was the dominant influence on European thinking for eight centuries, until AQUINAS combined Augustine's neo-Platonism with the Aristotelianism of Albert Magnus and moved into the ascendancy.

## The Saint

Aurelius Augustinus was a product of the Roman Empire, when it still ruled Europe,

Augustine encountered the Manichean religion as a student at Carthage and followed it for nine years, before eventually deciding it was a heresy. As a philosophy teacher in Italy (from 383 to 386 in Rome and Milan, the latter then being the capital of the Western Empire) he was inspired by the *Hortensius* by CICERO. His views hovered between scepticism and those of PLOTINUS and fellow neo-Platonists. Although much of his self-loathing is sexual in nature, he seems to have been pleased to become a father at the age of 19 when his mistress bore him a son, Adeonatus. He later recorded dialogues, in the manner of PLATO, featuring Adeonatus.

In his *Confessions* (ridiculed by Bertrand RUSSELL for the account of stealing pears – 'despite not even being hungry!') Augustine describes his journey from evil, ending with a confrontation with God in the garden of his house in Milan, part of an overwhelming emotional crisis. His conversion to Christianity, as his mother had expected from her 'dream', followed. He and his son were baptised in 387 by St Ambrose, Bishop of Milan. Augustine was then 32 years old.

Augustine records a conversation he had with his mother the following year, shortly before she died. They were in the garden of her house at Ostia and followed a pattern of meditation that became characteristic of Augustine: start with the nature of the outer world, pass to the inner world of SELF and on to abandonment to God. Words, even images of words, cannot convey profound EXPERIENCE. In conversation we use words, in thought images of words, but words are inadequate to express our deepest feelings. They cannot describe a sunset; a sunset is made insignificant in a word picture. When we meet a friend after long separation we are speechless with joy, words cannot convey our feelings. So it is in communion with God, now intermittent and transitory, but ultimately for eternity.

Augustine's honest response to being asked by a student what time is, with which he begins Book 11 of the *Confessions*, has become well known. He replies: 'I know well enough what time is, until someone asks me'. In fact, his view of time is that it is an illusion. Time is not objective, but a projection of the soul. The mind stretches out, catching the past and future in current attention, and then plays out the future, through the present, into the past. Aristotle's concept of the durationless instants used to measure motion, limits mind to the role of external observer and precludes eternity. Eternity is essential in Augustine's scheme of things.

The existence of the will as solution to the problem of evil, not to mention as precursor of DESCARTES, is found in Book VII of the *Confessions* (section 3, 5):

I knew myself to have a will in the same way and as much as I knew myself to be alive. Therefore when I willed or did not will something, I was utterly certain that none other than myself was willing or not willing.

Augustine had written his *Confessions* between 397 and 401; *The Trinity* during the following decade; and *The City of God* between 412 and 427. By then the Western Roman Empire was being overrun and the Byzantine Empire was drawing in on itself. The saint had laid the foundations for the persecution of many shades of Christian belief as 'heresies', but would have been dismayed that the lands of his youth would be swept by the new region of Islam some 250 years later.

Today, Augustine's thinking still attracts more innovative attention than the THOMISM that replaced it seven centuries ago.

Contributors: Colin Kirk and Martin Cohen

## Further reading

*The Confessions of St Augustine*

*The City of God*

### WICKED, GREEDY BABY!

In the Middle Ages, saintly experts such as Augustine saw human life as essentially a rather unpleasant sort of moral trial, with the unpleasantness a necessary part of achieving saintliness. Augustine saw mankind as a mass of corruption and sin proceeding inevitably towards hell. In Book I of the *Confessions* he describes the evil already there in the newborn baby, before going on to show how the adult is no better.

I have personally watched and studied a jealous baby. He could not yet speak and, pale with jealousy and bitterness, glared at his brother sharing his mother's milk... it can hardly be innocence, when the source of milk is flowing richly and abundantly, not to endure a share going to one's blood brother, who is in profound need, dependent for life exclusively on that one food.

(*Confessions*, Book I vii (11) p. 9)

## MARCUS AURELIUS (121–80)

See Stoicism.

## AXIOMS

The Greek word *axioma* literally means 'worthy of respect', and axioms claim to be that. Among ARISTOTLE's 'LAWS OF THOUGHT', for example, is the claim that factual statements (PROPOSITIONS) are either true or false, but not both (or indeed neither). LOGIC, MATHEMATICS and philosophical ARGUMENTS in general all are reliant on certain underlying assumptions, without which there can be no progression. Unfortunately, these assumptions are often anything but certain.

**B**

## BACHELARD, GASTON (1884–1962)

Gaston Bachelard started out as a philosopher of science, writing in France at the time of relativity theory and QUANTUM MECHANICS, and ended up as an iconoclastic critic of literary theory. His original argument, anticipating both Karl POPPER and Thomas KUHN, was that science cannot be understood as a smooth progression, but must be interpreted as inherently incomplete, with 'epistemological ruptures' or 'discontinuities' in its logic and progress. In *La Formation de l'esprit scientifique: contribution: une psychoanalyse de la connaissance objective* ('The Formation of the Scientific Spirit and the psychoanalysis of objective knowledge') published in 1938, he attempts to define the boundary between objectivity and SUBJECTIVITY in science. His study of fire, *La Psychoanalyse du feu*, published in the same year, illustrates the approach by showing that the image of fire as dangerous, purifying, destructive and 'passionate' not only affects but determines scientific thinking. He later applied the same approach to literature and poetry, saying that dreams and imagination are the essential complement to structured thought.

## BACON, FRANCIS (1561–1626)

Francis Bacon was the lawyer, philosopher and politician at the court of Queen Elizabeth (and later King James) in Tudor England who was traditionally counted as the first British 'empiricist'. He epitomised the Renaissance faith in scientific method, and devoted himself to developing a system combining data drawn from experience with a form of negative reasoning sometimes called 'eliminative induction'. The aim was to provide a solid base for certain knowledge, while allowing the widest possible range to ideas and research. For example, scientists looking into the relationship between heat and luminosity should concern themselves with cases where heat is present, such as in the sun's rays, and where it is absent, such as in phosphorescence. And the approach reflects Bacon's legal interests, in that English Common Law develops 'inductively', as it were, from the accumulation of past case law, before being applied as established doctrine to new cases.

Bacon never completed his project, and his most important book, *Novum organum* (1620) remained unfinished.

## BACON, ROGER (1214–1294)

### The essential Roger Bacon

Bacon is a rather prosaic name for a philosopher, and worse still, Roger falls somewhat in the shadow of his famous namesake, Francis, and so is not normally accorded much time (or space) in philosophy circles. But Roger Bacon's work was wide ranging and encyclopaedic in breadth: ranging across mathematics, the nature of knowledge, the geometry of prisms, language and the writings of ARISTOTLE. He ridiculed AQUINAS (they had been contemporaries in Paris) for basing himself on Aristotle without being able to read him in the original.

### First science

For Roger Bacon, Aristotle is important, but many other things are equally important, and not to be ignored just because they do not have Aristotle's authority. Dogma and DIALECTIC have their place, but are useless in the face of demonstration and mathematical proofs. He gives the example of fire, saying that we can hear any amount of information about fire, its light and heat, its destructive power, and so on, without being much the wiser. But once we have had the experience of fire, the mind is assured and appreciates the light of truth. Reasoning is not enough, one needs experience.

Roger Bacon was born in Somerset and died in Oxford. He studied in Oxford and in Paris, and is remembered both as 'Doctor Mirabilis' and as a Franciscan priest. He upset the authorities by pointing out that they celebrated Easter on the wrong day, in spite of the lengths they went to to ensure the date was correct, calculating the discrepancy between the solar year and the Julian calendar, which had accumulated to nine days by then. He was scathing about the ignorance of his colleagues, but the Oxford authorities banished him from the schools and he returned to Paris as an exile.

Bacon's work had been admired by Guy Le Gros Foulques, who became a priest in 1256 on the death of his wife. Foulques made meteoric progress. He was papal legate in England when he first became aware of Bacon's work. He then transferred to Paris as adviser to Louis IX (St Louis), himself a patron of learning. Having been elevated from bishop to archbishop to cardinal in eight years, Foulques was elected Pope as Clement IV in 1265. He had asked Bacon for a summary of his philosophy when cardinal, which the Franciscan order forbade Bacon to provide. But they could not block a papal mandate. Bacon's works had not previously been prepared for formal presentation. His *Opus Maius* was submitted in Rome in 1267. Publication, with papal approval, followed in 1268 and Bacon was allowed to return to Oxford.

Bacon is regarded, with Grosseteste, as a precursor of the scientific age. They valued objective demonstrable truth above repeated untried dogma: only the objectivity of numbers applied to demonstration exposes error. One of Bacon's important contributions was application of this to astronomy: the length of the solar year is less by some 130th part of one day. Hence, in 130 years there is 1 day in excess. Bacon was less concerned about the inaccuracy of the date on which Easter was celebrated, which he was nevertheless at pains to correct, than he was on the effect of trying to calculate dates of eclipses. He advised putting the date right and keeping it that way by dropping a day from the calendar every 130 years. PTOLEMY had made the same point in the *Almagest*, but Bacon's calculation is more accurate.

Roger Bacon's rhetoric was somewhat intemperate in condemning the ignorance of all the Pope's other advisors, which was unfortunate because the Pope, Bacon's only ally, died at the end of 1268. Bacon's real work was ignored. His assaults on others were not. Nevertheless, he was able to continue publishing his works on mathematics, LOGIC and philosophy until 1277. He pre-dates Leonardo in speculation about lighter-than-air flying machines, had the concepts of telescopes and microscopes, but not the skilled craftsmen to produce them, and, among many other things, seems to have discovered gunpowder, accidentally! In 1277 there was a reckoning: scholars were called upon to defend their views in order to stop wild speculation that was thought to have got out of hand. There was antagonism between the Dominican order, to which Aquinas had belonged (he had died in 1274), and the Franciscan order, to which Bacon belonged. In the event, hotheads of all parties were condemned, Bacon among them. He was jailed for 15 years and released just 2 years before his death.

There are too many similarities in the interests and dislikes of Roger Bacon in the thirteenth century and his namesake Francis, as a student in the sixteenth century, for the latter not to have had some acquaintance with the works of the scholarly friar. This is especially likely as regards the proposed change to the calendar. The continent went over to the Gregorian calendar on 4 October 1582, when Francis was at Cambridge and by which time the discrepancy had become ten days. At the command of Phillip II of Spain, who did not want a ruling of the Council of Nicaea (325 CE) upset, the vernal equinox remains the 21 March – in such ways is political power manifest. Protestant Britain refused to change its calendar on the say-so of the Pope; instead, it only followed suit on Wednesday 2 September 1752, which was thus followed by Thursday 14 September, as by then the discrepancy had become 11 days.

Contributor: Colin Kirk

## BAKHTIN, MIKHAIL (1895–1975)

Bakhtin was a Russian philosopher and philologist, educated at St Petersburg University, arrested in 1928 and 'internally exiled'. He was sent first to Kustanai (1930) and later to Saransk (1936), where he lectured at the Mordovian Pedagogical Institute, and became a head of the department of world literature. He was formally rehabilitated only in 1967, and he moved to Moscow in 1972, where he lived until his death.

He is counted, at least in Russia, as one of the greatest theorists of literature of the twentieth century; for revolutionising Saussure's linguistics and inspiring Jakobson and the philologists of the so-called 'Bakhtin Circle', who shared an ideal of cross-cultural dialogue.

But he was also a philosopher; and as a PHENOMENOLOGIST his main themes were intersubjectivity and responsibility. In 'Art and Answerability' he emphasises that the reality of responsibility is the condition of being human. Bakhtin also describes an AESTHETIC event as an experience of 'outsideness', adding a creative dimension to an act.

Like KANT, he considers that to be fully human requires that one should act as a responsible subject, as a self-conscious person. Like LEVINAS, Bakhtin considers that human subjectivity 'affirms oneself' as a response to 'the Other'. In an essay, 'Towards a Philosophy of Action' (originally written between 1919 and

1921, and sometimes translated as 'the Act'), he considers that the task for people is to complete themselves 'from without' through action, and rise above the general social consciousness as an individual, in so doing bestowing a kind of gift of completion of human singularity. But, he warns, one can find one's own SUBJECTIVITY only through a dialogue, in answering both to 'the Other' and to the 'I'.

> The dialogic nature of consciousness, the dialogic nature of human life itself. The single adequate form for verbally expressing authentic human life is the open-ended dialogue. Life by its very nature is dialogic. To live means to participate in dialogue: to ask questions, to heed, to respond, to agree, and so forth. In this dialogue a person participates wholly and throughout his whole life: with his eyes, lips, hands, soul, spirit, with his whole body and deeds. He invests his entire self in discourse, and this discourse enters into the dialogic fabric of human life, into the world symposium.
>
> *(Problems of Dostoevsky's Poetics)*

# BARBER PARADOX

The 'barber' paradox is a version of a very old PARADOX, which has been discussed ever since the philosopher Bertrand RUSSELL came across it in the early years of the last century. Russell rather inelegantly summed it up as the problem of the 'set of all SETS that are not members of themselves' – is it a member of itself? He was so appalled at the implications of the paradox, not only for LOGIC, but for mathematics and even ordinary language, that he wrote in his autobiography that his life work seemed dashed to pieces, and for weeks he could scarcely eat or sleep. He sent it to the mathematical philosopher, Gottlob FREGE, who commented: 'arithmetic trembles'.

In its more friendly form, the paradox is that of a barber in a particular town, charged with the responsibility of cutting the hair of everyone in the town – as long as they do not habitually cut their own hair. It sounds simple, except for the one problem case of the barber himself: if he in fact used to cut his own hair, then he is now forbidden to cut it; but equally, if he used to go to a friend's for a haircut, he is no longer allowed to, as the rule gives him responsibility for *everyone's* hair.

A number of solutions have been suggested. One is that the barber should try to arrange a nasty shock for himself, with the aim of making all his hair fall out. However, this device does not really get to grips with the fundamental problem.

In his *Principia Mathematica*, Bertrand Russell undertook to find solutions to no less than seven incarnations of the pesky paradox, and worked on his reformulation thus: Is the set of all sets that are not members of itself a member of itself, or is it not, and if it is not is it? Admirably precise though this specification of the problem is, it does not actually help resolve the contradiction and Russell took the drastic step of saying that all statements which refer to themselves should be 'outlawed', or at least treated as meaningless. Unfortunately, a great many meaningful statements are self-referential – like this one!

SEE ALSO

Paradoxes

# BAYLE, PIERRE (1647–1706)

As a Huguenot, Pierre Bayle experienced religious persecution at first hand in France, and his philosophy seems to reflect this. He argues that there are higher duties than that of 'maximising the good', in particular the duty to respect the individuality not so much of oneself, but of others.

Hailed for his *Historical and Critical Dictionary* of 1695–97, his critique was of RATIONALISM, or rather the overweening conceit of its followers, and in favour of belief, especially religious belief. He particularly criticised MALEBRANCHE for his attempts to explain why God should allow so much evil to exist in the world. Human reason, Bayle says, is excessively negative in approach, better at knocking down ideas than creating them, and equally, is unable to provide positive motivation. Bayle argued strenuously that Christian faith was contrary to reason. Some interpreters take him to have wanted to stress the *non-rational* character of the Christian faith, that is, you should be a believer, but should not expect to have your faith supported by, or even tolerated by, reason. Others, however, have taken him to have been stressing the *irrational* character of the Christian faith. So, you should not be a believer and to be one is to take leave of one's senses.

Whatever his view of believers, Pierre Bayle was the first advocate, or at least the most important in the modern era, of the view that religious 'unbelievers' can be good citizens and be morally upright, despite not having any expectation of rewards and punishments in the next world.

## BEAUTY

Philosophers agree very little on 'beauty', which is not in itself a very unusual thing (they agree very little on tables, on the colour of snow, and so on. . .). Some say assessing beauty is an aesthetic judgement, others say not. Some say beauty is both capable of definition and 'objective', like PLATO with his 'form of the beautiful'; others say it is entirely SUBJECTIVE and beneath serious consideration. If it is the former, then beauty is a quality 'out there' just as, say, a colour is; if it is the latter, then it is purely a matter of emotional response. Thomas AQUINAS defined beauty as 'that which pleases in the very apprehension of it', whereas KANT says beauty has 'subjective universality and necessity' by which he intends to give it some sort of solid foundation in our understanding of the world.

Nowadays, with artistic interest in the grotesque and the violent, the distinction is often lost, but beauty used to have an ETHICAL element, as to be beautiful was (in that respect) to be good, to be better than being ugly. It is because of this that we can describe actions as 'beautiful', or indeed, physically ugly people whose character is kind, as 'beautiful'.

SEE ALSO

Aesthetics

## DE BEAUVOIR, SIMONE (1908–86)

### The essential de Beauvoir

The conventional view of Simone de Beauvoir is that she is a minor figure, forever in the shadow of her lifelong intellectual confidant and companion Jean Paul SARTRE, with just a few forays into philosophy, such as in *Pyrrhus et Cinéas* (1944) and *The Ethics of Ambiguity* (1947). However, *The Second Sex* (1949) is now accepted as a key text in modern FEMINIST thinking.

### The inauthentic lovers

Curiously enough, most of de Beauvoir's EXISTENTIALIST philosophy appears in her fiction; in particular, in *She Came to Stay*, which was published in 1943, the same year as Sartre's celebrated *Being and Nothingness*. Here, Simone de

Beauvoir also describes various kinds of consciousness, in passages ranging from wandering through an empty theatre (the stage, the walls, the chairs, unable to come alive until there is an audience) to watching a woman in a restaurant ignore the fact that her male companion has begun stroking her arm ('it lay there, forgotten, ignored, the man's hand was stroking a piece of flesh that no longer belonged to anyone') – as well as this one:

'It's almost impossible to believe that other people are conscious beings, aware of their own inward feelings, as we ourselves are aware of our own', said Françoise. 'To me, it's terrifying when we grasp that. We get the impression of no longer being anything but a figment of someone else's mind.'

Indeed, although the two books came out in the same year, Simone de Beauvoir's was written some time earlier, and Sartre read the drafts avidly on his brief army leaves, before commencing *Being and Nothingness*. Sartre even records in his diary how de Beauvoir had to correct him several times for his clumsy misunderstanding of the philosophy. But then the Sartre–de Beauvoir relationship is both celebrated and completely misunderstood. It is itself a truly philosophical tale. On the one hand there is the well-known conventional plot of Sartre the womaniser, who denies the dutiful de Beauvoir marriage in order to preserve his 'existential freedom'. On the other, and much less well-known, is the reality that in 1930, Sartre proposed marriage to de Beauvoir, who as a radical feminist was aghast at both the conventionality of the proposal and the conventionality of Sartre's assumptions, and insisted instead on multiple relationships (with both male and female lovers).

One explanation for Simone de Beauvoir's disavowal of her own creation may be that de Beauvoir, unlike Sartre, acknowledged her sources, and through her study of HEGEL would have been aware that many of existentialism's elements can be found in the Eastern tradition of BUDDHISM for example, the notion of 'THE OTHER'. Here, the viewpoint tends (as one commentator, James Whitehill has put it), in matters of self and community, to be 'biocentric and ecological'. That said, de Beauvoir's later development of the notion to class all women as 'the other' in male-dominated society, was and remained her own, and her 1949 book *The Second Sex* is seen as groundbreaking. Her own attempts to get the ideas published were rebuffed by a French publisher, with the advice to stick to 'women's topics'. Perhaps she simply saw no reason to lay claim to anything in her lover's account which remained sadly inferior to her own. Not that it fits in very well with Sartre and de Beauvoir's great rallying cry through the 1960s of 'Authenticity'. . .

## Further Reading

de Beauvoir, S. (1949) *Le deuxième sexe* (*The Second Sex*)

Fullbrook, K. and Fullbrook, H.(1994) *Simone de Beauvoir and Jean-Paul Sartre*

## BEETLE BOX ANALOGY

This is the celebrated 'thought experiment' in which that old sceptic of the technique, WITTGENSTEIN, offers another way to consider the nature of language. He writes in *Philosophical Investigations:*

. . . Suppose everyone had a box with something in it: we call it a 'beetle'. No one can look into anyone else's box, and everyone says he knows what a beetle is by looking at his beetle. – Here it would be quite possible for everyone to have something different in his box. One might

even imagine such a thing constantly changing. But suppose the word 'beetle' had a use in these people's language? If so, it would not be used as the name of a thing. The thing in the box has no place in the language-game at all; not even as a something: for the box might even be empty. No one can 'divide through' by the thing in the box; it cancels out, whatever it is.

*(#293 Philosophical Investigations)*

Wittgenstein's beetle is supposed to show that people assume that because they are using the same words they are talking about the same thing, when in fact they may be discussing different matters, and what's more, doing so in quite different ways. There is a straightforward parallel between the beetle in the box and, say, 'consciousness', or perhaps a sensation like 'pain' in someone's personal 'beetle box' or 'head'. Everyone has such a sensation. But only they can look at it, and they cannot allow others to 'open the box'.

And the beetle is supposed to be like words and concepts generally. It is supposed to sever the link between concepts in our heads, and things in the world, by way of words. Today, the beetle is claimed by linguists, doctors and psychologists, artists and aesthetes to radically transform the conventional view of the stability of meaning and language.

Yet, in the best cryptic tradition of Wittgenstein, a little thought also shows that the beetle does not take any of the different positions claimed for it by philosophers, psychologists and so many others. If anything, it might even lend itself better to demonstrating the stability of language and communication.

SEE ALSO

Thought experiments

## BEGGING THE QUESTION

See Fallacies.

## BEHAVIORISM

Behaviorism (to use the US spelling) has several senses. The minor sense is philosophical, in which behaviour is explained by consideration of the action, rather than the INTENTION. The sense in which most people know it is derived from DESCARTES, who asserted that animals, far from thinking, merely react to stimuli. A dog, he thinks, cannot feel pain, it can only respond automatically in certain ways to being beaten. Animals were just automata, but human beings, supposed Descartes, also had this mysterious thing, 'the SOUL', which added a 'purposive' aspect to their behaviour. But since Descartes' soul was beyond scientific investigation, T.H. Huxley (1825–95), a younger contemporary of DARWIN, disagreed, saying that human beings had to be understood as automata too. This is an old idea, summed up in DE LA METTRIE's famous book, *Man a Machine* (1747). For Huxley, 'the feeling we call volition is not the cause of a voluntary act, but the symbol of that state of the brain which is the immediate cause of the act'.

This 'reflex' explanation of behaviour was taken a bit further by Pavlov with his experiments on dogs, who could be trained ('conditioned') to salivate at the 'stimulus' of a bell being rung (in anticipation of being fed); and J.B. Watson (1879–1958) theorised that thinking is only a kind of movement of the brain and larynx, and emotions likewise, while B.F. Skinner (1904–90) famously invented various kinds of electrified cage in order to test out the approach on animals as part of his demonstration that it is not necessary to understand what goes on in minds to be able to predict behaviour. 'Science often talks about things it cannot see or measure… the skin is not that important a boundary', he wrote in *Science and Human Behaviour* (1953).

## BELIEF

To believe something is to behave as though you know something to be the case, while acknowledging that you do not really have the logical proof or the empirical evidence for it. You might, for example, be relying on your intuition.

For philosophers, there is the notion of 'justified true belief', which is, near as dammit, knowledge. This says that something is 'known' if:

- we believe it to be the case;
- we have a good, relevant reason for our belief;
- and it is so.

However, consider the case of Farmer Field's cow, Daisy, the prize animal that he wishes to check is safe and sound in her field. He goes to the gate, looks over and sees a black and white shape moving in a copse of trees. He returns to the farmhouse content that he 'knows' his cow is safe in her field. However, when the farmhand goes to double check, he finds that Daisy is snoozing in a hollow out of sight of the gate, and there is a large piece of white and black paper flapping, caught in a tree in the copse. In Farmer Field's case, he satisfies all the conditions for 'justified true belief' – he:

- believed the cow was safe;
- had evidence that this was so (his belief was justified);
- and it was true that his cow was safe.

Yet we still might feel he did not really know that Daisy was in the field.

This problem is also set out in PLATO's *Theaetetus* (201c–210d), and, in slightly more formal language, has perplexed many philosophers ever since, particularly since the twentieth century interest in 'analytic' philosophy.

What this all suggests is that a different definition of 'knowledge' is needed. Although all knowledge may have to be 'true, justified beliefs', not all true, justified beliefs seem to be knowledge. This rejection of the three conditions as jointly still 'insufficient' encouraged a few philosophers to simply add an extra rule: nothing inferred from a false belief counts as knowledge, which certainly sounds plausible, but even so is not quite straightforward either. Other philosophers have tried to dispense with the first requirement, allowing someone to know without necessarily believing, while others wished to make the criterion for 'knowing' something more than just belief, suggesting instead that what is required is 'acceptance', whatever that is.

Belief is sometimes said to be the 'primary cognitive state', that is, 'perceiving things', 'knowing things', 'remembering things' all derive and are secondary to the original state of 'belief'.

## BENTHAM, JEREMY (1748–1832)

### The essential Bentham

Bentham was descended from two generations of lawyers and his approach is legalistic, although he himself decided that the more useful question was how the law ought to be, rather than what it actually was. He argues too that what his contemporaries were celebrating as 'natural rights' were little more than imaginary rights, and actual law created the only 'actual rights'. The French *Declaration of the Rights of Man* he described as 'nonsense on stilts', warning that to want something is not to supply it, that hunger is not the same thing as bread.

Bentham saw the world as torn between two great forces, the quest for pleasure and the avoidance of pain. From this, he intuited that it would be better to maximise the former and minimise the latter, and that all other considerations are irrelevant. This became known as the 'principle of utility', and Bentham's writings are a pure form of UTILITARIANISM.

Bentham even saw himself in the role of spiritual leader of a kind of utilitarian movement, and donated his body (after his death) to University College London (which he helped found), where it remains today, preserved in a glass case.

## Bentham's system

What sort of person was Jeremy Bentham? In some opinions he was a radical, an iconoclast and progressive, in others a reactionary, a die-hard and a killjoy. Probably the answer lies in his system – utilitarianism. It is a doctrine that allows no space for individual taste, just as it allows no room for rights or duties, although Bentham allows that these may have socially desirable roles as convenient fictions. As he puts it in the opening sentence of Introduction to *The Principles of Morals and Legislation*: (1789):

> The principle of utility judges any action to be right by the tendency it appears to have to augment or diminish the happiness of the party whose interests are in question... if that party be the community, the happiness of the community, if a particular individual, the happiness of that individual.

It is actually in *The Commonplace Book* (1774–75) that the phrase 'the happiness of the greatest number' can be found, Bentham writing that 'the greatest happiness of the greatest number' is the foundation of morality. The phrase actually originated slightly earlier with Frances HUTCHESON (1694–1746), who had said 'that action is best, which procures the greatest happiness for the greatest numbers'.

So Bentham's work ranges widely and it might seem erratically, at times. He spent much time and energy attempting to advance surveillance as the tool for a well-run society, even drawing up detailed plans for the construction of circular buildings, where the actions of many could be watched and controlled by just one: 'the Inspector'. He considered his invention to be particularly suitable for prisoners, but the 'Panopticons', or 'Inspection Houses', are also, as the title page of Bentham's account makes clear, applicable to any sort of establishment where people need to be kept 'under inspection', such as hospitals, factories, schools and 'mad-houses'.

The rewards from using 'the inspective force', as Bentham saw it, would be equally wide-ranging: 'Morals reformed – health preserved – industry invigorated – instruction diffused – public burthens lightened – Economy seated, as it were, upon a rock – the Gordian knot of the Poor-Laws . . . not cut, but untied'!

Bentham works it all out in enthusiastic detail.

> To save the troublesome exertion of voice that might otherwise be necessary, and to prevent one prisoner from knowing that the inspector was occupied by another prisoner at a distance, a small tin tube might reach from each cell to the inspector's lodge, passing across the area, and so in at the side of the correspondent window of the lodge. By means of this implement, the slightest whisper of the one might be heard by the other, especially if he had proper notice to apply his ear to the tube.
>
> *(Letter II)*

As for the 'inspection':

> It may be confined to the hours of study; or it may be made to fill the whole circle of time, including the hours of repose, and refreshment, and recreation. To the first of these applications the most captious timidity, I think, could hardly fancy an objection: concerning the hours of study, there can, I think, be but one wish, that they should he employed in study. It is scarce necessary to observe that gratings, bars, and bolts, and every circumstance from which an Inspection House can derive a terrific character, have nothing to do here. All play, all chattering – in short, all distraction of every kind, is effectually banished . . .

Jeremy Bentham also busied himself with a 'Plan for Universal and Perpetual Peace' (1789).

Jeremy Bentham's Panopticon was a product of utilitarian thinking

Undeterred by the lukewarm reception to his 'Panopticon', the plan is the same principle writ large, essentially relying on a supranational 'eye' to police the world – not by force, of course, but by the free exchange of information, shaming any transgressor nations into line. Still, doubtless mindful of the political non-response to his 'Panopticon', Bentham became an active campaigner for the reform of the British political system, arguing the then radical case of 'one man, one vote'. And although most of the 'philosophical' arguments for experiments on animals are 'utilitarian', that is, justified by saying that the benefits to humans outweigh the costs to animals, the 'father' of that school was firmly against such arguments. In 'The Principles of Morals and Legislation', Bentham says firmly:

> The day may come, when the rest of the animal creation may acquire those rights which never could have been withholden from them but by the hand of tyranny. The French have already discovered that the blackness of the skin is no reason why a human being should be abandoned without redress to the caprice of a tormentor. It may come one day to be recognised, that the number of the legs, the villosity of the skin, or the termination of the os sacrum, are reasons equally insufficient for abandoning a sensitive being to the same fate. What else is there that should trace the insuperable line? Is it the faculty of reason, or, perhaps the faculty of discourse? But a full-grown horse or dog is beyond comparison a more rational, as well as a more conversible animal than an infant of a day, or a week, or even a month old? But suppose the case were otherwise, what would it avail? The question is not, Can they reason?, nor Can they talk? but Can they suffer?

Contributor: Martin Cohen

## BERGSON, HENRI-LOUIS (1859–1941)

Bergson is remembered for two theories, the doctrine of *élan-vital* and the notion of 'duration'. The second is concerned that time is split into parts of set length by scientists, and parts of no length by mathematicians (for the purposes

of calculus), but Bergson says it needs also to be treated as indivisible, in the same way as a melody cannot be understood once you have broken it up into its separate notes. Bergson was born in the same year as DARWIN's (1859) *Origin of Species* was published and it is perhaps appropriate that his other concern was with EVOLUTION. In *Creative Evolution* (1907) Bergson says evolution, like time, is a single process that cannot be understood properly by being treated in fragments, and that animals change and develop constantly, not towards a particular predetermined 'end', but dynamically. The *élan* is the spirit of life, by which animals and humans too use their own power and resources to overcome difficulties.

In later life, Bergson concerned himself with morality, noting that in 'scientific time' we are reduced to merely responding mechanically to events, and it is only possible in terms of 'duration' that we regain our moral dimension. He argued against attempts to universalise morality, saying that such theories invariably based morality on the well-being of groups and must therefore impinge on the interests of those outside the group. Only through the leap of faith taken by those embracing 'all mankind' could people escape this problem.

## BERKELEY, GEORGE (1685–1753)

Bishop George Berkeley held the doctrine that *esse est percipi*, that material objects exist only through being perceived. To the objection that in that case, a tree, for instance, in a forest, would cease to exist when no one was around, he replied that God always perceived everything; in his opinion, this was a weighty argument.

Berkeley wrote his main works while he was in his twenties: *A New Theory of Vision* in 1709, *The Principles of Human Knowledge* a year later and the *Dialogues of Hylas and Philonous* in 1713. In this last, his argument against matter is set out best. 'Hylas' (the names all have particular meanings too) stands for scientific COMMON SENSE, and 'Philonous' for Berkeley's own view. After some amiable remarks, in the manner of PLATO and SOCRATES, Hylas says he has heard that his friend holds the view that there is no such thing as matter. Can anything be more fantastical, more repugnant to Common Sense or a more manifest piece of SCEPTICISM than this, he exclaims!

Philonous tries to explain that sense data are in fact mental, as is shown by considering lukewarm water. Put a cold hand in it and it appears warm – put a hot hand in it and it appears cold. Hylas accepts this point, but clings to other sensible qualities. Philonous then says that tastes are either pleasant or unpleasant, and are therefore mental, and the same can be said of smells. Hylas valiantly rallies at this point, and says that sounds are known to not travel through a vacuum. From this, he concludes, they must be motions of air molecules, not mental entities. Philonous responds that if this is indeed real sound, it bears no resemblance to what we know as sound, so that in that case, sound may as well be considered the mental phenomenon after all. The same argument fells Hylas when it comes to a discussion of colours, which it is realised disappear under certain conditions, such as when a golden cloud at sunset is seen close up to be just a grey mist.

Likewise, size varies, depending on the observer's position. Here, Hylas suggests that the object should be distinguished form the perception – the act of perceiving is after all mental, but there is still a material object. Philonous replies: 'Whatever is immediately perceived is an idea: and can any idea exist out of the mind?' In other words, for something to be perceived, there must be a mind somewhere perceiving it.

Berkeley's conclusion is that there are logical grounds for holding the view that only minds and mental events can exist. This view was adopted by HEGEL and other subsequent philosophers.

## BIOETHICS

Bioethics is a relatively new discipline concerned with the ethical, social and legal aspects of biological research and its applications, especially in medicine. It also seeks to apply broad ethical principles to areas of medical practice, and in this, it is the successor to a tradition in medicine that stretches from the Hippocratic oath, taken by physicians in ancient Greece, to the Geneva Convention in the twentieth century, which outlawed the participation of physicians and medical researchers in violations of HUMAN RIGHTS.

Bioethics addresses a number of secular or political themes, including rights, autonomy and justice. It represents a move from MEDICAL ETHICS that are based narrowly in either medicine or theology to one that draws on philosophical and legal traditions. These include UTILITARIAN and KANTIAN approaches, although these sometimes offer conflicting conclusions, utilitarianism attaching weight to welfare outcomes, Kantianism emphasising an unqualified respect for the human person. In some areas, an approach based on virtue ethics has been fruitful, marking a turn to the ARISTOTELIAN notions of TELEOLOGY and flourishing. Beyond these broad philosophical divisions, well-established principles such as beneficence and non-maleficence ('do no harm') continue to influence medical practice, and religious approaches, including Roman Catholic, Jewish and Muslim perspectives, are also influential.

Discoveries in the biomedical sciences have raised important questions at the margins of life which affect both research and medical treatment. On the one hand, science has brought unprecedented control over human life at the embryonic stage; on the other, it has raised many questions about death and dying, about ageing and deterioration, and about the use the living can make of the dead – from organ transplants to transplants of hand and face.

Key developments in the impetus to bioethics were the discovery of penicillin in the 1940s, the invention of artificial respiration in the 1950s, the first heart transplant in 1967 and the first test-tube baby in 1978. More recently, the decoding of the human genome has brought new ethical questions in genetics, both in patient treatment and research. A number of countries have set up bodies to advise politicians and public on ethical approaches to the new technologies.

### SEE ALSO

Medical ethics, Environmental ethics, Reproductive ethics

## BOETHIUS (C. 480–525)

Anucius Manlius Severinus Boethius was born in Rome, studied the 'liberal arts', including philosophy, and rose to become a consul (an honorary and actually rather expensive position). Boethius was part of the Roman 'establishment', entitled to be addressed as 'Your Magnitude', and was employed by the Gothic ruler, Theodoric, in various cultural pursuits, such as designing a sundial and waterclock for the King of Burgundy. Unfortunately, after dabbling in politically unwise areas, probably with the intention of overthrowing Theodoric for a more cultured fellow, he incurred Theoderic's displeasure and was arrested, tried on charges of conspiracy, imprisoned in Pavia, and executed around 525.

Boethius worked mainly in the area of LOGIC, translating many of ARISTOTLE's writings, particularly those on logic, into Latin, and writing commentaries on PORPHYRY's introduction to logic (suggesting that there is a difference between concepts (or 'universals') such as centaurs, which are imaginary, and ones like lines in mathematics, which are real, in the manner PLATO supposed his Forms were). He also achieved considerable medieval significance for his 'clarifications' of various religious matters, such as the logical status of the Trinity and of Christ. However, it is a work of ETHICS, the *Consolation of Philosophy*, written while in prison and lamenting innocent suffering at the hands of such as Theodoric, for which he is now remembered. Nature has made us all seek good, he says, echoing Plato, but error leads us astray. 'Despite a clouded memory, the mind seeks its own good though like a drunkard it cannot find its way home.'

Probably smuggled out of prison, the *Consolations* so appealed to Alcuin in the court of Charlemagne (some three centuries later) that they found their way to becoming a standard medieval textbook in schools. In England, Alfred the Great had it translated into Anglo-Saxon and Chaucer produced a version in the 'proper' English of the time. It is in the *Consolations* that Boethius tries to reconcile that age-old problem of free will and fate, as known and determined by God, by saying that God lives in 'an eternal present', so although God knows everything, God cannot be accused of 'causing' anything to happen.

## BOOLEAN ALGEBRA

Boolean algebra is so-called after the English mathematician George Boole (1815–64), who devised a new way of representing LOGICAL and mathematical relationships. The main idea is that a set can be represented by, say, 'x' and everything else not included by, say, 'x2'. Although LEIBNIZ had also been working secretively along similar lines at around the same time, it is Boole's system, with its logical operators of 'and', 'or' and 'not' that became the basis for modern logics and computing.

## BRADLEY, FRANCIS (1846–1924)

F.H. Bradley was an IDEALIST philosopher, which is not so much a reference to his having become a fellow at Oxford in 1870 and staying there for the rest of his life, as a shorthand for someone who thinks 'ideas' are what ultimately exists, and the world 'of things' perceived is secondary to them. Bradley was influential within British philosophy, at least until being disparaged by the LOGICAL POSITIVISTS in the inter-war period, arguing in *Appearance and Reality* (1893) that our ordinary understandings of the world include within them contradictions, and that instead truth can only be obtained through recognising that there is only one 'thing' and only that one thing (i.e. everything collectively in the universe) can perceive itself fully. This theory is said to have influenced T.S. Eliot (who wrote a doctoral thesis on Bradley) in his poetry. His critique of traditional LOGIC as failing to recognise the different ways arguments work, along with his insistence that it must be separate from PSYCHOLOGY, influenced the development of modern logics, and his METAPHYSICAL view of the necessity to treat both the universe and PERCEPTION in a holistic way led him to condemn what we might call the 'psychological egotism' of UTILITARIANS in general and J.S. MILL in particular.

## BRENTANO, FRANZ (1838–1917)

The Austrian academic philosopher Brentano is best known for his theorising around INTENTIONALITY and intentional inexistence. He is associated with the schools of phenomenalism, notably Edmund HUSSERL, and, contrarily, epitomises his time and context by advocating first of all a kind of HEGELIAN 'March of Philosophy' or knowledge, followed by a LOGICAL POSITIVIST turn in the early years of the twentieth century, in which he decides that all discussion of 'non-things' should and can be replaced with a discussion of 'things'. For example, since sounds and smells are not considered to exist, as such, in the world out there, but nor yet are considered 'mental phenomena', they should be replaced by 'immanent objectivity'. (Whatever that is. Is it a 'thing'?)

## BUDDHISM

### Essentials of Buddhism

Buddhism is a blend of philosophy, religious belief and educational principles that focuses on personal spiritual development. Although the distinction may be somewhat blurred, strictly speaking, Buddhists do not worship gods or deities, and the Golden Buddhas people pray to are supposed to be merely aids to understanding and contemplation. Because it is not a religion in the conventional sense, people are encouraged to question its teachings and to seek insight for themselves.

It is an education, one leading to insight into the true nature of life. The aim of Buddhist practices is to become free of suffering and to develop the qualities of awareness, kindness and wisdom. Originating in India, Buddhism gradually spread throughout Asia to Central Asia, Tibet, Sri Lanka, Southeast Asia, as well as the East Asian countries of China, Mongolia, Korea and Japan. The experience developed within the Buddhist tradition over thousands of years has created a great resource for all those who wish to follow a path – a path which promises ultimately to culminate in enlightenment, or Buddhahood.

There are around 350 million Buddhists and a growing number of them are Westerners. They follow many different forms of Buddhism, but all traditions are characterised by non-violence, lack of dogma, tolerance of differences and, usually, by the practice of meditation.

## Buddhism as education

In 1923, a well-known Buddhist scholar, Mr Jing-Wu Ou-Yang, gave a speech at Nanjing Normal University in China, entitled 'Buddhism is Neither a Religion, Nor a Philosophy, but the Essential for Our Modern Time'. It marked a turning point in the history of Buddhism. The much-documented speech offered a clear definition and analysis of Buddhism. Shortly afterwards, one of the greatest contemporary Buddhist scholars, Master Ching Kung, offered an interpretation of Buddhism as an education, not as a religion. He points out that we do not worship the Buddha, rather we respect him as a teacher, in the same way that the Chinese respect CONFUCIUS.

But what to some seemed a 'new-look' Buddhism, was also a return to an earlier kind of Buddhism. Buddhism is not a religion, because the Buddha is not a 'supernatural being or power'. The Buddha is a human being who has reached 'complete understanding' of the reality of life and the universe. And everyone, indeed every 'thinking thing', in this sense, can become a Buddha. The *sutras*, or epigrammatic teachings of the Buddha, tell us that 'all sentient beings can attain Buddhahood' as potentially, 'every being possesses the wisdom and virtuous character of the Buddha'. In other words, all beings are Buddhas by nature. However, as a result of our discriminations, our ever-wandering thoughts and emotional attachments, which are the root cause of all sufferings and disasters, we lose our original Buddha nature. Only once we completely free ourselves from this, abandon our fixations to certain ideas or objects, can we regain our lost Buddhahood, our original perfect enlightened state, our 'Buddha nature'.

The second difference between Buddhism and religion is that the 'belief', in the Buddha's teachings must not be 'blind belief', let alone 'blind faith'. Buddha asks his followers to test the teachings and prove them to themselves. The Buddha wants people to know, not merely to believe – to taste the truth for themselves.

Third, the 'rites and celebrations' in Buddhism are not centred on a supernatural being, but rather the people attending the assemblies. The ceremonies and celebrations in Buddhism serve an educational purpose, as a reminder of the Buddha's teachings and encouragement to all students who practise it.

Finally, advocates of Buddhism as education stress that the 'devotion' used in Buddhism is not one based on emotion, but rather one based on reason. Further evidence comes from examining the Chinese Way-preaching places where activities were (and are) held. The lessons included listening to lectures and discussions along with Buddha name-chanting or sitting meditation. Study and cultivation were used hand in hand to strive for the right and proper understanding and practice, to purify practitioner's minds and to eventually attain the state of enlightenment. These places continue to be educational institutions combining Buddhist teachings and art, a tradition stretching back almost 3000 years.

Yet if Buddhism is essentially education, this form is rarely seen today. Although originally it was not a religion, Buddhism has become one in the past few hundred years. It is difficult to deny this because the external form of Buddhism today is indeed that of a religion. It is no longer the education found in a traditional Way-preaching place, where cultivators had up to 16 hours a day for both lessons and cultivation. Since the monks and nuns spent 16 hours a day on study and cultivation, there was supposed to be little

## THE GREAT PERFECTION OF MAHAYANA BUDDHISM

The sequence of practice in Mahayana Buddhism is represented in China by the four Great Bodhisattvas: *Di Zang* (Earth Treasure) of Jiuhua Mountain; *Guan Yin* (Great Compassion) of Putuo Mountain; *Wen Shu Shi Li* (Manjushri) of Wutai Mountain; and *Pu Xian* (Universal Worthy) of Emei Mountain.

Earth Treasure means stored treasure of the great mother earth, which represents our mind. Without the earth, nothing could survive. So, the Buddha used the earth as a metaphor for our mind, which is the Great Perfection. It encompasses infinite compassion, wisdom, intuitive wisdom, auspiciousness, good fortune, merit and virtue. Therefore, all that the Buddha told us in the *sutras* is infinite, is the Great Perfection. Understanding this will enable us to find the boundless meanings within.

The Earth Treasure Sutra explains that we begin our learning and practice by being filial to our parents and respectful to our teachers and elders. Buddhism is an education of honouring teachers and revering their teachings, which is based on the foundation of filial piety. How can we expect a person who is not filial to his or her parents to respect his or her teachers? A teacher, regardless of learning and capabilities, cannot impart knowledge to a student who lacks respect and does not listen.

Therefore, only when we honour teachers and revere their teachings can we truly succeed in our learning of Buddhism. The Original Vow of Earth Treasure Bodhisattva *sutra* is the *sutra* of the filial piety, which is the very heart of the Great Perfection. All other perfections arise from it. From here, we extend this loving and caring for parents to respecting teachers and elders.

We keep expanding from here until we respect and care for all sentient beings without discrimination or attachment. This is the enhancement and extension of Earth Treasure Bodhisattva and is the teaching of Guan Yin Bodhisattva. Therefore, without filial piety, there would be no great compassion. In being filial to parents and showing compassion for all other beings, we should not use emotions. Rather, we need to base this compassion on rationale and wisdom. Only in this way can we attain positive results.

Next is the third Bodhisattva, Manjushri, who symbolises wisdom, and Universal Worthy Bodhisattva who symbolises the practice of filial piety, respect, compassion and wisdom in our daily lives. If we practise these principles when interacting with others, matters and objects, then we ourselves are Universal Worthy Bodhisattva.

The teachings of Universal Worthy Bodhisattva are perfect. As the Flower Adornment *sutra* tells us, we cannot attain Buddhahood if we do not follow this teaching, as this Bodhisattva is perfect in every thought, every vow and every deed. Without true wisdom, the great vow of Universal Worthy Bodhisattva cannot be fulfilled.

These four great Bodhisattvas exemplify this understanding and represent the perfection of Mahayana Buddhism. Therefore, from Earth Treasure Bodhisattva, we learn filial piety and respect, from Guan Yin Bodhisattva, we learn great compassion, from Manjushri Bodhisattva we learn great wisdom and from Universal Worthy Bodhisattva we learn the great vows and conduct.

time for discriminating or wandering thoughts, and so progress towards enlightenment could be attained relatively quickly. Nowadays though, as Venerable Master Jing Kung comments, this traditional form of Buddhism is seldom seen in Way-preaching places, which have become instead places to make offerings, to pray for blessings and to conduct memorial services. It is little wonder that people today regard Buddhism as a religion. Even so, it is perhaps a more appropriate religion for a modern world. After all, Albert Einstein considered Buddhism to have:

...the characteristics of what would be expected in a cosmic religion for the future: it transcends a personal God, avoids dogmas and theology; it covers both the natural and spiritual, and it is based on a religious sense aspiring from the experience of all things, natural and spiritual, as a meaningful unity.

Contributor: Yuli Liu

Siddhartha Gautama was a prince, born some 2500 years ago, in a small Indian kingdom in what is today southern Nepal. He renounced his royal heritage in order to escape the human cycle of birth, death and rebirth that he saw as inevitably leading to suffering, loss and pain. After six years of searching and putting his body through a variety of extreme practices, he finally gained enlightenment in his thirties. Motivated by a sense of profound compassion for suffering beings, Buddha shared his wisdom with them, and so embarked on a teaching career that would last for nearly 50 years. He travelled around India, teaching all who wished to listen, responding to the needs and mindsets of his listeners and skilfully adapting his teachings for each. Of his 79 years, he dedicated 49 to teaching.

SEE ALSO

Gautama

## BURKE, EDMUND (1729–97)

Irishman Edmund Burke was a British Member of Parliament who wrote a number of celebrated pamphlets on issues such as 'Conciliation with America' (written in 1775, the year before American Independence), the 'Causes of Present Discontents' and in 1790 some 'Reflections on the Revolution in France' – which he was (predictably) against. This last is quite a key text for political conservatives, setting out the merits of attitudes such as respect for traditions and suspicion of excessive theorising, with praise for institutions such as the monarchy and the Church, all of which, he writes, are the ingredients of a stable and prosperous society. (His feeling is that societies are not held together by calculations of self-interest but by an instinctive sense of shared bonds and community.) However, it is his *Philosophical Enquiry into the Origin of our Ideas of the Sublime and Beautiful* (1757) that has been of longer-lasting interest, suggesting that the former of these 'fundamental responses' is due to terror at the prospect of death, while the latter is a response caused by love of society.

## BUSINESS ETHICS

Business ethics is big business, and that justifies its inclusion here, at least on the sort of thinking often attributed to Adam SMITH. On one defi-

nition, if we might borrow some jargon from economics, *micro*-business ethics looks at the correct (the 'just') management and organisation of commercial enterprises: working practices, recruitment issues, management 'styles', financial accounting, and so on, as well as the effects of these enterprises' individual decisions on suppliers and the environment.

For managers and bosses, these additional 'ethical rules' for employees can be a powerful control tool, unlike ordinary rules and procedures for running a business, because the rules are 'grey' (that is, they are 'debatable', affected by context and detail). Employees may not be quite sure *what* they are supposed to do, and their autonomy and confidence as individual judges of their actions may actually be undermined. Sanctions and punishments may then follow supposed 'breaches' of the ethics guidelines.

The contemporary Australian ethicist, Trevor Jordan, says that there is too much of an emphasis on rules in business and professional ethics, too much talk of setting up 'ethics regimes' and giving ethics codes 'teeth'. Instead, he says, what we need more of are people who will do the right thing even without a rule book or manual.

Alternatively, although there is now a large and high-profile corporate world of 'ethics' specialists, and many governments have made the existence of such codes mandatory, many people see ethics codes as arbitrary, an imposition and perhaps also a waste of time. When the USA's third largest corporation, Enron, imploded, amid much shredding of internal memos, a culture of systematic deceit and fraud was found to have co-existed quite happily with some of the most sanctimonious and puritanical moralising.

Then, what might be termed *macro*-business ethics needs to consider notions of free will and of rationality as well as the dictates of HUMAN RIGHTS, as perhaps contrasted with that form of UTILITARIAN thinking known as PARETO OPTIMALITY – which is the attempt to arrange the world so that as many people as possible are 'satisfied'. Something is 'pareto-optimal' when no one can become better off without someone else becoming worse off.

## BUTLER, JOSEPH (1692–1752)

Joseph Butler is perhaps better known in philosophical circles as the Bishop of Durham, whose *Fifteen Sermons* of 1726 is praised by the contemporary UK philosopher, Timothy Sprigge, as 'the finest ethical work in English'. Joseph Butler argues that CONSCIENCE instructs us how to regulate our 'self-love' to satisfy our other impulses too, such as benevolence. Whatever his adherents' view of the theory, this looks very much like PLATO's old one writ large.

## BUTLER, SAMUEL (1835–1902)

Samuel Butler, a much more interesting character than his namesake Joseph BUTLER, being a satirist and vehement anti-Christian, is remembered as the author of *Erewhon* (which is 'nowhere' scrambled, and how's that for satire?). Here, he describes machines capable of evolving on their own, threatening their human masters, and a parallel currency to the normal Erewhon banknotes for shopping, and so on, which is solely issued in grand fashion in the most impressive buildings – and can buy nothing. (This all intended as a slightly amusing joust at Christianity.)

Stranger than fiction, Samuel also produced anonymously a sarcastic defence of the doctrine of resurrection in *The Fair Haven* (1873), which was so convincing that churchmen quoted it approvingly in sermons delivered from pulpits – until his authorship was exposed.

## CALCULUS

There are several types of calculus (including Hergé's excellent 'Professor'), but in philosophy the main ones are 'PREDICATE' CALCULUS and 'propositional' or 'sententional' calculus. Predicate calculus is used in LOGIC to formalise the relationships between its subject matter (its 'predicates'), although its most distinctive characteristic is probably the way it defines 'quantifiers'. Propositional calculus deals with the key operations introduced to logic, in earnest, by Boole and FREGE, of *not, and, or, if then* and *if and only if.* Predicate calculus deals with interesting statements like 'Some cats are black' and 'Some black animals eat mice at night', while propositional calculus works with, and also produces, statements like 'My cat X is not black if and only if X is a tabby cat.'

## CALVIN, JOHN (1509–64)

Calvin was the most autocratic of the Protestant reformers, yet had a democratising influence on the Christian tradition in that he made God (and God's grace, too) directly available to all believers, in that the scriptures, not Church officials, had authority in holy matters. He gave government and Church different areas of responsibility and allowed the development of the 'Protestant work ethic' by suggesting that hard work and production is a better service to God than monkish asceticism. The power of capital itself was released from the biblical prohibitions against moneylending by Calvin's radical discounting of scriptural guidance that, he said, related to circumstances which quite simply no longer existed.

Under his guidance, Geneva became a highly organised Protestant theocracy and the reformer was given absolute supremacy for life in 1555. Calvin considered everything to be 'predestined', but allowed scope during one's life for decisions all the same, since, after all, we are ignorant of our 'destination'.

## CAMUS, ALBERT (1913–60)

The French-Algerian philosopher and (rather better) novelist, Albert Camus wrote about the struggle of people in increasingly secular times to find meaning, to 'live and create without the aid of eternal values'. Among his writings are *The Plague* (1947) and *The Rebel* (1951). Like his friend, Jean-Paul SARTRE, he rehearsed in his writing his own feelings of guilt, failure and tragedy, including his and France's shame during the occupation by the Nazis in the Second World War. Camus' notion of 'the Absurd' is summed up in the tale of Sisyphus, the Greek mythological hero who has to push a rock up a hill everyday only to have it roll back down again later. Sisyphus, Camus says, is happy, once he accepts his fate and begins to scorn the gods.

## CANTOR, GEORG (1845–1918)

Georg Cantor developed mathematical 'set theory', with the observation that two SETS have the same number of members if they can be paired off one by one, like the animals in Noah's Ark. This leads on to a discussion of the nature of INFINITY, and Cantor realised that there are two kinds of infinity, not just one, as we conventionally think. There are 'countable' infinities (1, 2, 3, 4, . . .) and 'uncountable ones', such as the number of points on a line segment or what mathematicians call 'real numbers', such as those lying between 1 and 2, or 2 and 3 for that matter. These uncountable sets could be said to be bigger than the countable ones, although they are both infinite, just because. But there are some rather strange counter-intuitive properties of uncountable collections. For example, if you have two lines, one twice as long as the other – they still contain the same number of points. Which brings us back to the set theory.

Cantor's line-point diagram: every line has an equal number of points on it

## CAPITALISM

Capitalism is the economic system based on the production of goods, ultimately for consumption, by means of 'capital', that is, money capable of hiring people and buying land and machines. The term is used pejoratively by MARX and ENGELS, who predict that capitalism must finally dramatically implode, due to its 'fundamental contradictions'. It will then be replaced by COMMUNISM.

Certainly, even bourgeois economists do accept that capitalism has its 'cycles', with recurrent troughs and adjustments – in bad cases, economic depressions. But, on the crucial, factual claim of increasing absolute poverty, MARXISM seems simply to have been wrong. Marx and Engels did not perceive the almost inexhaustible ingenuity of the capitalist system in increasing production through technical progress, and generating within itself apparently unlimited financial resources, making possible high standards of living not only for the tiny minority of mill owners, and the ever-expanding ranks of the petty bourgeois, but for increasing numbers of the workers too.

Then again, perhaps, as suggested for exam-ple by the contemporary sociologist and former Marxist, André Gorz, the truly oppressed class of modern capitalism is not that of the workers any more – but of the 'unworkers' – the old, the unemployed and the very young (such as the street children of South America), who cannot work and must rely on state handouts or charity (or crime) for their sustenance. Even at the time that Marx and Engels were writing, this view was being expressed in Russia by Mikhail Bakunin (1814–76), who foresaw an uprising of the 'uncivilised', driven by their instinctive desire for equality. Bakunin predicted, in contrast to Marx, that the revolutionary instinct would be enfee-bled by 'civilisation', and that violence was part of a primitive urge.

The mechanisms of capitalism had been well described and explored earlier by the eigh-teenth-century philosopher Adam SMITH, in his incredibly popular book, *The Wealth of Nations*. For Smith, though, capitalism promotes the general good, and thus is not only the best possible system, but produces the best possible world, a view comfortably reflected today by Western politicians.

## CARNAP, RUDOLF (1891–1970)

Carnap was a student of FREGE's, the logician preoccupied with issues of 'sense and reference', and an influential member of the so-called VIENNA CIRCLE in the 1930s. His particular theme was that philosophical disagreements were really produced by differences between 'linguistic frameworks'. His approach is some-times called 'logical empiricism', and his ideas appeared as *Der logische Aufbau der Welt* (*The Logical Structure of the World*, 1928).

Questions in mathematics and LOGIC could be rationally discussed and objectively true answers obtained, but outside these areas only the methods of scientific observation were use-ful. However, he recognised that even logic and mathematics are based on assumptions which cannot be justified by anything more rigorous than a judgement of practicality or expediency, and that science, too, has its assumptions. In *The Logical Syntax of Language* (1934) he explains that 'It is not our business to set up prohibitions, but to arrive at conventions.'

## CARROLL, LEWIS (1832–98)

Lewis Carroll, the celebrated author of the Alice books (*Alice's Adventures in Wonderland*, 1865 and *Alice Through the Looking Glass*, 1871), was actually the Reverend Charles Lurwidge Dodgson, a mathematics don at Oxford. It is kept beautifully discreet, but his writings are full of mathematical and philosophical puzzles and observations. For example, when Alice 'falls down the rabbit hole', Dodgson is referring to a philosophical and mathematical debate over acceleration through a hole through the centre of the Earth, while his 'lobster argument', which runs: 'ALL red boiled lobsters are dead, AND all dead red lobsters are boiled, SO all boiled dead lobsters are red', is mimicking the LOGICIANS, an activity which is source indeed for many of the amusing elements in *Wonderland*. (The thing about the lobster argument is that it does not tell you anything, particularly as it is not even, in logicians' terms, deductively valid, which is his point. Try drawing a Venn diagram to see which bits belong where, if you are not convinced.)

Even a celebrated article for the staid British philosophy journal *Mind* in 1895, 'What the Tortoise said to Alice', is written in a light and entertaining style, while containing several 'deep' philosophical arguments.

## Further reading

Gardner, M. (1960) *The Annotated Alice*

## CARTESIANISM

See Descartes.

## CATEGORY MISTAKE

The 'error' of applying assumptions appropriate to one kind of thing, to something of a quite different 'category'. For example, saying that the colour blue is 'noisy' or 'heavy'. The term is associated with Gilbert RYLE, who thought that we made mistakes in applying certain words to activities of a purely mental nature. We might note, for example, the tendency nowadays to describe the mind in terms of a computer, but of course the real 'category mistake' may be in assuming that language has such tidy boundaries, when in fact it is much more metaphorical: a point which can be seen when reflecting (a term from optics) on our example of the 'noisy' or 'heavy' colour – the terms certainly seem to be meaningful.

## CAUSATION

### Essentials of causation

When DEMOCRITUS (460–370 BCE) said that he would rather discover one true cause than

gain the kingdom of Persia, he signalled both the difficulty and the value of gaining causal knowledge. It is arguably the acquisition of causal knowledge that is the primary goal of scientific enquiry; and within philosophy, causation has played a central role in recent theories of reference, PERCEPTION, decision-making, knowledge, intentional and other mental states, and the role of theoretical terms in scientific theories. Indeed, Samuel Alexander (1859–1938) suggested that causation was of the essence of existence itself, with his dictum that to be real is to have causal powers. Moreover, assumptions about the nature of causation structure a great deal of discussion elsewhere in philosophy. For example, debates over free will often take as their starting point the question of how we can be free if our INTENTIONS to act are themselves part of the causal order. Again, debates in the METAPHYSICS of mind often revolve around the claim that since every physical event has a physical cause, the mind must itself be in some sense physical in order to be the causal source of our actions qua physical events.

### Fundamentalism, reductionism and projectivism

What then is causation? The framework for contemporary philosophy of causation originates with David HUME (1711–76). Hume's empiricism dictated that all evidence for cause and effect relations must be ultimately reducible to evidence from the senses. Since causal relations cannot themselves be directly experienced, however, they must be constructions from some other kind of experience. Hume's proposal was that the concept of causation was a construction from the experience of the regular succession of spatio-temporally contiguous events. Similarly, the seeming necessity by which we think causes are connected to their effects is simply a product of the habits of expectation produced in us by the regular succession of events in the world. By taking this account of causation as our starting point, we can see a number of respects in which theories of causation may differ, and thereby isolate issues that continue to be debated today.

First, for Hume, causation was not part of the fundamental furniture of the world; rather, it was a concept we possess in order to organise our experience of a world which is not itself causal. There are in fact at least three views which might be taken on this first issue, what we might call the metaphysical status of causation:

■ *Fundamentalism.* Causation is a fundamental feature of the world.
■ *Reductionism.* Causation can be reduced to or identified with some (more) fundamental feature(s) of the world.
■ *Projectivism.* Causation is a projection on to the world.

Hume's view was closest to the third, so it is ironic that 'Humeanism' about causation is today generally used to refer to views of the second type.

Second, for Hume, any particular pair of (token) events was judged to be causally related only in virtue of being an instance of a general regularity among respective event types. The relationship between token and type causation (alternatively, singular and general causation) also permits a range of views: that token causation is primary; that type causation is primary; or that they are distinct kinds of causation, to be treated individually.

Third, for Hume, causation was a concept that related events. While this view remains popular, other proposals for the 'causal relatation' are facts, property instances (tropes), states of affairs – and also that causation is a relation that is independent of such metaphysical disputes.

Finally, for Hume, the difference between cause and effect consisted simply in identifying the cause with the temporally prior event of any constantly conjoined event pair. However, stipulating by convention that the asymmetry of causation is coincident with temporal order has several undesirable consequences: the fact that causes can be used to manipulate their effects does not seem to be merely a convention; it seems at least conceptually possible that there might be cases of backwards in time causation; and it rules out the project of giving an account of the direction of time in terms of the direction of causation (see TIME).

Most contemporary discussion of causation has been concerned with the metaphysical status of causation, and in particular the viability of various REDUCTIONIST analyses. The motivation for seeking such an analysis is no longer the constraint of an empiricist view of knowledge, but rather that since causal concepts do not appear in fundamental physical theories, the question is raised of the relation between our everyday causal concepts and the world as described by those theories. Reductionist theories include regularity theories, which start from the Humean idea that

causes arc regularly followed by their effects; and probabilistic theories, which start from the idea that causes raise the PROBABILITY of (but are not necessarily invariably followed by) their effects. COUNTERFACTUAL theories, originally proposed by David Lewis (1941–2001), start from the idea that, in general, if A causes B then it is true that if A had not occurred, B would not have occurred. Causal process theories have attempted to identify causation with various features of spatio-temporally continuous physical processes, such as the conservation of physical quantities, but have had problems accommodating intuitions about everyday cases of causation that seem independent of such features.

'Manipulationist' and 'agency' theories have started with the idea that causes can be used to manipulate their effects, and attempted to characterise causation in terms of facts about actual and hypothetical manipulations. These theories connect naturally with the Humean idea that consideration of how we acquire causal knowledge should play an important role in an account of causation, and it is an open question whether they can be developed in a reductionist way, or whether they lead to a form of projectivism.

A theory of causation should capture our intuitions about everyday cases of causation, explain how we come by this causal knowledge, why it is that causes tend to precede their effects and can be used to manipulate their effects, and show why causes can be used to explain their effects. It remains to be seen whether there is an account of causation that can satisfy all these criteria, and so it is an open question whether causation will turn out to be part of the fundamental furniture of the universe, or, as Hume thought, to be tied to our particular way of experiencing and interacting with the world.

Contributor: Brad Weslake

## CAVE, ANALOGY OF

In the seventh book of the *Republic*, PLATO uses the example of prisoners chained with their backs to a fire in a cave to illustrate his point about knowledge. The shadows thrown by the fire on the wall are interpreted by the prisoners as 'real' monsters, and the truth can only be ascertained by breaking their shackles and leaving the cave.

## CÉSAIRE, AIMÉE

See African philosophy.

## CETERIS PARIBUS

'Other things being equal', from the Latin. All scientific 'laws' are said to have a *ceteris paribus* clause implied.

## CHANCE

See Probability.

## CHAOS THEORY

According to chaos theory, the moving of a butterfly's wing in suburban Surrey can cause a tidal wave to engulf the unfortunate people of Polynesia, in the manner of one tiny thing leads to another, which leads to another, the whole connected certainly, but unpredictably. The unpredictability is not due to lack of knowledge, but is due to the inherent nature of 'non-linear' systems. 'Non-linear' is the mathematical way of describing a graph connecting two variables which cannot be connected by drawing a line. That is, the points, when plotted, produce a splattering of 'data points' with the location of each subsequent point seemingly random. For example, even the population of goldfish plotted against food in a pond is a non-linear system, in that if the amount of food in the pond goes up, so does the amount of fish – but only sometimes. At unpredictable points, the increasing of the amount of food results in an excess of fish which depletes oxygen levels in the water, so many fish perish. The example serves to illustrate that non-linearity has less to do with 'sensitive initial conditions' as some commentators put it, than to do with 'feedback'.

The implications of chaos theory are profound and very little accepted or understood. For example, despite the inherent impossibility of linking two variables such as '$CO_2$ levels' and 'global temperature', the two are now regularly treated as having a straightforward 'linear' relationship, with other factors and feedback effects (such as changes in ocean currents, in precipitation, in cloud cover, in vegetation cover) ignored. Several contemporary philosophers, such as Simon Blackburn, have attempted to rebut 'linear thinking' in climate change, but the political impetus to discount such complexities has been enough to stifle debate.

### Further reading

Gleick, J. (1987) *Chaos*

## CHARISMA

See Weber.

## CHINESE PHILOSOPHY

See Buddhism, Confucius, Chuang Tzu, Lao Tzu, Mencius, Taoism (but not the 'Chinese Room', below).

## THE 'CHINESE ROOM'

The 'Chinese Room' THOUGHT EXPERIMENT attempts to demonstrate that computers cannot be said to be intelligent, just because they may appear to be so. This was in a response to a challenge made by the celebrated Second World War code breaker, Alan Turing, who had suggested that when we are unable to tell the difference, after prolonged questioning, between talking to a machine or to a human being, we ought to consider the machine to have INTELLIGENCE.

This offended many philosophers. After all, intelligence is something hard acquired and jealously guarded. And it was in the celebrated 'Chinese Room' that they found their champion. It was there that the (contemporary) artificially intelligent philosopher, John Searle, sought to debunk such a generous interpretation.

Searle offers to be locked up in the imaginary room with a pile of Chinese hieroglyphs. He then asks us to consider what would appear to happen if, from time to time, someone outside the room were to post Chinese questions through the letter box for him to sort out. Now, as it happens, inside the room there are some instructions taped on the wall, written in English, which explain precisely which hieroglyph to post back, no matter which one is posted in. Searle's aim is to prove that such a person in such a room does not understand Chinese. Since computers operate in an analogous way, he then goes on to say that it is not really accurate to say they are intelligent or understand things, even if they produce intelligent-looking responses.

The experiment is fairly convincing at showing that the person in the room does not understand Chinese. After all, at the beginning of his example, he states that they 'know no Chinese, either written or spoken', and that for them, 'Chinese writing is just so many meaningless squiggles'. His conclusion may seem a bit like stating the obvious, but, well, analytic philosophers do that sort of stuff. The trick is to make the obvious seem not so obvious. Nonetheless, the philosophical problem is, as Searle puts it, that 'from the external point of view – that is, from the point of view of somebody outside the room in which I am locked, – my answers to the questions are absolutely indistinguishable from those of native Chinese speakers'.

But what Professor Searle *seems* to have missed is that it is not so much that the person in the room appears to understand Chinese, but that the whole 'system' – person in the room, sets of symbols on cards, plus instructions taped to the wall – gives the appearance of understanding Chinese. And this is much more plausible. After all, whoever wrote the instructions *did* understand Chinese.

What has happened in his example is that the expertise of the instructions' author has been transferred, via the written rules, to the person in the room.

Broadening the issue of whether computers really think, Lisa Wang of Qingdao University says the question, in any case, is not whether the machine demonstrates intelligence, but whether 'this human construct' demonstrates intelligence. Professor Wang notes that a picture, after all, may be said to be 'of a tree', or 'beautiful', or whatever, even if it is basically just bits of mineral squashed on to a piece of vegetable, a point made also by LEIBNIZ in the *Monadology* (1714), with his description of the mind as a kind of mill:

> Suppose that there were a machine so constructed as to produce thought, feeling, and perception. We could imagine it increased in size while retaining the same proportions, so that one could enter as one might a mill. On going inside we should only see the parts impinging upon one another, we should not see anything which would explain a perception. . .

SEE ALSO

Thought experiments

# CHOMSKY, NOAM

See Linguistics.

# CHRYSIPPUS OF SOLI (*C.* 280–207 BCE)

The third Head of the Stoa and perhaps the most important figure for early STOICISM. A prolific author (of some 705 books), almost all of whose works are lost. There have been some finds among the papyri uncovered at Herculaneum and there are extended quotations on psychology in Galen's *On the Doctrines of Hippocrates and Plato*. However, Chrysippus' greatest legacy is probably in LOGIC, and he is sometimes praised as the most important ancient logician after ARISTOTLE. In contrast to Aristotle's categorical SYLLOGISMS (e.g. all As are Bs; all Bs are Cs; so all As are Cs), Chrysippus developed a system of Stoic hypothetical syllogisms (e.g. if P then Q; P; so Q) that is generally considered the precursor to present-day propositional logic.

# CHUANG TZU (369–286 BCE)

One of the great sages of CHINESE PHILOSOPHY, Chuang Chou stressed the unity of all things and dynamic interplay of opposites. 'Good' and 'bad', he pointed out, are like everything else, interrelated and interchangeable. What is 'good' for the rabbit is 'bad' indeed for the farmer (to offer a rather limp example of our own). In contrast, the book, the Chuang Tzu, of which about a quarter is considered to be directly attributable to 'Master Chuang', is lively and playful, a mixture of stories and poetry as well as philosophical arguments, and has remained highly popular. His influence throughout the East, from BUDDHISM (which draws on his teaching that suffering is mainly a result of refusing to accept 'what is') to Zen philosophy (which reflects his love of PARA-DOXES or 'koans'), has been profound, while his message of nonconformity and freedom unshackled the Chinese mind from some of the effects of over-rigid CONFUCIANISM.

For example, here is how he attempts to show the relativity of moral judgements: If, as some sages said, killing was wrong, was it wrong to kill a hare when it was the only way to save yourself from starving? Surely not. Perhaps then it was always wrong to kill another human being? But what if that human being is a robber intent on killing and robbing a family? Surely it is then not wrong to kill him, if that is the only way to stop him?

All moral knowledge depends in this way on context and situations – it is relative. Chuang goes on to prove that in fact all knowledge – not just moral or AESTHETIC judgements – is equally rooted in context, and equally 'relative'. He puts it in this perfectly inscrutable way:

> Once I, Chuang Chou, dreamed I was a butterfly and was happy as a butterfly. I was conscious that I was quite pleased with myself, but I did not know that I was Chou. Suddenly I awoke, and there I was, visibly Chou. I do not know whether it was Chou dreaming he was a butterfly, or the butterfly dreaming it was Chou.

His conclusion was that we should strive to transcend the world of distinctions.

## CICERO, MARCUS TULLIUS (106–43 BCE)

Roman statesman, orator and important philosophical author, who knew and studied with some of the leading philosophers of his day. His philosophical works, the majority of which were written in just a single year (45–44 BCE) capture the doctrines and debates of HELLENISTIC PHILOSOPHY. These works are especially important, as they introduced Greek philosophy to the Latin-speaking world, and in the process Cicero laid the foundations for the Latin philosophical vocabulary in which philosophy was discussed in the West for the next 1700 years.

His principal philosophical works are: *De Finibus* (*On Ends*, on ethical theory); *De Officiis* (*On Duties*, on correct behaviour); *De Natura Deorum* (*On the Nature of the Gods*, on natural philosophy); *Academica* (*Academics*, on EPISTEM-OLOGY); *Tusculanae Disputationes* (*Tusculan Disputations*, on ETHICS); *Res Publica* (*Republic*, on politics – only fragments remain); *De Legibus* (*On Laws*, on politics); *De Divinatione* (*On Divination*).

Cicero frequently attacks the EPICUREANS and instead follows academic SCEPTICISM in epistemology, and is highly sympathetic to the ethics of STOICISM. His works remained in circulation during the Middle Ages and became especially influential in the Renaissance. While he remained an important source for ancient philosophy up to the eighteenth century, his reputation declined in the nineteenth century as scholars began to favour PLATO and ARISTOTLE over the Hellenistic schools.

## CIRCULARITY

See Fallacies.

## CIVIL DISOBEDIENCE

See Direct action.

## CLASS STRUGGLE

See Marx.

## CLASS, LOGICAL

See Logic.

## COGITO

The cogito, that is '*cogito ergo sum*', is the much misunderstood claim on which DESCARTES is supposed to have built his 'modern' philosophy of knowledge. Usually translated as 'I think, therefore I am', or sometimes, more inelegantly, as 'I am thinking, therefore I exist', it is more appropriately translated as 'where there is thinking there is a thinker', which was Saint AUGUSTINE's phrase, and Descartes was a student of Augustinian monks.

SEE ALSO

Descartes

## COGNITIVE SCIENCE

'Cogsci' emerged in the 1970s, along with the first computer labs for students, but actually encompasses much more than 'the thinking machines'. It is concerned with social, psychological and linguistic questions as well as some of the biological and chemical and physical scientific aspects of 'consciousness'. Nonetheless, the assumption underlying it is that the human mind works along the same principles as computers, being, as Stephen Pinker and John Searle put it, 'an information processing machine'.

SEE ALSO

The 'Chinese Room'

## COLOURS

Poor old colours – always 'SUBJECTIVE', always having secondary status in philosophical knowledge, trailing behind things like 'shape' or 'extension' and 'size' – even weight (which surely is very subjective. . .).

Sometimes, discussion has compared perception of colour with perception of 'pain' or indeed pleasure, and taste or smell. One way of resolving the issue of the proper status of colours for some philosophers has been to deny that colours really exist at all. Things appear to have colours, but this is misleading. Another idea is that things appear to have colours but only in relation to a perceiver. Snow is white only when someone is there to see it as white. Finally, there is the reassuring view that things really are coloured, in that they have certain 'physical properties' which we sense in the same way we sense weight, and so on.

The exact status and nature of colour perhaps help explain how David HUME got himself into such a tangle with his THOUGHT EXPERIMENT on the colour blue: the so-called 'Blue Shades'. 'Suppose some one has seen many colours', says Hume, 'but never one particular shade of blue.' Then,

> . . . let all the different shades of that colour, except that single one, be placed before him, descending gradually from the deepest to the lightest, and tis plain that he will perceive a blank, where the shade is wanting and will be sensible that there is a greater distance in that place betwixt the contiguous colours, than in any other.

And now is it not possible that they might 'raise up' to themselves, the idea of that particular shade, even 'though it had never been conveyed to them by their senses'?

The experiment appears to destroy the theory that 'simple ideas', like 'blue', are necessarily 'obtained from experience', which was indeed Hume's own view. Faced with this unpalatable possibility, Hume instead dismisses his own thought experiment as altogether too 'particular and singular' to be worth abandoning such an excellent general theory for.

## COMMON SENSE

PLATO had great contempt for the followers of 'common sense', although ARISTOTLE considered it the essential starting point. Later, David HUME and Thomas Reid used 'common sense' to guide their enquiries, while HEGEL elaborately spurned it. No one has yet defined exactly what we mean by 'common sense', but it seems to come down to consistency. It is all very well producing a philosophical theory, such as that nothing in the world really exists, for an essay, but if it does not connect to how we actually operate in the world, then there is what some would call an element of 'bad faith' in the assertions. So Reid used 'common sense' to criticise 'metaphysical' assertions and to praise instead the guidance afforded by common sense to conscience.

DESCARTES opens his *Discourse* with the observation that good sense is the most widely distributed thing in the world, which looks like a nice rallying cry for common sense, until you realise that he was copying the comment of MONTAIGNE, who continued humorously, that this is clear, since no one is dissatisfied with their own share of it.

## COMMUNISM

Communism is a timeless theory, which can be seen for example in the idealised life of the people in PLATO's *Republic*. In fact, there are many parallels between Plato's vision and both communist Russia and China, with the caste of Philosopher Guardians having a similar role – and authority – to the Communist Party apparatus. In the Republic, everything is held in common, even children, and each works for the weal (benefit) of all. Politically, though, communism only becomes a potent force through the writings of MARX and ENGELS, who describe in *The Communist Manifesto* how CAPITALISM fails, and how communism can be achieved.

The *Manifesto* explains that industrial society requires constant change, as opposed to the apparent tranquility of the feudal and other epochs. 'Constant revolutionising of production, uninterrupted disturbance of social conditions, everlasting uncertainty and agitation distinguish the bourgeois epoch. . .' it concludes, in one of its prolonged and rather tiring bouts of ironic, oxymoronic language.

Similarly, bourgeois society relies on a constantly expanding market, a claim borrowed from Adam **SMITH**'s earlier analysis of the creation of wealth. The industries demand raw materials from more and more obscure and remote sources, and must persuade consumers of new and exotic needs, thus creating a world market. The same applies in the intellectual sphere, with the rise of a 'world literature'. Legal systems, governments and methods of taxation must transcend any frontier. The 'most barbarian' nations are dragged into the impossible equation, with the cheap prices of commodities the 'heavy artillery' with which the bourgeoisie force the barbarians to capitulate. All nations, on pain of extinction, are compelled to adopt the capitalist mode of production.

> Modern bourgeois society, with its relations of production, of exchange, and of property, a society that has conjured up such gigantic means of production and of exchange, is like the sorcerer who is no longer able to control the powers of the nether world whom he has called up by his spells.

The insatiable forces of production even begin to threaten their bourgeois midwives, and, through continual crises, the whole of bourgeois society. But it is not only these forces that undermine the system. By creating the proletariat, the bourgeoisie have already 'forged the weapons that bring death to itself'.

At first, the counter-struggle is carried out by a few individuals (polite coughs from Marx and Engels), with the labourers still 'an incoherent mass'. But with the growth of industry, the strength of the workers increases, and as it grows the workers become more conscious of this strength and their power. At the same time capitalism is forced to worsen both wages and conditions for its workers, thereby inadvertently causing the growth of workers' clubs to protect their wages. Thus are unions born, who will be the bourgeoisie's eventual 'grave diggers'.

> Hitherto, every form of society has been based, as we have already seen, on the antagonism of oppressing and oppressed classes. But in order to oppress a class certain conditions must be assured to it under which it can, at least, continue its slavish existence. The serf, in the period of

serfdom, raised himself to membership in the commune, just as the petty bourgeois, under the yoke of feudal absolutism, managed to develop into a bourgeois. The modern labourer, on the contrary, instead of rising with the progress of industry, sinks deeper and deeper below the conditions of existence of his own class. He becomes a pauper, and pauperism develops more rapidly than population and wealth.

It is because the bourgeoisie is incompetent that it is unfit to govern (the *Manifesto* adds, with unusual reasonableness). Unfit, because it cannot stop its slaves sinking in poverty to such a point that it ends up feeding them. Communists are assured of eventual victory as the capitalist mode of production necessarily results in recurrent economic crises, perhaps creating wealth for a few, but increasing poverty for an ever-growing working majority. At the same time, Marxism predicts, equally optimistically, that there will be 'ever-growing' realisation among the proletarians of their exploitation – that 'law, morality and religion are . . . just so many bourgeois prejudices'. As a consequence, 'Its fall and the victory of the proletariat are equally inevitable.'

The *Manifesto* does not propose that communists form a separate party from the proletarian movement as a whole, as they should have no interests separate and apart from the whole. Communists are only the 'most advanced and resolute' part of the working class. They understand better than the rest that the abolition of the institution of private property is essential, for property represents (as Smith puts it) stored up, or (as the *Manifesto* puts it) expropriated, labour. However, with Marx's definition, since the wage labourer only receives the bare subsistence necessary to continue working, private property necessarily represents exploitation. Or, in the famous phrase of **PROUDHON**, Marx's contemporary and the first **ANARCHIST**: 'property is theft'.

Marx and Engels go on to describe the key points of the Communist revolution. They are:

- Abolition of landownership and rents.
- A heavy progressive income tax.
- Abolition of all inheritance rights.
- Confiscation of the property of all those who no longer live in the state, or who rebel against the new government.

- Centralisation of all capital and credit in a state bank.
- Central state control and ownership of the means of communication and transportation.
- Increased state production through factories and farming: development of underused land.
- 'Equal liability of all to labour'. New armies of workers, especially to work the land.
- Disappearance of the distinction between town and country: population distributed evenly over the country.

And, lastly:

- Free education for all in state-run schools, preparing the children for work in the new industries.

In the meantime, the *Manifesto* concludes, communists should support every 'revolutionary movement against the existing social and political order, bringing to the fore, as the main issue, the property question'. This should be done, 'no matter what its degree of development at the time', by which Marx and Engels mean the political aspects, rather than the economic stage prevailing. (It was left to MAO Zedong in China to make the important doctrinal changes necessary to allow communist theory to apply to pre-industrial peasant societies – the kind where it actually took root to some extent, as it had done earlier in Russia.) Otherwise, the *Manifesto* presses for unionisation and makes it clear that for communists the only way forward is the 'forcible overthrow' of existing social structures. 'Let the ruling classes tremble at a communistic revolution. The proletarians have nothing to lose but their chains. They have a world to win'!

## Further reading

Marx, K. and Engels, F. (1848) *The Communist Manifesto*

## COMMUNITY AND COMMUNITARIANISM

This is the notion that the 'community' should be the focus for political planning and ethical judgements. Communitarians emphasise that INDIVIDUALS are always linked to, defined by and part of a community, and thus (it is assumed) decisions are better taken when the community is considered, rather than the indi-

vidual. As a political force today, communitarianism is about creating societies containing relatively small groupings of people imbued by community spirit, for example, in the USA, building upon the churches which already play such a large part in many people's lives, providing both social welfare networks and political guidance. But taken as a whole, societies like the United States can be seen as excessively individualistic, whilst societies like China can be judged as excessively centralised, the community being more subtle than just saying 'everyone'. To be a community, people must share common ends and values, and *perceive* themselves as part of a shared community.

## COMPUTERS

See Artificial intelligence.

## COMTE, AUGUSTE (1798–1857)

Isidore Auguste Marie François Xavier, in full, the so-called 'father' of positivism, the theory of society which he outlined in 1842. Comte was a middle-class, French intellectual whom John Stuart MILL would later accuse of devising a 'despotism of society over the individual', although others would trace it (both the origins of sociology, and the despotism) to Jeremy BENTHAM's efforts to ground the authority of the law on the principle of maximising the happiness of the greatest number.

Whatever the truth of that, it is with Comte, who had been inspired by his study of medieval Catholic scholars into attempting to produce a new 'religion of humanity' and a blueprint for a new social order, that the science of society really starts. Comte apologetically coins the word 'sociology', which he calls a convenient barbarism (mixing as it does, Latin and Greek).

In the *Cours de Philosophie Positive* (1892), Comte, like René DESCARTES and many philosophers since, starts from a position of deep admiration for the precision and authority of the natural sciences, epitomised (at least in the public mind) by the advances in physics and chemistry. His 'positivist' idea was that the methods of natural science were the only way to understand HUMAN NATURE, both in individuals and collectively, and hence the only way to find out how to organise society. And Comte wanted to actually apply these 'scientific', quantitative methods to society itself, dissecting it to discover the laws and the principles governing it. Of these, he considered his most important discovery to be a 'Law of Human Progress', according to which, all societies pass through three stages: the theological; the METAPHYSICAL; and the scientific or positive.

The defining feature of each stage is the mental attitude of the people. During the theological stage, people seek to discover the 'essential nature of things' and the ultimate cause of existence, interpreted as God. Philosophers, Comte thought, were stuck at this stage, perpetually but fruitlessly pursuing these sorts of questions. Most people, however, were at the next, the metaphysical stage, which involves increasing use of abstract theory, although there is still a sense of the underlying essence of things, epitomised by broadly ethical notions of value. The final stage comes only when enough people put aside the illusions of opinion (echoes of PLATO) and confine themselves to logical deduction from observed phenomena. This is the so-called scientific (or positive) stage. 'Now each of us is aware, if he looks back on his own history, that he was a theologian in his childhood, a metaphysician in his youth and a natural philosopher in his manhood', Comte rather unconvincingly declares.

The stages are also supposed to correspond to periods of human history. The first relates to the pre-historical and medieval world, while the metaphysical stage is compared to the sixteenth, seventeenth and eighteenth centuries, a time when monarchies and military despots gave way to political ideals such as DEMOCRACY and HUMAN RIGHTS, including, most importantly, for social life, property rights. The last stage in history will be a scientific, technological age, when all activity is rationally planned and moral rules have become universal. It is as this final stage beckons that the science of society – sociology – comes into its own, with its task both of explaining and determining social phenomena and the history of mankind.

Comte was an IDEALIST who wrote of 'love' as the guiding principle and of bringing 'feeling, reason and activity into permanent harmony'. It was left to Emile DURKHEIM (born the year after Comte's death), Max WEBER, as well as, to some extent, Mill, to carry on to develop the science of society.

## CONCEPTS

Clearly, concepts are important. We need them to 'apply' words correctly, or to form meaningful sentences. In this sense, concepts lie behind language, enabling us to categorise the world. PSYCHOLOGISTS say concepts are 'internal representations', LOGICIANS think they are 'sets' of objects, and some philosophers use them as if they were a kind of 'rule'. 'Analytical' philosophers sometimes claim to be involved in 'conceptual analysis'; if so, they have yet to analyse the use of the word concept adequately.

## CONDITIONALS

See Logic.

## CONDITIONING

See Behaviorism.

## CONFUCIUS (551–479 BCE)

### The essential Confucius

Confucius was the essence of the ancient Chinese sage, a social philosopher, an educator, and the founder of the *Ru* School of Chinese thought.

It is recorded that altogether he had 3000 disciples and 72 of them were influential. Confucius presents himself as a kind of transmitter who invented nothing himself, and his greatest emphasis may be the one on learning from the ancient sages. In this respect, he is mostly respected by Chinese people as a Great Teacher or Master. His teachings, preserved in the *Analects*, form the foundation of much of subsequent Chinese speculation on the education, government and comportment of the superior man. Confucius' influence in Chinese history can be compared with that of SOCRATES in the West.

### Confucius and the unity of *li* and *ren*

To Western readers, Confucius is chiefly regarded as a wise man speaking in aphorisms or moral maxims, which hardly suffices to explain the depth of influence of Confucianism. Without a deeper unity of belief, no mere collection of aphorisms could dominate a nation's history as Confucianism has dominated China's. It would be impossible, therefore, to arrive at a full appreciation of the influence and the prestige of Confucius without an understanding of Confucian ideas as a system.

Confucius' social philosophy largely revolves around the concepts of *li* (rites or ritual rules) and *ren* (humanity). The system of ritual rules valued by Confucius came originally from the Western Zhou dynasty (1066–771 BCE) and lasted for 300 years until the Spring and Autumn Period (770–476 BCE). But in the Spring and Autumn Period, the authentic power of the royal house of the Zhou dynasty was declining and that of the princes of the feudal states was rising. Military wars between states and political intrigues within states were intensified by weak kings, ambitious princes and greedy officials. The old social order was destroyed and those rules of ritual lost their power and influence. This is what is often called 'the decline of Zhou rites'. Different schools, such as Confucianism, Daoism, Mohism and Legalism came into being during the time to deal with the problems generated by this decline. While other schools held a negative attitude toward Zhou rites, Confucius always took a positive approach towards them.

Mozi, the founder of the Mohist school, criticised the ritual of the Zhou because he evaluated the rites from a quasi-utilitarian point of view. Thus he judged that the funeral observances and music in Zhou rites were a waste of the wealth and energy of the people. He therefore was against music and advocated an economical approach to funerals.

The fundamental spirit of Daoism is a kind of high-degree freedom, which can be described as unfettered, integrated with the world and dependent on nothing. Daoism considered Zhou rites to be artificial, false, external and a formal constraint on our lives. Laozi stated that propriety is 'a superficial expression of loyalty and faithfulness, and the beginning of disorder'. For him, the Zhou rites are also superficial and forced: 'the highest propriety takes action, and in case no one responds, it turns up its sleeves and drags one near.'

Another school called Legalism opposed Zhou rites from a practical point of view. The goal of the legalists was a wealthy and powerful state, very different from the Confucian vision of an ordered world of peace, harmony and simple contentment. In a world where the great powers were girding themselves for battles, they offered themselves as experts in the arts of enriching and strengthening the state. In order to suit the great social changes at that time, legalism advocated the destruction of ancient hierarchical distinctions. The very idea of law, an impersonal and impartial force to regulate the relationship between the individual and the state, meant the overthrow of the **ETHICS** of Confucius with its hangover of feudalistic elements – Zhou rites.

But Confucius himself had great respect for the Zhou rites, believing they had attained a perfect state: 'The Zhou had the advantages of surveying the two preceding dynasties. How resplendent is its culture *(wen)*! I follow Zhou', he wrote. And Confucius saw the decline of the rites as a consequence of the effete lifestyle of the noble class. He argued that a system of perfectly designed rules of prosperity cannot be enforced by people without any virtue. If so, the Zhou rites became a kind of hollow **FORMALISM**. Confucius insisted that the problem was not in the rites themselves, but in the people who no longer followed them. In order to regain the validity of the rites, the people needed to be able to practise them in their daily life. Thus Confucius gave life to the Zhou rites by introducing a new concept – humanity *(ren)*. In this way, Confucius has turned attention from objective morality towards the moral subject. In the process, he integrates *li* (ritual rules) and *ren* (virtue of humanity) into one moral theory.

For him, on the one hand, *ren* is the essence and content of *li*. In performing the *li*, what must be emphasised is that one has to perform *li* with the correct attitude. For example, when performing a sacrifice, one has to feel reverence for the spirits; when carrying out the rites of mourning, one has to feel grief for the deceased. So when his disciple Lin Fang asked about the foundation of ceremonies (*li*), Confucius said, 'An important question indeed. In rituals or ceremonies, be thrifty rather than extravagant, and in funerals, be deeply sorrowful rather than shallow in sentiment.' Similarly, in serving his lord, a minister was to be respectful; in governing his people, a ruler was to be benevolent. Without this emotional component, ritual becomes a hollow performance. Confucius remarked: 'A man who does not have humanity, what can he have to do with ritual? A man who does not have humanity, what can he have to do with music?' Acting in conformity with the rules of proper conduct requires an inner dimension for its foundation. Otherwise, ritual will only be the mechanism of regulating people's behaviour.

In this respect, Confucianism contrasts with Legalism, which advocated bringing the masses into line by a severe system of penal law. As Confucius said, 'Lead the people with governmental measures and regulate them by law and punishment, and they will avoid wrongdoing but will have no sense of honour and shame. Lead them with virtue and regulate them by the rules of propriety, and they will have a sense of shame

## CONFUCIAN MUSIC

Confucius not only said interesting things, he sang them. It is said that Confucius accompanied himself on a 'qin' (a kind of zither) while singing the odes of the Classic of Poetry. We do not know what Confucius' zither may have looked like, but in popular accounts of his life, the image of the philosopher-musician became firmly established.

Confucius had clear ideas about the importance of music. He said: 'Let a man be stimulated by poetry, established by the rules of propriety, perfected by music.' For Confucius, not only does music reflect the feelings of man, it can mould man's character. This is because the harmony which is the essence of music can find its way into the depths of the human heart.

The nature of man is initially quiet and calm, but when it is affected by the external world, it begins to have desires. When the desires are not properly controlled and our conscious minds are distracted by the material world, we lose our true selves and the principle of reason in Nature is destroyed and man is submerged in his own desires. From this arise rebellion, disobedience, cunning and deceit, and general immorality. This is the way of chaos.

Music, which springs from the inner movement of the soul, can and should go into the inner recesses of the soul. Good music is that which leads to the introspection of one's mind and heart. The ancient sage-kings instituted ritual and music, not only to satisfy our desires of the ear and the eye and the mouth and the stomach, but to have the right taste or right likes and dislikes and restore the human order to normal.

Therefore, the superior man tries to create harmony in the human heart by a rediscovery of human nature, and tries to promote music as a means to the perfection of human culture. When such music prevails and the people's minds are led towards the right ideals and aspirations, we may see the appearance of a great nation.

According to Confucius, musical training is the most effective method for changing the moral character of man and keeping society in order.

and, moreover, set themselves right and arrive at goodness.'

On the other hand, for Confucius, *li* is concrete manifestation and expression of *ren*. Although *ren* as an inner morality is not caused by the mechanism of *li* from outside, it needs *li* to express itself. *Li* can be conceived as an externalisation of *ren* in a specific social context. No matter how abstract it appears, *ren*, almost by definition, requires concrete manifestation. To use the remark made by Mou Zongsan, *ren* needs 'windows' to expose itself to the outside world, otherwise it will become suffocated. *Ren* is expressed and fulfilled in actions in accordance with *li*.

It is said in the *Analects* that when Confucius offered sacrifice to his ancestors, he felt as if his ancestral spirits were actually present. When he offered sacrifice to other spiritual beings, he felt as if they were actually present. What Confucius values in ancestor worship is not any formal accordance with ritual rules but the unifying effects it has on the living to cultivate or find the feeling of love and reverence or, in short, *ren*-feeling in oneself.

This is why, on the one hand, Confucius warned his disciple Zizhang that *li* did not consist in playing about with sacrificial vessels, just as music did not consist in the mere beating of bells and drums; and, on the other hand, he thought that both ritual and music emanated from, and created, a state of mind, a state of God-fearing piety in the performance of ritual and a state of happiness and harmony in the performance of music.

Since performing *li* is not a process of following ritual rules mechanically, but a process that shows and embodies one's feelings, will and emotions, consciously performing *li* leads one to find and nourish *ren*-feeling in oneself and thus has a specific function in the cultivation of personal character.

Confucius emphasised both the importance of *li* to *ren* and of *ren* to *li* without assuming the primacy of either concept. The relation between *li* and *ren* could perhaps be described as approximating the relation between form and substance in Western philosophy. It seems that the distinction between virtue and rule becomes obscured and the conflict, between virtue ethics and rule-based systems in contemporary Western ethics, never becomes real in Confucius' moral theory.

Doubtless, Confucius, if living in our time and acknowledging this conflict, would think it fruitless and far detached from reality or moral practice. For him, it is unimaginable that moral rules and virtues can be understood separately. Or at least, he would agree with those Western moral philosophers who see the ethics of virtue and the ethics of rule as adding up, rather than as cancelling each other out. Indeed, it was the unity

of *li* and *ren* by Confucius himself that marked a qualitative break in Chinese intellectual history.

Contributor: Yuli Liu

## CONJUNCTION
See Logic.

## CONNECTIVE
See Logic.

## CONSCIENCE

In *Paradise Lost*, Milton has God declare: 'And I will place within them as a guide/ My umpire Conscience'. Others would say conscience is the 'voice of reason', perhaps the charioteer trying to regain control of the unruly steeds of the passions. The word comes from the Latin. 'con', with and 'scire', to know. Joseph BUTLER, the Bishop, describes conscience as 'a sentiment of the understanding or a perception of the heart', surely two quite different things.

## CONSCIOUSNESS, FALSE

DESCARTES left a legacy of consciousness as the crucial feature of knowledge, but also the problem of whether this crucial thing was a mental or a physical phenomenon. Certainly, consciousness is something hard to define. There seems to be some sense to the notion, but is it a form of inner speech or merely a series of automated reactions to stimuli? Descartes himself made all the processes of the human MIND activities of the SOUL, and hence part of being 'conscious', and all the activities of animals into the unconscious, pre-programmed reactions of machines, but nowadays such analysis looks superficial.

False consciousness, on the other hand, is a phrase that appears in a letter by ENGELS, who writes that 'ideology is a process accomplished by the so-called thinker, but with a false consciousness. The real motive forces impelling him remain unknown to him; otherwise it simply would not be an ideological process'. In a sense, all our consciousnesses (!) are false ones.

## CONSENT

The notion of consent is allowed great significance in both ETHICAL and political discussion, and the legal maxim, *violenti non fit injuria* (the willing are not harmed) may often be heard muttered by second-hand car salesmen as the customer drives their new purchase home. In

MEDICAL ETHICS, consent has to be sought for all actions except in the special circumstance where a person is unable to properly be consulted; and of course in political theory the 'consent of the people' is the bedrock of authority, be it through the apparently active process of voting and 'DEMOCRATIC' consultation, or through a more theoretical past granting of general consent, in the manner of Thomas HOBBES' social contract. In this, the people give up virtually (but not quite all) their rights in order to receive the protection of the ruler from anarchy, which he describes as the situation of the 'warre of all on all'.

Evidence of this sort of consent is not needed, and it also seems to be rather 'forced' in that the 'Hobbesian' alternative is probably death, but for more mundane transactions, we expect the persons consenting to have been adequately informed about both what they are consenting to and the alternatives.

# CONSEQUENTIALISM

See Utilitarianism.

# CONSERVATISM

For Edmund BURKE (1729–97), the Irish-born British Member of Parliament (writing partly in response to the shocking example of the French and their revolution), a good constitution is one decorated with 'pleasing illusions' to make 'power gentle and obedience liberal'. The term has a nice, reassuring ring, and makes some claim to 'conserve' or look after the environment, the old ways of doing things and the less fortunate in society. It is also one that supposedly seeks to 'devolve' power, wherever possible, away from the centre towards free-standing institutions. HEGEL is sometimes considered to be a key 'conservative' thinker, yet he was a great centralist whose ideas were adopted enthusiastically by both the MARXISTS and the FASCISTS, one who saw around him a desirable tendency for conflict to resolve itself in the eventual victory of the 'rational state'; and so if Hegel is a conservative, the doctrine is really little more than a name.

In Britain, the USA and Australia, for example, 'conservatism' seems to be a label applied to a set of political beliefs, crudely expressed as 'low taxes, strong defences, no foreigners', yet such a platform really has little more unifying it than the elevation of perceived self-interest over 'the OTHER'. In any case, just as Britain's great 'conservative', Margaret Thatcher, was a political radical and centraliser, so was Australia's 'White Australia' policy an initiative of the Australian Labor Party, and opposed as such by parties to the right. Nonetheless, in all three countries, 'conservatism' as a philosophy, whatever the party label, results in practice in military adventurism, widening social inequality, extreme ethnocentrism and cultural insularity.

# CONSISTENCY, LOGICAL

PROPOSITIONS are consistent if they can all be true together. They are inconsistent when it can be shown that one contradicts another, for example, by being its negation. As such, the charge of 'inconsistency' is a very precise and very serious one, although often loosely made in everyday debate. However, it is useful to remember that propositions (let us say ARGUMENTS) can be 'consistent' without that telling you whether they are true. Intriguingly, two propositions can be inconsistent even if they do not contradict one another.

**SEE ALSO**

Indeterminacy

# CONSTITUTIONALISM

For CONSERVATIVES, constitutionalism is the emergence of a set of conventions and institutions for governing the state; for LIBERALS it is more likely to be a series of foundational laws stated in a document, such as the American Constitution. The problem about such documents, as evidenced by the US case, with its seemingly regular 'amendments', is that they seek to be above and beyond political debate, while being central to them at the same time.

# CONTINENTAL PHILOSOPHY

The term 'continental philosophy' is a little passé today. It refers to the 'gulf' that emerged between the English language philosophy of the USA, Britain and elsewhere, and the rest of Europe after the Second World War. Language is important in the development of separate philosophical traditions, of course, but within Europe, Latin had been the unifying force of early philosophy, and the habit of writing in 'local' languages only took root much later. So, for example, both DESCARTES and KANT wrote in Latin as well as in (respectively) French and German. The central interests of this 'devolved' continental philosophy' are EXISTENTIALISM, STRUCTURALISM and MARXISM.

## CONTINGENCY, NECESSITY OF

See Logic.

## CONTRACT, SOCIAL

The 'Social Contract' is a theoretical notion, not a historical claim, relating to the ethical foundations of societies. According to Thomas HOBBES, writing in *The Leviathan* (1651), it is the implied agreement of the citizens to give up their 'freedom' in exchange for the protection of the STATE (and this is more from each other than from the State itself, of course). As such, the theory puts the individual prior to the social group, an assumption anthropologists challenge. Fellow Englishman LOCKE largely repeats Hobbes' view in his *Two Treatises of Civil Government* (1689), but Jean-Jacques ROUSSEAU, writing a century later offers a different kind of social co-operation in his book *Du Contrat Social* (1762), emerging out of an ill-defined 'general will'. A similar notion called 'contractarianism', explored by the contemporary philosopher John RAWLS, is traced back to Immanuel KANT and attempts to ground moral claims in a theoretical analysis of the agreements rational agents would make with each other, starting from an 'ORIGINAL POSITION' of perfect EQUALITY.

## CONVENTION

The view that human conventions, rather than independent realities, shape our most fundamental perceptions, theories and understandings, is one with which philosophers happily play, even at the expense of making themselves appear irrelevant. Yet conventionalism is also very much a practical issue, for science and mathematics. Scientific theories are recognised as ad hoc HYPOTHESES awaiting refutation, as Karl POPPER would say, rather than insights into the eternal harmonies of the universe, as the ancients might have preferred.

The French mathematician Henri POINCARÉ argued that mathematical theories remained part of a framework of ideas and assumptions, the choice of which remained arbitrary. For example, the Greeks imagined Euclid's geometry to be the exemplar of pure knowledge, 'parallel lines never meet', 'the angles of a triangle add up to 180°', and so on, yet Euclidian geometry is now recognised as just one possible kind of geometry, and there are others in which parallel lines do meet, and the angles of a triangle add up to rather more.

## COPERNICUS (1473–1543)

Copernicus, one of the great figures of science, was born in Torun and died in Frombork, both in Poland. There are many similarities between Copernicus and NEWTON, who lived a century and a half later and answered many of the questions Copernicus' works raise; such as why heavenly bodies fall to Earth if it is not the centre of the universe. Like Newton, he developed mathematical and scientific methods and was also a man of affairs.

Copernicus began his education in Krakow, but went on to Bologna, Ferrara, Padua and Rome. There he was influenced by Johan Muller's critique of PTOLEMY's Earth-centred model of the universe and Giovanni Pico della MIRANDOLA's attack on the foundations of ASTROLOGY. Pico questioned how variations in the powers of the planets could be known when astronomers did not even agree as to their order.

And of course, Copernicus continued with his astronomical observations that he repeated from the different vantage points of Eastern Poland and Northern Italy. He compiled data to support a theory that the sun is the centre of the universe, as well as a painstaking study of each of the planets, their sizes, orbits and relationships. The only model of the planetary system commensurate with his observations and calculations was one with the sun at the centre, with Mercury circling the sun in 88 days, Venus in 225 days, Earth with its moon in 1 year, Mars in 1.9 years, Jupiter in 12 years and Saturn in 30 years and the fixed stars beyond. Although he could not think of an alternative model capable of explanation of all his findings, he published them as a hypothesis with a dedication to Pope Paul III.

As important as his findings were his strict methods of observation and precision of calculation. Part of his major work was published separately as a work on trigonometry. Here was a model of scientific method.

*De Revolutionibus Orbium Coelestium* was published in full in 1543, shortly before Copernicus died. He himself was convinced of his demonstration that '*sol omnia regit*'. His book gave others opportunity to come to the same conclusion.

His scholarly work did not cause storms of protests from the inquisition, the thought police of the age, because it was academic work shared with and appreciated by like-minded people. It was not presented as a challenge to the teaching authority of the Church. In fact, in his own day it was only Protestant reformers who castigated him and wanted him silenced. Luther's colleague Melanchthon was one who went on the attack: 'There are those who think speaking nonsense like the Polish astronomer does, he moves the Earth and fixes the Sun, is excellent. In truth good government should shut up such rash talent.'

## COROLLARY

A corollary is a statement (philosophers prefer 'PROPOSITION') that can be shown to follow from another statement that has been shown to be true. In MATHEMATICS and LOGIC, this previously established proposition is called the 'theorem' and the proof of the 'corollary' is based on its proof.

## CORRESPONDENCE THEORY

This is the theory that whether a claim about something in the world is true must depend on whether it 'corresponds' to how the world actually is. It sounds promising, linking the truth of LANGUAGE to the facts of reality, but on closer examination, there are a lot of problems. But that's a long story.

## COSMOLOGICAL ARGUMENT

There a number of versions of the cosmological argument, but in essence it is the appeal to the supposed necessity of the 'unmoved mover' that ARISTOTLE wanted to set the heavenly spheres in motion. Thomas AQUINAS accepted that the law of causality requires every effect to have a cause, and since supposing God to be 'causeless' flouts this law, we simply have another reason to admire Him.

SEE ALSO

Ontological argument

## COSMOLOGY

The study of SPACE, TIME and the universe as a whole. The term comes from the Greek words for 'order' (*cosmos*) and study (*logos*). The term is used in physics to describe science that considers the physical structure of the universe taken as a whole. Cosmogony, confusingly, is the study of the origins or creation of the universe.

Cosmology considers issues such as whether space and time are 'absolute', as NEWTON thought, providing a set of fixed reference points for matter, or whether they are all bound together in a relative flux, as EINSTEIN decided.

## COUNTERFACTUALS

Counterfactuals are things that *could* have happened – but did not. After all, that is why they are called counterfactuals. They are often backwards looking, like *What if the Greeks had lost at Marathon? What if Hitler had won the war?*; but they can also be about the present or offer strange predictions like *What if we knew the world was going to end tomorrow?*

Philosophy has long been concerned with this subtle question of what is 'possible' as opposed to what is flatly impossible. And some philosophers hold that if something is possible then in some sense it already is part of the world of existence. Equally, if diametrically opposed, some philosophers say that 'facts' are created by people, so that they have no great status. Only things that are self-contradictory need to be distinguished, and in the case of a 'counterfactual', avoided.

Economists, for instance, interpret the question of 'what is possible' as a dynamic one, depending on the identification of various stable states for the economy. MARX and ENGELS constructed their 'science of materialism' on the assumption that there was a pattern to history, indeed an inevitable one. Geographers use similar notions when they talk of the earth having a tendency to return to its frozen state, with the ice and snow reflecting sunlight back into space, or speculate about the effects of rising global temperatures.

George Herbert's ditty about the horseshoe sums up the approach:

> *For want of a nail the shoe is lost,*
> *For want of a shoe the horse is lost,*
> *For want of a horse, the rider is lost,*
> *For want of a rider the battle is lost,*
> *For want of a battle the war is lost,*
> *All for want of horseshoe nail.*

This gives the attractive feel of a good counterfactual, with a small event operating, as one writer put it, a bit like a nineteenth-century railway points lever – switching the train of history with barely a jolt from one path to another.

## CRITICAL THEORY

A variety of social theory with MARXIST roots, considered to have originated with SOCIAL SCIENTISTS working at the University of

Frankfurt before the Second World War, and hence sometimes dubbed 'the Frankfurt School'. Exponents include Theodor ADORNO, Herbert Marcuse and, later, Jürgen HABERMAS. But what is the theory? It is that modern society is governed by administrators following a narrow and damaging creed of 'technological rationality'. To counter this, we need to consider moral, political and even religious values. But where is the Marxism in this? Only in the aim of the critical theorist not to 'interpret the world', but to 'change it'.

## CRITICAL THINKING, INFORMAL LOGIC

Critical thinking is concerned with the nature of ARGUMENTS; their structure, 'validity' and also their effectiveness. An argument can be logically 'invalid' but still effective. Critical thinking sees claims and arguments as part of a 'web of intercourse', which may involve partially competed and implied lines of reasoning, shared and hidden assumptions, vagueness, rhetorical devices and, of course, FALLACIES.

## CULTURE

### Essentials of culture

Not only does 'culture' itself often mean different things to different people, the word 'culture' also often means different things to different people. In anthropology, culture is often intended as the patterns of behaviour and thinking that people living in social groups learn, create and share. Culture also defines groups or societies. A group of people who share a common culture (common beliefs, rules of behaviour, language, some form of social organisation) constitutes a society. Two aspects of the relationship between culture and ethics are whether ethics are relative to time and space and the ethical and policy questions of whether 'culture' ought to be protected.

### Culture and ethical relativism

Traditionally, moral theories have considered moral agents as impartial actors, that is, building upon the premise that the moral agent ought to be impartial. By contrast, cultural relativism is the view that what is good or bad, or right or wrong, varies from society to society. The question of ethical RELATIVISM boils down to the question of whether the moral agent is impartial, or whether culture may inform the notion of moral agency.

Examples of cross-cultural moral judgements include the Western horror at the practice of female genital mutilation: one of its forms, infibulation, which is carried out in several African countries and in a few countries in the Middle East, with shards of glass and other unsanitary tools, can cause infections which may eventually result in death. Europeans reject the death penalty, yet it is widely used in both China and the USA. Several indigenous groups criticise the patenting of DNA and any forms of human life, based on the notion that DNA is a collective good that cannot be the subject of exclusive appropriation, while in Western countries patenting life forms is permissible both legally and morally. And abortion is legal in Canada, the USA and parts of Western Europe, but it is illegal in the majority of Latin American countries and in some EU countries (Ireland, Poland, Malta, Cyprus and Portugal). Cross-cultural judgements are also frequent with multicultural societies, in which minorities often decide to withdraw from the majority society and preserve their way of life. The question then becomes how society is going to cope with cultural practices that can conflict with the moral beliefs of the majority and, perhaps, national laws and regulations. For instance, in the USA, the Amish community's practice of having no lights on their vehicles conflicts with state law, not to mention other road users, while the tradition of Acoma Pueblo, a Native American tribe, of using eagle feathers in ceremonials conflicts with federal laws protecting bald eagles as an endangered species.

In the last 30 years, prominent scholars have argued that recognising cultural difference does not equate to ethical relativism, and that moral theory and cultural variations may be reconciled in advocating a political LIBERALISM within the HUMAN RIGHTS framework. Pluralism rejects the ideal of impartiality and seeks to preserve and strengthen group identity by including group differences in public reasoning. In its essence, this position – supported by contemporary philosophers such as Iris Young and Michael Walzer – claims that minorities and its members should be given individual and group rights that will enable them to develop and pursue a life plan that is consistent with their cultural values. Having your own culture is important for achieving this goal. However, certain cultural values are expressed by minority groups which, without protection (by the simple

Several international organisations have recognised the need to protect the culture of minorities. Among them, the United Nations Educational, Scientific and Cultural Organization (UNESCO) grants respect for cultural diversity and intercultural dialogue as one of the 'surest guarantees of development and peace'. To this end, UNESCO's Universal Declaration on Cultural Diversity defines culture as the 'set of distinctive spiritual, material, intellectual and emotional features of society or a social group and that it encompasses, in addition to art and literature, lifestyles, ways of living together, value systems, traditions and beliefs'. Traditional cultural expressions are considered to be part of cultural heritage and identity, and their protection and preservation are linked to the promotion of cultural diversity and human creativity.

The World Intellectual Property Organisation is active in addressing the issue of protection of traditional knowledge. However, the appropriation of local knowledge within the framework of existing global intellectual property rules is a major issue of contention today. A growing number of scholars and international organisations stress that local knowledge – and in particular folklore and indigenous culture – must be protected, and that governments have an ethical obligation to prevent developed countries from destroying local cultures. And recently people have to come to realise that indigenous and local cultures often transfer information that is beneficial outside the region where such culture is present, as in the case of drugs that are developed from observing traditional practitioners using local medicinal plants to satisfy the health care needs of the population.

role. The human rights framework brings back a role for impartiality in a multicultural world. A number of contemporary philosophers have argued – among them John RAWLS, Onora O'Neill, Martha Nussbaum and Amartya Sen – that the respect for human rights is a moral concept that has cross-cultural validity.

Contributor: Andrea Boggio

## Further reading

Arnold, M. (1869) *Culture and Anarchy*

## CUSTOMS

When the United Nations tried to agree a set of 'HUMAN RIGHTS' for its Declaration, it found it impossible to reach a complete consensus. The Saudis expressed the doubts of many other countries by objecting to the inclusion of women's rights and 'freedom of religion'. They thought these were not 'universal', or 'natural', and claimed instead the authority of customary practice. Certainly customs and 'rights' often tell a different story. The SOPHISTS (fifth century BCE) presented the opposition as between *physis*, nature, and *nomos*, law or custom, and it is hard sometimes to know which one is worse.

Herodotus famously described his tour of the Mediterranean region in which he contrasted different customs, concluding that it was impossible to prefer one system over another.

Perhaps Herodotus' most famous story is of the Massagetae, who boiled their old folk with beef, and ate the mixture as a treat, but there are many other equally strange stories. One tribe in Niger were said to kill their old people, smoke and pulverise the bodies, and then compress the powder into little balls with corn and water. These little burgers were kept for long periods as a basic food. Some would rationalise this today by saying that it reflected the cruel necessity of life in harsh conditions, perhaps citing stories of the Inuits in support of the theory (like the Hudson Bay Inuit, who strangled the old), or the Tupis (of Brazil, who killed any elderly person who became ill, and then ate the corpse), or the Tobas (of Paraguay, who were reputed to bury their old folk alive). However, these customs were never universal – some tribes had found other solutions. American Indian tribes like the Poncas and Omahas, as well as some Incas, created a role for the old and

reality of sheer numbers), would soon be pushed to abandon their traditions and to embrace the cultural values and practices that are expressed by the majority. Therefore, pluralism creates a duty to provide special protection to the cultural practices of minorities.

Moral pluralism does not mean, however, absence of ethical restraints. In fact, the practices protected under minority rights must respect wider human rights. Therefore, considerations of rights establish the boundaries within which considerations of partiality may play a infirm by leaving them at home, with supplies, while the rest of the tribe hunted or gathered. The old watched the cornfields and scared away birds.

# CYNICS AND CYNICISM

## Essential Cynicism

What is Cynicism? According to one ancient critic (Varro), Cynicism is not a proper philosophy at all, but merely a certain lifestyle, associated in antiquity with the image of the unwashed and unshaven philosopher in a dirty cloak. But this is merely a caricature. Cynicism offers a properly philosophical way of life, with the goal of attaining true happiness, based upon a distinction between what we actually need according to nature and what convention leads us to think we need in order to be happy.

## A way of life

Cynicism may have started with Antisthenes, an associate of SOCRATES, who appears in Xenophon's *Symposium* and whose life opens the book devoted to the Cynics in DIOGENES LAERTIUS. But it may be safer to say that while Antisthenes prefigures Cynicism in certain respects, the first Cynic proper was DIOGENES OF SINOPE, better known as simply Diogenes the Cynic.

At the heart of the Cynic philosophy developed by Diogenes is the distinction between what is according to nature and what is merely according to custom, a distinction first developed by some of the SOPHISTS of the previous century. Whatever is according to nature is necessary; whatever is according to custom is arbitrary. Cynicism argues that one should focus all one's attention on getting those necessary things that are according to nature (food, water, basic shelter and clothing), and pay no respect whatsoever to the unnecessary and arbitrary rules, regulations and assumptions of the particular culture in which one happens to find oneself.

This doctrine is memorably illustrated by a series of entertaining stories about Diogenes' own disregard for the customs of his day. It is reported that he masturbated in the Agora (marketplace) at Athens, proclaiming that he wished it were as easy to relieve his hunger simply by rubbing his belly. Diogenes' pupil Crates used to have sexual intercourse in public with his Cynic wife Hipparchia.

It is one thing to acknowledge that many things usually thought to be of value are in fact irrelevant to achieving happiness: it is quite another thing to put that doctrine into practice. The Cynics were well aware of this and so proposed the idea of philosophical training, or exercise. In order to train himself to become indifferent to external circumstances, Diogenes would roll in hot sand in the middle of summer and hug marble statues in the middle of winter.

Cynic indifference to conventions and circumstances was combined with a desire for complete self-sufficiency, so far as that is possible. Thus Diogenes reduced his physical needs to the bare minimum, pursuing only that which is absolutely essential. After seeing a child drinking water out of his hands, Diogenes threw away his cup, saying a child has beaten me in simplicity.

The task of mastering the life of independence and self-sufficiency, and so achieving a happiness that is secure in the face of all external circumstances, is both urgent and arduous. Consequently, Cynicism has little interest in the time-wasting abstract intellectual games of academic philosophy (although there is evidence that Diogenes had some interest in physics). When a philosopher tried to argue that there is no such thing as motion, Diogenes simply got up and walked around. He was equally contemptuous of PLATO's discussions of universals, saying: 'Plato, table and cup I can see, but your tablehood and cuphood I cannot see anywhere.' When one of his students asked if he could borrow some of his writings, Diogenes replied by saying: 'You would not choose painted figs instead of real figs, so why choose written training instead of true training', the latter being the living example of Diogenes, standing right in front of him.

Cynicism is indeed, then, a way of life, but it is a properly philosophical way of life, in so far as it is based upon philosophical arguments. The life proposed by Diogenes has not been chosen at random; it is the product of a philosophical meditation on what is truly necessary for a happy life and what is merely distracting paraphernalia. While many people chase after material benefits that they mistakenly think will bring them happiness, Cynicism proposes an alternative route to the same goal.

Contributor: John Sellars

## DARWIN (AND DARWINISM)

Charles Robert Darwin (1808–82) was born in Shrewsbury, England. He travelled widely, recording his findings and expanding on an already existing theory of evolution.

In his celebrated account *On the Origin of Species by Means of Natural Selection or the Preservation of Favoured Races in the Struggle for Life* (1859), to give it its full title, he used examples of newly discovered or little-known species to try to demonstrate that related species had at some point had a common ancestor, and that by a process of either successfully adapting to circumstances, and therefore flourishing, or failing to adapt, and therefore dying out, species evolved into the myriad forms we see today.

Darwin openly extended his theory to cover the human race, and therefore challenged many social, ethical and psychological assumptions. Moral values even, it now seemed to have been demonstrated, were just another form of randomly generated behaviour whose effect was to improve the chances of species preservation. Some philosophers have argued that because the theory rests on this random principle, application to human society and culture is inappropriate, but that seems to be missing the point.

## DEATH

Death has some significance in human affairs, even to philosophers, but it does not readily lend itself to examination. Traditionally, philosophers have not even managed to agree on what it means to be dead, a practical consideration for many in an age of artificial methods of bodily 'life support'. PLATO, for example, insisted that death was the point at which the SOUL separates from the body, which is surely not a measure of great practical utility. However, some things can be said about it: if humans (and animals) are considered to be no more than physical objects, death is not as final as it might sometimes seem, as in most cases, the human body does continue after what is conventionally considered the moment of death. In this happy case, there is 'life after death'. If the body is seen as not only an object but a 'machine', perhaps based on a heartbeat (as MATERIALISTS would have it), then of course with modern technology, the machine can continue to be artificially aspirated in ways that confuse the line between life and death even further. Alas, in both cases, the survival is of little apparent value, as all that survives is the body, which surely brings us to consider the alternative that the human being contains something mysterious that can indeed survive separate from the body.

Moreover, as Bernard Williams has observed, this notion has elements of illogicality inherent in it. If we are to survive after death in the spirit world, what age will we be? An eternity stuck in one state might become rather boring, he thinks, but an eternity of endles, slightly different 'cycles' or disconnected 'lives' (perhaps as the BUDDHISTS say, as various animals) seems to sever the link with our essential SELF (certainly there is no bodily one, and no conscious memory either) – so in what sense could it still be said to be the same individual?

That leaves the only thing that survives as a part of the 'cosmic spirit', in which case death truly is, as the Eastern tradition has it, an illusion.

## DECONSTRUCTION

See Derrida.

## DEFINITION FALLACY

See Fallacies.

## DEMOCRACY

The word 'democracy' is from the Greek, *demos*, or people, and *kratos*, or strength, hence the might or rule of the people.

Democracy has become a bit of a 'no-brainer' concept, in the sense that the term is used without any reflection on its essential essence or meaning. (Economists and political scientists, for example, are concerned that there is a conflict between individual preferences and collective ones.) Today, democracy is instead said to be more about respecting certain values, such as 'the rule of law', or it might be 'freedom of speech', or even 'property rights'. Certainly, the structures of all 'democratic systems' reflect the nature of CAPITALISM, by concentrating wealth (and hence power) in the hands of a minority. Athenian democracy, like Chinese COMMUNISM, was based on the principle that all citizens participated actively in all the decisions, although it should be remembered that in Athens the bulk of the populace, such as women and slaves, did not count as 'citizens', and in Chinese Commmunism the 'participation' was only at the bottom of a long chain of feedback and consultations to the governing elite. Certainly, the notion that a democracy is any society in which the government offers the citizens occasional opportunities to throw it out of office is not in itself democracy, although when the mechanism is not too blatantly manipulated it could be said to offer an 'element' of 'democratic oversight' or 'consent'. As has been observed, such democracies are really 'elective dictatorships'.

In recent years, the capitalist countries of the West, in which only a very small part of society has political power and influence, and, what's worse, uses it to further their own narrow agenda, have taken to asserting their 'democratic' superiority over countries, such as Communist China, in which mechanisms for achieving political influence are at least as open,

if not more so.

In PLATO's *Republic*, a useful list of different kinds of systems of government would identify what passes as 'democracy' today as in fact something between oligarchy and tyranny. Importantly, however, Plato himself would not like to see 'democracy' instead, as he considered it a recipe for poor decision-making.

## DEMOCRITUS (*C.* 460–370 BCE)

Democritus of Abdera, a city on the coast of Greece, was a student of LEUCIPPUS, who is credited by ARISTOTLE with the theory of 'ATOMISM'. Because Leucippus left only a few scraps of writing, but Democritus is comparatively well served, with some 50 extant fragments, it is with him that the theory is primarily associated. The problem with atoms, it had been argued, was that between one thing and another there must either be something else – or nothing. This nothing – 'the void' – was a problem: how could philosophers say that 'nothing' existed?

This, however, was precisely what Leucippus did do, and then went on to offer a new kind of explanation of how the world can appear to us via our senses. Democritus explains even that certain particularly fine and smooth atoms make up our 'SOULS', and PERCEPTION arises from the interaction between these and the slightly cruder world atoms.

## DENYING THE ANTECEDENT/ DENYING THE CONSEQUENT

See Fallacies.

## DEONTOLOGY

From the Greek *deon*, 'duty', or *dei*, 'one must'. Deontological ETHICS is concerned with duties, and considers certain acts to be right or wrong in themselves, not by consideration of their consequences.

## DERRIDA, JACQUES (1930–2004)

Derrida was born in Algiers, and after some bumpy educational transitions, ended up at the elite École Normale Supérieure in Paris, where he also taught. His book on HUSSERL, *Voice and Phenomenon* (1967), sets out most of his ideas, including his notion of 'Deconstruction'. This was coined as a philosophical term by Derrida in the 1960s (although its 'traces' can be found everywhere), at a time when the upturning of conventional structures was the position to be adopted by academics by default, if not already (to borrow a French word) a bit passé. Deconstructionists are intellectual radicals who say they must throw away all the fruits of philosophy: EPISTEMOLOGY, METAPHYSICS, ETHICS – the whole apple cart. After all, these are products of a view of the world rooted in false oppositions. False oppositions, that is, such as the 'is/is not' scientific one, the 'past/ future' chronological time one, the 'good/bad' ethics one. Derrida explains that all the other thinkers' and philosophers' claims and counterclaims, their theories and findings, are no more than an elaborate word game: they have been playing, as he puts it, 'jiggery pokery' with us.

Instead, deconstruction is concerned with the category the 'wholly other'. Derrida questions the 'metaphysics of presence', which, in characteristically French wordy and complicated style, he describes as the 'valuing of truth as self-identical immediacy, sustained by traditional attempts to demonstrate the ONTOLOGICAL priority and superiority of speech over writing'. And this approach, he says, can be sustained only by way of the violent exclusion of otherness.

Derrida takes apart Ferdinand de Saussure's attempt to describe the workings of language, and finds that in seeking to provide a list of distinctions between writing and speech, the father of STRUCTURALISM has inadvertently produced some – it is arbitrary in form, material and relative – that apply as much to speech as to writing. The difference between speech and writing is thus revealed as nothing more than a philosophical illusion. (This is a good illustration of how deconstruction cunningly takes the hidden assumption buried in a text – and turns it upon itself.)

Derrida instead tries to develop a supposedly radically different conception of language, which starts from the 'irreducibility of difference to identity', thereby bringing about a correspondingly different conception of ethical and political responsibility.

Following his successful deconstruction of the speech/writing distinction, comes the destruction of the soul/body one (vide DESCARTES); the collapsing of the difference between things knowable by the mind and things knowable by sense perception; the rejection of distinctions between literal and metaphorical, between natural and cultural creations, between masculine and feminine . . . and more.

From HEIDEGGER, Derrida also takes the notion of 'presence', the *destruktion* of which he says is the central task for philosophy. Heidegger's footprints are there too, in the concept of 'Being', and the difference between *beings* and *Being*, which he calls the 'ontico-ontological difference', and describes at heroic length in a book called *Identity and Difference*.

It was Husserl, however, who created the 'transcendental phenomenology', noting that 'Reason is the *logos* which is produced in history. It traverses *Being* with itself in sight, in order to appear to itself, that is, to state itself and hear itself as *logos*. . . In emerging from itself, hearing oneself speak *constitutes itself* as the *history of reason* through the detour of writing. Thus it *differs* from itself in order to *reappropriate* itself.'

And here we find the origins of 'différence', Derrida's favourite punning term, one in this case playing on the two senses of 'to differ' in position (in space) and 'to defer', delay, in time – that is, defer-ence.

## Further reading

Derrida, J. (1967) *L'Écriture et la différence* ( *Writing and Difference*)

Derrida, J. (1967) *De la Grammatologie* ( *Of Grammatology*)

# DESCARTES, RENÉ (1596–1650)

## The essential Descartes

Descartes, mathematician, scientist and philosopher, was born on 31 March 1596 in La Haye, France and died on 11 February 1650 in Stockholm, Sweden. He was educated at a highly religious Jesuit college, but joined the army in 1618 in order, as he put it, to travel widely for the next ten years. In 1628 he settled in Holland, where he would remain for most of his life.

Descartes' aim was to bring to philosophy the rigour and clarity of mathematics. His most influential book, *Meditations on First Philosophy* (1641), introduces what has become known as the 'method of doubt', the use of which requires all and any things about which it is possible 'to be deceived' to be rejected. Knowledge based on sense perception, from books or other authorities must be set aside, but so also must knowledge involving reasoning that is inadequately founded on certain 'indubitable' truths – all in order to arrive at something about which we can be absolutely certain. This point, it turns out, is

summed up in the famous Latin phrase, *cogito ergo sum*, usually translated as 'I think therefore I am', although that is, in itself, anything but uncontroversial; similarly, his doctrine of 'DUALISM', which splits the universe into two forever opposed parts: mind, the essence of which is thinking, and matter, the essence of which is what Descartes calls 'extension'. The problems this split raises for understanding consciousness, motivations and the world around us make Descartes a landmark figure in the history of Western philosophy.

## Descartes' Project for a Universal Science, suited to Raise our Nature

With Descartes, we are authoritatively told, 'modern' philosophy comes into being. 'Here we finally reach home', **HEGEL** wrote in his magisterial *History of Philosophy*, 'like a mariner after a long voyage in a tempestuous sea, we can shout "Land ho!", for with Descartes the culture and thought of modern times really begin'. Descartes, the crowned 'father of modern philosophy', is remembered for two things: for his dramatic proposition 'I think therefore I am', and for ushering in the scientific world with his rejection, as he says, as being absolutely false, everything of which he should have the slightest cause to doubt. But in fact, neither of these two philosophical monoliths stand up to close inspection.

But Descartes is a historical individual as well as a philosophical myth. And the work of the military gentleman who wrote the *Meditations*

(1641) and the *Discourse on Philosophical Method* (1637) can also be understood when seen as the product of an egotist, as well as the work of a 'genius'. So it was that Descartes can be found confidently predicting at the age of 23 that he had discovered an 'entirely new science', and announcing his intention to start writing a book. But then, ever wary of possible ridicule, he could not bear to commit himself and the book fell by the wayside after years of revisions. The same fate awaited his next project, of some 36 'Rules for the direction of the Mind', and indeed the one after that, 'Elements of Metaphysics'. In fact, by the middle of his life, Descartes had published nothing and was being ridiculed as a *celebris promissor* – a great promiser – who boasted everything but produced nothing!

So, at the end of his thirties, Descartes decided to cobble together (perhaps we had best say 'prepare'), a collection of all his unpublished works, to be entitled 'The Project for a Universal Science, suited to Raise our Nature to the Highest Level of Perfection'. And, at this point, he decided that perhaps it would be better if most of the first-person references were removed. Except, that was, in the preface, which instead became almost autobiographical in its account of 'the method'. In due course, the 'Preface' is upgraded and the scientific notes downgraded, making the title of the book the 'Discourse on the Method for the Correct Use of Reason and for Seeking the Truth in Science'.

And again, it is the mark of the egotist that has Descartes writing in the first person, not only as he mused in his oven room over the possibility of the Devil deceiving him or recalling his impressions of the wax as it melted and disappears, but also in the original scientific writings on light and geometry – throughout them all at centre stage is the young Descartes, holding forth on his discoveries.

This then was part of the charm of Descartes' highly personal style of philosophy – but even so, the novelty was less than it seems to those of us unfamiliar with the seventeenth-century French traditions. Descartes was in fact also mimicking the highly popular writings of **MONTAIGNE**, whose *Essays*, carefully self-deprecating, rambling observations had delighted French aristocrats for a good 50 years already. Nor does Descartes shrink from opening the 'Discourse' with a crafty reference to his predecessor, when he says that 'good sense' is 'the most evenly distributed thing in the world'. (Montaigne had gone on to say, 'as is clear since no one is dissatisfied with their own share of it'. Descartes offers no such humorous note.)

As befits one educated under the most stern and orthodox Jesuit masters, Descartes repeats many of St AUGUSTINE's credos in his philosophy. The 'method of doubt' does not include doubting those opinions that appear particularly plausible. St Augustine himself referred to the assistance of 'divine revelation' in coping with the uncertainties of human knowledge; this is recast as 'natural light' by Descartes, saying that all that appears obvious to us must be true. Alas, it leaves open the possibility for others to see by the natural light such truths as, say, the earth being flat.

In the opening summary for the *Meditations* he writes:

The whole of the errors that arise from our senses are brought under review, while the means of avoiding them are pointed out, and finally all the grounds are adduced from which the existence of material objects may be inferred. Not, however, because I deemed them of great utility in establishing what they prove, viz., that there is in reality a world, that human beings are possessed of

## DUALISM AND ANIMALS AS MACHINES

'I should like that those not versed in anatomy should take the trouble . . . of having cut up before their eyes the heart of some large animal which has lungs (for it is in all respects sufficiently similar to the heart of a man), and cause that there be demonstrated to them the two chambers or cavities which are within it. . . I wish to acquaint them with the fact that this movement which I have just explained follows as necessarily from the very disposition of the organs, as can be seen by looking at the heart, and from *the heat which can be felt with the fingers* . . . and from the nature of the blood of which we can learn by experience, as does that of a clock from the power, the situation, and the form, of its counterpoise and of its wheels . . . the *animal spirits* therein contained should have the power to move the members, just as the heads of animals, a little while after decapitation are still observed to move and bite the earth, notwithstanding that they are no longer animate; what changes are necessary in the brain to cause wakefulness, sleep and dreams; how light, sounds, smells, tastes, heat and all other qualities pertaining to external objects are able to imprint on it various ideas by the intervention of the senses; how hunger, thirst and other internal affections can also convey their impressions upon it; what should be regarded as the "common sense" by which these ideas are received, and what is meant by the memory which retains them, by the fancy which can change them in diverse ways and out of them constitute new ideas, and which, by the same means, distributing *the animal spirits* through the muscles, can cause the members of such a body to move in as many diverse ways, and in a manner as suitable to the objects which present themselves to its senses and to its internal passions, as can happen in our own case. . .

. . . And this will not seem strange to those, who, knowing how many different *automata* or moving machines can be made by the industry of man, without employing in so doing more than a very few parts in comparison with the great multitude of bones, muscles, nerves, arteries, veins, or other parts that are found in the body of each animal. From this aspect *the body is regarded as a machine* which, having been made by the hands of God, is incomparably better arranged, and possesses in itself movements which are much more admirable, than any of those which can be invented by man. . .

On the other hand, if there were machines (puff puff!) which bore a resemblance to our body and imitated our actions as far as it was morally possible to do so, we should always have two very certain tests by which to recognise that, for all that, they were *not real men*. The first is that they could never use speech or other signs as we do when placing our thoughts on record for the benefit of others. [And the other is] that although machines can perform certain things as well as or perhaps better than any of us can do, they infallibly fall short in others, by the which means we may discover that they did not act from knowledge, but only from the disposition of their organs.'

From the *Discourse on Method*

bodies and so on – the truth of which no one of sound mind ever seriously doubted; but because, from close consideration of them, it is perceived that they are neither so strong nor clear as the reasoning which conducts us to the knowledge of our mind and of God. . .

Nonetheless, deduction, in Descartes' new *Geometry of Knowledge*, is based on identifying such certainties, labelling them as clear truths and then enlarging and expanding on them. So, for example, having discovered it to be 'impossible' to doubt the existence of thought but entirely possible to imagine the non-existence of your body, Descartes concludes that the SOUL is a separate substance, entirely independent of the body (the philosophical notion known as 'dualism'). And expanding on this, he concludes that animals have no souls but are unconscious brutes, mere machines.

For Descartes, the essence of the everyday, observable world is 'extension', that is, height, width, place. And these attributes he makes literally universal: all matter must be the same everywhere in the universe. He thus offered science an apparently sturdy foundation for building on, although even with modest testing, the structure often began to shake. One example is his 'law of collision', which LEIBNIZ ably refuted.

If the *Discourse on Method* was originally a collection of practical writings on scientific matters, the *Meditations* was equally disguised as a collection of 'famous people' talking about a new essay – the *Meditations de Prima Philosophia* by 'Renatus Des Cartes' (as he now wished to style himself). Among these objections, lightly brushed off, is one from Thomas HOBBES, disputing the notion of 'doubting' everything, his objection dismissed as irrelevant since (Descartes explains tersely) he only mentions the 'disease' of doubt in the spirit of a medical writer intending a moment later to demonstrate how to cure it. (In any case, the preface to the *Meditations* explains that the book is not intended to be suitable for 'weaker intellects'.)

Montaigne constantly referred to himself as a way of both ridiculing and excusing his views – Descartes uses the same device to distance himself from anticipated criticism, and also to create the dramatic story of the author's 'enlighten-

## DESCARTES' LAW OF COLLISION

Descartes' Law of Collision stated that when a smaller object (like a rock thrown at a wall) hits a larger one it bounces straight back with equal speed, but when a larger object collides with a smaller one (like two careless ice-skaters), they move off together in a way that conserves the total quantity of motion. So far, so apparently obvious, but this, unfortunately, is not how other objects in the world operate, as a moment's thought suffices to demonstrate. Leibniz set out a simple but effective thought experiment in which he imagines a collision in which a ball strikes an ever-so-fractionally larger ball. In this case, according to Descartes' Law, the first ball must bounce back with equal speed to its approach while the other remains unmoved. Now, Leibniz says, suppose a tiny wafer is shaved off the second ball so that it becomes now fractionally the smaller of the two – what do we imagine happening if the experiment is rerun then?

According to Descartes' Law, if the collision is rerun, the first ball which previously bounced off the other at full tilt, will this time combine with it, and the two roll off together in the same direction at half-speed. Leibniz thinks it implausible that such a tiny change could have such a dramatic effect, and hence that there is a need for Descartes to review his Law (and, actually, some of his other notions, which, such as those of 'empty space' and 'motion', let alone the relation of the mind to the body, were also rather hard to explain). But the inventor of the method of doubt has no use for it himself here.

ment' after some six days reflecting on the nature of the world in a warm oven room. But it is only a device, the process of enlightenment seems to have taken as many years as the six days described in the book. But of course, if the whole enlightenment process has religious (Jesuit) undertones, so very particularly does the choice of six days.

The famous words *cogito ergo sum* never appear in the original version, only in a later and indeed rather casual translation (although there is a French language formulation in the *Discourses*). The words used are better translated as: '. . . let the Demon deceive me as much as he may, he

## DESCARTES MEDITATES IN THE OVEN ROOM

*On the first day,* Renatus Des Cartes enters the terrifying world of nothingness by allowing everything to be unknown and uncertain. . .

*On the second day,* Renatus Des Cartes calms his fears by reflecting that at least he knows one thing, that he is at least a doubting, fearing, thinking thing. . . 'What am I? A thing that thinks, what is that? A thing that doubts, understands, affirms, denies, is willing, is unwilling and also imagines and has sensory perceptions. . .' (*Meditations*)

*On the third day,* Renatus discovers that the existence of God is certain. . .

*On the fourth day,* he teaches himself some ways to avoid error. . .

*And on the fifth day* he furnishes himself with a superior proof of God's existence and. . .

*On the sixth and final day,* he throws aside any doubts and prepares to re-enter the world equipped with a new science for understanding it, a science that applies more carefully the very tools of sense perception originally jettisoned on day one.

will never bring it about that I am nothing so long as I think I am something. So, after considering everything very thoroughly, I must conclude that this proposition, *I am, I exist,* is necessarily true, every time that I say it, or conceive it in my mind'.

Descartes was clear to emphasise the difference between 'I think' and 'there are thoughts', a distinction that has got lost many times along the way ever since. And there are Augustine's saintly footprints all over the 'cogito' too. The saint had taught that 'He who is not can certainly not be deceived; therefore, if I am deceived, I am.'

Descartes said his intention was to create a 'geometry of METAPHYSICS' – but one built up not by putting one brick upon another in mental sequence, but by analysis of the various parts of the intellectual edifice, to see if they agree and can hold together. The whole LOGICAL approach, as with the philosophical narrative itself, was allowed to rest on the delayed effect of 'what is not yet known'.

His greatest works, the *Discourse* and *Meditations*, were in many ways afterthoughts – appendages intended to flatter the author, and not the attempt to overturn the fusty standards of French philosophy, let alone Church author-

ity, as they are sometimes reinvented as today. Even the 'method of doubt' is a mere device, speedily replaced by the author's ability to directly obtain true knowledge.

The tale told by Descartes of how he split the world into two separate parts, mind and matter, certainly ushers in the modern world of machines and dispassionate science, as well as sidelining mystery, feeling and compassion. Yet PLATO also has it that there are two kinds of substance, and strongly favours the separate existence of the soul (a fact which made him popular with Church Fathers like Augustine). In his dialogue, *Phaedo*, featuring SOCRATES in his condemned cell about to drink the hemlock, the case is set out for the separation of the soul from the body, firmly predicting that it alone will go to heaven. When Socrates is challenged to justify his faith in the soul's immortality, he uses the same sort of examples later used so effectively by Descartes – of the perishable world of substance and appearance, as opposed to the unchanging world of pure knowledge.

Descartes died a few years later in Sweden, that 'land of bears between rocks and ice' as he describes it unfondly, intent on his writings to the last – but not, as might be imagined, great philosophical treatises, rather a comedy and a ballet for the queen and her courtiers' amusement.

Contributor: Martin Cohen

## Further reading

Descartes, R. (1637) *The Discourse on Method*

Descartes, R. (1641) *Meditations on First Philosophy*

## DETERMINISM

Determinists think that events, including people's actions, do not happen by chance, but rather are caused, or predetermined, by something already decided. The chain of events leads back, until eventually we need a 'first cause', which is generally taken to be divine in character. The theory implies, of course, that the future is all decided, and the Greeks had the notion of the 'fates', even though EPICURUS modified the ATOMISM of DEMOCRITUS to include the random, 'undetermined' swerve of the particles of life.

After NEWTON elegantly demonstrated that

the mysterious movements of the cosmos could all be both explained and anticipated by measurements coupled with mathematics, the universe was reduced, it seemed, to a clockwork toy, and with it, humans seemed to lose their freedom to act.

These days, QUANTUM MECHANICS aims to explore whether there might really be something in Epicurus' 'swerve', but on the wider issues of determinism, the debate about what is and what is not really 'possible' to do otherwise remains firmly a philosophical question, and not a scientific one.

## DEWEY, JOHN (1859–1952)

Professor at Chicago and Columbia, John Dewey is remembered now mainly for his views on education, of which he favoured 'democratic' and progressive approaches. This is partly because he regarded HUMAN NATURE as being moulded by the circumstances we are surrounded by, and also that the best of such conditions are democratic ones. Education, he says, is a process of learning through freely discovered experiences, and not through officially devised and sanctioned routines.

Philosophically, Dewey reacted against his early HEGELIAN roots, instead rejecting all forms of DUALISM, not just between mind and body, but also between 'fact and value', thought and action', 'means and ends'. In its place, he used a kind of (DARWINIAN) evolutionary model, in which enquiries are modified and improved by constant 'testing', be it in the laboratory or in society.

SEE ALSO

The essay 'Individual Psychology and Education', under Education

## DIALECTIC

From ancient Greece to medieval Europe, the dialectic was a form of debate, that proceeded by challenging assertions of fact by posing questions, leading to modified assertions and more questions. Later though, KANT used the approach to show that science and philosophy alike contain contradictory elements, and HEGEL modified it slightly to emphasise the supposed progressive element of the dialectic – it should lead to ever better approximations to knowledge, and indeed (Hegel thought) eventually would reach a point at which all contradictions are resolved. Hegel considered this

stage to be that, in METAPHYSICAL terms, of knowledge 'knowing itself', and in practical terms, to be more or less there already in his contemporary Prussia. MARX and ENGELS considered it to be, on the contrary, yet to be achieved, in the very different society of the pure COMMUNIST state.

## DICHOTOMY

Everything in this encyclopaedia must be red or not red. Or indeed, read or not read. In LOGIC, a dichotomy is the division of an entity into two mutually exclusive parts. One use is for definitions, so for example, we might divide the encyclopaedia into 'key entries' and 'minor entries'. As ARISTOTLE observed, compared with the certainty of 'syllogistic deduction', the danger of such attempts to classify things, is that the criteria used may be faulty, and we may accidentally place things in one category which would have been better kept in the other.

## DIFFERENCE PRINCIPLE

See Rawls.

## DILEMMAS

There is a LOGICAL definition of a dilemma, which is something about hypotheticals, antecedents and disjunctions and too tedious to mention here. We might say in writing the encyclopaedia we face a little bit of a dilemma: on the one hand, we should mention the technical definition, and on the other hand, if we do, the reader will be confused, quite possibly put off and (worst of all) bored. However, it is not really a dilemma as, to be honest, it is not a choice that matters, and as everyone knows, dilemmas are choices which matter, and so only choices which matter are dilemmas. Nonetheless, the logical aspect does live on, for true dilemmas seem to have a contradictory quality – we cannot choose both options, and in choosing just one, we offend the other requirement.

The Greek word means 'two premises', but we also speak of finding a way 'between the horns of the dilemma', which, even if it sounds as if dilemmas were some kind of woolly goat, is faithful to the original sense of the term.

## DIOGENES LAERTIUS

Author of *The Lives and Opinions of the Philosophers*, an important source for ancient philosophy in general, but in particular for CYNICISM, STOICISM, PYRRHO and EPICURUS. Apart from being the compiler of the above-mentioned work, he is unknown. He is generally thought to date from the third century CE.

## DIOGENES OF SINOPE: 'THE CYNIC' (*C.* 400–325 BCE)

Born in Sinope on the southern shore of the Black Sea, Diogenes later moved to Athens and may have spent some time in Corinth. He is renowned for his controversial behaviour, recorded in Book Six of DIOGENES LAERTIUS and as the most important exponent of CYNICISM. His austere and uncompromising way of life led PLATO to call him a 'Socrates gone mad', by which he probably meant that Diogenes took SOCRATES' philosophy and pushed it to its logical extreme.

### DIOGENES AND 'THE DOGGIES'

Diogenes was expelled from his home town of Sinope, after his father was accused of having defaced the currency, and went to live in Athens and Corinth. Diogenes held that the only thing in the world that really matters is the distinction between right and wrong, or vice and virtue. As with Buddhists, he held that virtue is to be achieved through self-sufficiency, and this is best sought by the removal of want. The wise person thus has no use for property, goods, conventional values and the internal disturbance of desires and emotions. He is famous for illustrating his theories in practice, for example, by standing in the cold hugging a bronze statue in order to train his body to ignore cold, by courting insults in order to harden his emotions; similarly, generally living as a homeless beggar. His high point, at least in philosophy dictionaries, was the occasion of his masturbating in the public square, saying that if only it were as easy to be rid of the desire for food by rubbing his stomach! He is sometimes remembered by his nickname, 'the Dog', and occasionally his followers are called 'the Doggies'.

## DIRECT ACTION (NON-VIOLENT)

There are two types of political action, non-violent action, of which GANDHI was the chief exponent, and violent action, of which there are many forms and many advocates.

Mahatma Gandhi (1869–1948) was a *karma*

*yogin* (an action man) who based his actions on *satya* (pure existent truth), which demanded *ahimsa* (non-violence). His objective was to free the oppressed and those condemned to poverty from colonial tyranny. In one of the most famous acts of non-violent action in history, Gandhi's march to the sea and his ceremonial distilling of salt from the water, both the power and the limitations of civil disobedience are seen. The campaign was non-violent only on the protesters' part. In May 1930, a column of volunteers tried to march towards the salt heaps and the British toleration of protest came to an end: 320 Indians were injured after being beaten to the ground with steel-tipped bamboo sticks, and 2 died. Over subsequent protests, the violence escalated. India gained its independence in 1948, but much violence ensued. Gandhi fasted until the violence ended. He was assassinated shortly afterwards.

Gandhi's views can be contrasted with another twentieth-century opponent of colonialisation, the psychiatrist Frantz FANON (1925–61), who had exactly the same objectives as Gandhi but considered that 'decolonisation' must always be a violent phenomenon. His analysis of power politics is a convincing demonstration that without violent REVOLUTION the oppressed will remain oppressed. While Fanon was mainly engaged in the liberation of black Africa (coining the term 'NÉGRITUDE'), he applied his thinking to economic oppression generally. Becoming for many a hero of the poor and needy, he was equally also increasingly unpopular with the rich and greedy, who regarded his thinking as a serious threat, while the historian Eric Hobsbawm accused him of seeing action with gun or bomb as *ipso facto* preferable to non-violent action.

But then there is also inaction. Direct action is action that can be seen. Indirect action is action said to be taking place but which cannot be seen. Inaction is not taking place and cannot be seen.

With a few notable exceptions, philosophers have tended to favour non-violence over violence. In the last century, Bertrand RUSSELL graced protest marches by CND (the Campaign for Nuclear Disarmament) into his nineties, and Jean-Paul SARTRE led the 1968 protests against increasing state control by de Gaulle's exhausted government. When permission was requested from President de Gaulle to arrest Sartre, he replied, with suitable gravitas: 'In France one does not imprison VOLTAIRE'.

# Further reading

Gandhi, M.K. (1927) *An Autobiography, or the Story of My Experiments with the Truth*

Fanon, F. (1952) *Black Skin, White Masks*

# DOGMATISM

From the Greek *dogma*, for belief. As was neatly summarised by SEXTUS EMPIRICUS, in *Outline of Pyrrhonism*, 'Those who are properly called dogmatists . . . think that they have discovered the truth.'

# DOUBLE EFFECT, ETHICAL NOTION OF

In many cases, an action has two effects: one is the desired one and the other is, as it were, incidental, albeit still foreseeable. To use a contemporary example, the US attempt in 2002 to bomb the Iraqi president, Saddam Hussein, while he was thought (wrongly, as it turned out) to be dining in a restaurant, might have had the desired effect of killing the target, but it would also have had the effect of killing perhaps 50 innocent diners. Can such actions be ethically sanctioned? Thomas Aquinas thought that they could, as long as all three of the following mealy-mouthed rules are followed:

1. The evil result is not directly intended: no one wants to kill the diners.
2. The good result is not directly achieved through the bad result: it is not necessary for the diners to be killed, as the target could still be in the building and be killed. Note, actually, in this case, the proposed bombing falls at this requirement, as the likelihood of catching the target depends on his being surrounded by other people in the restaurant – making the bombing 'unethical'.
3. The good result outweighs the bad one: the target must be a very nasty piece of work, planning to kill many hundreds of innocent people, and the number of likely diners must be (in comparison) 'negligible'.

Like many philosophical theories (and Aquinas also has the much quoted one about 'Just Wars'), to assert that within such and such a system something is 'right', although useful for philosophy seminars, and indeed occasionally for politicians, does not actually make it so.

# DREAMS

Philosophers have always been very interested in what people are able to do when they are asleep. This is not because most people nod off during philosophical arguments, but because they think that, in sleep, the soul is freed, as it were, from the chains of earthly sense experience, to attain philosophical truths. (Well, that is what to say if you are caught dozing off.) KANT put it optimistically in the *Critique of Practical Reason,* that in 'deepest sleep, perhaps the greatest perfection of the mind might be exercised in rational thought'.

On the other hand, as Saint Thomas noted, if a man SYLLOGISES while asleep, when he wakes up 'he invariably recognises a flaw in some respect'. And PLATO himself records that SOCRATES asked Glaucon, 'Does not dreaming consist in mistaking the semblance of reality for reality itself?', a concern that continued to trouble WITTGENSTEIN in the mid-twentieth century, when, in his *Philosophical Investigations,* he worries that knowledge obtained in dreams was unreliable because it might not be remembered accurately.

But DESCARTES wrote, in the *Discourse on Method,* that 'all the same thoughts and conceptions which we have while awake may also come to us in sleep', adding later in a letter: 'I had good reason to assert that the human soul is always conscious in any circumstances, even in the mother's womb'. More recently, FREUD diagnosed, in *A General Introduction to Psychoanalysis,* that 'Dreams are the mode of reaction of the mind to stimuli acting upon it during sleep', which sounds like the view of ARISTOTLE, who had declared that someone who was asleep could both distinguish between a man and a horse, ugly or beautiful, white or not white.

Descartes ultimately decided, in the *Meditations,* that since God was 'supremely good and cannot err', any false information presented to the soul in the dreamlands must still be possible for a rational person to distinguish from the (supposedly) tidy, coherent knowledge of the world we live in. Neither LEIBNIZ nor Bertrand RUSSELL shared this confidence; Leibniz saying that 'it is not impossible, METAPHYSICALLY speaking, that there may be a dream as continuous and as lasting as the life of a man'. Or indeed, as the life of a butterfly, as described in a few lines of verse by the great exponent of life as a (butterfly) dream, the ancient Chinese sage, CHUANG TZU.

## DUALISM

Any theory of the world that divides it into two parts, neither of which can be reduced to the other, is called dualism. The most famous philosophical example is the so-called Cartesian dualism (of DESCARTES), wherein the world consists of two entirely separate entities, mind and matter, or 'extension' and 'thought', as he puts it. The obvious problem then is how one can affect the other; for example, how can the soul residing in a human being bring it about that they move their arm to have a drink – and why would the bodily need for a drink have caused the soul to want one too? The term is also used in other contexts.

## DUCK-RABBIT

In *Fact and Fable in Psychology*, J. Jastrow drew a strange, duck-like figure which also looks like a rabbit.

Is it a duck or a rabbit? (After Jastrow and Wittgenstein)

It is not a very good picture of either a rabbit or a duck, but nonetheless WITTGENSTEIN uses this example to argue that as the same thing can appear to be two different things, we must accept that PERCEPTION is a 'CONCEPT-laden' process, not a merely mechanical stream of SENSE DATA, as some would have it.

SEE ALSO

Perception

## DUNS SCOTUS, JOHN (C. 1266–1308)

As the name helpfully suggests, Duns Scotus was Scottish and probably came from Duns, although he spent most of his career as a philosophy lecturer in Oxford and Paris. Interestingly, his name also is the source for our word 'Dunce'. Philosophers at this time were concerned with questions such as how ARISTOTLE could be incorporated into Christian dogma. His own contribution was to say that human will is distinct from the intellect, and not bound by it. In fact, as we all know, the will does not necessarily choose the right thing, let alone the *'summum bonum'* (highest good), even when the intellect points it out to it very clearly!

Duns Scotus was a very careful thinker (for example, manoeuvring divine revelation out of philosophy into theology) and in so doing laid the ground for future, more sceptical approaches to conventional 'devout' philosophy.

## DURKHEIM, ÉMILE (1858–1917)

### The essential Durkheim

Born the year after COMTE's death, Émile Durkheim attempted to take Comte's work in developing a 'science of society' further, in particular by attempting to show how a new social consensus could provide the values of community and social order. These were values that had, Durkheim felt, characterised the pre-industrial era, and could also be called upon in his time to combat the increasing disorder stemming from the rapid changes resulting from industrialisation. Durkheim adopted a positive methodology, that is to say, he used the methods of natural science to understand social phenomena which were taken as essentially just another part of the natural world, to collect statistical evidence on suicides, on the labour force, on religion and on education. But Durkheim, like his fellow SOCIAL SCIENTIST and contemporary, Max WEBER (1864–1920), wanted also to build on this LOGICAL structure a more profound, METAPHYSICAL theory of social life, including an almost completely SUBJECTIVE moral and IDEALISTIC theory of social life. He says that:

■ individual morality and indeed consciousness are created from social life and the collective consciousness, and

■ social life is created out of a vast symbolism.

Unlike MARX, he tried to find a way to achieve this new social consensus without losing the benefits of individual emancipation and freedom.

## Rules and society

Durkheim's solution is centred around what he calls 'the collective consciousness' and the notion of 'social facts'. These last are 'ways of acting, thinking and feeling, external to the individual' – such as the customs and institutional practices, moral rules and laws of any society. Although these rules 'exist' in the minds of individuals, Durkheim says the true form can be found only when considering the behaviour of 'the whole' – of society itself. In this, not for the last time, he is echoing the words of PLATO and SOCRATES 2000 years before. Like Plato, Durkheim considered society to be essentially a moral phenomenon, created within a framework of overarching eternal values. And, like Plato, he rejected individualism and INTROSPECTION (and such approaches' attempts to create generalities out of particulars and to build social structures out of human atoms): instead, making society the cause and not merely the effect.

Durkheim rejects HOBBES' vision of the world in the 'state of nature', saying that if society were based, for example, on calculations of interest and social contracts, then the key social relationship would be the economic, 'stripped of all regulation and resulting from the entirely free initiative of the parties'. Society would simply be the situation 'where individuals exchanged the products of their labour, without any action properly social coming to regulate this exchange'.

Durkheim thinks this is not actually how society does function. 'Is this the character of societies whose unity is produced by the division of labour?' he asks rhetorically. And then, answering himself: 'If this were so, we could with justice doubt their stability. For if [self] interest relates men, it is never for more than some few moments.' Taking up Hobbes' challenge (as well as adopting his language), Durkheim goes on: 'where interest is the only ruling force, each individual finds himself in a state of war with every other since nothing comes to mollify the egos and any truce in this eternal antagonism would not be of long duration. There is nothing less constant than interest. Today, it unites me to you: tomorrow, it will make me your enemy.'

So we have to look elsewhere for explanation of the 'organic' solidarity of society. Durkheim chooses what he sees as Comte's 'organic' approach, in which everything is related to a whole. In the same way that an animal colony, for example, a beehive, 'whose members embody a continuity of tissue form one individual, every aggregate of individuals who are in continuous contact form a society. The division of labour can then be produced only in the midst of pre-existing society'. Individuals must be linked through material facts, but also by 'moral links' between them. As Durkheim explains:

> the claim sometimes advanced that in the division of labour lies the fundamental fact of all social life is wrong. Work is not divided among independent and already differentiated individuals who by uniting and associating bring together different aptitudes. For it would be a miracle if differences thus born through chance circumstance could unite so perfectly as to form a coherent whole. Far from preceding collective life, they derive from it. They can be produced only in the midst of a society, and under the pressure of social sentiments and social needs. That is what makes them essentially harmonious.

Societies are built up out of shared beliefs and sentiments, and the division of labour emerges from the structure created. Durkheim goes back to Comte, to remind the reader that, in Comte's words: 'co-operation, far from having produced society, necessarily supposes, as preamble, its spontaneous existence'. What brings people together are practical forces such as living in the same land, sharing the same ancestors and gods, having the same traditions. ROUSSEAU, Hobbes and even the UTILITARIANS are all guilty of disregarding the important social truth, that society pre-dates the individual.

> Collective life is not born from individual life, but it is, on the contrary, the second which is born from the first. . .
> Co-operation is . . . the primary fact of moral and social life.

People exist within and depend on only three 'types of milieu': the organism, the external world, and society. 'If one leaves aside the accidental variations of hereditary, – and their role in human progress is certainly not very considerable – the organism is not automatically modified; it is necessary that it be impelled by some external cause. As for the external world, since the beginning of history it has remained sensibly the same, at least if one does not take account of novelties which are of social origin. Consequently, there is only society which has changed enough to be able to explain the parallel changes in individual nature.'

Thus, Durkheim introduces the new science of 'socio-psychology'. And Durkheim considers our very awareness, our 'consciousness' to be not an individual but a social phenomenon. He argues that there are two types of symbol which create societies and cement the individual human beings into the social whole. These are collective representations, such as national flags and other shared symbols; and moral codes, such as notions of basic rights, and even unwritten, generally accepted, beliefs such as the idea that young children should be given toys to play with or that swimming in rivers should be free. Together, these written and unwritten rules create a 'collective consciousness'.

This consciousness is part of the psychological make-up of each individual in society, and is also the origin of more formal moral codes. Many things follow from this interpretation. For example, stealing from your neighbour is wrong not because of the affront to the neighbour, but because of the affront to the collective consciousness itself. And Durkheim draws from this, more generally, the conclusion that self-interest, or even considerations of the interests of the majority, (the goal assumed by utilitarianism), are incapable of producing moral behaviour. Instead, the 'collective consciousness' functions as a kind of watchdog for its own well-being as well as expressing a position based on certain principles.
Durkheim goes on:

It has often been remarked that civilisation
has a tendency to become more rational
and more logical. The cause is now evident.
That alone is rational which is universal.
What baffles understanding is the particular
and the concrete. . . the nearer the
common conscience is to particular things,
the more it bears their imprint, the more
unintelligible it is.

That is why we look on 'primitive civilisations' as we do. In fact, they are very like our own, and operate in a similar way. But, 'the more general the common conscience becomes, the greater the place it leaves to individual variations. When God is far from things and men, his action is no longer omnipresent nor ubiquitous. There is nothing fixed save abstract rules which can be freely applied in very different ways'. The collective conscience becomes more rational, and 'for this very reason, it wields less restraint over the free development of individual varieties.'

In essence, the key to social life is symbolism. It is the way that individuals communicate most effectively, and their social values are preserved and embodied in the sacred symbols.

Durkheim does make a special distinction between two types of possible society. There are 'simple' ones, where the population is small and dispersed within its limited territory, and 'complex' ones, with more members, closely packed, interacting and interdependent. The former are held together by traditions that operate uniformly on the various members, who are like little atoms – undifferentiated in themselves and interchangeable. The individuals in 'simple' societies have a powerful sense of shared purpose and function. This results in a type of social cohesion Durkheim calls 'mechanical'.

The other way of organising society, which Durkheim calls 'organic', is more complex. It involves a range of parallel institutions and traditions, with individuals falling into increasingly distinct subgroupings, each with its own traditions and 'social norms'. Within each grouping, individuals can become specialised and fulfil a particular function in the social whole. The division of labour, which Marx sought to abolish (as creating inequality), is seen by Durkheim as a desirable aspect of this evolution.

Because the cohesion of organic society is fundamentally one of interdependence, so even a malfunctioning part is valued. But there is a particular disease of complex societies that Durkheim identifies and gives a name to: *anomie*. This is the sense of futility and ALIENATION that leads individuals to, for example, take their lives, but also, perhaps, to attack their fellow citizens.

In all this, Durkheim's method for investigation was to try to find tangible instances of these admittedly immaterial social facts, through sophisticated analysis and interpretation of official statistics. These he found in fastidious trawls through collections of official statistics, population statistics, official descriptions of the nature of the workforce and professional groupings – even in the minutiae of the judicial codes. His most noted study is of the number of people committing suicide. For Durkheim, suicide was not just an individual activity (tragedy), but an action directly linked to and reflecting a general breakdown in social cohesion.

In *Suicide: a Study of Sociology*, Durkheim takes the discovery that self-destruction is more prevalent among certain religious groups – Protestants – than others, such as Catholics, to argue that this is because the 'collective consciousness' is stronger in Catholic communities. In a modern society, *anomie* (with its associated feelings of alienation from the whole, and individual futility) is such a threat that Durkheim says the various subgroupings in society, for example, the employees of a large multinational, or the vocational ones of professional groupings of academics, teachers, medical workers – or even politicians – need to be 'united and organised in a single body'. Taking the idea further, in *The Division of Labour*, Durkheim suggests professional groupings or unions should act almost as an extended family, taking an interest in all aspects of its members' well-being.

Contributor: Martin Cohen

# Further reading

Durkheim, E. (1912) *Social Rituals and Sacred Objects*

Durkheim, E. (1893) *Pre-contractual Solidarity*

# DUTY

'The moral law', wrote KANT, is 'a law of duty, or moral constraint'. In a general sense, duties are obligations that come with a role; in ETHICS, duties are those obligations that a person of 'good will' would feel. Kant attempted to show that they were all, in some sense, logically demonstrable. Central to his effort was dividing duties up between those dictated by law and those dictated by 'VIRTUE', those aimed at doing things for a positive reason and 'negative duties' – those dictated by desire to avoid doing something wrong.

More precisely, a duty is an action that one is under an obligation to perform, and to have an obligation is to be under a special kind of necessity ('moral' necessity) to perform a certain action. So 'duty' denotes an action, and 'obligation' denotes the moral necessity to perform it.

# *DVAITA* (DUALIST SCHOOL OF VEDANTA)

See *Madhva*.

# ECOCENTRISM

The currently rather fashionable new word for environmental HOLISM – the view that ethical and, in particular, environmental concerns need to be seen in the context of the whole of NATURE, of which humans, or indeed animals, are merely a part. So-called 'land ethics' and 'deep ecology' are merely a part of this all-encompassing ecocentrism.

# ECONOMICS

## Essentials of ethics and economics

Although economists like to portray their study as a precise kind of mathematical science, it remains firmly rooted in both social and individual psychology, as moulded by political institutions and norms. J.S. MILL's solution to this was to offer the reassurance of INTROSPECTION, a strategy largely accepted up until the 1930s. Yet economics both influences and is influenced by ETHICS. At its heart is the notion of human rationality and 'choice', and as in theories of UTILITARIAN ethics, judgements are arbitrarily considered to be of equal merit: it is not important why someone buys a tin of beans, only that they do so. Similarly, in terms of its modelling of actions and consequences, economics appears to offer, for some ethicists at least, tools for calculating and exploring the consequences of their suggestions.

## Economics: ancient and modern

The word 'economics' comes from the Greek *Oikonomia*, which itself is a combination of *Oikos* 'house' and *nemein* 'manage'. But this is a very different conception from the unlimited acquisitiveness endorsed in the modern economy. Instead, the ancients believed that nature places a natural limit upon the extent of necessary riches. **ARISTOTLE** writes, '. . . since no tool belonging to any art is without a limit whether in number or in size, and riches are a collection of tools for the householder and the statesman' (*Politics,* 1256b). Conceiving of wealth as a means for achieving our proper ends, he distinguishes natural acquisition from the perverse tendency to pursue wealth as an end in itself. And indeed, the ancients denigrated the life dedicated to manual labour and business dealings, since these activities diminish the time which might otherwise be directed towards the political or philosophic life. **SOCRATES** expresses this sentiment in Xenophon's work on economics:

'. . . for the base mechanic arts, so called, have got a bad name; and what is more, are held in ill repute by civilised communities, and not unreasonably; seeing they are the ruin of the bodies of all concerned in them, workers and overseers alike, who are forced to remain in sitting postures and to hug the loom, or else to crouch whole days confronting a furnace. Hand in hand with physical enervation follows apace enfeeblement of soul: while the demand which these base mechanic arts makes on the time of those employed in them leaves them no leisure to devote to the claims of friendship and the state.'

(Xenophon, *Economics* IV)

While cities may come into being to facilitate trade and preserve life, the ultimate goal of the political association, for the ancients, was to promote virtue and the 'good life'. It was nearly 2000 years later that John **LOCKE** was prepared to defend unlimited acquisition against the teachings of the ancients, in this case, based on his conception of the labour theory of value. Human beings, says Locke, in this following **HOBBES**, possess an inalienable claim to their body, and this, Locke argues, grants each of them a right to take possession of property in which they have invested their labour:

The labour of his body and the work of his hands, we may say, are properly his. Whatsoever, then, he removes out of the state that Nature hath provided and left it in, he hath mixed his labour with it, and

joined to it something that is his own, and thereby makes it his property.

(*Second Treatise of Government,* section 27)

Rather than understanding riches as a tool for achieving a definite and limited set of ends, Locke recognises money's ability to overcome nature's bounds. The farmer can only profit from hoarding excess produce as long as it is prevented from spoiling. If he exchanges his surplus for money, he can acquire without needing to ever again concern himself with spoilage. The body dies while wealth lives on.

While the modern economic system is liberating in so far as it recognises the fundamental **EQUALITY** of all human beings to own the work of their hands, it only accomplishes this by reducing the individual to a cog in the production process, a tendency praised by Adam **SMITH** for its gains in productivity. Whereas pre-market exchange forges bonds between individuals, industrial **CAPITALISM** fetishises the commodity, concealing the vast social nexus of workers that contributed to its production. Karl **MARX** writes:

A commodity is therefore a mysterious thing, simply because in it the social character of men's labour appears to them as an objective character stamped upon the product of that labour; because the relation of the producers to the sum total of their own labour is presented to them as a social relation, existing not between themselves, but between the products of their labour.

(*Capital,* Volume 1, Chapter 3)

With the fall of **COMMUNISM**, it seems increasingly that the world has imploded into a single industrial complex. Individuals in the Third World must abandon traditional cultures in search of the 'better' life promised by a world of competition for consumer goods. And if the First World may appear to benefit from global capitalism – particularly in contrast to the 'developing' world – all individuals in the economic system are impoverished inasmuch as basic human relations are reduced to the exchange of commodities.

Indeed, divorced from any religious connotation, Christ's recognition of money's ability to be worshipped as a deity may be instructive for orienting our comportment to the economic sphere: 'You cannot serve both God and Money' warned Saint Matthew (6:24).

If money assumes the position of a deity, all previous values will also be recalculated in terms of monetary worth. And, within this framework, human action will be directed increasingly by varieties of cost-benefit analysis – without regard for the ethical consequences.

Contributor: Daniel Silvermintz

## Further reading on economics

Xenophon, *Economics*

Locke, J. (*c.* 1681) *Two Treatises of Government*

Smith, A. (1776) *Adam Smith, An Inquiry into the Nature And Causes of the Wealth of Nations*

# EDUCATION

## Essentials of education

What is education? This great question was central to philosophy for thousands of years, although (to my knowledge) it is now considered either marginal or not philosophy at all. But here, to address the issue, is the first in a selection of essays originally published in the journal *The Philosopher* for the Philosophical Society of England. The Society was established in 1913 by what is recorded as 'a number of professional scholars and amateur philosophers' to promote the 'study of practical philosophy among the general public'. Its aim was (and still is) to bring together professional philosophers and non-professionals, to bring philosophical ideas and problems to the public attention, and to encourage wider discussion of both traditional and topical philosophical issues.

In its heyday, the Society numbered over 1500 enthusiastic members and received contributions from the great names of the subject, such as John DEWEY, justly celebrated as one of the great progressive educationalists of the twentieth century. His essay, 'Individual Psychology and Education' is reproduced below. In it, he outlines some basic principles for an education that is both democratic, effective and enjoyable.

## Individual Psychology and Education

The purpose of education has always been to every one, in essence, the same – to give the young the things they need in order to develop in an orderly, sequential way into members of society. This was the purpose of the education given to a little aboriginal in the Australian bush before the coming of the white man. It was the purpose of the education of youth in the golden age of Athens. It is the purpose of education today, whether this education goes on in a one-room school in the mountains of Tennessee or in the most advanced progressive school in a radical community. But to develop into a member of society in the Australian bush had nothing in common with developing into a member of society in ancient Greece, and still less with what is needed today. Any education is, in its forms and methods, an outgrowth of the needs of the society in which it exists.

No one is surprised that the educational methods in Soviet Russia are different from those elsewhere. That other methods will develop in a Hitlerized Germany is easy to understand. Yet even within as rigid and controlled societies as these two countries are at present striving for, there is and will be experimentation, discussion and difference of opinion amongst teachers as to the best methods of developing members of those societies. There will be satisfied parents and dissatisfied parents. There will be happy children who like the schools and adjust to them easily, and children who do not adjust and whose difficulties are blamed on the schools.

The Australian aboriginal, the Athenian, the Soviet citizen, the Hitlerite had, or have, societies that can be defined in definite terms; the aims of which, whatever we think of them, can be recognised by anyone. Accept these aims and there will be comparatively little difference of opinion about the kind of education that should be given youth in any one of the societies. In most democratic countries, aims have, until recently, been stated in terms of the individual, not in those of the society he is to be educated for. In the early days of modern education, all that seemed to be necessary for the attainment of the ideals of democracy was to give every child an equal start in life by furnishing him with certain fundamentals of learning, then turn him loose and let him do the rest.

Then life began to change. The things once made at home were now made in factories and the child knew nothing of them. The inventions and discoveries in science brought railroads, the telegraph and telephone, gas and electricity, farm machinery – a host of things about which one could not really know without far more training than was given by mere practice in using the finished product. Industrialisation brought the big city with its slums and palaces, its lack of play space, its sharp distinction between city and country. Finally, it brought the automobile, the movies and the radio, with their enormous influence in taking the family out of the home and making even the little child much more part of the great world than had ever been dreamed of in the past. These changes did not happen all at once. If they had, perhaps it would have been necessary to scrap the simple curriculum of the first schools and begin afresh with one that recognised all these new and tremendously different factors at once. Instead, what happened was that gradually, as one new need was felt, a new subject was added to the course of study.

The science of individual **PSYCHOLOGY** began to develop after the enrichment of the curriculum was well on its way, so that the two developments went on in parallel lines touching almost not at all. The discoveries of the former about the way people learn, about individual differences and the interrelation of effort and interest, were unknown to schoolmasters, or were thought of as too new-fangled for consideration. It was a little as if no one had been willing to put radios on the market, because it was obviously an absurd idea that sound can be transmitted for vast distances through mountains and brick walls without special means like wires. And although these psychological discoveries are many of them as well-established today as the facts of the radio, they are still temperamentally abhorrent to a great many schoolmasters and parents. A great many others are willing to admit them when stated in general terms, but feel the strongest emotional reluctance to giving children the benefit of them by applying them to teaching methods. In brief, these psychological discoveries may be stated as follows:

1. The human mind does not learn in a vacuum; the facts presented for learning, to be grasped, must have some relation to the previous experience of the individual or to his present needs; learning proceeds from the concrete to the general, not from the general to the particular.
2. Every individual is a little different from every other individual, not alone in his general capacity and character; the differences extend to rather minute abilities and characteristics, and no amount of discipline will

eradicate them. The obvious conclusion of this is that uniform methods cannot possibly produce uniform results in education, that the more we wish to come to making everyone alike the more varied and individualised must the methods be.
3. Individual effort is impossible without individual interest. There can be no such thing as a subject which in and by itself will furnish training for every mind. If work is not in itself interesting to the individual he cannot put his best efforts into it. However hard he may work at it, the effort does not go into the accomplishment of the work but is largely dissipated in a moral and emotional struggle to keep the attention where it is not held.

A progressive education movement has been the outgrowth of the realisation by educators of the fact that our highly complex, rapid, crowded civilisation demands and has been met by changes in school subjects and practice; that to make these changes effective something more is needed than simply the addition of one subject after another. The new subjects should be introduced with some relation to each other and the ways in which they operate and integrate in the world outside of school. It is also the outgrowth of the desire to put into practice in the classroom what the new science of psychology has discovered about individual learning and individual differences.

The desire to adjust a school curriculum to society results too from the use of the new psychology to increase the pupil's learning. When one tries to adjust a school curriculum to society, it immediately becomes necessary to formulate a conception of what that society is. What are its strengths that should be stressed in the schools, what its weaknesses that children should understand? Is it a good thing to bring up the young with desires and habits that try to preserve everything just as it is today, or should they be able to meet change, to weigh the values and find good in the new? How much of the background and development of our civilisation do children need to be able to understand what is in the world today? How much do they need to become cultivated individuals, able to enjoy leisure and carry on worthwhile traditions? The answers to these and many other questions, and the skill used in translating them into practice will determine the kind of school. Both these factors will differ according to the temperament, beliefs, background and experience of the individuals who answer them. In a world changing as rapidly as ours, expression of differences of opinion by different kinds of schools is a wholesome sign and an encouragement to progressive education.

Two instances of the kind of criticism that is commonly levelled at a progressive school are the matters of learning to read and of discipline. We know today that certain children have reading difficulties, due sometimes to eye peculiarities, sometimes to left-handedness, sometimes to other more obscure causes, or to a combination of all these possibilities. Experience has shown that if a child is mentally normal, he will learn to read anyway by the age of ten or so, and that in afterlife it is impossible to tell these late readers from the children who teach themselves when they are three. This shows that the fact that some children are backward about learning to read has nothing to do with the kind of school they go to. Similarly, there is absolutely no scientific objective evidence to support the view that behaviour problems are relatively more common in progressive schools than in traditional schools, or that the former are less successful in straightening out those that do arise than the latter. It is probably true that a progressive school seems disorderly to visitors who cannot imagine a school except as a place where rows of silent children sit quietly at a desk until told to do something by the teacher. But modern education does not aim at this kind of order. Its aim is the kind of order that exists in a roomful of people, each one of whom is working at a common task. There will be talking, consulting, moving about in such a group, whether the workers are adults or children. The standard for order and discipline of a group is not how silent is the room, or how few and uniform the kind of tools and materials that are being used, but the quality and amount of work done by the individuals and the group.

Progressive education, it is sometimes said, stresses individual development and the training of special abilities or talents at the expense of learning social adjustment, good manners, how to get along with adults. In fact, it is criticised because of its highly individualistic philosophy. If we confine ourselves to the philosophy, just the opposite seems to be the truth. It is the modern schools that have formulated their aims in definite social terms. It is they that are trying to work out some method of achieving harmony between the democratic belief in the liberty of the individual and his responsibility for the welfare of the group. To many, the mere fact that children are free to move about, to seek help from others, to undertake pieces of work in small groups, is taken as evidence that the aim of the methods must be to develop individualists, to let the children do as they please. These methods were, in fact, introduced because we know that physical freedom is necessary to growing bodies and because psychological investigation has proved that learning is better and faster when the child understands his problem as a whole and does his work under his own motive power rather than under piecemeal dictation from a master. Moral and intellectual powers increase in vigour when the force of the individual's spontaneous interest and desire to accomplish something are behind them. This is as true of children as it is of adults. It is these powers that progressive education seeks to release.

Progressive methods, some would say, may work with young children; but when the high-school is reached they must be given up and replaced by the old methods in order to allow pupils to pass college entrance examinations. It is true that these examinations require the accumulation of such a vast number of specific facts, that a great deal of drill and cramming is necessary if a pupil is to know enough answers to pass. This does not mean, however, anything more than to get into college a young person has to spend a great deal of time memorising details so that he can answer a great many detailed questions. This is so much true, that an interesting experiment is being carried out at present in the United States where nearly twenty progressive schools have completed arrangements with almost all the accredited colleges and universities to begin, in 1936, admitting their students on bases other than the passing of the regular entrance examinations. After a reasonable number of progressive school pupils have graduated from college, we shall have an authoritative answer as to whether progressive methods can be used in high schools with pupils who are going to college.

Meantime, change and experimentation will go on anyway because life outside the school is changing, because scientific knowledge of the nature of growth is developing, and because parents want things for the children that they did not obtain when they went to school. The real measure of the success of the progressive schools is the modifications that finally take place in conservative schools because of the experimental pioneering. For after all, every worthwhile education is a direct enrichment of the life of the young and not merely a more or less repellent preparation for the duties of adult life. Life is growth and while it involves meeting and overcoming obstacles, and hence has hard and trying spots, it is essentially something to be enjoyed now.

Dewey, J., in *The Philosopher*,
Volume XII, 1934

## PHILOSOPHY WITH CHILDREN

Matthew Lipman's work in the USA in the early 1970s was instrumental in creating the movement which became known throughout the world as 'Philosophy for Children' or 'Philosophy with Children'. Influenced by Dewey and the child psychologist Vygotsky, Lipman sought to introduce philosophical issues and problem solving into the classroom, both at elementary and more advanced levels. This has led to the introduction of philosophy as a subject into some countries' curricula, while in others it is practised more informally. Lipman's method uses 'informal logic' approaches similar to traditional rhetoric and also narrative or story-based approaches. It can be seen as having relevance both in epistemological and moral formation. Methodologies employed vary widely from country to country, from the more substantive or didactic approach, which has set answers, to the more procedural, which employs 'process' and allows children to come to their own conclusions.

The main aim of 'Philosophy with Children' is to improve 'first order thinking' or critical thinking in children, as opposed to the 'second order thinking' or memorisation approach, which is more prominent in traditional education. In more recent times, it has also been utilised to facilitate the development of 'anti-racism' and 'intercultural' programmes in schools. Here, it can be seen as developing the work of the Brazilian philosopher of education, Paulo Freire. It can be employed either as a stand-alone subject on the curriculum, or else as a supplementary method to be integrated into the curriculum more generally.

Contributor: Jones Irwin

SEE ALSO
Learning

## EGO, EGOISM

For Sigmund FREUD, the MIND has three parts: the *id*, the *ego* and the *superego*. The *id* has appetites but is not rational; it is what Freud originally called 'the UNCONSCIOUS'. The *superego*, on the other hand, is the body's 'moral' faculty; it is the 'CONSCIENCE', and is quite capable of acting not in the individual's interests but with regard to an idealised or general interest. But it is the *ego* that speaks for the real 'me': it has to try to decide between the opposed promptings of the *id* and the *superego*. It is, in a way, a bit like those cartoons of the drunkard looking at a bottle of whisky while two thought balloons pop up, one with a forked-tail devil saying, 'Go on – a little bit won't harm!', and the other with an angel saying, 'Remember your vow never to drink again while on duty!' In all this, the *ego* represents the compromise position dictated by prudence and responsibility.

In ETHICS, egoism (sometimes called NORMATIVE egoism or rational egoism) is the view that satisfying oneself is a sufficient justification for choosing one action over another. The case for egoism is made strongly by Thrasymachus in PLATO's *Republic*, and similarly is the founding principle of government for Thomas HOBBES in his *Leviathan*.

For some philosophers, there is an additional problem for 'egocentric statements' such as 'this book belongs to me', as both the terms 'me' and 'this' are hard to represent in a LOGICAL reformulation.

## EINSTEIN, ALBERT (1879–1955)

Albert Einstein was born in Ulm, worked as a clerk in the Berne Patents Office, and wrote an influential paper that attempted to build upon NEWTON's three-dimensional model of the universe, to include TIME itself. Often, his 'relativity' is taken as destroying Newtonian physics, but he himself was very clear that this was not the case.

Einstein originally called his 'Special Theory of Relativity', 'The Electrodynamics of Moving Bodies', a much more sensible title. He explained the germ of the idea later in very 'unrelative' terms:

From the very beginning it appeared to me
intuitively clear that, judged from the
standpoint of such an observer, (travelling
at the speed of light, relative to the Earth)
everything would have to happen according

to the same laws as for an observer who, relative to the Earth, was at rest. For how, otherwise, should the first observer know (i.e. be able to determine) that he is in a state of fast uniform motion?

Nonetheless, the paper starts with a simple THOUGHT EXPERIMENT designed to show that electrodynamics – studies of heat and light and magnetism – can dispense with the need for 'absolute rest', a theory found in Newton's bucket some centuries earlier. Einstein imagines a magnet and a wire spiral moving relative to each other. Doing this creates an electrical current in the wire. First of all, Einstein imagines the wire moving and the magnet at 'absolute' rest. Doing this, he points out, induces an electrical current in the wire. Then, in the second part of the thought experiment, the wire is stationary and the magnet moves. But doing this also induces an electrical current in the wire. This alone, he suggests, is enough to show that 'the phenomena of electrodynamics as well as of mechanics possess no properties corresponding to the idea of absolute rest.'

Instead, in the 'Special Theory', the first rule is that the speed of light is the same for all observers, regardless of their motion relative to the source of the light. The second one is that anyone (as long as they are not subject to different gravitational or acceleration effects) should observe the same physical laws. Putting these two ideas together, Einstein showed that the only way this can happen is if time and space themselves change. That, of course, flies against our everyday experience but it has nonetheless been shown to explain events in more rarefied circumstances. For example, scientists have shown that an atomic clock flying at high speed in a jet plane will tick more slowly than one left behind at the aerodrome, and during eclipses astronomers have detected starlight being 'bent' by the sun's gravity.

Philosophers today, who are often scientifically illiterate, despite the ancient history of philosophy as the investigation of the natural world, sometimes try to employ a notion of 'relativity' to back up radical philosophical doctrines of the arbitrary, 'SUBJECTIVE' nature of all judgements, be they factual ones about the universe, or psychological ones, or, of course, ETHICAL judgements.

## ELEATICS

The Eleatics were one of the key schools of ancient Greek philosophy, named after their base in Elea, on the southern Italian coast. (Elea was then a Greek colony.) PARMENIDES and ZENO were its most famous alumni, Parmenides arguing that fundamental reality consists of just one thing; a point Zeno was anxious to promote in his PARADOXES. These, typical of the school, rely purely on reason and not at all on the dubious evidence of the senses.

## *ELENCHUS*

Another name for 'Socratic Method', or indeed 'DIALECTICAL reasoning', *elenchus* is, essentially, the technique exemplified by PLATO in his description of SOCRATES' debates with other Athenians. The characteristic of it is that both parties are on a joint quest for TRUTH, and the inquiry proceeds by someone putting forward their belief, and the other challenging it by suggesting that their position entails another consequence, apparently incompatible with (contradictory to) the first. It is a very good debating technique, but because the points are neither trivial nor negative in intent, it should be distinguished from those methods which the Greeks came to disparage as 'SOPHISTRY'.

## EMOTION

From the Latin, *e*, or 'out', and *movere*, 'to move'. ARISTOTLE thought that emotion was indeed a kind of 'motion'. He describes embarrassment as the motion, or impulse, for revenge accompanied by pain, after an insult or slight is perceived. Both HUME and DESCARTES characterised emotions as 'feelings', not so different from the 'yellow' feeling that comes from seeing the colour 'yellow', for example, but as Descartes stressed, emotions having some sort of additional bodily response. This line was taken further by William JAMES and the Danish psychologist C. Lange, to the point that the emotion sorrow becomes simply the theoretical mental parallel to exhibiting bodily behaviour like crying, and to be 'afraid' is the theoretical mental state paralleling the state of having gone white and started to tremble. The feeling is thus secondary to the behaviour. In moral philosophy, emotions are important, as the notion of 'right' and 'wrong' is linked to the emotion of 'approval' and 'disapproval' in some way. The doctrine of emotivism in fact claims that the two things are interchangeable, that is, to say something is 'right' is 'only' to say that you feel positively towards it, you 'like' it.

## EMPEDOCLES (*C.* 490–432 BCE)

Empedocles was a philosopher-poet with a particular interest in the physical structure of the world, which he discussed in his poems that are known nowadays by the titles 'On Nature' and 'Purifications'. His philosophical contribution was to challenge the assumption of the ELEATICS (like PARMENIDES) that change was illusory, instead invoking two great agents of change, the well-named 'love' and 'strife'. These two forces combine to produce the flux of the everyday world, in a ceaseless cycle of creation and destruction. Empedocles himself was famously supposed to have leapt into the mouth of a crater of the volcano at Etna in a final, fatal act of philosophical purification.

## ENDS (MEANS)

In ETHICS, the distinction between ends and means is all-important: 'the end justifies the means', or, more often, 'the end does not justify the means'. But the distinction is not always so clear-cut. The 'end' of a walk is not merely where the car is parked, but getting some exercise. However, even in this example, the 'end' may actually be said to be 'being fit' or 'being slim', and getting the exercise is then merely the means to that end. Or indeed, conversely, it may be that I am not at all interested in being slim and fit, but happen to like walking, so the walk becomes the 'end' and not the means. Putting one leg after the other is perhaps then the 'means'. Nonetheless, many moral arguments are based on the distinction, and generally employed notions of 'UTILITARIAN' justifications rest on vaguely expressed (ill-defined) ends, such as the increased amount of happiness in the community.

## ENERGY

Although nowadays scarcely mentioned in philosophy, energy has a central role to play in the understanding of the universe. And the notion that energy can be measured by linking matter and motion can be found as early as ARISTOTLE. Not until the seventeenth century were philosophers of nature ready to try to put figures on such phenomena, with DESCARTES putting forward the theory that 'quantity of motion', or '*vis viva*', might be proportionate to mass multiplied by velocity, although LEIBNIZ insisted that it was much greater – mass times the square of the velocity.

With the new 'relativistic physics' of the twentieth century, it became clear that not only was energy interchangeable with mass (as $E=mc^2$), but that, in a sense, Friedrich SCHELLING had been right when he described matter in terms of 'frozen energy'.

## ENGELS, FRIEDRICH (1820–95)

Engels was the support system behind Marx, son of a textile manufacturer and owner of a factory in Manchester during the critical years following the failure of REVOLUTIONS in much of Europe (i.e. 1848–69). He himself originally wanted to be a writer of novels, but was obliged by his father to follow the family business instead. Of such things are revolutions made!

Although he met Marx originally in Berlin, in 1842, it was not until two years later, and in Paris, that they began their lifelong collaboration. And if Engels always plays second fiddle to Marx, that is not to say he was merely an assistant. Indeed, it was Engels who introduced Marx to the working-class issues and the new philosophy of political science, Engels who wrote and rewrote the 'Marxist' scripts, and Engels who developed the theory of 'dialectical materialism'. Nonetheless, Engels himself always credited Marx with that important but nebulous quality, 'originality'.

SEE ALSO

Marx and Marxism

## THE ENLIGHTENMENT

The Enlightenment period, from the end of the seventeenth century to the last decades of the eighteenth, is said to be the years of great scientific and artistic progress in Europe (NEWTON and LOCKE in England, HUME in Scotland, VOLTAIRE and DESCARTES in France, and Mendelssohn, LEIBNIZ and KANT in Germany). It is also known grandly as 'the Age of Reason'. This contrasts with the supposedly irrational and superstitious practices of the Middle Ages. Kant, and much of the philosophy of the period, was pleased to pronounce that humanity had now begun to think in a higher, 'more rational' (read logical) way, and indeed this notion was converted by HEGEL into what has been argued was the basis for the two totalitarian world systems that would tear apart the world during the twentieth century, FASCISM and COMMUNISM. Indeed, the Enlightenment period is conventionally said to have ended in the year of the French Revolution.

## ENTROPY

Entropy is a rather technical measure of the unavailable ENERGY in a system. By extension, it is also a measure of 'information' and has a related use within so-called information theory. But it all starts with the First Law of Thermodynamics, which says that the total amount of energy in the universe is constant, and all that ever happens is that it is transformed from one type (say, coal) to another, say, heat or light. The Second Law, with which MAXWELL's Demon plays around so diabolically, is the notion that the disorder of system cannot be reduced without outside intervention. (You can drop an egg on the floor and expect it to break, but not expect it to jump back together again.) In the nineteenth century, James Maxwell offered a THOUGHT EXPERIMENT to challenge this, saying that in theory a tiny demon operating a door between two chambers of air, one hot and full of fast-moving particles and the other cool, full of slow-moving ones, could in this way, over time, raise the temperature of the first chamber and lower the temperature of second, all without any expenditure of 'work', and contrary to the Second Law. And its overthrow is no small matter – effectively, entropy is the 'arrow of time', and the demon becomes a 'time lord'.

## ENVIRONMENTAL ETHICS

Conventional views of 'environmental ethics' look at changes caused by human beings to 'the environment', and at whether they are in the human interest. Concerns such as 'climate change', 'depletion of the ozone layer', over-pollution of the rivers, the seas and the air, are all essentially human-centred. Concerns about our propensity for destroying habitats, and with them animals and plant species, are also sometimes put in terms of the loss to humans – what if such and such a plant contained a cure for cancer? How will we feel if there are no more pandas to look at – even in cages? Often the degradation of the environment is more prosaic

(no song birds, fewer 'green spaces', more noise and fumes from cars) and it is not concern for the environment for itself, but rather concern for the ability of people to 'flourish' in such bleak, urban conditions. Other ethicists say self-interest, when it is fully understood, leads inexorably (in a sort of HOLISTIC way), to respect not only for other humans, but for all creation. Either way, much of environmental ethics is still the same sort of human self-interest as any other ETHICS.

The human perspective that taming of NATURE is 'good', and the dangerous or simply inconvenient activities of wild nature are 'bad' is what so-called 'Deep Ecologists' insist that we must move away from – and accept that what is good for us is not necessarily good for nature, and that we should instead begin to apply values such as 'freedom and autonomy' to rivers and animals, 'respect for others' to trees and mountains.

For other philosophers, questions about what we eat are both profound, pervasive and fundamental. Our attitudes and our whole approach to life stem from fulfilment of this basic need, they point out. 'There is nothing more intimate than eating, more symbolic of the connectedness of life, and more mysterious', as one 'Deep Green', Paul Callicott, has put it.

## EPICTETUS (C. 50–130 CE)

Epictetus was born a slave in Asia Minor and served in a noble house in Rome. His liberal owner allowed him to attend the lectures of the STOIC philosopher Musonius Rufus. Later freed, Epictetus began teaching in Rome, and when the philosophers were expelled from the city by the emperor he founded a school in Nicopolis on the western coast of Greece. Epictetus wrote nothing himself, but one of his pupils, the historian Arrian, compiled lecture notes that have come down to us as the *Discourses*, along with a shorter summary known as the *Handbook*. These works display a practically-orientated Stoicism, and focus upon what are and are not the proper objects of our own concern.

## EPICURUS (341–270 BCE)

### The essential Epicurus

Epicurus founded a philosophical community in his garden just outside Athens at the end of the fourth century BCE. His philosophy was marked by two central doctrines: ATOMISM in physics and HEDONISM in ETHICS. Although Epicureanism has entered the popular imagination as a synonym for sensuous debauchery, in fact Epicurus was far more concerned with minimising mental suffering than he was with maximising bodily pleasures. Epicureanism is neatly summarised by the Fourfold Remedy: do not fear god; do not worry about death; what is good is easy to get; what is terrible is easy to endure.

## Objects of desire

Epicurus was born in Samos, and founded his philosophical school in a private garden just outside the city walls of Athens. He is best known via three letters that have come down to us by being quoted in full in the biography by DIOGENES LAERTIUS. These are the *Letter to Herodotus* (on physics), *Letter to Pythocles* (on meteorology) and *Letter to Menoeceus* (on happiness). There are also a number of collections of sayings (*Principal Doctrines*, *Vatican Sayings*) and second-hand accounts of his philosophy (for example, those of CICERO). Excavations at the Villa of the Papyri in Herculaneum have uncovered parts of his previously lost magnum opus *On Nature*, and there will probably be further discoveries in the papyrus scrolls that are still waiting to be deciphered.

Epicurus was a proponent of atomism, following in the footsteps of LEUCIPPUS and DEMOCRITUS. He introduced into their mechanistic atomic theory the notion of the swerve in order to save free will. In EPISTEMOLOGY, Epicurus was an empiricist and offered a thoroughly physical interpretation of PERCEPTION, involving films of atoms continually leaving objects and entering the eye.

In ethics, Epicurus is most famous as a hedonist, proposing pleasure as the ultimate end for all human action (in contrast to his Hellenistic rivals the STOICS, who proposed VIRTUE). However, Epicurus was more concerned with minimising pain than maximising pleasure, and he observed that mental disturbances usually form a far greater obstacle to happiness than physical suffering. In particular, he argued that humans should not fear the gods and should not be concerned about death. For an Epicurean, death is nothing to us, for when we are dead we do not experience anything at all. While we might sometimes be anxious about what will happen when we or our loved ones die, that is literally concern about nothing: anxiety about a non-existence that none of us will ever, or could ever, experience. Echoing the CYNICS, Epicurus analysed objects of desire into the categories of the natural and necessary (simple food and water), natural but unnecessary (fancy food), and the unnatural and unnecessary (social status, great wealth). Epicurus argued that what we actually need to live well is easy to obtain and much human misery is due to desiring things that are in fact irrelevant to human well-being. While uninterested in traditional politics, Epicurus placed great value on friendship as a key component in a happy life.

Later Epicureans of note include Philodemus, Diogenes of Oenoanda (who set up a giant Epicurean inscription in his home town), and LUCRETIUS (whose *De Rerum Natura* presents orthodox Epicurean philosophy to a Roman audience in Latin verse).

Contributor: John Sellars

## EPIPHENOMENALISM

The grand-sounding doctrine that actually propounds a very down-to-earth theory, namely that states of consciousness, including 'feelings' and 'emotions', are just by-products of various brain states. As T.H. Huxley elegantly puts it, 'as completely without any power of modifying that working as the steam-whistle which accompanies the workings of a locomotive engine is without influence upon its machinery.'

## EPISTEMOLOGY

The branch of philosophy that enquires into the nature and possibility of KNOWLEDGE.

## EQUALITY

Two things are equal when they are the same, but equality in social terms is not so easy. People are not the same and it is not necessarily desirable that we should pretend that they are. For example, if everyone were to be paid the same, perhaps through ration books, the distinction between those virtuous souls who work hard and spend little, would be lost, and with it the CAPITALIST engine of development – the accumulation of savings that can then be 'invested'.

Nor is there universal agreement on ideals of 'equal treatment'. Many countries retain legal systems that formally restrict women's rights, particularly in crucial economic areas such as inheritance. Informal systems continue to ensure that age, gender, disability, sexual orientation, let alone 'optional' characteristics such as physical appearance, religion and political stance, are employed as factors justifying prejudicial treatment and discrimination. But then, for some people these factors continue to matter. Priests, they think, should not be women, let alone gay! Teachers should not be COMMUNISTS – let alone FASCISTS; movie stars and flight attendants should not be fat or old – and certainly not spotty. And of course, US Presidents must never be female or non-Caucasian.

For UTILITARIANS, in particular, equality is a secondary good, behind the happiness that may be achievable 'for the majority' by allowing inequalities.

## EQUIVOCATION

See Fallacies.

## ESP

Philosophy is full of dubious concepts and unprovable theories, so extrasensory perception should fit in well, yet apart from the celebrated Chair of it in Scotland, it attracts little serious attention. Outside academia, however, many people continue to believe that there are inexplicable instances – often in their own experience – of premonitions, telepathy, and so on, experiences that challenge the conventional notions, if not so much the rarefied quantum science ones, of causality and space-time.

## ESSE EST PERCIPI

Bishop George BERKELEY (1685–1753) held the doctrine that *esse est percipi*: that is, that material objects exist only through being perceived. To the objection that in that case, a tree, for instance, in a forest, would cease to exist when no one was around, he replied that God always perceived everything. In his opinion, this was a weighty argument.

## ESSENCE

Essence is a peculiar word for philosophers. About the only thing that is agreed upon is that if you take away the essence of a thing, you no longer have whatever it was.

PLATO thought the essence was to be found purely through INTROSPECTION, that is to say, by using one's mind to analyse CONCEPTS, while ARISTOTLE, agreeing that the essence of something was 'real' or objective, seemed to think it was really a matter of knowing its defini-

tion. John LOCKE derided Aristotle's contribution as 'wholly useless and unserviceable to any part of our knowledge' (Essay III iii 17), but then he was writing before modern LINGUISTIC approaches to philosophy moved the goalposts on uselessness somewhat.

For Locke, as for KANT, 'real real essence' (so to speak) is necessarily forever out of reach, and the best we can get at is an understanding of the arrangement of constitution of the world and its parts.

## ETERNAL RECURRENCE

The notion of eternal recurrence is an ancient one, employed for example by HERACLITUS, although seized upon by NIETZSCHE (in *Thus Spake Zarathusra*), who seemed to think it fitted in with the science of his time (although in fact it did not). The idea is that everything that happens is part of an endlessly repeated cycle of events. The logical weakness of it is that with even a finite number of entities, an infinite number of arrangements if perfectly possible, so there is no 'scientific' requirement to suppose that everything will someday, somewhere, be repeated. Nietzsche also used the notion as a way of measuring the worth of one's life. If you knew you were fated (like Dionysius, or indeed, for keen film-goers, like the hero of *Groundhog Day*) to repeat each and every day of your life again, would you not want to change things?

## ETHICS

One of the things people find most confusing about ethics is how exactly it is different from morality. And notwithstanding numerous offers to specify it, the answer is that the word ethics comes from the Greek (*ethikos*) while the word morality comes from the Latin (*moralis*) and, in the sense that CICERO picked *moralis* to be the Latin equivalent of *ethikos* at least, there is not any distinction to be made. Both are words for the study of GOOD and EVIL, which, as PLATO had no doubt, and as MARX would have applauded, is essentially a practical study. The ethicist is concerned with regulating behaviour, both their own as an individual, and more generally too, which means entering the political realm.

There are those who say that the right thing to do is determined not by individuals but by authority – perhaps by those with direct access to God, or perhaps merely by consideration of a rule. The Jewish Torah, the Christian Bible and the Muslim Koran all attempt to stipulate the correct mode of behaviour for all the essential stages of life, and couple this with threats of dire punishments. Some famous rules include the UTILITARIAN one concerning the correct thing being that which brings about the happiness of the greatest number; or the HOBBESIAN one, that right is whatever the most powerful individuals say is right; or the philosophers' evergreen favourite KANTIAN one, that we must act always as though our actions could be following a universal law. This, the 'Categorical Imperative', rules out borrowing money without paying it back, but still allows us all to commit SUICIDE (not that Kant wanted it to). A similar idea is at work in John RAWLS' more recent version, 'the veil of ignorance', where he seeks to remove the distorting effects of 'self-interest' from decision-making. Funnily enough, Adam SMITH makes selfishness the key to society learning to arrange itself in the way that both generates the most wealth and, incidentally, therefore, the most opportunities for its citizens.

In Plato's dialogues, the source of goodness is WISDOM, and 'the good' is described like a light that reveals truth. No one does evil, says Plato reassuringly, except out of ignorance. After all, doing something wrong makes someone less perfect, less harmonious, and who would do that knowingly to themselves? ARISTOTLE adds that the path to ethical health is a series of assessments of the middle option: not too much wine, nor too many slave boys, and, as he describes the magnanimous man in the *Nicomachean Ethics*:

. . . Such, then, is the magnanimous man; the man who goes to excess and is vulgar exceeds, as has been said, by spending beyond what is right. For on small objects of expenditure he spends much and displays a tasteless showiness; for example, he gives a club dinner on the scale of a wedding banquet, and when he provides the chorus for a comedy he brings them on to the stage in purple, as they do at Megara. And all such things he will do not for honour's sake but to show off his wealth, and because he thinks he is admired for these things, and where he ought to spend much he spends little and where little, much. The niggardly man on the other hand will fall short in everything, and after spending the greatest

sums will spoil the beauty of the result for a trifle, and whatever he is doing he will hesitate and consider how he may spend least, and lament even that, and think he is doing everything on a bigger scale than he ought. . .

Recently, Aristotle has had something of a revival on ethics courses for his so-called 'virtue ethics', that is, exhibiting virtuous character by evidence of your behaviour, the healthy practice of which over time causes you to become still better; but in fact this notion is really also Plato's.

The STOIC and Eastern traditions (as explored for instance by SPINOZA) of 'the good life' being a case of adapting and harmonising with nature and the 'times' offer a slightly different perspective, and indeed, both approaches try to avoid the 'right/wrong' duality of standard Western ethics, recognising that everything contains elements of both good and bad. Which is why ethical decision-making can seem so hard!

## ETHICS GAMES

See Games.

## ETHNO-PHILOSOPHY

See African philosophy.

## *EUDAIMONIA*

From the Greek, *eu* (good) and *daimon* (demon), albeit the nice kind that has the job of looking after people (Westerners would say 'guardian angel', perhaps). The word is sometimes shorthanded to 'happiness', but this loses its particular significance, which is that the happiness here is of the whole, and not merely that transient, 'illusory' happiness obtainable, for example, through the senses. For PLATO, ARISTOTLE and EPICURUS, *eudaimonia* was the state achievable only by living virtuously, which sounds bleak and indeed is.

## EUTHANASIA

From the Greek for 'good death', but usually translated as 'mercy killing'. There are three sorts: voluntary, where someone, perhaps a chronically ill person, asks for drugs to help them to die; non-voluntary, perhaps where doctors switch off a life-support machine; and involuntary, where the subject does not agree it is time for them to die and can say so! This is usually described as murder.

Related considerations for euthanasia are calculations of the individual's well-being (benefi-cence); the social interest (UTILITARIAN cal-culations routinely, if still not easily, made in modern hospital intensive care units); the prin-ciple of respect for autonomy; the need for informed consent (if only of relatives); and, for some, the principle of the 'inviolability' of life.

A limited form of euthanasia is available to citizens in the Netherlands.

## EUTHYPHRO PROBLEM

The problem is stated in the Platonic dialogue (of the same name) in which Euthyphro is con-sidering suing his father, in order, as he puts it, (to SOCRATES' dismay) to please the gods. It consists of the simple but profound question – is something 'good' (although note that here Euthyphro specifically is discussing 'piety') because the gods say it is good (in which case the gods can say anything at all is good and we must accept it), or do the gods say things are good because they (and doubtless gods are good judges) see that they are good – in which case their approval does not offer any explanation of why a thing is good or not?

## EVIL

### Essential evil

Like any term, and more than most, 'evil' is attended by a rich vocabulary of distinctions. This may result because there is such a wide vari-ance in perceptions of evil from place to place, from time to time, from tradition to tradition and from language to language, and because these traditions, languages and perceptions admit of dramatic transformations, adaptations and mutations, and an abundance of additions and omissions within each of these evolving forms along each of the trajectories of flow of the term. It has long been the tradition to per-sonify the notion of 'evil' and give it a name and a face – the devil, Beelzebub, Bin Laden, Saddam Hussein. Or, for many people, the notion may so defy conceptualisation that it must needs remain a nebulous ABSTRACTION.

### Let us speak evil. . .

In the English language, we speak of evil in a great variety of manifestations: sin, impiety, vice, malevolence, cruelty, immorality, criminality, pathology, abomination. Many of the terms employed to denote evil betray the pre-concep-tual origins of the notion in the ritual life of early human communities, naming the earliest wrongs that come to be regulated through a cul-ture's prohibitions. Incest, fratricide, patricide, cannibalism are examples of archaic notions of 'evil' construed early as extremely problematic because they were interpreted as crimes against the gods. Violation of these taboos did not remain a moral burden to the offender alone, but brought on a pollution that stretched across families seen to share in the offender's culpabil-ity. This cross-generational contamination could bring misfortune to family members generations removed from the original moral infraction (wit-ness Oedipus, and the ill fate of each of his chil-dren). In the worst cases, these gravest of crimes could even invite divine retribution against the entire community, in plagues, floods, feuds and like misfortunes. In short, the archaic world view deemed that the effects of the individual's actions were often felt by the larger community of which an agent is a part, affecting and threat-ening the welfare of family and friends, disrupt-ing the connection between the community and their ancestors and gods.

The words people choose in speaking about evil often tell us more about their group's METAPHYSICAL assumptions, their moral prej-udices and their orientation towards the world (as threatening or homely), than they tell us about the agent or event to which the term is attached. The choice of words meant to describe the agent or act often reveals whether their cul-tural group understands evil as breaching divine ordinance (sin, abomination); as a violation of social custom (disgrace, shame, dishonour); as a mistaken, wayward blunder (moral error, mis-take); or as a malevolent, purposeful deed of twisted desire (corruption, depravity, cruelty).

The word 'evil' comes to us from the Middle English term *evel* or *evill* from the Anglo-Saxon *yfel*. These words originally denoted the posses-sion of bad moral qualities (wickedness, corrup-tion, sinfulness, or badness) and signified the casting of bad effects upon others (whether by design, ignorance or ill luck). Evil was seen to cause pain or misery, to be injurious or threat-ening injury, or to bring misfortune to its vic-tims. Ironically, the term 'devil', the name often attached to personifications of evil, has connec-tions with a more positive history. Descending from the ancient Greek *daimon* or *daemon*, a demon was originally understood to be a median figure, messenger, arbiter or facilitator between disparate realms; benevolent connector of humans and gods. In the earliest Greek tales describing the advent of human beings, the first of the five races of human beings were so peaceful and harmonious in nature that when, after long and happy lives, they passed from their mortal flesh, they were named *daimons* to future, more troublesome races.

*Daemon* was also employed to signify a person's unique genius (in a certain art), or, used in a less personal way, the term denoted the moral aspect of the human being. One of the great innovations of **PLATO**'s dialogue, the *Phaedo*, was his employment of the term *psyche* as a replacement for the older term *daemon* in speaking of the moral aspect of the person, while yet maintaining the personal aspect of personality or individuality as well. The necessity for this move is clear when we remember that one of Plato's overriding purposes in his early writing was to establish the continuance, not of the soul, as such, in its general status of immortal breath of life (from *pneuma*), but to save from extinction the very personal and unique soul of the beloved **SOCRATES**. Without this curious amalgamation of psyche with its *daemonic* aspects intact, Plato indeed would have fallen prey to Gregory Vlastos' famed critique in *The Paradox of Socrates*. (The paradox is that if Socrates achieved the mirroring of the forms that he suggests as definitive of salvation, then his individuality, eccentricities – precisely what makes Socrates Socrates! – would be lost. Since Plato's whole reason for writing is to keep the beloved master alive, his success would be his failure.) In the hands of the Christian Church, the term 'demon' lost its divine linguistic linkages and came to mean median creatures serving forces of darkness, rather than human interests or the gods.

In his book, *The Devil,* Jeffrey Russell opens his historical treatment of personifications of evil with a useful general definition of evil that sets aside the metaphysical baggage generally attached to the terms 'evil' and '*daemon*'. Russell defines evil as: 'the infliction of pain upon sentient beings', adding some pages later that this is 'hurt deliberately inflicted'. The term 'evil', as employed in this secularised vein, echoes **ARISTOTLE**'s notion of cruelty, denoting a form of human wickedness distinguishable from (mere) violence and from unfortunate acts of nature (including animal aggressions) by the explicitly rational aspect of the act, that is, by the **INTENTION** invested in the agent. This (prior) reflective, deliberative feature narrows the scope

of the concept, restricting the use of the term 'evil' to an explicitly human range of activity, as the work of a rational animal. Only a human being, with its peculiarly rational component fully functional, can commit the 'calculated acts of outrage' that compose the 'evil'.

This definition of 'evil' not only refuses to hold blameworthy the gods or devils of popular belief for the violence effected by human agents, but it names evil-doers by the acts they commit and the harm that they cause, rather than by 'essentialist' allusions. The definition of evil as explicitly human excess avoids the many problems inherent in the view of evil as monstrous or subhuman. The latter designations serve well colonialist and **IMPERIALIST** agendas. White Westerners have traditionally employed such terms as 'savage' or 'primitive' to describe indigenous people who are exploited or slaughtered, even as they speak of 'progress', 'the spread of Christian virtues and values' and 'the advance of civilisation' in reference to their own violences.

The (false) distinction raised above, between 'civilised' and 'savage', expresses the prejudice that certain violences are a signal of cultural retardation, while others, far more lethal, are progressive and good for humankind. It is vested in the very language that was employed to speak of the treatment of the indigenous that it would be seen favourably by history, because those affected were only 'savages' in any case, while those responsible were brave adventurers to be celebrated. However, if we hold to a definition of 'evil' that looks at the harm done by the act according to the intention of the agent of the act – harm to sentient beings deliberately inflicted – then our language holds to account the perpetrators of harm on the basis of the suffering they cause to others.

To engage in a discourse about evil, then, even in the context of scholarly investigation, is to take up this language, with all its historical, **EPISTEMOLOGICAL** and metaphysical baggage. It means to participate in a narration that has itself proven the cause of a great deal of harm in the world. To speak of 'evil' is to work within a tradition that suggests the reality of its subject – the reality that evil things and evil people do exist, that we may know them, describe them, come to recognise them and take up scholarly discourse in regard of them.

Locating demons is a critical step on the way to the practice of the very thing that is being

WRITING ON EVIL

If I have been convinced of one thing through the course of my work as a violence scholar, it is that the intellectual act of locating evil, by word and by concept, and illuminating its location to others – the structure of the moralising gesture – composes a most ethically dangerous process. Illuminating the moral failings of others is a sure-fire way of eclipsing one's own faults, while legitimating the erasure of faulty others.

Thus, in the elaboration of the history of notions of 'evil' and the destructiveness that is legitimated by those notions, the scholar must chart an exceedingly convoluted route that navigates between a discerning appreciation of victim suffering and the moralising baggage that attends the history of the notion of 'evil'.

Contributor: WCH

demonised – the harming of sentient beings. To participate in the history of this illumination is an altogether foreboding prospect. On the other hand, to fail to take up the language, to fail to engage some things as 'evil', seems equally undesirable, since the denial that 'evil' has occurred seems to undermine the victim's experience of suffering and degradation.

Accounts of 'evil' derive from almost every discipline of study. Each has its unique approach to the problem, its own peculiar methods and terms of debate. Each begins from its own set of assumptions, and proceeds toward its unique set of 'truths' based upon these assumptions. Many discourses on evil will avoid the use of the term 'evil' for the problem of its religious baggage. They may instead speak of destructiveness, aggression, pathology, cruelty, violence or crime. In general, however, Jeffrey Russell's assessment holds true across the disciplines, no matter which of these terms is employed. The disciplines seem to agree upon this: 'intentionally doing harm to sentient beings' is a problem that requires explanation if we are to make headway in reducing that harm.

Evil is therefore often categorised into various forms, in service of the explanatory goal. Various experts speak of social evils, political evils, economic evils, crimes against humanity and the evils of aggression. Often the unique form of evil named 'genocide' is isolated for analysis, as an idiosyncratic evil that demands special examina-

tion. People speak of evil families, criminal groups, 'gangs', and 'communities of evil', while geneticists and anthropologists tell us evil inheres in the flesh. In this understanding, then, no human being escapes the disposition in favour of evil. Psychologists locate evil in the mind; so, where the mysterious paths of understanding can be disentangled from traumas past, there is hope for a cure for evil actions. Religious anthropologists and secular critics find the source of evil in the logic of belief systems; political analysts locate it in the state. Sociological accounts find individual acts embedded in the social structure; for them, evil is to be understood within the logic and by the terms of that structure. Thus, there can be no absolute 'evil' in this accounting.

There are many sound reasons for the lack of explicit philosophical attention to the problem

THE STUDY OF EVIL

The study of evil has been given relatively little attention by philosophers. Those philosophers, from Plato to Plotinus to Spinoza, who meditate copiously upon the excellence of 'Being', simply leave evil as the unspoken other, the unarticulated underside of the good – as a lack of perfection, an ignorance of what is good, or an incompleteness in the being of the thing. Even the most pessimistic philosophers who expect the worst from human beings have thought it quite reasonable that political and legal systems, carefully constructed, will suffice to keep at bay the devil at the heart of the human. Thomas Hobbes posited all men engaged in a 'war of all against all', but a strong Leviathan could hold them at arm's length from each other in the interest of good business.

Contributor: WCH

of evil. One is that evil does not make for pleasant rumination. Philosophers prefer to flee the mundane to ascend the lofty heights of abstraction. Wonder, says Socrates, in Plato's *Theaetetus*, brings a person to philosophy, where a thinker can soar above the darkness and, with the gods, feed upon the excellencies of Truth and Justice and Beauty.

Wonder's dark sister, suffering, can perform the same feat, but, as its attentions are focused upon much darker objects, those objects are less seductive to the enquirer. Indeed, philosophers and others may understand research into 'evil' to be senseless, since evil is an error and hence inexplicable. Monstrous acts are perpetrated by monsters. Monsters do not have reasons for their actions; their destructiveness is meaningless; and they offer no justifications for the harm that they do. For scholars to seek reasons for evil events and actions, they must first of all trust that reasons for evil exist, despite all popular prejudice to the contrary. Then they must be willing to plot a course across this abyss of prejudice. Worse, enquirers into evil, in their very attempt to understand 'monstrous' acts and events, must be ready to risk offending the victims of radical violences. The idea of offering justifications for the unjustifiable, and positing meaningfulness in place of the madness will, understandably, be offensive to many. Finally, precisely because evil acts are revolting, even to the scholarly observer, it is difficult to maintain the objective distance necessary to arrive at an unbiased analytic account of the problem. Socrates tells in the *Theaetetus* that philosophers gain a clearer vision of things because they climb above the world and look upon it from a thoughtful distance. But it can be difficult to maintain that lofty coolness when contemplating atrocity.

Thus it is hardly surprising that few philosophers have spent their intellectual energy obsessing about getting their definitions of 'evil' just right. However, some things can be inferred about 'evil' from what philosophers have left unsaid. For Socrates, to know the good is to do the good. All people seek happiness, and happiness is fullest when one seeks after the right kind of 'goods'. In the *Euthydemus*, where Socrates and Clinias investigate what things constitute the 'goods' that give happiness, Socrates argues that none of the things that we call 'good' are good in themselves, but only become good through right use. (Chocolate cake, for example, is good, 'used' a piece at a time, but the 'misuse' of eating the whole cake results in the 'evil' of a stomach ache.) The conclusion is that, without intelligence and WISDOM, one could possess plenty of these 'goods' – wealth, health and good looks are their examples – and yet be fully miserable. Even the things deemed to be the best of earthly goods have no absolute goodness – no 'natural' goodness – of their own, but if ignorance leads them, 'they are greater evils than their opposites, inasmuch as they are more able to serve the leader which is evil' (*Euthydemus* 281b-d).

Thus, evil results, at least in part, from the improper use of things. Socrates, the 'one-who-knows-nothing', understands the difficulty of acquiring the excellence or virtue of which he speaks, since such wisdom is a property reserved for the gods alone. So it seems that many of us are likely to fall prey to this ignorance that will cause us to do evil and to attach ourselves to evil leaders and help them to accomplish their designs. Even if we wish desperately to follow the good rather than the evil, it is clearly difficult to know the good when we see it. Only the form of Beauty shines brightly enough to capture the eye of the lover (*Phaedrus* 250b). However, surrounded by the imperfect as we earthly mortals are, it seems that there is far greater possibility that we may become practised in recognising 'evil' when we encounter it.

For Socrates, to know the good is to do the good; to be ignorant is to err or fall into evil. This explanation of evil resonates with everyday experience. We may not necessarily understand evil when we come across it, but we recognise it as such. But the universality implied in seeking definitions amid the infinite variety of worldly examples of evil things seems to deny the historical and experiential nature of the concept, as Herodotus demonstrates in his famous *Histories*.

It is clear that a thing or event passes through a certain conceptual framework before being named 'evil' or 'good,' a framework historically and experientially given. But this throws us into a kind of DILEMMA, since there are as many frameworks as there are cultures, and perhaps even as many as there are individuals. The same act can be regarded as good by one actor, and evil by another. Still yet, a single act can be deemed good by the perpetrator, and evil by the one suffering the act as its object. This problem has generally led philosophers to take up positions at two extreme poles, grabbing firmly at the horns of the dilemma: either evil is, as PROTAGORAS would have all things, measured by the man and different from perceiver to perceiver; or it is, as Socrates suggests, something stable, with absolute meaning, that is more and less perfectly understood from individual to individual.

Although NIETZSCHE argues that moralisations have their foundation in the moraliser and not the object of moralisation, many people believe evil to be ubiquitous of the world: that there is an evil in nature that is never fully controlled. There is an evil in the wild beast, and since humans derive from beastly origins, there remains a devil repressed inside each human being, struggling to get out and wreak havoc upon the world. In some, the beast is sublimated, lying dormant but always poised to resurface. In others, the beast is not far removed from the overt nature of the human thing. Nietzsche suggests that where people feel weak and threatened, they are likely to see evil in many things, whereas the strong Dionysian character celebrates life and can accept things as they are. If the desert can be turned by the right eye into lush farmland, then the evil, absurd and ugly can be made good, meaningful and beautiful by the beholder of generous spirit.

Nevertheless, the assumption that the beast resides at the heart of every person is a very common one. This assumption underlies any world view that defines 'humanity' as a goal to be achieved, rather than a species that we are. Socrates takes such a position when he defines justice as the definitive human excellence, leaving those of us without perfect justice (which is, on his own definition, all of us) definitively less than human (Plato, *Republic* 353e).

SPINOZA, in his *Ethics* (as Nietzsche), could be said to imply the ubiquity of evil when he names *conatus* (and 'will to power') as the potency through which human selves assert themselves over others in the world.

The view of evil as ubiquitous to the human world is counterproductive to the project of eliminating the ills of the world, since there is little point in trying to eradicate that which is utterly pervasive. Thus, the more popular view sees evil not as ubiquitous but as threatening ubiquitousness, creeping like a nasty infection

into pure and innocent things, befouling the good by its contaminating presence. This view permits moralising agents, as the identifiers of evil, to remove themselves entirely from the contaminating site of the evil forces they locate. When one has situated the source of 'evil,' one has already 'objectified' the object, separated it from the subjective space and placed it conceptually in the world 'out there'. It is only a short leap from a human observer's locating evil in the spatial 'out there' to placing it in the substantive 'out there', by categorising the alienated 'evil-doer' as something less than human – a monster!

A monster is thought of as another species of being that may assume the guise of a human being but is actually less than fully human, and does not follow the same life-affirming codes of behaviour and value peculiar to the human world. Monsters, like wild beasts, may inadvertently cause harm wherever they thoughtlessly lumber along or, more likely, they may be bent upon harming others. They may compose agents of some cosmic evil force or super-being – René DESCARTES' 'evil demon' – or they may themselves embody wholesale wickedness, deriving pleasure from the suffering that they cause to innocents they find in their path.

The view of evil-doers as monsters is also extremely functional to people. It means not simply that every declaration of the monstrous action reaffirms the wholesomeness of the human world, but this view further relieves the observer of any moral responsibility or intellectual duty to try to understand the 'evil' that is being witnessed. In fact, there is no point in trying to understand the violence of monstrous others. Monsters are by definition irrational, unreasonable entities driven by wild appetites and passions, propelled by 'evil' impulses we humans cannot possibly understand. Monsters take mad delight in random destruction. The myth about evil as the work of a monstrous other is a very common myth that not only obstructs the investigation and elimination of violence, but legitimates violent reactions to problems witnessed in the human world, construing counter-violence as a necessary and good violence that 'fights the good fight' for the sake of wiping out monstrous others.

In fact, Socrates contributed to the popularity of this view of evil by construing humanity as an ideal to be sought, rather than as something we are. Ironically, he also contributed to this with

## THE EVIL URGE

The psychiatrist Lionel Rubinoff takes a similar position in his *Pornography of Power* (1969). Rubinoff warns that human urges towards violence are so deeply embedded in our nature that our only hope of escaping their destructive effects is in facing them directly and working through our 'evil' impulses, rather than denying their existence. He warns that the repression of humans' demonic nature results in a search for substitute forms of gratification, in fantasies and in direct experiences of nihilism or violence.

Contributor: WCH

his generous dictum that no person does harm knowingly. Socrates, Plato and Aristotle agree that all men seek the good. Each of these ancient thinkers asserts that the problem of 'evil' is a function of human ignorance, occurring where there exists a lack in right knowledge of one's best interests. Evil-doers are, according to this view, people who do not understand that the harm they do to others is a moral debt to themselves, a wound or disfiguration that compromises the integrity of the agent's soul.

That debt composes a moral burden to be hauled throughout earthly life, not unlike the weighty and ugly barnacles that attach themselves to the hull of a sailing ship, obstructing its movement, marring its beauty, and encumbering its smooth intercourse with others. The debt-burden is destined to be paid in full in the all-too-exacting divine court-system of the next world. Evil-doing sullies the agent's soul and, since nothing in the world of becoming stays constant, its practice causes the soul to drift further and further from its best interests, from ignorance to brutality to tyranny over others. Since the tyrant is the unhappiest of men (729 times as unhappy as the good man, according to the *arithmos* of the *Republic*, in Book 8), one would have to be mad to prefer that end.

Appropriate knowledge and the practice of good habits, on the other hand, increasingly feed the 'wings' of the soul, raising it to lofty heights and truest happiness. Knowledge and practice of the good dispose the agent to increasingly prefer good to evil, sound judgements to unsound, and moral action to moral error. This right knowledge culminates in the realisation that it is better to be harmed than to do harm to others. This increasing moral knowledge composes the path that offers the best effects for the soul. So the evil-doer makes moral errors because he/she is without appropriate knowledge, because his/her reasons are less reasonable than they might be, and because his/her desires are askew and driving him/her to seek soul-damaging, wrongful courses of action. Since justice is, by Socrates' definition, the excellence or virtue definitive of the human soul, those who commit injustices are not simply irrational and unwise; they are less than human. We might even say they are monstrous.

While it may seem that this results in defining evil as monstrous, in fact, the Socratic position offers the most sympathetic launching ground from which to approach the problem of evil, since it demands that we assume an ignorant innocence in the agent, before a malevolent obsession. If we can locate the 'reasons' that persuade agents to do bad things, then we may be able to work with those reasons to convince the agents to change their ways in their future actions. So, with Plato, evil-doers are evil by epistemological (and even ONTOLOGICAL) position, but they can never be evil through malevolence.

This offers some interesting implications for the fight against evil. Where evil is seen to stem from mere ignorance, the solution is likely to be re-education. Therefore, it seems that Socrates' definition of evil as stemming from ignorance may lead to more enlightened and less violent 'cures' for evil than other views demand. However, to many people the optimistic view that claims 'no one does harm knowingly' may seem foolishly affirmative of human nature. After all, given the pervasiveness across the global arena of things that most people would agree to be 'evil', at least some of the people engaged in some of these events must be 'knowingly' causing harm to their victims.

Socrates' 'evil as ignorance' thesis can appear foolishly optimistic, and few victims of violence would respond to the acts of their perpetrators with so generous an acquittal. Yet the Socratic dictum is borne out with relentless and terrifying consistency when we consider accounts of past atrocities from the point of view of the perpetrators of those horrors. All too often, perpetrator accounts confirm that agents of evil do not consider their acts as evil. And, even where they do see their work as evil, they see it as the least evil among the available options for action under the given circumstances.

They may consider their acts as unfortunate, as harsh, but generally as necessary, as the best among available but limited options. Sometimes, they excuse the destructive fallout of their works as collateral effects of otherwise unambiguously good choices. Usually, perpetrators stay altogether away from the term 'evil' in describing their own works in the world.

The question, then, that must necessarily compel the scholar of violence concerns how it is that these people – those whose acts cause real harm to others and whose perceived benefits are irrefutably linked to other people's sufferings – reconcile their destructiveness with their good consciences. What is it that separates their accounts of an event from the testimony of their victims in those same events? How do they view their worlds, their acts, themselves, such that they are able to escape the seemingly inalienable fate of damaged self-esteem? How do they manage their 'knowledges' so as to remain ignorant of the harm that they do in the world (to thus satisfy Socrates' maxim, 'no one does harm knowingly'), while yet accomplishing such brazen acts of atrocity that witnesses and victims are compelled to describe them as 'evil' and 'monstrous'? What 'historical frameworks' and conceptual schemata govern their life-worlds and dictate their ideas of right and wrong such that atrocious actions come to be filed under the category of 'best of available options'? Where are the 'moral fault lines' in the perpetrator's moral system?

Contributor: Wendy Hamblet

## EVIL DEMON

See Descartes.

## EVOLUTION

In *Origin of Species* (1859), DARWIN asks: 'Can the principle of selection, which we have seen is so potent in the hands of man, apply in nature?' After some learned discussion of slim wolves and giraffes with long necks (and so on), he concludes that :

> under certain circumstances individual
> differences in the curvature or length of the
> proboscis etc, too slight to be appreciated by
> us might benefit a bee or other insect, so
> that certain individuals would be able to
> obtain their food more quickly than others,
> and the communities in which they
> belonged would flourish and throw off many
> swarms inheriting the same peculiarities.

The theory was by no means new when Darwin said it, but *Origin of Species* has nonetheless had a profound effect, not merely on understandings of biology and nature, but on views of human societies and morality. In Europe, the theory collapsed the pretensions of the Church to have the only explanation for how the world came to be the way it is, and even seemed to promise a similarly progressive trend to political systems, manifested through the destructive power of REVOLUTION.

Nonetheless, doubts have always challenged the theory's authority itself, questions about gaps in the so-called 'fossil record', about how the supposedly 'useful' traits spread from individuals across whole species, and so on; but the significant shift, whatever the eventual status of Darwin's 'theory', is that this sort of debate is, like the theory itself, now firmly about 'rational' ideas rather than the revealed knowledge.

## EXISTENCE

'To be, or not to be' is, for philosophers, not the question at all. For existence seems to be only a second-level property, behind things like being hot, or yellow, or soft. But not, it should be mentioned, for EXISTENTIALISTS following Martin HEIDEGGER, who insist contrariwise that 'existence precedes essence', meaning we are what we choose to be. Still, according to Gottlob FREGE and Bertrand RUSSELL, existence only tells us whether there are any actual 'existing' cases of a thing with certain properties. This is where Anselm went wrong in his argument for the existence of GOD, the philosophers think: God can have all the usual properties without needing the extra one of existing. But this line of argument cuts two ways, the fictitious King of the Potato People is no less important merely for not having any physical instantiation. After all, neither the past nor the future exist either.

## EXISTENTIALISM

Existentialism is a term associated with SARTRE, who in his philosophy emphasises the use of the imagination and what is not, over what is, the latter being a rather humdrum sort of affair consisting of the kind of facts that scientists examine, while the 'what is not' is really much more interesting. He sums up his view (if 'sums up' is ever an appropriate term in existentialist writing), thus: 'The Nature of consciousness simultaneously is to be what is not and not to be what it is'. This brings us back to our own natures, our own 'ESSENCES'. We exist, yes, but how do we 'define ourselves'? It is here that the waiter comes in:

> His movement is quick and forward, a little
> too precise, a little too rapid. He comes
> toward the patrons with a step a little too
> quick. He bends forward a little too eagerly;
> his voice, his eyes express an interest a little
> too solicitous for the order of the customer.
> Finally there he returns, trying to imitate in

his walk the inflexible stiffness of some kind of automaton while carrying his tray with the recklessness of a tight-rope walker by putting it in a perpetually unstable, perpetually broken equilibrium which he perpetually re-establishes by a light movement of the hand and arm.

*Being and Nothingness* (1943)

This spotlight on 'consciousness' is what made Sartre's name. Curiously, *She Came to Stay* (also 1943), by Sartre's lifelong intellectual confidant and companion, Simone de BEAUVOIR, also describes various kinds of consciousness, in passages ranging from wandering through an empty theatre (the stage, the walls, the chairs, unable to come alive until there is an audience) to watching a woman in a restaurant ignore the fact that her male companion has begun stroking her arm ('it lay there, forgotten, ignored, the man's hand was stroking a piece of flesh that no longer belonged to anyone').

Other 'existentialists' are Karl JASPERS, Gabriel Marcel, Martin HEIDEGGER, Maurice MERLEAU-PONTY and, perhaps, even Albert CAMUS. The definition is as fluid as the true extistentialist life – unbound, self-sufficient, responsible to no one.

So who really was the great existentialist? De Beauvoir, unlike Sartre, would have been aware that many of existentialism's elements, for example, the notion of 'the OTHER', can be found in HEGEL, where they were borrowed in turn from the Eastern tradition, with its 'de-emphasis' of individualism as a delusion born of ignorance – and, perhaps, conceit.

## EXPERIENCE

Experience is often equated with sensory PER-CEPTION, but there is considerable debate over whether it should properly be understood as coming before or after. That is, are our experiences to be understood as having been interpreted and arranged in our minds, or as being prior to such filtering. In the *Theaetetus*, PLATO describes images being imprinted on the mind like a block of wax takes an impression from a coin. LOCKE, in his second *Essay on Human Understanding*, expands the analogy to say the wax is like the passive sensory apparatus of the body. He calls this 'sensation', and for him, the mind that assesses or judges things is quite separate from the mundane world of 'experience'.

## FACT-VALUE DISTINCTION

Facts are supposed to be true statements about 'the actual state of the world'. For example, 'London is the capital of the United Kingdom' is one, and 'London is the centre of the world trade in endangered species' is another. The notion that statements of fact can be kept separate from statements of 'VALUE' is central to much anglophone, twentieth-century moral philosophy, particularly British, and indeed, seems to draw its inspiration from the Scottish philosopher, David HUME, with his advice that we should never confuse an 'ought' and an 'is'. But what of 'facts' like 'London is one of the most ugly cities in the world', or 'London is too expensive to live in'?

The 'fact/value' distinction is anything but straightforward, and even if we settle on what will count as facts, these may yet contain within them so many assumptions and judgements that the only 'value-free facts' may end up being TAUTOLOGIES.

## FALLACIES

In LOGIC, a fallacy is an invalid ARGUMENT, that is, one in which it is possible for all the premises to be true and yet the conclusion is false. As such, it is clearly to be avoided. People often use the term colloquially, to include arguments they consider 'false' because they disagree with one or other of the premises. 'It is a fallacy that paying people the dole encourages laziness' is probably a critique of the following informal argument: 'If people can get money without working then they will become lazy. The dole is a form of getting money without having to work for it; so, the dole encourages laziness.' Here, the argument hinges on 'if people can get money without working then they will become lazy', which looks plausible when understood as, 'sometimes, if people can get money without working then they will become lazy', but less so when understood as, 'in all cases'. . . (John Stuart MILL considered that this sort of argument was indeed correct, warning against the state attempting to aid sections of the citizenry.)

## More fallacious fallacies: fallacies and tactics in informal argumentation

Argumentation is the process of providing reasons to support a position. Reasons are, in practice, often limited to producing 'authorities' who are claimed to hold the same view, perhaps important people, important books or, of course, God.

Some legitimate tactics follow.

1. *Reductio ad absurdum*
   From the Latin for 'reduce to absurdity', the process of taking the other person's argument and showing that it leads logically to absurd consequences.
2. Affirming the antecedent
   An argument of the form, if P then Q. P, therefore Q. If it is autumn, then the leaves will fall off the trees. It is autumn, therefore the leaves will fall off the trees. Although 'valid', the argument is little different from the illegitimate tactic described below as 'begging the question'. ARISTOTLE called it the '*modus ponens*'.

   On the other hand, DENYING THE ANTECEDENT, that is, for example, saying: 'If it is autumn, then the leaves will fall off the trees. It is NOT autumn, therefore the leaves will NOT be falling off the trees', is a fallacy, as trees may lose their leaves for any number of reasons (such as a drought, for example).
3. Denying the consequent
   An argument of the form, if P then Q. P, therefore Q. If it is autumn... no, let's have another example! If you eat too many cream cakes you will get fat. You are not fat, therefore you have not eaten too many cream cakes. Although arguments of this from are technically 'valid', it is clearly more a logical truth than a practical one! Aristotle called it the '*modus tollens*'.
4. Analogies
   Some would say THOUGHT EXPERIMENTS are a form of analogy, and certainly, the term can be used that way. An analogy is simply a comparison in which one case is claimed to be 'like' another in some important respect.
5. Counter-example
   A special kind of analogy that challenges or even demonstrates the falsity of what has been claimed.
6. *Enthymeme*, or suppressed premisses

Arguments that have to have extra premisses added to make them valid, such as 'Smoking in bars affects people whether they are smoking or not, therefore it should be banned.' Here the extra premisses are that: 'The effect of smoking on people is bad' and 'bad things should be banned'.

The following are illegitimate tactics.

1. Affirming the consequent
   A surprisingly common error, of the form if P then Q. Q therefore P. If it is autumn, the leaves will fall off the trees. The leaves are falling off the tress, therefore it is autumn. It is a fallacy because the leaves could be falling off the trees for some other reason such as (mentioned in the legitimate tactic 'Affirming the antecedent', above) during a drought.

   A related common fallacy in argument, sometimes called 'correlation confusion', consists of assuming that because two things often go together there must be a link.
2. Begging the question
   The fallacy of assuming the very point at issue. In effect, the conclusion as one of the premisses in an argument supposedly intended to prove it. It is a form of circularity in argumentation.
3. The false DICHOTOMY
   Two choices are given when, actually, other alternatives are possible.
4. Equivocation and ambiguity
   Using a word or phrase that has two or more meanings as though it has just one. There are various types of ambiguity: lexical ambiguity refers to individual words; referential ambiguity occurs when the context is unclear; and syntactical ambiguity results from grammatical confusions.
5. Non sequiturs and genetic fallacies
   From the Latin, meaning 'that which does not follow'. Statements are offered in a way that suggests they follow logically one from the other, when in fact there is no such link. The important 'genetic fallacy' is both a kind of non sequitur and a product of ambiguity: this is where assumptions are drawn about something by tracing its origins back, although in fact no necessary link can be made between the present situation and the claimed original one.
6. Special pleading
   Employing values or standards against an

opponent's position, while not applying them to your own.

7. Wishful thinking
Assuming conclusions because we wish them to be so. An appeal to 'majority opinion' to back up a factual claim is a particular kind of wishful thinking.

8. Red herrings
Irrelevant topics or arguments brought into a discussion with the effect of allowing the real issue to go unexamined. Apparently, herrings were sometimes used to confuse dogs chasing after foxes.

9. STRAW MAN arguments
Introducing and attributing a weak or absurd position to an opponent and proceeding to demolish it.

10. Ad hominem attacks
From the Latin, meaning 'towards the man', these are comments directed not at the issue at hand but at the individual opponent. (The term is occasionally used to refer to the legitimate tactic of exposing an inconsistency in a person's argument too.)

Another variety of ad hominem attack, that takes place before the main argument has

## LYING – OR UNJUSTIFIED FALSE BELIEF?

Politicians rely on all the illegitimate tactics in argument, including equivocation, and ambiguity.

But then there is, of course, that 'nuclear bomb' tactic in argumentation: the downright lie. There are many examples in history of wars built upon falsehoods, but more recently, Britain's Prime Minister, Tony Blair, was accused of lying in making a case for the war in Iraq.

For example, Blair had told an American news station (NBC, 3 April 2002) that: "we know that [Saddam Hussein] has stockpiles of major amounts of chemical and biological weapons, [and] we know that he is trying to acquire a nuclear capability". But, after the war, it turned out that there were no stockpiles, and the Prime Minister was accused of lying.

Can philosophy shed any light in this sort of debate? Well, there is a notion in philosophy that we cannot say we know something unless we believe it to be so, we have a good, relevant reason for believing it, and (finally) it really is so.

As to the second of these, subsequent events showed that the 'reason' Blair offered for believing there to be Iraqi weapons of mass destruction, that is 'secret assessments' by the British intelligence services, rather than supporting his view, stated that intelligence on the subject was 'sporadic and patchy'. Rather than 'knowing' about Saddam's weapons, the most that British Intelligence claimed was that: 'Iraq retains some production equipment and small stocks of CW precursors, and may have hidden small quantities of agents and weapons' (JIC assessment, 15 March 2002, quoted in The Rise of Political Lying by Peter Oborne, 2005).

So was Blair lying? Not technically. He could simply have misread the evidence. Nonetheless, in the British Parliament an 'Inquiry' was called for, to find out. However, using a kind of Socratic or 'dialectical' reasoning, Parliament could already have deduced quite a lot:

1. Either the Prime Minister believed that there were weapons of mass destruction in Iraq, or he did not. If he did not, then he was lying when he said they were there.

2. If he believed there were such weapons then either he had secret evidence for it, or he did not. If he did not, then he was lying when he said he 'knew' they existed.

3. Since now there were no weapons to be found, either they were destroyed at the outset of war, or the secret evidence was wrong. If the weapons had been destroyed it would have been possible to demonstrate this. But as this had not been demonstrated, the evidence must have been wrong.

On this complex matter, which is less to do with lies than that old philosophical problem of 'knowledge', the Prime Minister eventually offered the justification that his claim was 'true' in that he 'believed it at the time'. This standard clears up many problems. He could have 'believed' there were weapons, as long as he 'believed' he had evidence for it. But it is also a dangerous tactic, which if considered legitimate, tends to destroy the distinction between truth and falsity itself.

In fact, it might be better if politicians lied more.

Contributor: MC

been introduced, is known as 'poisoning the well'. There is also the so-called 'bad company' tactic, where the opponent's position is criticised by its supposed association with some other view. The Nazis often appear in arguments, brought in for this purpose.

11. Humpty-dumptying

After Lewis CARROLL's egg-shaped character who sits on a wall (but not, it seems, a fence) and insists that a word can mean 'just what I want it to mean – neither more or less!'

12. Self-contradiction

And finally, the unfortunate tendency of a poor argument to inadvertently 'shoot itself in the foot'.

Contributor: Martin Cohen

SEE ALSO

Critical thinking, Intentional fallacy in art, in intentions and intentionality, Lying

## FAMILY RESEMBLANCE

This is a term associated with – and also attributed to – WITTGENSTEIN, who argued that attempts to provide LOGICAL or 'analytic' definitions were doomed to fail. Instead, he suggested, most things grouped together as a 'unity' really only share certain characteristics, and differ in others. They share a 'fuzzy', or as he puts it, a 'family' resemblance.

## FANON, FRANTZ (1925–61)

See Direct action.

## FARABI, ABU NASR AL- (C. 870–950 CE)

Al-Farabi was an influential ISLAMIC PHILOSO-PHER and a successful musician. His influence lies as a commentator on ancient Greek LOGIC, notably ARISTOTLE's, earning him the honorific 'The Second Master', for his trouble (Aristotle being the first.) He lived in Baghdad, travelled widely in Byzantium and died in Damascus.

He is little known, considering his contribution to the development of philosophy, notably the 'Virtuous City' (al-Madina al-fadila), which contains new arguments about divine omniscience and human free will, and what scholars call a NEO-PLATONIST account of GOD. This directly influenced the thinking of the next stage of Islamic philosophy, and, as their ideas returned to Europe, the thinking of Christian philosophers such as Thomas AQUINAS.

## FASCISM

### Essential fascism

Fascism, for most people, is the Nazis in Germany under Hitler (who himself was an Austrian), but in fact the roots of it are more complex. After all, 'Nazism' is shorthand for 'National Socialism' which is something quite different, and fascism is actually an Italian ideology, echoed in Spain and paralleled in Japan. Indeed, many, such as Karl POPPER, have seen PLATO as the original fascist, with the Republic providing a paradigm of totalitarianism. But this would be a misreading – both of Plato and of the fascist ideology, which can be summed up with two tenets:

- all life is a striving after power, with human beings important only as means to the ends of the exercise of this power;
- the state should be organised rationally, with individuals complying with and fitting in to its requirements.

Indeed, rarely has a creed been so swiftly and totally severed from its intellectual base. Yet to understand how the horrors of totalitarian states like Nazi Germany came about, it is necessary to take the philosophical roots seriously.

### Absolute freedom

Fascism, as an ideology, is not particularly repugnant. It is IDEALISTIC and, if its practical incarnations are appalling, it is always open to its adherents to say, as the supporters of COMMUNISM do of the experiment of the Soviet Union, that 'true' fascism has not yet been seen. Nazism bears the same sort of relationship to fascism, as Stalinism does to communism; that is to say, a historical rather than a logical one. Nor does fascism have much to do with the present-day holders of the name, who are motivated by a mixture of hatreds and resentments – racism, homophobia, xenophobia – which really do not add up to any kind of POLITICAL PHILOSO-PHY, other (perhaps) than an emphasis on conflict and 'recognition'.

The real roots of fascism are to be found in German thought, notably with the writings of HEGEL. That philosophy professor's dream of a Prussian State, run along strictly logical and rational lines, does indeed share some characteristics with Plato's, as does his emphasis on the 'universe of mind' existing somewhere apart from the 'universe of nature'. Unlike Plato, however, Hegel starts with the history of the world and a critical survey of Indian, Persian and Chinese thinkers, claiming that, in those societies, only the ruler himself had any freedom to think rationally, and that therefore their philosophers were suspect. It was only in ancient Greece that Hegel thought individuals began to be rational; and not until the protestant Reformation (which allowed each individual the ability to 'find their own salvation') that what Hegel calls the 'glorious mental dawn' occurs. It is then that 'the consciousness of freedom', which is the driving force of history, makes possible the first truly rational communities.

Hegel's new rational society aims to combine individual desires (for wealth, for power, for justice) with the social values of the community. This involves reclassifying all desires that are not compatible with the requirements of the social whole as 'irrational', hence not what the individual really wants. Instead, the collective will, the *Geist*, is given complete power and authority. This is what makes Hegel the founding father of two totalitarian doctrines: both fascism and communism. Hegel writes:

> The history of the world is the discipline of
> the uncontrolled natural will, bringing it
> into obedience to a universal principle and
> conferring subjective freedom. . . The
> German Spirit is the spirit of the new world.
> Its aim is the realisation of absolute truth as
> the unlimited self determination of freedom
> – that freedom which has its own absolute
> form as its purpose.

Hegel influenced much subsequent philosophy, but as a political theory his ideas really had to wait for the Italian philosopher Giovanni GENTILE and Benito Mussolini. Gentile, an academic like Hegel, carries the label of being a 'neo-Hegelian', as do, from their contrary stance, MARX and ENGELS. Gentile it was who wrote the manifesto for fascism, the *Dottrina del Facismo*, just as Marx and Engels had earlier composed *The Communist Manifesto*. Both doctrines adopt the Hegelian notion of individual self-consciousness being embodied in the state. Both manifestos led to the sufferings of millions of ordinary and extraordinary people, victims of ideologues with adopted Hegelian notions of 'the march of history', devised in the cloisters of a university.

Fascism, then, although widely bandied about as a term for any regime that people disapprove of, is more correctly identified as the ideology of the Italian Fascists under Benito Mussolini in the first half of the twentieth century. And Mussolini actually started his career as a SOCIALIST, gradually developing extreme syndicalist notions, centred around an all-powerful State.

Gentile gave fascism an idealistic and spiritual aspect. Where LIBERALISM and socialism sought to benefit each individual, fascism sought to benefit the nation. The well-being of the nation provided a high moral purpose for each individual, a purpose that took precedence over the squabbles of workers and unions on the one hand, and capitalists and libertarians on the other. Socialism and individualism served only to divide the nation and weaken it, the original fascists felt, so instead of trades unions and private enterprise, they created a single unifying force, capable of ensuring companies and workers alike worked in the interests of the state. The force was the Fascist Party, united behind a charismatic leader. In fact, the fascists created the German sociologist Max WEBER's ideal of the bureaucracy under the charismatic leader.

But Gentile's language in describing the benefits of this approach went further. Fascism was not just an economic theory, or a quasi-legal structure of rights, but (echoing Hegel) would restore the patriotic morality of 'service, sacrifice and indeed, death'. Fascism was much more: a way to live and a way to attain fulfilment. It was not enough to do what the fascist government said – the fascist citizen also had to want to do it, and to believe in doing it. That is why one of the most potent images of the fascist State is of massive parades lined with enthusiastically waving crowds.

Mussolini added in to this brew the notion of fascism as an 'action theory' – and the highest form of action (echoing NIETZSCHE) was violence. It was only through violence that individual fascists could fulfil themselves and it was only through wars that the fascist State could maintain its purity. When Mussolini used violence to seize power in Italy in 1922, the process was part of the new way of governing – not just a necessary prerequisite. For some, the courage of the fascists in fighting for power conferred nobility and cleansed the movement of the impurities of the shambling democratic State.

Like Hitler, Mussolini also stressed nationalism. For Mussolini, Bismarck was a great figure, who had succeeded in binding together the various elements of Germany into a powerful nation, and he also admired MACHIAVELLI for what he saw as Machiavelli's endorsement of power, especially military power, either missing or ignoring the earlier Italian's emphasis on justice.

But Mussolini's nationalism should not be confused with the German brand, which identified nationality with 'race'. Crucially, for Mussolini, it was the role of the State to create a people out of what in reality would be a mix of very different races. It was the failure of Hitler to understand this that led German fascism to the most grotesque irony of bureaucratic rules and structures, all aiming to make logical a doctrine of racial purity created out of irrational hatred and prejudice. Mussolini himself, the father of fascism, even wrote at one point explicitly that a people is not a race, instead it is a group united by an idea perpetuating itself. Nonetheless, over the period of the Second World War, Italian fascism soon adopted the various hate policies, notably the anti-Semitism, of the Nazis.

Contributor: Martin Cohen

## FATALISM

Fatalists believe that everything is predetermined, so really there is no point trying to change it. The notion is probably religious in origin, to do with being 'predestined' to go to heaven – or hell, in either of which case, you might as well enjoy yourself now.

## FEMINIST PHILOSOPHY

'Feminism' covers a range of perspectives, from notions of 'equal rights', to ones of socially constructed gender roles, and on to claims of (in some views) superior and unique characteristics for women. The term was coined in the late nineteenth century by the French utopian socialist Charles Fourier (yes, a man), with an eye on campaigns for basic social and legal rights for women.

The first level of 'feminism' is concerned with things such as non-discrimination: for example, equal access to education, training and employment, equal pay and, generally, EQUALITY 'before the law'. Then there are issues regarding both social and legal norms in terms of inheritance and the division of labour within a family.

The second level moves on to the role of ideas, such as ARISTOTLE's notion that women are 'mutilated males', and indeed the idea of Eve as being merely the 'spare rib' of Adam, which has both reflected and created a 'common-sense' view of women as somehow the

'deviant' form of men, and one furthermore that is different in being, inferior and lacking. By contrast, PLATO insists that the souls of men and women are the same, and that women can become 'philosopher guardians'. He also has Diotima as one of the major influences on SOCRATES' thought.

Yet, within philosophy, women traditionally have been held to 'lack' the logical tools necessary for philosophical insights (witness, for example, the dismissive views of KANT, HEGEL and ROUSSEAU), while a view of women as 'more emotional' and of 'dubious' moral tenacity have all been used as reasons to both justify and explain their low profile in intellectual history. Yet before we leap to the conclusion that these supposed characteristics must be rebutted one by one, we should also consider the possibility (which comes in perhaps as our 'third level' of feminism) that there may be different intellectual as well as physical characteristics between the two sexes. That, for example, the traditional LOGICS of philosophy may indeed reflect a peculiarly 'male' view of the world and how it 'ought' to work – even if it does not: that moral rules should be 'absolute' and not dependent on context; that 'emotion' is to be discouraged in preference to mechanical reasoning. Why should any of these attitudes be accepted? That there may be differences in male and female thinking certainly should not presuppose that one is superior to the other, and if we decide that one is indeed better than the other, it is certainly not to be taken for granted that gender alone tells us which one it would be.

SEE ALSO

De Beauvoir, Wollstonecraft

## FERTILISATION

See Reproductive ethics.

## FEUERBACH, LUDWIG (1804–72)

Feuerbach abandoned a promising career in Erlangen University, Germany when his authorship of a supposedly anonymous essay on IMMORTALITY (arguing against it as a possibility) became public knowledge. As an academic, he had been concentrating on the ideas of HEGEL, and the debate about the true nature of reality. He was increasingly doubtful of Hegelian abstraction and instead came to think that it might turn out that reality was something we find through sense perception. This doubt led naturally to his main thesis on theology, set out in *The Essence of Christianity* in 1841, and in particular, the notion that thinking about religion is basically a form of anthropology, that is, that religion is created by humans to fill a need left over by our physical limitations – such as dying. In this way, Feuerbach influenced MARX and ENGELS.

## FEYERABEND, PAUL (1924–94)

An Austrian who worked mainly in the USA, Feyerabend advocated a radical 'epistemological anarchism', in which he went further than Karl POPPER and Thomas KUHN, asserting that there is no such thing as scientific method, and that the scientific world view is no better than any other (for example, he suggests, astrology or voodoo). He says that the various scientific world views of the past were all quite 'rational' within their own framework, and only fall apart when one examines them from outside it. Paul Feyerabend is unusual among twentieth-century philosophers – his writings are fresh, lively and clear, even if not necessarily entirely persuasive.

## FICHTE, JOHANN (1762–1814)

Fichte came from a German peasant family, a fact that made his future career more remarkable. Aided by a local landowner, he went to Jena and Leipzig to study psychology, philosophy and theology. He met KANT in 1791, became something of a disciple and was rewarded with a teaching post. However, in 1799 he was thrown out (in good philosophical tradition), accused of teaching heresies, or ATHEISM in particular.

Fichte was an 'ardent' nationalist and urged the 'rebirth' of Prussia after her defeat by Napoleon, and he was soon back in favour, appointed to Berlin University in 1810. His philosophy posits that consciousness must be the starting point, as it is impossible to explain it in terms of anything else, whereas the world around us can be explained by referring to consciousness. Thus, Fichte rejected Kant's notion of reality as 'the-thing-in-itself', forever out of reach but still fundamental. This he sets out in *Theory of Knowledge* in 1797, and his ethical perspective is in a book a year later entitled, perhaps unimaginatively, *Theory of Morals*. Here he argues that the root of morality is CONSCIENCE, and we can either act so as to boost our self-esteem,

or so as to make ourselves feel ashamed. Thus, morality becomes rather self-centred and egotistical. Furthermore, Fichte says some individuals have such good judgement of these matters that others can and should take their lead from them. This is where religion can have a role – training and stimulating moral behaviour. The *Science of Rights* (1798) attempts to apply his theory to law (i.e. individuals, the family and the State) and international relations (i.e. relations between states).

There is also a role for the State in ensuring that people limit their actions not only to seeking to maximise their own interest, but to avoid trespassing on that of others. However, in order to judge one individual's proper sphere of action with regard to another person's, the individuals must all have equal rights and powers. In turn, this requires an economic revolution, allowing each to be autonomous: that a lesson doubtless drawn by Fichte from his own earlier experience.

## FICTION

Fiction raises some puzzling questions for philosophers – how can something 'not real' be important? What is going on when we react emotionally to fiction? On this last point, ARISTOTLE thought that dramas must always create the two feelings of pity and fear in the audience. PLATO thought that fiction was in principle objectionable, but if we must have it (for example, as poetry), then it should be wholesome and uplifting. But it is AUGUSTINE who writes most eloquently:

Stage-plays also carried me away, full of images of my miseries, and of fuel to my fire. Why is it, that man desires to be made sad, beholding doleful and tragical things, which yet himself would by no means suffer? yet he desires as a spectator to feel sorrow at them, and this very sorrow is his pleasure. What is this but a miserable madness? for a man is the more affected with these actions, the less free he is from such affections. Howsoever, when he suffers in his own person, it used to be styled misery; when he compassionates others, then it is mercy. But what sort of compassion is this for feigned and scenical passions? for the auditor is not called on to relieve, but only to grieve: and he applauds the actor of these fictions the more, the more he grieves. And if the calamities of those persons (whether of old times, or mere fiction) be so acted, that the spectator is not moved to tears, he goes away disgusted and criticising; but if he be moved to passion, he stays intent, and weeps for joy.

*(Book III, The Confessions)*

Second, philosophers have batted to and fro the question of 'truth; in fiction: 'King Lear has ungrateful daughters' looks like it is the same kind of statement as 'Queen Elizabeth II has several grandchildren', yet in the first one, as King Lear does not seem to really exist, or as philosophers put it (in the language of MEINONG and FREGE): there is no 'referent' out there to which we can tie the truth or falsity of the claim.

Funnily enough, as Jeremy BENTHAM pointed out, much of what passes as reality is actually 'fiction'. Motion, power, even matter are all 'made up' by us; they are not there in the world. David HUME joined in too, denouncing substance, the 'self' and space and time as all 'fictions'. (And that does not begin to consider the status of things like 'rights', values, duties and obligations. . . )

**SEE ALSO**

Narrative

## FILM ETHICS

Film ethics is quite the thing in philosophy departments these days, and some philosophers say that mass communications, such as films, are an essential tool for modern society; the ETHICAL cement that used to be provided by the great myths and religions. But what kind of cement is it? Matthew Arnold, writing in *Culture and Anarchy* (1882), says the responsible author or artist 'tries not to make what each raw person may like, the rule by which he fashions himself, but to draw ever nearer to a sense of what is indeed beautiful, graceful and becoming, and to get the raw person to like that.' Unfortunately, not many films are like that.

This brings us, of course, to censorship. Among film makers, it is sometimes said that if the use of music, the stylisation and the 'artistry' of the cinematography make the actual images acceptable, it is because there is some sort of 'distancing' of the audiences from the violence. This notion of 'distancing' is quite important outside films too.

It clearly applies to all types of cruelty where people create special terms for what they are doing to whom – perhaps street talk, perhaps racist jargon, perhaps 'technical terms' of scientists and administrators (or politicians). The language of police and military 'elite' squads is full of euphemisms; the two very media-savvy nations, Israel and the USA, not content to offer (the already rather mealy-mouthed) talk of 'assassinations of suspected subversives', invent terms like 'focused prevention', just as 'collateral damage' has taken the place of 'civilian casualties', for example.

Whether anyone can learn anything from watching films is a moot point. Many philosophers are sceptical enough about learning ethics from 'actual cases', much less imaginary ones. Movies that have so much 'incidental detail' and so little intellectual theory seem, for these philosophers, to creep in last of all as methods for considering ethics.

Neither Paul Ricoeur nor Martha Nussbaum, for example, two contemporary philosophers who advocate storytelling for ethics, consider films to be significant vehicles for this sort of storytelling, perhaps also because the watcher of a film is passive and the imagination is marginalised.

**SEE ALSO**

Narrative

## FINAL CAUSES

ARISTOTLE makes much use of the notion, saying that the 'final cause' of ducks having webbed feet is that they can swim better. This kind of explanation, assuming things have an 'end' or purpose, has a special name in philosophy, that of 'TELEOLOGICAL explanation', and despite it being anything but straightforward as an assumption, has characterised most philosophical and scientific thinking, especially in the West, since PLATO. Within science, however, starting with GALILEO and NEWTON, there has been a recognition that some things, such as the motions of the stars, are better explained without such 'teleology', but merely being described mathematically.

The 'first cause', or the 'prime mover', has played a role in much natural philosophy, and is always supposed to be God.

## FORGERY

The trouble with forged money is that you can get into trouble with it. The trouble for the State is that it may cause inflation. The trouble for philosophers about forgery is much more METAPHYSICAL. The philosophical debate in practice, though, tends to be focused on tangible things like forged paintings. If they look the same, what is the difference? Is the AESTHETIC perception of one real and the other deluded? In another situation, we may feel cheated by a plastic flower that we thought was a real one, or conversely, in a plastic orchid competition we may be shocked that someone tries to 'fool us' with – a real one!

## FORK, HUME'S

HUME seems to have had several forks, which is doubtless very useful. Two of the 'forks' are between relations of ideas and matters of fact, and between deductive reasoning and INDUCTIVE or 'probable' reasoning but the one that is most celebrated is the one that appears in Part III of his *Enquiry Concerning Human Understanding*. It is here that he proclaims: '*Does it contain any abstract reasoning concerning quantity or number?* No. *Does it contain any experimental reasoning concerning matter of fact or existence?* No. Commit it then to the flames, for it contains nothing but sophistry and illusion.'

## FORMALISM

Formalism is concerned with the essence of MATHEMATICS. One approach is concerned to debate to what extent mathematical proofs consist of following rules that are applied to written symbols, and to what extent maths is more like a game of chess in which understanding the rules is barely the beginning of understanding the game.

David HILBERT and his followers had high hopes of 'formalising' mathematics, that is, grounding it securely in rules, but GÖDEL's 'Incompleteness Theorem' pulled the rug from under that particular project's feet.

## FORMS

See Argument (logical forms), Plato ('the forms').

## FOUCAULT, MICHEL (1926–84)

Foucault was born in Poitiers, taught at the Collège de France from 1970, and died in Paris. A psychologist by training, with major interests in psychopathology, he was the leading philosopher of STRUCTURALISM, and wrote extensively on madness, crime, sexuality and religion

from a historical perspective, influencing both intellectuals and practitioners on social attitudes to mental illness and crime and the questioning of intolerance generally.

Foucault's method involved the structural analysis of the coded ideas that permeate society and the way it works, which is far more informative than the stated principles supporting the mores of society. In particular, he exposed the principles of exclusion, defining what really distinguished the sane from the insane in a society, the law-abiding from the criminal. He held that survey and analysis of social attitudes towards and within repressive institutions such as hospitals, asylums and prisons made overt the underlying apparatus of power.

He was concerned that he was very much a man of his times and so attempted to write himself out of his analyses, regarding 'SELF' and all it brought into play as SUBJECTIVE material that had to be eliminated. This is the JUNGIAN preliminary for the therapist in psychoanalysis. He examined the long historical perspective for explanation of current attitudes, particularly the change from the classical to early Christian attitudes to sex. The titles of his books are informative: *Madness and Civilisation* (1961), *The Order of Things* (1966), *The Archaeology of Knowledge* (1969).

One example of this last is his description of the workings of Jeremy BENTHAM's *Panopticon*:

Each individual, in his place, is securely confined to a cell from which he is seen from the front by the supervisor; but the side walls prevent him from coming into contact with his companions. He is seen, but he does not see; he is the object of information, never a subject in communication. . . If the inmates are convicts, there is no danger of a plot, an attempt at collective escape, the planning of new crimes for the future, bad reciprocal influences; if they are patients, there is no danger of contagion; if they are madmen there is no risk of their committing violence upon one another; if they are schoolchildren, there is no copying, no noise, no chatter, no waste of time; if they are workers, there are no disorders, no theft, no coalitions, none of the distractions that slow down the rate of work, make it less perfect or cause accidents.

*(Discipline and Punish: The Birth of the Prison*
Trans. Alan Sheridan. New York:
Vintage, 1977)

Initially the darling of FEMINISM, because of his exposé of the misogyny and repression of paternalism, he was later accused of ignoring the female contribution in his work on religion. *Confessions of the Flesh*, the final volume of his *History of Sexuality*, remains unpublished, under the terms of his will. He did not enjoy celebrity, was famously gay but never admitted it, valuing protection of self. The best quote from his final years is perhaps ' L'âme, prison du corps.' ('The soul, prison of the body.') He died of AIDS in 1984, one of its earliest European victims.

## THE FOUR FREEDOMS (ROOSEVELT'S)

They are: freedom from fear; freedom from want; freedom of speech and expression; and freedom to worship God in your own way. They were asserted in Roosevelt's State of the Union address in 1941, and were interpreted as the 'war aims' of the Allies.

## THE FOUR NOBLE TRUTHS

See Gautama.

## FRANKLIN, BENJAMIN (1706–90)

Franklin was something of a 'Renaissance man' in that his activities spanned the sciences, literature and, of course, politics. His *Autobiography*, the *Dissertation on Liberty and Necessity, Pleasure and Pain*, as well as his *Poor Richard's Almanac*, constitute his claim to be a philosopher, blending as they do a kind of ARISTOTELIAN ethics based on living as 'virtuously', following special

rules of good conduct and cultivating good habits, with a more scientific calculation of utility, based on the kinds of civic duties enshrined in the texts of American Independence.

## FREGE, GOTTLOB (1848–1935)

Frege's goal was to demonstrate that MATHE-MATICS could be reduced to LOGIC, and that it depended on nothing but pure 'reason'. This is claimed as the first 'formal system', distinguishing between 'axioms' and 'rules of inference'. In order to define NUMBERS, he produced some complicated logical statements such as, for 'cardinal numbers': 'the class of all classes which can be mapped one-to-one on to a given class. . .'; and many others that we need not go into here, other than to say that, in the process, he made a considerable contribution to both areas, and in particular the study of the fundamentals of ARITHMETIC. The statement above, incidentally, merely says that if you have as many things, say knives, on a table, as you have say, forks, you know you have the same 'number' of them even without counting them.

Frege's *Foundations of Arithmetic* (1884) is considered a 'philosophical classic' by logicians, and takes apart earlier efforts to explain number and mathematics by those such as John Stuart MILL. In the process of examining the nature of deductive ARGUMENTS, Frege also offers a way of looking at the nature of language, including his distinction between the sense of world (which is objective and determines its 'truth value') and its 'colouring', which is SUBJEC-TIVE and to do with the context in which the word appears. On top of that, there is its 'reference'. The evergreen example is the planet Venus, which is both the 'Morning Star' and the 'Evening Star': it has two senses, but only one referent.

# FREUD, SIGMUND (1856–1939)

## The essential Freud

Sigmund Freud was born in nineteenth-century Moravia, then part of the Austro-Hungarian empire, to a secular, middle-class, Jewish family. When Freud was four, the family moved to Vienna, where he remained for most of his life. He trained as a doctor and he always saw his theories as part of a scientific, empirical tradition. Freud viewed himself as extending the understanding of the human being, both normal and pathological. Freud has been immensely influential, both on the treatment of the mentally unwell and, more generally, on the modernist concept of the human self and mentality.

## Investigating the inner worlds

In the late nineteenth century, mental disorder had come to be understood in 'POSITIVIST' terms as something rooted in a disorder of the body. Treatment consisted in withdrawal to an asylum and various physical interventions. Freud, however, became interested in the use of hypnotism as a cure for hysteria.

In the 1880s, Freud and his medical colleague, Josef Breuer, treated a number of wealthy Viennese women using hypnosis. The most well-known of these cases is that of 'Anna O', a young woman who displayed a series of incapacitating physical complaints which appeared to have no organic origin. Anna O complained of paralyses, which at times were so severe that she could not walk. At other times she was unable to speak in German, but only in a variety of foreign languages. Breuer treated the patient by putting her into a hypnotic state and assisting her to talk through the memories which emerged. Anna O's treatment was abruptly broken off when Breuer finally realised that she had fallen in love with him and that this lay behind some of the pattern of her symptoms.

Anna O's case led Freud to develop the concept of the talking cure. He abandoned the use of hypnosis, thinking that what had effected an improvement was the slow, painstaking linking of each individual symptom with a specific event or memory. In other words, Freud began to develop a theory of the self as split, between a conscious, rational and social self and a hidden self, the inhabitant of an inner world without reason or social control that the conscious self strove to repress.

In Freud's theory, hysteria – the development of physical symptoms without organic origin – sprang from difficulties in the individual that arose when a wish conflicted with social or moral inhibitions. Freud's initial hypothesis is sometimes known as a 'hydraulic' or 'drive' theory. It sprang from nineteenth-century science, and was a way in which Freud attempted to link his innovative ideas with contemporary scientific theories of the human being as part of the animal world and of EVOLUTION. Freud argued that human beings were driven by libido, a powerful sexual impulse. He observed in his patients that libido could be directed towards many objects, which sometimes led to internal conflict. The attempt to repress what were felt to be forbidden desires could produce symptoms.

In a series of case histories, Freud presents a patient and her or his constellation of symptoms and describes the process of talking through the symptoms and the associated memories, often originating in early infancy. It is often not recognised that Freud was a very tolerant man, and did not judge his patients. He felt that their difficulties were an illness and that through his new science of psychoanalysis, patients would be helped to understand and recognise their desires and come to terms with them in a different, less self-destructive way.

Freud was initially struck by the number of his women patients who described themselves as seduced by their fathers or other male family figures. In 1897 Freud came to the view that these were, in fact, early childhood fantasies. He described these fantasies as the 'Oedipus complex' and argued that this was a phase which everyone has to go through. In simple terms, the child falls in love with the parent of the opposite sex and becomes a rival of the same-sex parent. In males, the boy is drawn to the mother but fears being castrated by an angry father. In a satisfactory development, Freud thought, the boy works through these feelings, renouncing his mother and identifying with his father. But if the boy is unable to do this, he will remain fixated at an earlier stage, and may, for example, identify with the feminine and become homosexual. In the case of the girl, she may be unable to move towards what Freud thought was a normal sexuality. For Freud, the woman's sexuality was essentially receptive, and the girl child had to accept her own, and her mother's, damaged status as lacking a penis. If she were unable to move towards this acceptance, the girl would adopt a masculine identity and interests and would be unable to experience what Freud saw as natural feminine sexuality.

These theories continue to be controversial, and for many professionals today are considered to be discredited. Freud's first female followers, analysts such as Helene Deutsch and Melanie Klein, challenged Freud's theories about women's sexuality. FEMINISTS in the 1970s argued that Freud's theories maintained women in a position of inequality. They argued that women expressed their dissent with conventional, circumscribed roles in a covert way through their symptoms, and that psychoanalysis acted as a means of inducing women to accept these roles through internalisation. The French feminist psychoanalyst Helene Cixous analysed some of Freud's key texts in a more sophisticated way. Cixous suggests that one of Freud's most famous patients, Dora, a young woman who suffered from hysterical symptoms, was in fact using the language of symptoms to express a critique of the sexual duplicity of the bourgeois Viennese society in which she lived. Cixous suggests we should read the case study as a historical, political and emotional text, which explores on many levels the nature of the family and of the place of women within it.

With the abandonment of the seduction theory, Freud located desire at the centre of the family and linked childhood to sexuality. These theories evoked disgusted rejection in many contemporaries, who saw childhood and the family as a haven of innocence. But his rejection of the seduction hypothesis has been condemned, most recently by Jeffrey Masson. Masson argues that Freud's women patients were indeed sexually abused and that Freud, in saying that these were fantasies, was unable to accept that the world of the family could include relationships of power and abuse.

In 1923, Freud presented a complex reworking of his theory of the self. He replaced the drive theory of the self with a tripartite model, in which the irrational and primitive world of emotions and libido, called the *id*, was checked by the EGO, the rational self, and by the *super-ego*, which was an internalised model of social and moral norms. The *super-ego* could itself be extremely punitive, and it was when a powerful and intolerant *super-ego* attempted to control the world of the *id* and there was no tolerant and understanding *ego* present, that the person fell ill. Freud was now concerned with the way these various parts of the self interact.

In *The Interpretation of Dreams* (1900) Freud described the unconscious world of the *id*. In the UNCONSCIOUS, there is no logic, but everything can co-exist and our most forbidden desires rule unchecked. The unconscious reveals itself in our dreams and through slips of the tongue. As the conscious mind attempts to repress transgressive desires, the unconscious reveals itself in distorted form, in symbols, which have to be decoded and interpreted. Surrealist artists attempted to represent the symbolic world of the unconscious in art.

In 1920, Freud had put forward another controversial theory, that we are pulled between a pleasure principle and a death instinct. He thought that within each cell of the body was an impulse which pulled the self towards ENTROPY, stagnation and death. This contrasted with an instinctual move towards life and creativity. This theory seemed to find support in the darkening of European life and culture at that time, with the growth of Nazism. EINSTEIN, among others, wrote to Freud expressing his sense of the truth of this account.

Freud was an extraordinarily creative thinker, whose ideas shifted over the course of his long life. His theories entered into the common language, and our modern or POSTMODERN Western concept of the self is shaped by his concepts of the divided self, of the conflicting worlds of desire and social and moral demands, and of repression.

Freud saw himself as in the tradition of empirical science. However, a devastating critique of psychoanalysis was made by fellow Viennese, Karl POPPER, who argued that psychoanalysis does not meet scientific criteria. It is not possible to prove or disprove a psychoanalytic statement about human behaviour through a predictive hypothesis. Popper and many other philosophical writers think there is no objective basis for any statement by Freud, or in his tradition. While many psychoanalysts would dispute this, even today, others, such as Adam Phillips, accept that psychoanalysis is not a science. What, then, is it? Some argue that psychoanalysis is a special kind of narrative, a way of making sense of and interpreting certain kinds of feeling and behaviour. It is also a therapeutic relationship, which many people find helpful and supportive.

The division between objective, measurable reality and the shifting, SUBJECTIVE world of the self remains. Neuroscience is currently hailed by some as a new way of finally pinning down what determines personality and behaviour. Many philosophers would argue that human beings are endlessly caught in a reflexive world, in which we can never quite glimpse ourselves. As a writer at the turn of the twentieth century, Freud describes some of the complexities of the human condition, caught between desire and social necessity, a prey to the internal world of irrationality and disorder, but seeking to make something of themselves and to contribute to human social and moral order. These ideas were expressed in much of twentieth-century literature, art and film. Freud captures some of our contradictions and, in turn, continues to shape how we perceive ourselves.

Contributor: Anna Cohen

## Further reading

Freud, S. (1900) *The Interpretation of Dreams*

Freud, S. (1905) *Fragment of an Analysis of a Case of Hysteria ('Dora')*

Freud, S. (1920) *Beyond the Pleasure Principle*

## FUTURE GENERATIONS

These are a problem for moral philosophers, and the problem is not only whether they should 'count' for anything (since they do not exist and may well never do so), but also, as Derek Parfit pointed out, the decisions we take determine who lives in the future. For example, pollution may adversely affect future generations – or stop them existing at all, in which case, it might seem, things would be 'better' as there would be fewer people to worry about things. Alternatively (more complicatedly), the pollution may adversely affect the future generations, but be necessary for their existence – perhaps it is necessary for me to pollute the river in order to earn enough money to have children, whatever the consequences for my neighbours.

## GALILEO (1564–1642)

Galileo Galilei was born in Pisa, Italy, where he pursued his first interest, medicine, before moving on to mathematics. From 1592 to 1610 he was professor of mathematics at Padua, applying the study to the mysteries of motion, of both the celestial and the earthly kind. From 1610 he became 'first philosopher' (as opposed to various lesser philosophers, presumably) and private mathematician to the Grand Duke of Tuscany, a position that seems to have enabled him to set about communicating his ideas through a series of books that changed the direction of both philosophy and science.

Despite, or perhaps because of, being charged with knowledge of such matters, philosophers ever since ARISTOTLE had advocated positions that were not only wrong, such as that heavy objects will fall proportionately faster than light ones, but were cumbersome and unproductive. In *The Assayer* (1623) Galileo concentrates particularly on 'deconstructing' Aristotle, separating out his notion of movement in the sense that plants, for example, 'move' towards the sun, for a more limited one, in which the physical and psychological worlds are separate and the physical world becomes amenable to mathematical analysis. *The Dialogue Concerning the Two World Systems – Ptolemaic and Copernican* (1632) sets out, in addition to the (well-known) arguments for the sun-centred solar system, a more interesting argument for the relativity of motion and space. This featured Galileo's celebrated 'Ship' THOUGHT EXPERIMENT, in which his two interlocutors discuss whether they would be able to tell if they were in the cabin of a boat moving 'in any direction you like', but steadily, from being in a motionless boat, for example, by taking a goldfish bowl with them and watching to see if the fish were affected, or by throwing a ball across the cabin to each other. This thought experiment, like the much misunderstood one of dropping the two balls off the leaning tower of Pisa (which proves logically, not experimentally, that all objects must be subject to the same acceleration effects from gravity).

It was the *Dialogue* that caused Galileo a year

after publication to be condemned by the Vatican and obliged to recant, but the reason for it seems to have been less to do with the affront caused by this debate concerning the two rival astronomical systems, than either the challenge to the orthodox view of matter (undermining the Church view on the Eucharist) or even, perhaps, a very blunt insult included by Galileo (who was nothing if not arrogant) to the sagacity of the Pope himself.

Galileo was also a careful empirical scientist, who made systematic and effective observation part of his method, most famously, using the new 'telescope'. But it was indeed Galileo who wrote that the book of nature is written in mathematics.

## GAMBLER'S FALLACY

The gambler's mistake (it is not strictly a 'FALLACY') is to assume that because the slot machine (say) has not given a jackpot for the last hundred goes – it is *more* likely to do so the next time. The fallacy is due to the fact that the machine neither knows nor cares what it has just done, and so is quite prepared to defy statistics and produce 101 or indeed 1001 'losing' combinations.

However, it is true that if you approach the machine intending to have a win, you are much more likely to hit the jackpot if you determine to put in coins up to the 1001st go than if you think to put in just one or two. Naturally, if the win does not appear until the end of your 'investment' it may not cover your losses. At any one time, the machine offers, like the toss of a coin, only the same odds as at any other time.

### See also

Fallacies

## GAME THEORY

Sometimes called 'decision theory', this is a mathematical theory about human choices. The 'rules' of the game or the facts concerning the situation are assumed to be known to all, and people are assumed to be 'rational', taking the strategies of each other into account. One application of the theory favoured by academic philosophy is to various boxes filled with varying rewards; but another is nuclear deterrence, where it is certainly desirable that all the 'players' should consider their rational interest to lie in not having a war at all.

## GAMES (IN ETHICS)

These days, the 'ethical awareness training' of many employees may be through playing 'board games'. These were originally developed in the USA for use by large multinational companies. Probably the best known was developed by Citicorp and called, efficiently enough, the *Ethics Game*. It consisted of a number of imaginary scenarios, printed on cards, with multiple-choice answers. The more ethical your answer, the faster you could move around the board, picking up rewards or forfeits as you did so. The game was popular enough to spawn versions in many different languages, including Spanish, French, German and Japanese.

The *Ethics Game* was similar to *Scruples*, a card game. But in *Scruples* there is no board and no pieces to move – just lots of cards, describing situations in which someone might be tempted to break some implied social rule or convention. The way to win is to correctly predict the answer (Yes, No or Depends) of another player. You do not need to enter into discussion of the answer, although people often did want to – that was part of the fun. All these games owe something to a much older board game called *The New Game of Virtue Rewarded and Vice Punished*. Produced in Britain in 1810, this one featured edifying images of 'The Stocks' and 'The House of Correction', as well as 'Faith' and 'Prudence'.

The approach was taken further by the armaments manufacturer Lockheed Martin whose ethics game it called *Gray Matters*. Lockheed Martin's interest in such matters was awoken after it had been prosecuted under the Foreign Corrupt Practices Act for attempting to bribe foreign legislators to secure new orders for military transport planes. At the time, an unrepentant Lockheed argued that their behaviour was not unethical, as they were acting with the interests of their employees at heart (who might otherwise be made unemployed). This piece of practical UTILITARIANISM fell on stony ground, and the company was fined $25 million.

And so the *Ethics Game* is played according to very strict rules. Although, in a spirit of 'greyness', in most cases it allows that there may be several acceptable answers, it also suggests there are some totally unacceptable ones. Allowing employees to address each other with endearments is one such example, meriting in the original game a penalty double the normal one for a 'wrong' answer. 'Stealing from the government' comes out more black than grey too. And the employee who 'learns' that any answer involving making a report to their supervisor or the ethics office is 'good', is also learning something which is not really ethics, but simply pragmatics. The employees are encouraged to accept company rules and company procedures as ethically pure, which is sometimes hard to square with the reality.

SEE ALSO

Business ethics

## GANDHI, MOHANDAS (1869–1948)

Mohandas (otherwise known as Mahatma – 'great-souled') Gandhi was a HINDU political leader and idealist who transformed the Indian Home Rule movement against the British Raj from an ineffective, Western-type, political movement into a spiritual force, which by non-violent means achieved Indian independence. In Gandhi's moral philosophy, means and ends are not separate but form a continuum. It follows that no 'end' can justify great violence and widespread killing.

Gandhi was born in 1869 at Poorbandar, West India, where his father was chief minister. His mother was a deeply religious Hindu, who taught Mohandas the spiritual value of fasting and that everything can be achieved by non-violent means. He was sent to London to learn law at the Inner Temple and subsequently practised law in Natal, South Africa. It was in South Africa, not India or Britain, that he first suffered the humiliation of colour prejudice.

He stayed in South Africa throughout his formative years, funding non-violent political activity on behalf of the Indian population there from his legal earnings. His first political activity was in opposition to legislation designed to disenfranchise Indians. In 1902 he was awarded the British Boer War Medal for organising a 1000-strong ambulance corps from among the Indian population.

Gandhi returned to India in 1914 after nearly 30 years abroad and was soon an activist on behalf of Indian Home rule within the National Congress Movement. He was jailed for two years after leading the civil disobedience campaign, which culminated in the Amritsar massacre of 1919, where the British army was responsible for the murder of 400 unarmed civilians. On his release he fasted for three weeks, as an example of non-violent intervention in a bitter dispute between Hindus and Muslims in Congress. He led the party from 1928. In 1930 he challenged the Indian government's salt tax by leading a multitude over 200 miles to the coast to pan for salt. He was arrested again, with over 60,000 of his followers.

India gained independence in 1948 after years of struggle, in which Gandhi suffered many disappointments and setbacks, but stuck to his non-violent principles. He was assassinated in Delhi in 1948.

## Further reading

Lyer, R. (various editions) *The Moral and Political Writings of Mahatma Gandhi*

Wolpert, S. (2002) *Gandhi's Passion*

SEE ALSO

Direct action

## GASSENDI, PIERRE (1592–1655)

Gassendi, a French priest, is sometimes only remembered for being one of the commentators on DESCARTES' mediations; his position being strongly against Descartes' 'RATIONALISM', in particular the optimistic assertion that if we *really* think we know something, or as Descartes says, 'clearly and distinctly perceive something', then it must be true. (This is because God, says Descartes, would not allow us to be deceived too cruelly.) Gassendi notes that what we observe may already be a product of what we expect to see, a point that John LOCKE would take up from him as part of his discussion of 'primary and secondary' qualities. Gassendi also dismisses Descartes' view of 'extension', which includes within it the dogma that there can be no vacuum, no 'void', preferring instead the idea of solid bodies (atoms) either moving or at rest. In the mid-seventeenth century, his arguments for the 'ATOMISM' of nature, advocating many elements from EPICURUS, were part of the new science associated with Robert Boyle and Isaac NEWTON.

## GAUTAMA, SIDDHARTHA (*C.* 567–487 BCE)

### The essential Buddha

Siddhartha Gautama, the founder of BUDDHISM, was born in Kapilavasthu, modern Nepal, son and heir of the chief of the Sakya

## THE FOUR NOBLE TRUTHS AND THE EIGHTFOLD PATH

Gautama claimed: I have taught just one thing: the four noble truths.

*The first noble truth: experience is impermanent, is transient suffering.*

Birth is transient suffering, ageing is transient suffering, illness is transient suffering, ecstasy is transient suffering and death is transient suffering. Joined to what you do not love is transient suffering. Separation from what you do love, not to have what you most want, is transient suffering.

*The second noble truth: it is wanting experiences that causes transient suffering.*

Wanting new sensual pleasures, wanting to perpetuate yourself, even wanting to end it all, each is a cause of transient suffering, each leads to reincarnation, rebirth to yet another cycle of transient suffering.

*The third noble truth: to halt transient suffering you must abolish all appetites.*

To abolish appetites, to stop wanting things, to avoid transient suffering is to achieve Nirvana, the chaff blown away.

*The fourth noble truth: to achieve Nirvana you must follow the eightfold path.*

Gautama has used Indian medical technique here. He has defined the disease, found its cause and now prescribes the remedy: the therapy of the eightfold path: the first path is just opinion, the second path is right thought, the third path is correct speech, the fourth is appropriate activity, the fifth is finding the best means of existence, the sixth is precise effort, the seventh is focused attention and the eighth path is total concentration.

The paths culminate in the yoga practice of holding positions that strengthen the body, of control of breathing that steadies the mind, of meditation that leads to increasing powers of concentration until all appetites are abolished, the self loses its individual essence as the subtle body fades away and release into absolute reality is achieved.

tribe, part of the Kshatriya caste, the ruling caste. His father, Suddhodana, tried to divert him from his destiny to be a great spiritual leader, as foretold in his natal stars, by protecting him from all signs of deprivation. As a young man, Siddhartha lived a luxurious and lascivious lifestyle. When eventually he did meet with poverty, he was horrified.

At about the age of 30 he left the rich life of his family and took up the life of an ascetic. He went to Vesali to learn an early form of Sankhya philosophy from the Brahmanic master, Arada Kalama. Then he went to Rajagrha, capital of Magadha, and was taught basic YOGA by Udraka Ramaputra. He moved to Gaya, Bihar in East India, where he lived in poverty, practising self-denial, yoga and meditation.

He awakened to the 'FOUR NOBLE TRUTHS' while sitting *padmasana* under a banyan tree in a garden outside Gaya, an event dated to 523 BCE. Commencing in the holy city of Benares on the Ganges, Gautama then proceeded to teach his 'noble truths', as well as the so-called 'Eightfold Path' to NIRVANA (by the blowing out of the flames of desire). He continued teaching the 'way of liberation' to converts for 40 years, attracting followers from all over India. He died at about 80 years of age in Kusinagara, Oudh.

## Placing the Buddha

Gautama Siddhartha's teachings fit within the Nyaya system of HINDU philosophy. The written *Nyaya Sutras* are attributed to him, but pre-date him as oral tradition. Hindu Brahmins make the attribution, but as if Gautama were a Hindu sage, distinct from Buddha.

The Sankhya, Nyaya and Yoga systems of Hindu philosophy, LOGIC and practice are the bedrock of Buddhism. They describe a dynamic relationship between essence with individual reality and activity in eternal interplay, with no primary cause. There can be no divine revelation. Buddha is not God, the son of God or the prophet of God, for there is no God. Buddha was the human being, Siddhartha Gautama, once awakened to reality. And this 'awakened' Buddha taught that philosophical treatise and ritual were barriers to understanding the essential methods of gaining release from the burdens of the day to appreciate the spiritual life and achieve freedom. He sought instead to make contemporary Hindu teachings on achievement of spiritual liberation readily available to all. His system was to be simple, practical, down to earth and accessible.

For these reasons he dispensed with Sanskrit and used the vernacular. In the process he alienated the Brahmins, the religious elite of the day. From his position as a member of the superior caste he taught that birth was of no significance, it was individual achievement that mattered. At the time, the Brahmins were scandalised and attempted to make Buddhism anathema in India. They were eventually successful. Buddhism all but died out in its birthplace, but had a solid revival in the twentieth century.

It is ironic, but not without parallel, that some of Gautama's followers, through to some present-day proponents of Buddhism, have turned his teaching into a mystery religion with its own complex jargon, rituals, vestments and, of course, a supervising elite. Even from the beginning, complex mythologies were woven around Gautama's life story, elaborate commentaries on the basic texts were produced and increasingly strange and exotic versions of the transmigration of souls.

Enlightenment is simplicity, the self unmasked, at one with the universe: the absolute reality of the natural world around us.

By example, Gautama convinced others of his four noble truths and the eightfold path to enlightenment. They recorded his teaching in the vernacular of his day. Gautama did not claim originality: *I saw the ancient pathway, followed by all awakening people; I have simply followed that path.*

Contributor: Colin Kirk

## THE MANY NAMES OF BUDDHA

Gautama is the family name of the original Buddha. Buddha means awakened. He is also known as *Sakyamuni*, the ascetic of the Sakya tribe; by his given personal name *Siddhartha*, which means goal attained; and as the *bodhisattva*, which means being awakened. The names *bodhisattva* and Buddha are not unique to Gautama; they are the names of spiritual states and, where appropriate, are applied to others.

SEE ALSO

Buddhism

## GEACH, PETER (1916–)

Peter Geach is one of the paradigmatic figures in British philosophy in the twentieth century,

and in later life turned to evangelical Catholicism. He is also one half of a rare philosophical couple, with the late Elizabeth Anscombe (also known as G.E.M Anscombe), translator and executor of WITTGENSTEIN and respected in her own right.

Geach is more generally remembered, however, for pioneering philosophy of the most uncompromising kind, dressed up in technical language, such as *Reference and Generality* (1962), in which he sought to demonstrate useful things, such as that the word 'every' in statements like 'every dog has four legs' does not refer to a special dog, the 'every dog', which might be supposed to have this interesting feature. His areas of study include the history of philosophy and the philosophy of religion.

## GENERAL WILL

The notion of the general will is that there are collective interests that can be supposed even if none of the individuals could be said to share them. KANT considered the general will to be what is left after throwing away all the individual idiosyncrasies and prejudices, partly reacting against ROUSSEAU, who seems to have coined the term and used the idea in a biological sense, seeing society as a kind of organism, while more recently, John RAWLS uses it as a purely hypothetical notion for calculating optimal outcomes.

## GENETIC FALLACY

See Fallacies, esp. section 5: illegitimate tactics

## GENTILE, GIOVANNI (1875–1944)

Gentile was a distinguished 'new HEGELIAN' philosopher, author of *The General Theory of Spirit as Pure Act* (1916), which has the IDEALISM as well as the sinister quality of FASCISM within it. He was Minister for Education in Mussolini's fascist government and was influential enough to be assassinated in 1944 by partisans.

SEE ALSO

Fascism

## GENTZEN, GERHARD (1909–45)

The German LOGICIAN who developed 'natural deduction' as a new way of doing logic, both 'classical' and what is called 'first order'. Rather than start with some small set of rules, 'AXIOMS', the method of natural deduction, allows you to introduce assumptions as you go along, with the assumption being stated openly as an inference from one of the arguments' premisses, or to 'eliminate' assumptions in the sense of later on finding a justification for them so that they no longer need be counted as such. For example, if the premises are A and later on B, then you can introduce the assumption (wait for it!) 'A and B'.

The advantage of the approach is its flexibility, although it is still subject to the same limitations of certainty as any other logic.

## GESTALT PSYCHOLOGY

The school of PSYCHOLOGY founded by Max Wetheimer, Wolfgang Kohler and Kurt Koffka in Germany in the early twentieth century. A 'Gestalt' is a pattern that has features not present in the individual parts. For example, a melody is not present in each individual note, but only once they are combined. A flashing light is just a flashing light, but combined with others can become a figure throwing a ball, or indeed anything, given the sophistication of today's 'flashing lights'.

SEE ALSO

General will

## GEULINCX, ARNOLD (1624–69)

Geulincx was born in what would later become Belgium. He was a follower of DESCARTES and, particularly concerned to explain the problem of how mind can affect matter once the distinction between them has been drawn, argued for the possibility of there being two synchronised but otherwise wholly unconnected clocks striking the hours, a possibility which then allows there to be two different areas governed by the same laws, despite there being no causal connection between them. God acts like this on a universal scale, in being able to arrange everything everywhere without being subject to normal LOGICAL or causal limitations. Human minds are indeed unable to interact with their bodies, but it does not matter as our minds are part of the divine, and the divine consciousness propels all events. The comparison is made (if all this sounds a bit implausible) with a nation's money. For the many coins in circulation are indeed merely brute lumps of metal; it is only the collective assumptions of value that turn them into 'money' and hence give them their purpose and power to act.

## GHAZALI, ABU AL- (1058–1111)

The Persian theologian whose autobiographical account, *Deliverance from Error*, and *Incoherence of the Philosophers*, called on theologians to use philosophy to undermine philosophers and their heresies. The first work is sometimes compared to AUGUSTINE's *Confessions*. Among his 20 questions for theology to answer were eternity, IMMORTALITY and causality. This challenge was taken up by Averroës, among others.

## GOD (AND ARGUMENTS FOR AND AGAINST EXISTENCE OF)

### The essentials of God

The supreme idea, concept or entity that, for some, still regulates the universe, and, for many, still regulates ETHICS.

### God as a concept

Philosophers have described the nature of God as the Creator, the Generator, the Principle, the Infinite, the Good, the Being, the One, the Perfect, the Absolute or the Transcendent. The history of these definitions has made of God the common ground among theology, META-PHYSICS, ONTOLOGY, ethics and EXISTEN-TIALISM, for, as KIERKEGAARD pointed out, any question about God is a question about existence. The Pentateuch already speaks of a God that *is*, an ontological statement that coincides with the mysterious definition of an eternal Being by PARMENIDES. Centuries before KANT, Saint Anselm understood that any intellectual discussion on God is A POSTERIORI to his Idea, an intuition that studies of isolated non-Western societies have corroborated.

God is a concept as malleable as the history of mankind. Before the Mesopotamian distinction between good and evil was established, primitive cultures associated God to the creative and destructive forces of nature, a conception that was anthropomorphised by the Assyrians and that the soldiers of Hernán Cortés discovered as late as the sixteenth century, in their conquest of the Aztec Empire. PLATO, under the influence of the Indian philosophers, referred to the supreme God as the Demiurge, that is to say, as the maker and ruler. ARISTOTLE rather understood it as his alter ego, an immobile motor who ponders eternally about himself.

As early as the fifth century BCE, XENOPHANES argued for the ethical nature of God, far more compelling than the capricious behaviour of the anthropomorphic gods of Ethiopia, Egypt and Thrace. In the same vein, SOCRATES disdained polytheism and worshipped a single God, an attitude that eventually contributed to his forced suicide. And indeed, Christianity was born as ethics, rather than as religion. In the Sermon on the Mount, Jesus does not bless a race or a group of believers, but instead those who he calls the poor of spirit, the meek, the merciful, the peacemakers, the persecuted, the righteous and the mournful.

Moses and the prophets of Israel had already associated the concept of justice to God, but, as Plato proved, 'justice' can be as imprecise a word as 'God'. Jesus objected to the *lex talion* stated in Exodus and Deuteronomy ('An eye for an eye, and a tooth for a tooth'), and demanded love and forgiveness in the face of violence and oppression. Jesus, nonetheless, abstained from formulating love as mere compassion – as Buddha did. Persuaded that self-sacrifice was the only solution to a continuous circle of retribution, he set up a precedent of his teachings in his own trial, crucifixion and death. As late as 1953, secular spectators could hear the lament of one of Samuel Beckett's characters: 'All my life I've compared myself to him' [that is, Christ].

The first Christian writers (in particular, Saint John) presented Jesus not only as the Christ, but also as the incarnated God whose main attribute was love. Centuries later the MYSTIC and shoemaker Jacob Boehme would go even further, declaring love to be more important than God, a statement that coincides with FEUERBACH's remark that Christianity must sacrifice God as God has sacrificed himself out of love. The cult of the Virgin Mary responds to the Christian appraisal of motherhood as the highest manifestation of love, a veneration that has raised eyebrows among purists since the iconoclastic upheaval, and that prompts postmodern FEMINIST scholars to debate in a neo-Byzantine spirit the true gender of God.

But the definition of God as selfless love conflicts with the morals of the *Realpolitik*, and the concept of God has been ably adapted to the needs of the world by popes, priests and theologians. The intolerant God of sixteenth-century Spain has more in common with the stern God of the Roman emperors than with the cosmopolitan God of the Renaissance popes. Under the shadow of an optimistic Industrial Revolution, the nineteenth-century death of God was also the death of ethics. Two world wars

and the rise of religious fundamentalism have demonstrated that secular governments cannot underestimate the new conceptualisations of God. Whereas the existential horizon of physics and science is death, the TELEOLOGICAL nature of any secular or religious ideology inspires believers to accomplish deeds beyond their capacities and even against their own instinct of survival. Thus the God of the Old Testament encouraged a community of runaway slaves to build an empire in Canaan, a deed emulated by the first followers of Muhammad and the seventeenth-century American pioneers.

In one of his epigrams, Goethe wrote that those who have art and science have religion, whereas those who do not have art and science should have religion. In the same vein, Carl JUNG understood that religion supplies to common folk what educated men receive from art and philosophy. The sudden discredit of the Scriptures, which until the rise of COMMUNISM had been the ethical reference of millions of workers and peasants, left an ethical gap that was filled with the writings of LENIN, MAO and Hitler, demagogues who clearly understood that the main function of religion was not metaphysical but moral, and who organised their ideologies as creeds. Days before committing suicide, a delirious Hitler prophesied the coming of another Führer. After Lenin's death, Stalin presented himself as the Messiah, announced by MARX the Father under the guidance of Lenin's writing – his Holy Ghost.

And many sceptics and reformers have played a role in the history of religion. Recently, the confessed ATHEIST Luis Buñuel questioned through his films the nature of God in a universe ruled by interests and passions, while displaying the heroism of sainthood in a selfish world. Meanwhile, the apparently 'objective' accounts of the mass media have made scientists the new priests of our time. 'Science' and 'reason' have become the voice of God. Not surprisingly, we hear a new theory of the origin of the universe every year, as provisional and improbable as the arduous speculations of the long-forgotten, pre-Socratic metaphysicians.

Contributor: Hugo Santander

## Further reading

Morris, T.V. (1991) *Our Idea of God*

# GÖDEL, KURT (1906–78)

Gödel's name is synonymous with his 'incompleteness theorem', which may sound airy, but is in fact very mathematical and precise. Gödel was born in Austria, but spent most of his career in the USA, where he counted EINSTEIN as a great friend. In the 1930s he produced a LOGICAL proof demonstrating the 'completeness' of what is called first-order PREDICATE CALCULUS – that is, the logic of sentences beloved of philosophers, such as 'A is an apple', 'A is red', 'A is round', and so on. But following on this work he found that the logical systems being explored by contemporaries, such as Gottlob FREGE, Bertrand RUSSELL and Alfred North Whitehead, were necessarily unprovable or 'incomplete'. This indicated that mathematics itself, inasmuch as it depends on logic for its certainty (or 'consistency'), is also incomplete. Gödel's theorem, as it is called, put more formally, is:

> for any consistent formal system S,
> containing a certain part of arithmetic, a
> sentence in the language of S can be
> constructed which is neither provable nor
> disprovable within S.

The implications for mathematics and logic are profound, in that it means that there is no system in which every mathematical truth can be proved, hence 'justified'. The system contains claims that are neither provable nor disprovable by consideration of the original AXIOMS.

# GODWIN, WILLIAM (1756–1836)

William Godwin was a moral and POLITICAL PHILOSOPHER, and the author of a number of 'political novels', such as *Caleb Williams* (1794) – and the husband of Mary WOLLSTONECRAFT. His *Enquiry Concerning Political Justice* (1793), advocating a radical version of ANARCHISM with UTILITARIAN underpinnings, was sufficiently controversial as to risk prosecution. Among his arguments was one that government (power) corrupts both the governments and the peoples governed, while creating and aggravating inequality and injustice. By contrast, a completely free, 'non-political' structure allows the essential benevolence and community-mindedness of people to emerge.

In his personal life, he advocated a radical kind of freedom, which left Mary Wollstonecraft to an early and lonely death shortly after the birth of their child.

# GOLDEN RULE

The golden rule is said to be 'do unto others as you would have done unto you', or similar (and vice versa). CONFUCIUS offers a very similar warning, and the Bible presents it as a Christian teaching at Matthew 7:12. But how good a principle is it? Its virtue is that it supposes a kind of impartiality in behaviour, but that, in another sense, is a rather weak ETHIC. I might wish that no one should bother me and just leave me to get on with my own life – but when I stop my car to offer a lift to someone who has broken down, have I broken the rule? Then, as philosophers love to point out, there are those such as masochists who wish to be tortured: is it right that they should tie up and torture their neighbours? KANT dismissed it as trivial in a footnote of his *Metaphysic of Morals*, and Sidgwick worried that it is both too 'general' and weakened by exceptions to be a useful rule.

# GOOD

PLATO, in the *Republic*, considers 'the Good' to be a kind of 'FORM', indeed the most important of all the forms, the source of 'being' and 'knowledge' itself. Thus it was that all life centred around the search for the Good, and this was the highest form of wisdom. ARISTOTLE gave 'the good' a central role, as being that to which everything aspires, but then spoilt this by saying that everything aspires to a slightly different version of the good. A knife aspires to be good in a different way to a monk. Indeed, the same thing appears to be capable of being good in a confusing array of ways – a good dog may be good in that it obeys instructions, or in that it can run fast; for a hooligan it may be good in that it bites people, but for others in that it does not do so.

Certainly, it seems as if we do use the term in such different ways that it might be wise to set off the sense in which good relates to something like 'making most people happy'. So, for example, 'that is a good action' means 'that is an action that will increase the amount of happiness'.

In the twentieth century, G.E. MOORE attempted to rule out use of the word 'good' as being 'unanalysable' and accessible only to intuition – a 'non-natural' property. To use the word 'good' to describe things in the same sort of way that they might be called 'yellow' or 'heavy' is a 'NATURALISTIC FALLACY'. Later in his life, he joked that he had never himself worked out why his objection applied more to 'being good' than to any other property. John RAWLS offered what he called a 'thin theory' of things as 'good', if they were things that everyone in a community wanted.

## GOODMAN'S PARADOX

See Grue.

## GRAMMAR

See Linguistics.

## GRAMSCI, ANTONIO (1891–1937)

Gramsci was born in Sardinia, Italy, to a middle-class but impoverished family. As a young man he was an active SOCIALIST, working as a journalist on the leading socialist newspaper. In 1920 he was one of the founders of the Italian Communist Party. This coincided with the rise of FASCISM. Mussolini seized power in 1922 and in the following years socialist and COMMUNIST organisations were suppressed and their members arrested. Gramsci was arrested in 1926 and sentenced to 20 years in prison. Gramsci had always suffered from ill health and while in prison became seriously ill. He died in 1937 while imprisoned.

Gramsci's main contribution to political and cultural thought was the development of the idea of HEGEMONY. From 1929 he began to write a series of essays on themes connected to history and MARXISM. These are known as the 'Prison Notebooks'. Gramsci elaborated Marx's view that ideology arose secondarily to economic and political power. Gramsci drew attention to the role of ideas in political power and argued that they were not secondary. He thought that a political and economic group or class needs to instil in other groups its own way of seeing the world in order to gain and maintain itself in power.

These ideas influenced the development of the Italian Communist Party in the decades after the Second World War. They were also taken up by left-wing historians, such as E.P. Thompson in Britain and Ferdinand Braudel and E.P. Ladurie in France, who developed a continuing strand of history which explores mentalities, or the emergence, dominance and decline of particular world views, and their relationship to economic and political power struggles. Gramsci's influence can also be seen in FOUCAULT's work linking discourses of knowledge and power.

### Further reading

Gramsci, A. (1947) *Prison Letters* (*Lettere dal carcere*) posthumously published

## GROTIUS, HUGO (1583–1645)

While DESCARTES meditated in the comparative luxury of his warm oven room ostensibly as a soldier in the Dutch army, Delft-born Grotius was meditating as a political prisoner on what would become a highly influential political treatise, *De Jure Belli ac Pacis*, titled in translation, *The law of war and peace* (1625). A lawyer and theologian, with poetical leanings, he wove medieval and classical legal theory together with the new ENLIGHTENMENT political ideas and emerging legal principles. Among his arguments was that morality remains valid even if one discounts the existence of God, because 'natural rights' emerge from rational judgements made in the context of social life. Rights are 'powers' or 'freedoms' to do things, and political society is about providing the framework for citizens to exercise these rights.

Grotius also argued that as there is no such framework for governing conflict between states, countries could justify going to war in order to rectify any wrongs.

## GRUE (GOODMAN'S PARADOX)

Named after the US philosopher Nelson Goodman, the paradox defines the colour 'grue' as 'having the property of being' green up to a certain time (the example frequently offered was, of course, the year 2000) and blue forever afterwards. Goodman's point (if that is not too strong a word) was that although the empirical fact that all the emeralds we have seen so far have been green, this would appear equally to confirm their being 'grue'. But come the Year 2000 (or whatever time) we would find that the previous instances counted for. . . not a lot.

This is really an old philosophical point about 'INDUCTIVE reasoning', especially associated with David HUME.

SEE ALSO

Paradoxes

## HABERMAS, JÜRGEN (1929–)

One of the so-called Frankfurt School of CRITICAL THEORY, which numbered among it philosophers such as ADORNO and Herbert

Marcuse, Habermas was proclaimed as 'Germany's leading intellectual' after the publication of *Knowledge and Human Interests* in 1968. (And that is a 'good thing'.) In *The Theory of Communicative Action* (1981), he goes on to pinpoint the causes of various crises confronting modern society (political, economic and cultural) as a perverted form of rationality, driven by the vested interests of money and bureaucracy at the expense of genuine collective decision-making and social values.

## HAECCEITY

An obscure philosophical term meaning 'this-ness', or standing for the property that something has that makes it what it is. For example, Socrates has the property of being Socrates. Futile though this tactic may appear, some philosophers (notably Roderick Chisholm) have attempted to prove that no entities have such properties, that is to say, individual ESSENCES, but only the properties of being 'self-identical'. Alas, there we must leave 'this' in its full haecceity.

## HAPPINESS

### Beauty is the guide of happiness

There are five parts to my guide to happiness.

1. In times of philosophical explanations, philosophy should be used as the conductor that directs the symphony of thoughts, so that the harmony of wisdom is also adorned with truth.

   For when we try to consider happiness, the whole effort of our attention is directed on what we see in life, and how we comprehend it, as well as by which method we shall be able to distinguish beauty. For such visions of beauty bring to light a mystical loveliness that blends the perceived world in the mind with the already existent.

   Perhaps it does not cast a great shadow that the fruit of happiness embodies the achievement of that elusive harmonic perfection of the body and soul, the combining of their two worlds in one where beauty leaves the reflection of its eternity. For the nature of our mortal selves is that we are predestined in time, and the contemplation of genuine beauty represents the only chance, the only way, to look upon the eternal fruit that can be comprehended by a mind.

This, then, is the way in which the true orientation, the proper direction of cognition is as the mediator between us and a philosophy rooted in the nature of space and time.

Otherwise, the mind is like PLATO's shackled prisoner, condemned to a lifetime of thirst, even as the vision of happiness with its eternal promise surpasses all in space and time – in other words:

2. Happiness is the fulfilled beauty of the eternal instant that celebrates victory over the few remaining minutes in space and time.

   Within this dimension of happiness, one wearing the triumphal wreath of love is victorious over the soul's emptiness, which gives birth to the abyss that leads to the death of the heart, and to an emptiness that follows a human being through all their days.

   Because constantly searching for pleasure, our bodily nature predestines us to be slaves to the temporal senses, and simultaneously it rushes onward towards beauty perceived by the mind. At the same time, this nature insists on its right to define independently the attractiveness of pleasure.

   So it is this that ruins the true world, for happiness defined by the passions of the body, is, as should now be admitted, a degradation of the mind. (An event unfortunately all too ordinary in the wider society of today.) So, such definition of happiness may be said to aspire towards a happiness without a consciousness – to try flying without wings.

   Consider, for example, how the body's passions manage to conquer the mind. Life emphasises its existence in space every minute. Yet every shape or thing connected with this minute is separated from perfection and exists in emptiness. Yet this momentary life is the only hope of existence (as there is nothing beyond this emptiness). As for consciousness in general, without philosophical thinking, existence would be nothing but a world in only shades of grey.

   And then without colours the world begins to lose its beauty and must grow ever poorer in our thinking that adds up to devaluation of life. From this point of view we can now take the chance to reach out to some conclusions:

3. Beauty is one of the main pillars of the value of life and philosophy.

Obtaining the true harmony of the body and soul in its relations with the world requires the latter transformation by that which comes from holiness – for it is these things only that embody the soul's eternal nature, that are articulated by the mind – and through which it becomes possible to transform the momentary pleasure into the eternal senses.

Or, as HEGEL put it, 'beauty shares in this higher world. So regarded it is a Reflection of the beauty of Mind.' His are, as ever, very impressive words, but I would like to emphasise that beauty includes in itself and reveals each thought, an idea of love, a sound, a shape and colour – these are all elements that create art. So beauty both discloses itself through art and acts within it. Accordingly, beauty is accompanied with art that portrays the fascinating picture of happiness. Hence, the fourth point can be said simply:

4. Beauty perceived by the mind of a human being personifies the idea of happiness.

For the attractiveness of beauty is being disclosed in art, its brilliance without holiness cannot be beautiful – and seeing that the depth of a thought represents the elevated which accords with beauty, their sacred chain expresses the treasure of universal concept, from where might be seen the value of happiness which is coming from the dimension of love.

So it should be admitted that the knowledge described with the pen of art is elevated over the sensual senses and together with it, it expresses the soul's beauty that guides the heart's desire... To go deeper:

5. Happiness is the true art of love.

Contributor: Zura Shiolashvili

## HAYEK, FRIEDRICH (1899–1902)

Hayek was an influential economist whose main theme was that the collective wisdom of individuals, as expressed through the 'free market', was far superior to that of governments. This, of course, was an old theme, made most effectively by Adam SMITH in the eighteenth century. However, Hayek explained a bit more why it might be so, saying that when individuals try to understand a mammoth and complex entity like modern society, their understanding and knowledge base will be quite inadequate, not as a

matter of practical reality, but because much of the decision-making depends on guesses as to what individuals will do in the future, which is of necessity unknown. Worse still, governments attempting to make judgements themselves affect and change decisions, so there is a potentially disastrous form of feedback in the system.

Hayek was the 'darling' of the political right in the USA and the UK in particular, and his writings on political freedom became influential especially during the Reagan/Thatcher years towards the end of the twentieth century.

## HEDONIC CALCULUS

See Utilitarianism.

## HEDONISM

From the Greek *hedone* or pleasure. It is the creed advanced by Aristippus of Cyrene (435–356 BCE) of the nobility of the pursuit of pleasure-seeking. However, even the most selfish hedonists face the problem of how to balance their pleasure (for example, eating cream cakes) against their own later pain (for example, feeling a bit sick). This problem about choosing short-term pleasures over long-term ones lies behind the preferences of EPICUREANISM and the very long-term pleasure of wanting next to nothing. Epicurus also distinguishes between pleasures that come from making good a deficiency (eating when desperately hungry) and those which can increase the pleasure of a person who has everything, which is where the virtuous pleasure of 'doing without' comes in.

UTILITARIANISM, in contrast, rests on a rather unsophisticated measure of pleasure in the sense of 'whatever makes people happier'. J.S. MILL tried to produce a guide to higher and lower forms, echoing PLATO in the dialogue, the *Protagoras*. In the process, he criticised his father's friend and his own educational guardian, Jeremy BENTHAM, as a man who equated the pleasures of 'push-pin' and 'poetry'. (Of course, push-pin is much more fun!)

There are distinctions drawn these days between 'psychological hedonism', the theory about motivation that says that pleasure is necessarily the only thing we can desire; and 'evaluative hedonism', which is concerned rather with values and what we ought to want.

# HEGEL, G.W.F. (1770–1831)

## The essential Hegel

Georg Wilhelm Friedrich Hegel was born in Stuttgart and educated at Tübingen seminary, alongside the epic poet Friedrich Holderlin and fellow philosopher Friedrich SCHELLING. The three of them together watched the unfolding of the French Revolution and collaborated in a critique of the IDEALIST philosophies of KANT and his follower, FICHTE.

With the exception of a brief period as a newspaper editor, Hegel devoted his life wholly to teaching, first at Jena, then at Nuremberg and Heidelberg, and finally at Berlin. The first two posts were in schools, and only the latter ones (after 1816) were as a university 'professor' as he is invariably depicted. In fact, his key works date from his grammar school rather than his university life.

Hegel's first, and most celebrated, major work is the *Phenomenology of Spirit* (or '*Mind*'). During his life he also published many other works, including the *Encyclopaedia of the Philosophical Sciences*, the *Science of Logic* and the well-named *Philosophy of Right*.

Many consider Hegel's thought to represent the summit of nineteenth-century Germany's movement of philosophical idealism; it led to the 'historical MATERIALISM' of Karl MARX as well as to the development of the FASCIST ideology, via Giovanni GENTILE, in Italy, Spain and Germany.

## Hegel, and the rise of totalitarianism

Hegel's writing is notorious for being hard work, and he is certainly ambitious in the range of topics he attempts to cover.

In his book, *The Open Society and its Enemies*, Karl POPPER criticises Hegel, arguing, among other things, that his 'system' is in reality a fairly thinly veiled paean to Prussia's then ruler, Frederick William III. In striving to show that the ultimate goal of history must be to reach a state approximating that of early nineteenth-century Prussia, he dabbles in HISTORICISM even in, as at the time, Arthur SCHOPENHAUER sneered, 'pseudo-philosophy'.

Hegel's most characteristic contribution to philosophising is the use of an ancient technique that is now associated with him, called 'the DIALECTIC'. This is introduced by Hegel in various guises, but most famously as a system for understanding the history of philosophy and the world itself. His thesis is that history is a series of moments evolving successively out of the conflicts inherent in the previous one.

So it is that for Hegel, the origin of society is in the first conflict between two humans, a 'bloody battle', with each seeking to make the other recognise them as master and accept the role of 'slave'. (We may suppose that the apparently relevant conflict between male and female, resulting in the subordination of the latter, is less significant here. It is not part of Hegel's analysis, anyway.) In Hegelianism, it is the fear of death that forces part of mankind to submit to the other, and society is perpetually thereafter divided into the two classes: slaves and masters. However, it is not material need that propels one class to oppress the other – it is a conflict borne solely out of the peculiarly human lust for power over one another. And the French Revolution was simply the slaves revolting. Hegel, unlike, say, Thomas HOBBES, approves of the motivation, he calls it the 'desire for recognition'. For many, this risks death, but that is the way towards 'freedom'. During the French Revolution the ideal of freedom is accompanied (and then consumed) by brutal terror. Out of this conflict, however, emerged a new kind of State, in which the power of rational government combines with the ideals of freedom and equality.

*The Science of Logic* (*Wissenschaft der Logik*, 1812–16) and *Encyclopaedia of the Philosophical Sciences* (*Die Encyclopedie der Philosophischen, Wissenschaften im Grundrisse*, 1817) attempt to apply this approach to all areas of human knowledge. Hegel's *Nature and Statecraft* (*Naturrecht und Staatswissenschaft*) develops the political ramifications stressing the desirability of the individual being subservient to the State, which alone has moral worth and encapsulates 'the Spirit'. In the *Philosophy of Right* (1820), Hegel explains in excellent headmasterly style that the State does not exist for the individual, but rather the individual exists for the State.

Hegel's new society aims to combine both individual desires (for wealth, for power, for justice) with the social values of the community – a kind of early 'third-way' politics. But Hegel's solution also involves reclassifying all desires that are not compatible with the requirements of the social whole as 'irrational', hence not what the individual really wants. Instead, the collective will, the *Geist*, is given complete power and authority. This is what makes Hegel the founding father of the two totalitarian doctrines: fascism and COMMUNISM. Hegel writes:

> The history of the world is the discipline of the uncontrolled natural will, bringing it into obedience to a universal principle and conferring subjective freedom: The German Spirit is the spirit of the new world. Its aim is the realisation of absolute truth as the unlimited self determination of freedom – that freedom which has its own absolute form as its purpose.

Lying behind this totalitarian concept of society is a view of the universe not as a collection of fundamental particles, whether atoms or souls, but as a whole, an organic unity. 'The True is the Whole', Hegel explains in *The Phenomenology of Spirit*. It is an illusion to think of anything as separate from anything else, and, inasmuch as we do so, our thinking is flawed. Actually, even 'the whole', which replaces all these imagined separate objects, is not essentially one substance, but many, just as an organism, such as the human body, is made up of different parts with their own characteristics and functions. Even that most basic distinction – between space and time – results in us misguidedly splitting up the world and thereby losing touch with reality. Hegel calls reality – this whole – 'The Absolute', and it is his contention that all that is true of the world can be formally deduced from consideration of the Absolute, using LOGIC.

The Absolute is also rather like God (a rather austere kind of God, like ARISTOTLE's). A quote, from Hegel's lectures on the Philosophy of History, gives the flavour:

> That this Idea or Reason is the True, the Eternal, the absolutely powerful essence; that it reveals itself in the world, and that in that world nothing else is revealed but this and its honour and glory – is the thesis which, as we have said, has been proved in philosophy, and is here regarded as demonstrated.

Perhaps paradoxically, Hegel opposes all forms of world government, explaining in the *Philosophy of Right* (which contains the Hegelian version of the march of World History, as it progresses from the 'Oriental' via the 'Greek' and the 'Roman' to arrive ultimately at the 'Germanic') that war is crucial: 'Just as the blowing of the winds preserves the sea from the foulness which would be the result of a prolonged calm, so also corruption in nations would be the product of prolonged, let alone "perpetual" peace.'

Hegel, out of all the Western philosophers, is one of the most clear about the educational foundations of his system. He wrote voluminously on the methods for teaching and learning, both in the form of manuscripts and as letters, and reflected on numerous 'pedagogical matters'. These included the conflict between the need to achieve discipline, and the advantages of 'student-centred' learning, the bad practice of 'spoon feeding' on the one hand, and the desirability of obliging children to imbibe from the deep well of the classics.

Here, in its earliest form, is the Hegelian play of the dialectical reasoning. Everything has two sides, creating tension that must be resolved. In fact, Hegel is, in general, locked into a conflict between the two poles of traditional and progressive ideas of education. So it is that Professor Hegel bans duelling and fighting while introducing military drill into the school day, considering that it would help students both to learn quickly and 'to have the presence of mind to carry out a command on the spot without previous reflection.'

In keeping with his admiration for the discipline imposed in the classroom of PYTHAGORAS, who demanded that his pupils keep silent for the first four years of their studies, Hegel favours (as his school address of 1810 puts it) 'quiet behaviour, the habit of continuous attention, respect and obedience to the teachers.'

But Hegel also writes that teachers should not:

induce in children a feeling of subjection and bondage – to make them obey another's will even in unimportant matters – to demand absolute obedience for obedience's sake, and by severity to obtain what really belongs alone to the feeling of love and reverence. A society of students cannot be regarded as an assemblage of servants nor should they have the appearance or behaviour of such. Education to independence demands that young people should be accustomed early to consult their own sense of propriety and their own reason.

Hegel had an illicit liaison with a young woman and had a child with her. It is known that Hegel later 'legitimised' the child as his own, although he would not marry the mother. Probably she came from a 'lower' social class.

In 1831, cholera was epidemic in Berlin and Hegel's colleague and intellectual enemy, Schopenhauer, despite or perhaps because of being famously pessimistic, quickly left the city for the healthier climes of Italy. Schopenhauer thus survived the epidemic. Hegel stayed, perhaps out of his preference for his own nation, contracted the disease and died.

Contributor: Martin Cohen

## Further reading

Lowith, K. (1941, trans. 1965) *From Hegel to Nietzsche: The Revolution in Nineteenth-century Thought*

## HEGEMONY

See Gramsci.

## HEIDEGGER, MARTIN (1889–1976)

SARTRE may be 'the father of EXISTENTIAL-ISM' for the general public, but it is Martin Heidegger who holds this proud title among the European philosophers. Naturally, he rejected 'existentialism' as a gross over-simplification, admitting only to the rather airy study of 'being'. *Being and Time* (*Sein und Zeit*) paved the way in 1927, following on several journal articles

broadly concerned with rejecting the 'IDEAL-ISM' of KANT for a more modern 'critical realism'. It is here that Heidegger explains that the problem for humanity, with its conscious awareness of its existence ('Dasein', as he puts it), 'lies in its always having its being to be'. The problem about time is that 'being' excludes past and future, elevating the present.

The approach is built in part out of the 'destruction' of Edmund HUSSERL's 'neo-Kantian' writings and views. (Heidegger was one of Husserl's students, and the book was – initially – dedicated to him. Interestingly, in the light of his later activity in the Nazi party, not least the cancelling of this dedication, Husserl was, by ethnicity, a Moravian Jew.)

For Heidegger, truth is found by starting from everyday understandings and linguistic usages, and discarding things you do not agree with, things such as science and technology, which he saw as neglecting 'being'. For the same sort of reasons, LOGIC was none too welcome either. 'No other thinker so unsettles the analytic enterprise', declares David Krell, one of his admirers today. In fact, Heidegger ranges widely, and is unusual in elevating poetry and art above traditional analytic philosophy as a guide to the true nature of the world and reality.

'Dasein', he says, is definitely part of 'the world', the world that is of everyday things, not of science or philosophy with their abstractions and theoretical entities. Heidegger borrows an example from Tolstoy's novel, *The Life of Ivan Ilyich*, to illustrate a further point: Ilyich images his house to be the epitome of individual good taste – the furniture, the paintings on the walls, even the conversations over dinner, are all (he believes) unique to him. But they are rather, or so Tolstoy cruelly reveals, 'all the things people of a certain class have in order to resemble other people of that class'. (In passing, it might be said that perhaps there is an element of 'circularity' in Tolstoy and Heidegger's reasoning here.) This is an example of 'inauthenticity'. Another, discussed by Heidegger, is the human tendency to discount the inevitability of their own death.

Large sections of his works, including *Being and Time*, are left uncompleted. Silence, he tells us, is also part of discourse, and his style of philosophy is deliberately obscure. He uses words in old, obsolete ways that they are no longer understood as meaning, and coins new words as and when he feels the urge. Needless to say, among many philosophers today he is revered.

His support for Nazism through the entire period of its reign – the period of intellectual fear, during which he became rector of his University, the Gestapo state and, of course, the time of the concentration camps – has made him a controversial figure. After the defeat of the Nazis he lost his post as head of the University of Freiburg.

## HEISENBERG, WERNER

See Uncertainty principle.

## HELL (AND HEAVEN)

Those who commit mortal SINS (or simply fail to be baptised) go to hell, which is a nasty place, traditionally underground, where they are subjected to everlasting torments. Numerous warnings about what happens to bad people when they die are to be found in ancient myths and the Christian New Testament merely offers a new 'systematic' account. Although today hell is less prominent in the Christian message, this in turn raises the question of the afterlife itself – if there is nowhere to go, what does it mean to say there is one?

Both Christianity and Islam still use this incentive to better behaviour while alive. Indian philosophies have concentrated rather on heaven, with many different realms postulated, described and debated. BUDDHISTS, by contrast, tend to stress the highest form of happiness comes to us while still here on earth – the state of 'NIRVANA'.

## HELLENISTIC PHILOSOPHY

Hellenistic philosophy is the collective name for the schools of philosophy that flourished in the Hellenistic period, that is, from the death of Alexander the Great (323 BCE) to the fall of the last of the kingdoms founded by Alexander at the battle of Actium (31 BCE). Traditionally, there are three Hellenistic schools: STOICISM, EPICUREANISM and SCEPTICISM, the latter divided into two traditions: Academic Scepticism, which dominated PLATO's ACADEMY for part of this period, and PYRRHONIAN Scepticism. Recent scholars have started to use the phrase post-Hellenistic philosophy to refer to the period that immediately followed, ending around 200 CE.

## HÉLOÏSE COMPLEX

The French philosopher and writer, Héloïse, was seduced and later betrayed by her tutor, the medieval philosopher and logician, Peter Abelard. Described by Michèle le Doeuff in *Hipparchia's Choice* (1991), the Héloïse complex is the tendency 'since the days of antiquity' for women to be 'admitted into the field of philosophy chiefly when they took on the role of loving admirer'.

## HERACLITUS (OF EPHESUS)

Heraclitus lived in the sixth century BCE, 'flourishing', as it is often put (like some sort of exotic philosophical flower), in Ephesus around 500 BCE. According to later writers, he also buried himself in dung, but alas, as so often, this seems likely to be more apocryphal than a historical fact. Like all the other 'pre-Socratics', little remains to record his thoughts and ideas, just a few 'fragments'. (There are about 100, the longest just 55 words. )

His preference for composing short, almost paradoxical philosophical epigrams later earned him the sobriquet 'the Dark'. But it is an innocuous-looking theory about rivers that has made his reputation: 'The waters that flow over those who step in the same river will be different.' Cratylus, a late fifth-century self-styled follower of Heraclitus puts it, 'You could not step twice into the same river.' Elsewhere, Heraclitus says: 'All is flux.' ARISTOTLE says that PLATO's familiarity with 'the Heraclitean theories that all sensible things are for ever flowing' led him to doubt that we can know the sensible world, and hence to the theory of FORMS.

Heraclitus himself was not at all MYSTICAL, saying for instance of the origin of the universe, that it was not created by anyone, but had existed always, and that what was important about it was to be found not through examining its parts, but by studying its arrangement, its structure. He himself thought it was essentially made of fire, which was also the essential ingredient of the soul.

The point about the river seems to have been a more prosaic one, to do with the nature of human experience. We encounter things all the time as being different, but behind the appearance of diversity is a more important and more fundamental unity: 'cold things grow hot, the hot cools, the wet dries, the parched moistens'. Not that Heraclitus is saying that the senses are deceived, for 'whatever comes from sight, hearing, experience, this privilege'.

Day and night are one, as are life and death. 'The same living and dead, what is awake and what sleeps, young and old: for those changed are those, and those changed around are these.' The opposites are united by change: they change into each other. And change is the fundamental reality of the universe. The highest, 'divine' perspective sees all the opposites: 'day and night, winter and summer, war and peace, plenty and famine', as the same. With the divine perspective, even good and evil are the same.

Two thousand years later, HEGEL found in Heraclitus' theory of the unity of opposites the kernel of a new 'world philosophy', a historical notion of perpetual change (thesis, antithesis, synthesis), which led directly both to MARX's DIALECTICAL materialism and to FASCISM and the notion of the purifying powers of conflict and war. But then Heraclitus had also declared: 'You must know that war is common to all things, and strife is justice.'

## HERMENEUTICS

The 24-carat word 'hermeneutics' derives from the Greek god Hermeneia, who is charged with delivering messages for Zeus. Thus hermeneutics is concerned with understanding and interpreting texts. The notion became important after the Protestants decided they needed to reinterpret the Bible, developing a system of four levels of meaning: literal, allegorical, tropological (or moral, not to be confused with topological) and anagogical or eschatological. (Hermeneutics is the study of long words.) Modern hermeneutics, as it calls itself, starts with Friedrich Schleiermacher (1768–1834), who, in addition to understanding the Bible, wished to reinterpret PLATO. Besides grammatical interpretation, there is a need to understand the psychological aspects underpinning the texts, and later philosophers, such as Martin HEIDEGGER and his student Hans-Georg Gadamer, have attempted to build on this an edifice of human existence seen as a text to be hermeneutically deconstructed.

## HERMETIC CORPUS

A number of ancient texts, dated between 100 and 300 CE, that were reputed to contain ancient wisdom – supposedly that of the ancient Egyptians that had been the source of both Moses' and PLATO's knowledge. They were translated by Marsilio Ficino in 1463, when they provided a spur to the view that human beings had access to the divine realm through their ability to use reason.

## HERO OF ALEXANDRIA (FIRST CENTURY CE)

Author of several scientific treatises, written in an accessible style, perhaps for students (including many examples of 'fun things' that can be done with science), his works include one on pneumatics in which he suggests gases must consist of a mixture of atoms and emptiness, as they can be compressed; and one on optics, in which he advances the thesis that the best explanation for natural phenomena, such as the behaviour of light, is the simplest one.

## HILBERT, DAVID (1862–1943)

The German mathematician who proposed a way (by assuming a series of formal AXIOMS) of defining mathematical CALCULUS without needing to worry about the reality or otherwise of certain fundamentals that were traditionally the object of philosophical debate. Unfortunately, this effort was shown to be futile by Kurt GODEL in 1931 (the 'Incompleteness Theorem').

## HINDUISM

### Essential Hinduism

Hinduism, like BUDDHISM, is neither a philosophy nor a religion. Rather, it combines them both, becoming a complex and multifaceted phenomenon, with social, cultural and religious manifestations. Its teachings, as much as its rituals, reflects the myriad geographical, social, racial and linguistic perspectives of the vast Indian subcontinent

There are highly intellectual varieties of

Hinduism, just one part of the deep pool of Indian philosophy, with its investigations of the nature of perception, of space and time, and of the correct way to live; alongside the simple, even naïve practices of the millions of villagers, who together form the bedrock of Hinduism.

Hinduism is eclectic and tolerant, pluralistic, full of contradictions and thrives on creative antagonism. The key texts common to all forms of Hinduism are the *Vedas*, ancient and anonymous texts which originated as part of an oral tradition of knowledge, between 1500 and 500 BCE. The oldest parts are in the form of hymns or prayers, while the more recent writings, including the UPANISHADS, written between 400 and 200 BCE, become more philosophical in nature and content.

## The play of God

The popular literature of Hinduism is made up of epic tales based on the Vedic Triad, and are a free mix of monotheism, polytheism and PANTHEISM. However, there is one fundamental reality – Brahman – underlying the many (approximate and changing) things which we see. Brahman is beginning-less, supreme, beyond what-is and what-is-not. All the gods of Hinduism are but different aspects, reflections, of this single underlying reality. In this sense, Hinduism is monotheistic.

Brahma is the creator among the Vedic Trinity. Much more prevalent in the beliefs and temples of Hinduism are the other members: Vishnu, the preserver and Shiva the destroyer.

When Brahman appears as the human spirit or soul, it is called 'Atman', when as part of the mundane physical world it is 'Lila', the 'play of God'. Hindus see this manifestation as a kind of sacrifice by Brahman, in the original sense of that which becomes 'sacred'. The force driving the 'play of God' is '*karma*', 'the force of creations, wherefore all things have their life'.

The most widely read book of Hindu philosophy is the *Bhagavad-Gita*. Every system, every sect, claims it teaches exactly what they believe. It also has a wide international readership. It tells how Arjuna, in the middle of the field of battle, immediately before fighting commences, hesitates, concerned about taking part in a fratricidal war. He questions whether victory over his enemies is worth the inevitable slaughter. Krishna appears in the tale in the form of charioteer and teaches Arjuna the philosophy of

### HINDUISM AND SOCIAL LIFE

Hinduism is integral to the life of its followers. In Hindu thought, philosophy detached from practice has no meaning. It is not organised or taught, but the daily custom and practice surrounds everyone from the cradle to the grave. Worthy as this is, it is unquestioning. It permitted development of customs such as child marriage, polygamy, sati (burning live wives on the funeral pyre of their dead husband), idolatry, animal sacrifices and the pernicious caste system.

Despite its many restrictions on women, Hinduism offers a great contrast to Western notions of propriety, in its celebration of sex. Sexuality is considered part of being human, and the medieval branch of Tantrism specifically celebrates the enlightenment brought about through imaginative sexual union. Hindu goddesses are far from being 'virgins', they are erotic beings of great sexual power.

Two hundred years ago, the Raja Ram Mohan Roy (1774–1833), familiar with Western as well as Eastern philosophy, attempted to reform Hinduism. He hoped that as Baconian philosophy had been used in England to displace the ignorance of the Schoolmen, similar liberal and enlightened instruction would serve reforms needed in India. Many practices were abolished as a result.

However, one part of the traditional religious system has proved highly resistant to reform. Like the class system in England, the caste system lingers on. As with extreme codes followed by other faiths, the caste system has no foundation in the original holy books. The *Vedas* and *Upanishads* are caste free. Only the Code of Manu ( the Brahmin sage Vishnu saved from the flood) is claimed as the authority for teaching the superiority of the Brahmins and the strict regulation of the lives of all strata of society. Like the British notion of social class, the caste system is too deeply rooted to be easily reformed.

action. On the battlefield it is too late to debate the morality of war, one must fight. Everyone is destined to die anyway and the philosopher need not fear the change of form others call death. The soldier is but an instrument in the hands of God.

## THE *DASAVATAR*

Vishnu, the preserver, is lithe, handsome and has four arms. He usually sleeps with Lakshmi, the female aspect, massaging his feet and the serpent Ananta, representing eternity, sleeping on his couch. Other deities alert them when the existence of the universe has to be preserved in the face of threats from the powers of evil. This has happened on nine out of ten predicted occasions.

Vishnu is incarnated on these occasions in various forms or Dasavatar. There are elaborate accounts of each Dasavata:

- As Matsya (fish) Vishnu saved the universe from the flood, with only the sage Manu surviving.
- As Kurma (tortoise) Vishnu supported mount Mandhara on his back to stop it sinking into the ocean so that the other deities could continue churning milk into ambrosia.
- As Varaha (boar) Vishnu dived into the sea where the demon Hiranyaksha was drowning the earth, stabbed him to death with his tusks so the earth floated again.
- As Narasimha (half-man, half-lion) Vishnu destroyed the demon Hiranyakasipu, who had prohibited worship of Vishnu and could be destroyed by neither man nor beast but was by a composite.
- As Vamana (a dwarf) Vishnu tricked the Asuri king Bali into giving back to the deities their native land by being granted three paces of land so he could sit and mediate: his request granted he grew until three paces covered all the land.
- As Parasurama (a Brahmin) Vishnu fought 21 campaigns to destroy the Kshatriyas who had persecuted the Brahmins.
- As Rama (the hero Bhagiratha) Vishnu destroyed Ravana, demon king of Sri Lanka, by bringing the Ganges down from heaven.
- As Krishna (in the eighth Dasavatar) Vishnu destroyed the demons Kansa and Shishupala. Krishna was the ideal child, youth, lover, soldier, statesman and philosopher. He became a role model for everyone. Krishna is the philosopher of action. Wisdom has to be attained living with people, not meditating alone.
- As Buddha Vishnu is an enigma. Indeed, for some, Buddhism is a heresy. Here is one of the glaring contradictions of Puranic Hinduism. The Brahmin argument that Vishnu taught heresy so they had heretics to convert is unconvincing, although Buddhism is a minority religion in India.
- As Kali (the outstanding tenth Dasavatar) Vishnu will bring the present age, Kaliyuga, which is seen as evil, to an end. At the moment, people degenerate generation by generation until a point is likely to be reached when even Vishnu will be unable to save the world. Then, mounted on Garuda (the man-bird), brandishing his sword of destruction in his right hand, Vishnu Kali will destroy the present age and bring in the next one. (As a consequence, both humans and deities try not to disturb Vishnu's present slumbers.)

Kill therefore with the sword of wisdom the doubt born of ignorance – be one in self harmony, in Yoga and arise great warrior, arise.

Out of the Vedic triad, Shiva is the most popular. Although nominally the destroyer, he is also a regenerator, who manages to be an object of worship by both sex cults and ascetics. Shiva is also lord of the Cosmic dance, and can assume many forms and sustain the universe through the endless cycle of creation and destruction. The contemporary philosopher and physicist, Fritjof Capra, has claimed that Hinduism offers many powerful insights, with its fundamental conceptual framework, far better attuned to the workings of the universe than that available to those following the Christian and CARTESIAN world view.

Shiva lives in the wilds. For company, he prefers ghosts, imps and devils. Nandi, the bull, is Shiva's sacred charger. Once, in an argument with Brahma(n), Shiva called the sacred cow as witness. She was caught out in a lie. Shiva cursed her mouth, which remains unclean, while all the rest of her, together with her milk, dung and urine, are for ever sacred.

Shiva and his wife Parvati are worshipped together in temples sacred to them both and to their sons. Their eldest son Ganesha is the elephant-headed personification of prudence and the remover of obstacles by reason. His help is sought by every Hindu at the start of each new project. The younger son Kartikeya is the war god.

These are just the deities arising from the Vedic trinity. There are countless others, each with their own story, form and characteristics.

Contributors: Colin Kirk and Martin Cohen

## HIPPOCRATES (FIFTH CENTURY BCE)

Hippocrates of Cos was a physician who maintained early on that epilepsy and other illnesses were not the result of evil spirits or angry gods, but due to natural causes. He has been called the 'Father of Medicine', and the 'wisest and greatest practitioner of his art'. Hippocrates taught the sanctity of life and called other physicians to the highest ETHICAL standards of conduct. According to the anthropologist, Margaret Mead, the Oath of Hippocrates marked a turning point in the history of Western civilisation, because for the first time it created a complete separation between curing and killing. (Throughout the primitive world, the doctor and the sorcerer tended to be the same person.) The Oath says:

> I swear by Apollo Physician, by Asclepius: I will use treatment to help the sick according to my ability and judgement, but never with a view to injury and wrong-doing. I will neither administer a poison to anybody when asked to do so, nor will I suggest such a course.

No support there for EUTHANASIA. And similarly, it continues, 'I will not give to a woman a pessary to cause abortion.' Nonetheless, under Hippocrates, medicine emerged as the prototype of the learned professions.

## HISTORICISM

Historicism is the view that there is a pattern to events, to history, and often also the assumption that there is a progression to be discerned. Famous 'historicists' include HEGEL, who saw history as a process leading to the triumph of reason; MARX, who saw it as a series of class conflicts leading to COMMUNISM; and, finally, Hitler and Mussolini, who believed they had tapped into the tide of history with their FASCIST states. Karl POPPER rejected such thinking in his post-Second World War book, *The Poverty of Historicism.*

Only, of course, we must not say 'finally' as that implies both a process and an 'end' to the process. Indeed, recent Western politicians, notably George Bush Junior and his eternal 'ally', the British Prime Minister, used to cite their role in facilitating the 'spread of freedom and DEMOCRACY' in much the same way as these older theoreticians. After the fall of the Berlin Wall, an academic analyst for the US government, Francis Fukuyama, wrote an influential treatise at the end of the twentieth century, confidently predicting that democracy was the final end of human development and there would be no more social conflict.

## HISTORY OF PHILOSOPHY

Most histories of philosophy are misleading. They are either preoccupied with 'METAPHYSICS' and 'EPISTEMOLOGY', or with a supposed march of LOGIC and reason – because today that is what academic philosophers write on. They over-emphasise philosophers who deal with those subjects, such as ARISTOTLE and KANT, and they marginalise philosophers who deal with life itself, such as MONTAIGNE and DE BEAUVOIR, THOREAU and Benjamin Lee WHORF. Indeed, they refuse to recognise some of these as 'philosophers' at all. They insist on grand systems and despise the philosophers who write in prose, in aphorism, in riddles or in poetry. We shall not make that mistake here!

## HOBBES, THOMAS (1588–1679)

### The essential Hobbes

Hobbes' influence is profound. For the first time, individual RIGHTS are deduced and derived from a supposed 'fundamental right' to self-preservation. Together with the works of the Dutch lawyer and politician, Hugo GROTIUS, he both set the style and laid the foundations for future work in the areas of political theory, social ethics and international law.

Thomas Hobbes provides an antidote to the high-minded reasoning of the schoolmen and, indeed, the ancients. Starting from a pragmatic assessment of HUMAN NATURE, he strengthens the case for a powerful political and social organisation organising our lives. And with his interest in the methods of geometry and the natural sciences, he brings a new style of argument to political theorising that is both more persuasive and more effective. But from Hobbes we

also obtain a reminder that social organisation, however committed to fairness and equality it may be intended to be, being motivated by a struggle between its members, is also inevitably both authoritarian and inegalitarian. Modern societies today reflect his view that people are motivated by selfishness, and, left to their own devices, they always come into conflict.

## Hobbes' wicked world

**ARISTOTLE** thought that people, being rational, would be naturally inclined to organise themselves voluntarily in societies. Thomas Hobbes, writing nearly 2000 years later, thought that people, being rational, would not.

Thomas Hobbes has a more cynical (he would say realistic) view of human nature than the Greeks. While he agrees that people have regard for their self-interest, there is little else Hobbes will accept from the ancients. Where Aristotle and **PLATO** imagined that (at least some) people were virtuous (and even **MACHIAVELLI** that at least it was important to appear so), Hobbes considers that society is only a mixture of selfishness, violence and fear, topped with a healthy dollop of deceit, the last there to make things work more smoothly. Hobbes even has the temerity to describe this as the 'State of Nature', a shocking phrase calculated to arouse the wrath of the Church, directly conflicting with the rosy biblical image of Adam and Eve in the Garden of Eden before the Fall.

How had Hobbes come to such a negative view of society? After all, for most of the Middle Ages in Europe, virtually the only theorising on these matters had been that of the Catholic theologians in their monasteries and convents. In his commentaries on Aristotle, Saint Thomas

**AQUINAS** (1225–74) had built upon Aristotle's notion of rationality the necessity of a virtuous and divinely inspired social order, that none could challenge without challenging **GOD**. For doing this (among other reasons) Hobbes was considered by many of his contemporaries to be, if not actually an **ATHEIST**, certainly a heretic. Indeed, after the Great Plague of 1665, when 100,000 Londoners died, and the Great Fire of 1666, a parliamentary committee was set up to investigate whether heresy might have contributed to the two disasters. The list of possible causes specifically mentioned Hobbes' writings.

But what is certain is that Thomas Hobbes was born in middle England into a Tudor society which was beginning to collapse into the acrimony of the English Civil War. Much has been made of this fact, as explaining Hobbes' desire for one all-powerful authority, and perhaps it is too easy to explain away retrospectively Hobbes' unique contribution to the development of the Western model of society. After all, the Greeks lived in circumstances in which governments were continually coming and going, and yet they produced theories favouring quite different aims. It might as reasonably be said by psychological **BEHAVIORISM**, that Hobbes' approach stems from emotional distress at being separated from his father, a vicar, who lost his job after quarrelling with another pastor at the church door. (Which certainly would explain his own tendency to battle with the Church, yet not disown it.) After that event, the young Hobbes had to be brought up by his uncle, eventually becoming an accomplished scholar at Oxford. After university, he travelled widely with the Earl of Devonshire, moving in increasingly aristocratic circles and even meeting the celebrated Italian astronomer, **GALILEO**, in 1636.

Hobbes' books are a strange mixture of jurisprudence, religious enthusiasm and political iconoclasm. The legal points are innovative and frequently perceptive, even if occasionally dubious in the logic of their argument. But of it all, it is the political theory, the first significant one since Machiavelli's, that is most interesting and, historically, the most influential.

Commentators later made much of Hobbes' lack of academic and, indeed, scientific rigour, perhaps reflecting the prejudices of his contemporaries who despised his lowly origin, but Hobbes ploughs his own furrow, himself mocking the philosophers. Yet perhaps the most striking aspect of Hobbes' **POLITICAL**

## THE *LEVIATHAN*

The starting point for Hobbes' theory of society is a mechanistic view of both the universe and of human life within it. 'Nature (the Art whereby God hath made and governs the World)', Hobbes writes, by way of an introduction to his great work, the *Leviathan* (1651): this being the term he offers for the intended all-powerful State. People themselves are just machines, moved by 'appetites' and 'aversions'.

These small beginnings of Motion within the body of Man, before they appear in walking, speaking, striking, and other visible actions are commonly called ENDEAVOUR. This Endeavour, when it is toward something is called APPETITE or DESIRE; the later, being the general name, and the other often times restrained to signify the Desire of Food, namely Hunger and Thirst. And when the Endeavour is fromward something, it is generally called AVERSION.

Hobbes thinks the 'human machine' is programmed to direct its energies selfishly. He doubts if it is ever possible for human beings to act altruistically, and even apparently benevolent action is actually self-serving, perhaps an attempt to make them feel good about themselves. In human beings, the primary motion is towards power:

. . . in the first place, I put for a general inclination of all mankind, a perpetual and restless desire of Power after power, that ceaseth only in Death.

PHILOSOPHY is that, at a time of elaborate respect for the various authorities of God, the Pope, the high-born or whoever, it is resolutely rational in its approach. And, in his theory of motions, Hobbes is reflecting the popular view of science in his time, impressed by Galileo's rediscoveries of the mountains on the Moon (DEMOCRITUS had written of them, too), the phases of Venus and the movements of the planets, as well as by biological discoveries such as that by Harvey of the circulation of the blood, all of which tended to challenge established opinion. His arguments are based on clearly set-out grounds, his reasoning shown in clear, step-by-step terms with no waffle or 'fluttering', and no appeal to mystic or traditional authorities. This is a conscious aim, too, for as he writes of the 'abstruse philosophy' of the Schoolmen:

When men write whole volumes of the stuff, are they not Mad, or intend to make others so? So that this kind of Absurdity, may rightly be numbered amongst the many sorts of Madness; and all the time that guided by clear Thoughts of their worldly lust, they forbear disputing, or writing thus, but Lucid intervals. And thus much of the Virtues and Defects Intellectual.

Much of the *Leviathan* is legalistic in tone, as befits a theory based on constructing order out of anarchy. Crucially, there are even restrictions on the all-powerful sovereign. Similarly, 'no man... can be obliged by Covenant to accuse himself much less to 'kill, wound, or maim himself.'

Covenants entered into out of fear are obligatory, just as, Hobbes says, with Machiavellian pragmatism, if someone has agreed to pay a ransom, then they must pay it. 'For it is a contract wherein one receives the benefit of life; the other is to receive money, or service for it.' If it were not so, then it would invalidate the supposed contract between the individual and the sovereign, for this is precisely that of one motivated by fear. However, there is one exception to this, and that is a covenant not to defend yourself from force: to forego the 'right to self-defence.' This is always void, for 'no man can transfer, or lay down his Right to save himself from Death, Wounds, and Imprisonment.' For the same reason, most sound systems of law do not compel an accused person to testify against their own interests – the citizen has what today we would value as 'the right to silence'.

Hobbes even defends the man who flees the Court, a position which seems to be based on a low opinion of judges rather than any philosophical consistency.

Nor can anyone be bound to kill another. Even a soldier may refuse to fight the enemy 'though his Sovereign have the right to punish his refusal with death'. This may seem to be inconsistent, but there, that's autocracy for you! At least Hobbes is more generous than the generals of the First World War to their shell-shocked conscripts, in saying: 'Allowance may be made of natural timorousness, not only to women: but also to men of feminine courage.'

Indeed, if a man is in danger of dying, 'Nature' compels him to 'break the law'. On the other hand, Hobbes has no time for 'the poisonous doctrine' that 'every man is a judge of Good and Evil actions', and that listening to your conscience takes higher priority than following the law. Judges should have a sense of 'equity', contempt of riches, be dispassionate and capable of listening patiently and attentively. Hobbes bases his law on what he supposes to be the reality of human psychology, even rejecting the commandment not to 'covet', saying that this makes a sin out of human nature.

Certain technical repercussions of a system of laws, such as what happens when someone does not know of the law, are considered. Ignorance of the 'Law of Nature' is no excuse, for the law of nature is simply that one should not do to others what one would not like done to oneself. However, ignorance of a civil matter, perhaps like that of a traveller in a strange country, is an excuse. Ignorance of the sovereign is never allowable, for the sovereign is always the citizen's protection, nor is ignorance of the penalty. Ideally, children should be brought up to obey the law instinctively. On the other hand, no law made 'after a Fact done', can make something a crime.

In general, premeditated crime is worse than that arising 'from a sudden Passion' and crimes undermining the law are worse than those of no effect. Punishment must be sufficient to deter a rational criminal, while being essentially positive in its aims, a notion which includes, for example, the deterring of others.

Hobbes recommends a series of limitations on the power of the law to punish. Punishments should not constitute revenge, but only restitution, that is, righting wrongs. They should inflict no pain unless it can be offset against some future good – perhaps persuading others not to behave similarly. But the punishment must be greater than the benefits of the crime, and any ill effects that by chance strike the wrong-doer are not to be offset against the eventual sentence, for these are not 'inflicted by the Authority of man'.

> The final Cause, End or Design of men, (who naturally love Liberty, and Dominion over others,) in the introduction of that restraint upon themselves... is the foresight

## THE SOCIAL CONTRACT

Hobbes is often presented as a social contract theorist, with people thinking of words like:

> I ground the Civil Right of Sovereigns, and both the Duty and Liberty of Subjects, upon the known natural Inclinations of Mankind, and upon the Article of the Law of Nature; of which no man... ought to be ignorant.

But in another way, it is a bit of a misnomer to call this a contract. Hobbes has no use for such a notion, which is clearly more 'metaphorical' than practical. His position is that it matters not what the people think, the 'commonweal' simply is to cede absolute power to a sovereign authority – the State, the 'Leviathan'.

If people were able to choose, they might take John Locke's view, expressed a century later, that Hobbes' social contract is actually worse than the state of nature it is supposed to help them to rise above, because of the arbitrary powers it gives to the sovereign. Who, Locke asked, would sign a contract to escape from 'polecats and foxes', if the result was to be put 'at the mercy of lions'?

of their own preservation and of a more contented life thereby; that is to say, of getting themselves out from that miserable condition of War, which is necessarily consequent to the natural Passions of men, when there is no visible Power to keep them in awe, and tie them by fear of punishment to the performance of their Covenants. . . Covenants without the Sword are but Words.

Contributor: Martin Cohen

## D'HOLBACH, BARON (1723–89)

Paul-Henri Thiry d'Holbach was one of the celebrated 'encyclopédistes' in France, along with VOLTAIRE and, erratically, ROUSSEAU. His book, *Système de la Nature* (1770), described a world constructed as a great machine, a system of particles eternally in motion, with no space at all for God to play a role. Humans are just organic machines, whose thoughts are just different kinds of sensations. Like plants seeking the sun, we seek happiness, in whatever form, and once collected into groups of humans, or societies, this produces ethics – the science of co-operation). At root though, ethics is there solely to ensure that the individual can achieve happiness, which of course was also the UTILITARIANS' view.

Despite, or perhaps because of, being a baron, d'Holbach was a political radical and opposed both hereditary privilege and absolute monarchies.

## HOLISM

Holism is really 'whole-ism', a way of looking at issues which seeks to understand them through consideration of their relationship to everything else. For example, an environmentalist may seek to understand individual species by considering their role within the ecological cycle. A philosopher of language may say that the meaning of a sentence can only really be grasped by consideration of the whole of that language, as each word and each sentence is connected to each other, and meaning resides ultimately in the 'whole'.

## HOLINESS

One definition of 'holiness' is that something is holy if people worship it. Some people worship statues, some trees, some cows, but are the statues, trees and cows really 'holy'? Another is that something is holy if it has great and mysterious powers. Indeed, the traditional gods were awesome, causing earthquakes and plagues and such like; only recent Christian ideas have reduced being holy to the rather damp sociability of saints who look after the sick. In the Christian sense, holiness is to do with 'reverence', which is due to that which is wholly and absolutely 'GOOD'. In the words of XUNZI, when people revere objects or animals or people, in the limited sense of social ornaments, respected but not magical, then this is 'fortunate' and a positive thing. But when people revere them as divine, it is 'unfortunate'.

## HOMOSEXUALITY

A homosexual is someone who has erotic relations with someone of the same sex. It has traditionally been considered immoral, and condemned by the Christian Church as a sin meriting eternal damnation. Although there are many references in PLATO to his love of his boyfriend, and indeed Greek society was generally sympathetic to a whole range of sexual practices, there is a discussion in one of his dialogues (the *Laws*) in which SOCRATES argues that birds and animals are not homosexual so neither should humans be. (Actually, biologists now say that homosexuality does exist among some species.)

Thomas AQUINAS considered the practice to violate 'NATURAL LAW', and thus to be a form of 'rape', not so much of the partner (assuming voluntary activity, of course), but of God. Almost alone among philosophers (prior to the twentieth century), Jeremy BENTHAM defended the practice on UTILITARIAN grounds, but even he shied away from including such arguments in his major works. WITTGENSTEIN was actively homosexual, but considered the trait to be a 'weakness', and subsequent philosophers have tried to protect him from being identified as such.

Since the publication of various studies claiming that homosexuality is both widespread and 'genetic', the ETHICS of it have shifted, and Michel FOUCAULT and others have argued that homosexuality is a 'social construction', created in order to serve the ends of a minority – he points the finger at the medical establishment in particular. Today, homosexuality is socially recognised in many countries by the existence of various laws 'protecting' homosexuals from 'discrimination', in employment or in receipt of services. At the same time it remains illegal and disapproved of in countries supposedly following Islamic law. The Christian Church is still split over whether or not homosexuals can become priests.

## HOMUNCULUS FALLACY

The homunculus or 'little man FALLACY' simply observes that many philosophical theories of how the mind works end up by supposing that a little bit of the body or of the mind acts as though it were a 'little man' in itself – with its own thoughts and mental states. Such a little man would then need to be analysed too, and we would end up with a 'vicious regress', of Russian dolls awaiting unpacking. Daniel Dennett offered the weak defence of 'homunculi' that are progressively simpler and more specialised, saying that then they do indeed help explain the way the mind works.

SEE ALSO

Fallacies

## HSUN TSU

See Xunzi.

## HUMANISM

PROTAGORAS said that 'man is the measure of all things', but it was only really during the Renaissance period in Europe that education began to shift away from the study of God towards the study of humanity. There was interest in the relationship of humans to nature, a confidence in the judgements and the abilities of the human mind, and a conviction that it was better to consider ETHICAL issues from the point of view of humanity, rather than from one claimed as divine. Petrarch is generally considered the first humanist, while Erasmus is counted as its greatest exponent.

## HUMAN NATURE

The view taken of the 'essence' of human beings, that is, what their true nature is, affects many questions in philosophy. The legacy of ARISTOTLE and Christianity, relayed faithfully by philosophers such as DESCARTES over the centuries, is that the true essence belongs to the SOUL and not the body, that man is essentially different from animals and that this difference is to be celebrated through the eschewal of things animals do (such as eat and have sex) and the pursuit of things peculiar to humans (such as discussing ABSTRACT ideas). PLATO held (as usual) a slightly more ambiguous position, where human nature seems to vary from person to person (thus defeating the search for one), yet also, we are assured, it is fundamentally the same in sharing the same virtuous goals.

Another related question is whether people are essentially 'good', 'evil' or 'neither'. The view taken is obviously significant for questions of education and law. Here, the responses range from the optimism of CONFUCIUS and Plato, who both insisted that people started off good, but could be corrupted, to the pessimism of XUNZI and MENCIUS in China, and AQUINAS, AUGUSTINE and HOBBES in the West, who all, in different ways, assumed that the selfishness and fleshy appetites of humanity would, if unchecked, always lead to sin.

## HUMAN RIGHTS

### The essentials of human rights

In recent years, the moral doctrine of human rights has come to occupy centre-stage in our understanding and evaluation of both national and international political affairs. Indeed, one might reasonably argue that human rights are fast becoming the dominant global moral vocabulary for the twenty-first century. Human rights offers the promise of finally reconciling the profound moral differences and cleavages which continue to divide humanity and have been the cause of so much conflict and suffering.

Philosophers tend to be less concerned with speculating on the potential practical consequences of adhering to human rights principles, and prefer instead to focus on the underlying rationale of this particular moral commitment. A philosophical examination of human rights restricts itself to concerns over the basis and justification of human rights. What, then, are human rights, and how have philosophers sought to convince us that they are worthy of the claims made on their behalf?

The moral doctrine of human rights aims at identifying the fundamental prerequisites for each human being to lead at least a 'minimally good', in the sense of 'virtuous', life. Human rights have been defined as basic moral guarantees that people in all countries and cultures allegedly have simply because they are people. Calling these guarantees 'rights' suggests that they attach to particular individuals who can invoke them, that they are of high priority, and that compliance with them is mandatory rather than discretionary. Human rights are frequently held to be universal, in the sense that all people have and should enjoy them, and to be independent, in the sense that they exist and are available as standards of justification and criticism, whether or not they are recognised and implemented by the legal system or officials of a country.

### Rights and principles

Human rights aim to provide the basis for determining the shape, content and scope of fundamental, public, moral norms. While it is claimed that all human beings share in the responsibility to protect and promote human rights, primary responsibility falls upon those national and international institutions considered most capable of discharging this duty. The principal site for the establishment and promotion of these duties has been the United Nations, beginning with the UNIVERSAL DECLARATION OF HUMAN RIGHTS (1948), which was subsequently augmented by a comprehensive plethora of legally binding, international instruments and covenants. The doctrine of human rights has been progressively assimilated within the legal codes of many individual nation states through their membership of the United Nations and legal ratification of the various human rights norms.

Philosophical justifications of human rights typically contend that human rights are based upon principles which are trans-historical and trans-cultural. The doctrine of human rights is grounded upon moral universalism. While specific attempts to justify the universality of human rights have identified varying grounds or human attributes deemed capable of sustaining the doctrine, all have shared a basic commitment to the belief that there exist rationally identifiable, universal, moral truths. Thus, contemporary theories of human rights tend to focus upon the need to satisfy certain fundamental human interests as compelling evidence in support of human rights.

Alternatively, other philosophers have identified our capacity for the exercise of a rational will as entailing a commitment to the provision of human rights. These two positions have been labelled the 'interest theory' and 'will theory' approaches respectively.

Philosophical justifications of the universality of human rights characteristically draw a distinction between legal rights and moral rights. The former refer to all those rights found within existing national and international legal codes. As such, legal rights cannot be said to exist prior to their passing into law, and the limits of their validity are set by the jurisdiction of the body which passed the relevant legislation. The latter are rights which, it is claimed, exist prior to and independently of their legal counterparts, owing their recognition not to the actions of lawmakers, but the rational identification of universally valid moral principles. An appeal to human rights as moral rights has been essential to combating many politically repressive regimes. Thus, the racially discriminatory policies of apartheid in South Africa were entirely 'legal' and could not LOGICALLY be condemned as violations of the legal rights of the black majority. Nevertheless, an appeal to human rights was essential to the anti-apartheid campaign and could only be philosophically sustained by appeal to human rights as moral rights, which belong to all human beings everywhere, irrespective of the legal systems to which they are exposed. Legal rights and moral rights, however, should not be seen as mutually exclusive. The passing of various human rights norms into national and international law is essential to the protection and promotion of individuals' human rights. Justifying why these rights should be enshrined, however, entails an appeal to moral rights, which itself emanates from the doctrine of moral universalism.

## Challenges to the universality of human rights

The philosophical defence of human rights as founded upon universally valid and objectively true moral principles has been subject to consistent criticism from a diverse array of critical perspectives, including MARXISM, FEMINISM, legal POSITIVISM, philosophical SCEPTICISM and moral RELATIVISM. This last, arguably, has had the greatest resonance for non-philosophers and raises some serious concerns for human rights.

Moral relativists argue that universally valid moral truths do not exist, that there are no trans-historical and trans-cultural moral truths. Moral relativists view morality as a social and historical phenomenon. Moral beliefs and principles are therefore presented as socially and historically contingent, valid only for those cultures and societies within which they both originate and enjoy widespread recognition. Relativists point to the vast array of diverse moral beliefs and practices apparent in the world today as empirical support for their claims. Even within a single, complex society, such as the USA or the UK, there exist a wide diversity of fundamental moral beliefs, principles and practices, many of which may be in direct conflict with one another. There certainly exist cultures which reject the importance that human rights supporters attach to the individual as the principal bearer of human rights. Cultures which prioritise communal or collective values over individualist ones have come into direct conflict with attempts to uphold various human rights. Based upon the claims to universality and objectivity, advocates of human rights have characteristically sought to resolve this kind of conflict by insisting that recalcitrant cultures accept the force of human rights and change their practices and institutions accordingly. Many relativists have sought to characterise this strategy as revealing the role of the exercise of power in the articulation and attempted promotion of purportedly universal moral doctrines.

From this perspective, human rights have been condemned for allegedly promoting a form of cultural IMPERIALISM, which fails to pay due respect to cultural integrity, while simultaneously mistaking the cultural basis and character of its own beliefs for trans-historical and trans-cultural moral truths. Advocates of this form of criticism typically proceed to argue that human rights are a predominantly Western phenomenon and, as such, cannot avoid the articulation of Western values and ideals. The universal aspirations of the human rights project are thereby condemned for being ethnocentric; the promotion of a set of culturally contingent values as universally valid entails the repression of alternative moral belief systems.

There can be little doubt that power has influenced the development and implementation of human rights. Similarly, the philosophical development of human rights has mostly occurred within Western universities and academies. It would also be futile to attempt to deny that this development has been significantly driven by individualist values, which are not universally shared. However, the charge of ethnocentrism is often too easy. Indeed, it is itself motivated by a moral commitment to tolerating and respecting cultural differences. Many advocates of human rights are similarly motivated. One can only hope that adhering to the spirit and principles of human rights will help guide and sustain the peaceful dialogue necessary for reconciling humanity with itself.

Contributor: Andrew Fagan

# HUME, DAVID (1711–76)

## The essential Hume

Hume was born into a devoutly observant Scottish Presbyterian family, and initially was intended to take up law. But from the age of 17 he instead began work on a great philosophical project that would, in due course, wake the philosophical world from its 'dogmatic slumber', as KANT aptly put it, recording his own debt to Hume.

Six years later, at the age of 23, Hume left Scotland for La Flèche, a small town in France, home to the Jesuit college attended by DESCARTES a century before, and set out the bulk of the *Treatise on Human Nature* on paper.

Although written in the 1740s, *Dialogues Concerning Natural Religion* had to await publication until several years after his death, owing to its controversial views, and although Hume's *Political Discourses* (1752) and efforts on an epic

history were reasonably popular, his lifelong ambition to be considered a great writer was never fulfilled. He had to be content instead with increasing recognition for his scrupulous integrity and determination. Adam SMITH commented after his death that Hume approached 'as nearly to the idea of a perfectly wise and virtuous man, as perhaps the nature of frailty will permit'.

## Against miracles

In his introduction to the *Treatise on Human Nature*, David Hume advises the reader to be wary of philosophers who 'insinuate the praise of their own systems, by decrying all those, which have been advanced before them'.

Then he proceeds to denounce the weak foundations of everyone else's philosophical systems, replete with 'incoherencies' which are 'a disgrace upon philosophy itself', and instead to propose, 'a compleat system of the sciences' of his own.

Hume's most important ideas, set out in his *Treatise on Human Nature* (1739), were, like BERKELEY's writings, published before he reached the age of 30. In 1744 he made an unsuccessful attempt to become a university professor, and on failing to achieve this, became first of all, as Bertrand RUSSELL pithily puts it, tutor to a lunatic and then secretary to a general. Despite an anonymous *Abstract* (by himself) promoting its ideas, the *Treatise* fell, as he put it himself, 'stillborn from the press', and later revisions of it, the two '*Enquiries*': *Concerning Human Understanding* (1748) and *Concerning the Principles of Morals* (1751) also failed to receive the attention they really deserved, and the portion of the original *Treatise* dealing with 'the Passions' fared still worse, despite being in some ways the most original.

Hume is a profoundly modern thinker. He bases his arguments solely on, as the famous quote has it, **ABSTRACT** or experimental reasoning:

If we take in our hand any volume of divinity or school metaphysics, for instance; let us ask, Does it contain any abstract reasoning concerning quantity or number? No. Does it contain any experimental

## HUME ON ETHICS

Hume is a humbugger of ethics. 'Tis an object of feeling – not of reason!', he scoffs, in his *Treatise on Human Nature*. Although initially Hume had tried to make the notion of 'sympathy' the keystone of his moral theory, he decided it better to abandon the attempt to base morality on logic.

He explains:

. . .when you pronounce any action or character to be vicious, you mean nothing, but that from the constitution of *your nature* you have a feeling or sentiment of blame from the contemplation of it.

Vice and virtue are merely qualities which we see in things, just as we see colours. And Hume continues:

I cannot forbear adding to these reasoning an observation which may, perhaps, be found of some importance. In every system of morality, which I have hitherto met with, I have always remark'd, that the author proceeds for some time in the ordinary way of reasoning, and establishes the being of a God, or makes observations concerning human affairs; when all of a sudden I am supriz'd to find, that instead of the usual copulations of propositions, is and is not, I meet with no proposition that is not connected with an ought or an ought not. This change is imperceptible; but is however of the last consequence.

(Book III, *Of Morals*, part I)

reasoning concerning matter of fact and existence? No. Commit it then to the flames: for it can contain nothing but sophistry and illusion...

Religion has no place and no role in his philosophy. Knowledge, ethics and God are all obliged to return to earth for Hume's scrutiny.

Hume sees us as essentially animals, with the additional facility of a sophisticated language. 'Reason' is merely a product of our use of language, and animals too can reason, albeit in simpler ways. He offers accounts of both emotions and ideas as if we were essentially machines, motivated by pleasure and pain, or, as Thomas **HOBBES** had put it earlier, by appetites and aversions. His observation that 'an is does not imply an ought', also stresses that, sooner or later, we all fall back on our feelings in order to make any choices.

In his later writings he accepts the label 'SCEPTIC', and certainly that is how his contemporaries saw him. First victim of his approach was 'consciousness', or 'the SELF', as an entity. Hume observed that consciousness is always of something, of an impression of some sort (feeling hot, cold or whatever), and so the self is a bundle of **PERCEPTIONS**. No one can perceive 'the Self' as such, certainly not in anyone else. Hume, thus, went one step further than Bishop Berkeley, who had demonstrated that there was no matter, by proving that there was no mind either.

Hume examined the notion of cause and effect, which Descartes took to be a necessary truth, and decided it could yield only probable knowledge. When we see an event constantly followed by another, we 'infer' that the second event has been caused by the first. However, 'we cannot penetrate into the reason of the conjunction'. For instance, if we eat apples, we expect them to taste a certain way, If we take a bite and it tastes, say, of banana, we would consider it anomalous. Hume says that this is sloppy thinking. It is, in fact, another aspect of the problem of induction. 'The supposition that the future resembles the past is not founded on arguments of any kind, but is derived entirely from habit.'

From that, we might conclude that all knowledge is flawed, and that we can believe nothing. Hume sees this, but, in the manner of the gentleman philosopher he was, suggests that 'carelessness and inattention' offer a remedy: we should neglect the flaws in our arguments and continue to use reason whenever we find it suits us. Philosophy remains, then, only as an agreeable way to pass the time (he found, anyway), not a reason to change your views.

Hume might also have found philosophy an agreeable career, had it not been for the controversy raised by his critique of religion. Even his great friend (and then much more famous philosopher), Adam Smith, acting as a referee for Hume's candidature for the post as professor of 'Ethics and Pneumatic Philosophy' at Edinburgh, wrote advising against appointment!

Contributor: Martin Cohen

## HUMOUR

There is no humour in philosophy. Where there is humour in a text – for example, PLATO offers some witty asides in his dialogues – assuredly, it is no longer philosophical.

## HUSSERL, EDMUND (1859–1938)

Edmund Husserl was born in Prossnitz, now a town in today's Czech Republic, but then part of the Austro-Hungarian empire, and is remembered as the German philosopher who founded PHENOMENOLOGY. He read mathematics at Berlin and psychology at Vienna, but identified philosophy as the 'a priori' discipline.

Phenomenology holds that everything known to us is derived from consciousness. Objects of consciousness, or PHENOMENA, be they things or information, are accessed through one or other sense organ. Consciousness recognises these phenomena by PERCEPTION, BELIEF, thought or desire. All these acts of consciousness derive from the objects of consciousness and must therefore also be phenomena.

Husserl uses the term 'intentionality' for the relationship that exists between objects of consciousness and acts of consciousness. Assumptions are made about a new phenomenon, which is inevitably experienced against the background of existing information and experience, acquired through teaching, circumstances, and so on. Such prior knowledge and prior experiences cannot be eradicated, so account must be taken of them, otherwise all future phenomena will be received as more of the same, and we are trapped in the same mindset.

So, in order to expand comprehension, critical analysis of presupposition is essential. One method of critical analysis is called fantasy

variation. Recalled experiences are submitted to review in various appropriate and inappropriate circumstances in order to determine a critical essence that remains permanently present, however analysed.

*Logical Investigations* (1901) sets out a 'science of essences', or phenomenology, and was particularly influential in France, Germany and the USA. MERLEAU-PONTY, SARTRE, DE BEAUVOIR, DERRIDA and HEIDEGGER all drew on his ideas. Phenomenology influenced the development of ideas in many SOCIAL SCIENCES, including anthropology, sociology, forensic psychiatry and psychology, as well as giving rise to GESTALT PSYCHOLOGY.

## HUTCHESON, FRANCES (1694–1746)

Hutcheson was born in Ireland, but counted as Scotland's great ENLIGHTENMENT moralist. Using the same sort of language as John LOCKE had for describing 'sense perception', Hutcheson elaborated a theory, advanced earlier by the Earl of Shaftesbury, that human beings have a moral sense that enables us to distinguish between right and wrong, and (as if this were not already implausible enough) that we are always inclined to prefer the virtuous path. We also have a 'beauty sense' that works in harmony, as good things are more beautiful than bad things. Thus, virtue is a matter of AESTHETICS, and Hutcheson also reflects the language of PLATO, linking goodness with BEAUTY. Hutcheson was part of the Adam SMITH/David HUME 'Glasgow teahouse' circle and also influenced KANT and BENTHAM. His most important works are the *Inquiry into the Origins of our Ideas of Beauty and Virtue* (1725) and the posthumously published *System of Moral Philosophy* (1755).

## HYPATIA (370–415)

One of the few acknowledged women philosophers, Hypatia was known for her public talks on philosophical matters in general, and astronomy and sex in particular. She shared the same 'IDEALIST' view on matters as PLATO, and hence is counted as a 'NEO-PLATONIST', and also shared with Plato an interest in practical politics and a commitment to living the virtuous life. Doubtless because of both these views, she was killed by a Christian mob, and became, like SOCRATES, one of philosophy's noble martyrs.

## HYPOTHESIS

A hypothesis is a theory that requires a little more work before it can be considered proven. It is better than a hunch, in being more systematic, and weaker than an 'ARGUMENT', which is generally a thing advanced by someone who holds their words to be true. A hypothesis can be advanced without any such commitment.

As part of his critique of science, Karl POPPER relegated all scientific theories to the status of 'hypotheses; impossible to ever prove, and most of them likely some day to be falsified'.

KANT has a 'Hypothetical Imperative', which is weaker than his more famous 'Categorical' one, being linked, like UTILITARIAN calculations, to some supposed positive outcome.

## IDEALISM, IDEALS AND IDEAS

Idealism, in philosophy anyway, is the view that 'ideas' are the proper study of philosophy, as it is only ideas that we are aware of, and indeed, that ideas are quite possibly all that there are. Idealism is opposed to what might be considered the common-sense view that there is a 'real world' out there and that, however imprecisely, we create the ideas out of it.

---

### IDEA-ISM

Which philosophers are idealists? Since Plato argued that the fundamental aspects of reality were the ideas, and our sense perceptions mere shadows, he might be thought to be a good candidate, but most philosophers insist, contrariwise, that his approach is not strictly 'idealist' as he seems to think the ideas exist outside of our minds. (Notably in the dialogue, *Parmenides*. In passing, it might be said to reflect the erratic nature of progress of philosophical debate, that Plato's notion of idea itself is a more sophisticated one than that which is used nowadays.)

Leaving aside Plato's status in this matter, conventional philosophers instead seize upon that most conventional of thinkers, Descartes, as their example of 'an idealist', with his comfortable distinction between the world 'out there' of 'extension' and the world of our minds, populated solely by ideas. Indeed, as a term, 'idealism' does not appear until after Descartes. The view was part of what motivated Leibniz (1646–1716) to posit the existence of Monads, as Descartes' kind of matter seemed to him to be too passive and inert, in need of some spiritual element to bring it into 'actuality'.

Bishop Berkeley (1685–1710) represents another pure form of 'idealism' in that he firmly asserts that since all we are aware of is ideas, anything that is not an idea cannot be said to have any existence, assertions to the contrary being just that – assertions. Immanuel Kant attempted to impose some structure on the idealists (hence his school is sometimes called 'critical idealism'), objecting to the use of the word 'ideas' to cover things like 'being red' as well as things like 'justice', (accepting only the latter kind as true ideas) as well as arguing that since certain concepts, such as space and time, structure our ideas, they must be prior to them, and indeed that all our other ideas are also based on 'something' – although this, he says, must always remain unreachable to us.

German philosophers (notably Fichte, Schelling and Hegel) took this last view forward, producing increasingly metaphysical theories of fundamental reality and the paramount importance of the human mind within it. British philosophers (notably Hume and Bradley) took the opposite view and attempted to resurrect sense perception as producing the true ideas, with the other abstract ones being manufactured later, as it were, from this raw material.

Contributor: Martin Cohen

## INNATE IDEAS

Innate ideas are ideas which, at least according to René Descartes (1596–1650), are inborn to the mind and they exist there from birth. In Descartes' system, ideas – a term which covers both concepts and truths – are divided into three types: innate, adventitious (entering the mind from some outside source) and fictitious (i.e. created or invented by the mind). Adventitious ideas include ideas of particular things, pains, sounds, colours and other sensible qualities which are ultimately acquired by the use of the senses. Such ideas could not be the material of certain knowledge, since the senses are fallible and potentially deceptive. Fictitious ideas are products of fancy and again play no part in scientific knowledge. Innate ideas are contrasted with the other two types, in that they are highly general and their clarity and distinctness enables them to provide the foundations of certain knowledge. Ideas in this type include those of God, freedom, immortality, substance, mind and matter, circle, triangle and other mathematical concepts, as well as a set of (allegedly) self-evident truths that are never set out exhaustively.

Descartes presents his theory of innate ideas as a kind of reasonable hypothesis. As he writes in the *Principles of Philosophy*:

... It seems reasonable to think that a mind newly united to an infant's body ... has inside itself the ideas of God, itself, and all such truths as are called self-evident, in the same way as adult human beings have when they are not attending them. It does not acquire these ideas later on as it grows older.

In a number of passages Descartes asserts that these ideas are implanted in the mind by God, but he does not press the point. In at least one minor work he claims that even sensory ideas are innate, on the grounds that nothing reaches our mind from external objects except certain bare corporeal motions, but then these motions are not conceived by the mind exactly as they occur in the sense-organs. The suggestion seems to be that adventitious ideas themselves must be treated or coordinated by the mind's innate powers.

Descartes' theory of innate ideas constitutes a rejection of the medieval doctrine that 'there is nothing in the intellect unless it was previously in the senses' and harks back to Plato's doctrine of reminiscence. In the *Meno*, Plato put forward the view that our knowledge of Ideas is acquired by the soul before birth, when it is in a state of communion with these entities, but forgotten when it joins the body at birth. As a person grows up, he is able to recollect these ideas and develop a progressively clearer understanding through a process of questioning and discussion.

John Locke rejected any theory of innate ideas and substituted the doctrine that the mind at birth is like a blank paper and all the diverse materials of knowledge are acquired by means of sense-experience of the external world and reflection of mental operations. He was in turn criticised by G.W. Leibniz, who argued that the mind at birth is nothing like a blank paper, but it is more like a block of marble with veins and fissures, which predisposition it towards a certain shape and place constraints on how the block can be sculpted into a statue. In an analogous manner ideas are innate to the mind as 'inclinations, dispositions, tendencies or natural potentialities and not as actualities'. Sensory experience must strike the mind to 'reveal' the shape of its ideas, but at the end our understanding of how the world works will have to be structured by the inner dispositions of the mind.

In the twentieth century, Noam Chomsky proposed that the human mind has an innate structure, a kind of universal grammar which enables children to learn to speak through a limited exposure to their native language and learn to tell an unlimited number of grammatical from badly constructed sentences.

Contributor: Zenon Stavrinides

# IDOLS

Idols are false gods, things that people worship, but should not. For Christian philosophers such as Bishop BERKELEY, Nicolas MALEBRANCHE and even Francis BACON and Robert Boyle (better known for his scientific views), widely held beliefs in the independent existence of astronomical and even ordinary objects were 'idolatrous', as were the powers often attributed to 'Nature'. Bacon's *Novum Organum* (1620) warns against the fictions created by conventions surrounding not only traditions and customs, but the use of words themselves. NIETSZCHE's *Twilight of the Idols*, written in 1888, which was the last year before he went officially mad, warns that the 'apparent world is the only one: the "real" world is merely a lie', and Nietzsche generally rails against all the various false idols of his time, notably God and morality.

This concern with the social role of idols is also an important part of both FREUDIAN psychology and MARXIST politics.

## ILLUSION (ARGUMENTS FROM)

The evergreen case of the straw in the glass of fizzy lemonade which appears to be bent is an example of the argument 'from illusion'. The straw is not really bent, yet it appeared so. Therefore, appearance is misleading and cannot be relied upon. Another old favourite is the possibility that we might imagine we are sitting in the garden reading a book, when in fact we are lying in bed, asleep, dreaming of sitting in the garden reading a book.

### SEE ALSO

Naïve realism, including the 'Argument from illusion'

## IMMORTALITY

For Christians, GOD is immortal, as he is outside such limiting things as 'change' and 'time'. God is unchanging, everlasting and timeless. Angels and SOULS are immortal in that God has made them so. (God could even choose to close heaven down. . .) This is also the kind of immortality that PLATO outlines in the *Phaedo*, where he says that the soul is immortal as it has no physical aspects, and so cannot be affected by physical events or time. Another kind of immortality, though, is the 'eternal cycle' of REINCARNATION, where the soul is reborn into various different forms.

## IMPERIALISM

Modern notions of imperialism are drawn from LENIN, who saw it as an economically motivated process, involving the export of capital and the centralisation of production and distribution. The First World War was, on this view, the CAPITALIST camps falling out and fighting over the spoils. Nowadays, to speak of imperialism is a bit passé, except in the form of 'cultural imperialism', the all-too-obvious phenomenon where profit motives spur the spread of a few limited cultural icons, usually at the cost of destroying small, local, cultural artefacts, ideas and tradi-

tions. (Even if the European Union has insisted on the 'cultural exception' to its otherwise fairly total acceptance of market forces. . .)

Instead, 'globalisation' is the preferred term, still meaning the tendency of the richest companies in the richest countries to divide the world up for their own financial benefit. In this, often economically naïve, view, the developing countries are made to surrender their assets (such as land and minerals) to Western companies, who then sell them on at vast profits to their rich domestic markets. Another claimed variant is when the transnational companies process the goods in the West and sell them back to the original countries at inflated rates, while the last diabolical effect appears when the countries not only offer the raw materials but also produce the goods, which are then either exported or sold to their own internal markets! In this case, the undesirable element is said to be the inevitability of low wages and poor safety and environmental standards, evidenced for example by the worst-ever industrial accident at the Union Carbide chemical factory in Bhopal, India, which was indeed a plant run on lower wages and lower safety standards than would have been acceptable in the company's home country, the USA.

At the same time, however, the MARXIST critique of international trade, which was precisely the virtuous beacon of capitalist economics for Adam SMITH, is increasingly challenged by the successes of various developing countries. There are now too many counter-examples of 'Third World' economies that have managed to change from being weak and exploited to being major forces in global markets in their own right, with sophisticated, highly educated and wealthy workforces.

## IMPLICATION (LOGICAL)

The relation between two PROPOSITIONS or statements of fact, such that if the first one is true, the second one will be as well. In the early twentieth century Bertrand RUSSELL complicated things by talking of 'material implication', where the two propositions have no connection. For example, a false proposition, such as 'All cats are green', implies 'All dogs are blue' because a false proposition (any false proposition) 'implies' every other possible proposition. This strange effect is because, in LOGIC, the only time we can say 'p does not imply q' is when the first statement is true and the second one is not, and as the claim about cats here is never going to be true, it is permissible to say that it does imply all the other possible statements.

G.E. MOORE, Russell's colleague and chum, then suggested a new term, 'entailment', which attempts to retain a sensible link between the two propositions. Essentially, this says that if q is deducible from p, then p entails q. Unfortunately, the connection cannot itself be satisfactorily explained.

SEE ALSO

Truth tables

## INCOMPLETENESS (THEOREM)
See Gödel.

## INDETERMINACY, LEGAL
See box under Law.

## INDIAN PHILOSOPHY

### Essentials of Indian philosophy

Indian philosophers apply reason in their search for truth and teach means of achieving salvation, which they regard as the justification for philosophy; what it is all about. Without action, philosophy is nothing. Thus all Indian philosophies combine ONTOLOGY and soteriology in totally integrated ways. Central to Indian philosophy is how to achieve emancipation from suffering, which is caused by the delusion of separation from the absolute. During a lifetime it is possible, by following the right path, to throw off this delusion and be reunited to the absolute at death. Failure to do so results in staying in the cycle of rebirth and death, continuing to suffer.

### How to reach *Nirvana*

Indian philosophy is ancient and perennial philosophy. It has an unbroken history of at least 3000 years. Restatements of ancient truths are made as language dulls and, as a result, concepts wear thin. Often startlingly dramatic restatements are hazarded, which superficially appear to be in complete contradiction to what has gone before. They never are. Rather they are re-illuminations of ancient truths because they share a common primary source: the *Vedas*.

All systems of Indian philosophy rely on the ancient *Vedas* as revealed wisdom, revealed in the sense that wisdom pervades everything. The *Vedas* are hymns from around 1500 BCE, com-posed in praise of the Vedic deities. The hymns are more valued than the deities themselves, for all wisdom is contained within the *Vedas* and each of their statements is held to be true. The *Vedas* are written in Sanskrit, a sophisticated language which is older than Greek or Latin. In India, Sanskrit is now used exclusively for philosophical writing and debate. It probably always was.

The *UPANISHADS* attached to the *Vedas* are the source documents of the different philosophical systems. Originally, all philosophical study was orally transmitted in metrical aphorisms, called *Sutras*. The various series of *Sutras* were written down between 400 and 200 BCE and it is in this form they are known collectively as the *Upanishads*. They are studied along with commentaries written on them several hundred years later, which are now the interpretations on which each of the philosophical systems relies.

The orthodox Indian philosophical systems are *Sankhya*, *Nyaya* and *YOGA*: now regarded as the philosophical, LOGICAL and practical aspects of the same system. *Purva Mimamsa* and *Uttara Mimamsa* are separate systems thought by Westerners to have been influenced initially by Christianity and Islam. The influence may have been the other way round.

*Kapila* is acknowledged as the originating sage of *Sankhya* philosophy. The existing *Sankhya-karika* was written by Isvarakrishna in the fifth century CE. This classic of Indian philosophy, with only 70 stanzas, holds the accolade for brevity. It is also pellucid, the clarity of style and meaning unsurpassed.

Everything throughout the universe, be it a grain of sand or heroic sage, is of two fundamental parts, *purusha* and *prakriti*, which are eternal, with no primary cause. *Purusha* is individual reality, all that identifies an individual as itself, but inert, inactive, without desire or experience of pleasure or pain. This natural state of *purusha* is permeated by *prakriti*, universal dynamism, which brings into play time, space and causation.

The qualities of *prakriti*, known as *gunas*, are considered in three groups:

- *satva gunas* are refined, pure, luminous, intelligent characteristics
- *tamas gunas* are coarse, vulgar, static, obscure characteristics
- *rajas gunas* are all forms of motor, physical and mental activity.

However, none of them exists separately, always simultaneously. Furthermore, there are endless variations of each of these *prakriti gunas,* and possible combinations of them all. The precise combinations account for the manifest differences of everything throughout the universe.

Each individual phenomenon in the universe consists of its *purusha,* with its unique combination of prakriti gunas, which comprise the gross body. In addition, living things have *lingasarira,* or subtle body, the product of the senses, influenced by *buddhi,* the intellect, in conflict with *ahamkara* or egoism.

*Ligasarira* stores *karma,* the result of chosen actions (like habits). *Karma* determines the future, even beyond death – especially beyond death. *Lingasarira* escapes from the dying *purusha* and clings to the next available *purusha* appropriate to the quality of its *karma.* Life is essentially suffering, is painful. The objective of the *buddhi* is escape from endless cycles of life and death, achieved when *purusha* is freed from *prakriti.* Freedom is gained by the ability to resist *lingasarira.* When *lingasarira* is resisted successfully it fades and falls away, and is sloughed off like a dead skin, a mask removed, with *purusha* remaining in its natural state.

*Sankhya-karika* records a philosophy only. *Yoga Sutras* by Patanjali, written at the same time, provides a method of achievement. *Sankhya* is the basis of BUDDHIST philosophy, whose exponents differ as to whether liberated *purusha* remains in existence or not. *Sankhya* originally taught ritualistic methods of escape, but these became passé as *Yoga* became popular and gained the ascendancy. Subsequently *Sankhya* was further developed alongside *Yoga,* so that the two systems, although separate, are complimentary.

*Nyaya* is now regarded as a system of logic and EPISTEMOLOGY because it concentrates on correct reasoning. Things can be known through perception, INFERENCE, comparison and testimony. GAUTAMA, the HINDU sage who founded Buddhism, is credited with compiling the *Nyaya Sutras.* Gangesa wrote the *Tatva Chintamani,* a commentary on them which is recognised by Hindu scholars as authoritative, during the twelfth century.

Life is held to be inseparable from pain. Pain is stronger and more persistent than pleasure. It makes life a burden. Self, attached to life, causes *Moha* – the delusion that pain and pleasure are attributes of self. The adept seeks *Mukti,* which is

release of self from life, the cycle of deaths and rebirths. True knowledge of the nature of *Atman,* or eternal freedom, achieved only by experience through self-discipline and meditation, is rewarded by *Mukti,* which is possible during life, and finally by *Apavarga* at the moment of death, when *Nirvana* is achieved.

Buddha is said to have rejected philosophy when he awakened from delusion. He certainly rejected Sanskrit in favour of the vernacular and used homely allusions in place of philosophical concepts. When asked philosophical questions he likened it to asking a man pierced by a poisoned spear how it happened, when it happened, what was his adversary like, what kind of poison, when what was important was treating the man as soon as possible. Buddha now concentrated on the cure: how to reach *Nirvana.* The answer was by the eightfold path, which was *Yoga.*

*Yoga* philosophy describes practical methods of achievement of escape or realisation. The fifth century CE *Yoga Sutras* of Patanjali are the definitive work on liberation, acceptable alike to Orthodox Hindus, Buddhists and JAINS.

*Vairagya* detaches self from worldly attachment in preparation for *Yoga* meditation. Detachment requires non-injury, truth telling, non-stealing, celibacy, poverty, purity, contentment, courage, study and devotion to liberation. Once the guru, the trainee's teacher, is satisfied on these counts, the practice of *Yoga* begins. First, the preparation stage of *Asanas,* which are the postures commonly thought of as *Yoga,* *Pranayama* breath control and *Pratyahara* insight, which overlaps with the meditation stage. Steps in the meditation stage are *Dharana, Dhyana* and *Samadhi,* which are increasingly demanding forms of concentration. In *Samprajnata Samadhi,* the first sub-stage of *Samadhi,* all distraction is eliminated, but because *lingasarira* still attaches to *purusha, satya* is experienced as ecstasy. In *Asamprajnata, Samadhi* consciousness of the world and self are eliminated, and at death *purusha* is liberated to *Atman.*

*Purva Mimamsa,* which means earlier investigation, applies to study of the *Brahmanas,* the rituals laid down at the end of *Vedas.* It is distinguished from *Uttara Mimamsa,* or later investigation of the *Upanishads,* which come after the *Vedas. Purva Mimamsa* emphasises ritual and ceremony. It was important when sacrifices and the rituals that accompanied them were popular, but is not so now. There was conflict between those who sought liberation through sacrifice and ritual and those who sought liberation through *Yoga*, and the latter won out. Basically the difference is between mystery religions with initiation ceremonies and secret rites of all kinds, where the adept is essentially passive, and techniques of personal development, control and fulfilment through one's own efforts.

*Uttara Mimamsa* is commonly called *VEDANTA*, the end of the *Vedas*, because that is where the *Upanishads* are found. *Vedanta* is used to mean Hindu philosophy generally. The *Vedanta sutras* are attributed to Badarayana of the fourth century CE, but Vedantins claim Vyasa, the mythical author of the *Vedas*, as founding father. By far the best known commentary is from the eighth century CE and is by SANKARA, one of the most subtle Indian philosophers. Sankara's commentary advocates *Advaita* – the philosophical statement of MONISM.

*Advaita* is the mirror image of the *Sankhya* system, which denies the existence of God. *Advaita* denies the existence of anything else; nothing exists but God. All things are *Maya* illusions, the result of ignorance. The phenomenal world is a figment of the imagination. Beyond *Maya*, there is the Real; it is in you, that is, it is yourself. All that was, is and will be, either has already passed or will soon pass into oblivion. It is *Maya*. It exists because you make it exist. The object of life is not release but realisation. You cannot be released from the Real but grow into it through *Jnana* knowledge.

*Vedanta* training requires a period of detachment from *Maya*, followed by *Srvana*, the study of the *Upanishads* with a guru. Then *Manana*, unassisted meditation on the *Upanishads*, which finally leads to *Nididhyasana*, meditation into oneness with the Real. Such an adept is a *Jivan-Mukta*; they live in the world but are no longer part of it, and they work tirelessly for others with great exuberance and energy.

Some see the *Advaita* system as having an amoral intellectualism that links back to Shiva with his mix of erotic energy, asceticism and those above the moral mores of society. In this case, *Vishishta Advaita* brings the *Advaita* system down to earth. The system is traced back to the *Vedartha Samgraha*, Ramanuja's eleventh-century CE commentary, and has much in common with the theistic Tamil poetry of the period. In it, God maintains the soul in existence and the matter it controls; a qualified monism. The object of life is deliverance from the cycle of births and deaths, a deliverance in which the soul finds God. *Bhakti* – or loving devotion to God – is one means of deliverance, but better is *Parapatti* – total surrender to God. Even an untouchable can be freed from his *karma* by *Parapatti*.

Finally, *Ramanuja* was writing when both Christianity and Muhammadanism were gaining converts in India and he may have been, in part at least, influenced by them. The system was and is popular. It is linked with Vishnu, the preserver member of the Vedic triad of Hinduism.

Contributor: Colin Kirk

## INDIVIDUALS AND INDIVIDUALISM

In LOGIC, an 'individual' is something that can be considered as the subject for a statement in PREDICATE CALCULUS, because, as it is put rather nicely, 'all particulars are individuals, but not all individuals are particulars'. After which rather fruitless aside, we might proceed to 'individualism', which in social theory and ETHICS is the assumption that not only does it make sense to abstract an individual from their context, history and relationships, from the group, from the environment, but that after doing so, the individual has their own interests, rights and values. The famous phrase of Immanuel KANT that individuals are 'ends in themselves' sums up this view.

Indeed, ethical individualism is the view that only individuals have moral values or ethical obligations.

## INDOCTRINATION

Indoctrination is the style of teaching in which it is intended that certain beliefs, such as 'helping other people is good', or 'the largest country in the world is Russia', or 'dropping the atom bomb on Hiroshima saved tens of thousands of lives', should be accepted without question. As such it is part and parcel of everyday education. Nonetheless, there is a fairly common feeling that 'indoctrination' is bad, and that learners should be encouraged to develop their own powers of judgement, to exercise their autonomy as 'individual learners'.

In an effort to combine both the practical reality of 'indoctrination' with this lurking ETHICAL doubt about its appropriateness and effects, teachers may attempt to provide within the curriculum areas which are offered as 'open to debate'. But even this apparently satisfactory compromise is prone to problems. In the USA, efforts by Christian 'fundamentalists' to make the teaching of the theory of EVOLUTION 'open to debate' are fiercely resisted by many, who despite often being LIBERAL in disposition, here prefer to add to the theory the additional stamp of being 'indisputable'.

## INDUCTION

The term comes from ARISTOTLE, and the Latin *inductio* or 'leading to', and describes the kind of reasoning that proceeds from examination of a few cases to a general rule. For example, as the sun came up every day for the last hundred thousand years, it will come up tomorrow. It is the kind of reasoning that we use in practice all the time, despite it being, in LOGICAL terms, 'invalid'. To illustrate this, Bertrand RUSSELL offered the example of the chicken who expects a handful of corn each morning because the farmer's wife in the past has always provided one. But one day, the farmer's wife wants chicken for dinner, and the hen's reasoning will be to no avail.

It is the opposite to deduction, in which particular conclusions are drawn from more general statements. Philosophers use the term 'deduction' differently from, say, Sherlock Holmes, who can deduce from the traces of heather and the smell of whisky (or some such trifling observations) on the man sitting opposite in the train, that the man is from Scotland and has just sold his house to an American. In philosophy, deduction is more rigorous, and literally 'non-informative', as all the information has to be there in the original general statement.

## INEQUALITY

Because people are different – prettier or uglier, stronger or weaker, good at logic or bad at logic – and circumstances vary, 'equality' is both impossible and undesirable. However, certain types of equality are considered to be both realistic and positive, such as 'equality of opportunity' or of 'rights'. Egalitarianism also seeks to reduce the economic differences between groups and individuals in society. Within education, many of the problems with inequality can be seen. Individual children and indeed social groups of children, arrive at primary schools with very different abilities, due to personal dispositions and talents, and to the effects of early-years rearing (whether their parents talk constructively with them, for example). If all the children receive the same education, the ones already lacking the basic skills will be permanently disadvantaged. So should some children get more attention in order to help them 'catch up'? And if it is desirable that all children should do 'as well as they are capable of', then there can be no objection to allowing those who can afford it to send their children to elite schools which will enable them to gain access to elite colleges and the top jobs in their countries.

It is not easy, in practice, to choose between equality of treatment and equality of outcome, and often the two are opposed. In France today, for instance, large numbers of French youths of African origin face actual discrimintion when applying for jobs, yet the idea of 'affirmative action' or 'positive discimination', as enacted by the USA to combat racism in employment there, is anathema to the French ideal of every individual being 'equal'. In any case, within a competitive culture predicated on measuring and then 'failing' most people, and within economic structures based on the principle that it is desirable to encourage consumption by offering better goods and services to those prepared and able to pay more for them, inequality is seen as both inevitable and desirable (but politicians hesitate to say this too often).

## INFERENCE (LOGIC)

Inference is the process of drawing a conclusion from one or more other statements. There are two types of inference, inductive, which gives conclusions that are merely probable, and deductive, which is certain. LOGIC seeks to give the rules for 'valid inference'.

## INFINITY

The ancient Greeks considered infinity to be a most undesirable concept, incomplete and imperfect. ARISTOTLE wrote in the *Physics* that the universe must therefore be finite, and infinity was merely a potential. (Much later, this notion was revived by Georg CANTOR in his mathematical distinction between 'countable' infinities and 'uncountable' ones.) Through his famous PARADOXES, infinity was discussed by ZENO, raising fundamental issues in physics and astronomy, not just for rabbits and tortoises. For NEWTON, space had to be both infinite and unbounded, while for EINSTEIN it became finite but still unbounded – something which is possible for any sphere. Einstein added that, in any case, space-time does not have to obey the rules of geometry. (Although it may be modelled using alternative geometries, such as Riemannian.)

However, the age of the universe is a bit of a problem too. It would seem obvious that either the universe had a beginning – or it did not. The trouble with it having a beginning is that something must have come of nothing, and what is nothing without something anyway? (The sound of one hand clapping?) On the other hand, if the universe has always existed, then it must be infinitely old – and that means it is getting older than that infinitely old every minute – which is not really very LOGICAL either.

This was the first of Immanuel KANT's four 'ANTINOMIES' or contradictions. Kant followed Zeno and other philosophers by giving examples of how 'infinity' can lead our normal thinking processes astray. True to his predecessor's challenge, HEGEL, in his *Logic*, attempts to unite both finite and infinite (in the manner of all his 'DIALECTICAL reasoning'), offering as an example the 'ABSOLUTE', which he says is both finite and infinite – like a circle, which is finite from one perspective and unbounded from another.

There is a political aspect to infinity too. For the Christian Church, for instance, it is a very good thing, and God is more perfect because of being infinite, both in extent and in time, and indeed anything else we are to think of, such as goodness, wisdom, and so on. Conversely, the world is finite, and 'limited', which is 'bad'.

## INFORMAL LOGIC

See Arguments.

## INSUFFICIENT REASON, PRINCIPLE OF

According to the Principle of Insufficient Reason, whenever we are faced with a question which we have no definite information to help us deal with, a question such as 'are there giraffes on one of Alpha Centauri's planets?', the possibilities are 50-50 that either there are or there are not. We have no information to say more definitely one way or the other. The economist J.M. KEYNES called it the 'principle of indifference' and spent a whole chapter of a book attempting to refute it.

## INTELLIGENCE

Despite numerous efforts, no one has yet produced a widely accepted definition of 'intelligence'. Some think it is the ability to solve problems, others the ability to remember and produce information appropriately. Some talk of LINGUISTIC intelligence, others of spatial, others of 'kinaesthetic' (that is, to do with touch and ability to deal with objects) and then, of course, the much neglected 'EMOTIONAL intelligence'. Nor is there any agreement on the extent to which intelligence is fixed and determined at birth, and the extent to which it develops, as a result of circumstances and surroundings – the 'nature/nurture' debate. Every so often the spectre that there are gender or racial characteristics in 'intelligence' raises itself, and has to be knocked down again by the statistical observation that even if one group *is* 'substantially' better at something than another group (let us say, they measure ten points higher on one of the tests – and as E.G. Boring (no really, a real name!) put it, intelligence is 'what the tests test'), it will still remain true that the 'general rule' will tell you absolutely nothing about the 'intelligence' of any one individual as compared to another.

## INTENTIONS AND INTENTIONALITY

The word 'intention' comes from the Latin for 'to stretch', the idea being that your action stretches out towards some end. Intentions are important for explaining actions; and for ascribing praise, or more often, blame. Thomas AQUINAS made the distinction between two kinds of state of being – *esse naturale* and *esse intentionale*, and there are further philosophical distinctions made between intentions taken as being instantaneous, such as: 'I stole the bread because I was hungry, m'Lud', and in the future, such as: 'He bought the philosophy dictionary intending to memorise it by heart, but never got past the letter B.'

Franz BRENTANO argued that every mental phenomenon could be understood as 'intentional', that is, directed towards an object. Things such as sounds and colours are not perceived as spatial objects, but nor are they considered to be solely mental constructions. But things such as joy, sorrow and hope, or disapproval, admiration and envy were different, containing 'an object intentionality within themselves'.

The 'intentional fallacy in art' is concerned to distinguish between the 'intentions' of the artists and what the great work actually communicates. The FALLACY is that the author's intentions and what the work of art actually says may be quite different things.

# INTROSPECTION

William JAMES defined introspection as 'the looking into our own minds and reporting what we there discover'. James adds that in psychology it is only 'introspective observation' that we have to rely on, an approach resisted by some as making the study necessarily SUBJECTIVE and unable to achieve (the supposed) full rigour of a science. John LOCKE called introspection 'reflection', talking of the 'notice which the mind takes of its own operations, and the manner of them'.

# INVISIBLE HAND

(Smith's market forces)
See Smith.

# IRRATIONALITY

Since ARISTOTLE declared that 'Man is a rational animal', irrationality has been thought of as the mode of operation solely of deranged and deficient people. Yet man is not a 'rational animal' at all. If anything, man is quintessentially an irrational animal. Animals marshal the information at their noses to find food, shelter and reproduce, human beings do a little more than this. That is why the Chinese sages called man a 'moral animal'. PLATO certainly thought that the highest processes of thought were not simply a mundane business of processing information, even if these processes were achievable only for a few (philosophers) and that in a rather MYSTICAL (irrational) way. Saint Thomas AQUINAS too was sure that some important conclusions relied not on reason but on 'faith alone'.

With the ENLIGHTENMENT, rationality came back into favour, and thinkers such as LOCKE, LEIBNIZ, BENTHAM and SPINOZA all set about trying to achieve well-ordered systems for processing information and obtaining sound conclusions.

# IS/OUGHT DISTINCTION

See Hume.

# ISLAMIC PHILOSOPHY AND ETHICS

## Essential Islam

Islam has become a global faith numbering today nearly one person in seven (some 800 million people in over 75 countries) as Muslim. In fact, it is the fastest-growing religion in the world today. Within a century of its being introduced among the Arabs in the seventh century CE, Islam governed and regulated an empire larger than that of either Rome or (ARISTOTLE's errant pupil) Alexander. The word 'Islam' means 'submission' – to God, and there is no God but Allah, of whom Muhammad is a messenger, as was Jesus too. A solemn recitation of faith is required of every Muslim every day, facing Mecca.

## Unambiguous philosophy

The importance of Islamic philosophy can be seen in the context of the decline of the Hellenic civilisation. By 300 BCE Athens was already being rivalled by Alexandria in Egypt as the cultural centre of the ancient world. The great leader of NEO-PLATONISM, PLOTINUS, although often viewed as a Greek philosopher, was actually an Egyptian. The eclipse of Greek philosophy, however, began with the closing of the School of Athens by the Byzantine Emperor Justinian, which heralded an eastern migration of Greek thought to Persia, which was more sympathetic to philosophers at this time. This heralded a period of great ignorance of Greek philosophy in the West, with PLATO's *Timaeus* and Aristotle's LOGICAL treatises, alongside the work of neo-Platonism, being the only extant works of the original masters.

The next significant period of philosophy is the so-called Arab-Islamic period, which began in 750 (and lasted until 1258), when Baghdad inherited from Alexandria and Athens the title of cultural centre of the world. Through Baghdad in the East, and the Western capital of the Islamic empire, Cordoba in southern Spain, Islamic thought was to exert a massive and determining influence on the history of civilisation. Any analysis of MEDIEVAL PHILOSOPHY must take account of the extraordinary relationship that existed between philosophy and theology during this entire period. Whereas Early Christianity was primarily Platonic in orientation (under the influence of both Plato's works and those of his neo-Platonic disciple, Plotinus), later medieval thinking began to look to Plato's successor, Aristotle, for philosophical guidance. Centres of Greek learning in Mesopotamia, Syria and Egypt were responsible for the survival of Aristotle's works in the West during this time. Most texts were translated from the original

Greek into an intermediate Syriac version and then into Arabic. When later, many of the original Greek texts were lost, it was these Arabic translations which were to provide the foundation for re-translation back into late medieval Latin. When one considers the immense influence of Aristotelianism on later medieval Christianity and Judaism, and indeed on succeeding Western history, it is instructive to remember this historical debt to the East. But the real intellectual contribution of medieval Islam to Western culture is less in terms of translation and more in terms of independent philosophical analysis.

There are three great Islamic philosophers before Averroës (1126–98 CE); these being al-FARABI (c. 870–950), Avicenna (980–1037) and al-GHAZALI (1058–1111). Al-Farabi is the least important of these, primarily significant because he is a pioneer in the invocation of Aristotle as a philosophical authority (thus paving the way for the Golden Age of Muslim Aristotelianism). He is said to have believed in the unity of the thought of Plato and Aristotle and his work shows a confluence of their theories, for example, in his claim that God is simultaneously identical with the neo-Platonic One and Aristotle's Self-Thinking Thought. With Avicenna, however, one has the development of a Muslim philosophy more independent of theological constraints and an Aristotelianism less apologetic to Platonic doctrine. Thus, Avicenna rejects the conception of a divine creation of the world in time (God is contemporaneous with the world) and follows Aristotle in considering the primary aim of philosophy to be the study of being *qua* being.

Al-Ghazali, writing at the end of the eleventh century, represents a critical backlash against the Aristotelianism of Avicenna, within the Islamic tradition. In his famous *The Incoherence of the Philosophers*, he attacks the inconsistency of the philosophical positions of al-Farabi and Avicenna with orthodox Koranic interpretation. What makes this work philosophically significant is that it does not rule out the possibility of philosophy *de jure*, but rather points to the misuse of philosophy by both of his predecessors. In particular, he was concerned with the philosophical theories of the eternity of the world and the denial of bodily resurrection, theories which he regarded not simply as theologically heterodox, but as the result of a misapplication of Aristotelian logical methods. For reasons which

are more political, to do with power struggles between various Islamic sects, al-Ghazali's defence of theological orthodoxy was to become associated with a form of theological traditionalism, which refused to enter into dialogue with theological or philosophical rationalism. Thus, al-Ghazali's philosophy and theology are an important influence on the movement which will later be termed Islamic fundamentalism. It can also be said that the upshot of al-Ghazali's and his followers' influence in Baghdad was the virtual death of philosophy in the East, although it was soon to receive a new lease of life in the Western part of the Islamic kingdom. This was to be primarily through the work of Averroës.

Averroës is generally regarded as the greatest of the Islamic philosophers of the medieval period and one of the greatest philosophers of the medieval period as such. Nicknamed 'The Commentator' (because of his incisive commentaries on Aristotle), Averroës' thought has two main strands. On the one side, he seeks to rid Islamic Aristotelianism of what he reads as a neo-Platonic bias which conflates the very different philosophies of Plato and Aristotle. Here, he is critical of both al-Farabi and Avicenna. It is important to note here, in sympathy to these early Islamic philosophers, that part of their difficulty in interpreting Aristotle correctly lay in the incorrect attribution of some neo-Platonic texts to Aristotle; thus works of both Plotinus and PROCLUS became known as works of Aristotle and thus led to a misconception of his thought as inconsistent. It is also worth noting, however, that Averroës was the first philosopher to point out that these texts were wrongly ascribed to Aristotle, given their inconsistency with his general thinking.

Averroës is not simply in conflict with preceding Islamic philosophy, but also with a kind of theological traditionalism present in al-Ghazali's criticisms of Aristotelianism, which Averroës seeks to undermine. In his ironically titled (but nonetheless intently serious) response to al-Ghazali, *The Incoherence of the Incoherence* (a direct response to al-Ghazali's *Incoherence of the Philosophers*), Averroës seeks to defend philosophically a consistent Aristotelianism, freed from neo-Platonic residue and theological prejudice. In so doing, he creates a complicated relation between his philosophy and his religious tradition.

In defending a consistent Aristotelianism, Averroës is critical of philosophical compromises made in the name of theological ortho-doxy. What is most significant about this defence of philosophy is that Averroës defends it through recourse to the Koran. Averroës argues that the study of philosophy is imperative according to Islamic doctrine. He begins by defining philosophy as the investigation of exist-ing entities, in so far as they point at or 'exhibit' the Maker. He then cites two passages from the Koran: verse 59:2, which urges 'people of under-standing to reflect'; and verse 7:184, which asks have they not considered the kingdom of the heavens and the earth and all the things God has created?'

He distinguishes between two different kinds of passage in scripture; those which the Koran refers to as 'unambiguous' (which must be inter-preted literally) and those which are 'ambigu-ous', which must be reflected on and interpreted. The Koran refers to the interpreta-tion of ambiguity as 'imperative' and also clari-fies that this interpretation can be done by 'only God and those well-grounded in knowledge'. This phrase allows Averroës to introduce his very important distinction between different dis-courses on truth and interpretation: his so-called three-tiered conception of truth. This privileges what he terms 'demonstrative truth' (that is to say, philosophical truth) over what he terms 'DIALECTICAL' and 'RHETORICAL' truth (both the latter being under the province of the-ology). Simply described, it is only philosophical or demonstrative discourse which proceeds from first principles; theological or dialectical dis-course proceeds from assumptions; while rhetor-ical discourse refers to the use of allegory or narrative to make difficult truths palatable to the public at large. Here Averroës again resorts to the Koran for justification, citing verse 16:125, 'call to the way of your Lord with wisdom and mild exhortation and argue with them in the best manner'. It is also worth noting here that this threefold division of discourses is a develop-ment of Aristotle's own classification of dis-courses and truths in the *Topics* and the *Rhetoric*.

With regard to al-Ghazali, the latter for Averroës confuses the category of religious or even rhetorical truth with that of philosophical truth, seeking to subordinate the category of rea-son to the category of revelation. But this is sim-ply to repeat the dogmas of Islamic theology, with little philosophical relevance. For example, Averroës rejects al-Ghazali's defence of a divine creation of the universe in time. Although many

Koranic verses seem to suggest the creation in time, here, according to Averroës, Scripture has resorted to what he terms 'sensuous representa-tion', that is, the third category of rhetorical dis-course which frames truths in terms palatable to the many (in this context, rhetorical embellish-ment is required because the idea of creation *ex nihilo*, or 'out of nothing', is an idea which com-mon people are unable to grasp, according to Averroës). Similarly, Averroës rejects al-Ghazali's orthodox claim of the personal immortality of the soul after death, again arguing that the philosophical truth consists in impersonal immortality, but this has to be made more bear-able for the common people, who find it diffi-cult to accept that their individuality does not survive death. In both these cases, Averroës is defending Aristotle's claims; both that the uni-verse is eternal and not created in time and also that the soul is only impersonally immortal, but also significantly claiming that these views are compatible with Islamic orthodoxy, in so far as the real truth of the Koran lies not in theological embellishment but in philosophical rationalisa-tion.

In contrast to al-Ghazali's work, the work of al-Farabi and Avicenna lays claim to philosophical relevance and seeks to distance itself from the mere repetition of theological orthodoxy. Nonetheless, according to Averroës, the philo-sophical systems of al-Farabi and Avicenna both fall into the category of theological rather than philosophical truth. This is perhaps more clearly the case with al-Farabi, whose work shows a cer-tain caution in its attempt to be consistent with Islamic orthodoxy (this is most notable in al-Farabi's defence of the doctrine of creation of the world in time). However, Avicenna had already begun to distance himself from these theological residues and, for example, is explicit in his avowal of the Aristotelian theory of the eternity of the world.

Despite this apparent philosophical progres-sion, Averroës remains critical of what he sees as implicit deferral to orthodoxy on crucial philo-sophical points. Thus, he censures Avicenna's theory that essence precedes existence. Rather, for him, existence precedes essence. He is also critical of Avicenna's proofs of the existence of God from the relation of necessity to contin-gency, as this argument imports too much METAPHYSICAL baggage for Averroës' liking. Rather, any proofs of God's existence must avoid metaphysics and rely on physical CAUSATION

## ISLAMIC ETHICS

The Koran is revered by Muslims as the literal word of God, superseding all previous revelations, such as the Bible. It forbids gambling, the consumption of animal blood, foods offered to pagan gods and idols, pork and alcohol and the eating of carrion. It describes at length punishment in hell and reward in paradise. To many in the West, but also to many educated Muslims, much that at least masquerades (for as with the Bible, there are many competing interpretations) as *Sharia*, or Islamic Law, is cruel and barbaric. In some 'Islamic' countries, for example, the penalty for habitual thievery may be loss of a hand, that for premarital sex may be 100 lashes in public, while for adultery – a 'sin' now all but completely absorbed into Western lifestyles – it can be death. All this sits uncomfortably with stories of the prophet's own life, such as that telling how, on awakening from his rest one afternoon, Muhammad found a small, sick cat sound asleep on the fringe of his cloak. The Prophet cut the corner off his garment, allowing the cat to sleep on, undisturbed.

As Islam is an all-embracing, comprehensive approach to living, covering all aspects of both individual and social life, there is no distinction between material and spiritual, physical and mental, religious and political, and the most minute act is seen as being subject to guidance by ethical experts, who are, by definition, religious leaders. Fortunately for the practicality of such a totalitarian doctrine, Good (*Hasan*) and bad (*Qibih*) are subdivided into imperative, recommended, allowed and forbidden or disapproved, with vagueness entering into many decisions.

Almsgiving to the poor, the aged and orphans is an obligation, as is a yearly 2.5 per cent *zakat* tax on your total assets. As for the treatment of women, the Koran is ambiguous. Muhammad instructed his followers to respect those 'who have borne you as mothers' and gave Muslim women civil and property rights – still a revolutionary step in the Arab world. The practice of wearing a *chador* or a veil is not mandated by the Koran; this practice appeared centuries after Muhammad. Women are merely injuncted to dress 'modestly'. The role allowed for women is hard for Westerners to see as anything other than oppressive and second-best, although there are female advocates of it, who say that, in fact, it provides a superior and honourable role for women. Whether this is true or not provides problems for those who take human rights as being universal, but none, of course, for relativists.

The Islamic way relies on a harsh system of punishment for transgressors, rather than simply the free choice of individuals. But then that is part of the doctrine: the equality of all believers is combined with a hierarchy based on 'piety, knowledge and hard work for society'. At least man is seen as 'a source of potentiality', not sufficient as he is, certainly, but at least not 'fallen', as in the Christian stories of the Garden of Eden, of Cain and Abel and of Noah and the Flood. Nor does the Koran allow for collective punishment – that anyone can pay for the crime of another – as is repeatedly suggested by these biblical stories, an Islamic ethical principle that sadly seems to have been lost somewhere along the way.

*Contributor: Martin Cohen*

alone. In both these cases, it is arguable that Avicenna is in fact closer to the literal meaning of Aristotle's original texts than Averroës and that Averroës is already moving beyond mere commentary on Aristotle to something approaching an independent philosophical system.

Whatever the truth of this, it is undeniable that Averroës has certainly succeeded in releasing Islamic philosophy from the fetters of Islamic theological dogma. In this context, it is perhaps not surprising to find that Averroës did not find too many disciples within Islam itself. In fact, in later life he was accused of 'irreligion' and temporarily exiled from Morocco where he

had gone to live, and sent back to Spain. However, this was less the result of intolerance of philosophy and more the result of infighting between Islamic tribal factions.

Averroës was eventually pardoned, although in the meantime his books had been burned and his exile used as an excuse to ban the study of Aristotle. He was allowed to express his views freely and with influence, but in the intermediate future period his influence was to be greater beyond the boundaries of his own culture than it would be within it, in particular his influence on the development of Christian philosophy.

*Contributor: Jones Irwin*

# JAINISM

Jainism is a religion and an ancient school teaching the **ETHICAL** principle of non-violence. It follows the teachings of its founder, Vardhamana; as expounded in the sixth century BCE. The name of the system is derived from Vardhamana's nickname, Jina – the conqueror. Vardhamana is believed to be the 24th and final Thirthankara. Like the Buddha he gave up wealth and power at the age of 30 and spent 12 years living as an ascetic until he became Jivan-Mukta, living in the world but no longer part of it, working tirelessly for others with great exuberance and energy.

Jainism has all the usual prohibitions but is unique in taking them literally. The prohibition against killing applies to all living things, including plants. You can eat leaves, flowers, fruit and nuts, but must leave the root and growing point of the plant to flourish. One extreme sect, the Digambaras or 'sky-clad', wear nothing because ownership of clothes is implied by wearing them. The sect is for men only, as, according to its precepts, women cannot reach *NIRVANA*. Suicide is permitted in order to reach *Nirvana* – but only after 12 years of mortification of the flesh and only by means of starvation and exposure. Jainism, let alone the Digambaras, is too demanding to be a popular system.

In Jainist theology, there are many deities but no God. The deities are lower than the Thirthankara or 'ford-finders', prophets who have found the route across the fateful river, not dissimilar to the Styx. As the deities have not yet reached *Nirvana* they have to take on human form to do so. Worship of the Thirthankara and deities is good in itself and beneficial to the worshipper for that reason alone; neither party can help the worshipper in any way. The **YOGA** path to liberation and enlightenment is yours alone.

Although Jainism rejected Brahminism it is otherwise similar to orthodox **HINDUISM**; its philosophy, logic and practice being akin to the Sankhya system. The main difference is that the *jiva*, the Jain equivalent of the *purusha*, is itself active and has a subtle body, made up of numerous enumerated and named particles. Casting away these particles by appropriate austerities releases the *jiva* to become *Jivan-Mukta* in life and to reach *Nirvana* at the point of death.

# JAMES, C.L.R. (1901–89)

## The essential C.L.R. James

Cyril Lionel Robert James was a radical figure whose ideas had revolutionary implications, not just for the West Indies, but also throughout a world that continues to be divided by race and prejudice. Journalist, sports writer, historian, critic, cultural theorist and **POLITICAL PHILOSOPHER**, he was born in Tunapuna, Trinidad and died in London, England.

## A philosopher often misread

James saw the Caribbean of his childhood as a **HEGEMONIC**, social imitation, still in the Victorian era. Trinidadian history and people were not discussed in schools. Instead, Trinidadian education projected a picture of faraway Britain as the source of everything that mattered, and insisted that the British ideal was to be admired, imitated and aspired to.

James wrote about the impossibility a person faced when their country had become a mere colony of another — they could not preserve their culture, nor could they completely assimilate into the coloniser's society. Although he was one of the world's first post-colonial intellectuals and a forefather of a rich Caribbean tradition of radicalism, he himself had to progress through the colonial structures,

In *The Black Jacobins* (1938), his epochal biography of Haiti's revolutionary leader, Toussaint L'Ouverture, a work now regarded as a founding text of post-colonial studies, he showed that the abolition of slavery in the West Indies was not (as Europe supposed) the result of direct intervention by enlightened Europeans, but rather owed everything to the actions and minds of the slaves themselves. *The Black Jacobins* also attempted to demonstrate that hegemony is never a complete and closed system, and that while Western values, contained in the writings of French revolutionaries and the 'Declaration of the Rights of Man', can be exported, they must still be recreated anew by each colonised people.

James also challenged what he saw as an elitist European assumption that world revolution would begin in Europe, becoming instead increasingly conscious of black struggles around the world. He wrote that 'the Negro represents potentially the most revolutionary section of the population', and emphasised that black struggles did not require the leadership of the white labour movement, contradicting a view he attributed to many white radicals.

During the Second World War he wrote articles about the struggle against racism in an army that was supposed to be fighting FASCISM, and stressed the need for blacks to create a brand of MARXISM particularly tailored to their needs. The 'Free French' Army was largely composed of black soldiers from the French colonies, yet the 'Free French' Army that marched through liberated Paris was almost entirely composed of white soldiers.

Imprisoned on Ellis Island at the height of McCarthyism, he was deported for 'un-American' activities. On his return to Trinidad in 1958 he called for a West Indian Federation, arguing that independence offered colonial peoples a unique opportunity to chart their own future and form a new society distinct to the colonial centre: a concept that was never grasped by Trinidad's leadership, unfortunately.

Appreciating that all bodies of thought rooted in human experience need to renew themselves constantly and draw from other currents of thought in order to remain relevant and viable, James, once an active Trotskyist, later developed his own interpretation of Marxism. He decided that radicals and intellectuals simply could not afford to cut themselves off from popular culture, or what he preferred to call the 'popular arts', with its immense political relevance; noting that even the most absurd Hollywood movies, comics and sports were expressive of larger social forces and trends, even if these expressions of creative form were sometimes distorted.

Yet what sets him apart from his intellectual contemporaries in Europe and the so-called 'Frankfurt School' in particular, is not merely that he was broad-minded enough to find such virtues in popular culture and mass entertainment — in calypso, comics, popular literature, jazz and television soap operas. It is rather that he used HEGEL and TROTSKY, alongside Thackeray's *Vanity Fair* and cricket, to understand all of them the better. For him, discovering MARX did not mean dismissing Thackeray or cricket, it meant appreciating new dimensions of them. And it was his love of cricket, the enjoyment and meaning 'mass' audience discovered there, that required him to work with the people as well as write about them.

## SPORT AND SOCIAL JUSTICE

In 1963, C.L.R. James published what is widely regarded as the greatest sports book written anywhere in the world, *Beyond the Boundary*. Unlike Trotsky, his intellectual mentor, who disapproved of sport because it distracted the working class from the political struggle, James always believed in the realm of pleasure, beauty and spirit, and had little problem with the so-called unruly distractions of aesthetic competition or play.

In cricket, he saw a game that had been a central part of colonial education and proved significant in bringing down racial barriers by making competition possible between different classes and ethnic groups without disrupting the social fabric. But cricket was more than that. It was also an original performance, a spectacle that exemplified the movement and tactile values of the arts. Set in context against more significant matters, it became a cultural unifier, a supplier of ethical principles, an instrument of social justice.

On every level of interaction with its audience, cricket expressed the relentless aspiration of human beings for genuine democracy and fairness. As such, the terrain of sport became a space, where organic, anti-colonial discourse could be viewed.

When the skill of local players surpassed that of their British counterparts, cricket was something new, as much a West Indian sport as a British one, subverting the colonial project and eroding its social reality. 'Calypso' cricket became the best in the world at a game that Lord Harris, a governor of Bombay, once argued required the 'doggedness of the English temperament' for success.

Contributor: DK

From his early experiences of being brought up in Trinidad under the British, James recognised a separation existed between the 'educated colonised' and the 'uneducated colonised'. Though he himself was part of the educated elite, he was always able to appreciate the genius and vitality of everyday people and the ways in which they subvert power.

From the 'negro question' in America to the problem of 'DIALECTICAL materialism' in the writings of LENIN and Trotsky, to his interventions in issues of civil rights, class and race antagonism, COMMUNISM, CAPITALISM, Marxism,

West Indian self-determination and pan-Africanism, James never yielded himself fully to the empire's centre and so is often overlooked today, precisely because this independence of thought left him a political and intellectual outsider (though one who questioned established modes of thought and sought to make a different world).

Contributor: Dylan Kerrigan

SEE ALSO

'Negritude', in African philosophy

## JAMES, WILLIAM (1842–1910)

William James has an interesting (and possibly confusing) family tree, being the son of Henry James, the religious philosopher, and brother of another Henry James, the novelist. He himself was a philosopher and psychologist who taught at Harvard, publishing *The Principles of Psychology* (1890), an account of how the brain is related to the mind, or rather 'consciousness'.

Taking DARWIN's view that consciousness has an EVOLUTIONARY origin and purpose, he dismisses the idea that we are all effectively automata or machines, and considers instead the possibility that we may have some sort of 'soul', before rejecting that too on the grounds that consciousness seems to be a transient state of the brain, continually being destroyed and refreshed. This is what has become famous as the 'stream of consciousness'.

Another influential element of his analysis is the distinction between the 'I' and the 'me'. James says that the 'I' is the 'thinker'; while the 'me' is made up of a 'material me', essentially preoccupied with bodily concerns, and the 'social me', which is concerned with how others perceive it in social situations. Our personal identity consists in the 'I' remembering the demands of the various 'me's. In this sense, James is a 'PHENOMENOLOGIST' as he sees mental states being based on physical processes. The exception is 'free will', which James hopes is indeed 'free', since the 'I' is able to choose 'freely' the thoughts it wants to think about.

His version of the 'will to believe' is that even if we lack any 'rational' basis for believing something, we can reasonably allow the emotional consequences to determine our decision. He is, after all, considered one of the leading 'PRAGMATIST' philosophers.

## JASPERS, KARL (1883–1969)

### The essential Jaspers

Jaspers was originally a psychiatrist, but became one of the founders of EXISTENTIALISM. His argument was that the great philosophical systems have all collapsed since it is the nature of human existence to be limited and uncertain. Science offers only limited knowledge, and existence is always in flux, affected by interaction with other 'existences'. Like some of the other later existentialists, Jaspers supposes there to be a higher mystical ESSENCE that transcends this world.

### Existence and being

Karl Jaspers, psychiatrist and philosopher, was born in Oldenburg, Germany and died in Switzerland. After studying medicine (psychiatry, psychopathology) he joined the philosophical faculty at Heidelberg University and so began to study and teach philosophy, and become a philosopher. However, during his apprenticeship in the psychiatric clinic in Heidelberg, he made and published some studies on jealousy, on homesickness and on dementia. In 1937, under Nazi dictatorship, Jaspers was forbidden to teach at the University of Heidelberg, due to his marriage to a Jewish woman. After 1938 his works could no longer be published in Germany. In 1945, with the defeat of the Nazis, his professorship was reinstated.

In *Allgemeine Psychopathologie* (*General*

*Psychopathology*, 1913), Jaspers used the 'PHE-NOMENOLOGICAL method' of Edmund HUSSERL to study the different manifestations of human pathology. *Psychologie der Weltanschauungen* (*Psychology of World Views*, 1919) follows the transition from psychology to philosophy and the birth of European existentialism. In *Philosophie* (*Philosophy*, 1932), Jaspers starts from the conviction of philosophy as a way of life in which thought and behaviour are inseparable, and seeks to demonstrate the limits of scientific and philosophical knowledge, which he thinks are both doomed to fail because of their incapacity to comprehend reality, whole and complete.

He writes that existence (*Existenz*) can only be realised through experiencing the possibility of being different from the natural or unconscious 'mere being', which he terms *Dasein*. As this reveals itself as impossible and fails, people can only overcome the defeat with an attitude of philosophical faith in 'Transcendence'. That discloses itself through symbols and 'cyphers', although it is always beyond the boundaries of the cyphers and thus remains unobjectivised.

By acknowledging that each cypher contains its own truth, just as each existence has a personal relation with the 'Transcendence' (the Encompassing), Jaspers seeks to avoid any form of DOGMATISM (by claiming only one truth) or RELATIVISM (by professing the existence of many truths).

After the Second World War, Jaspers moved to Basel and dedicated himself more actively to political issues. Influenced by Max WEBER, he sought to combine the strong LIBERAL values of liberty, responsibility, education and HUMAN RIGHTS with elements drawn from the intellectual aristocracy, such as spiritual hierarchy, the need for leaders and the assertion of the primacy of philosophy. His book *Die Atombombe und die Zukunft der Menschen* (*Atom Bombs and the Future of Humanity*, 1962) reflects his MODERNITY by dealing with the most pressing political topics of the day: technology, state sovereignty and international organisation – all explored within the context of a firm belief in the power of human reason.

Contributor: Elena Alessiato

## JEFFERSON, THOMAS (1743–1826)

Thomas Jefferson, third president of the USA, was responsible for the 'Declaration of Independence' and other important political documents, such as an act providing for religious freedom in the state of Virginia. Jefferson himself was a Christian, but his philosophical position was strictly 'LOCKEAN', that is to say, he considered all the members of the nation to be bound by an assumed 'covenant' in which they gave up some of their freedoms in return for the state assuming certain responsibilities, notably, responsibility for their safety and (in his view) education, too.

## JUNG, CARL (1875–1961)

### The essential Jung

Jung was born in Kesswil, Switzerland and died in Zurich. He was the founding father of analytical PSYCHOLOGY. He met FREUD in Vienna in 1907 and initially collaborated with him. Jung was president of the International Psychoanalytical Society from 1911 to 1914, but became increasingly critical of Freud's method. They parted completely in 1913 after publication of Jung's *The Psychology of the Unconscious*.

### Understanding the unconscious

The methodology of Freud, Jung and Adler had similarities, but their resulting concepts of the structure of the psyche and its motivations varied. Simplistically, Freud's psychoanalysis laid major emphasis on sexuality, whereas Jung's analytical psychology emphasised religion. Adler called his theory 'individual psychology' and concentrated on power.

Jung described psychological types (extroverts and introverts); identified and described the collective UNCONSCIOUS with the archetypes pervading it; and regarded the psyche as a self-regulating system seeking individuation. He was a clinical psychiatrist who developed his own treatment method: analytical psychology, a therapy requiring intermittent rapport between clinician and patient over a matter of months. He emphasised the importance of the analyst bringing only analytical attention into the relationship. The analyst was to be divested of SELF and limited to prompting continuation of the patient's monologue. All ideas, images, verbal constructs, and so on, were to originate with the patient to avoid contamination by the analyst.

But, first and foremost a doctor, Jung used his method to help many patients through crises in their psychological development. In the process he discovered a widespread use of symbols that led him to posit a collective unconscious. Unlike the subconscious of Freud's construct, which was a repository of repressed desires, Jung's concept of the unconscious is inhabited by symbols that are communicated in dreams.

Jung, the most positive of the analysts, considered the psyche a self-regulating creative system striving for individual identity, which he termed 'individuation'. DREAMS convey practical advice from the unconscious to the conscious self, assisting achievement of individuation. In *Modern Man in Search of a Soul* (1933) Jung suggests that the modern world causes ALIENATION by severing humanity from its roots, which are essential to psychological growth and hence to satisfaction. This has resulted in unprecedented levels of depression, despair and suffering. Humanity must understand its symbols and allow them to inform the creative development of the conscious mind. For this reason, Jung placed great emphasis on dreaming to allow the unconscious to communicate with the conscious mind. This is a natural process.

The individual unconscious is an integral part of the personality, with its unique capacity to dream, form, select, make symbols and present them for interpretation by the conscious mind. The analyst is needed only to help correct the interpretation of dreams in times of psychological crisis and in the context of training programmes for future analysts. Here, the role of the analyst is to focus on recurring symbols and the various possible representations of them, until the patient's conscious mind can interpret them in a positive and satisfying way.

He made a comment that all scientists should have inscribed over their desks: 'Nothing is more vulnerable than scientific theory, which is an ephemeral attempt to explain facts and not an everlasting truth in itself.'

Contributor: Colin Kirk

## Further reading

Jung, C.G. (1964) *Man and his Symbols*

Jung, C.G. (1933) *Modern Man in Search of a Soul*

## JUSTICE

Traditionally, justice sits at the heart of ETHICS, but it is not necessarily so, as the UTILITARIANS decided in the nineteenth century. Indeed, for many 'practical' ethicists today, justice must defer to 'utility' in working out policies. Decisions about organ donations, for example, will be taken on the basis of how many years of life each potential recipient may be expected to have, rather than on the basis of how socially worthy or noble that life might be expected to be. So the term 'justice' these days tends to be the prerogative of the courts; indeed they have, in a sense, usurped the term. But legal justice is only the application of the law, and the laws have to be written by human beings operating with a sense of . . . justice.

Philosophically speaking, justice is easily summed up as 'to each his own' – you get what you deserve. But how do you decide what someone deserves? People *all* seem to think they deserve better than they have, and at least some of them must be wrong! Lawyers are concerned with 'corrective' justice, which is punishment, but moral philosophers are usually more concerned with 'distributive' justice, which is that complicated calculation of laws, RIGHTS and HAPPINESS that is (evidently) so difficult to make.

PLATO's best-known dialogue, the *Republic*, is primarily concerned with the nature of justice, for the assumption Plato makes is that justice can be seen more easily in considering the larger organism (a community or city) than the smaller (the lone individual). And Plato argues that justice is essentially that which follows from having everything well organised and harmonious; the philosophers rule the city, giving orders to the 'spirited ones', the police and army, who stop the workers from indulging their natural tendency towards squabbling over material goods.

Thucydides too discussed the relation of 'justice' and 'expediency' with the much larger case of a city's inhabitants in mind, the case of Mytilene on the island of Lesvos, just off the Turkish coast. In 427 BCE, Mytilene's inhabitants had revolted against their Athenian masters and the Athenian assembly (all male citizens) decided the just punishment for this would be to execute every single male of the city and enslave the women and children. Thucydides poses the issue as a debate between a 'hawk', Cleon, and a 'dove', Diodotus, and the arguments are essentially practical – which policy in the long term will produces the most obedient cities in the Athenian empire? But Diodotus makes the essential point in all debates about punishment: the correct penalty is the one that never needs to be used.

# KABBALAH

A kind of Jewish MYSTICISM that reached its apogee during the Middle Ages, with various Christianised variants following afterwards. As well as the interpretation of sacred writing, the Kabbalah includes magical and esoteric knowledge relating to alchemy, ASTROLOGY and numerology, for example, not to mention speaking with spirits of the dead; but the main quasi-philosophical interest these days is in its approach to knowing and understanding God, who is said to be linked to the world through ten special 'hypostatic' numbers.

# KANT, IMMANUEL (1724–1804)

## The essential Kant

Kant's philosophical career reflects the breadth of his teaching and his interests. When, after 1770, he finally came to write the works for which he is most famous, namely the three 'Critiques', he addressed what he saw as the fundamental questions that cover human concerns: 'What can I know?', 'What ought I do?' and 'What may I hope for?' His answers to these questions are marked by the changes he bequeathed to EPISTEMOLOGY, ETHICS and AESTHETICS. Writing in the *Critique of Pure Reason,* Kant himself described these changes as a 'Copernican Revolution'. Some of his many other works focus upon the consequences of these foundational revolutions for moral behaviour, law, physical science and religious belief.

## The genesis of the Critical Turn

Kant was born and lived all his life in the town of Königsberg (present-day Kaliningrad). His childhood was uneventful, chiefly marked by a pietistic family background. At school, he mainly learnt theology and the classics, and was particularly fond of Lucretius. He only discovered the exact sciences, mathematics and philosophy on entering the university at the age of 16. He soon settled upon the idea of pursuing an academic career in the exact sciences, and indeed, he was awarded a doctorate for his thesis 'About Fire' (1755). A year later, Kant started teaching at the university, finally obtaining a chair in philosophy in 1770. Although philosophy had become the focus of his research, he taught an impressive range of subjects: mathematics, anthropology, natural sciences, physical geography, LOGIC, METAPHYSICS, moral philosophy, natural theology, fortification construction and pyrotechnics.

Kant was a very sociable man who enjoyed regular meals with a number of intellectual but non-academic friends. This number was always at least three (the number of Graces) and never more than nine (the number of Muses). The conversation at Kant's table spanned a broad range of topics, and Kant always showed a keen interest in the latest political, economic and scientific developments. He was known for his wit and his memory for detail, so that he could expound at length upon the impression made by a foreign town, even though he had never visited it.

But to understand the nature of Kant's critical thought, we must first examine his early writings. These are characterised by an important scientific publication, that of Kant's COSMOLOGICAL theory in *Theory of the Heavens* (1755). Here, Kant is the first to attempt to give a completely mechanistic explanation of the formation of the solar system and, more generally, of the whole universe on NEWTONIAN principles. Kant leaves no place for any divine intervention in the process. This theory was later validated by Laplace's calculations, and is now known as the Kant-Laplace theory.

A second important characteristic of the writings prior to 1770 is the particularity of Kant's contribution to the metaphysical debates of the day. This is chiefly one of debunking flawed metaphysical constructions that rely upon mere logic (in its ARISTOTELIAN form) to derive substantial conclusions about the world, God and the soul. In 1763, he thus publishes 'An attempt to introduce the concept of negative quantities into science'. This treatise seeks to identify internal contradictions in abstract metaphysical theories derived from pure logic. Essentially, Kant points out that, although in logic either 'A' or 'not-A' is true, in reality, something can be both 'A' and 'not-A'. For instance, a body can be both in motion and still since it depends with respect to what point of reference the position of the body is measured.

Among the other topics dealt with by Kant, we note the examination of the nature of causality and the proofs for the existence of God.

In dealing with causality, Kant, announcing famously that HUME had 'awoken him from his dogmatic slumbers', takes on board much of Hume's SCEPTICISM by pointing to the difference between the necessity that connects the conclusion to the premises it is logically derived from, from the necessity connecting a cause and an effect.

Kant examined the three proofs of the existence of God that were common currency in the metaphysical treatises of the day. In these proofs, God is viewed as the ultimate Cause of things (cosmological proof); as a Being whose existence can be deduced from the perfection of the universe He created (the physico-theological proof or 'argument from design'); or as a Being whose existence is necessary in light of the perfection that characterises Him (the ONTOLOGICAL proof). Here, the pre-critical Kant finds it at least possible that a combination of the ontological and the physico-theological proofs should enable the construction of a 'well-grounded' demonstration of the existence of God, since the existence of such a necessary being can be argued to be required by the world.

These two issues of causality and the existence of God are interesting, as they illustrate the transitional nature of Kant's pre-critical writings. He is taking on board some of the scepticism that originates in British empiricism (in particular, in the work of Hume), but is still very much anchored in the metaphysical tradition. However, what is determining for the 'Critical Turn' of his thought is the chasm that becomes more and more apparent between the success of a scientific understanding of the world and the unresolved nature of all the speculations of the metaphysicians. Kant was particularly well placed to be aware of this chasm, as he was at the forefront of the science of the day (and particularly impressed by the success of Newtonian physics), and wrote extensively about diverse shortcomings of the use of pure logic in metaphysical enquiry.

And then comes 'the Critical Turn'. The first publication that indicates the way Kant's philosophy will approach the problem of this chasm is his inaugural 'Dissertation' (1770) as professor at the University of Königsberg. There, he identifies the problem of knowledge as that of accounting for the possibility of what he terms 'synthetic *a priori*' truths. SYNTHETIC JUDGEMENTS are ones such as 'bachelors usually live longer than married men', and are informative, unlike logical statements such as 'bachelors are unmarried men'. A priori statements such as '2 + 3 = 5' are known to be true, independent of experience. Another feature of them is that saying the opposite is

## KANT'S GOD

In *Religion within the Bounds of Reason* (1793) Kant introduces a notion of faith that is grounded in reason. Since happiness is not fully achievable in the empirical world, it is rational for the moral agent to postulate an endless progress towards it, and that requires the immortality of the soul. The progress implied by a convergence towards the Highest Good, in turn requires an original good, the existence of God as ultimate cause of the natural world.

Kant distances himself from the ritualistic dimension of religion to emphasise the primacy of a religion centred around morality. Although this may involve beliefs in historical facts (such as the resurrection of Christ), religion ought not require more of people than that they behave morally. This understanding of religion was clearly not to the liking of the Prussian Protestant Church. Under pressure from Friedrich-Wilhelm II, Kant agreed to abstain from further expressing his opinions on the subject of religion.

Contributor: CO

absurd or self-contradictory. The problem with statements such as 'all events have a cause' is that it makes an a priori claim that holds universally, although it cannot be derived from mere conceptual analysis. Prior to 1770, metaphysicians had happily written treatises full of such claims. Kant was now questioning the validity of the arguments they used.

Kant used mathematics as the paradigm of synthetic a priori knowledge. In geometry, the drawing of a triangle in the mind's eye generates what Kant calls an intuitive representation. Such intuitions constructed under the guidance of a concept (like that of a triangle) form the basis for the acquisition of mathematical knowledge through the formulation of judgements about these concepts. The case of scientific knowledge may prima facie seem quite different as we have to apply concepts to what is in the outside world.

This is where Kant makes what he describes as the 'revolutionary' move of suggesting that, since little success has been reaped from attempting to account for knowledge as conforming to the objects of our experience, it may be more promising to consider these objects as having to conform to our cognitive faculties. This so-called 'Copernican Revolution' in philosophy amounts to a radical rethink of what it is to be an object, for an object is therefore defined in terms of a subject of knowledge. The *Critique of Pure Reason* (1781) examines the fruitfulness of this approach, and provides grounds for the metaphysical position it represents, 'Transcendental Idealism'.

In this work which, Kant himself confessed, is difficult (and which he substantially revised for the second edition of 1788), Kant examines in detail how synthetic a priori knowledge is possible. The conditions for cognition are of two types: intuitions and concepts. In both cases, there are a priori versions of these. In the case of intuitions, by claiming that space and time are forms of our sensibility that are prior to any experience, Kant is providing a justification for TRANSCENDENTAL idealism. For this entails that what we perceive are appearances. By this, he is not suggesting that our perception is in some sense illusory, but rather that what we know is partly the product of our own manner of perceiving.

The concepts that we require 'prior to experience' are categories and their seat is the faculty of the understanding. An object of knowledge is constituted by the application of such categories to a diversity that is given in space and time, thus bringing unity to it. In the case of mathematics, this diversity is generated by the subject thinking under a given concept (for example, that of a triangle). In the case of empirical knowledge, that which is presented in space and time originates outside the subject. Thus, in viewing the movement of a piece of iron towards a magnet as caused by the latter, I am bringing the diversity I perceive under the unity of the category of causality. The objective structure of the empirical world is thus that which I bring to it by applying certain basic concepts.

The faculty of reason is the cognitive faculty which brings further unity to the empirical knowledge acquired by the understanding. The ordering which reason introduces in the diversity of specific elements of knowledge (for example, Newton's theory of universal attraction) is driven by its search for unconditioned knowledge. The errors of metaphysics consist in assuming reason can obtain the unconditioned. These take three generic forms: knowledge of oneself as a substantial soul, of the world as a totality (for example, whether it has a beginning) and of God (for example, that God exists). Metaphysics makes knowledge claims although it does not respect the conditions for knowledge, which are that some diversity be unified in intuition under a category. By pointing out the source of the errors of metaphysics, Kant seeks to put a full stop after a whole era in the history of metaphysics.

But he also points to the vocation of reason as lying not in knowledge, but in the practical domain. In the *Groundwork to the Metaphysics of Morals* (1785), and later, the *Critique of Practical Reason* (1786), Kant extends this 'Copernican Revolution' to the practical realm. Morality is not connected with the inclinations that we are subjected to as a result of our empirical nature. Rather, our duty is to give ourselves the law of our conduct, that is to say, to be autonomous. By reflecting upon what could stand as universal duty for any rational agent, Kant derives the famous formula of the categorical imperative: '*Act only on a maxim that you can at the same time will to be a universal law.*'

In this formula, we see that what is crucial is not the success of the outcome of an action, but the intention formed in acting. This does not mean that consequences are irrelevant, since they are precisely that which has to be weighed up when assessing the moral worth of a purported form of action. But, once a maxim of action is formed that is universalisable, one's duty is fulfilled by acting upon it on the ground of this universalisability.

The way in which this is to be applied can be illustrated by considering the case of the duty not to make false promises. We are asked to consider a world in which the practice of making false promises when convenient is a universal law. In such a world, the institution of promise-making would collapse in so far as no one would trust any promise-making. The question is then whether we could will such a state of affairs. The fact that we could not is not to be understood as motivated by self-interest, for the only motive here must be duty. Rather, the problem lies in the contradiction there is for someone who universalises a maxim of making false promises when convenient. For he will only be in a position to derive any advantage from breaking his promise if the practice of promise-making is alive and well, which will not be the case if the maxim of making false promises when convenient is universalised. That is, this agent would both will the existence of the institution of promise-making and will a situation in which it cannot exist. This contradiction entails that it is not possible to universalise the maxim in question, so that the maxim of not making false promises is morally binding.

Much as the categorical imperative is sometimes associated with a form of 'rigorism' connected with Kant's Prussian upbringing, it can hardly be said to tie down the agent to precise forms of action. The duty to provide help when needed, for instance, can be implemented in a variety of ways. But it does appear to unconditionally exclude certain forms of action, such as lying, in ways we might find unacceptable in the face of the complexity of moral life.

There are indeed certain passages in Kant's texts which suggest such an interpretation. We thus find him (considering the possibility of lies prompted by **ALTRUISTIC** motives) declaring that a servant lying to the murderer at the door about his master being at home is morally forbidden – even though telling the truth would put the master in mortal danger. Kant also seems to bring apparently irrelevant factors into consideration, suggesting that there may be circumstances enabling the master to escape, and that, were the master to be killed because,

## KANT'S *CRITIQUE OF JUDGEMENT*

Kant's critical work was not over after the publication of the critiques of pure and of practical reason. For the unity of Kant's system required that the ground of appearance which lies beyond the realm of the knowable be connected with the intelligible world in which the moral subject exercises his autonomy. This issue is the motivation behind the *Critique of Judgement* (1790). His solution is found in the examination of the notion of 'purposiveness'. This says that the unity of our knowledge of the natural world is guided by the idea that it is *as though* nature had a purpose. It is this idea that accounts for the way in which scientific knowledge is meant to evolve towards an ever greater integration of disparate bodies of knowledge. This teleological grasp of the natural world can then be brought together with the teleological notion of the Highest Good in morality. The purpose of the natural world becomes something that can only be fulfilled through the moral agent.

The judgement that something is 'purposive', however, can mean one of two things. It is either that the object is indeed viewed as though there were some objective purpose at work, and this leads to the kind of judgements that characterise our grasp of living organisms, for instance. Or it is the judgement that the way in which something is presented is purposive for our cognitive faculties. Typical of the latter is the aesthetic judgement that something is beautiful. By that is meant that what is presented enables a harmony between my imagination and my understanding, as though it were destined for my appreciation. To say something is beautiful is therefore not to bring it under a concept, so there are no canons of beauty. Rather, it is to indicate that the presentation has a form which is particularly adapted to my being able to find structure in it. It is the *purposiveness* that I judge to be present in the presentation of the rolling hills before my eyes, which grounds my judgement that they are beautiful.

Contributor: CO

unbeknown to the servant, he had actually gone out and subsequently encountered the murderer, the servant could rightly be accused of being responsible for his master's death.

Many rigid interpretations of the categorical imperative, however, follow from considering simplified examples of moral choices and extending them without clear warrant to more complex cases. That Kant himself was not blind to the complexity of moral issues can be seen by looking at how he deals in detail with practical problems in the *Metaphysics of Morals.* Thus, in dealing with the tradesman who is honest from self-interest (*Groundwork to the Metaphysics of Morals*), or in describing avarice or beneficence (*Metaphysics of Morals*), he shows us how aware he was of the variety of subtle moral distinctions which make up the fabric of our lives.

The dominant role of reason in morality, however, does not stand in opposition to human inclinations merely for the sake of crushing them. On the contrary, Kant recognises the drive to seek happiness and does not condemn it, as long as it does not take the driving seat in determining human conduct. Indeed, he sees the notion of Highest Good in which happiness accrues to those who act dutifully and in proportion to their so doing, as providing the dutiful agent with a goal for his endeavours.

Contributor: Chris Onof

## Further reading

P. Gruyer and A.W. Wood (ed. and trans., 1998) *Critique of Pure Reason* (Cambridge University Press). This edition includes Kant's notes to the original 1781 edition.

## KEYNES, JOHN MAYNARD (1883–1946)

Keynes' *General Theory of Employment, Money and Interest* (1936) was a key part of the post-Second World War consensus on the State management of economic life. In it, Keynes attempts to explain and to justify economic laws, and the desirability of State intervention in economic affairs. His earlier, more obviously philosophical work, *A Treatise on Probability* (1921), tries to offer a LOGICAL basis for judgements of PROBABILITY. An establishment figure, fellow of King's College, Cambridge, as well as Baron Keynes of Stilton, he held many UK government posts.

## KIERKEGAARD, SØREN (1813–55)

### The essential Kierkegaard

Søren Kierkegaard was born and died in Copenhagen, where he studied philosophy, theology and literature at the university. He was in Berlin when SCHELLING was teaching against the prevailing dominance of HEGEL's philosophy, and from him derived the notion that purely speculative systems of thought are irrelevant to life choices. But Kierkegaard went further than him in rejecting the Hegelian rationale and arguing that philosophical systems are irrelevant, the search for objectivity is a false trail and that SUBJECTIVITY is truth: '*What is truth but to live for an idea?*'

### Truth is my truth

Kierkegaard's life coincided with Denmark's golden age. The period between the disasters stemming from the Napoleonic wars (Denmark lost Norway and suffered national bankruptcy in 1813–14), to the achievement of constitutional monarchy in 1849, was one of artistic and scientific achievement for Copenhagen.

Kierkegaard's parents had both started life in serfdom, as the children of crofters, but had become wealthy. His father, Michael, had prospered in the city and benefited from the national bankruptcy. By the sale of his businesses and inheritance from an equally successful uncle, the elder Kierkegaard was a wealthy man before he started a family at the age of 40. His second wife was a girl in service, who was four months pregnant when he married her. They had seven children, but only the eldest, Peter, who became Bishop of Aalborg, and the youngest, Søren, outlived their parents.

Søren was very attached to his mother, who could read but never learned to write, but Michael Kierkegaard was a revered authoritarian. He dominated Søren's youth. (Søren was 25 when his father died, aged 82.) The family were traditionally pietist-Moravians and Michael was a firm believer in God who, in the hardship of his youth as a shepherd boy out on the exposed Jutland marshes, had cursed God for his miserable lot. He had done so in all seriousness.

In rapid succession, his newly enriched uncle summoned him to Copenhagen, Michael started his own successful enterprises, his first wife died and he got a girl pregnant instead of having a bride allocated by the pietist-Moravian community. Five of their seven children predeceased their parents and his much younger wife predeceased Michael.

Throughout his life Michael interpreted these happenings as the result of his curse on God. God, in his turn, had cursed Michael with a love of Mammon and by taking away his loved ones, including his love of God. He became an intellectually committed Christian, a God-fearing man.

Søren himself went to the best school in town, the Borgerdydskolen – the School of Civic Virtue – and on to Copenhagen University, where he studied theology. As a student, he lived the life of a man about town, ran up debts and spent more time on philosophy and literature than on theology. At home, he relied on his father's wealth and spent his time in intellectual discussion with his father, elder brother and many of the eminent thinkers of his day. Much of Kierkegaard's writings are directed at intellec-

tuals who reduced Christianity to a formal pillar of state control. Ironically, it was from the family house in Nytorv, living among those who ran the kind of highly organised State that Hegel designed as his ideal for the good of the individual, the community and society, that Kierkegaard rejected Hegel's philosophy of State control. At the time, Denmark was an autocratic monarchy with an established Lutheran Church, which was an essential part of the apparatus of State control.

Søren went to the pastoral seminary in 1840 and submitted his doctoral thesis *On the Concept of Irony* in 1841. He became engaged to be married but he decided against it, citing 'family secrets', thus avoiding any marriage. Nor did he pursue the religious career he had embarked upon. He was to be 'free to be himself'.

He attended Berlin University briefly through the 1840s, while Schelling was lecturing there. Schelling held that philosophy begins conceptually and switches to a realisation that it is existence that matters. Hegel had failed to make the change, building an ever more complex conceptual system in an attempt to explain reality. Nevertheless, it was a system with which Schelling had a deal of sympathy.

Kierkegaard accepted Schelling's criticism of Hegel, but wanted to proceed to demolish the entire edifice as irrelevant to existence. In the *Concept of Anxiety* (1844) he generalised from Hegel's concept to all others. Philosophical systems are empty; they do not equip one to face the reality of existence. In addition, Kierkegaard had an emotional objection to Hegel. His philosophy was coldly inhuman. In fact, the whole of ENLIGHTENMENT literature read like the cold, abstract thoughts of passionless men. The passions of the soul were important to Kierkegaard. His next step was to deny there was such a thing as objective truth. Concepts are empty; the objective truth sought does not exist.

To paraphrase Kierkegaard, truth is my truth, it is specific to me. Truth is subjective. The only unavoidable imperative is to live by my truth. A leap in the dark is involved away from the protection of shared ideas, which are a ritualistic common bond, to whatever is essential and vibrant in my existence. In this way I find myself and live honestly according my subjective truth. This is both Socratic, in SOCRATES' sense of divine madness, and modern in psychological terms – in EXISTENTIALIST terms.

This is certainly how Kierkegaard's thinking is

often presented. In fact he was a formal Christian, who became a SCEPTICAL observer and then, when he made his leap in the dark, it was into his own Christian truth, which he lived by for the rest of his short life.

Another way of presenting Kierkegaard's thinking starts with his period as a sceptical observer, without any commitment. He calls it the AESTHETIC phase, when there is no continuity, no fixed values, no moral commitment. He also calls it the Don Juan stage, by which he means people who want to sample all experiences, seek a 'false INFINITY'. In this phase he himself became increasingly cynical, then totally disillusioned, and considered suicide.

He rejected the idea of suicide and underwent a moral conversion, in 1836, into the ETHICAL stage. Here, meaningless 'individualism' gave way to behaviour in accordance with universal moral law, which gives shape and definition, a continuity to the individual life, which was missing in the aesthetic phase. But ethics offers no more than happiness, temporal satisfaction, with no affirmation of the transcendent.

It is affirmation of the transcendent that Kierkegaard craves, where the individual does not submit himself to impersonal universal values, but stands in direct relationship to his supreme 'Subject': his personal values, world view, life affirming reality. He chooses himself in the deepest sense, affirms his self before God and transcends the universal.

These stages are not part of a smoothly developing thought process, but a series of breaks with the past, an affirmation of a new life, not knowing where one's personal truth will lead until arrival there.

There are parallels in Socratic thought, or in the achievement of NIRVANA, or in the life of the Jivan Mukta, but Kierkegaard made his own discoveries within a particularly narrow Christian tradition. These parallels suggest that his generalising from supposedly subjective truths to humanity in general is in fact justifiable, even if somewhat illogical.

Kierkegaard's third stage, the 'leap in the dark', involves humanity launching itself into the unknown and finding itself in the process. This act of the spirit does not require God, which is why it is acceptable to AGNOSTICS and ATHEISTS.

Kierkegaard was a prolific writer. There is still uncertainty as to the extent of his output, as he wrote particularly contentious works under pseudonyms, both because of his many inconsistencies and because his views were regarded as subversive by powerful State and Church elites. He mainly kept a low profile, but wrote for the satirical paper *The Corsair* during the 1840s. After the change to a constitutional monarchy he looked for a Christianising of the Danish State Lutheran Church and openly attacked the Church hierarchy; indeed friends, neighbours and relatives too. It was at the height of this controversy, with publication of his *What Christ's Judgement is about Official Christianity* that he died, in November 1855.

His work influenced the development of later European thought, through the writings of Karl JASPERS, Martin HEIDEGGER and the other existentialist philosophers of the mid-twentieth century.

Contributor: Colin Kirk

## Further reading

Kierkegaard, S. (1843) *Fear and Trembling*

## KILLING

Killing has always had a poor reputation in ETHICS, although it is a much-applauded part of social and political life. For countless millennia, killing has been celebrated in conflicts and tournaments, the basis for 'law and order' and the imposition of social organisation. At the same time, once a society has been established, there seems to be a widely shared prohibition on killing members of one's social group. The extension of this anthropological state over the years has been slow but steady. If killing of one's immediate family was first to go, followed by this disapproval of the killing of other members of the same immediate community, protection was then extended to members of the same 'racial' group, the same 'nation'; while today the debate is on in earnest about whether to extend the privilege of not being arbitrarily killed to non-humans.

The supposed prohibition on killing finds expression in the debates on SUICIDE, 'mercy killing' (EUTHANASIA) and abortion.

## KINESIS

ARISTOTLE discusses *kinesis* in his *Metaphysics*, using it to mean a kind of motion, but an 'incomplete' one, since it must have its final 'end' outside itself. In contrast, *energia* is a movement which is complete.

## KNOWLEDGE

The problem of how to find rock-bottom certainty is the underlying theme of much Western philosophy, as practised by the ancient Greeks and epitomised by René DESCARTES in his questions to himself while meditating in his sixteenth-century oven room. He thought he had found the answer in the certainty of his own existence as a thinking being, famously encapsulated as '*Cogito ergo sum*' – 'I think therefore I am'. This, René believed, was something that he definitely did know – not just believed to be the case. In a sense, just as this is an encyclopaedia of philosophy and ethics, it is an encyclopaedia of 'knowledge'.

## KOJÈVE, ALEXANDRE (1902–68)

The Russian social philosopher Alexandre Kojève was born into a rich merchant family and was nephew to the celebrated Russian artist, Wassily Kandinsky (and about whom he wrote: 'The Concrete Paintings of Kandinsky').

He was arrested and was due to be sent to the scaffold by the Soviets, but escaped, and emigrated to Germany in 1920. Under Karl JASPERS' supervision he studied philosophy in Heidelberg and then moved to Paris. He taught at the *École Pratique des Hautes Études* where he gave celebrated seminars on HEGEL's *Phenomenology of Spirit*. Some of the participants at the seminars became his 'disciples'; among them ALTHUSSER, Bataille, Breton, LACAN, MERLEAU-PONTY, Queneau and SARTRE. This is why Kojève is a key figure in POST-MODERN philosophy.

In 1945 he suddenly left philosophy, and for 20 years after 1948 he was an officer in the Ministry of Economic Affairs of France. His civil career was enigmatic, and included a spell in the French intelligence service, the DST probably for his Soviet connections.

In his estimation of the philosophy of history he combines three authors, Hegel, HEIDEGGER and MARX, synthesising social theory with PHENOMENOLOGY. As with many Russian thinkers, he was a MARXIST and initiated a period of fashionable philosophical discussion of Marx. He borrowed from Hegel to develop an idea of a universal historical process that would result in the synthesis of oppositions,

and he also drew on Heidegger. He followed Marx's thesis that as desire is the centre of historical process, it is necessary to reject desire in order to overcome ALIENATION. Kojève's ideas found an extension in Sartre's EXISTENTIAL Marxism, and his interpretation of the 'master-slave DIALECTIC' was developed by Lacan in the 1950s. Finally, his thesis that to be a human being is to be desirable was the starting point for Bataille's writing, and his idea of 'the end of history' was echoed in the title of the contemporary American SOCIAL SCIENTIST Francis Fukuyama's bestseller.

## KOREAN PHILOSOPHY

The prevailing theme of Korean philosophy is 'irenic fusionism', which is not very well noted outside Korea and China, but important to mention here. Despite its off-putting name, 'irenic fusionism' is only a different kind of way of looking at the workings of the mysterious TAO. The Tao's image is of water, but in Korea it is the flow of the wind, or *poong-ryu-do*. It is indivisible, yet everywhere, and unites everything. The BUDDHIST monk Wonhyo (617–86) tried to use this unifying principle to unite not merely the various schools of Buddhism, but also Taoism and CONFUCIANISM, saying that just as all the streams will combine in the river and flow into the sea, so much as the various schools of thought.

In the sixteenth century, Korean philosophers debated the unification of the virtues and the emotions, the so-called 'four-seven' debate, after the traditional Chinese definitions of the four virtues (humanity, righteousness, propriety and wisdom) and seven emotions (joy, anger, sadness, fear, love, hatred and desire). However, the fusion of the METAPHYSICAL and the physical worlds is brought about best through action, and it is here that Korean philosophy moved furthest away from its Confucian and Buddhist roots, creating the characteristic emphasis on practical learning over 'speculation'.

## KORZYBSKI, ALFRED

See Visualisation.

## KROPOTKIN, PETER (1842–1921)

### The essential Kropotkin

Kropotkin was both a political writer and ANARCHIST, arguing against the prevailing 'social-

Darwinist' view that society progresses by allowing the strong to destroy the weak, and that co-operation is a natural feature of society that does not need to rely solely on coercion.

## Freedom and collectivism

Prince Peter Alexeievich Kropotkin was born into a rich, powerful family that served the Romanov dynasty. He joined, as a commissioned officer, the Tsarist army and served in Siberia, where he later undertook survey work for the Russian Geographical Society. It was during these trips that he became aware of the injustices of Tsarist autocracy (such as the labour camps and salt mines), and of alternative models of social organisation. Impressed by the collegiality of tribal communities on the Manchurian border, and the examples of ALTRUISM and co-operation in his zoological studies of the natural environment, Kropotkin became convinced that mutual aid and co-operation were essential traits for survival.

This tendency towards social solidarity was based on Kropotkin's account of humanity's 'species being': the requirements for the thriving individual. Humans, he argued, needed not just the satisfaction of basic material needs, but also luxuries and a harmonious society. Thus, Kropotkin's ETHIC has been criticised for its essentialism by post-anarchist thinkers like Saul Newman and Todd May.

As a result of his radical political views, Kropotkin soon came into conflict with the Russian authorities. After escaping imprisonment and experiencing periods of exile in Switzerland and France, he settled in the East End of London. While there, he set up the anarchist newspaper *Freedom* and worked to support industrial workers and fellow refugees. He also developed and publicised his distinctive version of politics, of anarchist-COMMUNISM that followed from his earlier commitment to the other dominant forms of anarchism (mutualism and collectivism).

While originally a follower of Michael Bakunin's collectivism, Kropotkin rejected this form of anarchism because of its reliance on 'labour vouchers' for its system of redistribution. Collectivism was criticised by Kropotkin because it reintroduced arbitrary social divisions (between supposedly productive and unproductive labour) and recreated CAPITALIST forms of exchange. Kropotkin's alternative form of anarchism was based on freely undertaken labour, with production and distribution being co-ordinated by federated voluntary organisations. As such, Kropotkin has been dismissed as a 'utopian', although he pointed out that many such successful organisations are run on these principles.

Kropotkin's work continues to be admired by contemporary anarchists and heterodox MARXISTS, as well as EVOLUTIONARY biologists, geologists, artists and activists.

Contributor: Benjamin Franks

## Further reading

Kropotkin, P.A. (2003) *Ethics: Origins and History*

Kropotkin, P.A. (1991) *Memoirs of a Revolutionist*

Kropotkin, P.A. (1987) *Mutual Aid: A Factor in Evolution*

## KUHN, THOMAS (1922–97)

Cincinnati-born Thomas Kuhn was the philosopher of science whose theory of 'PARADIGM SHIFTS' became something of a SOCIAL SCIENTIFIC standby. The theory claims that scientific knowledge proceeds in fits and starts, with theories fighting to the death, as it were, against each other, rather than as a smooth process of the accumulation and refinement that we tend to imagine.

In it, Kuhn says that problems and weaknesses in a theory accumulate, with a process of accommodation (either by modification for the theory or by plain suppression of conflicting information) sustaining it, until one day either a completely incompatible finding destroys its credibility, or people simply decide to move to adopt a new and supposedly better theory instead, perhaps for reasons of fashion. The modification of the PTOLOMAIC System, that is, the ancient Greek theories of how the heavenly bodies might be on crystal spheres, is a 'paradigm' example of this, as the number of spheres kept having to be increased each time observations showed a problem for the general theory.

Nonetheless, his own theory is not without problems itself, as other parts of knowledge have remained resolutely 'modifiable'; a fact of which, as a scientist, Kuhn would have been more aware than many of his earnestly 'RELATIVISTIC', non-scientific followers.

# LACAN, JACQUES (1901–81)

Lacan was a French psychoanalyst who attempted to combine FREUDIAN and Saussurean theories of how the MIND uses LANGUAGE. He writes that the UNCONSCIOUS mind is structured like language, and that language creates and governs the world through its rules, as well as forming the basis of our own identities. On this topic, he makes much of the pleasure the young child has in recognising its reflection in the mirror. 'Slips of the tongue' are really the unconscious mind communicating directly. Following Saussure, he argues that there are two aspects to symbolism: speech and language. Social relations are determined by speech, but LOGICAL relations are to be found in the rules of language. His key ideas are set out in *Ecrits I and II* (1966) and *The Ego in Freud's Theory* (1978).

## LANGUAGE

Language is philosophy. It is the medium in which we carry out the study, and it is the subject. For just as 'sense perceptions' can seem to stand between us and the world, words can seem to stand between us and our CONCEPTS. LEIBNIZ summed up this view when he wrote that 'languages are the best mirror of the human mind, and that a precise analysis of the significations of words would tell us more than anything else about the operations of the understanding'. And just as some philosophers have sought to telescope things together, by making the world only what we sense, other philosophers make our concepts only the words we use. But not many, as for most philosophers, the 'problem' of language is that it is 'imprecise', and so a perennial theme of philosophy has been both the examination (analysis) of language, and the quest for better, usually more 'LOGICAL' ways of expressing our findings. (Such was the approach of Leibniz, RUSSELL, FREGE, the LOGICAL POSITIVISTS and WITTGENSTEIN, to mention just a few.)

Probably the first philosophical treatment of the issue comes not from the Western tradition, but from the Indian, seen in Panini's Sanskrit Grammar, *Astadhayi* (*c.* 350 BCE), with the 'Great Commentary' of the Patanjali, perhaps 400 years later. The ancient Greeks were preoccupied with the question of 'universals' and how a word might describe something to which it really only approximates – like 'justice', or even 'perfect tables' (as in 'chairs', not mathematical tables). The Greeks also enquired into how words might come to be joined together and, most importantly, how they could be used correctly to make claims about the world. With this aim, ARISTOTLE produced the basis of Western philosophical logic.

Twentieth-century philosophers, such as G.E. MOORE and J.L. Austin, investigated the 'play' of words, the latter also contrasting everyday usage with a supposedly more rigorous philosophical one, while philosophers concerned with AESTHETICS have made much of the use of metaphor, which is seen by some (such as Suzanne Langer) as the essence of art, conveying meaning by symbols; and the same could be said of the operations of language, in the sense that many 'abstract' words derive from ones designating (originally) 'common or garden' objects. Others have considered language, gender and sexism; languages and animal exploitation; or language and euphemism, the baleful consequences of which allow some of the worst atrocities to be carried out 'with a clear conscience'. For example, people are very quick to learn new words to describe other people: historically we have had 'niggers', 'Jews', 'Commies', or conversely, 'bourgeoisie', and so on: all used as terms to designate people as 'the OTHER', and outside the protection of ETHICAL norms.

SEE ALSO

Linguistics

## Further reading

Everson, S., ed. (1994) *Companions to Ancient Thought 3: Language*
(An unlikely title, but an interesting source book of ancient perspectives on the philosophy of language.)

## LAO TZU (*C.* SIXTH CENTURY BCE)

Lao Tzu seems to have been a contemporary of CONFUCIUS (sixth to fifth century BCE), and is traditionally viewed as the author of the classic of **TAOISM**, the *Tao Te Ching*, or the 'Classic of the Way and Its Power'. He is revered in China as one of the three great sages, but barely acknowledged in the West. The story goes that one day Lao Tzu was unhappy with China and wanted to leave it to travel, but at the frontier a guard recognised him as the great sage and refused to let him pass unless he first recorded all his wisdom on parchment. Because of, or perhaps despite, being indubitably very wise, Lao Tzu managed to do this in just a few weeks, producing a volume of a little over 5000 Chinese characters. An early chapter reads:

Something amorphous and consummate
existed before Heaven and Earth.
Solitude! Vast! Standing alone, unaltering.
Going everywhere, yet unthreatened.
It can be considered the Mother of the
World.
I don't know its name, so I designate it,
'Tao'.
Compelled to consider it, name it 'the
Great'.

Handing the completed text to the guard, he famously mounted his bull and disappeared off, heading westward. (Images of Lao Tzu riding his bull are still popular in China to this day.)

The earliest known manuscript copies date back to the second century BCE, but for many (like the Bible) it was assumed to have a divine origin in any case, with Lao Tzu revered not merely as an author, or even a prophet, but as an immortal. Yet for those who place Lao Tzu somewhere between immortality and complete nonexistence, he was born in the sixth century BCE at Juren, in the State of Chu.

And whatever its origins, the *Tao Te Ching* is a repository of enormously powerful ideas. Just one of these is the notion of '**YIN AND YANG**'. These are the two aspects of everything in reality. Yin, the feminine aspect, is dark, soft and yielding. Yang, the masculine aspect, is bright, hard and inflexible. Everything in the world consists of both elements, and everything is in a state of flux, changing to become more yin, or more yang.

*Human beings are born soft and flexible; yet*
*when they die that are stiff and hard...*
*Plants sprout soft and delicate, yet when they die*
*they are withered and dry...*

*Thus the hard and stiff are disciples of death, the*
*soft and flexible are disciples of life.*
*Thus an inflexible army is not victorious, an*
*unbending tree will break.*
*The stiff and massive will be lessened, the soft*
*and fluid will increase.*

Another message of the *Tao Te Ching* is that everything follows certain patterns: 'the way'. Human beings should also 'follow the way', and yield to the times and influences. However, the lessons of this are not as passive and negative as many seem to assume. It is part of the philosophy that the 'way' applies to the very small as much as to the great things.

## LAW

### Essentials of law

Law is an acknowledged and enforceable body of rules governing the conduct of citizens and officials. A system that aims to set norms and standards of behaviour (and only this is capable of being identified as a legal system) must possess de facto authority, an authority that a particular society recognises as binding on itself. This applies whether the body of law is drawn from formal legislative enactment or simply from custom.

In this way, the authority of the legal system exists as a matter of fact rather than deriving itself from the right to rule. Legal systems, however, can also possess *de jure* authority, whereby the authority of the system exists as a matter of right. The structure and function of law and legal systems, the purported connection between law and morality and other human relationships and institutions, play a pervasive and important role in our everyday lives.

### Law and public morality

It is characteristic of law's origins and its nature as a social phenomenon that it involves restrictions on personal autonomy, limits individual freedom and imposes sanctions. When we ask why people ought to do things, or in the case of particular areas of law, why people should refrain from doing particular things, we are primarily concerned with their reasons to act (or refrain from acting). But what might count either in favour of or against acting, and reasons why these considerations are authoritative, are complex and much disputed. The fact that, for instance, a particular action has been prohibited by the state purports to provide individuals, not only with a justification for why they should refrain from such activities, but guidance on how one should behave. Criminal laws, for instance, provide us with reasons to *refrain* from acting by penalising the performance of such actions with fines or imprisonment. Civil laws provide us with reasons *to* act, for instance, to take particular precautions not to injure others and to honour contracts.

A number of important implications follow from how close the connection, if any, there is between law and morality. In particular, there is the question of to what extent the state can legitimately restrict the freedom of its citizens on moral grounds. If 'legal moralism' is justified, the law can be employed legitimately to prohibit conduct that conflicts with society's shared morality, possibly even in cases where such conduct does not result in harm to others. If 'legal paternalism' is justified, the law can be employed legitimately to prohibit the actions of individuals that are judged to cause harm to citizens themselves.

According to CONSERVATIVES, there is no distinct division between the notion of law and morality. The purpose of political COMMUNITY is to support the moral good of its citizens; to foster habits of good conduct and to promote valuable basic goods, such as life, health, knowledge and religion. Conservatives hold that society has a right to preserve its moral values by outlawing conduct it deems to be a violation or threat to society's shared morality. Immoral acts, such as murder, rape, theft, and so on, are prohibited in law as an expression of society's commitment to condemn conduct that is not in accordance with the moral values of the community. As such, the proper scope of the law is only limited by the community's shared sense of moral outrage and disgust. By contrast, according to the LIBERAL tradition bequeathed by J.S. MILL and others, the proper purpose of the law is only to forbid conduct that is liable to cause harm to persons. On this view, immoral conduct that does not cause others harm is not sufficient to justify using the law to prohibit the act. Liberals contend that it is questionable, and likely dubious, to believe that the criminalisation of conduct can be successfully used or normatively justified as an instrument to support a shared community morality.

Of course, questions arise concerning the legitimate limits of law in relation to the scope of the state's coercive powers. If there is no close connection between law and morality, some

## LEGAL INDETERMINACY

Legal issues are 'indeterminate' to the extent that the legitimate sources of law cannot provide a single correct answer to the question they have been asked to adjudicate. To say this, at least with respect to easy cases, is to hold that there are legal cases in which (legal) rules for their adjudication do not clearly apply. When consideration is restricted to hard cases where it is unclear which legal rules clearly apply, indeterminacy arises when it is ambiguous or controversial which legal rules should be applied, or what is required by law under the rules of the existing legal system.

Take, for example, a legal rule that forbids you to take a vehicle into a public park. This most certainly forbids an automobile, but what about bicycles? Skateboards? Toy automobiles? It is unclear whether the legal rule should classify these objects as 'vehicles', and reveals that we often have terms that have core meanings, which are generally incontrovertible, as well as terms with penumbral meanings, in which it is not entirely obvious whether the term is applicable or ruled out by the legal norm in question.

The indeterminacy of law may be caused by a number of factors, such the open texture of language used in law, vagueness and legal gaps. In these cases, the law is either silent on what is legally required or speaks with many voices, such that judges cannot decide on legal grounds which legal norms (for example, social facts concerning a law's promulgation, judicial decisions, administrative regulations and other relevant interpretative considerations) should be applied to the case at hand.

When courts cannot adjudicate hard cases on legal grounds, such cases could and may be decided only on extra-legal grounds (for example, by employing moral or political justifications). Where judges have judicial discretion to employ extra-legal grounds to decide such cases, concerns arise about whether courts are extending beyond their role of applying law on to breaking new legal ground by acting in a quasi-legislative capacity. Legal theorists have argued that this form of judicial discretion does not have to be arbitrary or unfair; instead, adjudication along these lines should employ characteristic judicial qualities, such as neutrality, impartiality and principled decision-making.

Contributor: AV

philosophers have argued that it is hard to understand how there can still be a moral obligation to obey the law. Other theorists argue that a general moral obligation to obey the law need not exist to have a reason to obey the law. There is also a concern relating to the justification for the state's ability to impose sanctions — in particular, the moral purpose and justification for punishing individuals for violating legal directives.

As well as these broader questions concerning the legitimate conditions in which the state can intervene in the lives of citizens, there are many occasions when laws play an integral role in everyday life. Indeed, it is this integral role that makes the problem of the limits of law acute. There is little agreement on how to regulate medical questions such abortion, EUTHANA-SIA, purchasing organs for transplantation and genetic engineering, or on the limits of the freedom of consenting adults to engage in activities such as the consumption of narcotics, adultery and pornography, while views on the conditions under which we can treat and kill non-human animals remain widely divergent – and this is just to name a few issues in which law and public morality are entwined.

Contributor: Adrian Viens

## LAWS OF NATURE

There is some debate over whether there really are any 'laws of nature'. EINSTEIN thought there were, saying, famously, 'God does not play dice'. NEWTON made up a few, such as the law of gravitation, which seemed to work, but still required a bit of invention, notably the concepts of 'Absolute Space' and 'Absolute Time' (neither of which anyone now thinks really exists, handy as concepts though they may continue to be). So there are two views possible: one is that the universe follows precise laws, and we make limited observations of them, learning a bit more as we go along; the other is that the universe is a mess, and we impose upon it regularities which to some extent are creations of our own.

SEE ALSO

Paradigm shifts

## LAWS OF THOUGHT

### Essential laws of thought

Western philosophy has been founded, to a very large extent, upon laws of thought. We believe

that our thinking should strive to eliminate ideas that are vague, contradictory or ambiguous, and the best way to accomplish this, and thereby ground our thinking in clear and distinct ideas, is to strictly follow laws of thought.

Ones like:

- the law of identity $(A = A)$,
- the law of non-contradiction (A does not equal ~A), and
- the law of the excluded middle (either A or not A but not both A and ~A).

In spite of how dominant these laws of thought have been, they have not been without their critics, and philosophers from HERACLITUS to HEGEL have levelled powerful arguments against them. But the issue does not seem to be whether the laws are applicable or not, but where and when they are applicable. Certainly, the laws of thought have a place, but what is that place?

### A philosophical history of the laws of thought

The laws, and the opposition to them, can be traced to the pre-Socratic philosophers. It was PARMENIDES who first formulated the law of non-contradiction. 'Never will this prevail, that what is not is.' PLATO also refers to this in the SOPHIST: 'The great Parmenides from beginning to end testified. . . "Never shall this be proved that things that are not are."' (Plato, *Sophist*, 237A)

It may seem strange that the principle of non-contradiction was not part of a natural way of thinking that had its origins deep in our prehistory, but rather was introduced by Parmenides in the fifth century BCE. Even more surprising is the fact that Parmenides' law of non-contradiction represented a radical break from the Ionian philosophy of nature, which preceded it. The Ionian philosophy was based on observation or experience in the ordinary sense. On the basis of such experience, Heraclitus argued that contradictions not only existed but were essential and the basis of a thing's identity: 'Not only could it be stated that identity is the strife of oppositions but that there could be no identity without such strife within the entity.'

Heraclitus argued that since things changed, they had to contain what they were not. Only such contradictions could account for change. As Heraclitus says, 'Cold things grow warm; warm grows cold; wet grows dry; parched grows moist.'

In opposition to Heraclitus, Parmenides claimed that identity involved the idea of non-contradiction. What made for the difference between Heraclitus and Parmenides was what they respectively believed were the proper objects of thought. For Parmenides, the things we encounter in our experience make for poor objects upon which to fix our thoughts. Indeed, the things we experience are not suited to provide the kind of knowledge that Parmenides, and so many others who were to follow him, wanted. The kind of knowledge they desired was a knowledge that was fixed and certain. Such knowledge would require objects of thought that were equally fixed and certain. Thus, Parmenides settled on the idea of being itself, into which all change would collapse.

The PYTHAGOREANS, too, desired objects of thought that were fixed and certain. For them, mathematics provided those kinds of objects. Plato also sought similar objects of thought and settled on other-worldly FORMS that were eternal and immutable. With the Platonic forms, as with Pythagorean numbers and Parmenidian being, the laws of thought are certainly applicable. Thus, Plato endorsed the laws of non-contradiction and 'excluded middle' in the *Republic* when he has SOCRATES say: 'It is obvious that the same thing will never do or suffer opposites in the same respect in relation to the same thing and at the same time' (4:436b).

Of course, Plato was well aware that in order for the laws of thought to work they needed to be restricted, for if left unrestricted they could lead to absurd conclusions. In the *Euthydemus*, Euthydemus' brother, Dionysodorus, argues that Socrates must be the father of a dog, since the dog had a father, and Socrates has admitted that he is a father (298d–299). Since one cannot be a father and not be a father at the same time, Socrates must be the father of the dog. Although Socrates is obviously not the father of the dog, it was not so obvious, in Socrates' day, where Dionysidorus' thinking was going wrong. Thus, Plato attempts to sort out where and when the laws of thought apply, and where and when they do not apply.

The restrictions Plato places on the laws of thought (that is, 'in the same respect' and 'at the same time') are an attempt to isolate the object of thought by removing it from all other TIME but the present and all respects but one. Thus, although we are involved in many relationships, when we think about ourselves relationally, we must restrict our thinking to one relationship, at one time, in order for the laws of thought to be applicable. Thus, it is not only the Platonic forms that are abstract and apart from the world of experience, but any idea to which the laws of thought are to be applied must also be abstracted from the reality of our experience, which is multi-relational and multi-temporal.

Like Plato, ARISTOTLE also believed that the laws of thought, in spite of being controversial, were cornerstones of all right thinking. He argues for them in several places (*Metaphysics*, 3&4; *De Interpretatione* 11, 21a32–33; *Topics* IV 1, 121a22–4; *Sophistical Refutations* 5, 167a1–6). It is, however, not so much that he argues for them, as he sets them in a proper light. That is, he shows where they are appropriate and where they are not appropriate. Basically, what he says is little different from Plato. He argues that such laws apply only to attributes, and attributes at a particular time and in a particular respect: 'The same attribute cannot at the same time belong and not belong to the same subject and in the same respect' (*Metaphysics* G, 3,1005b18–20).

By limiting the laws of thought in this way, Aristotle overcomes Heraclitus' claim that identity contains contradictions because the attributes of a thing change over time. By isolating identity in one moment of time, Aristotle abstracts the objects of thought, just as Plato had done. Thus, identity is set in a different light than it had been for Heraclitus, who understood identity as dynamic and thus involving change and, equally, contradictions.

But Aristotle also introduces another element to support the laws of thought further. The principle he introduces concerns the way we formulate our concepts or ideas of kinds. According to Aristotle, to establish a clear concept of the species 'man', we combine the genus 'animal' and the differentia, or that characteristic which distinguishes man from other animals, for example, that he is rational. Thus, the species 'man' is conceptualised as, 'rational animal'. Our desire for clear and distinct concepts has made Aristotle's model for conceptualising species enormously influential in Western thinking. In biology we classify and understand species under a single lineage, whereby each concept or idea of a species belongs to only one genus. Every family of living things belongs to only one order, and every order belongs to only one class, and every class to only one phylum and kingdom. Such ordering gives us neat and clear concepts and satisfies our desire to conceptualise things in as simple and clear a way as possible. But the platypus does not fit neatly into a single genus, or, more precisely, into the class designated as 'mammal'. In fact, many species do not seem to fit such a neat Aristotelian model, and might better be conceived if we understood them to belong to more than a single genus.

This Aristotelian model for conceptualising species has not only been applied to biological species: we attempt to organise all our experience in a similar fashion. In spite of the fact that many of our concepts might be better conceived if we understood them as descending from multiple genuses, the Aristotelian model of concepts that descend from a single genus is deeply entrenched in our thinking. One of the reasons behind its entrenchment is that such a principle allows the laws of thought to work consistently and appear universal. On another model in which concepts are thought to descend from multiple genuses, the laws of thought are not as applicable because, as a member of more than a single genus, a concept could contain contradictory attributes.

With the modern era, a mechanical view of the universe replaced Aristotle's biological paradigm. Things were no longer organic wholes, but composites and, as such, more compatible with an analytic way of thinking that broke things down into ever smaller parts until all contradictions disappeared and the laws of thought prevailed. Basic to this mechanical view, known as the 'corpuscular philosophy', was an apparent distinction between the kinds of qualities that we attribute to physical entities. Qualities such as shape, extension, motion, and so on, were thought to exist within the objects themselves, while tastes, smells, COLOURS, and so on, were said to exist within us. The former kind were referred to as 'primary' and the latter kind as 'secondary', as John LOCKE argued in his *Essay Concerning Human Understanding* (II. viii. 17). So, a physical thing like a strawberry, while not actually possessing anything that resembles the taste or smell of the strawberry, does have the power to produce those sensations within us because of the arrangement and motion of the insensible corpuscles that make up the strawberry's internal structure. By contrast, when we perceive that the strawberry is extended, we are perceiving a quality that represents the thing itself, since the strawberry is made up of corpuscles and corpuscles are extended.

Thus, the claim of the corpuscularians was

that primary qualities were more real than secondary qualities. Of course, what is meant by 'more real' is that primary qualities seem to be more objective than the subjective, secondary qualities. But why should we privilege the objective over the subjective? One reason, perhaps the most important reason, is that the laws of thought are more applicable when SUBJECTIVITY is removed. Subjectivity certainly undermines the laws of thought. While a thing can be sweet and not sweet at the same time, it cannot not be square and round, nor in motion and at rest, at the same time. Consequently, primary qualities make better objects of thought, in the sense that the laws of thought apply better with them than with secondary qualities. *What has in fact taken place, however, is that the objects of thought have been made ever more abstract and removed from the reality of the world we actually experience.*

Traditional logic, then, seeks a realm over which the laws of thought can assert sovereign rule. Once proper objects of thought have been created through ABSTRACTION, the laws of thought certainly apply. Others such as Hegel would argue, however, that these laws of thought do not apply when the objects of thought are not such abstract entities. Thus, the laws of thought do not rule universally over all thinking, but are only universal when the objects of thought are abstracted from the reality of the phenomenal world. If we turn our attention to the world of experience, 'everything is inherently contradictory.' Thus, Hegel posits the law of contradiction, rather than the law of non-contradiction.

As it was for Heraclitus, reality for Hegel (as for later 'EXISTENTIALISTS') is something that moves, thus making any fixed, abstract identity impossible. Things are always 'becoming', and so they must contain within themselves that which they are not. Contradiction is the root of all movement and vitality; it is only in so far as something has a contradiction within it that it moves, has an urge and activity.

A little later, Hegel says something that is even more shocking to those who strictly adhere to the traditional laws of thought and imagine them to be the basis of all right thinking:

Something moves, not because at one moment it is here and at another there, but because at one and the same moment it is here and not here, because in this 'here', it at once is and is not.

Hegel even attacks the law of identity and claims that the law of identity says very little in itself. The fact that A = A is no more than a TAU-TOLOGY and has little meaning. It tells us almost nothing about the identity of a thing. The only way a thing truly takes on identity is through its otherness, or what it is not. What a thing *is not* is as necessary to the identity of a thing as what it *is*, in that what it *is not* is what gives boundaries, definition and meaning to a thing. Thus, its otherness must be contained within the very identity of the thing.

When Plato and Aristotle qualify the law of non-contradiction and say 'in the same respect', and 'at the same time', what they are doing is breaking a thing down into its parts. If we focus on ever smaller parts, we can eventually eliminate all contradictions and thus preserve the law of non-contradiction and the law of the excluded middle. When, however, we deal with the whole, rather than the parts, we are treating all the respects or parts together, and then we certainly may encounter contradictions and the truth is often both/and, rather than either/or.

When we say that life is full of joy and sorrow, we can eliminate that contradiction, or any such contradiction, by analysing life and dividing it into joyous parts and sorrowful parts. That is, in one respect it is joyous and in another respect it is sorrowful. If, however, we leave life (or anything else) whole and do not analyse it into this respect or that respect, we see myriads of contradictions because that is the nature of the reality in which we live. We have been taught to think analytically about abstracted parts of our experience in order that the laws of thought can be neatly applied, but that is only one way of thinking. We can also think about wholes rather than parts and when we do, the laws of thought do not always apply.

This does not mean that there is no place for analytic thinking and the laws of thought. Analytic thinking is a mode of thought we use all the time. The problem lies in the fact that Western intellectual history has been intent on creating an understanding that is founded upon universal laws, and, in order to create such universal laws, we have attempted to eliminate all objects of thought to which such laws do not universally apply. And that is itself 'irrational', since there are obviously such dynamic and HOLISTIC objects of thought.

Twentieth-century science has discovered the bicameral nature of the human brain, and although pop psychology might be too quick to draw hard and fast lines between the two hemispheres of the brain in assigning analytic thought to the one and synthetic thought to the other, there certainly is something to the fact that the physiology of our brains allow us to think in different ways. Analytic thinking, based upon one hemisphere of the brain, has dominated in the West. Thus, it is no wonder that the laws of thought seem so absolute to so many.

But to apply the laws of thought strictly to all our thinking is perhaps to use only half your wits.

(This is an edited version of an article originally printed in *The Philosopher*.)

Contributor: James Danaher

# LEARNING

## Essentials of learning

Learning is the 'acquisition of knowledge', or perhaps the development of skills in the application of already existent knowledge. Reassuringly, perhaps, HEGEL said that even if we do not remember what we have learned, it is nonetheless still there within us. On the other hand, PLATO seems to show that a lot of things we might want to learn, for example, how to be good, can only be achieved if we do, 'deep down', know all about them already.

## Learning and gateways to hidden knowledge

The human mind, as FREUD famously put it, is like the iceberg: mostly submerged, with only a small portion appearing above the waterline. The 'submerged area' of the iceberg that is the mind is very hard to access and, as a result, has often been neglected both by philosophers and educators. It has been described as the area of 'psychological blindness'.

Conventional learning is carried out by the individual, either, as many philosophers would have it, by INTROSPECTION and analysis of eternal truths already written in their hearts or, as modern schooling assumes, by 'absorption' of already discovered knowledge, usually by institutional, mechanical means. But the much greater resource of 'intra-personal' knowledge can only be explored by means of human interaction.

The PSYCHOLOGICAL aspects were explained graphically by the Johari Window, developed by Joe Luft and Harry Ingham in the USA in the 1950s. The word 'Johari' was intended as rather a silly play on 'Joe' and

'Harry', signifying the nature of interaction, but it emerged, to the authors' surprise, that it is a word with many more subtle and profound connotations, meaning in Hindi: 'one who knows the value of gems'; and in Swahili: 'someone who is brave and strong'. According to Dr Luft's model, when Joe and Harry interact, there are four aspects to their awareness of the behaviour, feelings and motivations of each other, which he represented in the four quadrants of the 'Johari window' (see figure).

|  | Known to self | Not known to self |
|---|---|---|
| Known to others | 1 Open — I know, you know | 2 Blind — You know, I don't know |
| Not known to others | 3 Hidden — I know, you don't know | 4 Unknown — Neither of us know |

The Johari window (after Luft and Ingham)

When two people are engaged in a trusting relationship (quintessentially, the 'learning relationship') their interaction in the 'open area' of shared knowledge or awareness will be extended and the 'hidden area' will be shrinking. And as a result of mutual disclosures by the two people, light is thrown onto each other's 'blind' area.

Although the 'unknown' area is difficult to penetrate on their own, if the two people work together, they may be able to make a breakthrough and disclose something hidden, and something previously unknown to their awareness.

Conventionally, knowledge is regarded as received, academic and research-based, and as fixed and eternal rather than tentative and temporary (a view of the world sometimes called the 'the technical rationalist model'). Scientists attempt to find laws and principles which should apply 'universally. In the process, we take a REDUCTIONIST view of human life, assuming that it could be easily reduced to categories, and that these will then be generalisable and applicable to practice. The denial of human values by the 'technical rationalists' must neglect the soft, practical wisdom of 'the-person-in-the-world' as opposed to the hard, superior knowledge of the expert. Real learning, then, is supposed to lie in the theories and techniques of basic and applied science. Knowledge and skills are accessible only through external intervention. But this kind of learning is often of value *only to a world that has already been passed by.*

This kind of learning neglects human values, the central role of human relationships and the myriad effects of social settings and context. In so doing, it creates a gap between theory and practice and ultimately leads to the dehumanisation of knowledge. In schools and colleges, teachers are reduced to mere technicians, deprived of power, with the tasks of the production and distribution of knowledge. Power is placed instead into the hands of politicians and 'expert' researchers who set the criteria for

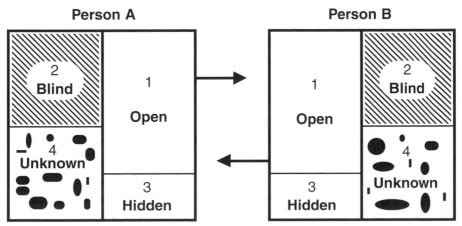

Human interaction windows

assessing the success of their own projects. The teachers' personal knowledge and strategies are seen as slow, unpredictable and excessively individualistic, to the point of being self-indulgent, and so are ignored. But without teachers' own idiosyncracies, intuitions and, yes, values, a key reality of the long development of EDUCATION and learning also drains away.

Contributor: Lisa Wang

# LEIBNIZ, GOTTFRIED (1646–1716)

Leibniz was born in Berlin and later became one of the founders of its academy. A LOGICIAN and mathematician, he is remembered today mainly as a 'RATIONALIST' philosopher, whose name is often linked with DESCARTES and SPINOZA. He lived a bachelor existence in the service of the Archbishop of Mainz and at the court of the Elector of Hannover, while energetically corresponding with most of the other thinkers in Europe at the time, as well as with many of the 'names' in high society. He famously fell out with Isaac NEWTON in England, over the question of which of them had invented CALCULUS. His theories of space and time were important historically, but were not ultimately convincing to others working in the field.

Gottfried Leibniz, 'an elegant man in a powdered wig', as one contemporary summed him up, spent most of his life deep in philosophic contemplation, revealing himself to the world only through learned correspondences with several hundreds of other philosophers and scientists. Even so, his influence in seventeenth-century intellectual circles was great, much to the envy of Sir Isaac Newton.

Newton also wanted to make not only matter and time 'real', but space as well, otherwise, without 'absolute space', his theory of mechanics could not function. Instead, MIND becomes of dubious reality, an anachronism in an increasingly mechanical world, even if Newton himself searched lifelong through the alchemical works of the ancients for just such a unifying element. Leibniz, by contrast, while accepting that matter and time exist, disputes 'absolute space'. Instead, he unified the cosmos with the mind of God.

. . . To conclude. If the space (which the author fancies) void of all bodies, is not altogether empty; what is it then full of? Is it full of extended spirits perhaps, of material substances, capable of extending and contracting themselves; which over therein, and penetrate each other without inconveniency, as the shadows of two bodies penetrate one another upon the surface of a wall. . . Nay, some have fancies that man, in the state of innocency, had also the gift of penetration; and that he became solid, opaque, and impenetrable by his fall. Is it not overthrowing our notions of things, to make God have parts, to make spirits have extension? The principle of the want of a sufficient reason does alone drive away these spectres of the imagination. Men easily run into fictions, for want of making a right use of that great principle. . .

I don't say that matter and space are the same thing. I only say, there is no space where there is no matter; and that space in itself is not an absolute reality. Space and matter differ, as time and motion. However, these things, though different, are inseparable.'

*(From Leibniz's fifth letter to Samuel Clarke)*

Leibniz, like many other philosophers before and since, sought to make the world more rational, by rearranging the universe into fundamental and eternal 'simple facts' (logical atoms, as Bertrand RUSSELL similarly describes it). These are then the ultimate building blocks of reality, and Leibniz gives them a special name: the 'MONADS'. Knowledge is essentially a matter of analysing these 'building blocks' of reality.

Leibniz also thought that it was possible and desirable to construct an artificial language to better exhibit the logical form of ARGUMENTS. In describing his famous 'monads', Leibniz explained they do not appear, but we must postulate them in logic – in order to explain reality and understand the meaningfulness of language.

In the *Discourse on Metaphysics* (1666) and the *General Inquiries* (1681), as well as the *Monadology* (1714), he explores his theory and described possible complex arrangements of his 'monads'.

His conclusion from all this was that the world was in fact perfect, the 'best of all possible worlds', as VOLTAIRE sarcastically put it, and needed no supervision from God or anyone else.

# LENIN, VLADIMIR ILYCH (1870–1924)

Lenin was a POLITICAL PHILOSOPHER as well as a practical revolutionary who wrote mainly on MARXISM, moving on to political action in the role of leader of the October Revolution in Russia in 1917. It was Lenin who converted MARX and ENGEL's writings into the official 'dialectical materialism' philosophy of the Soviet Union, emphasising as he did the role of the Party and the need for constant reaffirmation of revolutionary principles through action. He was DOGMATIC by nature, but after reading HEGEL, accepted the philosophical point that ideas are part of an evolutionary process. His writings became a kind of 'road map' for COMMUNIST revolutionaries, identifying just where a society was in terms of its economic and political development, and the strategies needed to move forward, both in pre-revolutionary and post-revolutionary society. Ultimately, Lenin thought, SOCIALIST society would produce the creative freedom of all.

# LEUCIPPUS (FIFTH CENTURY BCE)

Leucippus was the first of the ancient Greek philosophers to suggest that the world might be made up of tiny atoms. Like other great philosophers, there is some dispute about whether he really existed, and if he did, what he might have said. Of his one known work, an overview of how the universe works, entitled *The Great World System*, only one tiny fragment remains, which asserts that everything is predetermined, as in a machine.

SEE ALSO

Democritus

# LEVIATHAN

See Hobbes.

# LEVINAS, EMMANUEL (1906–95)

## The essential Levinas

Born into a Jewish family in Lithuania, Levinas moved to France at the age of 17, where he remained for the better part of his life. His university studies brought him into personal contact with two of the key figures in early twentieth-century German philosophy: Edmund HUSSERL and Martin HEIDEGGER. While highly indebted to both, it was Heidegger who would become the central target of Levinas' own, distinct philosophy. He is frequently credited as the major impetus behind what has come to be called the 'ethical turn' in contemporary European thought. It is a measure of Levinas' ability to speak to a diverse readership that his writing has influenced not only fellow European philosophers like Jacques DERRIDA, but also thinkers far removed from the European tradition, such as the American ANALYTIC philosopher, Hilary Putnam. Beyond philosophy, Levinas' ideas concerning the relationship between 'SELF' and 'OTHER' have had a considerable impact in fields as diverse as education, psychotherapy and religious studies.

## Ethics as the encounter with 'the other'

Prior to Levinas, continental philosophy seemed to demonstrate a deep-seated aversion to ETHICS. This lack of interest in ethics had much to do with Heidegger's influence. Heidegger privileges what he calls the 'question of being' (*Seinsfrage*) over ethics. For him, addressing this question is the principal task of 'fundamental ontology', by which he means the study of being as it unfolds in time. By contrast, traditional ONTOLOGY, according to Heidegger, had misconstrued being as something timeless. In his mind, ethics is a branch of traditional ontology. And if the trunk – that is, traditional ontology – is virtually lifeless, then the branch is even more so. In his *Letter on Humanism* (1947) Heidegger hints at the possibility of recovering a more primordial ethics. But he still subsumes such an enterprise under what he claims to be the more original task of thinking through the problem of being and time. In his view, a proper understanding of ethics is possible only once we have a better grasp of the complex temporal unfolding of being.

Not surprisingly, given the priority placed on the question of being by Heidegger, and given his influence, ethics would receive little attention in Europe for several decades to come. Levinas, however, would eventually break with his teacher on the question of the place of ethics in philosophy. This dissatisfaction was finally made explicit in 1947 when Levinas declared that his own thought was 'governed by a profound need to leave the climate of [Heidegger's] philosophy'. In pursuing his own path, Levinas would, in time, challenge a new generation of philosophers to think more deeply about the nature of ethics.

Levinas sought to demonstrate that Heidegger's suspicion of ethics, while superficially correct, betrays a blind spot typical of the Western philosophical tradition. Heidegger is correct in arguing that ethics is a mere branch of ontology if by 'ethics' we mean rules, norms and moral theories. But the error that Levinas thought Heidegger made here is to assume that these categories exhaust the significance of ethics. Levinas reserves the term 'ethics' to refer to the non-ontological source of moral prescriptions, laws and theories about morality. This source, as Levinas shows, is neither an idea nor an entity. Nor can ethics, as Levinas understands the term, be understood as that which emerges from within the temporal horizon of being. Ethics – to borrow the title of Levinas' well-known work – is 'otherwise than being'. And since both traditional philosophy and its critics (including Heidegger) are so preoccupied with ontology (the problem or question of being), neither can do justice to ethics.

Levinas would spend the greater part of his career describing ethics as that provocation of 'the other', which eventually leads us to develop and conceive of customs, laws and moral theories. By the 'other' (or 'neighbour'), Levinas means the singularly unique person who stands before me in the guise of a disappointed friend or lover, a dependent child, a stranger in my midst who seeks orientation, the homeless person I encounter on the sidewalk, and so forth. Only 'the other', Levinas contends, has the power to personally obligate me. This power was formerly understood as a facet of impersonal ontology; for example, PLATO's 'Good' (the Form of Forms) or KANT's 'Categorical Imperative'. But as Levinas argues, ideas and principles, however sublime or noble, lack the binding force hoped for by philosophers.

Impersonal principles are simply too abstract and general to solicit my finite being. Levinas repeatedly underscores the fact that it is other human beings who disrupt the EGO's narcissism, and not philosophical notions, no matter how sophisticated the latter might be. That 'the other' has this remarkable power over me testifies to a feature of his or her nature that remains outside my grasp. This is what Levinas means by the 'alterity' of 'the other'.

Ethics, thus conceived, with an emphasis on the irreducible strangeness of 'the other', cannot be understood adequately in terms of ontology. Levinas' original contribution to philosophy is to show that the true nature of ethics eludes the classical categories of ontology: 'whatness', power, appearance and visibility. When Levinas identifies ethics with 'the other', it is important that we do not imagine that this has something to do with the physical being of the other person. Even before I notice the colour of her eyes, 'the other' silently commands me not to harm her, nor to force her to conform to my image of her. In this respect, Levinas notes, I hear 'the other' before I see her.

Levinas himself fully acknowledges the difficult task of describing the ethical encounter. How does one articulate that which by definition eludes ontology and, by extension, cognitive understanding? Levinas adopts a strategy of deploying the terminology and signposts of classical philosophy, but he does so in a peculiar manner. For example, when he employs the word 'transcendence' to describe the encounter with 'the other', he does so without suggesting the classical connotation of this term. For Levinas, transcendence does not refer to some separate, more perfect, reality behind our world, but rather the transformative force that others have on us. That I undergo transcendence in relation to 'the other' means for Levinas that 'the other' draws me out of my self-centred being.

Similarly, Levinas reinterprets the ideas of certain classical philosophers in a novel manner to reflect his conception of the ethical encounter. Thus Descartes, while correct in noting that we intuit the presence of God by way of the Infinite, was, Levinas thinks, wrong to frame it in EPISTEMOLOGICAL terms. (According to Descartes: I have the idea of the Infinite within me. As a finite creature I cannot possibly be the author of this idea. Only some entity that is equally infinite could account for that idea.

Therefore, God exists.) In Levinas' version of this argument, the divine comes to mind whenever I am confronted by the disquieting presence of 'the other'. In my dealings with 'the other', what remains is the awkward sense that 'something,' an 'infinite' presence, not of my own making, nor of this world, has effectively displaced my centre of attention. In this way 'the other's' inexorable capacity to call me into question insinuates the divine without ever positing it as such.

This last point might remind some of the philosophy of another important twentieth-century Jewish thinker, Martin Buber. But whereas Buber emphasised the reciprocal character of the 'I-Thou' experience, saying that both self and 'other' are mutually transformed by such experiences, Levinas insists that the nature of the ethical encounter is not symmetrical, and that when 'the other' impinges on my space, I am the one who is called to account for myself in his or her presence. This may eventually prompt dialogue and reciprocity, but it can happen only after the fact. Prior to reciprocation, I find myself completely beholden to 'the other'.

It is Levinas' strong conviction that if the ethical moment were truly reciprocal in character it would not be able to account for the intense sense of obligation that I feel personally – for example, in the form of a guilty conscience. In this respect, Levinas is often fond of quoting Dostoevsky's famous line from *The Brothers Karamazov*.

Every one of us is guilty before all, for everyone and everything, and I more than others.

Contributor: John Caruana

## Further reading

Levinas, E. (1961) *Totality and Infinity*

Levinas, E. (1974) *Otherwise than Being*

## LÉVI-STRAUSS, CLAUDE (1908–)

Claude Lévi-Strauss originally studied law and philosophy. He lived for a number of years in South America and subsequently became one of France's foremost anthropologists. His work was extremely influential on English and American anthropology and, to some extent, entered a wider cultural domain. Lévi-Strauss saw himself as a KANTIAN idealist.

Lévi-Strauss argues that the world exists in a chaotic state, onto which ideas impose structure and significance. The world itself cannot be directly apprehended. He was greatly influenced by the work of the LINGUIST, Ferdinand Saussure. In much of his writing he explored myth and ritual as a series of arbitrary signs, which order reality. In his monumental work, *Mythologiques*, Lévi-Strauss developed the theory of STRUCTURALISM, the idea that complex patterns of symbol and myth can be decoded into a series of binary oppositions.

Lévi-Strauss developed the key opposition between NATURE and CULTURE, to which earlier writers, such as Van Gennep, had drawn attention. For Lévi-Strauss, human beings are poised between the two contradictory states of nature and culture. Subsequent anthropologists have been concerned with how human myth and ritual are concerned with marking the difference between these states. However, Lévi-Strauss himself accepted that structural analysis ultimately did not arrive at any underlying significance. He thought that the world of signs eventually only reflected the cognitive structures of the human mind.

## Further reading

Lévi-Strauss, C. (1962) *The Savage Mind* (*La Pensée Sauvage*)

## LÉVY-BRUHL, LUCIEN (1857–1939)

The French social anthropologist Lévy-Bruhl argued, following his countryman Auguste COMTE, that a science of society should regulate behaviour and social norms, instead of METAPHYSICAL and religious notions. It is only at the higher levels of theoretical thought that we can see things properly, and members of primitive societies are 'pre-logical', as a result of their social context. Emotions, to put it very loosely, cloud judgement. Levy-Bruhl is interested in the irrational and emotional behaviour these pre-logical societies allow, but over the period of his career, he came to realise that the same kinds of irrationality exist in even the most technically advanced society.

## LIAR PARADOX

The 'All Cretans are liars' type of PARADOX has kept philosophers, from ARISTOTLE to AQUINAS, and back again to ZENO, busy for countless years. The paradox originated with the ancient Greek philosopher, Epimenides, who is supposed to have claimed that people from Crete always told lies. This was not only somewhat racist, but somewhat inexplicable, as he himself was from Crete. If it was true, then what he himself was saying should have been a lie, but if it were a lie, then. . . The truth of the claim affects the circumstances it is uttered in, which affects the truth of the claim, which . . . and so on and so on: an infinite twisting and turning of the truth. Effectively, the statements are neither true nor false, although they look like they ought to be.

SEE ALSO

Paradoxes

# LIBERALISM AND LIBERTARIANISM

Liberalism is unquestionably one of the great survivors of political theory. It is, essentially, an English doctrine with four English philosophers, HOBBES, LOCKE, BENTHAM and MILL, as its founding figures. At its heart, though, is a contradiction: there is the UTILITARIAN ethic, adopted from Jeremy Bentham, in opposition to the appeal to fundamental rights of John Locke. Yet despite different starting points, both arrive at the characteristic set of individual rights and freedoms.

Liberalism offers individuals equality before the law, and at the same time, it accords individuals secondary status to that law, and the institutions and authorities embodying it. The free market vision of society is rooted in fear, the central justification behind the state, at least in Thomas Hobbes' and John Locke's brand of 'DEMOCRACY'. In Hobbes' case, fear of death or exploitation; in Locke's, and many contemporary CAPITALIST societies, fear of loss of their material possessions (or fear of the consequences of attempting to steal other people's goods). Liberalism does not even suggest any positive purpose for human existence: perhaps thinking individuals should find it for themselves.

While Thomas Hobbes, John Locke and the architects of the American Declaration of Independence held that rights were largely a means of protecting the individual from the rapacious desires of their neighbours, the rights also appeared to include more positive freedoms to create and develop just the sort of freedoms that lay behind the economic expansion spearheaded by the Protestant entrepreneurs who created the European Industrial Revolution.

If Mill himself writes that 'after the means of subsistence are assured, the next in strength of the personal wants of human beings is liberty'; today, liberalism is increasingly inadequate as a response to the all-seeing, all-powerful State, the preoccupation with which is the province of libertarians. But then liberalism was always essentially freedom from, rather than freedom to. Freedom from arbitrary laws or taxes, from being made to work against one's will, freedom from being told what to believe and freedom from being obliged to participate in social activities that cannot be justified by being necessary for the well-being of the community. It is not freedom to work, or to live in a home, or to be healthy – as the ever widening underclasses of the consumer societies can vouch. F.A. HAYEK, in *The Road to Serfdom*, his influential book, written in the aftermath of the Second World War, specifically warns that 'nothing has done so much harm to the liberal cause as the wooden insistence of some liberals on certain rough rules of thumb, above all the principles of *laisser-faire*'. Instead, the correct attitude of the liberal towards society should be more like that of good gardeners towards their plants – they tend them carefully and try to create the conditions in which they can flourish.

# LIBERTY

'Liberty' needs to be treated slightly differently from freedom. Liberty is essentially legalistic, about who makes the laws, and whether these laws are 'proper', in the sense that they do not go beyond their proper scope; for example, if they assert the rights of one group over another (as in the USA, laws banning black people from white buses prior to the Civil Rights movements of the 1960s) or in curtailing rights, such as freedom of speech, or limiting 'activities', as in restrictions on religious freedom. There are thus two questions: Who shall govern me? and, What shall be governed?

Although the original French revolutionary rallying cry of 'liberty, equality and fraternity' made liberty very much one of the socialist goals, today the term often implies INDIVIDUALISM, which is in opposition to notions of social life, and is used as such to criticise societies governed by the ideal 'one-mindedness' of traditional CONFUCIANISM, such as Chinese society today.

SEE ALSO

Freedom

## LIFE, THE MEANING OF

What is the meaning of life? Or: What is the purpose of existence? Once upon a time people looked to religious teachings for the answer, but today, most philosophical pundits cluster around the vaguely 'scientific' view that the purpose of being alive is simply to pass on your 'genetic material', through sex, and producing children.

There is actually quite a lot of circumstantial evidence for this. First, the sexual drive is very strong, and seems to achieve little other than the production of children. Second, at least among some of the population, there is a tendency to look after these children and make sacrifices for them which really cannot be explained in any other way than as an investment in their own genetic future. (Certainly not ALTRUISM, as other people's children do not arouse the same interest!) This is the 'selfish gene' determining behaviour. All our other behaviour (football, art, killing other people – and their children) can be explained this way. And we are even designed to die shortly after the children have grown up and finished with us. It's tidy, even if not very nice!

Perhaps the drawback with this argument is that it only seems to put the question one stage further off. For what is the point of our children's existence?

## LIFEBOAT ANALOGY

The lifeboat THOUGHT EXPERIMENT, as made popular by the contemporary philosopher, Garret Hardin, simply asks: 'If there is an overcrowded lifeboat and the only way to prevent the boat from sinking is to throw one or two people overboard – is it justified?' The scenario is not straightforward. Hardin used the example to make a point about the 'overpopulation' argument that mass death of people in third world countries is the price necessary for the survival of the rest. There are various arguments that may be made, one is that to kill is worse than to 'allow to die'; another is that you cannot be sure that the 'rescue vessel' is not about to turn up and overturn (so to speak) the calculations. In the wider world case, there is no reason to accept the analogy at all; indeed, since the USA consumes one-third of the world resources

yet constitutes only 3 or 4 per cent of the population, it would seem perverse to 'sacrifice' the world's poor. Another US philosopher, Tom Regan, used the scenario with a dog in the boat to make a similarly weak case against animal rights.

## LIGHT

The understanding of light was rightly considered a central question for philosophers, up until the point when NEWTON seemed (annoyingly for the true philosophers) to have solved it. PLATO suggested it was to be taken allegorically as rays from the 'fire in the eye', illuminating all that they fell upon, albeit for some reason aided by the presence of the greater fire, the Sun. ARISTOTLE then made this literally the case, despite the observed peculiarity of the ray sending its rays to the stars and back in a trice. Today, you will not find 'light' discussed at all in the standard dictionaries of philosophy, even though it remains central to many historical texts. Despite this, the importance of light was re-acknowledged in EINSTEIN's theory of relativity.

## LINGUISTICS

Some philosophers maintain (absurdly) that linguistics is a branch of ANALYTIC philosophy, even crediting WITTGENSTEIN with its creation, and indeed at Oxford, Humpty-Dumpty-like (for Humpty is remembered for saying that words mean whatever he wants them to mean), that is the way the term is used. Yet in reality, the analysis of how language works has always been one of the central themes of philosophy, clearly evident in PLATO and ARISTOTLE. In the nineteenth and twentieth centuries, linguistics flowered into a separate, quasi-scientific discipline. Its key figures include Ferdinand de Saussure (1857–1913), who said that language was a system of signs which were in themselves entirely arbitrary; Benjamin Lee Whorf (1897–1941), who is remembered for arguing that the particular language we use influences the way we see the world; and the contemporary sociolinguist Noam Chomsky, who – *au contraire!* – is celebrated for claiming that all humans share a kind of 'hard-wired' fundamental GRAMMAR, seen as a sort of metaphorical or actual 'language learning organ', and different languages are merely superficially different, constructed using it. Thus we have the 'deep structure' of the hard grammar, and the 'surface structure' of the individual languages.

In fact, Chomsky's deep structure begins to look a bit like that ancient world of Plato's 'FORMS', with its perfect 'justice', 'beauty', 'tables' and 'chairs'. Anxious to avoid this conclusion, modern sociolinguistics offers a baffling array of technical jargon and supposed biological evidence of the linguistic connections in the brain, notwithstanding the perennial problem of explaining how even a 'synapse firing' can represent say, a colour, if colours are themselves defined solely by the ability to make certain synapses fire in the brain.

# LOCKE, JOHN (1632–1704)

## The essential Locke

John Locke was born in a quiet Somerset village into a Puritan trading family, and into a (rather less quiet) period of Civil War between Parliament and Royalists. His interests ranged widely, with his 1689 *Essay Concerning Human Understanding* reflecting the mechanistic science of the time, by detailing how the mind might take in 'simple or complex ideas' via the senses to assemble knowledge, which he describes as 'nothing but the perception of the connexion and agreement... of our ideas' (IV i 2). Since this rules out the possibility of innate knowledge, his philosophy was seen as an antidote to DESCARTES'.

However, it is his political theory, set out in the *Two Treatises on Government* (1690), that has been,

over time, the more influential. Like PLATO, this starts with a search for moral authority. And like Plato, he makes human conscience behoven only to God for judgement on all matters, placing individual judgement firmly above that of both Church and State, and limiting the latter's role to protecting property. 'All being equal and independent, no one ought to harm another in his life, health, liberty, or possessions', he proclaims.

John Locke fitted the times so well (Bertrand RUSSELL even described him as the 'apostle of the Revolution of 1688') that his philosophy was actively adopted by contemporary politicians and thinkers, and his ideas were transmitted to eighteenth-century France through the medium of VOLTAIRE's writings, to inspire the principles of the French revolution, and on then to America, too.

Locke creates a picture of the world in which 'rationality' is the ultimate authority, not God, and certainly not, as HOBBES had insisted, brute force. He argues that people all have certain fundamental 'rights' and also attempts to return the other half of the human race, the female half, to their proper, equal, place in history, the family and in government. His is the first, essentially practical, even legalistic, framework and analysis of the workings of society.

## Life, liberty and the pursuit of wealth

John Locke is the intellectual forebear of much of today's political orthodoxy, a role that befits a thinker of a naturally orthodox turn of mind. Like Thomas Hobbes, the upheaval of the English Civil War is the background to his writings and it no doubt had its influence. But, notwithstanding this, Locke seemed to enjoy a placid enough childhood, undisturbed by the activities of the rebellious Parliamentarians, including among their number his father. Even the execution of King Charles in 1649, while he was a schoolboy, failed to radicalise him. Instead, Locke rose steadily up through English society until well into middle age, particularly after rather fortuitously saving the Earl of Shaftesbury's life by performing a hazardous but successful operation on him. (At this time, of course, any successful operation had the nature of something of a miracle, requiring lavish rewards.)

The Earl of Shaftesbury went on to three notable political achievements: he led the opposition to Charles II; he founded the Whig Party, the forerunner of the Liberals; and he pushed Locke into politics. Locke would become one of the most influential POLITICAL PHILOSO-PHERS of all time.

The Civil War itself represented a flare-up in the perennial dispute between the king and his parliament of aristocrats (and bishops), who were always seeking a greater role, particularly in the setting of tariffs and the levying of taxes, as well as in the conduct of religious affairs. Eventually, the dispute was resolved on the battlefield by Cromwell's New Model Army, in favour of the Independents. After a period of increasingly less democratic parliaments, the rule of the 'Lord Protector', and with it England's first republic, rapidly descended into a personal dictatorship. By the time of Cromwell's death, most English were relieved to have Charles' son return as, effectively, their first constitutional monarch, bound to parliament by the principles of habeas corpus and the need to seek its approval for new taxes. And perhaps there was another, more subtle, legacy of the Civil War – a fear and dislike of over-powerful individuals.

Locke's political writing is mainly presented in academic style as a response to issues raised before him by writers such as Hugo GROTIUS, the Dutch lawyer and statesman with a special interest in ETHICS and international law; or by the English political theorist (pundit, we might say today), Sir Robert Filmer. Filmer's royalist tract, *Patriarcha* (1680), earned the author his knighthood. It also earned him a particular notoriety in the eyes of the Parliamentarians, who later vented their pent-up frustration during the war by ransacking his house, not just once, but ten times.

It is with an eye to Sir Robert's comfortable, traditionalist thesis that people are *naturally* born unfree and unequal, and rulers are equally naturally over them – directly descended from the First Man (Adam, who had been given dominion over all creation by God himself) – that John Locke begins his political writings. The *Essay Concerning the True, Original Extent and End of Civil Government* starts by declaring that:

> . . . it is impossible that the rulers now on earth should make any benefit, or derive any the least shadow of authority, from that which is held to be the fountain of all power, Adam's private dominion and paternal jurisdiction, so that he that will not

give just occasion to think that all government in the world is the product only of force and violence, and that men live together by no other rules but that of the beasts, where the strongest carries it, and so lay a foundation for perpetual disorder and mischief, tumult, sedition and rebellion. . .

At this time, the prevailing view, exemplified by Sir Robert, was that the State (personified in the monarch), through its officers, had the same sort of authority over the citizen as a father (in a patriarchal society) had over his children, or a squire over his servant, a lord over his slave – or a man over his wife. Locke takes them all on, outspoken and unusual in his firm advocacy of women's rights.

Like Hobbes (who published the *Leviathan* while Locke was preparing to study at Oxford), Locke goes back to consideration of the 'state of nature', where there are no laws and all may do as they will, without 'asking leave, or depending on the will of any other man'. Yet Locke also notes that it is a state of equality, and not total anarchy, and there is one rule – the 'sacred and unalterable law of self-preservation':

> The state of nature has a law of nature to govern it, which obliges everyone: and reason, which is that law, teaches all mankind, who will but consult it, that being all equal and independent, no one ought to harm another in his life, health, liberty or possessions.

Since we are all the work of the 'one omnipotent Maker', and 'furnished with like faculties, sharing all in one community of nature', there 'cannot be supposed any such subordination among us, that may authorise us to destroy one another, as if we were made for one another's uses, as the inferior ranks of creatures are for ours'. This 'state of nature', as Locke notes, still existed then, and continues to do so today, in international relations, between states.

If once one transgresses another's rights or property, then, be warned, everybody has a right to 'punish the transgressors of that law to such a degree, as may hinder its violation'. But this punishment must still be 'proportionate', only just inasmuch as it serves to undo the original harm, or to prevent future occurrences. For Locke's state of nature has two faces. It is a benign, cooperative existence originally, until an individual or group (like Cromwell and the Independents) seeks power over others. Then it becomes a state of war, with the individual entitled – nay, obliged – to use any means to regain their freedom.

This freedom is the kernel of his philosophy: 'The freedom . . . of man and liberty of acting according to his own will, is grounded on his having reason which is able to instruct him in that law he is to govern himself by. . .' It is freedom from 'absolute, arbitrary power', not necessarily freedom to do anything, but liberty to follow one's own will and volition, except where a rule, 'common to everyone of that society, and made by the legislative power erected in it', prohibits such action. To which extent his doctrine is an early kind of UTILITARIANISM, the engine of a machine with the aim of increasing the sum of human happiness. Locke has in mind only the *enlightened* self-interest of individuals. But in the priority he gives to individual rights, Locke appeals to a moral conception which is beyond self-interest, and which lies at the heart of political LIBERALISM.

This new morality starts with the institution of property. In Locke's philosophy, property is the key to 'civil' society, and the key to property is labour. The more you work, the more you own. Initially, however, the earth, and 'all inferior creatures' belong to everyone in common – with one important exception. Each individual does own one thing, they have property in their own person. 'This nobody has any right to but himself', Locke adds (neglecting, it would seem, the issue of slavery and indeed his own investments in the Royal Africa slaving company, doing a profitable trade for him at the time). Second, 'the labour of his body, and the work of his hands', are rightly considered to belong to each individual. 'Whatever people produce through their own effort, using the commonly owned raw materials of nature, are also (properly) theirs'. This apparently SOCIALIST principle, anticipating MARX's Labour Theory of Value by some centuries, Locke amplifies further:

. . . for 'tis labour indeed that puts the difference of value on everything; and let anyone consider, what the difference is between an acre of land planted with tobacco, or sugar, sown with wheat or barley; and an acre of the same land lying in common, without any husbandry upon it.

Locke sails close to the wind here, as on other occasions, for the rights of 'non-landowners' to 'commons' in seventeenth-century England was a sensitive matter. Common ownership had already been taken rather further by the Diggers, active during the first part of Locke's life, with their 'alternative' communities. 'Commons', by definition, unenclosed areas available for grazing or, indeed, collecting acorns, were always being threatened by the aristocracy, who wished to appropriate the common land to themselves. In the rest of Europe, where there was no equivalent tradition of common land, the suggestion that people had a 'right' to the products of their labour would have been even more scurrilous and revolutionary. Even so, all Locke has in mind is a limit on appropriation. No one should take 'more than they are able to make use of' before it spoils. Whatever is beyond this, 'is more than his share, and belongs to others'. Happily, Locke hastens to add, gold and silver do not 'spoil', and therefore there is no harm in their accumulation.

Locke also assumes an effectively unlimited supply of property (as with the gold and silver), thereby avoiding the more problematic issues his theory raises:

Nobody could think himself injured by the drinking of another man, though he took a good draught, who had a whole river of the same water left him to quench his thirst. And the case of the land and water, where there is enough of both, is perfectly the same.

But although property is the foundation of political society, Locke traces its origin back not to commerce, but to 'the conjugal union'. The first society was between man and wife, and later, their children.

Conjugal society is made by a voluntary compact between man and woman: and though it consists of right in one another's bodies, as is necessary to its chief end, procreation; yet it draws with it mutual support, and assistance, and a community of interest too, as necessary not only to unite their care, and affection, but also necessary to their common offspring, who have a right to be nourished and maintained by them, till they are able to. . . shift and provide for themselves.

Locke has no particular view over the form government should take, as long as it is based on popular consent. It may be a republic, but it could be an oligarchy and there might still be a monarch. But whatever form it takes, Locke says it does need to include some 'separation of powers', and sets out fairly precisely the distinction to be made between the lawmaking part of government – the legislature – and the action-taking part – the executive. The executive must have the power to appoint and dismiss the legislature, but it does not make the one superior to the other, rather there exists a 'fiduciary trust'.

Despite the fact that 'rigged justice' was very much a central issue of the 'Glorious Revolution' (and Locke himself lived through the 'Cavalier Parliament', after all, from 1661 to 1679, which did little other than pass increasingly totalitarian and repressive laws – mainly against religious freedom), it was left to Montesquieu to argue (in his *Spirit of the Laws* some half a century later, 1748) the need for the additional separation of judicial power characteristic of the American constitution. Before the Civil War, judges could be dismissed at will by the king. After, they were removable only with the consent of both Houses of Parliament.

Locke argues, too, that because self-defence is the foundation of the law of nature, people must always be allowed to protect themselves from an unjust or tyrannical government. (Observers of the changes of 1989, and later, in Eastern Europe have claimed that these were 'Lockean' revolutions in that the people – a political community, not just a class – withdrew their assent from their governments after years of waiting and biding their time.) Locke's 'social contract' is different from Hobbes', in being not a once-and-for-all act, but an ongoing bargain between people and sovereign.

If a king sets himself against the body of the commonwealth, whereof he is head, and shall, with intolerable ill-usage, cruelly tyrannise over the whole, or a considerable part of the people; in this case the people have a right to resist and defend themselves. . .

But not to go any further: for example, not to revenge themselves or to lose their sense of respect for the royal authority.

Contributor: Martin Cohen

# LOGIC

ARISTOTLE's *Prior* and *Posterior Analytics* are generally taken as the first fully systematic logic. Here, he introduces terms such as 'PROPOSITION' and 'INFERENCE', together with a taxonomy of all the acceptable SYLLOGISMS and all the unacceptable ones. On the basis of Aristotle's rules of reasoning, which state that there are some 256 different possible types of ARGUMENT, of which only a few, given that they start off with true assumptions, will always produce true conclusions. His is a 'formal' or quasi-mathematical logic of terms, concerned with the structure of arguments rather than their content, and is opposed to the STOIC logic, which is one of propositions, and the criteria for deciding whether they were true, or not – or 'in between' (for Stoic logic, unlike Aristotle's approach, allowed the third option). Aristotle invented a new notation for his reasoning, and used letters to stand for 'the terms', thereby creating the impression of great things being said that subsequent philosophers have always been indebted to him for.

Philosophers have been attracted to logic – the attempt to impose order on our concepts, language and ideas – ever since Euclid's elegant mathematical proofs, which certainly seemed so much better than ordinary language discussions. And certainly, Aristotelian logic is a mathematical way of looking at the world, which bears only a rather flimsy resemblance to it, entirely based on the assumptions you start with.

Nonetheless, most philosophical logic proceeds that way. LEIBNIZ thought that logic would enable humankind to construct a machine to solve all its problems ('Come, let us calculate'), a delusion all the more popular since the invention of the computer.

Logic, however, still has its disadvantages, as G.K. Chesterton once pointed out. It can send quite normal people into a twilight world of their own:

Poets do not go mad; but chess-players do. Mathematicians go mad, and cashiers; but creative artists very seldom. I am not, as will be seen, in any sense attacking logic: I only say that this danger does lie in logic, not in imagination.

(*Orthodoxy*, 1908)

## SYLLOGISMS

Syllogisms are arguments with two premisses, followed by a conclusion. In medieval times they were all given names, like 'Barbara'.) An example of one is:

- Premiss 1: All apples grow on trees.
- Premiss 2: All Golden Delicious are apples.

## Conclusion: All Golden Delicious grow on trees

The process of inference is an 'argument', and arguments are either valid or invalid, depending upon whether they follow the rules of reasoning. This is not the same as being 'true' or 'false', which is a matter of facts, to be decided upon after investigating the actual assumptions or premisses. All that is necessary for an argument to be valid is that it must follow the rules of logic, which to some extent are also the rules of reasoning, such as the Law of Non-contradiction and the Law of Excluded Middle.

Aristotle defined four types of 'claim':

1. All S are P.
2. No S is P.
3. Some S is P.
4. Some S is not P.

These can be arranged in various ways in the syllogism, leading altogether to the 256 different possible syllogistic arguments. The great majority are invalid, and Aristotle concentrates on the valid forms. But how does he prove that the valid forms are valid? After all, the idea is to show that arguments are valid because they are one of the valid forms. It does not seem to be possible to apply this to the argument form itself. However, Aristotle argues that there are indemonstrable starting points to any chain of reasoning. The notion of being 'self-evident' is central to his approach, but the question always lurks: 'self-evident' to whom?' In any case, 'self-evident' is a psychological statement, not a logical one. A different kind of objection to his logic is that Aristotle assumed that the subject of a premiss, as in 'all cats have whiskers', existed. Later logicians have wanted to avoid this, and have changed the sense to:

- For any x, if that x is a cat, then that x has whiskers.

This in itself produces a gap between ordinary language and logic.

## Modern logic

Modern logic is often taken as having begun in 1879, credited to Gottlob FREGE (1846–1925), with additional work by Bertrand RUSSELL (1872–1970) in the twentieth century. Where Aristotle was interested in the structure of sentences (within sentences), much of modern logic tries to treat sentences as propositions and units, which are then manipulated, usually via symbols and notation. The main ones required are:

- AND          CONJUNCTION
- OR           DISJUNCTION
- NOT          NEGATION
- IF. . . THEN  CONDITIONAL
- IF           BI-CONDITIONAL

(The small print: There are all sorts of funny symbols used to represent these, depending on the philosophers' fancies. The 'or' in logic is 'inclusive' – both possibilities are allowed to be true. If a logician asks you if you would like orange juice OR tea, do not be surprised to get an unappetising mixture. And the conditional does not imply any sort of relationship, causal or otherwise. . .)

The question to what extent logic really is the way we reason is at the heart of much of contemporary Western philosophy. For example, the definition of VALIDITY used in a standard 'formal logic' is that it must not be possible for the premises of an argument to be true and yet the conclusion to be false.

Two strange and slightly ridiculous consequences have to be swallowed, even with this fairly modest assumption. The first is that any argument with inconsistent premises is valid, irrespective of what the conclusions of that argument are. For example, if snow is always white is the first premise, and the second is that snow is sometimes not white, it follows logically that the moon is a balloon, because anything at all follows from inconsistent premises.

The other is that if a conclusion is necessarily true, then the argument is valid, irrespective of what the premises were. This is because there are no circumstances in which the conclusion can be false and the premises true, because the conclusion itself cannot be false. Likewise, if cats can fly on broomsticks, then dogs can drive buses, is a perfectly *valid* inference, as a false statement implies any statement whatsoever. (Because the only way 'If P then Q' can be falsified is by finding a situation where P is true and Q is false, which cannot ever happen here.)

#### SEE ALSO

Truth tables, Fallacies

## LOGICAL POSITIVISM

### Essentials of logical positivism

In 1922, Moritz SCHLICK, a philosopher-scientist who had made something of a name for himself translating EINSTEIN's theories into 'philosowaffle', was made Professor of Philosophy at the University of Vienna. Around Schlick formed the so-called VIENNA CIRCLE, of very dry, very scientific philosophers, who described themselves as 'logical positivists'. The Circle would only admit those who agreed that nothing anyone says has any meaning unless it can be checked up on using scientific procedures of 'verification'. Philosophers, of course, are still very important, as they can check that the verified claims and indeed the unverified ones, are expressed nice and logically.

### Unanswerable questions?

It is natural that humankind should take great pride in the steady advance of its knowledge. The joy we feel in the contemplation of scientific progress is fully justified. One problem after another is solved by science; and the success of the past gives us ample reason for our hope that this process will go on, perhaps even at a quicker pace. But will it, can it, go on indefinitely? It seems a little ridiculous to suppose a day might come when all imaginable problems would be solved, so that there would be no questions left for which the human mind would crave an answer. We feel sure that our curiosity will never be completely satisfied and that the progress of knowledge will not come to a stop when it has reached its last goal.

It is commonly assumed that there are other imperative reasons why scientific advance cannot go on forever. Most people believe in the existence of barriers that cannot be scaled by human reason and by human experience. The final and perhaps the most important TRUTHS are thought to be permanently hidden from our eyes; the key to the Riddle of the Universe is believed to be buried in depths, the access to which is barred to all mortals by the very nature of the Universe. According to this common belief, there are many questions which we can formulate, and whose meaning we can grasp completely, though it is definitely impossible to know their answer, which is beyond the nature and necessary boundary of all knowledge. In regard to these questions a final ignorabimus is pronounced. Nature, it is said, does not wish her deepest secrets to be revealed; God has set a limit of knowledge, which shall not be passed by his creatures, and beyond which, faith must take the place of curiosity.

It is easy to understand how such a view originated, but it is not so clear why it should be considered to be a particularly pious or reverent attitude. Why should Nature seem more wonderful to us if she cannot be known completely? Surely she does not wish to conceal anything on purpose, for she has no secrets, nothing to be ashamed of. On the contrary, the more we know of the world the more we shall marvel at it; and if we should know its ultimate principles and its most general laws, our feeling of wonder and reverence would pass all bounds. Nothing is gained by picturing God as jealously hiding from his creatures the innermost structure of his creation: indeed, a worthier conception of a Supreme Being should imply that no ultimate boundary should be set to the knowledge of beings to whom an infinite desire of knowledge has been given. The existence of an absolute ignorabimus would form an exceedingly vexing problem to a philosophical mind. It would be a great step forward in philosophy, if the burden of this bewildering problem could be thrown off.

This, one may argue, is evidently impossible, for without doubt there are unanswerable questions. It is very easy to ask questions the answers to which, we have the strongest reasons to believe, will never be known to any human being. What did Plato do at eight o'clock in the morning of his fiftieth birthday? How much did Homer weigh when he wrote the first line of the *Iliad*? Is there a piece of silver to be found on the other side of the moon, three inches long and shaped like a fish? Obviously, men will never know the answers to these questions, however hard they may try. But at the same time, we know that they would never try very hard. These problems, they will say, are of no importance, no philosopher would worry about them, and no historian or naturalist would care whether he knew the answers or not.

Here, then, we have certain questions whose insolubility does not trouble the philosopher; and evidently, there are reasons why it need not trouble him. This is important. We must be content to have insoluble questions. But what if all of them could be shown to be of such a kind as not to cause any really serious concern to the philosopher? In that case, he would be relieved. Although there would be many things he could not know, the real burden of the ignorabimus would be lifted from his shoulders. At first sight there seems to be little hope for this, as some of the most important issues of philosophy are generally held to belong to the class of insoluble problems. Let us consider this point carefully.

What do we mean when we call a question important? When do we hold it to be of interest to the philosopher? Broadly speaking, when it is a question of principle; one that refers to a general feature of the world, not a detail; one that concerns the structure of the world, a valid law, not a single unique fact. This distinction may be described as the difference between the real nature of the Universe and the accidental form in which this nature manifests itself.

Correspondingly, the reasons why a given problem is insoluble may be of two entirely different kinds. In the first place, the impossibility of answering a given question may be an impossibility in principle or, as we shall call it, a logical impossibility. In the second place, it may be due to accidental circumstances that do not affect the general laws, and in this case we shall speak of an empirical impossibility.

In the simple instances given above, it is clear that the impossibility of answering these questions is of the empirical kind. It is merely a matter of chance that neither Plato nor any of his friends took exact notes of his doings on his fiftieth birthday (or that such notes were lost if any were taken); and a similar remark applies to the questions concerning the weight of Homer, and things on the other side of the moon. It is practically or technically impossible for humans to reach the moon and go around it, and such an exploration of our earth's satellite will never take place. *[Well, it seemed a good example then. Ed.]* But we cannot declare it impossible in principle. The moon happens to be very far off; it happens to turn always the same side towards the earth; it happens to possess no atmosphere which human beings could breathe – but we can very easily imagine all of these circumstances to be different. We are prevented from visiting the moon only by brute facts, by an unfortunate state of affairs, not by any principle by which certain things were deliberately held from our knowledge. Even if the impossibility of solving a certain question is due to a **LAW OF NATURE**, we shall have to say that it is only empirical, not logical, provided we can indicate how the law would have to be changed in order to make the question answerable. After all, the existence of any Law of Nature must be considered as an empirical fact which might just as well be different. The scientist's whole interest is concentrated on the particular Laws of Nature; but the philosopher's general point of view must be independent of the validity of any particular one of them.

It is one of the most important contentions of the philosophy I am advocating that there are many questions which it is empirically impossible to answer, but not a single real question for which it would be logically impossible to find a solution. Since only the latter kind of impossibility would have that hopeless and fatal character which is implied by the ignorabimus and which could cause philosophers to speak of a 'Riddle of the Universe' and to despair of such problems as the 'cognition of things in themselves' and similar ones, it would seem that the acceptance of my opinion would bring the greatest relief to all those who have been unduly concerned about the essential incompetence of human knowledge in regard to the greatest issues. Nobody can reasonably complain about the empirical impossibility of knowing everything, for that would be equivalent to complaining that we cannot live at all times and be in all places simultaneously. Nobody wants to know all the facts, and it is not important to know them: the really essential principles of the universe reveal themselves at any time and any place. I do not suggest, of course, that they lie open at first glance, but they can always be discovered by the careful and penetrating methods of science.

How can I prove my point? What assures us that the impossibility of answering questions never belongs to the question as such, is never a matter of principle, but is always due to accidental empirical circumstances, which may some day change? There is no room here for a real proof; but I can indicate in general how the result is obtained.

It is done by an analysis of the meaning of our questions. Evidently philosophical issues – and very often other problems too – are difficult to understand: we have to ask for an explanation of what is meant by them. How is such an explanation given? How do we indicate the meaning of a question?

A conscientious examination shows that all the various ways of explaining what is actually meant by a question are, ultimately, nothing but various descriptions of ways in which the answer to the question must be found. Every explanation or indication of the meaning of a question consists, in some way or other, of prescriptions for finding its answer. This principle has proved to be of fundamental importance for the method of science. For example, it led Einstein, as he himself admits, to the discovery of the Theory of Relativity. It may be empirically impossible to follow those prescriptions (like travelling around the moon), but it cannot be logically impossible. For what is logically impossible cannot even be described, i.e. it cannot be expressed by words or other means of communication.

The truth of this last statement is shown by an analysis of 'description' and 'expression' into which we cannot enter here. But taking it for granted, we see that no real question is in principle – i.e. logically – unanswerable. For the logical impossibility of solving a problem is equivalent to the impossibility of describing a method of finding its solution and this, as we have stated, is equivalent to the impossibility of indicating the meaning of the problem. Thus a question which is unanswerable in principle can have no meaning; it can be no question at all: it is nothing but a nonsensical series of words with a question mark after them. As it is logically impossible to give an answer where there is no question, this cannot be a cause of wonder, dissatisfaction, or despair.

This conclusion can be made clearer by considering one or two examples. Our question as to the weight of Homer has meaning, of course, because we can easily describe methods of weighing human bodies (even poets); in other words, the notion of weight is accurately defined. Probably Homer was never weighed, and it is empirically impossible to do it now, because his body no longer exists; but these accidental facts do not alter the sense of the question.

Or take the problem of survival after death. It is a meaningful question, because we can indicate ways in which it could be solved. One method of ascertaining one's own survival would simply consist in dying. *[In both the negative and positive cases there would be alternative possibilities making this certainty elusive! You might survive as a snail rather than a philosopher, or not survive at all but be unable to tell yourself the fact. Probably not a good method at all. Ed.]* It would also be possible to describe certain observations of scientific character that would lead us to accept a definite answer. That such observations could not be made thus far is an empirical fact which cannot entail a definite ignorabimus in regard to the problem.

Now consider the question: 'What is the nature of time?' What does it mean? What do the words 'the nature of' stand for? The scientist might, perhaps, invent some kind of explanation, he might suggest some statements which he would regard as possible answers to the question; but his explanation could be nothing but the description of a method of discovering which of the suggested answers is the true one. In other words, by giving a meaning to the question he has at the same time made it logically answerable, although he may not be able to make it empirically soluble. Without such an explanation, however, words 'What is the nature of time?' are no question at all. If a philosopher confronts us with a series of words like this and neglects to explain the meaning, he cannot wonder if no answer is forthcoming. It is as if he had asked us: 'How much does philosophy weigh?' in which case it is immediately seen that is not a question at all, but mere nonsense. Questions like 'Can we know the Absolute?' and innumerable similar ones must be dealt with in the same, way as the 'problem' concerning the nature of Time.

All great philosophical issues that have been discussed since the time of **PARMENIDES** to our present day are of one of two kinds: we can either give them a definite meaning by careful and accurate explanation and definitions, and then we are sure that they are soluble in principle, although they may give scientist the greatest trouble and may even never be solved on account of unfavourable empirical circumstances, or we fail to give them any meaning, and then they are no questions at all. Neither case need cause uneasiness for the philosopher. His greatest troubles arose from a failure to distinguish between the two.

From an original essay by Moritz Schlick,
published in *The Philosopher* in 1936

## *LOGOS*

The word comes from the Greek, but its exact meaning is obscure. Often, it is used as a synonym for 'word', but it can be used to mean the faculty of speech. **HERACLITUS** uses it to stand for an objective universal principle that is true for all, while the **STOICS** saw *logos* as a kind of force responsible for both knowledge and the predictability of events, and **PLATO** and **ARISTOTLE**, following Stoic discussions, also stressed the role of *logos* as respectively the rational part of the **SOUL** and the essence of definition. The word lives on today in its commercial guise of the 'logo' or symbol.

## LOTTERY PARADOX

See Paradoxes.

## LOVE

### Essentials of love

'Love, in its true and finest meaning, seems to be the way in which is manifested all that is highest, best and beautiful in the nature of human beings', or so wrote Harriet Taylor to John Stuart **MILL** in the nineteenth century. This is surely the philosophical ideal of love. Yet the strength and undisciplined nature of love is also depicted by **PLATO** in the *Phaedrus* as the struggle of a charioteer to control two horses, one representing physical desire and uncontrollable passion, the other a more intellectual and compassionate kind of love.

Worse still, in the dialogue the *Republic, eros* is denounced as a 'tyrant'! Yet, in another dialogue, the *Symposium* (drinking party), Plato takes up the theme again, describing how **SOCRATES**, in a rather different mood, recalls that the wise woman, Diotima, had once told him that love was a step on the way to the under-

standing and appreciation of beauty and goodness: indeed, not only that, but of the ideal **FORMS** of beauty and goodness themselves. Looked at in this way love provides the foundation for Plato's *Theory of Forms*. In the *Symposium*, too, Socrates praises personal love in a way that makes a surprising contrast to his normally stern words. At one point, shortly after describing the psychological fevers that the physical presence of a lover can create, he says that this alone prevents the 'wings of the soul' from becoming parched and dry.

### Friends and lovers

In its most virulent form, the form the Greeks called '*eros*', the word that has given us the concept of the erotic, love can be unpredictable and uncontrollable. It comes out of the blue to strike its innocent and unsuspecting victim, like the dart of a playful god. The Roman philosopher, **LUCRETIUS**, describes this kind of love as capable of shocking acts of sadism and aggression.

But friendship is both a more common and a more manageable condition than love, a broader but less interesting relationship. Not that **ARISTOTLE** sees it quite that way. In Book I of the *Nicomachean Ethics*, he describes three lives, one constructed around what he calls 'bovine pleasure'; one around pleasure from social activity – particularly on behalf of the community, but also from socialising with friends; and one of the refined scholastic pleasures of philosophical contemplation.

Aristotle thinks only two of these kinds of life can truly be considered 'happy', especially praising the pleasure that the social life can bring. (It need not be said here which of the three he dismisses!) But, he says, the 'human being is a social animal, and the need for company is in his blood'. And in Book viii, he goes on to consider various definitions of 'friendship'. One, in terms of beneficence or good will is 'wanting good for another'; another is the suggestion that friendship might be simply valuing someone's company and sharing one another's joys and sorrows.

The third and best is the friendship of equals, people who share an equality of goodness. While later, the **STOIC** philosophers recommended emotional detachment from loving, since all the objects of our affection are transitory, Aristotle said that loving is the distinctive virtue of friends and that loving is more important than being loved. Even for Immanuel **KANT**, writing long after, friendship offers release from the prison of the loneliness of the SELF, a prison, he adds sternly, from which we have a duty to escape.

So the ancient Greeks distinguished the kind of love that exists in families between parents and children or among siblings, as well as affection between friends, from the more passionate or sexual love between people who are physically attracted to each other. The word for the first was *philia*, the root of the word, philosophy, meaning the love of wisdom.

The second kind of love, *eros*, or sexual love, is remembered mainly as the rather dangerous god who took malicious pleasure in implanting in people irrational passions for each other, as depicted by Plato in the *Republic*. This kind of passion could exist between male and female, between males, or between females. A third word, *agapein*, was used as the verb, 'to love'. As the noun *agape*, this word later became the notion of Christian love or charity, meaning the kind of love GOD has for humanity, that humans may have for God, and that they are urged to have for each other. This was the type of love recommended by Jesus and later by Saint Paul. Saint Paul's 'Letter to the Corinthians' sums it up:

> Love is patient and kind; love is not jealous or boastful; it is not arrogant or rude. Love does not insist on its own way; it is not irritable or resentful; it does not rejoice at wrong, but rejoices in the right. Love bears all things, believes all things, hopes all things, endures all things.

Philosophers have also wondered about the possessiveness of love, for example, the love of one's country. Indeed, is it really possible to 'love' one's country, and, if so, are the patriotic feelings because of its particular virtues, because it has good laws and nice countryside (if it does) or is it simply because it is 'mine'? If the former, why not also love other countries that are similar (or better); if the latter, what kind of 'patriotism' is this? Similarly, if I have feelings of romantic love towards someone in response to their qualities of kindness, humour, attractiveness, and so on, would it not make sense to feel the same love for any other individuals I meet who have the same desirable qualities? It seems not: the reason being, as with patriotism, that this form of love, unlike the others, is exclusive, its object is necessarily one particular country, one particular person.

## PLATONIC LOVE

Plato gave his name to the concept of love without sex: the Platonic relationship, illustrated by Socrates' description in the *Symposium* of a night passed in company with the desirable young Alcibiades. The dialogue reveals that he chose to use the occasion for companionship and conversation rather than a togetherness of a more physical nature. In other dialogues, however, Plato portrays Socrates as recognising the dangerous force of passion and its power to overcome its victim. In the *Phaedrus*, the image is of a charioteer trying to control two horses pulling in different directions, one representing physical desire and uncontrollable passion, the other a love that is love of a person expressed in a more intellectual and compassionate way.

But if this kind of love, whether for a particular person or place, provides a gateway to a broader, more comprehensive love, then, paradoxical though it may seem, love can be both individual and universal. In other words, there is a sense in which the real and complete love of one individual is the love of all.

Contributor: Brenda Almond

## LUCRETIUS (*C.* 95–54 BCE)

*De Rerum Natura (On the Nature of Things)* is an unusual book, let alone poem. Lucretius describes his poem as a 'honey-coated' pill containing some unpalatable truths about the universe. These truths were discovered by the great philosopher EPICURUS, such as that everything in the universe is made up of just two things: empty space and tiny, invisible particles; and that these particles can neither be created nor destroyed. His celebrated THOUGHT EXPERIMENT of the spear is intended to demonstrate that the universe is infinite and contains all possible things and all possible worlds.

> Suppose for a moment that the whole of space *were* bounded and that someone made their way to its uttermost boundary and threw a flying spear. Do you suppose that the missile, hurled with might and main, would speed along the course on which it was aimed? Or do you think something would block the way and stop it? You must

assume one alternative or the other. But neither of them leaves you so much as a loophole to wriggle through. Both force you to admit that the universe continues without end. Whether there is some obstacle lying on the boundary line that prevents the spear from going farther on its course, or whether it flies on beyond, it cannot in fact have started from the boundary.

Book I, Matter and Space, in *De Rerum Natura*

In fact, the view set out in the poem was far and away the best description of the universe, at least up to the twentieth century, and, for all our sophisticated models today, maybe it remains in some ways superior to present thinking. For example, Lucretius, or rather Epicurus, specifically added a little 'swerve' to the movement of the particles, so as to allow for the possibility of free will in our human lives. Otherwise, the universe and everything in it was no more meaningful than the ceaseless playing of the tiny motes in a sunbeam.

## LYING

Lying is as old as speech; it could hardly be otherwise. Everyone does it. God, doctors, teachers, philosophers – even some clever birds lie to each other. They hide their store of food in one place, knowing other birds are watching, and secretly return later, dig it up and hide it in another place. Winston Churchill once said that truth was so important and so valuable, that it must always be accompanied by a bodyguard – of lies.

But the philosophical status of the lie is another matter. With the tale of the 'mad knifeman', SOCRATES argues with Glaucon over the conflict between the ETHICAL imperative to always be truthful and the negative practical consequences that may follow. That is to say, if your honesty leads the mad knifeman to the person he is seeking, and they are then stabbed to death, your honesty would appear to have somewhat undesirable consequences. But PLATO insists that the prize of honesty is greater than any apparent costs. Although, funnily enough, he does allow the founders of his *Republic* 'one little lie', that of deceiving the citizens about their origins – the 'gold, silver or iron' in their souls. Perhaps, like 'Sir' Robert Armstrong, in Court in New South Wales to explain the British government's position on the suppression of a book, he would stress that is not exactly a lie anyway.

It contains a misleading impression, not a lie. It was being economical with the truth.

In the Middle Ages, the issue still rated highly in learned debate, with Thomas AQUINAS writing at length 'On lying' and also making a case for it, occasionally. Although Aquinas agreed with the earlier warnings of Saint AUGUSTINE that 'the mouth that belieth killeth the soul', that 'every lie is a sin', and that generally 'lying is in itself evil and to be shunned', he then, like so many of us, went on to muddy the waters a bit. In fact, Augustine's ability to take a firm stand on lying depended mainly on his decision to put the emphasis entirely on the individual (soul)'s self-interest in all these matters – any consequences be damned!

Another device, for liars, as the ancient equivocator SENECA observed, is to appeal to the flux and change of the universe:

for a man to be bound by a promise it is necessary for everything to remain unchanged: otherwise neither did he lie in promising – since he promised what he had in his mind, due circumstances being taken for granted – nor was he faithless in not keeping his promise, because circumstances are no longer the same.

(*De Beneficence*, IV)

Meanwhile, a lone figure on the other side, brandishing the trusty sword, KANT warns that the liar causes contracts to be voided and to lose their force, and 'this is a wrong done to mankind generally'. A lie does not need to cause harm directly to be wrong, and even when it appears to do good, it instead must be judged by this general collapse of the truth. 'To be truthful in all declarations, therefore, is a sacred and absolutely commanding decree of reason, limited by no expediency', he concludes.

SEE ALSO

Fallacies

## MACH, ERNST (1838–1916)

Mach was the Austrian physicist whose name is immortalised in relation to the speed of sound

(Mach 1). He also made original contributions to the science of 'light waves', optics and the Doppler effect, and was interested in the methodology of science itself, writing that sensations and physical objects themselves were as 'preliminary as the objects of alchemy'. He advocated the use of the intellect to move science forward in bold steps, including the use of THOUGHT EXPERIMENTS, saying that no theory really represented 'reality', but merely existed to offer predictions.

He was an inspiration to the 'LOGICAL POSITIVISTS' of Vienna and elsewhere, impressed EINSTEIN, and merited special derision in LENIN's *Materialism and Empiriocriticism* (1908). His own key work is the *Science of Mechanics* (1883).

## MACHIAVELLI, NICCOLI (1469–1527)

### The essential Machiavelli

Ironically perhaps, for one writing of 'Princes', Machiavelli was the first writer to move away from the paternalism of traditional society towards something closer to our own notions of 'DEMOCRACY'. In his writings, the masses, ignorant and vulgar though they may be, are better guardians of stability and liberty than individuals can ever become. And despite his reputation for CYNICISM, Machiavelli reminds us that injustice threatens the foundations of society from within, and urges that it always be combatted – wherever it appears and whoever it

affects. His reputation comes from two of the most notorious political works ever written, *The Prince* (1532) (*Il principe*) and the *Discourses* in 1531 (*Discorsi sopra la prima deca di Tito Livio* – Discourses on the first Ten Books of Titus Livy). Prior to Machiavelli, medieval writers had based legitimacy on God, who expressed His will through the hierarchy of Pope, bishops and priests or, alternatively, through the emperor and the royal families of Europe. Machiavelli, in contrast, has no doubt that power is available to all and any who are skilful enough to seize it. Popular government is better than tyranny, not for any overriding 'moral' reason, but by reason of its success in bringing about certain political 'goals': national independence, security and a well-rounded constitution. This means sharing power between princes, nobles and people in proportion to their 'real' power. (For maximum stability, Machiavelli thinks, the people's share should be substantial.) Machiavelli is the first major European figure to praise freedom as a primary virtue, writing variously that 'those who set up a Tyranny are no less blameworthy than are the founders of a Republic or a Kingdom praiseworthy. . .' and that 'all towns and all countries that are in all respects free, profit by this enormously'. The year of Machiavelli's death, 1527, was the year the Emperor Charles V's armies reached and sacked Rome, marking the passing of the Renaissance period itself.

### The psychology of the State

Sixteenth-century Italy contained a number of elements that made it, like Greece centuries before, peculiarly fertile ground for all types of arts, philosophy and political thinking. Out of the whole of Europe, it was the least feudal, the most wealthy and the most politically diverse land. Its culture was sophisticated, urbane and secular, its administrative structure made up of city states or 'communes' presided over by their own 'Princes', and governing cliques. As a result, the country was a patchwork quilt of oligarchies, tyrannies – and a handful of democracies.

One such was Florence, the magnificent Italian city where Dante had written some centuries earlier not only of his vision of hell, the 'inferno', but of the politics of human society. Dante had asked the question why people should want to live peacefully and collectively together, when they could often gain more by either striking out alone, or by competing one against the other, before answering it by suggesting that they realised that social life was the best, indeed the only way, for them to develop their rational nature. But by the fifteenth century, the ruling family in Florence, the Medici, had become a byword for over-indulgence and corruption, stoking conflict between small traders and large powerful guilds as a means to gain and retain control.

The Medici were displaced by a Dominican Friar, Savonarola, who was concerned only with morality and not at all with politics, let alone consolidating his own position, and indeed, in 1498, he was executed. His democratic experiment, however, lasted a bit longer – until 1512 when the Medici themselves returned to power. Niccoli Machiavelli worked for this new Florentine democracy as a middle-ranking civil servant, gaining during this period all his experience of government.

During the purge following the Medici's return, Machiavelli was arrested and tortured by the triumphant new administration. Only when finally acquitted was he allowed to retire peacefully and concentrate on writing up his political ideas. *The Prince* is often said to have been an unsuccessful bid to regain favour and indeed is dedicated in glowing terms to 'Lorenzo the Magnificent', son of Piero dei Medici. Machiavelli introduces the work with the words: 'It is customary for those who wish to gain the favour of a prince to endeavour to do so by offering him gifts of those things which they hold most precious, or in which they know him to take especial delight. In this way princes are often presented with horses, arms, cloth of gold, gems, and such-like. . .' But Machiavelli finds nothing among his possessions which he holds so dear 'as that knowledge of the deeds of great men which I have acquired through a long experience of modern events and a constant study of the past'.

Having set out his stall in this respectful manner, and set the style for his investigations, Machiavelli announces his intention to leave discussion of republican government to 'another place'.

This is, in fact, the *Discourses*, which, although less celebrated, is his longer and more substantial work. It even contains some additional, **LIBERAL**, ideas, which are at odds with pleasing the Medici, but there is no essential contradiction between the works. Indeed, there is a great deal of duplication. Today, Machiavelli is often narrowly portrayed as simply promoting the ruler's use of force and fraud, but his intention was highly moral: to protect the State against internal and external threats and ultimately to promote the welfare of the citizens, not simply the interests of the Prince. In the *Discourses*, Machiavelli advocates 'civic virtue', putting the common good ahead of selfish interests, and identifies that curious feature of collective decision-making, that the judgement of the masses may be sounder than that of even enlightened individuals.

He argues that as people are all a mixture, none much superior to the other, and as no system is perfect either, so even a good Prince can become corrupt, and it is best to design the State with a series of checks and balances. And since the State is only as good as its citizens, the rulers must be aware of the dangers of allowing civic spirit to wane. Despite his reputation, even on the subject of the 'many ways to gain power', he advises that only a few of them are worth following.

Machiavelli's most important and original points are usually considered these days to relate to the dry matter of the analysis of the conditions for republican government, but he also allows himself to spend much time and wordspace discussing military tactics. 'When an Enemy is seen to be making a big mistake it should be assumed that it is but an artifice', he warns, before describing 'the rival merits of fortresses and cavalry', all the while utilising his main literary device of much self-serving name-dropping.

Despite these other personal aims and interests, his analysis of government is still far more detailed than that of either **PLATO** or **ARISTOTLE**, and there is, after all, no one (in the European context) to compare him with in the centuries in between. And indeed, his writings have stood the test of time too. If Machiavelli writes of, and for, a pre-industrial society, his notions are still – sometimes strikingly – relevant. In sixteenth-century Italy, society and power were split between three groups: the land and peasantry, industry (such as it was) and the bureaucracy, of which Machiavelli had been a member; all of which is a surprisingly timeless arrangement. Even Machiavelli's discussion of military adventures can be taken as a metaphor for the strategies and effects of economic competition today.

Taken literally, Machiavelli may be 'off-message', but taken more thoughtfully (reading between the lines, as all medieval texts need), his discussions are often not far from today's needs. Unfortunately, Machiavelli has rarely been read thoughtfully – or even been read at all – before being condemned. His reputation is far worse than he merits: rather than being a 'doctor of the damned', recommending immoral behaviour whenever necessary or convenient, his name a synonym for what some dictionaries today record as 'cunning, amoral and opportunist' behaviour, there is much in his writings to suggest a fundamentally moral man trying to understand human society in its political form.

Of Agathocles the Sicilian, who rose by means of wickedness from 'the lowest and most abject position' to become King of Syracuse, by means of trickery, such as the occasion he called the Senate to discuss a proposal, and then gave a signal to his soldiers to have them all murdered, he writes that he may have succeeded in achieving power, but surely not 'glory'.

One of his strongest and most consistent themes is the perils of ignoring injustice, urging Princes to '. . . consider how important it is for every republic and every Prince to take account of such offences, not only when an injury is done to a whole people but also when it affects an individual'. Not that he is not ruthless. Machiavelli advises that if a Prince must choose to be either feared or loved, it is better that he be feared, for 'love is held by a chain of obligation which [for] men, being selfish, is broken whenever it serves their purpose; but fear is maintained by a dread of punishment which never fails.' In this sense, he is HOBBES, writing a century later, or even MAO Zedong in the twentieth century.

Actually, much of Machiavelli's notoriety probably relates to his attacks on the Roman Church, the body that he blames for the political ruin of Italy. Pre-dating NIETZSCHE by some 400 years, Machiavelli writes: 'Our religion has glorified humble and contemplative men, rather than men of action. It has assigned as man's highest good humility, abnegation, and contempt for mundane things...': even though, on his deathbed, he asked for – and received – absolution (although this could have been just a ploy, of course!). The advice Machiavelli offers to would-be rulers in Renaissance Europe instead is that: 'it is as well to . . . seem merciful, faithful, humane, sincere, religious, and also to be so; but you must have the mind so disposed that when it is needful to be otherwise you may change to the opposite qualities . . . [and] do evil if constrained.'

Here, Machiavelli heralds the tactics of the emerging secular societies in redefining their relationship with the moral authority of the Church, and he is very clear: the Prince has a 'higher' morality rather than no morality at all. Machiavelli gives some examples of 'justice in practice', describing the curious time in ancient Rome when women started poisoning their husbands, and the difficulties of coping with mutinous armies.

His solution is random executions: 'For when a great number of people have done wrong, and it is not clear who is responsible, it is impossible to punish them all, since there are so many of them; and to punish some, and leave others unpunished would be unfair . . . the unpunished would take heart and do wrong at some other time – but by killing the tenth part, chosen by lot, when all are guilty, he who is punished bewails his lot, and he who is not punished is afraid to do wrong lest on some other occasion the lot should not spare him.'

Advice like this leads even sympathetic commentators like Bernard Crick to say that Machiavelli would not have recognised the merits of the famous words inscribed on the Old Bailey in London: 'Let justice be done though the heavens fall.' But in another sense, Machiavelli is insisting precisely that justice *must* be done. Machiavelli may be immoral, but surely history is wrong to condemn him as simply amoral.

Contributor: Martin Cohen

## Further reading

Machiavelli, N. (1531) *The Discourses*

## MADHVACÁRYA (1197–1276)

### Essential Madhvacárya

Madhvacárya, or Madhva, in the template of Indian philosophy, holds a pre-eminent position as the exponent supreme of the *DVAITA* (dualist) school of VEDANTA. Born in Pajáka, near the modern temple-town of Udupi, Karnataka, India, Madhva traced back dualist thought to some of the *UPANISHADS*. His system, also called *Tattvaváda* (Realism), encompasses the most tangible and unrelenting disapproval of Vedantic MONISM (ADVAITA).

Madhva's philosophy glorifies five differences (*bheda*). It refutes the monists' stand (of God and man being one entity) in a novel way, saying that: God is different from the universe; God is different from 'I'; 'I' is different from 'you'; and, 'I am' is different from (say) the table, which is different from the chair. In so doing, Madhva cogently rejects the venerable monistic-Hindu theory of *maya*, or illusion, which infers that only spirituality is eternal; the material world being merely delusory, or deceptive.

## Dvaita philosophy

Madhva believed that philosophy per se could fulfil its purpose, and attain its apogee, by allowing every mortal to realise the eternal, indivisible or indissoluble connection of *bimba-pratibimba-bhava* – a reflection as a trans-empirical entity that exists between God and man.

Madhva admitted three ways of knowing: PERCEPTION, INFERENCE and verbal testimony. His basic assertion of the reality of God is of an independent nature, with all of us (mortals) being dependent on God's continued benevolence. In like manner, souls, Madhva testified, conform themselves implicitly not only upon an inherent, distinctive gradation, among themselves, from 'me', 'you' or 'someone else', but also on pedestals related to varying degrees of one's knowledge, power and bliss.

Madhva believed in eternal damnation, and offered a concept of heaven and hell, with a third alternative: a HINDU purgatory of endless transmigration of souls; of REINCARNATION, or rebirth. His doctrine is, indeed, the philosophical touchstone intended to argue, validate and bring about a sort of rapprochement between the presence of the sinister dimension with divine perfection in the light of our own responsibility, or understanding, of goodness and evil. This, says Madhva, is further dependent on the moral freedom born of diversity in the nature of our souls, which are themselves eternal and uncreated in time.

In Madhva's oeuvre, bondage and release are real. So, devotion, Madhva emphasised, is the only way to release, albeit God's kindness is more than a primal requirement that will save us, in the ultimate analysis. Scriptural duties, Madhva added, when performed without any ulterior motive, purify the mind and help one receive God's blessings and grace.

Madhva thought of knowledge as being relative, not absolute. He spurned the universal as a natural consequence: of a principal sense of belief, or the uniqueness of a particular person or a thing. To know a thing, said Madhva, is to know it as distinct from all others in the general sense, and from some (others) in a specific way. Mere appearance, Madhva argued, is not reality, while objective experience is. And, so, he emphasised, every new relation changes, or modifies, its consequence, or substance, to the extent possible. This, he said, is greater in some than in others.

In Madhva's canon, reality is one of the more certain aspects of what could be defined as existence, consciousness and activity, expressed in space–time relationships through the eternal idea of matter, mind and/or soul. Madhva further maintained that plurality, or the basic disparity, in the nature of souls themselves, is based on a much more fundamental concept than *karma* with its myriad garbs and influences. His riposte: 'If that fundamental "model" was only an illusion, the law of *karma* would not have been what it is in its essential context (today).' It would have just remained a chimera. *Karma*, according to Madhva, was a predestined event. Why? Because, God (re)creates the cosmos, and sets 'born-again' souls once more on their paths, in tune with the inherent characteristics which each one of us possesses. It is also God that determines how each soul fares in its journey through time.

The first INDIAN PHILOSOPHER to have introduced the new doctrine of *visesas* (speciality), and its relationship with the underlying perception of difference between individuals; the individuality of each person, as it were, and objects, Madhva did not dispel the pre-eminence of the doubt conundrum: the idea of doubt in our thought and action. Where doubts arise, he said, they must be put down to the perception of difference. This, he said, could be done simply by way of examples in terms of related differences between objects, or from a few high-altitude counter-comparisons, with their close association of resemblance, or otherwise, to the object in question.

The principal thrust of Madhva's philosophy lies in its palpable concept of atoms, where all atoms have taste, colour, smell and touch: this alludes, most notably, to the fact that atoms may differ in their qualitative structure. To draw an example: air has just one attribute: touch; while fire has two: touch and colour; water has three: touch, colour and taste; and earth has all four,

Madhva attempted to explore the deep nature of reality as being present in the mind of God, even in terms of realities that are far beyond human perception. He implied, through his doctrine, that all acts of consciousness (of the dependent selves) are finally reliant on God's will. He also observed that God's will is the essential condition and sustaining principle; the Brahman being the only independent Real, the source of all reality – who represents the consciousness and activity of the infinite. In other words, it is an idea that epitomises perfect happiness, the eternal of the everlasting, including the realities of our existence and awareness of our entire being itself.

'Existence', said Madhva, 'is a test of reality'. Put simply, this means actual existence, at some place, at some time. It bears ample evidence to separating the real from the unreal, or what is categorised as 'illusion' in monistic parlance.

including smell. In other words, Madhva's philosophy envisages that scientific descriptions are generally postulated to be objective, and quite independent of the human observer and the process of knowing. It also holds the view that consciousness is a social phenomenon.

Madhva left a great corpus of work: 37 books in all. His writings also include ten philosophical monographs expounding his LOGIC and METAPHYSICS, commentaries on the ten *Upanishads*, the *Gita* and the *Brahmasutras*, not to speak of the *Rig-Veda* and an epitome of the *Mahabharata*, including the *Bhagavata*. His magnum opus is the *Anu-Vyakhyana*; an exposition of the *Brahmasutras*. His writings (in Sanskrit) are characterised by exceptional brevity of expression and simplicity of thought: they also espouse a strong note of MYSTICAL fervour and rationale.

Contributor: Rajgopal Nidamboor

## MAIMONIDES, MOSES (1135–1204)

Maimonides was the Jewish lawyer and philosopher who fled his native Spain after its conquest by Almohad, to settle in Egypt. Here he became physician to Saladin's 'wazir' and wrote the *Guide to the Perplexed* (1190), in Arabic, along with many other commentaries on theological matters. His guide, which is written as though to a philosophy student, strips down the theological texts to offer a series of LOGICAL arguments, supposedly demonstrating God's perfection. In the process, Maimonides argues that neither ARISTOTLE's nor yet the Bible's approaches are sufficiently rigorous, although the Bible is to be preferred, as it improves our behaviour. Paradoxically though, the effect of the work was to increase interest in Aristotle in Europe, particularly influencing AQUINAS and SPINOZA.

## MALEBRANCHE, NICOLAS (1638–1715)

Malebranche was highly regarded once, particularly for his efforts to prop up DESCARTES' theory of DUALISM, in particular the problem of how the mind could influence the body, when the two were said to be completely separate. His answer, which became known as 'occasionalism', was that GOD causes every event 'necessarily', but other than that, there is no connection. Similarly, problems with Descartes' notion of 'ideas' is solved by saying that they arise, not from the material world at all (only 'sensations' are from there), but only from our souls participating in God's knowledge of things.

LEIBNIZ and LOCKE tore into the two arguments, Locke calling the latter 'an opinion that spreads not, and is like to die of itself', which indeed it soon did.

## MANICHAEISM

An influential doctrine founded by Mani (*c.* 216–277) in Persia (but deriving from Zoroastrianism), which says the world is forever being fought over by two powerful forces, Light and Darkness. This battle, or the 'strife', is what creates moral conflict. Each human is made up of both forces, the soul partakes of light, and the body of darkness. . . Happily, as the body dies, the soul wins eventually. In the meantime, Manichaeism advocates living very simply, like an ascetic monk.

## MANTRA

Mantra is sound equivalence, a universal concept of great antiquity. It is a tool of YOGIC action leading to realisation of reality. All things have sound equivalence. Sound equivalence is not the name of the thing. Names are merely labels. Sound equivalence is the thing itself. For example '*Lam*' is supposed to be the sound equivalence of earth, the first cosmic element.

Mantra are available only as oral tradition. The 'yogin' is taught mantra sounds by his guru. The importance of being given a mantra is the auditory communication of it, making the sound(s) correctly being all important. Concentration and repetition of a thing's mantra is a means of approaching planes of reality of that thing not otherwise appreciated. Repetition of the mantra is initially used to hold concentration until appreciation is realised, when the mantra links the 'yogin' to the thing itself.

As the Buddha said: '*With his ear clearly awakened, far surpassing the dormant ear of men, the awakened one hears mortal and immortal sounds both far and near, penetrating to the core of other beings, other men, Wisdom herself.*'

# MAOISM

## Essential Maoism

Mao Zedong, for all his later obsessions, delusions, excesses and cruelties, left a legacy of commitment to the rights of the rural poor, to women, and set new minimum standards for education and health across the 'developing' world. By addressing himself to the uneducated, agrarian poor, Mao also changed the perception of class struggle and society in both COMMUNIST and non-communist societies.

Mao declares that 'the history of mankind is one of continuous development from the realm of necessity to the realm of freedom'. This is an old story, told also by MARX and HEGEL, and other earlier philosophers, too. But Mao says the process is never-ending, as in any society in which classes exist, class struggle will never end, and even in the classless society the struggle will

continue 'between the new and the old and between truth and falsehood'.

## The Red Book

Maoism is a mixture of the writings of Marx and ENGELS, of the subsequent interpretations of LENIN and TROTSKY, and the two distinctive Chinese philosophies of CONFUCIANISM and TAOISM. In Confucianism, the primary function of government, apart from details such as raising taxes, is education. All officials, from the emperor and the Mandarins down, have a sacred duty towards the masses of educating them, particularly in a moral sense. Li Dazhao, one of the early Chinese communists, influenced the development of MARXISM in China away from historical determinism, by allowing countries to 'telescope' their progress from an agrarian society to communism, by education, that is, through a consciousness of the class struggle. This doctrine also translated in Maoism as the policy of 'permanent revolution'.

Another element in Confucianism is the desire to create a 'one-minded' society. So also Mao. The people should all think the same on any important matter. Mao himself included egalitarianism as such a 'one-minded' goal. The challenge of this orthodoxy by Liu Shaoqu contributed to the destructive conflict of the Cultural Revolution, Mao's flailing attempt to reassert his philosophical dominance and political supremacy. Following Mao's death in 1976, and Deng Xioping's succession, egalitarianism was abandoned in place of something closer to the Western CONSERVATIVE notion of 'trickle-down' – some people must get rich first, creating wealth that later benefits the others.

In the West, surprisingly few consider Maoism a distinct philosophy, calling it 'Chinese Marxism' or ignoring it entirely. Yet within China, for many years, the little Red Book of 'Quotations from Chairman Mao Tse-Tung' had almost the status of a bible or holy work, carried around for reference at all times, and even touched for protection at moments of strife (or for good fortune at others).

The originality of the Red Book starts with its structure – set out as a series of REVOLUTIONARY phrases, short statements designed to be learnt and recited. For example, it starts:

If there is to be revolution, there must be a revolutionary party. Without a revolutionary party, without a party built on the Marxist-

Leninist revolutionary theory and in the Marxist-Leninist revolutionary style, it is impossible to lead the working class and the broad masses of the people to defeat imperialism and its running dogs.

Written originally just as the Second World War came to an end in April 1945, this opening section is intended to link the revolution to economic progress, and appeal to the patriotism of a people who had recently suffered so greatly and so brutally under the Japanese invaders (and before them, the Western ones). Recognising that it will be 'an arduous task' to ensure a better life for the people of China and to turn an 'economically and culturally backward country' into a prosperous and powerful one with a high level of culture, Mao makes education the priority. And Mao thinks there is one good thing about China:

Apart from their other characteristics, the outstanding thing about China's 600 million people is that they are 'poor and blank'. This may seem a bad thing, but in reality it is a good thing. Poverty gives rise to the desire for change, the desire for action and the desire for revolution. On a blank sheet of paper free from any mark, the freshest and most beautiful characters can be written, the freshest and most beautiful pictures can be painted.

Revolutionary theory and history are straightforward to teach. But two of Mao's most famous essays – 'On Practice' and 'On Contradiction', both from 1937 – are concerned with a theoretical belief about the nature of knowledge. Knowledge starts with sense-perception, it is distilled into ideas and theory, and then tested through practice. Essentially, 'Maoism' is learning through experience, through experiment even. As the Red Book goes on, 'Only through the practice of the people, that is, through experience, can we verify whether a policy is correct or wrong and determine to what extent it is correct or wrong.'

And this task is complex, as everything has to be understood as containing its opposite. The 'unity of opposites' is a blend of Marxist **DIALECTICS** and Taoism.

To regard everything as positive is to see only the good and not the bad, and to tolerate only praise and no criticism. To talk

as though our work is good in every respect is at variance with the facts. It is not true that everything is good; there are still shortcomings and mistakes.

We must not be like the 'frog in the well'. In a speech at the Chinese Communist Party's National Conference on Propaganda Work (12 March 1957), Mao declared that:

In approaching a problem a Marxist should see the whole as well as the parts. A frog in a well says, 'The sky is no bigger than the mouth of the well.' That is untrue, for the sky is not just the size of the mouth of the well. If it said, 'A part of the sky is the size of the mouth of a well' that would be true, for it tallies with the facts.

Such '**HOLISM**' even brings Mao to muddy the holy water of Marxist **MATERIALISM**: 'While we recognise that in the general development of history the material determines the mental, and social being determines social consciousness, we also – and indeed must – recognise the reaction of mental on material things, of social consciousness on social being and of the superstructure on the economic base'.

Mao made enormous social changes to the traditional Chinese social pattern (albeit with exceptions), but the old patriarchal model outlived him. Today, many Chinese women, particularly in the rural areas, like many Western women, let alone those in Middle Eastern and developing countries, are still second-class citizens, with limited autonomy and economic rights.

Post-Mao, China is flirting with competition, entrepreneurship and profit, all of which it tries to include in the definition of '**SOCIALISM**'. Yet for many the question is whether this is possible or whether in fact the forces of the 'free market', once unleashed, will bring the whole edifice of socialism crashing down. As the third millennium – China's fifth millennium – begins, voices are increasingly predicting the end of the Maoist experiment; that Chinese Communism will merge seamlessly into Western-style **CAPITALISM**. But when Mao looked ahead to the turn of the next century, in 1956, he saw an industrial utopia and a new powerful China.

It is only forty-five years since the Revolution of 1911, but the face of China has completely changed. In another forty-five years, that is, in the year 2001, or the beginning of the 21st century, China will have undergone an even greater change. She will have become a powerful socialist industrial country. And that is as it should be. . .

For, indeed, as Mao foresaw, it would take 'several decades' to make China prosperous. The road to communism is and was an uphill and bumpy one, to use a metaphor which Mao comprehensively exhausts. The way is complicated too, by tempting-looking alternative turnings. Even during the first years of the People's Republic, Mao observed a 'falling off in ideological and political work among students and intellectuals', and some unhealthy tendencies appearing in society. 'Some people seem to think that there is no longer any need to concern themselves with politics or with the future of the motherland and the ideals of mankind.' Mao sighs towards the end of the Red Book, that 'it seems as if Marxism, once all the rage, is currently not so much in fashion'. His solution, offered to young people in particular, is a tempting recipe entitled: 'Self-reliance and arduous struggle'.

Contributor: Martin Cohen

## MAPS, PHILOSOPHICAL

Innovative ideas interest and stimulate individual minds. New ideas are passed on enthusiasti-cally, person to person. This simple natural diffusion of ideas has always gone on, unless barriers have been set up to prevent it.

The explanation of the same ideas occurring across Afro-Eurasia within years in the early centuries of rapid human development is that there was nothing stopping their movement. People traded across the entire land mass. Plants propagated in China crossed Persia and reached Europe. Ideas spread as quickly as people moved by land and sea. Simultaneous emergence of ideas obviously can and does occur and the collective unconscious can no doubt recycle ideas over millennia. But in general we learn from each other, taking advantage of original thinking from wherever it emerges. There is evidence of Greek philosophers moving around the Mediterranean world, visiting cultural centres in Egypt and Persia. Similarly there is evidence of Indian and Chinese presence in Babylon. The parallels in the emergence of ideas and their development in Eastern and Western philosophy are marked from the earliest times.

Barriers were set up with the establishment of the long-lasting Roman, Parthian, Gupta and Han empires. Augustus Caesar and his government made sophisticated use of propaganda. The Roman Empire effectively cut itself off from barbarians, apart from trade in commodities from the Far East that used increasingly narrow trade routes.

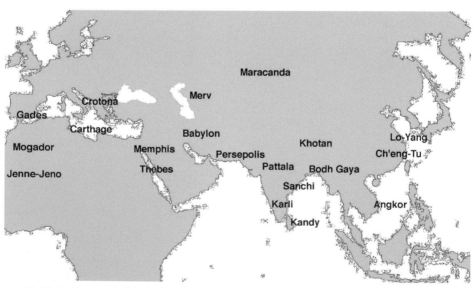

A world of the free movement of ideas, prior to the fourth century BCE

Empires and barbarians: the development of empires creates political barriers to the flow of ideas and knowledge

Much more developed were the methods of censorship of the theocracies of the Middle Ages. Between about 400 CE and about 1550, the political structures gave way to religious divides. The process can be said to have started with the burning of books that did not support religious orthodoxy by the 'Christian saints' in fourth-century Milan, and included the piece-meal destruction of the library at Alexandria by a variety of bigots over many decades.

The emergence of empiricism in Northern Europe at the end of the sixteenth century chal-lenged religious orthodoxy and Tsarist Russia at a time when Christian and Muslim theocracies cut off the area from the rest of Afro-Eurasia, leaving only sea routes to new lands as the way

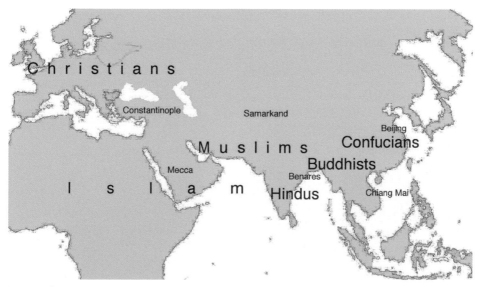

The Age of Faith creates religious barriers

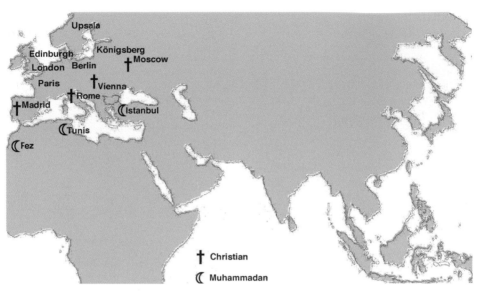

A new empiricism is trapped by theocracy

out for the dissemination of new ideas, inventions and political dissenters.

The twentieth century was dominated by the separate development of **CAPITALIST** and **COMMUNIST** zones with minimum communication and understanding between the two. Similarly today, political, religious and business propaganda machines attempt to restrict and control ideas. Often it seems the press is merely the tool of a rich and powerful elite. However, perhaps more optimistically, the internet may in a way have recreated a world more like that of ancient times, with innumerable sources of information, both large-scale official agencies and individual-scale postings. The twenty-first-century world may be one again without barriers to innovative ideas and, what is more, one without the need to cross continents on foot to search them out.

Contributor: Colin Kirk

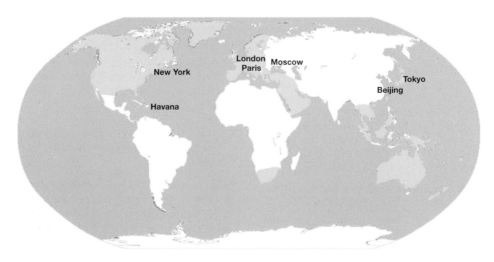

Capitalist and communist ideological zones in the twentieth century

## MARRIAGE

The definition of 'marriage' is very much a source of philosophical interest, but traditionally it had a simple definition: a contractual union with the purpose of raising a family. Built into it of course were other factors, such as the economic status of women and children, and the 'control' of sexual activity by the authorities.

PLATO regarded the worst sort of arrangement to be that which is considered 'normal' today (that is to say, the nuclear family of a man and a woman who live together with their children); recommending instead (in the interests of social cohesion) that children and wives should be held in common.

## MARX, KARL (1818–83)

### The essential Marx

Karl Heinrich Marx was born in Trier (then in German Rhineland) and died in London 1883. He studied law at Bonn and Berlin, but became enthralled by philosophy and history, applying HEGEL's 'DIALECTICAL' method, where everything generates its opposite, followed by a conflict in which a 'synthesis' emerges, to economic life, the so-called 'dialectical MATERIALISM'. He edited a radical German newspaper, until it was suppressed for sedition in 1843, when he moved to Paris, before being obliged to move on again after just two years, to Brussels, where he began his collaboration with ENGELS, his disciple, financial backer, editor and translator.

They reorganised the COMMUNIST League for its meeting in London in 1847 and co-wrote *The Communist Manifesto* in 1848, the year of revolutions. Expelled from Brussels in 1849, they moved to London where Marx studied economics. He and Engels pioneered and organised the First International from 1864 until Marx exiled it to Philadelphia in 1872. *Das Kapital* was intended to be his major work: the first volume appeared in 1867, the second the year after he died and the third in 1894, the year before Engels died.

### Marx, Revolutionary Marxism, and the Communist Manifesto

*The Communist Manifesto* opens with the famous promise: 'Let the ruling classes tremble at a communistic revolution. The proletarians have nothing to lose but their chains. They have a world to win!'

Alas, of course, reality was never so simple, as many failed communist societies could testify, not to mention failed 'anti-communist' dictatorships. But for a century at least, it seemed as though Marx was right and it would be a straight fight between the workers' forces calling for common ownership of 'the means of production', and an increasingly beleaguered and unpopular elite clinging to private ownership. It also seemed it must be true that certain macroeconomic factors were all that created and defined societies and the lives of their citizens.

The *Manifesto* describes society as a whole already increasingly 'splitting up into two great hostile camps, into two great classes directly

### REVOLUTIONARY INGREDIENTS

The 'generally applicable' requirements of communist revolution, as offered by the *Manifesto* in pocket summary form are:

- Abolition of landownership and rents.
- A heavy progressive income tax.
- Abolition of all inheritance rights.
- Confiscation of the property of all those who no longer live in the State or who rebel against the new government.
- Centralisation of all capital and credit in a State bank.
- Central State control and ownership of the means of communication and transportation.
- Increased State production through factories and farming: development of underused land.
- 'Equal liability of all to labour'. New armies of workers, especially to work the land.
- Disappearance of the distinction between town and country: population distributed evenly over the country.

And, lastly:

- Free education for all in State-run schools, preparing the children for work in the new industries.

In the meantime, the *Manifesto* concludes, communists should support every 'revolutionary movement against the existing social and political order, bringing to the fore, as the main issue, the property question'.

Contributor: MC

## THE MATERIALIST THEORY OF HISTORY

In the introduction to *The German Ideology*, like Hegel, Marx explains that the history of mankind is one, non-repeatable process, each stage unique but dependent on what went before, governed by laws capable of identification. He rejected Hegel's universal Spirit, whose internal conflicts are embodied in self-realising Ideas, which manifest themselves in the clash of war between nation states. These Spirits and Ideas are capable of being seen and understood only by sublime minds, akin to Hegel's! They faded to oblivion in Marx's mind when he read the materialist Feuerbach's theory of human evolution extended into recorded history, which, though comprehensible to more mundane mentalities, Marx subsequently rejected as a further abstraction.

Saint-Simon's view that the need for survival is the basis of all social relationships led Marx to regard political economy as the basis of civil society. History is the struggle of people to attain their full human potential by mastery of both external constraining forces, and of themselves, in order to attain freedom. The laws governing the history of this struggle are inherent in ownership, work, production of necessities and distribution of surpluses. The clashes of interests between the different social groups involved, as agriculture, trade, industry, and so on, gain in importance, govern historical development. The rules identified in these historical developments can be used to predict future developments. According to these rules historical materialism determined a future where workers would control the distribution of surpluses, which they would do on the basis of social justice.

Contributor: Colin Kirk

facing each other: bourgeoisie and proletariat.' (Even if, today, 150 years on, the proletariat, or full-time workers, often are the bourgeoisie too. But the words still strike a chord, for even as the workers are 'embourgoiseified', there develops what contemporary Marxists have described as the new 'unworking class', of casual labourers, the unemployed, the old, the mad and the sick – together making up a new underclass.)

And as Marx continues, when we examine the characteristics of the new industrial society, we see that the bourgeoisie has established itself as the supreme power in the modern State, running the government, turning it into 'but a committee for managing the affairs of the whole bourgeoisie'.

Karl Marx and his supporter and collaborator, Friedrich Engels, wrote a great deal, of a largely rather turgid quasi-economic variety. There is not just the three voluminous parts of *Das Kapital;* but also the *Critique of Hegel's Philosophy of Right*, in which Marx and Engels declared that religion was 'the opium of the people', and the publication of the *Theses on Feuerbach* in which it is observed that 'philosophers have only interpreted the world in various ways – the point is to change it'. Not to forget the numerous essays *On Religion, On Literature and Art, On Ireland*, and so on, nor other documents such as letters and correspondence.

But it is the relatively short and colourful *Manifesto* for the embryonic Communist Party, written in German, printed in London and speedily translated into French in time for the insurrection in Paris of June 1848, which made his mark on history.

Produced as revolutions rocked Europe, in Paris, Rome, Berlin, Vienna, Prague and Budapest, the *Manifesto* optimistically heralds the new era. Its 'fundamental proposition' is that 'in every historical epoch' the prevailing 'mode of economic production and exchange' and 'the social organisation necessarily following from it' determine the political structures of society, along with the intellectual beliefs and ideas. That is, economics determines social life, and that decides political positions. In one of the *Manifesto*'s memorable phrases, Marx and Engels argue that it therefore follows that 'the whole history of mankind has been a history of class struggles, contests between exploiter and exploited, ruling and oppressed. . .'

This idea, as Engels ambitiously puts it in the preface to the English version of the *Manifesto*, is comparable to DARWIN's theory of EVOLUTION. Marxism is the theory of the evolution of societies. It is as impersonal and its conclusions as inevitable as Darwin's biological model of the development of species. The *Manifesto*'s emphasis is on the class struggle, and its consequent call for revolutionary action indeed led to Marx being arrested in Cologne in 1849, after the crushing of the 1848 revolutions, and tried for sedition. Although acquitted, Marx spent the rest of his life as an exile in London, supported financially by Engels' Manchester textile business. There he pored over books in the reading room of the British Museum, leaving the front-line action to others. Indeed, Marxism began to stress the inexorable changes in economic production over the role of the proletarians.

Marx lived a rather sad and lonely life of (if not true poverty) straitened circumstances, apparently deeply affected by the early deaths of four of his seven children, from malnutrition and poor living conditions. The son of a wealthy German lawyer, who had renounced his Jewish faith in order to progress in his career, he married the 'most beautiful girl in Trier', the daughter of the Baron of Westphalen, Jenny, to whom in due course it fell to pawn the family silver (marked with the crest of the Dukes of Argyll), and cope with Marx's unfaithfulness, which produced an illegitimate child by one of their servants. She also had to edit and write out many of the revolutionary scripts. (How great an input Jenny Marx may have had into the *Manifesto* is unknown, but it may well have been more than is conventionally acknowledged.) All the while, Marx vowed never to allow 'bourgeois society' to make him into a 'money-making machine', and money that was given to him or otherwise came to the family was frequently expended rather ineffectually on either revolutionary projects, school fees or just parties. In many ways Marx's writings are a substitute for physical activity – revolutionary or otherwise. And in a way, he was a great snob, embittered by personal experience. Just before his death he observed that he was 'the best hated and most calumniated man of his time.'

Contributor: Martin Cohen

## Further reading

Marx, K. (1846/6) *The German Ideology*

Marx, K. and Engels, F. (1848) *The Communist Manifesto*

## MARXISM (AS PHILOSOPHICAL METHOD)

Although MARX himself famously derided philosophy, saying the point is not to 'interpret' the world, it is to change it, he has influenced many schools of philosophy ever since. The publication of his *Economic and Social Manuscripts* (in the 1930s) led to many schools of academic 'Marxism' springing up, notably those following the interpretations of Gyorgy Lukaks (1885–1971), who focused on ALIENATION and 'Marxist AESTHETICS'; the Italian radical, Antonio GRAMSCI (1891–1937), who spent most of his time in prison and attempted to offer a Marxism that allowed moral and cultural values to be preserved by an elite; the 'CRITICAL THEORISTS' of the Frankfurt School (such as Theodor ADORNO, Herbert Marcuse and Jurgen HABERMAS); EXISTENTIALIST Marxists (such as Jean Paul SARTRE and Maurice MERLEAU-PONTY); and the 'STRUCTURAL' interpretations of Louis ALTHUSSER (1918–90) – who claimed that Marx had contaminated his theory of history by his ideological stance, and that a more dispassionate approach was better – and all this just to mention a few, now rather faded-looking, blooms.

## MATERIALISM (AND MATTER)

Materialism has several slightly confusing senses in philosophy. The first is that of philosophers such as DEMOCRITUS and LEUCIPPUS, who explained the world as atoms (that is to say, indivisible bits of matter) in motion; as well as HOBBES, who is in touch with modern views of how the brain works, by claiming that the body was a machine propelled by appetites and aversions. LEIBNIZ imagined the 'extensionless' centres of energies, the 'MONADS', were the reality, with SPACE and matter the illusion. Similarly, BERKELEY was definitely an 'immaterialist' as he thought that matter did not have any significance, and that the only reality was the conceptual one. Hence, the world might as well be considered not to exist when it is not being perceived. DESCARTES is usually lumped in with the other materialists (and, of course, created the great division in schools in the first place), but really, his argument is that there are two substances to the universe, mind and matter, and since he considers the former to be the more important, it seem perverse to call him a 'materialist' (although philosophy books conventionally do.)

The hypothesis that the things that people like LOCKE used to call 'ideas' are really 'brain states' – PHENOMENA created by chemical reactions in the tissue of the brain – is a twentieth-century elaboration of this old Hobbesian doctrine. Today it may also go under grand-sounding titles such as the 'contingent mind-brain identity hypothesis' or 'central state mechanism'. Indeed, Locke writes in the second book of his *Essay Concerning Human Understanding* that 'perception, thinking, doubting, believing, reasoning, knowing' are all aspects of a kind of 'internal sense', not in principle different from those of smell, touch, taste, and so on.

REDUCTIONISM is the view that 'thinking' is best reduced in any case to a process of stimulus/response, the behaviour is a complicated 'reaction to a stimulus, while 'eliminitativism' consigns the notions of mind and thought to the dustbin in their entirety as outmoded expressions relating to a superstitious pre-scientific era.

## MATHEMATICS

The rise of Greek philosophy was on the wings of mathematics, so to speak, and mathematics has continued to exert a fascination for philosophers ever since, not least in the efforts of the logicians to reduce human thought to a kind of symbolic notation. Indeed, PYTHAGORAS taught that all learning was ultimately about 'number', and Euclid's *Elements*, in which he sets out definitions and AXIOMS in order to demonstrate a wealth of geometrical facts, was for a thousand years the epitome of pure knowledge, so desired by philosophers.

KANT was concerned by the apparent paradox of a mathematics that was both true 'by necessity' (2+2 must = 4) and yet 'informative' – in that it appears to offer new information. Kant expressed this by saying that mathematics is 'synthetic *a priori*' in nature, that is to say, it is true by definition (a priori), yet it yields new information (synthetic findings). Unlike later philosophers, and writing uncritically of Euclid's claims of universal applicability to his theorems, he considered geometry and ARITHMETIC to be essentially two aspects of the same type of knowledge.

Yet the facts of mathematics are not so certain after all. Philosophers and mathematicians such as POINCARÉ have accepted that not only are the many different geometries possible, but they are mutually incompatible and impossible to choose between, other than by 'convention'. Indeed DESCARTES, LEIBNIZ, RUSSELL and FREGE turned out to be more use as mathematicians than as philosophers, even though Russell and Frege, in fact, held that LOGIC was superior to mathematics, which they attempted to reduce to a number of logical principles, without success.

## MAXWELL, JAMES CLERK (1831–79)

The philosophically trained Scottish scientist, James Maxwell, unified the theories of electricity, magnetism and light, invented statistical dynamics and coined the term relativity. Although he never wrote anything specifically 'philosophical', his use of analogy, classifications and relations created a language for modern theoretical physics.

## MCTAGGART, JOHN (1866–1925)

McTaggart is remembered for saying that time is unreal. His confusing argument of the 'A series' and the 'B series' runs like this: The 'A series' consists of the terms past, present and future, while the 'B series' has terms like 'preceding', 'simultaneous with' and 'following afterwards'. At any time, say, 'teatime', there must be a time before it, let us say, 'lunchtime'. If lunchtime comes before teatime, then at some point lunchtime was in the past and teatime was in the present. In fact, says the Cambridge professor, any event has all three 'A series' properties; that is, it is in the future, the present and the past, albeit at different times. In adding the qualification, 'at different times', claims McTaggart, we enter an 'infinite regress', the only way out of which is to deny the existence of time.

SEE ALSO

Time

## MEAN, DOCTRINE OF THE

The 'goldilocks' doctrine of everything 'in moderation' is central to ARISTOTLE's discussion of character in the *Niomachean Ethics*. This extract is from Book IV, passages 1120–1135 .

> Now the man is thought to be proud who thinks himself worthy of great things, being worthy of them; for he who does so beyond his deserts is a fool, but no virtuous man is foolish or silly. The proud man, then, is the man we have described. For he who is worthy of little and thinks himself worthy of little is temperate, but not proud; for pride implies greatness, as beauty implies a good-sized body, and little people may be neat and well-proportioned but cannot be beautiful. . .

[for] . . . it is hard to be truly proud; for it is impossible without nobility and goodness of character. It is chiefly with honours and dishonours, then, that the proud man is concerned; and at honours that are great and conferred by good men he will be moderately Pleased, thinking that he is coming by his own or even less than his own; for there can be no honour that is worthy of perfect virtue, yet he will at any rate accept it since they have nothing greater to bestow on him; but honour from casual people and on trifling grounds he will utterly despise, since it is not this that he deserves. . .

## MEANING

Philosophy is concerned with various questions of 'meaning', and the way language relates to reality. Words, it seems, look to other words and grammatical rules for their correct usage, but also to 'the world'. FREGE attempted to split meaning into two parts, 'sense' and 'reference', while W.V. QUINE goes back to the old view that observing behaviour is the only way of obtaining the 'meaning' of words. Other twentieth-century philosophers, including WITTGENSTEIN and TARSKI, attempted to investigate the 'semantic structure' of sentences to pin down the criteria for 'meaningfulness'.

## MEDICAL ETHICS

Medical ethics started with HIPPOCRATES and his oath to 'do no harm'. Today, the term covers a range of issues in health care and other related fields. In the 'hospital context' these include the relationship of patient and doctor, the need to obtain 'informed' consent before undertaking treatment and, related to this, the degree to which the doctor can depart from the truth when it appears in the patient's interest to do so; the allocation of health care resources; EUTHANASIA and withholding of treatment (perhaps from the newborn, perhaps from the very old); confidentiality of medical information, and so on. In a research context they may include the limits of acceptability of experiments on ANIMALS – or on humans; the use of genetic information (particularly in relation to choices affecting families); the relationship of private profit to public health. The term 'BIOETHICS' is often used interchangeably.

The idea behind medical ethics is that there is a particular kind of moral expertise that belongs not in the area of medicine but in philosophy, and that either philosophers can be asked to express their opinions on medical matters, or medical people can be given training as philosophers. In practice, this leads to the dominance in the field of two narrow interpretations of ETHICS: the UTILITARIAN calculations, epitomised by such things as the QALYs system for allocating resources (where the number of Quality Assessed Life Years for patients is counted up and compared under various treatment options – so, for example, a hip transplant programme may be 'better' than an expensive ear operation); and a residual notion of 'rights' in which certain treatments (for example, being treated for a rare disease) are funded anyway, whatever the potential costs: part of a sense of a fundamental 'right to life'. These approaches are often described as 'KANTIAN'.

### SEE ALSO

Reproductive ethics

## MEDIEVAL PHILOSOPHY

Medieval philosophy starts with Saint AUGUSTINE (354–430 CE), even though he really belongs to the era of Rome, not the medieval period. Nonetheless, it is his writings that shaped much of the later thinkers, with his attempt to co-opt the Greek philosophical tradition into the edifice of Christian revelation. Concepts such as good and evil, time and eternity, the origins of the universe (Creation) and its likely future (endless?) are central, as of course is GOD. In consequence, the key figures of medieval philosophy are the 'Saints', that is ANSELM (1033–1109 CE) and Thomas AQUINAS (1224–74 CE), alongside the Arabic (Muslim) philosophers such as AVICENNA (980–1037 CE) and Averroës (1126–98 CE), who used the same method, but with a rather different perspective.

## MEINONG, ALEXIUS (1853–1920)

Alexius Meinong was an Austrian historian and student of Franz BRENTANO, appointed 'Estraordinarius of Philosophy' at the University of Graz, who challenged the prevailing opinions about the way language worked (in particular, the attempts of LOGICIANS such as RUSSELL and FREGE to treat the 'meanings of words' as if they were objects). His most celebrated work, *On Assumptions*, appeared in 1902, with a more detailed second edition eight years later. Meinong is concerned about the properties of things that may or equally well may not actually exist, such as 'Golden Mountains' or even 'Round Squares'. Russell objected that the notion of round squares was logically contradictory, but Meinong was unmoved, merely considering being logically self-contradictory to be another kind of property.

# MEMORY

## Essentials of memory

How can something from the past that is no longer in existence remain present in our memory? PLATO described memory as a storage system fashioned out of wax. Expanding on this metaphor, ARISTOTLE claimed that it was made up of traces of experiences, which in some way record and represent them. Similarly, British empiricist philosophers, such as John LOCKE and David HUME, thought of memory as a storehouse of ideas copied from previous impressions, Hume insisting that they differed from both perceptual impressions and ideas of the imagination only in their degree of vivacity. This view, though challenged by WITTGENSTEIN, remains prevalent to this day.

## Remembering: recognition, recollection, reminiscence and retention

Although the details of this traditional 'storage view' of memory are constantly being modified to meet the results of neuroscientific research, the view has been held by the majority of philosophers and cognitive scientists to this day. Thus, according to the GESTALT PSYCHOLOGIST Wolfgang Kohler (1887–1967) and the renowned neuroscientist Antonio Damasio (1944–), our experiences are stored inside the brain as codified physiological traces, which are in some way 'isomorphic' with the original experience. That is, for Damasio, that our memories are stored and indexed as 'neural representations' somewhere at the back of the brain. When we remember or recall something, our brain 'looks it up' in the index and then decodes and recovers the relevant memory-data stored.

Such clouds of philosophy were condensed into one drop of grammar by Ludwig Wittgenstein (1889–1951), who argued that they were literally nonsense. Although Wittgenstein himself never gave the topic of 'memory' any systematic treatment, his scattered remarks on memory would inform careful work by his pupil Norman Malcolm (1911–90), and more recently by leading Wittgensteinian scholar P.M.S. Hacker. Malcolm and Hacker persuasively argue that it makes no sense to try to locate in which hemisphere of the brain our long-term and short-term memories are 'stored', though we might of course have empirical evidence for saying that one part of the brain is particularly active when performing a general task, such as trying to recall something from the distant past or giving an account of what one did five minutes ago.

Bertrand RUSSELL (1872–1970) and William JAMES (1842–1910) followed Aristotle and Hume in thinking that imagery is a necessary, but not sufficient, condition for memory, but Wittgenstein and other Wittgensteinians have disputed the assumptions lying behind the whole approach. Wittgenstein argued that it was an illusion to think that that there may be such a thing as a picture which contained its interpretation in itself. This would be like suggesting that an arrow signpost points only because one joins to it a picture of an arrow. There is nothing about a complex image (or state) that could make it refer to one and only one state of affairs. Even if a mental image does accompany X, it cannot explain it, for one would in turn have to recognise that it is an image of X. If I remember the Parthenon at dawn it does not follow (as the representational theory would have it) that the 'content' of one's memory is just an image or representation of what is being remembered, let alone that the Parthenon is in any shape or form 'inside' anything which we might call my memory.

Extended-mind theorists, such as Andy Clark (1957–) and David Chalmers (1966–), claim that our mind is ONTOLOGICALLY complex, spreading out over space and time and including bits of the world, such as notebooks. Accordingly, Clark and Chalmers argue that in the future we may be able to plug into our brain modules for additional memory, much as one can plug an additional hard drive into a computer. But we consult notebooks precisely because we cannot remember – it makes no sense to talk of our consulting our memory to see what we find there. Having a notebook implanted in us would no more enhance our memory than swallowing a dictionary would improve our vocabulary. We do indeed use external things to aid us in remembering, but in so doing we are not storing memories in our fingers or notebooks anymore than we ordinarily store them in our brains, though of course one can record one's memories in a diary and read them later on in life, when we have forgotten the incidents recorded.

Memory is essentially the retention of knowledge, and as such can exist independently of causal connection (as when something has lost its original colour). By contrast, if – as Russell thought – our memories have been implanted in our brain, we lose not only the sense in which it is our duty to remember an appointment, but also to ensure that past human achievements – and atrocities – are not forgotten.

Contributor: Constantine Sandis

## Further reading

Aristotle, *On Memory*

Malcolm, N. (1977) *Memory and Mind*

## MENCIUS (371–289 BCE)

### The essential Mencius

As CONFUCIUS, in the Eastern tradition, might be to SOCRATES in the Western philosophical tradition, so Mencius is to PLATO. For Mencius is the communicator of Confucian philosophy, known for his insistence that human nature is basically good. His views, set out in the 'Book of Mencius' or Mengzi, were adopted as the basis for the Chinese civil service exams in the four-

---

**MENCIUS AGAINST UTILITARIANISM**

Challenged by followers of Mo Tzu to justify elaborate funeral traditions, Mencius replied:

In ancient times there was no burial of one's parents. When a man's parent died, he simply threw the body into a ditch. When he later passed by, what he saw was that the body was being eaten by the foxes or bitten by the gnats or flies. . . He could not bear the sight. The feeling of the heart flew out to his face. He then hurried home and came back with baskets and a spade for covering up the body. If the covering up of a human body was the right thing for primitive man, it is quite right today for a filial son or man of *ren* to prepare the funeral for his parents.

Contributor: Martin Cohen

---

teenth century, and remained the core texts for the next 600 years.

### On benevolence

Mencius, known as 'the Second Sage' of Confucianism, was born in the State of Zou, located in what is now the province of Shandong, only 30 km south of Qufu, the town of Confucius. Mencius is the first Confucian philosopher who explored the question of HUMAN NATURE systematically. During his time, it was popular to explain human nature in terms of life.

Mencius argues against this: if understanding human nature in terms of life, then it follows that the nature of a dog is the same as the nature of an ox, and the nature of an ox is the same as the nature of a man. So instead, he explains human nature in terms of its moral quality and declared definitely that human nature is originally good. He argues, when a person sees a child about to fall into a well, invariably he will feel a sense of alarm and compassion, and will rush to save the child. And this is not for the purpose of gaining the favour of the child's parents, or seeking the approbation of his neighbours and friends, or for fear of blame should he fail to rescue it. It is rather due to the spontaneous response of human nature.

From this it follows that the sense of sympathy, the sense of repentance, the sense of courtesy and the sense of judgement on what is right and wrong are the four beginnings of humanity, righteousness, propriety and wisdom. So it is said that these virtues are not drilled into us from outside. They are rooted in human nature and are found in all persons. Unfortunately, many people cannot develop them.

Thus Mencius sighed, 'When person's fowls and dogs are lost, they know enough to seek them again; but if they lose their human heart/mind, they do not know to seek for it.' According to Mencius, the goal of moral cultivation is to return to one's innate nature. This is also the aim of his ideal State, as Plato attempted to build in his *Republic*.

So when King Hui of Liang asked Mencius what benefit he would bring to the kingdom, Mencius answered: 'humanity and righteousness, and these shall be the only themes. Why must you use the word "profit"?' Mencius spent his life bouncing from one feudal State to another, trying to find some ruler who would follow his teachings, but he was largely unsuccessful in his endeavour. But later in Song Dynasty, Zhu Xi (1130–1200) included the *Book of Mencius* as one of the *Four Books*, which became canonical texts of the Confucian tradition.

Mencius came to be regarded as the greatest Confucian thinker, after Confucius himself, and his teachings have been very influential on the development of Confucian thought in the Song, Ming (1368–1644), Qing (1644–1912) and up to modern times.

Contributor: Yuli Liu

## MERLEAU-PONTY, MAURICE (1908–61)

Merleau-Ponty is counted as one of the great French EXISTENTIALISTS, which may be true, but still his contribution to knowledge is very slim. He seems to have thought that what we experience is not entirely a product of what is out there, nor yet entirely a product of our own creation. This is counted as a 'rejection of Cartesian DUALISM'. In the *Phenomenology of Perception* (1945) he adds that without perception we would not have any views on anything.

## META-ETHICS

This is the study not of what is actually right or wrong, but our reasons for thinking that there might be a question there to be answered at all. It includes questions about the 'meaning' of moral terms, whether judgements are objective or purely SUBJECTIVE, and pinning down (in G.E. MOORE's phrase) what 'goodness is' rather than what things are good.

## METAPHYSICS

David HUME scared the horses when he wrote in *An Enquiry Concerning Human Understanding* (1748):

If we take in our hand any volume of divinity or school metaphysics, for instance; let us ask, Does it contain any abstract reasoning concerning quantity or number? No. Does it contain any experimental reasoning concerning matter of fact and existence? No. Commit it then to the flames: for it can contain nothing but sophistry and illusion.

Yet originally, 'metaphysics' was very respectable – the chapter after 'physics' in ARISTOTLE's philosophy. It can be defined as 'beyond science', or even 'before science', depending on taste. Thomas HOBBES and other philosophers before and since railed against the 'Metaphysicians', and the public assessment of the study is rather the way H.L. Mencken (1880–1956) defined it in his 'Notebooks: Minority Report'. For Mencken, it is merely one way of increasing 'the capacity of human beings to bore one another', along with the dinner party of more than two, and the epic poem.

## DE LA METTRIE, JULIEN OFFRAY (1709–51)

The French philosopher de la Mettrie is remembered for his mechanistic model of human existence, *L'Homme Machine* (*Man, the Machine*, 1747). Mental activity is explained therein as various changes in brain state, and behaviour is reduced to a series of causes and their effects. Religious belief and free will are dismissed. The implications for ETHICS, he suggests, are that the only value is HEDONISM, or the pursuit of pleasure, and the only virtue is self-love, as described in another of his books, the *Discourse on Happiness* (1751).

## MILL, JOHN STUART (1806–73)

### The essential Mill

Mill was born in London, son of James Mill, and worked at the East India Company, with a brief

spell as a Member of Parliament, with a particular interest in women's rights, constitutional reform and **ECONOMICS**. In 1830 he met Harriet Taylor, to whom, he says in his *Autobiography*, he owes none of his 'technical doctrines' but all of the liberal ideas. Mill holds that allowing people to decide for themselves as much as possible increases the general happiness, thereby arriving at a philosophy arguing in favour of liberty of thought, speech and association. And it is these ideas, on the roles of individuals and society, set out in *On Liberty* (1859) and *The Principles of Political Economy (with Some of the Applications to Social Philosophy)* (1848), that are indeed where his legacy lies, as a great political thinker.

## A British Liberal

*The Principles of Political Economy (with Some of the Applications to Social Philosophy)* was written in 1848, around the same time as **MARX** and **ENGELS** were attempting to foment proletarian revolution. It is essentially an attempt to emulate Mill's illustrious Scottish predecessor, Adam **SMITH**, in setting out the workings of the modern State. Unlike Smith, however, Mill is a poor writer and lacks both the insight and subtlety of the Scot. Despite, or perhaps because of, his famous education at the hands of his father (Greek at age 3, Latin at 8 and **LOGIC** at 13), where Smith has pace and acuity, Mill has leaden prose and plodding mathematics.

Mill's strength is less in the analysis, particularly not the economic one, than in the **ETHICAL** system building and the **IDEALISM**, where he places economic and social claims in a new framework of political rights. For example, he writes, following Smith, that only labour creates wealth, but capital is stored up labour and may be accumulated – or even inherited – quite legitimately. Then he goes on, inheritance is acceptable, even when initially based on an injustice, once a few human generations have passed, as to remedy the injustice would create worse problems than leaving the situation alone. On the other hand, the inheritance of wealth beyond the point of achieving 'comfortable independence' should be prevented by the State intervening and confiscating assets. People who want to live more than 'comfortably' should work for it.

Mill thought that this '**BENTHAMITE**' part of his book would cause more than a little stir, and indeed hoped to become notorious for it. However, as it was tucked away in nearly half a million other words, it attracted little interest. Still, as he himself wrote in a letter to a friend,

The purely abstract investigations of political economy are of very minor importance compared with great practical tensions that the progress of democracy and the spread of socialist opinions are pressing on.

It is these elements, largely confined to the end portion of Book V, which make for the most original parts of the whole work. Mill is one of the first writers to consider himself a '**SOCIAL SCIENTIST**', and was firm in his conviction that the social sciences were justly related to the natural sciences and could be pursued using similar methods. Mill distinguished between the study of individuals, which would be largely psychology, and the study of collective behaviour, which would be largely economics and politics. He tried out various terms for summing up his study, such as 'social economy', 'political economy' (which he thought might belong on its own somewhere), even 'speculative politics', but eventually returned to what he called **COMTE**'s 'convenient barbarism' – sociology.

And his finding, really drawn from Smith, is that it is this element of 'co-operation' that is the key to modern societies. From it characteristically follows a great 'flowering of co-operatives' and joint-stock companies. But Mill adds to it this distinctive rider, that:

Whatever theory we may adopt respecting the foundation of the social union, and under whatever political institutions we live, there is a circle around every individual human being which no government, be it that of one, of a few, or of the many, ought to be permitted to overstep. . . That there is, or ought to be, some space in human existence thus entrenched around, and sacred from authoritative intrusion, no one who professes the smallest regard to human freedom or dignity will call into question: the point to be determined is, where the limit should be placed; how large a province of human life this reserved territory should include.

Mill's LIBERALISM is grounded in the UTILITARIAN ethic adopted from Jeremy Bentham, rather than on the appeal to fundamental rights of that other great liberal Englishman, John LOCKE. Yet despite different starting points, both arrive at the characteristic set of individual rights and freedoms.

Contributor: Martin Cohen

# MIND

The key question for philosophy of mind is not the practical study of how the mind works (which is now separated off as PSYCHOLOGY), but whether there is anything worthy of the name anyway. If there is a sense to the term, then when we say, 'I think I can see the sun coming out', we report not merely some sense data, but a 'mental event'. The mind/body problem is one such concern: if there is a difference, how does one affect the other? Another question is, if human beings evolved from simpler life forms – did they have minds too? If not, at what point did 'minds' appear? According to 'panpsychists', even stones have minds, but as humans became more and more complex, our 'simple minds' combined to form the present, slightly more impressive ones. Philosophers have contemplated the possibility of the mind being separated from its sources of sensory information, and the possible effects of that. If we are merely processing sense information in our minds, and we reach a point (death) when this stops, it would appear to be much less likely that we carry on in any sense.

Philosophers of mind today focus on areas such as the different kinds of 'content' that mental phenomena may include, such as pains and itches; seeing COLOURS and smelling flowers; after images and DREAMS; and so on; or rather different kinds of thoughts involving views and BELIEFS; MEMORIES of facts; attitudes and the famous 'INTENTIONS', as discussed by BRENTANO.

SEE ALSO

Consciousness

# MODERNITY

One of the crucial disagreements between modernity and POSTMODERNITY is centred on the ENLIGHTENMENT clarion call, 'Liberty, Equality, Fraternity'; the postmoderns ask: 'But for whom?' Taking its cue from the initial FEMINIST critique of modernity as misogynistic and patriarchal, there has been a developing critique of modernity on race or ethnic grounds. Modernity, so the argument runs, is not simply misogynistic, it is also RACIST and monocultural. Thinkers such as Cornel West have employed the genealogical method of NIETZSCHE and FOUCAULT to point to a consistent 'white supremacist bias' at work even in such apparently civilised thinkers of Enlightenment as KANT. Frantz FANON's work on the political implications of this bias as manifested in colonialism has also been highly influential. Fanon reads racism as a 'psychopathology', a view strongly supported by SARTRE in his preface to Fanon's *The Wretched of the Earth*.

Thinkers such as Fanon and West have provided the inspiration for the development of what is now termed 'intercultural philosophy', a philosophical approach alert to a specific cultural bias in apparently neutral philosophical methods and practices. Such interculturalism has been keen to stress the need for philosophy to link to 'praxis', most especially political contexts requiring intervention and critique. It has also had, in various forms, a huge influence on educational policy and programmes. Anti-racism and multicultural programmes in schools, for example, can be said to operate within an intercultural philosophical framework, and the very move from the previous 'multicultural' paradigm to an 'intercultural' one was made on philosophical grounds: the former was seen as simply allowing cultures to 'tolerate' each other side by side, whereas the latter paradigm of 'interculturality' is seen as inspiring genuine questioning and dialogue between cultures and value systems. The relevance and necessity of such philosophical work is clear. Intercultural philosophical approaches are also strongly committed to an interdisciplinary research method and ethos.

**SEE ALSO**

Postmodernism and Post-rationalism

## MODUS PONENS AND MODUS TOLLENS

*Modus ponens* is the Latin term for the rule of INFERENCE that says that given a relationship, if p, then q; and also 'p', we can conclude 'q'. It is also called 'affirming the antecedent' or 'the affirming mood'. If someone 'affirms the consequent', that is, they argue: if p then q; q; therefore p, they commit a dreadful FALLACY. (The antecedent is the first clause, the consequent is the one that is being 'concluded'.)

The *modus tollens* is the negative case: also known grandly as the 'destructive hypothetical SYLLOGISM'. If p then q; not q, therefore not p. And similarly, the fallacy of 'DENYING THE ANTECEDENT' is to assume that if there is no 'p' there is no 'q', as there might be, but for a different reason.

**SEE ALSO**

Logic

## MONADS

A term used by LEIBNIZ originally in a letter to mean something that has no parts, in effect, a kind of conceptual 'atom'.

**SEE ALSO**

Leibniz

## MONISM

A term contrasted with DUALISM and pluralism, covering views based on there being 'one' substance only. For example, someone who argues that the universe consists ultimately of one basic substance (SPINOZA used God in this way) is a monist.

## MONTAIGNE, MICHEL EYQUEM DE (1533–92)

The French HUMANIST aristocrat whose witty essays inspired DESCARTES to write his philosophical essays in a more popular style. One such, in 1588, *Apology for Raimond Sebond*, for example, was SCEPTICAL about the claims of theologians such as Sebond that faith could lead to knowledge, and indeed about the possibility of knowledge in general. Montaigne was himself echoing the scepticism of SEXTUS EMPIRICUS, whose writings in Greek and Latin had at this time become fashionable in France. Among the questions Sextus had discussed were the criteria for knowledge, and what makes humans different from animals, both of which questions were thus transmitted through Montaigne to Descartes and became the central issues of the so-called 'modern' philosophers.

## MOORE, G.E. (1873–1958)

George Edward Moore was the Cambridge philosopher known for his 26-year editorship of *Mind*. His 'naturalistic FALLACY' denied that the 'is' in the sentence 'pleasure is good', was a real 'is', a real is, like, for example, 'snow is white'. Moore said 'is' should only be used for 'natural' properties. Funnily enough, years later, Moore admitted to never having given 'any tenable explanation' of what he meant by saying 'good' was not a natural property.

**SEE ALSO**

Naturalistic fallacy, Good, Language

## MORAL CONFLICT

### Essentials of moral conflict

Moral conflicts arise when we are faced by two conflicting obligations. In their extreme form they are 'ethical DILEMMAS'. Many contemporary philosophers argue that such conflicts are only apparent, and that careful analysis with reference to some sophisticated moral theory will resolve the matter, by either providing a clear hierarchy of moral obligations (so that one of the prima facie obligations is overridden and therefore falls away), or by showing that one of the obligations need not, after all, concern us. However, there are a number of strong reasons why it is plausible to think that real moral conflict does indeed exist.

## Moral conflicts and the fragility of ethics

An example of moral conflict often quoted within philosophy circles, is found in Jean Paul SARTRE's *Existentialism and Humanism*. Sartre describes a young man who has to decide whether to stay with his elderly mother or leave to join the Free French Forces in England, to make the point that there is no ETHICAL standpoint that can resolve this conflict without 'bad faith'. These conflicting obligations arise because finite human beings find themselves in situations where they acknowledge and feel the force of two conflicting obligations, yet are unable to fulfil them both no matter how much they would want to do so. A second aspect of this kind of moral conflict seems to be that people (or groups) often hold different and irreconcilable purposes, values and ends.

Isaiah Berlin, for example, insisted that certain cherished and central political values simply cannot be adhered to without compromising or undermining another set of equally cherished and fundamental values. My desire to live in a free and equal society might be impossible, since to allow a very high degree of genuine liberty leads inevitably to deep inequalities, and vice versa. A variant of this argument focuses on the inevitable moral conflicts which arise due to different ways of life, or different incommensurable goals within one life. Leading a pious existence as a practising Catholic, for example, cannot sit easily with fellow citizens who are enthusiastic pornographers or libertine bohemians.

These kinds of clashes are evident when we observe the mixing of ethnic or religious groups within a pluralist society (although such conflicts also arise in largely homogeneous societies) and their irresolvability can be traced to deep and enduring differences in world views or, as the influential contemporary political philosopher, John RAWLS, put it, 'conceptions of the good'. However, a third, and perhaps the most interesting genesis of moral conflict, arises from the different claims and emphases of competing NORMATIVE moral theories.

Different approaches privilege different categories, some emphasising the moral importance of the agent's intentions, while others focus on the action's consequences; and this inevitably leads to different advice on how we ought to act as moral persons. UTILITARIANS such as BENTHAM and J.S. MILL, for example, take consequences as all-important in deciding between right and wrong actions. In stark contrast, KANTIANS insist that moral actions must accord with a universal, explicit and rule-governed moral law independent of particular outcomes, rendering the consequences of our actions irrelevant to their status as right or wrong.

But even if one holds to a DEONTOLOGICAL (rule-governed) or CONSEQUENTIALIST (consequence-focused) account of what makes an action right or wrong, there are still complications. The universal nature of moral imperatives can clash with our particularistic duties (such as obligations to friends or family), duties that characterise special relationships which are essential to any notion of the good life.

The principle of partiality (or 'agent-relative' principles) captures these special obligations, which sometimes trump universalistic 'agent-neutral' principles that would otherwise hold sway. The very nature of commitments and obligations towards significant others, such as our children, parents or friends, are in large part constituted by, and meaningful because of, what Steven Lukes calls 'a refusal to engage in the very kind of trade-off that full commensurability would require'. A parent's contemplation of general utility calculations, which treat strangers and kin alike, is morally grotesque because it undermines the very essence of the special child–parent relationship. Similarly, to consider friendship entirely in terms of a reciprocal formal set of duties and obligations manifestly fails to grasp what is constitutive of being a true friend.

What we find here is disagreement at the most basic level of moral theorising, and with it the inevitable conflict in deciding which obligations or duties apply in specific situations. The basis for moral conflicts, then, is the sheer diversity of our values, aims, aspirations, and an ineradicable tension between different kinds of moral judgements – ones particular to the agent, as opposed to those that go beyond any particular moral agent and seek to be univeralisable. If we accept that there can be real moral conflict, then this provokes more questions about the status of the duty overridden and the allocation of praise or blame.

Does the overridden value or duty leave, as Bernard Williams suggests, a 'moral residue' or 'moral remainder'? It may be the case that no matter what an agent does in the face of moral conflict, she will be left feeling morally polluted by failing to fulfil a cherished moral duty. This problem takes on an even stronger focus in cases where a clash of moral duties cannot be resolved even from a practical point of view, because there can be no commensurability (or trade-off) between conflicting duties. Here an agent faces a moral dilemma, which in itself spawns a host of difficult philosophical questions about the nature of morality itself.

Second, does the existence of real moral conflict open the way for the emergence of what has become known as the 'dirty hands' problem? Here we find situations (most commonly in politics) where the immoral actions of others can leave good and moral persons facing circumstances where they are forced, in order to bring about the lesser evil, to commit moral violations. In short, can we coherently talk about agents being forced to do wrong in order to do right, and if so, what impact does this have on their character and moral status?

In sum, if the arguments for the existence of real, rather than merely apparent or prima facie, moral conflict are persuasive, then this has ramifications for ethical theory itself. Ethical systems that reject the existence of genuine moral conflict must be challenged for failing to properly capture our moral reality. The view that there is always an unambiguous right or moral action in any set of given circumstances becomes problematic and unpersuasive. Perhaps the contemporary philosopher, Martha Nussbaum's claim that good and moral persons can be destroyed by circumstances, and that there is 'fragility to goodness', better fits with our deepest reflections on the ethical life.

Contributor: Stephen de Wijze

# MOTION

Motion presents a number of problems to philosophers. When does something start to move? How long does this 'starting' last? Is 'change' motion? Is change (and motion) an illusion? (As PARMENIDES, and hence ZENO, argued.)

# MURDOCH, IRIS (1919–99)

## The essential Murdoch

Born Jean Iris Mudoch in Dublin, Murdoch spent most of her life in England, particularly around Oxford, where she was a philosophy tutor from 1948. Before that, she worked in London as a civil servant at the Treasury and for the United Nations in Brussels. She might have gone to the USA to study instead, but was banned under the McCarthyite restrictions against 'COMMUNISTS'.

She is remembered now as a novelist, but in fact her first published work was the non-fiction, *Sartre, Romantic Rationalist* (1952). She had met SARTRE, and although she later considered him 'dangerous' for his views on individual freedom, EXISTENTIALISM is a theme of several novels, including *Under the Net* (1954). *The Bell* (1958) combines humour with a study of religion and the human psyche, while other books explore psychoanalytical theory and ETHICS.

## Seeing 'human goodness': Iris Murdoch on moral virtue

One recent advance in contemporary moral philosophy is Iris Murdoch's unique understanding of the concept of the moral SELF. The attempt to improve the account of the moral self she associates with traditional ethics, which mainly focuses on the 'will', is the motif of her view of ethics. Iris Murdoch's historical criticism of the moral self as developed by LIBERALISM, ROMANTICISM, existentialism and linguistic empiricism is, though debatable among philosophers, nevertheless significant in the development of contemporary ethics. In various ways, she says, an overall cast of romanticism marks these philosophies, in that they strengthen the role of the will in becoming moral, at the expense of other faculties such as consciousness. The focus on the will makes the moral self solipsistic and does not dismantle selfishness.

Drawing from the world of art appreciation, Murdoch holds AESTHETIC perception to be the necessary component of moral regard for others. She claims that a moral person becomes suitably other-directed through the practice of aesthetic perception and EGO 'unselfing'. In contrast to the ARISTOTELIAN emphasis upon the rewards of virtue, Murdoch posits the self-interested 'ego' as the chief obstacle to correctly seeing others and, following from this, not rightly exercising virtue towards them, for it cannot love.

The problem of selfishness, the main ethical DILEMMA, could be solved if virtues in general, and particularly the virtue of love, Murdoch suggests, were to become central to moral life, for in loving, we focus on others. The non-judgemental love for particulars, so characteristic of Murdoch's view, helps to explain her emphasis on the relation between virtue and consciousness through love and art. Hence, Murdoch's concept of virtue is a rigorous one, since it advocates the perfection of one's moral vision as an end-in-itself, thus presenting a concept of virtue which comes much closer to the HOLINESS of the saint than to the excellence of a hero. Instead of viewing morality as a system of principles to be grasped by the detached intellect, her aim is to correlate an account of the moral self as other-directed, with the idea of the good through aesthetic perception. Love as a virtue is a response to the perception of value; sensibility suffuses it, and this love contents itself with an awareness of the importance of others.

Murdoch offers a more situational account of the moral self in contrast to both traditional and contemporary ethics. She argues that these theories lack a sufficient development of what it is to have a regard for others through aesthetic perception, which is the most important aspect of the moral self. To have regard for others demands a responsiveness that can also be explained in terms of aesthetic sensibility. Murdoch's process of obtaining aesthetic 'seeing' through development of a 'virtuous consciousness', is a process of empathic experiencing that provides the only true path of practising virtue towards others.

Contributor: Ana Lita

# MUSIC

## Essential music

From **PYTHAGORAS** and **ARISTOTLE**, to **HEGEL** and **NIETZSCHE**, music has been studied by philosophers while, in a similar spirit, some composers have wanted to include philosophical reflection in their works.

In fact, Aristotle, Plato, **DESCARTES**, Hegel, **KANT**, Nietzsche, **SCHOPENHAUER** and **ADORNO** all mentioned music in their works. Aristotle, for instance, wrote extensively on music as 'Mimesis' in his *Politics*, arguing it was vital in education; he also condemned the flute as being 'not moral' and 'too passionnal'. For Pythagoras, the harmonies of music were also the essence of the cosmos, and he ingeniously devised a tuning system inspired by **MATHEMATICS**.

## A short composition

Jean-Jacques **ROUSSEAU** (1712–78) composed classical cantatas, motets and ballet music, such as *Les Muses galantes* and *Le Devin du village*. He also contributed entries on music theory for Diderot's 'L'Encyclopédie', which later became Rousseau's *Dictionnaire de musique* (1767), after 15 years of research and work.

Nietzsche first admired, before later rejecting, Richard Wagner's music. In a tragic gesture about the unavoidable nature of destiny, Beethoven wrote 'Muss es sein?' and answered: 'Es muss sein!' ('Must that be? It must be!)

The twentieth-century composer Richard Strauss (not to be confused with the Waltz composer Johannes Strauss) wrote a flamboyant cantata inspired by Friedrich Nietzsche's philosophical work 'Zarathoustra', entitled 'Also Spracht Zarathoustra', and Nietzsche himself composed short pieces for piano and an opera.

Artists related to the musical sphere can be divided into creators (composers, lyricists) and performers (musicians, singers). Far fewer artists manage to combine both composing musical works and performing with a musical instrument. However, in the realm of classical music, Frederic Chopin, Franz Liszt and Leonard Bernstein are examples of composers who were also piano soloists or orchestra conductors.

In his essay 'The Work of Art at the age of the Mechanical Reproduction' (1936), Walter Benjamin argued that the way art is perceived has changed now that technology has made its near perfect reproduction both possible and often more convenient. Just as art galleries are no longer the sole place to see art, concert halls are no longer the only places that one can listen to music in. Since the 1920s the gramophone has brought bands playing music into simple homes, and so, appreciating music is no longer the exclusive preserve of the elites.

Philosophers and sociologists interested in music (like Pierre Bourdieu) have also questioned tastes in, or the **AESTHETICS** of, art and music, and questioned how people have (or do not have) access to various musical genres – through radios, music stores, advertising. For instance, why are some musical expressions fashionable in one country and not in another? Why do certain social classes tend to listen to classical music? Why does choice of music seem to be as predictable for marketing experts as our taste in any consumer goods?

**SOCIAL SCIENTISTS** and anthropologists have studied traditional music and questioned social identity through musical expressions. For instance, ethno-musicologists have theorised on original, unusual ways to conceive music, singing and rhythm in some isolated groups and tribes, mainly in Africa and Asia. The fact that many Third World countries cannot export or diffuse their musical culture remains an ETHICAL issue, particularly when one considers how Anglo-American music has become globalised through both the English-language media and the sophisticated techniques of corporate marketing. The choice of music in films, television dramas or even advertising and spots confirms the commodification of music. This can explain why European countries promote cultural diversity in music, movies and on television, refusing to 'let the market decide by itself'.

Some philosophers from the Frankfurt School had a strong interest in popular music, jazz and radio. As Theodor Adorno and Max Horkheimer have explained (while they lived in the USA during the mid-1940s), mass culture does not emerge from the masses; it is rather conceived for massive audiences, produced and distributed as any industrial process. Cultural studies today question distinctions between 'high art' and 'low art' in terms of music, and focus on how elements of a specific popular culture can be appropriated by audiences and individuals for building their own identity. And so, music is still a not wholly controlled part of social identity and systems of fashion.

Contributor: Yves Laberge

## Further reading

Aristotle, *Politics*. Book V.

Bourdieu, P. (1979) *Distinction*

Rousseau, J. (1767) *Dictionnaire de musique*

## MYSTICISM

Mysticism (from the Greek, *mystikos* or secret) has always been a part of Greek philosophy, with secretive cults such as at Eleusis. Similarly, there are mystical elements in the religious doctrines of Judaism, Islam and Christianity, although in the last case, mystical elements have also been sought out and condemned as 'heretical'. William JAMES and WITTGENSTEIN discuss mysticism sympathetically, but HEGEL (in his *Logic*), despite being a bit of a mystic himself, condemned it as a cover for incomprehensibility and superstition.

## NAESS, ARNE (1912–2004)

Naess is the Norwegian rock climber who founded the so-called 'Deep Ecology' movement. The human perspective that taming of nature is a 'good', and the dangerous or simply inconvenient activities of wild nature are bad, is what the 'Deep Ecologists' insist that we must move away from – and to accept that what is good for us is not necessarily good for nature, and that we should instead begin to apply values such as 'freedom and autonomy' to rivers and animals, 'respect for others' to trees and mountains.

Funnily enough, Naess' philosophical origins lie in the 'LOGICAL POSITIVISM' of Moritz SCHLICK and the VIENNA CIRCLE, and with his development of the view that the meaning of words is simply the way they are used, and hence that meaning is amenable to empirical study in just the same way as other natural phenomena are.

## NAGARJUNA

Nagarjuna is the most famous and mysterious figure in medieval BUDDHISM. His actual dates were *c.* 243 to 300 CE, but his real life is hidden within a mythic personage. Whole TANTRIC, alchemical and magical literatures now make up his biography. He taught *Sunyatavada*: the doctrine of universal emptiness, or the 'middle way', which influenced Buddhism and the direction of philosophy in the East.

Nagarjuna also taught that all contraries are illusory; extreme evil coincides with extreme good. Philosophical systems are demolished by the realisation that it is not possible to express the ultimate truth through language. Instead, he offers two kinds of truth: the conventional one judged by practical usefulness, and the 'ultimate' truth, which leads to deliverance. Definitions, categories and LOGICAL manipulations are but activities of the imagination.

To this end, he refers to Buddha's teaching that everything is in the one category, the void. But the second conclusion is that there is no distinction between the sense world, *samsara*, of phenomenal experience, and the ideal world attained on *NIRVANA* or liberation. For *nirvana* is itself a fabrication of the mind.

So the ultimate truth is complete indifference to both things and the antithesis of things: their cessation. Nagarjuna says Sunyatavada is not a philosophy but a DIALECTICAL and contemplative practice that rids the adept of every theoretical construction there is in the world, enabling achievement of imperturbable serenity and freedom. In this state the *bodhisattva* can be devoted to ALTRUISM and charity, although he considers there are no beings to serve, that all is universal emptiness.

## NAÏVE REALISM

The view that our everyday perception of the world is direct, rather than subject to some mental intermediaries. The chair really is there, the snow really does look white and the stone really does hurt when you kick it. Tastes, sounds and colours all reflect the world out there, rather than the world inside the head of the person perceiving them.

### Naïve realists

In the long-standing philosophical controversy on what sense-perception involves and how far it provides knowledge of the external world, the term 'naïve realism' has been used by a number of philosophers, who considered themselves to have a sophisticated understanding of perception (Bertrand RUSSELL, H.H. Price, A.J. Ayer and some logical empiricists), to represent their *opponents'* position, which they judged to be a remnant of untutored COMMON SENSE and, as such, badly mistaken, indeed naïve.

The self-consciously sophisticated theorists have held that when a person uses his sight, touch and the other senses to find out how things are in his environment, what he becomes immediately aware of are not, as it may be innocently supposed, physical objects existing in space and time independently of anyone perceiving them; rather they are entities of a mental or mind-dependent character referred to by various technical terms, such as 'ideas of sense', 'impressions', 'appearances', 'sensations' and, in the twentieth-century term, 'sense data'. These sophisticated philosophers, who may be generically called 'sense-datum theorists', have supported their central contention by various lines of argument, three of which may be briefly indicated.

### Argument from perspectival relativity

A physical object presents different appearances to different observers, depending on the angle of vision and perspective of the observers relative to the object. The same penny or (to modernise the old stock example) compact disc may appear to observers looking at it at different angles to have different shapes: to X it is round, to Y it is elliptical and to Z it is a thin and straight bar. Therefore it cannot be true that the visual data given to all three observers are *all* identical to the real shape of the object. And so, if Y and Z judge the object to be round, there must be a sense in which their respective judgements go beyond their respective visual data. The suggestion here is that in perception we are aware of momentary sensory glimpses or aspects of the appearances of things, but somehow the 'real' thing and its permanent properties are forever hidden from the senses, and could only be reached by some kind of imaginative INFERENCE.

### Argument from the causal conditions of perception

When a person has a visual experience of the kind that is ordinarily described as 'X sees a red tomato', what really happens is that light strikes a certain physical object and is reflected on X's eyes, causing a complicated pattern of stimulation of the receptors, which in turn causes a sequence of events in the optic nerve and brain, with the result that X has a visual experience that should, strictly speaking, be described as the awareness of a red tomato-like patch. The content of his immediate visual awareness – the visual sense datum – is the end result of a causal process and it cannot be identified with the physical object 'out there', which is a relatively distant factor in the causal chain. In changed circumstances, for example, when the very same object reflects light from a blue electric lamp, or X wears dark glasses, or if he suffers from an impairment of the eyes, the visual awareness would be in certain respects different from how it is now. Therefore, X perceives the tomato not directly, as it is commonly supposed, but *indirectly*, through the immediate awareness of visual data which provide the bases for inferential knowledge of the existence of the physical object, the tomato itself.

### Argument from illusion

When a straight stick is immersed in a bucket of water, it will appear to be bent, owing to the familiar phenomenon of refraction. When X looks at the immersed stick, the content of his immediate awareness is very similar to what he would obtain if he were to look at a really bent stick outside the bucket; hence the possibility of deception. Again, travellers in deserts report that occasionally they get the illusion of seeing an oasis where none exists. In this case, as in the previous one, it is argued that the illusory experience is qualitatively indistinguishable from the veridical experience. To put it another way, in both cases the two sets of experiences, considered as states of immediate awareness, have the same characteristics. Therefore, each of the experiences in each of the two cases is distinct from any objects existing in physical space and time. These two versions of the 'argument from illusion' are held to show that the immediate content of perceptual awareness is never part of a physical situation. However, in cases of veridical experiences, the experience provides inductive justification for the existence of the relevant physical objects.

The preceding lines of argument are developed with considerable ingenuity by empiricist philosophers to show that immediate awareness consists of private sense-data, and so ordinary people and philosophers who are not unhappy with the common-sense view that in perception we directly perceive physical objects are being naïve.

Philosophers on the other side of the controversy, far from accepting that they are being naïve, try to show in a mostly polemical fashion that the arguments invoked by sense-datum theorists are themselves invalid, fallacious or confused. For example, they point out that:

- The argument from 'perspectival relativity' trades on the fallacy of treating the different ways in which a thing appears to us when we see it from different angles and perspectives as being themselves *things* which somehow stand between us and the 'real' object. (This fallacy underlies the PHENOMENALIST effort to define the 'thinghood' of an object in terms of all the sense-data that perceivers would experience if they were placed in various hypothetical circumstances and positions vis-à-vis the object in question.)
- The 'scientific account' of the causal processes involved in seeing, hearing and generally perceiving things about our environment in no way shows that what we perceive are never 'real' physical objects. Indeed, to say that the presence of any visible physical object before my eyes under adequate non-distorting lighting is a condition of my (having the experience of) seeing it – seeing *it* and not a hypothetical intermediary before my mind — is to say no more than that in normal circumstances I (and all other normal persons) see things as they are. There is an internal relation between the conditions for something being a physical object, the conditions for a person establishing the existence and properties of a physical object by means of perception, and our conception of the circumstances under which the two sets of conditions are normally deemed to be realised.
- And finally, the 'argument from illusion' is based on the assumption that what a person sees when he sees an object as it is and what he sees when he falls victim of an illusion or hallucination are 'qualitatively indistinguishable'. The idea that there is a single experience that is common to both perception and the corresponding hallucination — what was labelled by John McDowell 'the highest common factor conception' of perceptual experience – came under intense scrutiny by several REALIST philosophers in recent decades.

The negative conclusion of these negative arguments is that there are no valid reasons for positing the existence of mental or mind-dependent intermediaries, such as sense-data, between the sensory awareness of the perceiving person and the tomatoes, the table, the people or whatever else the perceiver has acquired knowledge about. It is, therefore, in order to retain the common-sense view that, for example, the red tomato one sees and takes in one's hand and mouth, the green grass one sees and walks on, the brown, smooth desk one sees, touches and leans on, the people one sees, hears and shakes hands with, and so on, *are* real things; specifically, they are the real and direct objects of one's perceptual experience, and their mind-independent reality cannot be undermined or doubted by any philosophical arguments. This acceptance of the common-sense and instinctive view of sense-perception may be expressed in general terms – in terms which suggest something like a philosophical 'theory': thus, a person's sense-perception normally consists in his awareness by means of the senses of physical objects and events and their properties and relations.

These philosophical defenders of common sense sometimes call their 'theory' of perception – the 'theory' that the sense-datum theorists call 'naïve realism' – by the name of 'direct realism' to indicate that in perception we gain direct visual, tactual, auditory, and so on, awareness with mind-independent physical objects. Among the best-known twentieth-century philosophers associated with direct realism are J.L. Austin, Peter STRAWSON, Hilary Putnam and John McDowell.

Contributor: Zenon Stavrinides

## NARRATIVE

### Essential narrative

Narrative is often the interweaving of real or imaginary conflicts according to the principle of causality. Traditionally associated with story-telling, narratives express individual perceptions of reality, which is a weakness or strength for critics seeing themselves as the chosen heralds of meaning and truth. For some, truth itself appears to be a narrative, as SCHOPENHAUER understood in the appropriate opening sentence to his epic *Die Welt als Wille und Vorstellung*: 'The World is my representation.'

### Three discourses

A narrative differs from a statement in that it is structured in compliance with the principle of causality, that is to say, it refers to its own possible causes and consequences. When Shakespeare, for instance, has Gertrude utter the words: 'He is mad' (Hamlet, III, IV), it is at a moment when the audience is preoccupied with questions about the causes and aftermath of Hamlet's madness, and the words have additional depth.

That we conceive a narrative in terms of causes and consequences, recreating unexpressed and unspoken conflicts and identifying with or opposing the players, our interest reflects our desire to know the resolution of the narrative puzzle, be it a sporting contest or a murderous nightmare. Equally, some narratives, such as *Waiting for Godot* by Samuel Beckett, excel by virtue of their deliberate incompleteness.

Although the boundaries between knowledge and narrative are tenuous – the former term itself comes from the Latin *noscere* (to know) – narrative is distinguished from discourse on account of its intentionality. While narratives do not intend to prevail over each other, a discourse will attempt to regulate meaning under the façade of claimed objectivity. NIETZSCHE's reaction against philosophy can be understood as the reaction of a narrator against dominant discourses – or 'meta-narratives', as Lyotard called them. That said, there are no technical differences between narratives and discourses – the reader who follows the plots and characters of Dickens and Dostoyevski applies the same understandings, even if the authors differ in INTENTION and sensitivity – the one enticed by the ideas and developments of Saint AUGUSTINE, the other by HEGEL.

The ETHICS of narrative was one of PLATO's main concerns. In the *Apology*, he has SOCRATES denounce Aristophanes as a playwright who has distorted his, Socrates', way of living, a misrepresentation in due course that contributes to Socrates' death. Seeing narrative as a feeble representation of reality, and fearful of its influence on children, Plato advocated instead censorship as a mean to force poets to write according to the dictates of morality.

ARISTOTLE, on the other hand, did not seek to censure what he perceived as mere entertainment; in his *Poetics*, the most cited technical assessment of narrative, action and plot are praised over thought, a subtle move that challenged Plato's assumptions over the role of narrative in philosophy.

Narrators, according to Aristotle, did not hinge their discourse on sensitivity, but on their ability to move audiences to feelings of fear and compassion. Later, Longinus, in *On the Sublime*, corrected Aristotle and underlined the DIALECTICAL value of narrative by ranking thought and emotion over plot-making and diction.

In the medieval period, going even further, the young poet and courtier Sir Philip Sydney (1554–86) claimed the ascendancy of poetry over philosophy, for the latter 'replenisheth the memory with many infallible grounds of wisdom, which, notwithstanding, lie dark before the imaginative and judging power, if they be not illuminated or figured forth by the speaking picture of poesy'. Sydney understood ethics as a discourse that required to be consolidated by the narratives provided by the poets.

So, in spite of the apparent diversity of creative writing and cinema, we can consider there to be three 'essential' ethical discourses articulated by contemporary narratives, as follows.

## The 'vindictive discourse'

The 'vindictive discourse' represents the irreconcilable confrontation of two forces, in which the hero – an incarnation of the prevailing conception of 'good' – is offended by the antagonist, a beast or inhuman character that performs 'evil'. Horror pictures, thrillers, summer blockbusters, animated films, computer games and even sport competitions enact the narrative of the puritan hero that must eliminate his perverse antagonists in order to save his honour or his life. The discourse dates back to Babylon, where the most intolerant passages of the Pentateuch were written under the influence of Zoroastrianism, a religion that divided the world into two distinct and independent reigns: the reign of light and good, and the realm of dark and evil.

## The 'submissive discourse'

The 'submissive discourse' stages the struggle of the hero who attempts to adapt to the demanding conditions of his world or society. Soap operas, light comedies and family dramas are examples of the submissive discourse in modern times. It can be traced back to India, where early writers ascertained Brahma as the true maker of their society, whose origins were superior to any man or woman – individuals born according to the deeds and misdeeds of their previous lives. In spite of its METAPHYSICAL insight, several UPANISHADS convey a discourse of submissiveness, suitable to the contrivers of the ancient caste system that still prevails in India today. In the *Isavasya Upanishad* we read, 'Be happy and self-resigned, and do not covet the riches of your neighbour.'

Brahmanism greatly influenced BUDDHISM, a doctrine that describes suffering as a devious state of the mind caused either by desires or *karma* (a punishment due for offences committed by previous lives).

The Chinese mandarins also consolidated a society of infallible hierarchies ruled by emperors exempt of guilt. The philosopher Han Fei (who died in 233 BCE) wrote that 'Nothing is more worthy than the royal person, more praiseworthy than the throne, more influential than the position of the ruler.' The films by Japanese film makers such as Ozu, Mizogushi and Kurosawa (most of them adaptations of short stories and novels) are strongly influenced by the submissive discourse. In the West, such discourse found expression in the STOIC philosophers, but also in the comedies of Menander, Plato and Terence, in which the main characters struggle to comply with the conventions of society.

## The 'compassionate discourse'

Narrators influenced by the 'compassionate discourse' represent the drama of the outcast or the defeated, whose sufferings are caused by chance or by their own will. In a compassionate narrative, recrimination is deadened by compassion, hate by understanding, and revenge by forgiveness. The New Testament, which Coleridge used once as a tool of moral indoctrination, appears to be the most influential compilation of compassionate narratives: the prodigal son, the good Samaritan, the passion of the Christ.

The most sensitive poets and novelists have been compassionate narrators: in *The Persians* Aeschylus stages the Greek victory of Salamis from the standpoint of the defeated, whereas in *Macbeth* and *Hamlet* Shakespeare drives spectators to sympathise with murderers. By sympathising with the foolish and the grotesque, Cervantes structured the modern novel, a narrative in which existence overcomes characters, plot and diction; such a move encouraged narrators to explore their own lives as their main source of inspiration.

The nineteenth-century French poet Charles Baudelaire was, according to Walter Benjamin, the first narrator to make his own experience the main subject of his work. Modern novelists such as Proust, Mann, Joyce and Beckett have widened the abysms of the self by producing autobiographical, self-compassionate works.

In spite of the LIBERAL claims of POSTMODERNISM, most universities still regard narratives as raw materials that require the expert eye of the scholar in order to render their full meaning. Bernard Shaw was so outraged by this practice that he himself wrote exhaustive analysis of his plays, with the outcome that his works are now rarely taken into consideration by scholars. But as long as narrators present ideas as a by-product, or even sub-product, of the passions and follies of fallible individuals, narratives will remain closer to readers than the discourses of omniscient philosophers.

Contributor: Hugo Santander

## Further reading

Noreña, Carlos G. (1970) *Juan Luis Vives*

# NATIONALISM

Literally, nationalism is a political or legal doctrine about the recognition of the political rights of certain groups of people, usually, but not exclusively, defined geographically, which is again often taken as reflecting ancestry. (Other factors might be religious, linguistic or historical and cultural.) The most important of these rights is the right to decide all the other ones, that is to say, the right to 'self-determination'. This is usually taken as requiring self-government as an independent entity. Nationalism has an ambiguous quality, in that it can be a positive expression of cultural diversity, of a desire of a group of people to continue and to develop in a way of their own choosing, and it can be a highly negative, counter-cultural phenomenon, calling upon simplistic, at best, or bigoted, at worst, invariably divisive notions of ethnic and religious identity in order to exclude others.

The pride or patriotism of nationalism, for which 'National Socialism' is the most authentic voice (not that everyone would agree with that), must eventually express itself in conflict with other nations, necessarily seen as inferior. Such friction is often accompanied by campaigns of virulent hatred. For that reason, philosophers, such as HOBBES and KANT, have traditionally favoured the withering away of the nation state and the creation of supranational institutions.

## NATIVE AMERICAN PHILOSOPHY

Many American Indians do not like the term 'Native Americans', saying that the term is meaningless and would cover all people born in America.

There are, of course, many different variations of American Indian tradition, but the shared emphasis is on animism, that is, the view that everything in the universe and not just things we normally consider to be 'alive', possess a mental aspect, a kind of consciousness. (LEIBNIZ, SCHOPENHAUER and SCHELLING are philosophical exponents of similar views.) Language and reality (as investigated by Benjamin Lee WHORF) are intimately and dynamically related, hence ritual ceremonies are seen as having the power to affect events. Analogy and metaphor are central to the structures of thought (as LÉVI-STRAUSS discusses). Dreams and premonitions are accorded equal status to conventional senses as ways in which mind interacts with reality.

ETHICAL consideration is extended to this more complex world of animals, plants and rocks, as well as to the spirit world inextricably linked with it.

## NATURAL DEDUCTION

A method of formalising LOGIC attributed separately to Gerhard Gentzen and S. Jaskowski in the 1930s. Unlike the previous logical systems, natural deduction makes no claims about the 'TRUTH' of its starting points or 'AXIOMS', but only about the 'VALIDITY' of its procedures in manipulating the claims. It is 'truth preserving'. In this way, the emphasis is shifted to the question of the reasoning used to get from the premisses to the conclusion, rather than the premisses themselves.

SEE ALSO

Logic

## NATURAL LAW

Natural law consists of a few sweeping general claims about what is politically and ETHICALLY acceptable. For example, HOBBES used the term to say that the 'LAW OF NATURE' allows, above all else, self-preservation, and that this law can be defended LOGICALLY, as its corollary would appear to allow not only an individual, but a society made up of individuals, to destroy itself, which would be in a sense 'self-contradictory'. In international law, the term is used in discussion of 'crimes against humanity' or 'just wars'.

Hobbes also distinguishes between *jus naturale*, in the sense of liberty, and so on, and *lex naturalis*, which are precepts or commands.

---

### THE LAW OF NATURE

The right of nature, which writers commonly call *jus naturale*, is the liberty which each man hath, to use his own power, as he will himself, for the preservation of his own nature; that is to say, of his own life; and consequently, of doing anything, which in his own judgement, and reason, he shall conceive to be the most apt means thereunto.

(Hobbes, *Leviathan*)

---

## NATURALISTIC FALLACY

See Fallacies.

# NATURE

## Essential nature

Nature stands in contrast to the artificial world, that is, things made by human beings. It refers to the whole universe, and to the whole of time. Philosophical views of nature have fluctuated: it is sometimes seen as random, messy and imperfect. The 'ROMANTIC' writers and philosophers such as SCHELLING reacted against the recent 'taming' of Nature by NEWTON (reducing the planets themselves to mere lumps of rocks circling the sun) and suggested that, instead, nature has a higher state which determines all our values.

## (Human) nature

'Nature' means so many things that at times it might seem an empty notion. And yet it retains a special force. Claims that something (an attribute, an event, a need) is 'natural' will aim to make us look at that something in a different way – perhaps as a 'given', or as immutable, or as existing at an especially fundamental level. Take these phrases: 'Let's face it: people are *naturally* competitive.' 'But I can't help it – it's in my nature.' 'Nature will always catch up with us in the end.' The point of each is that there is a kind of finality about nature which means that, in the end, we cannot escape its clutches. It is part of the furniture of reality – something to be sought, respected and valued. Call something 'natural', and it seems we should embrace or at least accept it. 'Unnatural' may seem to have inevitably negative undertones. But equally, the sense of the term 'nature' can be stretched in different directions and put to malleable uses. If it has force, it might be dangerous: while some may favour 'natural' childbirth or 'natural' remedies, many will recoil at the idea that social hierarchies reflect some kind of 'natural' order of superiority between genders or races. Nature may open up a dazzling wealth of opportunities, and offers us profound, perhaps indescribable beauty; it also gives us mortality and the often aggressive and bloody relations within and between the species that populate our planet.

But *does* it? Is nature itself the author of these things, be they good or bad? What are we actually talking about when we talk about nature? In philosophy, just as in everyday discourse, the term is elastic. It has covered pretty much everything, from the ultimate nature of the universe, to the living world, to the non-human world, to (at its broadest) everything that exists. Nowadays 'natural philosophy' is the province of scientists, not philosophers.

To most ancient Greeks, including PLATO and ARISTOTLE, NATURAL LAWS are revealed by both of the disciplines which the modern age calls 'philosophy' and 'science' – and, indeed, by religion as well. Viewed like this, nature has a kind of intelligence, a mind of its own, which we need to tune into in order to understand the subtle regularities of its workings. To understand nature is, in this sense, to understand the patterns of the intentions of God. This is one influence on the association of nature with things of *value*, whether ETHICALLY or AESTHETICALLY speaking. The natural is good: true art represents this goodness, or taps into its rhythms; true morality captures the goodness in us, and provides principles by which it might flourish. This general hunch surfaces in different ways down through Western history, from medieval theology to the Romantic poets.

While nature might be regarded as being at the very basis of human life, it is also, in another familiar sense, contrasted with it. While the Greeks sought the elements which would link human existence to the machinery of the wider universe, others have used 'nature' to describe precisely all that is separate from human life. In this sense, *nature* is contrasted with *CULTURE*, or society. In this sense, being 'unnatural' might, for us humans, be a kind of compliment. For modern thinkers from DESCARTES down, to be human is to be capable of *transcending* the constraints of nature, through reason. For KANT, our capacity for autonomous action means that we can never simply explain our behaviour by recourse to the putative laws of biology. Even more so for EXISTENTIALISTS like SARTRE, the idea that 'nature', human or otherwise, might have any bearing on the value of our lives, or the decisions we make in shaping them, is both wrong-headed and morally degrading. Viewed this way, nature is a kind of threat to human agency – a mechanistic order which we need to escape in order to be free. A view emerges in sociobiology and evolutionary psychology that what we experience as free choices, or as value judgements, are in fact the operations of nature itself, with the purely functional purpose of enabling us to survive better. Evolutionary theory has grown dominant in the natural sciences; whether it can transcend age-old philosophical disputes is a matter for debate.

In **POLITICAL PHILOSOPHY**, the idea of a 'state of nature' has formed the basis for considerations about social and political justice. Social contract theorists (**HOBBES, LOCKE, ROUSSEAU** and, more recently, John **RAWLS**) have sought to consider how society should be run, by viewing it from the perspective of a world without the fabric of laws, rights and social conventions to which we have grown accustomed. Of course, they differ about what life before 'civil government' was like. For Hobbes, **HUMAN NATURE** is the source of the conflict, aggression and acquisitiveness which would dominate without the order provided by a heavily powerful state. For Rousseau, the pre-social human is an altogether more cuddly being. Rawls, like many modern philosophers, attempts to avoid a 'thick' conception of human nature in devising social rules, and appeals instead to the priorities which individuals would have *regardless* of knowledge of their own particular preferences or orientations. His critics argue that despite its ambitions, such a theory fails to be 'neutral' between alternative models of what is good for the sort of being that humans are.

But the very idea of a 'state of nature' throws up a fundamental ambiguity about the way in which nature is discussed. It tends to be presented in contrast to something else – culture, human rationality, 'the unnatural' – as if there were clear dividing lines between such categories. But what is nature, in and of itself? If we look at the 'natural' world, we find that (for better or worse) it is everywhere shaped and changed by human influence. Many might say the same of human nature, too: that because we can describe ourselves, and our projects, in such a wide range of ways, it really does not make much sense to talk in terms of 'natural' ways of human living, or authentically 'human' needs or priorities. Does it make a difference whether systems of '**HUMAN RIGHTS**', for example, reflect real, universal aspects of what it is like to be human? Often, the 'natural' is contrasted with the 'artificial' or 'manufactured'. From many different angles, recent thinkers have questioned whether this distinction is viable at all. Which is the 'true' depiction of nature: a biology textbook or a landscape painting? Is Nazi ideology at odds with the true nature of humanity, or just currently unfashionable? Can we ever decide whether **CAPITALISM** allows human nature to flourish, or prevents this, or a bit of both? Must 'essentialist' claims about the nature of human-

ity, or the world, always end up being exclusionary, and prejudiced against that which does not fit the norm? And is any such 'norm' not just, in the end, a human construction rather than anything given in the 'nature' of things?

Yet one does not have to be an ecologist to appreciate that there is a value of the concept of 'nature'. As critics of Hobbes and Rawls have shown, assumptions can be all the more consequential when they are hidden, or even unintentional. Not all the world is human culture; and aspects of that non-cultural world are themselves, in terms of the causal powers they furnish, preconditions of there being a rich, varied, immeasurably valuable human culture in the first place. We can choose to deconstruct the idea of nature, or to downplay its significance for human life. But even so, not least in the form of our mortality, nature is indeed likely to catch up with us in the end.

Contributor: Gideon Calder

# NATURE (MYTHOLOGY)
## Essentials of nature and mythology

**ARISTOTLE** considered the origins of philosophic enquiry to stem from our innate desire to understand the causes behind the natural world. He thus links mythology and philosophy, in as much as they both attempt to explain the forces of **NATURE**.

## Nature according to myth, science and philosophy

The harmony and turbulence of the natural world was understood by early religion and mythology to be caused by the compassion or wrath of one of the gods. Individual worshippers who experienced nature's wrath first-hand believed that they had brought on the deity's anger through their misconduct. Fearing the consequences of divine retribution, the followers of mythology were motivated to order their lives in such a way as to receive their gods' countenance. The systems of mythology were thus able to provide a primitive means of explanation, as well as an ethical imperative for good behaviour.

Notwithstanding the artistic genius employed in crafting the various mythological systems, the explanations offered by poetry must ultimately be recognised as abandoning real enquiry by appealing to irrational stories. While mythology might encourage ethical action, the attempt to derive norms from the unpredictability of nature's forces results in a notion of **ETHICS** that is just as capricious. SOCRATES notes the inability of the poets to defend or explain their conceptions of nature:

> . . . they do not make their work by wisdom, but by some kind of talent and by inspiration, like the seers and the 'oracle-mongers'. These people, too, say many things, wonderful things, but they know nothing about what they are saying . . .
>
> (*Apology* 22c)

In contrast to the irrational but beautiful stories of the poets, scientific enquiry emerges as thinkers begin to forward explanations of the natural world that can be defended through argument and demonstration.

Although we have little more than fragments expressing the seminal ideas of early natural scientists, we see how they depart from the tradition of storytelling and, for the first time, advance rational arguments. THALES, typically reckoned as the first philosopher and natural scientist, boldly propounds water as the sole cause underlying the entirety of nature. The ability of water to assume the different states of matter (liquid, solid, gas) suggests how the seeming multiplicity of phenomena might be reduced to a single substance. Simple experiments might bolster this claim as vegetables could be pulverised and reduced into liquid.

Yet there are consequences that emerge as a result of the scientific revolution. The persisting order of the cosmos is now understood as preserved by the unvarying forces of nature. Fire, for example, exhibits the same nature, regardless if it burns in Greece or Persia. In contrast, ethical norms vary widely from one city to the next. The variability of religious practices, political systems and social conventions led the SOPHISTS to conclude that the realm of human affairs was wholly arbitrary and without a natural basis. This position is nicely summed up by HERACLITUS: 'To God all things are fair and good and right, but people hold some things wrong and some right. . .' (fragment 61). The new conception of the divine enacted by the scientific revolution understands nature's forces as wholly indifferent to the entire moral order. Just as the lion is not censured for preserving its life when it eats the lamb, nature does not judge the strong from trampling over the weak in the realm of human affairs. When compared with the unvarying principles of nature, the distinction between just and unjust actions appears as arbitrary and conventional.

Responding to the upheaval in the ethical realm, Socrates sought universal definitions for ethical concepts, contending that they do possess unvarying natures. He tells us in an autobiographical reflection in *Phaedo* that he was only able to pursue this sort of enquiry by focusing on human affairs and abandoning his previous investigation into the entirety of nature. The inability of Socratic philosophy to address the cosmic order relegates it to be just as one-sided as the pre-Socratic natural scientists.

For several thousand years, Aristotle's *Physics* had provided a solution to the schism between natural science and ethical enquiry. Rejecting the disembodied world of Platonic FORMS, Aristotle engaged in extensive biological studies of living, breathing organisms. In these studies, the individual parts of the organism and all its motions were understood as purposively contributing towards the attainment of the organism's final end. The internal striving of living beings to preserve their own existence ultimately culminates in the contribution of the individual towards the preservation of the species. One can then investigate the goal of ethical action in a similar fashion as one can study the consistent trajectory by which the acorn strives to be an oak tree. The failure of some acorns to achieve their end when they become fodder for the squirrel does not negate the innate striving of the acorn towards its end. While the acorn is only prevented from becoming an oak tree by the intervention of outside forces, human beings are peculiar, in so far as they actively cultivate deleterious habits, leading them to pursue ends contrary to human nature and the life of virtue.

The modern scientific revolution, inaugurated in the seventeenth century by BACON, DESCARTES and NEWTON, shares certain features with the scientific revolution of the sixth century BCE, though now nature is treated as a force to harness for the sake of relieving man's estate. In the twenty-first century we are presented with advances in medicine and technology heralded by the prophets of the modern scientific revolution. Notwithstanding the many ways in which technology has improved our lives, the ethical sphere once again emerges as lacking any natural basis. Rather than understanding the natural world as purposive, DARWIN assumes that species EVOLVE through random mutation and the survival of the fittest. Postmodern RELATIVISM can thus be seen as the ethical complement of modern science. Contemporary ethical theory once again awaits an Aristotle who can ground ethics by providing a unified framework for understanding both the natural world and the world of human affairs.

Contributor: Daniel Silvermintz

## Further reading

Aristotle, *Physics*

Bacon, F. (1620) *The New Science* (also known as the *Novum Organum*)

Darwin, C. (1859) *The Origin of the Species*

## NECESSITY

That without which we cannot do. For LEIBNIZ, God is METAPHYSICALLY 'necessary'; the truths of mathematics are 'absolutely necessary'. But more recent philosophers have recognised that both mathematical and LOGICAL necessity are rooted in mere conventions. Statements are only 'necessary' because of the way we define our terms, and that in turn is just a result of the way we want them to be.

## NEGRITUDE

See African philosophy.

## NEO-PLATONISM

Neo-Platonists such as PLOTINUS and PORPHYRY attempted to reconcile the works of the two great masters, PLATO and ARISTOTLE, generally by seeing Aristotle's practical approach as a way into the 'higher wisdom' of Plato. Of this, the MYSTICAL view that the 'GOOD' is the ultimate and 'transcendent' truth is the end product and characteristic.

## NEWCOMB'S PARADOX

Also known as the prediction PARADOX. There are two boxes, A and B, and a wise Being with a record of always predicting human behaviour. Although popular, the paradox is at best inelegant and at worse completely unintelligible, which would of course explain its popularity among philosophers. In any case, it seems not worthy of the attention it has received. (So it can have a bit less here!)

## NEWTON, ISAAC (1642–1727)

Newton was born into a rural family and only his inability to keep track of the cows led to him eventually being allowed to go to Oxford as a kind of assistant scholar to richer students. But once there he feasted upon the knowledge revealed in the libraries, drawing up a list of great questions spanning the whole range of human knowledge that he intended to investigate.

In the event, he was woefully unsuccessful, scarcely proceeding beyond the first half-dozen matters, such as the nature of motion, chemical change, gravity, light – and time. Despite many secretive years searching for the 'philosopher's stone', he never came up with that either.

Nonetheless, Sir Isaac is sometimes said to have been to science what Euclid was to mathematics. His *Philosophiae Naturalis Principia Mathematica* (1687) systematised the science of mechanics, that is, the science of objects and how they move, just as Euclid systematised the study of geometry. Both provided the terms and definitions for all the rest. Newton found it necessary to deal with otherwise apparently philosophical issues such as those of the nature of 'space' and of 'true motion' (in particular the views of DESCARTES) in order to address PARADOXES such as that of how the Earth could both be 'accelerating' away from the Sun at any moment and yet be motionless. If his nostrums of 'Absolute Space', let alone 'Absolute Time', seem to have been collapsed by relativity theory, EINSTEIN was the first to acknowledge that it was Newton who gave the world the framework for investigations.

## NIETZSCHE, FRIEDRICH (1844–1900)

### The essential Nietzsche

Friedrich Nietzsche was born in the Prussian town of Rocken in a period of political and economic ferment. His central interests were the 'death of God' and, with it, he claimed, the 'slave morality' of Christianity with its elevation of self-sacrifice and pity over what he considered the true virtue: the pursuit of power. He read SCHOPENHAUER's *The World as Will and Representation* as a revelation, which he adapted to his own, rather dubious, ends.

Nietzsche interpreted the world from the point of view that human beings, and indeed all life, are engaged in this struggle to increase their

*power.* Declaring himself to be the 'first immoralist', he promised to 'revalue' all values, starting with the unmasking of Christianity and literally making 'good' 'bad', but was unable to complete this task as, in 1889, he descended into a twilight of his own, never emerging from madness.

## Of supermen and super battles

Nietzsche was a philosopher-poet who wrote of supermen and battles, yet Nietzsche, the historical man, was prone to ill health, headaches and chronic short sight, along with intestinal problems, cutting, in many ways, a tragic figure. At one point, Nietzsche rather feebly blames the weather for making him a 'narrow, withdrawn, grumpy specialist' instead of a significant, brave 'spirit'. Then again, he says that his sickness 'liberated me slowly', by forcing him to give up his teaching and books, and to break his habits, above all, to 'put an end to all bookwormishness'.

His father was a Lutheran pastor, and died before Nietzsche was five, leaving him to be brought up solely by his mother and other female relatives. Psychologists may see the origin of his two themes, hatred of Christianity and contempt for women, in this biography.

He became professor of classical philology at Basel in Switzerland at the early age of 24, but his first book, *The Birth of Tragedy* (*Die Geburt der Tragoedie*, 1872), which he dedicated to the composer Richard Wagner, was not particularly well received. More successful was *Thus Spake Zarathrustra*, which was even produced as a

pocket edition for German troops during the First World War; and later, *On the Genealogy of Morals.*

In all his work, Nietzsche rails against morality, which he saw as a form of weakness. Instead he favours what he called 'anti-morality', as where a great man (and it had to be a man) enjoyed his power to the full, untrammelled by dreary notions of 'responsibility', 'duty', 'pity', let alone (of all things) 'being "good"'. After all, as he puts it at the end of *Ecce Homo*, 'Behold the Man', a semi-blasphemous title in itself:

> . . . in the concept of the good man common cause [is] made with everything weak, sick, ill constituted, suffering from itself, all that which ought to perish – the law of selection crossed, an ideal made of opposition to the proud and well-constituted, to the affirmative man, to the man certain of the future and guaranteeing the future.

Nietzsche also wrote that the goal of humanity is not in some supposed general strategy or

### THUS SPAKE NIETZSCHE

*On atheism and the death of God:*

In *Thus Spake Zarathustra*, a madman carrying a lantern announces that: 'God is dead'.

'Where has God gone?' he cried. 'I shall tell you. We have killed him – you and I. We are all his murderers.'

*On being good:*

'What is good?' he writes in *The Anti-Christ*, and answers, 'All that heightens the feeling of power, the will to power, power itself in man. What is bad? – All that proceeds from weakness.'

*On himself:*

In the concluding chapter to *Ecce Homo*, 'Why I Am Destiny', Nietzsche writes:

> I know my fate. One day, there will be associated with my name the recollection of something frightful – of a crisis like no other before on earth, of the profoundest collision of conscience, of a decision evoked against everything that until then had been believed in, demanded, sanctified. I am not a man, I am dynamite.

process, such as the maximisation of happiness, but is to be found in the activities of its 'highest specimens'. These men (and it is only *men*) transcend history, and are bound to no laws other than that of their own pleasure.

> The man who would not belong in the mass needs only to cease being comfortable with himself; he should follow his conscience which shouts at him: 'Be yourself!' You are not really all you do, think, and desire now.

His discussion of the 'master/slave' relationship, as later summarised in *The Will to Power*, was politically influential.

His writing is part prose, part poetry, with a sprinkling of philosophy. Always egocentric, as mentioned above, he went clinically insane in 1889. Opinions differ as to whether his work constitutes either good literature or good philosophy. However, he has been able to retain a largely undeserved reputation for profundity and originality.

Although Nietzsche loudly trumpets that he has 'transcended' all other values, he overstates the radicalism, as he has only reversed the conventional ones. Nonetheless, Nietzsche is important within ETHICS, for providing an alternative position to the usual, rather sanctimonious one.

Contributor: Martin Cohen

## NIHILISM

The rather negative doctrine that nothing is true, and that nothing matters. Ethical nihilism says that in ETHICS nothing is true and nothing matters. In scope, it is not completely unlike ethical RELATIVISM, and prompts the same sort of response. For example, if someone challenged a nihilist thus: 'Well, you would not like it if I cut off your toes – just for malicious fun!', the nihilist will say (correctly) that although *they* certainly would *not* like it, some masochistic soul might, and hence it cannot be said to objectively 'wrong'.

## *NIRVANA*

*Nirvana* is a BUDDHIST term for the ABSOLUTE, the goal to which all things ultimately aspire, the liberation achieved by following the path taught by the Buddha, the enlightened one. This follows Buddha's four great truths, that:

- pain dominates life;
- pain is caused by desire;
- pain can be ended by loss of individuality in *Nirvana*;
- one must follow the right path to reach *Nirvana*, which is the eightfold path to enlightenment.

Buddha was down-to-earth. His language and allusions were all simple. He said he was awakened, the source of the word Buddha, rather than the more profound-sounding 'enlightened'.

He used the Sanskrit words *nir*, meaning 'out' or 'away', and *vana*, meaning 'blown', in two contexts; with reference to chaff and flames. In the first passage, the husks of the corn are blown away, leaving the grain. In the second, the flames of desire are blown out. In the final stages of meditation, leading to merging with absolute reality, a roaring wind is heard, followed by the absence of all sensation.

*Nirvana* is liberation from *samsara*: experience of the phenomenal or finite; the trap of the cycle of births and deaths; transitory existence. Nothing can be said of it because, according to Buddha, one cannot say he is or he is not, as he neither is nor is not. This being a restatement of the *Neti! Neti!* of the *UPANISHADS*.

## NON-BEING AND NOTHINGNESS

'Nothing shall come of nothing, speak again.' Thus advised King Lear to his daughter Cordelia, but like many philosophers before and since, she heeded him not. Controversy over whether 'nothingness' really exists can be traced back certainly to the pre-Socratic philosophers in ancient Greece or, to be more precise, to Asia Minor, southern Italy and Sicily.

Foremost among them, PARMENIDES of Elea, in the early fifth century BCE, warned that to speak of 'Not Being' was to take a '. . . wholly incredible course, since you can not recognise Not Being (for this is impossible), nor speak of it, for thought and Being are the same thing.'

Parmenides, and his followers, the ELEATICS, were challenging the teachings of PYTHAGORAS, who claimed that 'Nothing', a kind of 'Not-Being', does indeed exist. But others, such as DEMOCRITUS of Abdera, remembered for his theory of the world as being made up of atoms, who were teaching a few decades after Parmenides, still insisted, like Pythagoras, that

Not-Being must in fact be, whatever Parmenides' reasoning. And so it is too that PLATO can be found, in the *Sophist* dialogue, coming down on the side of Nothingness, and saying that what 'is not' in some sense also 'is'. For Plato, 'not-being' is a necessary part of creating distinctions in the first place. If it were not possible to have nothing in the cupboard, it would not be possible to have something in it either. This is the same sense that persuades medieval theologians, such as Thomas AQUINAS, in the *Summa Theologica*, to say that it is necessary that GOD brings things into being from nothing, or LEIBNIZ to insist on the nothingness of empty SPACE as a precursor to arranging his MONADS in it.

Even HEIDEGGER has a place for nothingness in his system, saying that 'das Nichts selbst nichtet', which is German for 'the Nothing nihilates'. The LOGICAL POSITIVIST Rudolf CARNAP (1891–1970) used this as one of his examples of METAPHYSICAL nonsense. But it is not true to say that nobody believes nothing does not exist – Henri-Louis BERGSON offered a nineteenth-century version of Parmenides' argument, saying that the concept of nothingness is indeed 'self-contradictory', offering as an example the claim that 'no contingent beings exist'. This, he protests, is also to say 'every existent being has some property that is incompatible with being existent'. This is indeed food for thought.

## NORMATIVE

The term is used by philosophers as an adjective, meaning 'to do with 'norms' or standards. And 'norms' are, in effect, rules.

## NUMBERS

The first numbers seen in written records were the positive integers, I, II, III, IIII, IIIII, and so on, derived from heaps of pebbles, or marks on sticks, expressed only later in Arabic notation as 1, 2, 3, and so on. Positive integers are all very useful and practical for keeping records: for example, how many sheep you have, and for measuring out fields and buildings. The Egyptians and Mesopotamians soon complicated things, however, by introducing fractions, also called 'rational numbers', with the inevitable consequence that PYTHAGORAS and his school soon after discovered the 'irrational numbers'; those such as the square root of two. Legend has it that a member of the school was drowned for revealing the

existence of such untidy numbers to a horrified public.

MATHEMATICS could not advance much before the invention of 'zero', which is indeed a strange number. It was Indian mathematicians who systematised its use, around the seventh century, and shortly afterwards it became possible to work with negative numbers and even the first imaginary numbers (the square root of a negative number is called an imaginary number). Numbers that are so small they cannot be expressed (infinitesimals) were conjured up by both NEWTON and LEIBNIZ, in order to create the mathematics of CALCULUS, and the manipulation of INFINITY, soon split into 'countable' and 'uncountable' varieties took place in the nineteenth century, largely as a result of Georg CANTOR.

Most of ZENO's PARADOXES and quite a lot of the philosophy of space and time involves number theory, and just as Zeno challenged the assumptions of his time with his paradoxes of MOTION, much of the orthodoxy of modern philosophy and mathematics rests on certain agreed numerical conventions that are certainly not as ancient or indeed perhaps as inevitable as we have become accustomed to thinking.

## *OBLIGATIONES*

The *obligationes* were a popular spectacle in medieval times, essentially a kind of public debate structured upon the best principles of the 'Socratic dialogue', or indeed 'DIALECTICAL' reasoning. One person would argue a position, for example that the movement of a lance when thrown through the air is due to the pressure of the air rushing in behind it and pressing it forward. Another would then say, if the lance is thrown with its blunt end forwards and its sharp end at the back, will the pressure of the air on the lance be greater at the tip or at the back? And so the first HYPOTHESIS would fall, to great amusement.

More formally, the proponent sets out their position through detailing the PROPOSITIONS, which the 'respondent' then 'concedes', 'denies' or 'doubts'.

# OCKHAM, WILLIAM (1285–1347)

William Ockham was a Franciscan monk, who was born near Guildford, England, but worked mainly near Oxford. Although nicknamed the 'More than Subtle Doctor', it is 'Ockham's razor' that has immortalised him. This is the rule of reasoning also known as the 'technique of parsimony', which, simply put, says that, given a range of possible explanations, the most simple is to be preferred. It reflects his approach to ARISTOTLE, who freely generated new categories and distinctions. Another aspect of this 'razor' was his emphasis on 'nominalism', or the appropriateness of our use of LANGUAGE. This runs that when we call things 'chairs' it is because they all conform to the rules governing the use of the word 'chair', rather than having some strange quality, 'chair-ness', perhaps in the world of the FORMS. Ockham was indeed an early semiologist, or scientist of the use of signs, distinguishing between intuitive 'signs', which are words 'labelling' impressions derived from the senses, and mental signs, such as 'man' in the (evergreen) sentence 'man is a rational animal', which are abstract and suitable for philosophical manipulation.

Ockham was thus the forerunner of much of traditional Western philosophy of language, and directly influenced the theorising of other English philosophers such as Thomas HOBBES and John LOCKE; and his critique of the ancients' concept of matter as 'potentiality' encouraged DESCARTES to describe matter as simply 'extension', as well as offering the distinction between supposedly 'primary' and 'secondary' qualities. Finally, Ockham challenged Aristotle over the notions of 'FINAL CAUSES' and 'ESSENCES', preparing the philosophical ground for the scientific revolution of the seventeenth century. All of this was against the conventional opinions of the time; and indeed, lectures he gave on Peter Lombard's *Sentences*, dealing with the issue of empiricism, were so unorthodox he was summoned to Rome in 1324 to face charges of heresy. Further differences with the Church over the policy of praising absolute poverty led to him being excommunicated in 1328 and – as if this were not bad enough – he contracted the black plague and died.

# ONE-OVER-MANY PROBLEM

How can different things, such as this red apple, this red car, this red light – all be the same things – red? The solution has been to create the 'universal', that is, 'redness', but that useful invention in turn creates many problems.

# ONTOLOGICAL ARGUMENT

The classic expression of the ontological argument for the EXISTENCE of GOD is that of the eleventh-century Archbishop of Canterbury, ANSELM, who says God is 'that Being than which nothing greater can be conceived'.

Yet if God is defined as that thing of which nothing greater can be conceived, then one of the qualities of God must be existence, as it is possible to imagine God exists, and such a God is clearly superior to one who does not exist.

KANT objected that this treats 'existence' in the same way as other attributes, such as being omniscient, or popular, or even bearded, or as Kant puts it, 'as a predicate'. Even within the Catholic Church, the argument was abandoned early on, in favour of the 'first cause' argument, sometimes called the COSMOLOGICAL ARGUMENT, which says that everything in the universe that we know about has a cause, but something originally must have had no cause – and that thing can only have been God. The weakness with this argument is that it is self-contradictory, in that it makes the rule about everything needing a cause, only it breaks it in the case of God. We might instead say everything needs a cause except the universe as a whole!

# ONTOLOGY

A woolly term, probably intended to cover theories of EXISTENCE, but also used to describe theories of 'being' or 'reality'. The term is used unhelpfully nowadays in conjunction with other bits of jargon, such as 'the ontology of my theory is . . .' or 'the ontology of events is . . .' Appropriately, the term was adopted by the Polish LOGICIAN Lesniewski (1886–1939) to be the official name of his system for manipulating terms.

# ORACLE (DELPHIC)

Oracles are a way of obtaining advice about proposed plans and strategies. They usually contain two elements: a human interpreter and a physical device ostensibly enabling that interpreter to access usually hidden knowledge, often of the future.

The physical aids range from the throwing of yarrow sticks for the *I Ching*, dipping a piece of lead into a pot of coloured beans, reading tea-leaves or crystal balls or (for the Azande in Africa) the poisoning of chickens. Perhaps the most famous of all oracles however was the Pythia of Delphi, on the slopes of Mount Parnassus in Greece.

Throughout the fourth, fifth and sixth centuries BCE Greeks undertook pilgrimages in large numbers to Dephi to consult the Oracle, paying a considerable sum each time to the priests who decoded the strange pronouncements of the mediums, who were necessarily disorientated, often in a trance state, as they were partly in this world and partly in another. PLATO and ARISTOTLE refer to the Delphic Oracle occasionally, but as they disliked competition for wise pronouncements they attempted to discredit it.

The fame of the Delphic Oracle rested on occasions such as that in the sixth century, when King Croesus asked the Oracle what would happen if he attacked the Persians. The Oracle wisely replied that 'a great empire would be destroyed'. Croesus took this as an endorsement of his plan, attacked the Persians, and lost both the battle and his empire.

In terms of human PSYCHOLOGY, oracles often work (like ASTROLOGY) by being ambiguous. In reading meanings into their opaque pronouncements, we can in fact find out what we ourselves actually think, perhaps obscured to us under a layer of other assumptions. Many oracles, however, were also repositories of considerable practical wisdom. That at Delphi, for instance, drew on the considerable accumulation of knowledge of both the priests and mediums. They received enquiries and information from people all over the ancient world and were often in a good position to make guesses about the future. In the same way, the text of the *I Ching* and the many writings on astrology contain many thousands of years of collected wisdom.

## ORIGINAL POSITION

See Rawls.

## ORIGINAL SIN

Saint AUGUSTINE invented 'original SIN' later than one might have supposed, claiming that the biblical story of Adam and Eve eating the 'forbidden fruit' in the Garden of Eden conveys the origin of our departure from grace; a departure which is then passed on to all descendants, with nothing much to be done about it, except

for praying for GOD's forgiveness. The view is significant in that it insists all human beings are wicked and sinful, right from birth, as opposed to the view that sees us as born innocent but in danger of becoming contaminated by EVIL in the world.

## OTHER, THE

In modern European philosophy, such as that of Edmund HUSSERL, the 'Other' is everyone except oneself, the 'EGO'. Emmanuel LEVINAS argues that the whole of ETHICS rests on respecting the absolute 'otherness of the other'. 'The absolute other is the Other. He and I do not form a number. The collectivity in which I say "you" or "we" is not a plural of "I"', wrote Levinas in *Totality and Infinity* (1961).

The 'other minds' problem is slightly different and relates to the much more significant question of how we can know whether plants or ANIMALS or even other people think, or are conscious, or, as we say, have MINDS. After all, it is hard to explain how we know ourselves that we have one. Though we think we do. . .

### SEE ALSO

The 'Chinese Room'

## PAINE, THOMAS (1737–1809)

### The essential Paine

Thomas Paine was historically the key conduit for John LOCKE's new ideas of EQUALITY and freedom. Through his book *The Rights of Man* (1791), Locke's liberal INDIVIDUALISM became something much more potent, contributing the ideals as well as the language of the two events that heralded the modern world – the French and American Revolutions.

### Rights and common sense

Born in Norfolk, the young Paine worked variously as a 'staymaker', a civil servant, a journalist and a schoolteacher. It was while working for the Excise board in Lewes, Sussex that he became interested in politics, serving on the town

It was only a journalist like Paine who would write:

Why is it that scarcely any are executed but the poor? The fact is a proof, amongst other things, of a wretchedness in their condition. Bred without morals, and cast upon the world without a prospect, they are the exposed sacrifice of vice and legal barbarity. The millions that are superfluously wasted by governments, are more than sufficient to reform these evils, and to benefit the condition of every man in a nation. . . It is time that nations should be rational, and not be governed like animals, for the pleasure of their riders. To read the history of kings, a man would be almost inclined to suppose that government consisted in stag-hunting, and that every nation paid a million a year to a huntsman . . . It has cost England almost seventy millions sterling, to maintain a family imported from abroad, of very inferior capacity to thousands in the nation. . .

(*The Rights of Man*, 1791)

council, and holding heated political discussions of Locke's ideas in the White Hart Inn. Actually, Paine once remarked rather dismissively of his debt to his political forebear, that he had 'never read any Locke, nor ever had the work in my hand', but it was certainly Locke's ideas that made the running in those political debates in the White Hart.

Paine soon left quiet, half-timbered Sussex for the New World, on the recommendation of Benjamin FRANKLIN himself, whom he had met in London, and at the same time moved from talk to action. On settling in Philadelphia, Paine immediately began to set out his ideas on paper: Lockean ideas of equal RIGHTS for men and women, for African and European – and even on the fair treatment for ANIMALS. Paine was thus one of the first in America to press for the abolition of SLAVERY. His book *The Rights of Man* (1791) is rightly considered a political classic, even overshadowing Locke's ponderous prose, whose ideas Paine so largely borrowed. But it would be the novel issue of national self-determination that made the name of Thomas Paine historically significant. The issue that John Adams, second President of the United States,

once described as a dreadful 'Hobgoblin', 'so frightful . . . that it would throw a delicate person into fits to look it in the face'.

In the seventeenth century, uprisings such as the revolt of the Netherlands against the Holy Roman Emperor in Spain had been driven by religious differences, not by NATIONALISM as such. Even the discontent of the American colonists was directed against unjust treatment by the English King, not against royal authority in itself. Paine's nationalistic pamphlet *Common Sense* (1776) was a spark in a tinderbox which started a fire that would eventually sweep away far more than the English claim to America.

And it was Paine who had the practical suggestions for the management of the new societies:

In the first place, three hundred representatives, fairly elected, are sufficient for all the purposes to which legislation can apply, and preferable to a larger number. They may be divided into a number of houses, or meet in one, as in France, or in any manner a constitution shall direct.

And, as representation is always considered, in free countries, 'the most honourable of all stations', the 'allowance made to it is merely to defray the expense which the representatives incur by that service, and not to it as an office.' (A principle sadly lost somewhere along the line.)

Paine even worked out neatly, in double entry bookkeeping form, exactly how much the government would cost, which was not to be very much. In fact, when finances are done his way, there is, happily, enough to pay all the poor people of the country some money. This money, Paine pointed out, is no more than remission of their own taxes, from hidden taxation imposed by duties on imports, and so on. Furthermore, those who cannot work deserve State support as, Paine calculates, the benefits of relieving parents of the twin burdens of paying for the very young and the very old (and the sick – all right, three burdens) enables them to cease being dependent on others, and society is restored to its natural state of being an engine for the production of prosperity.

Contributor: Martin Cohen

# PANTHEISM

First coined in 1705 by John Toland, the term covers theories that everything is united and contains in equal parts, a spiritual and material aspect. SPINOZA summed it up by stressing that there was only one substance, and that substance was divine.

## PARADIGM SHIFT

See Kuhn.

## PARADOXES

From the Greek for 'beyond belief'. A paradox is a contradiction, where reasonable assumptions and sound reasoning lead to a ridiculous, or otherwise unacceptable, conclusion. ZENO's Paradoxes of MOTION are an example of this use of the term. Another important one in philosophy is the paradox of the LIAR, also known as the 'Cretan Paradox', attributed originally to Epimenides, which simply runs 'All Cretans tell lies all the time'. The paradox arises when this claim is made by a Cretan – is the statement true or not?

The point is that the truth of the claim affects the circumstances it is uttered in, which affects the truth of the claim, and so on, in an infinite twisting and turning of the truth. Effectively, the statements are neither true nor false,

'The Liar' is actually rather an untidy paradox, as it would appear to be possible just to say that the statement is not true, but nonetheless it is a philosophical favourite and has spawned a fair literature on its own. Better formulated is

Bertrand Russell

the version to do with a prisoner and a Hanging Judge, which is too long to go into here, but is discussed in the editor's book, *101 Philosophy Problems* (2001).

There is also a version of RUSSELL's paradox (also known as the 'BARBER PARADOX') in which a barber is obliged to cut the hair of everyone in the city 'who does not normally cut their own hair'. Does he cut his hair or not? Russell offers the formal statement of this as: the problem of the 'SET of all sets that are not members of themselves' – is it a member of itself? He was so appalled at the implications of the paradox, not only for LOGIC, but for MATHEMATICS and even ordinary LANGUAGE, that he wrote in his autobiography that his life work seemed dashed to pieces, and for weeks he could scarcely eat or sleep. So he sent it to his co-worker, the mathematical philosopher, Gottlob FREGE, who commented: 'arithmetic trembles'.

SEE ALSO

Liar paradox

## PARALLELISM

This is the theory dredged up by DESCARTES, having irrevocably separated MIND and matter, to explain how the two things can then possibly work together. The idea is that they simply operate in parallel. SPINOZA considered body and mind to be two aspects of the same underlying 'substance' and so had no qualms about also adopting the approach to explain everyday appearance of mental events causing physical actions.

## PARETO OPTIMALITY

The principle named after the Italian economist Vilfredo Pareto, which refers to the state of affairs where no one can be better off without making someone else worse off.

## PARMENIDES (FIFTH CENTURY BCE)

Parmenides was a radical Greek poet who appears in the PLATONIC dialogue of the same name. In the one poem we have of his, he describes the 'Way of TRUTH' and the 'Way of Seeing' being shown to him by a goddess. 'The Way of Truth' is said to be the earliest example of sustained philosophical argument in the Western tradition. Parmenides presents an unchanging and timeless universe, discounting the possibility of things both being and not-being as self-contradictory. In any case, only that which *is* can be spoken of.

'The Way of Seeing', on the other hand, looks very much like the Eastern tradition of cyclical change, with light and dark, hot and cold forming each other, but the goddess seems to be offering this approach to the world as an inferior, common-sense one.

## PARTICULARS

Particulars are to be contrasted with 'universals', which sounds straightforward, or at least it was until recent work by P.F. STRAWSON and other philosophers of the ANALYTIC tendency started positing a distinction between particulars and 'INDIVIDUALS'. Particulars are spatio-temporally existing individuals, but 'other individuals' such as the number '3' or the fact 'that there is no King of France anymore' are not particulars, after all.

## PASCAL, BLAISE (1623–62) AND PASCAL'S WAGER

Pascal was born in Clermont-Ferrand in France and soon became a celebrated 'philosophe', whose *Pensées* (Thoughts) were eventually collected together and published shortly after his death. The recurrent theme of these is the wretched and sinful nature of human life, and for a time he followed the theological approach of Jansenism, producing the polemical *Lettres Provinciales* (1656–57). Both his MATHEMATICAL thinking and his philosophical essays are models of elegance and precision. He once wrote apologetically to a friend to explain that his letter was so long 'because he did not have the time to write a short one'.

Despite – or perhaps because of – being a mathematician first and foremost, and contributing to the development of geometry, number theory and PROBABILITY, as well as devising an early kind of COMPUTER, Pascal insists that the foundations of KNOWLEDGE still rest on faith, rather than on reason. This renders all knowledge uncertain, the famous example being knowledge of GOD. His 'wager' is that since we cannot be sure God really exists, we should assume He does, as the consequences of error in this case are none, but if we assume He does not exist and are wrong, the consequences are eternal damnation.

## PASSIONS

The word 'passion' originally meant 'suffering', and the ancients usually considered passions to be a kind of madness. Aesop stated firmly that reason should be the master of the passions, a view that reappears in PLATO's analogy of the chariot. DESCARTES uses the term to indicate a dangerous subset of the EMOTIONS. Yet David HUME, the great iconoclast, states equally firmly that 'reason is and ought to be the slave of the passions', and HEGEL too admits that 'nothing great' has ever been done 'without passion'.

## PATERNALISM

Paternalism comes from the Latin for 'father', and describes the situation where power or authority is exercised by a person, or institution, over others. It is supposedly done with the latter's interests in mind, but it also inevitably must diminish their 'autonomy' as well as their freedoms. Modern states exhibit a paternalist taste for LAWS against alcohol, drugs, smoking, unconventional SEX, gambling, and so on.

## PERCEPTION

Perception covers both our sensory 'perception' of the world – and our mental organisation of it. The former may or may not involve 'direct' receipt of 'SENSE data', while the latter may be supposed to be by the means of LANGUAGE, by use of mental CONCEPTS – and so on. 'Perception' is central to the brand of philosophy known as 'EPISTEMOLOGY', and illusions and hallucinations, in particular, offer many interesting examples to ponder on the status of KNOWLEDGE.

### SEE ALSO

Naïve realism, including the 'Argument from the causal conditions of perception'

## PERENNIAL PHILOSOPHY

'Perennial philosophy' is the title that the English author Aldous Huxley (1894–1963) gave to his work on MYSTICISM. There are four fundamentals:

1. The phenomenal world is manifestation of Divine Ground, in which are all partial realities and without which they would not be.
2. Human beings are capable of knowing about the Divine Ground both by inference and direct intuition, which unites the knower with the known.

3. Human beings as well as a phenomenal ego have an eternal self with which they can identify themselves with the Divine Ground.
4. Humanity's purpose on Earth is identification of and with eternal self in order to come to knowledge of the Divine Ground.

For some at least, this states the unifying principles of all religions, which differ only in the unessentials: mythology, ritual or expression.

## PERSONAL IDENTITY

### Essential identities

What makes something 'something'? What makes me, 'me', or the ship of Theseus, the ship of Theseus – as opposed to any other? Questions of identity, especially 'personal' identity, have preoccupied philosophers over the centuries and continue to raise new problems today, as advances in medicine create ever more possibilities, and with them questions.

### Chimeras of personal identity

In PLATO's dialogues, the *Republic* and the *Symposium*, only the immaterial, divine FORMS never change in themselves, because they are complete and perfect. Everything else, including persons, must change in TIME or SPACE, in order to become what they are.

After all, without the idea and shared assumption that each person has a fixed identity, our systems of ETHICS, LAW, medicine, and indeed our everyday personal, social interactions and interdependency would be endangered. It may be enough for the GOD of the Hebrew Bible to pronounce the answer to the question, 'Who Am I?' with the response: 'I am who I am', but the rest of creation seems to require more differentiation.

And so, over the centuries, philosophers have returned again and again to the problem, focusing on different aspects. Some look to explain the nature of name; numerical and spatial identity; others, SOULS. Some wonder about the essential elements of the body or of DNA; some of the nature of the brain, the MIND, consciousness; MEMORY; EXPERIENCE. Classic cases include 'The Ship of Theseus' (physical contiguity in time or space); the medieval debate over survival of the soul that led to Thomas AQUINAS' 'THOUGHT EXPERIMENT' (mocked by Bertrand RUSSELL) of the family of cannibals who appear to have no

atoms rightfully of their own in order to enter heaven; and 'The Prince and the Cobbler', part of John LOCKE's (1690) *Essay Concerning Human Understanding*, this last looking at mental and PSYCHOLOGICAL continuity in consciousness.

In an attempt to lay the debate to rest, David HUME (1739–40), in *A Treatise of Human Nature* (IV. I. 6), concluded that personal identity is nothing more nor less than a composite of one's lifetime activities and experiences, taken altogether, not separately.

And that is not even to mention the views of Plutarch; Thomas HOBBES in *De Corpore*; Gottfried LEIBNIZ in his *Discourse on Metaphysics*; or Thomas Reid's *Essays on the Intellectual Powers of Man*. Starting with Amelie Rorty's anthology, *Identities of Persons* (1976), many recent efforts, by such as Derek Parfit or Bernard Williams, have fed into legal and moral debates concerning personal agency and accountability.

The LOGIC, ethics, CONCEPTS and terms of identity must and do change with each historical epoch, and from CULTURE to culture. Today, genetic manipulation, biotechnology, surgery or drugs may affect someone's personal identity. These may undergo dramatic radical alterations in cases of physical and mental enhancements and reductions: change of eye colour, sex change, bionic and robotic bodily insertions, artificial and transplanted body parts, including animal and manufactured parts and materials. Recent 'chimerical' experiments, which seek to create new species by mixing other ones, or the transplantation of human and animal stem cells in embryonic research, have made the issue far more than a topic of philosophical interest.

Contributor: Mary Lenzi

## PHENOMENA AND NOUMENA

Literally 'things that appear' and 'things that are thought'. PLATO's FORMS seem to be a kind of 'noumena'. KANT uses the terms to argue that we can see the world of phenomena only imperfectly via the senses, as well as being obliged to distort any PERCEPTIONS through the obligatory wearing of a kind of 'perceptual spectacles'. Alas, he thinks the world of 'noumena' is even worse – these objects of 'pure KNOWLEDGE' are denied to humans limited to a world of phenomena.

# PHENOMENOLOGY

Literally, the 'SCIENCE of appearances'. Or perhaps not so literally, for phenomenology is not scientific but one of the most obscure and esoteric of the branches of philosophy. ARISTOTLE speaks of 'phainomena', but really, the first use in the sense of studying appearances and illusions was by J.H. Lambert, following the work of Christian Wolff, in the *Neues Organon* of 1764. KANT joined in with his distinction between the 'noumenal world', forever out of reach, as opposed to the world of appearances, while HEGEL's *Phenomenology of Spirit*, which argues that PHENOMENA are the expressions of ideas or KNOWLEDGE that the MIND is in the process of developing, brought the term into the philosophical mainstream.

After Hegel, phenomenology became the study of the development of 'consciousness' from its simplest (animal-like) forms to its supposedly highest (logical male, Germanic) form. Today, phenomenology counts as one of the major strands in CONTINENTAL PHILOSOPHY, and looks to Edmund HUSSERL, who sought, like DESCARTES, to explain 'EXPERIENCES'; Martin HEIDEGGER, who offers a 'HERMENEUTICAL phenomenology' and saw his task as continuing Hegel's work of bringing about a pre-ordained historical process of achieving a higher state of self-awareness, '*Dasein*' or Being; and Max Scheler in Germany (who adopted this as his task too); as well as the French 'EXISTENTIALISTS', such as Jean Paul SARTRE, Maurice MERLEAU-PONTY and Gabriel Marcel.

> Phenomenology is accordingly the theory of experience in general, inclusive of all matters, whether real or intentional, given in experiences, and evidently discoverable in them.
>
> Edmund Husserl (1901), *Logical Investigations*

# PHILOSOPHER'S STONE, THE

The substance reputedly capable of turning base metals into gold. Alchemists in North Africa and Europe, by way of China and India, devoted much labour to searching for it. Perhaps the most famous alchemist was Isaac NEWTON, although he kept this part of his research even more to himself than his gravitational theories.

Even if neither Newton nor anyone else really ever found the secret, much useful chemical and physical experimentation was certainly done in the process.

# PHILOSOPHY

Philosophy is (at least) one of the subjects of this book. It is sometimes defined as 'the love of WISDOM', from the Greek, *philia*, love, and *sophia*, wisdom. Some people say it began with the Greeks, a couple of centuries before the birth of Christ, but this would be to ignore the subtlety and insights of the INDIAN and CHINESE traditions, in particular. However, if we accept a narrower definition of philosophy for a moment, it might more accurately be paraphrased as the love of contradictions. These are obtained by creating artificially rigid distinctions, starting from the fundamental 'is/is not' one, which is central to Eastern philosophy. Since philosophers like to split everything into two, they proceed from 'is/is not', to 'true/false', 'good/bad', and, increasingly these days, to the dull distinctions of LINGUISTIC philosophy: 'subject/predicate', 'objective/subjective', formal/informal', 'content/object', and so on. Predicates can then be conjoined with PROPOSITIONS, and so on.

PLATO termed those who used to baffle others through empty tricks with words as 'SOPHISTS', and much that passes for philosophy is also sophistry. But there is another sense in which the word 'philosophy' can be used, and that is something to do with the search for VALUES and human MEANINGS. And that is why the subject of this book is equally ETHICS.

# PIAGET, JEAN (1896–1980)

The Swiss PSYCHOLOGIST and EDUCATIONALIST, who developed a theory of the way the MIND works. His careful observation of young children led him to conclude that KNOWLEDGE was constructed as a result of the interaction between humans – or indeed any 'organism' – and their environment. For children, though, it followed that the environment should be as interesting and intellectually stimulating as possible, educational advice which, sadly, sometimes appears to have been lost somewhere along the way.

# PIERCE, CHARLES SANDERS (1839–1914)

Charles Pierce was the American originator of 'PRAGMATISM', which is the view that the significance of statements lies simply in their practical consequences. Things are meaningful only in as much as they affect our lives. He offers a sort of 'consensual' view of the structure of KNOWLEDGE, which he thinks is how SCIENCE works. He also coined the term 'abduction' for the process in which theories are developed out of supposedly theory-neutral observations.

Following the style of KANT, Pierce offers several categories for making sense of the world. 'Firstness' concerns individual EXISTENCE; 'Secondness' concerns the relations between things; while 'Thirdness' is the operation of LAWS and rules.

# PLATO (427–347 BCE)

## The essential Plato

Plato was born, studied, taught and died in Athens. His dialogues, apparently recording historical conversations between SOCRATES and various fellow citizens of the city, range widely, from the distinction between MIND and matter (echoed later by DESCARTES), to the strange theory of heavenly ideas, or FORMS, one of which exists for every CONCEPT we have. However, it is clear from his elevation of the 'Form of the Good' and his metaphor of the CAVE (both in the Republic), that ETHICS is the central concern to which he always returns. The shackled prisoners can only be 'set free' when they let the light thrown out by knowledge of the GOOD illuminate their miserable earthbound existence.

## The ambiguous Plato

Plato's family was a distinguished Athenian one with political connections, particularly with the DEMOCRATIC and oligarchic movements, and he had aristocratic lineage (perhaps even seeing himself as of 'kingly' stock). His real name was Aristocles, but in his school days he received the nickname 'Platon' (meaning 'broad') because of his broad shoulders, and that is how history has remembered him. As was normal at the time, Plato trained as a soldier as well studying poetry. He himself had political ambitions, and the Republic, like all Plato's dialogues (which was written in the form of a little playlet, starring Socrates), is not only a central text in Western philosophical thought, but a political manifesto. It seems plausible that his contempt for democracy, which he condemns as the rule of the unwise, limited his options at home, as Athens was then a 'democracy' (that is, for well-off Greek males). In 399 BCE the execution of Socrates seemed to bear out the erratic nature of the beast. After this, Plato left the city, declaring that things would never go right until either 'kings were philosophers or philosophers were kings'.

For several years he visited the Greek cities of Africa and Italy, absorbing PYTHAGOREAN notions, and in 387 BCE returned to Athens. One story has it that he was captured by pirates and held for ransom. Whether that is true or not, the second half of his long life is much more placid, with Plato establishing the famous 'ACADEMY' for the study of philosophy in the western suburbs of Athens, that some like to consider the first 'university'.

There is one exception to this scholarly existence, however. During the 360s he travelled twice to Syracuse, the capital of Greek Sicily, to advise the new king, Dionysius II. This, perhaps, was his attempt to put the ideals sketched out in the Republic into practice. Yet the reality was disastrous: Plato fell out with the King, who preferred his own opinions, and only just managed to extricate himself from the situation to return to the relative tranquility of life as Head of the Academy. He is reported to have died in his sleep at the age of 80, after enjoying the wedding feast of one of his students.

Whereas Socrates' life and works are something of a mystery, Plato's seem to be clear. As Richard Robinson, writing in The Concise Encyclopaedia of Western Philosophy and Philosophers, puts it: 'Plato's publications are all preserved, and make five large modern volumes. They constitute not merely the greatest philosophical work there is, but also one of the greatest pieces

Above the doorway to the Academy it was famously written:

LET NO ONE IGNORANT OF MATHEMATICS
ENTER HERE

For that reason, the story (in the *Meno* dialogue) of Socrates teasing out Pythagoras' theorem from an apparently ignorant slave boy is an interesting social comment, for it offers a more 'inclusive' definition of educational competence.

Astronomy was experimental in a sense, but the heavens were considered to exhibit the geometry of the gods, which was why it was necessary to insist on the stars and planets circling the earth on perfect crystal spheres, making music as they turned (whence the phrase 'the music of the spheres'), long after observations undermined the hypothesis. The dialogue the *Timaeus* echoes this perspective, with the five geometrical shapes – or solids – representing the four elements, while the fifth, the dodecahedron, represents the universe as a whole. Here too, Plato deplores the fact that 'the great mass of mankind' regard geometrical and mechanical descriptions of phenomena 'as the sole causes of all things'. But such causes are 'incapable of any plan or intelligence for any purpose'.

A story (also told of Euclid) shows both a harsh and dogmatic Plato, but also an idealistic one. Asked by a student to explain the practical application of the courses he was being taught, Plato, the story goes, instructed a slave boy to give the student a small coin so that he might appreciate better the value of the knowledge – and then threw him out of the school!

'early dialogues', are thought to be the ones written in his youth, when he is supposed to be still reflecting Socrates' influence. These are thought to be the most 'factual' accounts of Socrates' own views. The key dialogue from this period would be the *Apology*, apparently written shortly after Socrates' execution.

The second period, the middle dialogues, includes what are now thought to be the most important philosophical works, with Plato, it is said, at the peak of his brilliance. These are the dialogues of the *Republic*, the *Symposium* and the *Phaedrus*. The *Republic*, as already mentioned, deals not only with the design and organisation of the 'ideal STATE', but also with the nature of KNOWLEDGE and the 'Forms'; the *Symposium*, or 'Drinking Party', deals with the nature of BEAUTY, LOVE and the 'meaning of LIFE'; and the *Phaedrus* deals with the question of IMMORTALITY and the SOUL.

Some people would place the *Symposium* later in the chronology, and the convention is that the 'late dialogues' have left the historical Socrates far behind, while an increasingly poetic Plato is preoccupied with more 'METAPHYSICAL' questions and even starting to challenge his own earlier views, for example, on the nature of the 'Forms'. Certainly, nothing in Plato can be taken at face value. Although in the *Republic* we have an apparently clear condemnation of poetry and even SEX (children are to be produced in the *ideal state* in a more controlled and logical way); in the *Symposium*, an entirely different view is given. After describing the PSYCHOLOGICAL fevers that the physical presence of a lover can create, the fevers condemned in the *Republic* as a 'tyrant', Socrates here says that it is only this that prevents the 'wings of the soul' from becoming parched and dry, and proceeds, scandalously, to credit *eros* – sexual love – as a god!

The little that seems to be clear about Plato's own views is that he (like Socrates and indeed the other Greeks, notably Pythagoras) had a hierarchy of knowledge in which ethics comes out on top, pure MATHEMATICS comes second and 'practical' knowledge, of the kind obtainable by experimentation, trails in last.

Contributor: Martin Cohen

of literature in the world.' Indeed, if anyone asks what philosophy is, he continues confidently, 'the best answer is: "read Plato".'

Plato's works consist of a series of little playlets, starring Socrates, in which conversations between Socrates and various interlocutors are recorded, often with wit, always with subtlety. Plato himself never appears in any of the dialogues – as such – but it is impossible to say whose views are really being rehearsed in them, or where.

Scholars conventionally divide Plato's dialogues into three main periods. The first, the

## PLEASURE

For many ancient Greeks, the desire for pleasure was something to be sated, like water for thirst. The 'HEDONISTS' have given us the term for this attitude towards life. ARISTOTLE saw pleasure as a guide to achieving the correct natural balance, yet the STOICS thought that, far from being a guide, it actually distracted. In the *Philebus*, PLATO, wise as ever, says pleasure is a kind of 'intermediate state' and cannot be measured. If he is right, that would destroy the basis for UTILITARIAN calculations.

## PLOTINUS (*C.* 204–270 BCE)

Plotinus joined the Roman Army hoping to learn more about Persian and INDIAN thought, but his military career was curtailed and he ended up in Rome instead, where he spent his life teaching and writing, becoming the initiator of what is now called 'NEO-PLATONISM'. His writings, short and lively in style, were gathered together by PORPHYRY and called the *Enneads*. Plotinus takes PLATO's vision of the 'GOOD' (also called 'the One') a bit further, saying that uniting with this is the true aim of the philosophers. Religion, of course, is no use in achieving this, but even reason will tend to produce 'false IDOLS' (he uses the word 'phantoms'), just as it is reason that produces the SENSE world we imagine around us all the time. The true FORMS remain out of reach to reason.

Plotinus offers three universal principles or 'hypostatases' to describe the levels of reality. The foundation of the triad is SOUL, which, at least in the case of humans, is said to contain various parts, that is, some plant parts, some animal parts and some parts capable of reaching the next level, which is 'intellect'. Intellect, in turn, is linked to the One, the 'Good'. But the One is beyond all intellectual terms, such as whether it exists or not.

## PNEUMA

The breath of the cosmos. The STOICS considered *pneuma* to be a mixture of air and fire that pervaded the universe. It was held to link the elements of water and earth together, and to be essential both for creating change and permitting EXISTENCE. Later philosophers called a similar linking force the 'aether', and it has some similarities to physicists' notions of invisible forces, or indeed energy fields.

## POETRY

Poetry and philosophy go together like chalk and cheese, for poetry claims to convey MEANING in a distinctly 'non-rational' way that challenges philosophers to think a bit harder.

Nonetheless, many philosophers, of whom PLATO is only the most famous, were also poets. Although in the *Republic* we have an apparently clear condemnation of poetry (along with SEX); in the *Symposium*, an entirely different view is presented, with the poetry of love now said to be able to convey insights into the most profound truths.

## POINCARÉ, JULES HENRI (1854–1912)

Although primarily a MATHEMATICIAN, Poincaré also wrote on many other matters, such as astronomy, theoretical physics and the philosophy of SCIENCE and mathematics itself. He is remembered for demonstrating 'mathematical conventionalism', that is, the view that the geometry of SPACE is neither 'Euclidean' nor even 'non-Euclidean', neither 'true' nor 'false', but basically anything we choose to make it. On the other hand, like EINSTEIN, he did not offer an 'anything goes' universe, he just highlighted an aspect that was rooted in SUBJECTIVITY. Much of science, he thought, was entirely objective, grounded in one very sober reality.

## POLITICAL PHILOSOPHY

Political philosophy potentially covers all areas of social life, from the family and the PSYCHOLOGICAL character of people, to the STATE and the institutions and rules that should govern it. However, if we restrict it to the latter, the great political philosophers are the 'authoritarians', such as PLATO, HEGEL, MARX and ENGELS, CONFUCIUS and MAO Tse Tung; the PRAGMATISTS, in the sense that they argue that the 'end justifies the means', such as MACHIAVELLI, HOBBES and even BENTHAM; and the 'LIBERALS', such as LOCKE, ROUSSEAU and MILL. Issues that political philosophy addresses include RIGHTS and LIBERTIES, EQUALITY, welfare and ECONOMICS, the origins of authority and the doctrines of consent, civil disobedience and REVOLUTIONARY change, and representation and DEMOCRACY.

## POPPER, KARL (1902–94)

### The essential Popper

Karl Popper is counted as one of the greatest philosophers of SCIENCE of the twentieth century. He was also a social and POLITICAL PHILOSOPHER of considerable stature, a staunch defender of liberal DEMOCRACY (and the principles of social criticism upon which it is based), as well as of the 'open society', and an implacable opponent of authoritarianism or what is nowadays sometimes called centralised, 'big government'. His arguments against the classical view of scientific methodology, based on inductive reasoning, that is, drawing general conclusions from a limited number of instances, and his espousal of 'falsifiability' as a criterion of demarcation between science and non-science, set the parameters for further debate.

## Falsification and totalitarianism

Karl Raimund Popper was born to middle-class assimilated Jewish parents in Vienna, then capital of Austro-Hungary, and completed a PhD in philosophy at the University of Vienna in 1928. He became for a time a schoolteacher and cabinet maker, but was also an active participant in the vibrant intellectual life for which Vienna was then famous. FREUD, MARX, Adler and EINSTEIN were among those whose work influenced him, and he then became quite closely involved with a group of scientists, scientifically-minded philosophers and MATHEMATICIANS, which focused around Moritz SCHLICK, who had been appointed professor of the philosophy of the inductive sciences at Vienna University in 1922. This was the famous 'VIENNA CIRCLE' of LOGICAL POSITIVISTS, whose work dominated ANALYTIC philosophy between the two world wars. Popper, who shared the Circle's esteem for science and distaste for speculative METAPHYSICS, was nonetheless never offered membership of the group, and grew increasingly critical of both its aims and its methods. He took pride in the title 'the official opposition', which some members of the Circle bestowed on him, and in later years was to claim that he had been responsible for the death of the movement.

Concerns about the growth of Nazism and the threat of the *Anschluss* obliged him to emigrate in 1937, and he took up a position teaching philosophy at Canterbury University College in New Zealand. He first sprang to prominence in the English-speaking world with the publication of the *Open Society and its Enemies* in 1945, a work which was written in New Zealand and to which he liked to refer as 'his war effort'. In 1946 he returned to Europe to teach at the London School of Economics, and was appointed professor of logic and scientific method at the University of London in 1949.

Popper is widely viewed as one of the pre-eminent philosophers of science of the twentieth century. He was also a social and political philosopher of considerable stature, a staunch defender of the democratic principles of the 'open society' and an implacable opponent of all forms of political authoritarianism. The publication of *The Logic of Scientific Discovery* in 1959 (a translation of the 1935 *Logik der Forschung*), brought Popper's innovative ideas in the philosophy of science into prominence, though his Viennese origins and association with the Vienna Circle gave rise to a long-standing misconception that he was a logical positivist.

In fact, Popper was hostile to the 'LINGUISTIC turn' in philosophy, and was critical of what he saw as analytic philosophy's obsession with the nature of LANGUAGE and the question of MEANING, dismissing it as 'trivialising'. Short in stature, Popper was a brilliant but rather pugnaciously aggressive and mercurial thinker, who distained contemporary philosophical fashions in favour of a neo-classical concern with the nature of human rationality as manifested in science and political life. For this reason, he was destined, in Britain as in Vienna, to become a victim of those very fashions. Thus, just as membership of the Vienna Circle had eluded him, so too, he never achieved the kind of recognition from the Oxbridge academic establishment in Britain which, it is fair to say, he craved. In both cases, he attributed this to the influence of one man, his fellow-Austrian, Ludwig WITTGENSTEIN, whom he met only once in an encounter that has entered philosophical legend (this was the famous 'Poker' incident at the Cambridge Moral Science Club in October 1946), but whom he viewed, nonetheless, as his lifelong nemesis.

As his reputation and influence grew, Popper became the recipient of many honours, including a knighthood and fellowships from the Royal Society and the British Academy. He retired from academic life in 1969, though he remained intellectually active until his death in 1994.

## Reason and science: the demarcation

Popper described himself as a 'critical rationalist'. This represented a conscious alignment of his position with that of such RATIONALIST thinkers as DESCARTES, LEIBNIZ and, above all, KANT, on the key issue of the genesis of human KNOWLEDGE. It also signified his rejection of the classical empiricism of BACON, LOCKE and HUME, which had been revived and refined by the logical positivists; and of the inductivist account of science which had grown out of it. Against it, Popper argued that: (a) There are no theory-free, infallible observations as empiricists assume: all observation is theory-laden, and involves the application of a conceptual scheme to particular experiential situations; (b) INDUCTION, conceived of as process of logical INFERENCE from the particularity of experimental evidence to the generality of scientific law, is a myth: such inferences, he held, play no role in scientific investigation or in human life generally; (c) It is logically impossible to secure the verification of a universal statement. Since all scientific theories are universal in form, Popper contended, they are unverifiable, and can be tested only indirectly, by references to their implications.

Popper thus set his face firmly against the notion that positive experimental results can ever permit the investigator to inductively infer that a scientific theory has been verified. Following Hume, he argued that no number of positive outcomes at the level of experimental testing can confirm a scientific theory, but crucially, a point which he believed Hume had missed, that a single genuine counter-instance is logically decisive: it shows the theory from which the implication is derived to be *false*. In other words, Popper argued the view that scientific theories are not logically derived from experience, nor can they be confirmed by it. Such theories, given their universal nature, are rather irreducibly conjectural or hypothetical, and are generated by the creative imagination in order to solve problems which have arisen in relation to a pre-existing field of knowledge. The critical role of experimental testing in science, he held, is to show us which theories are false, not which theories are true, though a theory which has successfully withstood critical testing is thereby said to be 'corroborated', and may justifiably be regarded as having a higher explanatory power at a given time than its falsified rivals.

In this respect, the central thrust of Popper's EPISTEMOLOGY was SOCRATIC, and contained an interesting emphasis on the importance of the negative: the actual falsification of a scientific theory is itself a positive contribution to human knowledge, which precipitates and guides the search for a better theory. His account of the logical asymmetry between verification and falsification was crucial to Popper's philosophy of science, and inspired him to take

falsifiability as his criterion of demarcation between what is and is not genuinely scientific: a theory, he proposed, is to be accounted scientific if and only if it is falsifiable. This view formed the basis for his dismissal of the claims of both psychoanalysis and contemporary MARXISM to scientific status: the former because it has never been stated in terms which opened it to the possibility of falsification; the latter because it had been reformulated to make it consistent with facts which would otherwise have demonstrated its falsity.

The recognition of the fallibility of human knowledge, and, with it, the willingness to subject even one's most cherished theory to a critical test which could conceivably show it to be false, thus became, for Popper, the defining characteristic of the true scientific mentality. As he put it in *The Logic of Scientific Discovery*: 'The wrong view of science betrays itself in the craving to be right.'

## Reason and the open society: the critique of historicism

His emphasis on the fallibility and limitations of human knowledge was one of the key links between Popper's philosophy of science and his social and political philosophy. In both *The Open Society and Its Enemies* and *The Poverty of Historicism* he developed a powerful critique of the view (which he termed 'HISTORICISM') that historical processes are goal-directed and have a LOGICAL or DIALECTICAL structure, a view which he believed to be the central theoretical assumption underpinning forms of political authoritarianism in both the ancient and contemporary worlds. He took this as being particularly clearly evidenced in the social and political theories of PLATO, HEGEL and Marx. Associated with it, he held, is 'the historicist doctrine of the social sciences', the view that the principal task of the SOCIAL SCIENCES is predictive, the yielding of knowledge of future social and political developments.

Popper attacked the latter by arguing that it is founded upon a mistaken view of the nature of prediction in natural science, in which the unconditional prediction of events such as eclipses is wrongly taken as typical and constitutive. In fact, he held, unconditional prediction of this latter kind is relatively rare, and applies only to systems which are well isolated, stationary, and recurrent. Moreover, since the growth of human knowledge is a causal factor in the evolution of historical processes, and since it is impossible in principle to predict future states of knowledge, it follows, he argued, that there can be no predictive science of human history. For Popper, metaphysical and historical indeterminism go hand in hand.

On the positive side, Popper advocated the rather sinister-sounding 'piecemeal social engineering' as the central vehicle for generating social policy and reform, against the 'largescale social planning' which has frequently characterised authoritarian regimes. By this he meant that in an open society intentional political policies should ideally be directed to the achievement of a limited number of objectives at any given time, with the rights of citizens to evaluate their consequences being formally safeguarded. In such circumstances, policies which have unacceptable or unanticipated implications can be abandoned or modified in the light of such scrutiny. This parallels the critical testing of theories in scientific investigation, and these were argued by Popper to be two of the central critical functions of reason in human life. Popper also had a strong ETHICAL commitment to negative UTILITARIANISM, and was strongly affirmative of the ideals of individualism, market ECONOMICS and a LIBERAL democracy in which the key RIGHT of citizens is to change the ruling order through the electoral process.

Popper has had no shortage of critics. These range from classicists who contend that his interpretations of Plato and ARISTOTLE are ill-grounded, to those who seek to vindicate the claims of psychoanalysis or of Marxism to scientific status. However, perhaps the single most serious challenge to him comes in the philosophy of science, in the shape of the Quine-Duhem thesis. This argues that theories cannot be tested in isolation, but only in complex 'clusters', and that the observation of an anomalous PHENOMENON can thus logically show no more than that something is amiss with the cluster, rather than falsifying any particular element of it. Popper himself endeavoured to meet this challenge by acknowledging that, methodologically, a single conflicting or counter-instance is never sufficient to falsify a theory, but his position came under further attack from the work of Thomas KUHN, who held that science is essentially a paradigm-governed activity, and that there is little evidence in favour of falsificationism to be found in actual scientific practice. Popper's student, Imre Lakatos, attempted a reconciliation of Popper's position with that of Quine-Duhem and Kuhn by arguing that scientific theories are abandoned, not as a result of falsification on the Popperian model, but rather as a consequence of the research programmes with which they are associated becoming degenerative with respect to their explanatory value.

It is arguable that, within contemporary philosophy of science, the consensus would lie in the direction of Lakatos' approach: while generally conceding the logical significance of falsifiability, few would now accord it the canonical status attributed to it by Popper. However, even Popper's most trenchant critics would acknowledge the dominant, agenda-setting position occupied by him in the philosophy of science since the decline of POSITIVISM, and few would question his status, with Bertrand RUSSELL, as one of the twentieth century's most passionate rationalist thinkers.

Contributor: Stephen Thornton

## Further reading

Popper, K. (1945) *The Open Society and Its Enemies* (2 vols)

Popper, K. (1959) *The Logic of Scientific Discovery* (translation of *Logik der Forschung*, 1935)

Popper, K. (1961) *The Poverty of Historicism*

## POPULATION

In recent years, the question of how many people there ought to be has perplexed ETHICISTS, trying to weigh up different UTILITARIAN calculations. More people, more HAPPINESS; or is it too many people, less overall happiness? Or even, too many people now, less happiness for FUTURE GENERATIONS? But then why should non-existent people come into any sort of calculation of happiness?

Certainly, we need to distinguish between people who may or may not exist, perhaps depending on our actions now; and 'future people' who we are prepared to state will exist, despite the very obvious uncertainties about such predictions. 'Predicted people' might be a useful shorthand.

SEE ALSO

Lifeboat analogy

## PORPHYRY (*C.* 232–305 BCE)

Porphyrius Malchus spent most of his life in Rome, although he studied in Athens and was brought up in Tyre. Among his writings are fragments of *Against the Christians*, and commentaries on PLATO, looking at the *Timaeus* and the SOUL; on ARISTOTLE, especially the *Categories*, and on PTOLEMY's discussion of the celestial harmonies. His work was considered to be the best source on Aristotle's LOGIC; and the *Isagoge*, Greek for 'Introduction', became a kind of logic textbook throughout the Middle Ages. *De abstinentia* was another much praised work: a kind of vegetarian tract, not unlike those of PYTHAGORAS earlier.

The 'Tree of Porphyry' is a way of showing the structure of CONCEPTS and ideas, by means of a 'branching' diagram. For example, 'ANIMALS' might be split into 'rational' and 'irrational', and one of the branches of 'rational animals' would be labelled 'man'.

## POSITIVISM

Positivism can be said to have formally commenced in the year 1842, with the publication of the *Cours de Philosophie Positive*, by Auguste COMTE (1798–1857), although its ancestry goes back further, some would say to Francis BACON. Comte was a middle-class, French intellectual, whom John Stuart MILL would later accuse of devising a 'despotism of society over the individual' (although others blamed Jeremy BENTHAM's efforts to ground the authority of the LAW on the principle of maximising the HAPPINESS of the greatest number).

Whatever the truth of that, it is with Comte, who had been inspired by his study of medieval Catholic scholars to attempt to produce a new 'religion of humanity' and a blueprint for a new social order, that the science of society really starts.

In the *Cours*, Comte, like DESCARTES and many philosophers since, starts from a position of deep admiration for the precision and authority of the natural sciences, epitomised (at least in the public mind) by the advances in physics and chemistry. His 'positivist' idea was that the methods of natural science were the only way to understand HUMAN NATURE, both in INDIVIDUALS and collectively, and hence, the only way to find out how to organise society. The positivists wish to actually apply these 'scientific', quantitative methods to society itself, dissecting it to discover the laws and the principles governing it. Comte thought he had discovered the 'Law of Human Progress', according to which, all societies pass through three stages: the theo-

logical; the METAPHYSICAL; and the scientific, or positive.

The defining feature of each stage is the mental attitude of the people. During the theological stage, people seek to discover the 'essential nature of things' and the ultimate cause of EXISTENCE, interpreted as GOD. Philosophers, Comte thought, were stuck at this stage, perpetually but fruitlessly pursuing these sorts of questions. Most people, however, were at the next, the metaphysical stage, which involves increasing use of ABSTRACT theory, although there is still a sense of the underlying ESSENCE of things, epitomised by broadly ETHICAL notions of VALUE. The final stage comes only when enough people put aside the illusions of opinion (echoes of PLATO) and confine themselves to logical deduction from observed PHENOMENA. This is the so-called scientific (or positive) stage, and this is also the ideological source of 'logical positivism'.

Comte's stages are also supposed to correspond to periods of human history. The first relates to the pre-historical and medieval world, while the metaphysical stage is compared to the sixteenth, seventeenth and eighteenth centuries, a time when monarchies and military despots gave way to political ideals such as DEMOCRACY and HUMAN RIGHTS, including, most importantly for social life, property RIGHTS. The last stage in history will be a scientific, technological age, when all activity is rationally planned and moral rules have become universal. At this final stage, the science of society – sociology – comes into its own, with its dual task of explaining and determining social phenomena and the history of mankind.

## POSSIBILITY

There is a view, known as 'actualism', that says only the world that actually exists – exists. This dull scenario offers only 'concrete individuals' and 'actual instantiations' – even of ABSTRACT ideas. Against that is the idea that there are other 'possible' worlds. Confusingly, in 'common-sense language' (which is where the words have been borrowed from), 'possible' means just that, 'possible', but not actually existing. In philosophy, 'possible worlds' are said to exist in a new sense of the term. Everything 'possible' exists, and the only things 'not possible' are things that are self-inconsistent, logically contradictory, and so on. Thus the notion of 'possibility' has an important role in LOGIC and, more generally, in generating 'COUNTER-FACTU-ALS' or analysing PROPOSITIONS.

In one sense, saying that something 'X' is possible carries the implication, be it logical or conversational, that 'X' is not actual. On the other hand, in a different sense, universally accepted by philosophers, and indeed by the radicals of 1968, everything is possible – that is, both that which is actual and that which could be, but is not. *Ab esse ad posse valet consequentia*: 'X is actual' implies 'X is possible'.

But then there is a *different* thesis, promoted primarily by David Lewis, that everything possible exists in some sense of 'exists' – it exists in some possible world, which is different from, but as real as, our world, the one that we think of as the actual world.

In ETHICS, one view of 'possibilism' is that the best course is the one that it is 'possible' to take, rather than the one that is best 'in theory'.

## POSTMODERNISM AND POST-RATIONALISM

Modernism and its nemesis, postmodernism, are terms that started in New York among artists to indicate a rejection of the assumptions behind the 'modernist' art of the early twentieth century. Neither school makes much sense, but oppositions can be presented such that 'modernism' represents experimentation and inner TRUTH, distinctions drawn between the mundane and the exalted or between the common and the elite – and postmodernism the opposite. In the 1970s, CONTINENTAL PHILOSO-PHERS took up the task of constructing 'postmodernism', seeing DESCARTES as the original 'modernist'. They thus reject 'rationality' and 'LOGIC' with what they call 'NARRATIVE' and unpredictable change.

Post-rationalism is less well known, but has emerged as a term among CRITICAL THEORISTS and academic specialists in continental philosophy. Interestingly, however, the term was originally created speciously to parody the pretensions of just such circles, the first known example being a spoof talk given at Sussex University in the mid-1980s. Despite its authors' intentions, in the best tradition of postmodernism, the term has gone on to mean many different things to many different people.

SEE ALSO

Modernity

## PRAGMATISM

The term comes from the USA and the work of Charles Sanders PIERCE, William JAMES and John DEWEY, in particular. Simply put, pragmatism is the view that philosophy should not try to investigate reality as such, but only to serve humankind in its practical attempts at living in the world. The pragmatists see the error stemming from DESCARTES, with his elevation of KNOWLEDGE obtained through 'INTROSPECTION' and intuition. Dewey criticises Descartes for imagining the thinking SELF somehow detached from not merely the body, but from its cultural and social context, including the social web of LANGUAGE. In *Pragmatism* (1907), the 'father' of the subject, William James, declares that 'TRUTH' itself is 'only the expedient in our way of thinking'.

## *PRAXIS*

Greek for 'action', used by ARISTOTLE to mean 'doing something', as opposed to 'thinking' or 'wondering', but adopted by MARXISTS to mean thinking – about social change.

## PREDICATE CALCULUS

A predicate is what is said of the 'subject' in a sentence (literally, 'before-spoken'), for example, being big, if the sentence is 'Rex is a big dog', or even, 'Rex is bigger than Tibbles'. Predicate calculus is sometimes called the 'CALCULUS of Relations', and aims to systematise and formalise the LOGICAL relationships between 'PROPOSITIONS'.

## PRE-SOCRATICS

The term covers a period roughly from the first half of the sixth century BCE to SOCRATES' lifetime (469–399 BCE). Loosely considered all as 'Greeks', the thinkers normally counted as 'pre-Socratics' include THALES, Anaximander and Anaximenes, together comprising the so-called 'Milesian school' based in today's Turkey; the PYTHAGOREANS; PARMENIDES, ZENO and Milissus, comprising the ELEATIC school in today's Italy; EMPEDOCLES and Anaxagoras; and the 'ATOMISTS' DEMOCRITUS and LEUCIPPUS. Some of the pre-Socratics lived at the same time as Socrates, but they are allowed as such if they were not apparently influenced by his teachings.

## PRESCRIPTIVISM

The ETHICAL theory known as 'prescriptivism' is credited to Oxford philosopher, Richard Mervyn

Hare (1919–2002). In books such as *The Language of Morals* (1952), he says that moral statements are different from others because they imply compulsory guidance on behaviour of some sort. 'It is wrong to kill animals' means you should not kill them. Also, they imply that the prescription is universal – it applies to everyone. Moral statements are different from, indeed superior to, mere orders, in this last respect.

## PRIMARY AND SECONDARY QUALITIES

The distinction can be traced back to the ancients, but is mainly associated with John LOCKE, who thought things like shape, size, mass and even texture were 'primary', while things like COLOURS, sounds and tastes were not so much to do with the 'things themselves', but more to do with our PERCEPTIONS of them. The former merit the term 'real'; the latter only exist as long as someone's mind creates them. Which is where BERKELEY comes in. . .

## PRIVATE LANGUAGE

A term used by WITTGENSTEIN, particularly in *Philosophical Investigations* (1953), sections 243–315. There, he 'apparently' argues that they are not possible, as LANGUAGE is dependent on shared rules of use. His BEETLE BOX thought experiment is part of this debate.

Ludwig Wittgenstein

## PROBABILITY

To say something is 'probable' is to put it somewhere between 'possible' and absolutely certain.

Pierre Simon Laplace, who set out his LOGICAL theories of the subject in his 'Essai philosophique sur les probabilités' (1814), once said that the most important questions in life were those involving calculations of probability.

KANT was interested in distinguishing between things that were 'empirically' possible and 'logically' possible, while DESCARTES was more inclined towards what could be imagined as 'possible', which is a kind of psychological POSSIBILITY. ARISTOTLE was particularly interested in 'potentiality', which he summed up with his example of a block of marble which he thought might have the 'potential' to become a statue of Hermes.

Although the STOICS, and HOBBES too, thought that if something was possible, then that meant it had to happen, as otherwise it was not really 'possible', MATHEMATICAL theories of probability superimpose a grid of certainty upon the partially unstructured – upon the comparative judgements of likelihood of naïve COMMON SENSE. Nothing in the mathematical

### JUST FANCY THAT!

Consider the statistical odds of a well-shuffled pack of cards being dealt out to four whist players (the game where one suit is trumps and you try to win 'tricks') and each player ending up with all the cards of just one suit. It is actually very unlikely: about one in 2,235,197,406,895,366,368,301,600,000, according to a calculation made in 1939 by Horace Norton of University College London. How unlikely is that? Well, put another way, if everyone in the world, that is, about a billion people, played an enthusiastic 100 games a day, every day of the year, for a million years, the odds against it are still a hundred to one. Yet, more than once, it is recorded that such hands have been dealt. One such case involved the pensioners of the Bucklesham Village Whist Club, who, in January 1998, were highly amused when, after Mrs Ruffles (aged 64) had given the cards a good shuffle, one of the players announced they had thirteen trumps! Curiouser and curiouser, each of the players discovered they too had complete hands of just one suit, as of course did the 'dummy' hand, face down on the table.

theory of probability can settle the proper 'values' of possibilities. 'Logical theory has to explain how *a priori* truths can have any bearing on the practical problem of anticipating the unknown on the basis of non-demonstrable reasons', wrote LOCKE in his look at probability in the *Essay Concerning Human Understanding*. Frequency calculations, as taught in maths class, fall apart with situations which only occur occasionally from out of a range of possibilities.

It was PASCAL who introduced the MATHE-MATICS of probability to philosophy, through his examination of games of luck, or perhaps we should say CHANCE. It is much misunderstood, even in practical areas like allocating health resources, with the effect, for example, that trivial probabilities of succumbing to obscure diseases can be met with mandatory programmes of treatment with high and real likelihoods of side effects. Or (more positively) that people continue to buy lottery tickets.

## PROCLUS (*C.* 411–485 CE)

### The essential Proclus

Proclus was a METAPHYSICIAN, SCIENTIST, theologian, theurgist and devout teacher. He was born in Byzantium, died in Athens and was buried with his mentor, Syrianus. He intended to become an attorney like his father, but after a 'conversion' experience, took up philosophy. He attended the Platonic ACADEMY at Athens, where he studied under Plutarch and Syrianus, eventually becoming the next 'Diadochus', or Head of the Academy.

Marinus, Proclus' student and biographer, relates that he had a full teaching schedule, wrote about 700 lines of prose a day, and worshipped the gods without fail. In *The Elements of Theology* and *The Theology of Plato*, his central concern is 'the One', also known as 'the GOOD'. This is absolute simplicity, transcendent, strictly unknowable in itself and, properly, unnameable. Proclus' metaphysics was not only important for the development of science, but it is also MYSTICAL. By offering a grand systemisation of the science and spirituality of the ancient world, he directly influenced many later thinkers, such as Kepler, COPERNICUS, William of OCKHAM, AQUINAS, DESCARTES, HEGEL and KANT.

### Proclus and the search for 'the One'

Proclus (and NEO-PLATONISM in general) has been neglected by the majority of philosophers

> ## OF PROCLUS
>
> His language flows like a torrent, inundating its banks, and hiding the dark fords and whirlpools of doubts, while his mind full of the majesty of things of such a magnitude, struggles in the straits of language, and the conclusion never satisfying him, exceeds by the copia of words, the simplicity of the propositions.
>
> Johannes Kepler (1571–1630)
>
> . . . the most beautiful and orderly development of the philosophy which endeavours to explain all things by an analysis of consciousness, and builds up a world in the mind out of materials furnished by the mind itself, is to be found in the Platonic theology of Proclus.
>
> Samuel Taylor Coleridge (1772–1834)

for the last century, which is not surprising, given the fashionable suspicion of metaphysical systems. But this neglect is unjustified. Proclus' analytical and logically rigorous systematic writing, for example in *The Elements of Theology*, which contains 211 intricately interdependent PROPOSITIONS, is unparalleled in the ancient world, and arguably unmatched in modern times. He is often the only or major source of important historical information, such as in his *Commentary on the First Book of Euclid's Elements*. His direct influence (and often indirect influence) is immense. Kepler found in Proclus a way of understanding rationally how MATHEMAT-ICS is the intermediary between the divine and the physical world. DUNS SCOTUS and William of Ockham both tried to understand and interpret the first proposition of the *Liber de causis* (or *The Book of Causes*), a small book containing ideas and theses extracted from *The Elements of Theology*.

Around 1245 Roger BACON taught the *Liber* in his lectures and on 19 March 1255 it became required reading at the Faculty of Arts at Paris. The contemporary neo-Platonist Wayne Hankey writes that the form Aquinas gave his principles of spiritual hierarchy can be traced to Proclus. Hegel followed Proclus in attempting to create a comprehensive philosophical system, and both he and SCHELLING, in their 'Philosophy of

Nature', used a 'neo-Platonic' 'triadic DIALEC-
TIC' in unfolding unity into a polarity of forces
with differing levels of potency. Even Shelley's
*Adonais* reveals Proclus' influence: 'The One
remains, the many change and pass.' Today,
'new age' and 'green' concerns find expression
in such concepts and terms as 'levels of meaning', 'HOLISTIC', 'organic', 'oneness' and 'illumination', which are rooted in Proclus and
neo-Platonism.

Proclus' metaphysics unifies scientific and
spiritual knowledge through seeking absolute
simplicity and the most general principles or
causes. But modern science, the familiar story
goes, is at odds with religion. Science is supposed to give us facts; religion or spirituality, if
they give us anything at all, merely provide a
SUBJECTIVE and relative sense of VALUES that
are superfluous appendages to 'real' scientific
KNOWLEDGE. But facts are only possible
within an understanding or interpretation that is
itself based on the prior acceptance of a theory.
This theory, in turn, is based upon fundamental
AXIOMS or postulates that cannot be or have
not been verified or falsified by empirical investigation (and are often never even explicitly
stated or known by its believers).

These assumptions can only be supported
rationally by metaphysical reasoning, and applying metaphysical reasoning is essential when trying to discover and understand new areas of
science. The essential need of metaphysics in
conjunction with empirical observation has
been recognised and often explicitly stated by
the greatest 'natural philosophers' or physicists,
including many of the most significant in the last
hundred years, such as Max Planck, James Jeans,
Erwin Schrodinger, Louis De Broglie, Arthur
Eddington, Albert EINSTEIN, Niels Bohr and
Werner Heisenberg. In *My View of the World*,
Heisenberg writes, 'a real elimination of metaphysics means taking the soul out of both art
and science, turning them into skeletons incapable of any further development'. And, in
*Across the Frontiers* he adds that 'The Search for
"the one", for the ultimate source of all understanding, has doubtless played a similar role in
the origin of both religion and science.' He also
recalls that Niels Bohr told the VIENNA
CIRCLE that banning metaphysics 'would prevent our understanding of quantum theory'. If
metaphysics has received unjustified prejudicial
treatment in recent times from various philosophers, we might instead do better to recognise

Proclus' ability to clarify the underlying unity of
scientific and spiritual knowledge through metaphysical reasoning. Indeed, Heisenberg reminds
us that PYTHAGORAS and PLATO anticipated
'the entire program of contemporary exact science'; and Max Planck remarks that Kepler's
'faith in the existence of the eternal laws of creation' allowed him to become the creator of the
new astronomy.

In *The Elements of Theology*, Proclus gives us a
metaphysical landscape that can be inferred to

## PROCLUS ON MATHEMATICS

In *A Commentary on the First Book of Euclid's
Elements*, section 22, Proclus explains that
mathematics:

> . . . contributes things of the greatest
> importance to the study of nature, both
> revealing the orderly nature of the reasoning,
> in accordance with which the whole has been
> constructed, and so on, and showing that the
> simple and primary elements, by means of
> which the whole of the heaven was completed,
> having taken on the appropriate forms among
> its parts, are connected together with
> symmetry and regularity.

Mental endeavour is the preparation for
theology. For those features which to the
uninitiated in the truth of divine matters seem
difficult to grasp and lofty are by mathematical
reasoning shown to be trustworthy, manifest
and uncontroversial, by means of certain
images. For they show proof of the
supernatural properties of numbers; and they
make clear the powers of the intelligible forms
in reasoning. Thus Plato teaches us many
remarkable things about the nature of the
gods through the appearance of mathematical
things; and the Pythagorean philosophy
disguises its teaching on divine matters with
these, so to speak, veils. For of this kind is the
whole of that sacred writing, both Philolaus on
the Bacchae, and the whole Pythagorean
system of teaching about God.

Kepler uses those exact quotations in his book,
*The Harmony of the World*, but few philosophers
appreciate how deeply Kepler was influenced by
Proclus because few of them have read Kepler.

follow from the experience of divine luminosity (or radiance), and which leads us to that which is beyond all predicates, the One or the GOOD itself. As SOCRATES says, 'the good is superior to being' (*Republic* 509–B). Proclus systematically considers the nature of reality by showing that alternatives lead to absurdities or impossibilities. For example, Proposition One states that:

Every manifold [many-ness or plurality] in some way participates [in] unity.

This seems simple enough, but what are the implications, and what reasoning supports it? Assume that a plurality or manifold does not participate in unity, then, as Proclus writes, 'Neither this manifold as a whole nor any of its several parts will be one; each part will itself be a manifold of parts, and so to infinity.' Therefore, only by being unified in some way can anything be a 'one'. For example, one pen, one person, one piece of hair, one electron or one universe all share in common their ability to participate in unity because they are all a 'one'. The EXISTENCE of anything, including the universe, is only possible by being unified through participation in unity, and what is responsible for unity, the One, is also the Good (Proposition Thirteen). Consequently, scientific knowledge or 'facts' (and all things) are possible because the fundamental nature of reality is Good. Facts are possible because of moral values.

Proclus was respected by his peers as much, or perhaps even more, for his way of life than for his intellectual prowess. He was so devoted to the spiritual life that, as Marinus writes, 'In general, he observed the important holidays of all peoples and of every nation in the way proper to each; and he did not make them an excuse, as others do, for idleness or feasting, but celebrated them entirely by sleepless (prayer) meetings, singing hymns and things like these.' Proclus wrote many hymns, which, as has been suggested, should be understood as a form of theurgy.

Theurgy is the priestly art and translates as 'divine-working' or 'operating on the gods'. The contemporary neo-Platonist, Lucas Siorvanes, writes that the 'theurgist-priests can share some of the creative power and channel it to good deeds for their fellow human beings, and also to elevate their own soul.' Theurgy involves personal experience rather than simply intellectualising, and it comes in many forms, such as the manipulation of symbols, prayer, hymns and

## THE ONE REMAINS UNDIMINISHED

The One gives birth to Bound and Infinity, Being-Life-Intellect, Soul, Nature and Body. Proclus' metaphysics was not only important for the development of science, but it is also mystical. All things have a 'desire' for reversion to the original cause, to the One itself. Yet, even while generating a procession to duality and multiplicity, the One remains undiminished. The One is beyond knowledge, and beyond everything since it is the cause of everything. We ourselves can only revert to our original cause and achieve mystical union by transcending discursive reasoning (useful though Proclus acknowledges it is for science and for elevating us towards contemplation of the one). Only 'divine madness' can transcend the distinction between the knower and the known. Plato's 'divine madness' seems essential to transcend the distinction between the knower and the known, allowing unification with the One, at least as far as we are able.

incantations. The lower level is related to magic and miraculous healing, but these practices should give way to the higher level of approaching unification with the One, the real goal.

Select initiates would be taught Orphic Hymns, Pythagoras' Golden Verses and Exhortations, and the Chaldean ORACLES. If philosophy is the love of WISDOM, and the source of wisdom is the One, then it would seem that, in the end, we need to go beyond philosophy to reunite, as far as we are able, with the One. This act of unification, the final goal of theurgy, is mystical. Theurgy may seem difficult to understand, but they meant for their teachings to be cryptic, as their actual practices were only for initiates. But this transcendence of rationality or discursive thought is *not* anti-intellectual; on the contrary, it provides the foundation of the Intellect itself. Siorvanes reminds us that 'Proclus often cautions that we must not allow imagination to run riot, but exercise our mind with logic and science before we are ready to attempt unification with the One.'

Contributor: John Spencer

## Further reading

E.R. Dodds (trans. 1963) *The Elements of Theology* (Oxford University Press)

G.R. Morrow (trans. 1970) *Proclus: A Commentary on the First Book of Euclid's Elements* (Princeton University Press)

M. Edwards (trans. 2000) *'Neo-Platonic' Saints: The Lives of Plotinus and Proclus by their Students,* (Liverpool University Press)

## PROPOSITION

A proposition is usually (but not of course always) defined as sentences which 'convey truth'. Euclid's kind of MATHEMATICAL claim is a favoured example. My dog is called Fritz, is not. (And nor is she called Fritz.) If philosophers got out more they would know that a proposition is also a proposal (perhaps a marriage one! or at least a business one). In this form of everyday use, propositions are not 'propositions' after all.

## PROTAGORAS (*C.* 485–415 BCE)

Protagoras of Abdera was the master SOPHIST, an expert in the arts of RHETORIC and politics. However, only a few fragments remain of his excellent prose, such as 'Man is the measure of all things', the view challenged by PLATO in his dialogue (of the same name), where it is said that it is self-refuting, although the more plausible response is that it is an extreme form of RELATIVISM, and therefore is simply saying nothing.

### Protagoras' problem

Protagoras' problem is the paradox of whether Euathlos needs to pay Protagoras for his training as a lawyer, if it was entered into under the generous arrangement whereby he does not need to pay anything for his tuition until and unless he wins his first court case. The puzzle arises supposedly because Euathlos decides to become a musician and never takes any court cases. Protagoras demands that Euathlos pay him for his trouble, and when he refuses, decides to sue him in court. Protagoras reasons that if Euathlos loses the case, Protagoras will have won, in which case he will get his money back. Furthermore, even if he loses, Euathlos will then have won a court case, despite his protestations about being a musician now, and will therefore still have to pay up. Euathlos can reason a little differently, however. If I lose, he thinks, then I will have lost my first court case, in which event, the original agreement releases me from having to pay any tuition fees. And

even if I win, Protagoras will have lost the right to enforce the contract, so I still will not need to pay anything!

## PROUDHON, PIERRE-JOSEPH (1809–65)

Proudhon was a French POLITICAL PHILOSOPHER, whose answer to the question used as the title of his book, *What is Property?* was: 'Property is theft'. Proudhon argues that man is by nature social, and a searcher for justice, but the institutions of property destroy this good nature, particularly as they become larger and more impersonal. His compromise is to suggest that small groups of workers join freely together, which influenced the new movement of syndicalism and trade unions.

## PSYCHOLOGY

Psychologists offer four explanations for moral behaviour (as they put it). It may be to please (or to avoid shocking) other members of our social group; it may be as a result of the promptings of our CONSCIENCE; it may be because of a good upbringing, one that rewarded good behaviour and punished bad; or, finally, it may be because good behaviour is recognised by the (SOCRATIC) rational individual as simply the best way to live in the world.

Studies have found little difference between the stated moral beliefs of delinquents and non-delinquents – if anything, the delinquents may be more indignant and intolerant of what they consider to be 'bad' behaviour. (Some psychologists say that 'bad behaviour' is the result of too strong a conscience.) However, there may be a failure on the part of delinquents to accept responsibility for their own actions. The classic FALLACY obtains something like: All people who steal envelopes from work are bad people. I steal envelopes from work. I am not a bad person. The ability to 'circle this square' is a necessary response to what psychologists call 'psychological dissonance'. At its extreme, this dissonance can lead to a nervous breakdown, which is why SOCRATES was sorry for anyone who did anything wrong.

## PTOLEMY (87–150 CE)

The ancient Greek (one who, however, lived in Egypt) astronomer, MATHEMATICIAN and geographer. His THOUGHT EXPERIMENTS may not be much (such as the one to prove the earth must be absolutely stationary, otherwise objects when dropped would fall slightly to one side), but his 13–volume book of the heavens, based on at least 80 interacting heavenly spheres, was actually more accurate in calculating positions than the COPERNICAN one that replaced it.

## PUNISHMENT

The philosophy of punishment is conventionally summed up as restitution, retribution, deterrence and reform. The first involves forcing the criminal to 'make amends' for the harm that they have done, to try to undo the damage and put things right again. It is not a very practical response to many crimes, even those involving damage to property or theft of goods or money, but it is certainly a minimal sort of justification for fines and community work orders or suchlike. Reform may be an unpleasant process too, but it is often the aim of punishments for younger offenders.

More serious crimes tend to be impossible to 'undo', just in terms of the emotional and PSYCHOLOGICAL harm to the victims. However, a punishment that makes other people 'think twice' before repeating the crime is also justified under certain UTILITARIAN measures. With 'retribution', society recognises the desire of law-abiding citizens to 'get their own back' on criminals. In nineteenth-century England, the system allowed a powerful sense of involvement: the public were allowed to sit in judgement on their fellows, ultimately with the power of life or death over them, and also to witness the executions.

Of course, at some point, the general social desirability both of 'making an example' (deterring) and satisfying the need for retribution has to be set against the individual RIGHTS of the prisoners. Today, many countries have rejected the use of the death penalty as a violation of prisoners' fundamental rights, but the USA carries on – citing the 'deterrence' factor particularly (although the 're-election' factor is also pretty evident). Deterrence is also part of a general justification for punishment as a way of 'protecting' the good people from the bad.

## PYRRHO (FOURTH TO THIRD CENTURY BCE)

Pyrrho was a priest whose radical SCEPTICISM led him to refuse assent to any BELIEF. Stories tell of his detached attitude, such as the occasion he was on a ship in a tempest, and rather than rush about as everyone else was doing, merely observed that as the pigs, also on board, were continuing to eat quite happily, so would he. Needless to say, Pyrrho wrote nothing.

SEE ALSO

Scepticism, ancient

## PYTHAGORAS (*C.* 570–*C.* 500 BCE)

### The essential Pythagoras

Pythagoras was born on the island of Samos. He not only made important contributions to MUSIC, astronomy, METAPHYSICS, natural philosophy, politics and theology, he was the first person to bring the concepts of REINCARNATION, heaven and HELL to the Western world, declaring that the doctrines were a personal revelation to himself from GOD. Driven from Samos in 529 BCE when the tyrant Polycrates declared him a subversive, he went to Italy, where he established a school of philosophy at Croton in southern Italy and a monastic order based on practising vegetarianism, poverty and chastity.

### The harmonious life

Pythagoras is often misrepresented. A recent description has him part priest, part philosopher, part conjurer, who wore a white robe,

---

### THE HARMONY OF THE HEAVENS

In his notes to propositions 4 to 9 of *Principia Mathematica*, Newton says the mathematics of the laws of gravity were known to Pythagoras, who had applied harmonics to the heavens:

By means of experiments he ascertained weights by which all tones on equal strings were reciprocal as the squares of the lengths of the string. . . The proportions discovered . . . he applied to the heavens and . . . by comparing those weights with those of the planets and the lengths of the strings with the distances of the planets he understood by means of the harmony of the heavens that the weights of the planets towards the Sun were reciprocally as the squares of their distances from the Sun.

trousers and a coronet and appealed to the authority of Orphic poetry. All this can be derived from the ancient literature, but is misleading in its selectivity.

Perhaps it is because of the strict rules governing study at his school: centrally, vegetarianism. One pupil, Empedocles, records that he considered the KILLING of ANIMALS to be murder and eating them cannibalism. This followed from Pythagoras' belief in reincarnation. Certainly, he implored men not to eat animals. Instead, Pythagorean meals consisted of honeycomb, millet or barley bread and vegetables, and the philosopher himself would pay fishermen to throw their catch back into the sea, once even telling a ferocious bear to eat barley and acorns, and not to attack humans any more. Pythagoras not only showed respect for animals, but also for trees, which he insisted were not to be destroyed unless there was absolutely no alternative. Lesser plants too merited concern: on one occasion an ox was injuncted not to trample a bean field.

The crucial event in Pythagoras' life seems to have been the conquest of Egypt 525 BCE, while Pythagoras was there, learning from priests, architects and musicians. He was taken to Babylon as a prisoner of war and in so doing was introduced to a rich tradition of geometrical and mathematical wisdom.

The famous 'Pythagorean theorem' was in use long before Pythagoras, but what was significant about it was the method of deduction. The modern tradition of mathematical proof, the basis for Western SCIENCE, thus originated with Pythagoras, replacing the approach of classical Indian mathematics which tended to be intuitive. Pythagoras showed (in the manner made famous by PLATO in the SOCRATIC dialogue with Meno) that the world could be investigated and explained using human reason; that the LAWS OF NATURE could be deduced purely by thought alone.

Pythagoras believed that MATHEMATICS offered a glimpse of a perfect reality, a realm of the gods, of which our own world is but an imperfect reflection, and contrasted this pure, incorruptible and divine realm with the corruptible, earthly sphere. Sadly, it was in this sphere that the human SOUL was trapped, caught in the body as in 'a tomb'. He considered NUMBER was at the root of all creation.

---

**PYTHAGOREAN POLICY**

Honour the immortal Gods, famous heroes, parents, family.

Choose friends for their virtue. Appreciate their counsel.

Learn from their actions. Do not easily take offence.

Grow strong by bearing all you can. Control your habits:

stomach, sleep, anger, love of luxury. Avoid arousing envy.

Cause no shame to others or yourself. Honour of self is the highest duty. Practice justice in word and deed.

Never act inconsiderately. Remember death comes to everyone.

Possessions are left behind. Bear all sorrows patiently.

But observe: few sorrows befall people who act well.

Don't be over anxious what people say about you. They are fickle.

Don't be afraid, practice patience. Don't let anyone persuade you to do or say anything evil. Think before you act.

Inconsiderate acts are the mark of a fool. Having decided how to act, carry it through. Do nothing beyond what you know.

Before you sleep review your actions from the start to the end of the day, grieve over errors, rejoice over successes.

Learn this, repeat it with joy and for ever walk the path of virtue.

Contributor: Colin Kirk

---

He demonstrated this convincingly in the case of sound. NEWTON credited him with understanding the mathematics of gravity, from his study of the various distances of the planets from the Sun.

Pythagorean ideas were constantly referred to at both the ACADEMY and Lyceum, and there are many references in the works of Plato and ARISTOTLE.

Contributors: Colin Kirk and Martin Cohen

## *QUALIA*

Experienced sensations, 'raw sense data' or 'phenomenal' properties. (Not 'phenomenal' as we normally use the word, of course, but merely as in 'relating to phenomena'.)

## QUANTUM MECHANICS

Philosophers like quantum mechanics as, supposedly, normal rules do not apply in it, in particular, NEWTON's rules about mechanics, like cause and effect. And then there is the 'indeterminacy principle', which makes it impossible – even in theory – to know both the exact energy state or the exact position of a particle. The quantum world is seen as 'indeterminate' and knowledge about it is 'relative'. Yet the great RELATIVIST himself, EINSTEIN, would have none of this, saying that 'God does not play dice', and that it is our understanding of the quantum world that is at fault, a position also taken by Karl POPPER and Hilary Putnam.

## QUINE, WILLARD VAN ORMAN (1908–2000)

Quine exercised quite a thrall on ANGLO-AMERICAN PHILOSOPHY for much of the second part of the twentieth century. The Harvard logician's writings are sometimes so obscure and indigestible as to have merited satirical parody, but essentially, his aim was to show that the division between 'analytic' and 'synthetic' statements was at best fuzzy. The so-called Quine-Duhem thesis says that empirical methods only apply to networks of HYPOTHE-SES and not to single theoretical sentences. Following on from this, for example, is the view that accurate translation is never really possible, as each particle depends on the rules of the foreign language, which depend on having grasped all the particles already. He merits inclusion here as his name begins with 'Q'. Not many other philosophers can claim that!

## RACISM

Racism, as an activity, is as old as human society itself, built upon the ancient prejudice against 'the OTHER', the stranger', the fear of the wolf. But racism as a theoretical justification for this deeply rooted hostility towards others is rather more recent. Perhaps the notion of a superior white race evolved in the context of the drive to exploit and enslave the peoples of other countries as the Europeans expanded across the globe, borne on the crest of a wave of technical and military power. Throughout this imperial period, philosophers and others debated possible differences between the various peoples they had found, producing ill-founded and prejudicial categories of humanity, in the manner that DARWIN had recently demonstrated for animals and plants, a study known as polygenesis.

Racism has an important role in personal ETHICS, making acceptable (for the individual racist) things that otherwise would be unacceptable. Thus, the SLAVE trade between Britain and America spawned a new philosophy of 'Negro' (literally 'black') infantilism and inferiority, to explain what otherwise appeared contrary to the 'Christian values' of the time. The term seems to have been conjured up by the Europeans with the effect of 'dehumanising' those it was used for. The same attitudes were necessary to allow the formal apartheid of pre-Civil Rights America, and of course South Africa.

One institutionalised system of racial discrimination, appealing as ever to apparently rational and SCIENTIFIC criteria such as differences in average height and ownership of horses (which was said to reflect different tribal origins, although in fact it merely reflected different amounts of family wealth), is the case of the central African region, known today as Rwanda. This theoretical racial division was then formalised by the Belgians, who instituted a system of identity cards detailing each individual's 'race', to create a governing caste of Africans, the Tutsi, as distinguished from the Hutu majority. The Hutu were demoted socially, intellectually and physically. This theory, based on nothing more than a handful of colonial prejudices, would later lead to the genocide of 1994.

The watershed for theories presenting themselves as scientific justifications of a hierarchy of supposed racial groups was the twentieth century: in the USA, preoccupied with its black slaves and dispossessed Indians; and then later in Europe, where they were formalised, investigated and implemented by the Nazis.

## RATIONALISM

Rationalism comes from the Latin for 'reason', and being rational is, conventionally at least, the highest goal of philosophy. Yet built into the search for rationality are value judgements and prejudices. Why, after all, is the world obliged to be 'rational' just because we want to be? Rationalists seek to apply their powers of reason and their LOGIC and ANALYTICAL skills to attaining complete understanding. (Empiricism, unlike rationalism, claims not to prejudge issues, but merely to take notes, to observe and deduce.) The term has been used in many ways, but this is the dominant one, famously encapsulated in ARISTOTLE's claim that 'Man is a rational animal'.

Nowadays, not only psychologists but economists, too, have made great play of how in fact the human animal is anything but rational, and a branch of philosophy known as 'GAME THEORY' attempts to explore situations where deciding what is 'rational' in various cases depends on what other people decide, with all the confusing problems of feedback that implies.

## RAVENS, PARADOX OF

A problem of KNOWLEDGE or, precisely, philosophy of science, or so-called 'confirmation theory'. We may see a lot of black ravens and draw from this the reassurance that each black raven corroborates the claim that 'all ravens are black'. 'If something is a raven, then it is black', and, 'If something is not black, then it is not a raven'. Yet (or so argued the twentieth-century 'logical empiricist' Carl Hempel) if we think *that*, then 'logically', every example of a not-black thing, such as white handkerchiefs or red apples, even black puddings, anything that is not black and a 'non-raven' is also confirmation for the thesis – which seems absurd.

SEE ALSO

Paradoxes

## RAWLS, JOHN (1921–2002)

The twentieth-century American philosopher John Rawls attempts to sketch out rules for a LIBERAL, egalitarian society in his influential book *A Theory of Justice* (1971). The main idea, which he sees as bolstering the Western model of DEMOCRACY, is that society should be governed from under a 'veil of ignorance', a veil which prevents those taking decisions knowing how to benefit either themselves or any other portion of society. Hence they will, out of self-interest, arrive at a respect for 'basic liberties' (each individual, he says, should have as much freedom as is compatible with maintaining other people's liberties too) and seek to reduce INEQUALITIES. A policy that favours one section of society over another will only be acceptable if it raises up the poor to the level of the rich. He calls this the 'difference principle'.

And equal LIBERTY (he hopes) will result in the routing of the forces of persecution, RACISM and discrimination. Rawls considers his approach to be better than UTILITARIANISM, which could allow the position of minorities to deteriorate in pursuit of the 'maximisation' of the HAPPINESS of the others. This awareness is part of the method of 'reflective equilibrium', he says.

SEE ALSO

Liberalism

## REALISM (VARIETIES OF)

### Essentials of realism

In everyday terms, realists urge us not to be seduced by ideals, but to focus on the 'reality' of life as it is lived, whether it is beautiful or dirty or unsettling. Philosophical realism is quite separate. It is a position about the *way* reality comes to be reality in the first place. Realists about *x* believe that *x* exists, and is the way it is, independently of how we think of it. One can be a realist about pretty much anything: life, death, the external world, evil, the LAWS OF NATURE, colours, social structures, moral values, human need, numbers, other minds, the past, the future. And in connection with each of these, philosophers have suggested that realism is either naïve, untenable or wildly extravagant.

SEE ALSO

Visualisation

## The fallacy of anti-realism

Realism really gets going in the face of these other arguments generally called 'idealist', which *deny* that whatever is in question exists independently of its **PERCEPTION** or description by human minds. From these other directions (sometimes called 'anti-realist', sometimes 'nominalist'), the idea that the world exists independently of all the intermediate forces through which we come to appreciate it – perceptions, language, social processes, or whatever – is just that: an idea (or a piece of language, or a side-effect of social processes). And as with any other, the idea either creates, or makes possible, or in some other way exists prior to, the world with which we engage. At one extreme, the 'anti-realist' case is epitomised by **BERKELEY**'s suggestion that the existence of the physical objects around us really depends on our perceiving them. Looked at this way, realism and anti-realism are opposing **METAPHYSICAL** positions about the ultimate nature of reality.

Realism says that this nature, or this reality, does not depend exclusively on *other* factors, like ideas or discourse, to make it what it is. Put like this, it might just seem like a modest reminder that we do not simply create what is around us in our own image, or our conceptual schemes. There is a kind of 'common-sense' appeal about the insistence that if science is explaining the world, it is explaining the workings of what is already, independently there, rather than simply bringing a new world into being. It seems important that perceptions or descriptions of the world could be out of phase with the way the world itself is structured. If not, it seems hard to see how scientific knowledge might get more accurate – or indeed how descriptions of the world could be *wrong*, or give a false representation of it.

One way of looking at **PLATO**'s 'myth of the **CAVE**', in the *Republic*, is that it rejects reality in preference for the world of ideas, or **FORMS**. Yet another way of looking at it is that it offers us a kind of realist model, in which the unenlightened are transfixed by 'mere' appearances, without access to the true reality of the Forms. On this picture, true ideas map, or reveal, the ultimate nature of reality itself. And one need not be a Platonist to think that claims should be judged, at least in part, by their success in describing or explaining the way things really are.

In any case, the trend in recent philosophy of science, and of language, has been to challenge the idea that anything can 'track' an independent reality in the way Plato suggests. The reverse has been argued: that the objects of science, or the referents of language, are in fact constructed through the ways in which they are approached. If observation is, in the common phrase, 'value-laden', then the perspective from which we view the objects of enquiry, or the symbols through which we interpret it, will condition the reality we then accept as true. This applies elsewhere, too. Take judgements about moral value. For the moral realist, such values are 'discovered', rather than just being invented, or willed into existence, or constituted by our judging them in this way or that. Yet *is* extracting information out of people by pulling out their fingernails (or some such) 'wrong'? Is it *true* that it is wrong? If so, is this not more a matter of the way we have come to class such activities as 'torture' which includes within its definition being 'wrong', rather than the very nature of the acts themselves? What if other individuals, or cultures, think the opposite, or conceptualise those acts differently?

Some worry that realism leads inevitably to **SCEPTICISM**, but realists tend to have the reverse worry: that the question of what reality is might simply be settled by the person with the biggest research grant, or the greatest access to the media. For them, there is a **FALLACY** involved in reducing **ONTOLOGY** (questions about what there *is*) to **EPISTEMOLOGY** (questions about what we can *know*).

Contributor: Gideon Calder

# REASON AND
# PRACTICAL REASON

**KANT** thought reasoning was essential to finding the 'right way', and indeed a requirement to be imposed on all decisions. Hence his rather rule-bound existence. David **HUME**, however, famously said that reason is 'and ought to be' the slave of the **PASSIONS**. Hume goes on to explain that what he calls 'demonstrative reasoning', for example that used by a mathematical proof, has no effect on the passions, while 'probable' reasoning only attempts to persuade the passions of the most efficacious route to fulfilment. In similar vein to Hume, the political writer, Edmund **BURKE** (1729–97), also criticised the dominant role of 'reason' in political life, saying that society needs 'prejudice' more than reason to function (see also the entry for 'reform'). Prejudice, in this sense, is instinctive feelings of love and loyalty, and the sense of community. Reason, instead, elevates the individual's notion of their own self-interest.

## REDUCTIONISM

Reductionism is concerned to 'reduce' a complex theory or procedure to a simpler one. MARXISTS have objected that in so doing, elements (such as the hierarchical nature of society, or of knowledge) may be lost, resulting in a false and misleading simplification. However, anti-Marxists have complained that their rejection of forces within the 'superstructure' of societies as superficial consequences of materialism (for example) is also 'reductionist'. In METAPHYSICAL matters, reductionism may involve jettisoning entities that appear not to have effects, perhaps not even exist – such as GOD. Again, the discussion becomes political.

In 'theory reduction', reduction seems to mean 'replacement', and the concern here might be that the 'old theory', say Newton's model of the universe, if superseded in some matters, continues to be needed in all but certain areas, so that the desire to reduce the number of theories is pointless.

## REFORM

Reform has been defined as 'an attempt to improve something without altering its essential character'. The 'something' might be a social institution, such as health care provision, education or pensions – or it might be an individual who has misbehaved. Edmund BURKE (1729–97), the Irish-born political thinker and Member of Parliament, introduced the distinction between 'reform', in this sense, and 'change'. To change a person or an institution is also to alter their fundamental character.

Nowadays 'reform' is a much abused word as it relates to changes made for any number of motives, the 'reform' of the pension system may be to redirect money towards new weapon systems or tax breaks; the 'reform' of the immigration system may be to keep out black people; the 'reform' of the schools system may be for any number of political reasons including worsening education for some children in pursuit of some other ideological aim.

## REICH, WILLIAM (1897–1957)

From the same era and with many of the same concerns as his fellow Austrians, WITTGENSTEIN and Weininger, Reich worked

as a psychiatrist as well as a social theorist. He developed the idea of 'character armour', that is, the set of attitudes that people develop to protect themselves both from the world around them and the nasty human beings in it – and from their own feelings, especially anger, doubt and worry. In *Character Analysis* (1933) Reich describes the pain and tension he could see in the faces and postures of his clients: hunched, worried shoulders; squinty, suspicious eyes; contemptuous grimaces – and so on. From this he deduced that conventional approaches to MIND (driven astray, as ever, by DESCARTES' philosophy), such as what he calls the 'feudal individualism' of FREUD, had to be abandoned, and instead the human treated as a whole, both mind and body together. The face does not merely reflect the mind, it interacts dynamically in forming the 'character'.

Similarly, the social character of society as a whole is dynamically related to its physical manifestations, an idea he explores in *The Mass Psychology of Fascism* (1933).

## REINCARNATION

Reincarnation is life after DEATH, but unlike the Christian version, it is a completely new life, with a new body and new MIND. It might even be as a new species – or as a rock. The idea is important in both ancient Greek thought and in the Eastern, especially Indian tradition, but for today's philosophers, the most pressing question is how this 'new me' could be said to have anything in common with the 'old me'. And if it cannot, then what sort of 'life after death' is this, anyway?

Like a 'heavenly afterlife', the idea probably facilitates social structures based on INEQUALITY, as those suffering as, say, the lowest caste in India, can be considered to be merely paying their dues for past transgressions in an earlier incarnation.

## RELATIVISM

### Essentials of relativism

'Man is the measure of all things' said PROTAGORAS, and that is the heart of philosophical relativism. What is good for you may not be good for me, if, say, you are a cannibal and I am a vegetarian. What is big to you may not be big for me, if you are an ant and I am an elephant. In fact, Protagoras was particularly concerned with his latter kind of 'perceptual relativism', while PLATO and many since have searched 'high and low' for exactly those kinds of truths that are 'eternal and unchanging'.

Philosophically speaking, relativism is the doctrine which holds that judgements, positions and conclusions are relative to individual CULTURES, to divergent situations and to differing PERCEPTIONS. It denies the existence of universal or absolute criteria, holding instead that what we know and what there is to know is relative: to our own tastes, experiences, culture and attitudes. It substitutes the variability of our vantage point and 'perceptual mechanisms' for universals when considering moral propositions and in the realms of EPISTEMOLOGY, including science. Relativism ranges from its strong version, which maintains that all truths are relative, to its more limited version, which highlights and refers to the great number of divergent standards in etiquette and custom.

## Ethical and scientific relativism

Relativism, in regard to ETHICAL judgements, holds that moral positions do not reflect absolute truths. Instead it stresses that these judgements unfold from social customs, cultural tendencies or personal preferences. Relativism disallows a single, 'objective' standard by which an ethical claim can be evaluated. Thus, according to some relativists, one person's view has no more truth value, and is not better, than any

### RELATIVISM AND PHYSICS

In a paper entitled 'Geometry and Experience', Einstein wrote: 'As far as the propositions of mathematics refer to reality, they are not certain; and as far as they are certain, they do not refer to reality.' In fact, he said, mathematics and physics operate with different rules, and should be kept apart, to some extent. Physics is empirical, based on measurement, but mathematics is based on 'axioms' that are assumed at the outset.

Nonetheless, Einstein's Special Theory replaced Newton's Absolute Space and Absolute Time, both eternal and unchanging, for more complex, fundamentally relational systems. The surprising consequences of the Special Theory are that bodies have different lengths, clocks run at different speeds and the same event can occur at several different times – depending on the relative motion of the observer.

other. Rather, moral positions can be traced or reduced to certain cultural or individual biases.

Although the ancients were well aware of 'cultural relativism', Herodotus' *Histories* describing the range of 'customs' he encountered in his travels still shocked them. Similarly, for example, we still wonder whether the fact that the Cashibo tribe in South America, who considered it essential, out of religious sentiment, to eat their dead, undercuts the view in our own culture that this practice seems gruesome. And even if cultures share a religious sentiment, expressions of that sentiment can differ widely. One practice or another cannot determine motive or viability, yet nor can simple observation of practices, such as abandoning the elderly, as Inuit people do, necessarily show differing 'ethical values'.

The Finnish philosopher-anthropologist, Edward Westermarck (1862–1939), formulated a theory of moral relativism that argued that the moral ideas involved in ethical decisions are subjective judgements that reflect one's upbringing. Ethical thought and action rely on a correspondence between the better and the more metaphysically true, and strong relativism has great weakness in denying a standard against which issues such as terrorism, genital mutilation, genocide, racial discrimination and the sex trade can be judged.

Science seeks knowledge about phenomena; while 'cognitive relativism' asserts that truths in general are relative and cannot be determined 'objectively'. Thus relativism presents a challenge to the community of scientists, who, while at least grudgingly prepared to admit that many scientific conclusions get overturned in light of new data, are not, on the whole, prepared to accept that no real knowledge is possible. They say instead that many objective facts have indeed been ascertained, none of which change 'depending on the angle of perception'. Yet as science increasingly accepts, for instance, that the observer is implicated in the observed, it remains an open question whether the scientific method as practised can legitimately claim immovable facts or universal reliabilities.

Relativism has grown alongside a historical trend. The main tenor of the modern and POSTMODERN eras has challenged and, in large measure, ousted ideas such as the animism of nature and the ultimate authority of God; parallel to this, a diversity of cultures and angles of perception came to light, especially in the nineteenth and twentieth centuries, and this has infused relativism with a resolution that judgements are a matter of custom and local interpretation, failing to be descriptive of any universal or unconditional truth.

And it is easy to see why relativism often goes hand in hand with SCEPTICISM. But relativism has more than a sceptical eye; it holds that 'better' and 'worse' – in testing procedures or in ethical resolutions – are without grounding beyond the box of perception, extending no further than a particular individual or culture. It maintains that norms and standards remain in a non-privileged status in relation to other norms and standards.

Some hope that, in an ethical realm, the authority of a universal good, grounded in a newly discovered greater whole of nature, may also make relativistic stances untenable, and science speaks loudly of its quest for the final 'Grand Unifying Theory'. Relativism, even in the midst of these pursuits, is constructive in taking account of divergent ways of being and emphasising the presence of diverse modes of evaluating.

Plato also quotes the sophist, Protagoras (c. 481–420 BCE), as saying, 'The way things appear to me, in that way they exist for me; and the way things appear to you, in that way they exist for you' (*Theaetetus* 152a). Yet this also highlights a problem for relativism: there cannot be such a thing as falsehood.

SEE ALSO

'Argument from perspectival relativity' under Naïve realism

Contributor: Andrew Porter

# REPRODUCTIVE ETHICS

Until the late twentieth century, human reproduction was linked to two apparent immovables: one, the biological fundamentals of male and female; and the other, the idea of the family as the basic building block of human society. But work on the fertilisation of animal and later human eggs in the laboratory led to new and unforeseen possibilities in manipulating human genetic material – and, in particular, to the birth of the first test-tube baby in 1978.

In the early stages of the reproduction revolution, the emphasis was on helping couples to have their own children, but the new developments meant that it was now possible to transfer human gametes, first sperm, then sperm and eggs, from person to person without the need for sexual intercourse. Reliable contraception, bolstered by relatively easy access to abortion, which had also been introduced around the same time, had made sex possible without reproduction. Now embryology made possible reproduction without sex.

But these developments brought new and unfamiliar ethical dilemmas. Parenthood became a divisible concept: a new threefold division made it necessary to distinguish between genetic, social and legal parenthood, with motherhood facing a further possible division as the mother who supplies the egg from which the child develops is no longer necessarily the mother who gives birth to the child. In fertility treatment, the freezing of embryos meant that a child might be born years after conception and even after the death of one or both of its biological parents. And although in many countries regulation was introduced to prevent male donors fathering large numbers of children, in practice gamete transfer has produced many half-siblings, most unknown to the others.

Some believe that a child's genetic origin is irrelevant and that parenthood is a purely social concept. But while this may be a legal convenience, the science of genetics is providing strong medical reasons for acknowledging the importance of biological connections. Socially, too, individuals are increasingly interested in understanding their own complex genetic inheritance as part of their conception of their own identity.

Another aspect of the new possibilities is that they make possible new kinds of child-raising arrangements: for example, for single parents, older women, lesbians, gay men or cooperating groups to bring children into the world. HUMAN RIGHTS to privacy and the right to found a family may be cited in support. Whatever objection is raised, it is always trumped by those who favour this extension of adult choice with the argument that a child conceived under whatever circumstances would not have existed otherwise, and life is always to be preferred to non-existence. But there is also a child's perspective, when children created in extraordinary ways are deprived of the biological network that children conceived and born in the ordinary way are able to take for granted.

But the importance of genetic relations – grandparents, aunts, uncles, cousins, and so on, to say nothing of ancestors and descendants – cannot simply be written off. Not only are they often important in the lives of individuals, they have also historically supplied the webbing underpinning a culture.

While these are matters of continuing controversy, reproductive possibilities do not end here, as scientific developments open up new and equally contentious frontiers for exploration. In particular, embryos can have other uses, including supplying stem cells for some dramatic new medical possibilities.

Contributor: Brenda Almond

# REVENGE

In ancient Greece, vengeance and JUSTICE were the same thing, but PLATO has SOCRATES offer the opinion that 'the return of evil for evil' is itself evil, that is to say, unjust. Similarly, while the Old Testament demands 'an eye for an eye' and 'a tooth for a tooth', Jesus appears in the New Testament counselling the superiority of 'turning the other cheek'. The modern mind is supposed to rise above feelings of revenge, or even retribution, as they are rooted in just that – feelings. Yet KANT draws a distinction between the two, and argues that the latter is not only excusable, but essential.

# REVOLUTION

The word 'revolution' appears to have two quite distinct senses: the political one, meaning radical change or upheaval; and the geometrical one, meaning 'turning a complete circle'. Yet the two senses are not so far apart. The Greeks understood political revolutions as a kind of great circle, starting with tyranny, which creates opposition among the people, which becomes civil conflict and finally leads to a new government. And that, naturally, will soon become a tyranny.

# RHETORIC

PLATO is credited with coining the term, in order to distinguish between persuasive arguments in general, and philosophical ones in particular (philosophy, of course, being far superior, irrespective of any lack of persuasive force). Rhetorical activity was central to ancient Greece, considered essential to playing a role in public affairs, and it is the topic and title one of ARISTOTLE's key works, examining and cataloguing the way language and arguments work.

The STOICS took this latter aspect further and treated rhetoric as a branch of LOGIC.

# RIGHTS

See Human rights, Animals, Environmental philosophy.

# ROMANTICISM

## Essential romanticism

Romanticism is notoriously difficult to define, both as a historical movement and a school of thought. It has no definitive beginning or end points, and its influence spans several disciplines. Writers, painters, musicians and philosophers all refer to it, but mean different things. However, the commonality that all of romanticism shares is an aversion to the extreme RATIONALISM that characterised the Age of ENLIGHTENMENT, and this aversion brought about a new era and a new way of thinking. And philosophical romanticism certainly plays an important role in the history of Western philosophy, and continues to develop even today.

## The perfect medium

During the eighteenth century, Europe experienced an 'Age of Enlightenment', in which many intellectuals began to feel that humans must be coming close to knowing all that is knowable in the scientific world. However, this focus on objective, scientific discovery was not entirely enlightening; it also made people feel small and unimportant, without purpose or design. This sentiment led a small, underground group of 'anti-rationalists' to create what became known later as the Romantic Movement.

Romanticism, in the most general sense, takes emphasis away from objective reason and places it with the EMOTIONS, intuition, NATURE, faith or other 'irrational' concepts. By this definition, romanticism has been alive in some degree for nearly all of our intellectual history. ARISTOTLE, for instance, dedicates Book VIII of the *Nicomachean Ethics* to a discussion of friendship, and PLATO devotes the entirety of his *Symposium* to a long discussion of the nature of LOVE. However, the Romantic Movement is radical in its overwhelming emphasis on the irrational. While Plato and Aristotle were willing to spend a single chapter or dialogue on specific romantic issues, the prevailing feeling in their work is quite rationalistic. In fact, both Plato and Aristotle argue that the proper role of reason is in control of the irrational PASSIONS, resulting in a harmony, or 'golden mean' that can only be achieved through this particular order. This idea can then be followed through history (especially present in the Enlightenment) up to present day, where concepts such as intuition and the emotions are demonised in favour of objective reason. The romantic era, however, reversed these roles, and began to place favour with many different forms of irrational expression.

The first seeds of the Romantic Movement were planted in the works of Jean-Jacques ROUSSEAU, who wrote on the glory of 'natural man', the superiority of the 'noble savage', and the corruption of culture. This emphasis on the natural and disdain for the manufactured greatly influenced many of the poets to follow, including William Wordsworth and Samuel Taylor Coleridge. Although both were products of the Enlightenment, the two began writing poetry that shunned the prevailing intellectual attitudes – focusing on themes like nature, idealism, imagination, freedom and emotion. They also rejected the stiff, intellectual verbiage favoured by the poets of the time, in favour of common language about common people. The influence of these two poets quickly extended into the wider literary community, as well as music, the arts and philosophy.

While poetry, music and the arts seem the perfect medium for conveying anti-rationalist sentiments, it is somewhat more difficult to imagine what form romanticism might take within philosophy. In fact, the label of 'romantic philosophy' is not always easy to assign. For instance, Immanuel KANT is sometimes called the 'Father of Philosophical Romanticism', although his total philosophy was not really very romantic. His claim to this title came from his famous division between 'reason' and 'understanding', which he used largely as a way to allow faith into his personal philosophy – a goal very much in line with the larger romantic community. However, the rest of his philosophy is so rigorously rationalistic that to label Kant a 'romantic' sounds strange indeed (consider his famous 'Categorical Imperative', which argues that the barometer of right action is to consider whether the rule which one is following could be, without contradiction, applied universally). John Stuart MILL, too, is often considered a romantic philosopher, due to the central role of HAPPINESS within his ethics. Mill, who was greatly influenced by both Wordsworth and Coleridge, argues that it is human nature to desire happiness, and that happiness is the presence of pleasure and the absence of pain. However, despite having this romantic account of the human condition, he never entirely escapes UTILITARIAN upbringing, even as he acknowledges the narrowness and limitations of the approach.

It was not until very late in the romantic era (most likely after the artistic movement had more or less ended) that the philosophical community got its first taste of a fully romantic philosophy, provided by the EXISTENTIALISTS of the nineteenth century. For anyone who had wondered what a philosophy which shuns reason would look like, the answer was put forth in a book entitled *Fear and Trembling*, by Søren KIERKEGAARD. In this text, Kierkegaard argues that there are three basic ways of existing, the highest of which can be achieved only through an absurd, wholly irrational 'leap of faith'. In this way, he gives primary value not to reason, which can take one only to an 'ethical' level of existence, but to the romantic concept of faith. Similarly, Friedrich NIETZSCHE, writing shortly after Kierkegaard, also creates an intensely anti-rationalist philosophy, but rejects the value that Kierkegaard places on faith. For Nietzsche, faith and human reason are equally without foundation in human experience, and so he creates a system of ethics based on a creative force that he calls the 'Will to Power'.

Even with this interest and support from the 'great', philosophical romanticism never became more than a hiccup in the history of Western philosophy. Contemporary philosophy has remained dominated by an analytic approach, which claims its lineage from the most extreme of the rationalists, and considers philosophical romanticism to be no more than a brief, historical oddity. Yet romanticism is enjoying a kind of minority revival in the writings of contemporary philosophers like Robert Solomon and Martha Nussbaum, who, instead of shifting the emphasis away from reason towards emotion, are beginning to question the traditional dichotomy between the two. In addition, there are those who believe that the emotions are essential components of humanness, but that they have been demonised because of their traditional label as feminine virtues. If these contemporary romantic views are no more widespread than their nineteenth-century predecessors, they do at least provide alternatives for those who suspect that the use of 'pure reason' is not entirely the noble goal within philosophy that it pretends to be.

Contributor: Travis Rieder

## Further reading

Rousseau, J.J. (*c.* 1770) *The Confessions* (posthumously published)

Coleridge, S.T. and Wordsworth, W. (1802) *Lyrical Ballads*

Kierkegaard, Søren (1843) *Fear and Trembling*

## ROSENZWEIG, FRANZ (1886–1929)

### The essential Rosenzweig

Franz Rosenzweig was born in Cassel, Germany, to assimilated German Jewish parents. He finished his doctoral dissertation on 'Hegel and the State' at Freiburg in 1912. He almost converted to Christianity, but on Yom Kippur (the Day of Atonement) in 1913 he went to an orthodox synagogue where he describes having 'a conversion experience', after which he became instead an observant Jew. He was a soldier in the First World War, afterwards marrying Edith Hahn, with whom he had one son (Rafael), and lived in a small apartment in Frankfurt where Rosenzweig was the principal of the Jewish Lehrhaus (Free School). The Lehrhaus was attempting to restore assimilated and secularised Jews to Hebrew language and learning, which it saw as a redemptive education. He is credited with a new way of explaining and relating GOD, the world and humanity, which starts from a 'dialogue of I and thou', a phrase he borrows from FEUERBACH's critique of HEGEL.

### Philosophy as commentary

Rosenzweig is a religious philosopher. He thinks religion is integral to philosophy. Of religions, he argues that only two, Judaism and Christianity, are of particular significance in this regard. *The Star of Redemption* (*Stern der Erlösung*), 1921, stands at the centre of Rosenzweig's importance as a philosopher. The work is famously difficult to read. It rose to visibility in a post-Holocaust, post-Christian world, which in itself tells us something about it.

Rosenzweig wrote *The Star* during the war years while serving on the Balkan front, on army postcards sent back home, which he put together into a book after the war. The book is composed of short sections or set pieces, grouped and finalised into broader chapters and whole parts. While the short sections have an aphoristic quality, they interlink; therefore *The Star* does have a narrative; a narrative that would move us from death to life, with the full spiritual connotations these words carry.

*The Star* posits the absolute difference of God, world and man. These three are names of different origins of reality as a whole – of all that is thinkable and of all that really exists. We cannot know God, world and man as if they were empirical objects; for our relation to them is not simply empirical. We know God, world and man because they reveal themselves. God, world and man have the quality or energy of being self-revealing or revelatory. As things in themselves they remain unknown and unknowable.

Creation, revelation and redemption are the key words of Rosenzweig's philosophy. They are what he calls 'ways' between God, world and man, in which they coalesce. Creation, revelation and redemption are realities of God, world and man respectively, as well as categories of understanding, and concepts we can use. Creation, revelation and redemption name horizons of understanding, with respect to God, world and man.

A year after *The Star*, Rosenzweig produced a simplified interpretation of it, *Understanding the Sick and the Healthy* (1922). In 1925 he published a long essay entitled 'The New Thinking', which he believed *The Star* gave rise to.

In 1922, Rosenzweig began to suffer from symptoms of the degenerative illness which would leave him paralysed until he could only communicate by blinking, and Edith alone could understand him. During the seven years of decline and slow death he translated and published 92 hymns and poems of Jehuda Halevi, a medieval Jewish poet writing in Hebrew. In essays, Rosenzweig developed important theories of translation and scriptural interpretation. With Martin Buber, whose dialogical philosophy Rosenzweig influenced, he began to translate the Bible. They reached the Book of Isaiah together and Buber completed the translation on his own.

Rosenzweig died in Frankfurt-am-Main on

## ROSENZWEIG'S SPEECH THINKING

Rosenzweig's work has considerable relevance to understanding the ethical implications of the Holocaust, although it was written before the events. The (post-Holocaust) Jewish writer, Elie Wiesel, has argued that the Holocaust goes 'deep into the nature of man and has extraordinary implications abut the relationship between man and men, man and language man and himself, and ultimately, man and God.' It is the seriousness of *The Star* on these very questions, pervasive questions, about man, language and God, which mark its importance – its unavoidability – today.

The 'new thinking' of Rosenzweig explicitly affirms common sense; by common sense, Rosenzweig thinks of a healthy, life-affirming, world-affirming and godly thinking, with others, in response to them and with a sense of responsibility for them.

The new thinking is speaking-thinking, or speech-thinking (Sprachdenken); that does not mean the thinking is not written. It means that philosophy is always, with respect to truth and wisdom, commentarial; it is commentary on creation, revelation and redemption. And philosophy is dialogue, between man, world and God, but dialogue that supposes a teacher–student relationship. Speech-thinking is educational, moving us from the sources of our speech in ourselves, the world and God, through dialogue and example to truthful action. The context of truthful action is one where 'Truth is not God. God is truth'. Philosophically, speech-thinking presupposes the infinite difference between man, world and God. Rosenzweig's translations of Jehuda Halevi's poems come with short interpretations appended to each. Rosenzweig offered these as examples of speech-thinking.

9 December 1929, at the age of 43. Philosophy was a way of life for Rosenzweig. This way of life is ethical, social and liturgical. The contrast is with paganism, in which the world is divided against itself in a hundred ways. Our postmodern condition is one like paganism, with relative and self-aggrandising agendas on one hand and syncretism on the other. It might be said that what Rosenzweig gives us is not a philosophy of **ETHICS**, but an ethics of philosophy.

## Further reading

Rosenzweig, F. (1985) *The Star of Redemption* (translated by W. Hallo)

Contributor: Matthew del Nevo

# ROUSSEAU, JEAN-JACQUES (1712–78)

## The essential Rousseau

Born in Geneva, Rousseau was educated at home by his father, Isaac, a watchmaker, and his aunt, after the untimely death of his mother following his birth. Unfortunately, he soon lost his father too, after the latter unwisely challenged a gentleman to a duel, and was expelled from the city as a result. Jean-Jacques went into the care of his uncle, to become an apprentice engraver. But Rousseau considered this to be a demeaning trade and, using a tactic his city had demonstrated some years before to gain its independence, changed his religion to became the ward of some benevolent Catholic aristocrats, the de Warens of Savoy. It was in their library of the great political philosophers that he imbibed the ideas of **HOBBES**, **MACHIAVELLI** and **LOCKE** that would later inspire his influential, even revolutionary, works.

In his most polemical essay, the *Discourse on Inequality* (1753), he ridicules the pretensions of 'civilisation'. Nor is he impressed by the achievements of science. Instead, he argues that primitive peoples had been happier and better off without it. He demands that people be measured not by their social position, not by their possessions, but by the shared divine spark that he saw in them all, the immortal soul of 'Natural Man'. In his influential work on education, *Emile* (1762), he outlines a way to bring up children to recreate this supposed vanished world, and to bring out the spirit of free co-operation. His philosophy offers a more spiritual, romantic view of the world.

Rousseau marks a radical shift in philosophy, away from the search for authority and towards uncertainties of 'freedom'. As the eighteenth century drew to an end, new ways of looking at the world were needed, and Rousseau, despite his personal aristocratic pretensions, seemed in his writings to offer a complete reversal of the values of the time. His views were, of course, also anathema to many. **VOLTAIRE** refused to abandon 'civilisation' to accept what he called an invitation to 'go down on all fours', saying that after 60 years or so, he had lost the habit. Dr Johnson said of Rousseau and his supporters: 'Truth is a cow that will yield them no more milk, so they have gone to milk the bull.' But many others were entranced and inspired.

## Natural Man

At the age of 32, Rousseau arrived in Paris, where he began to move in the sort of circles he felt he belonged in, being, after all, a citizen of Geneva and, as he never tired of telling people, born free. He became secretary to another aristocratic family, found a mistress and began to write.

His first major work was an attack on the ideas of the encyclopaedists, and indeed the whole basis of the **ENLIGHTENMENT**. In the *Discourse on the Sciences and Arts* (1750), Rousseau takes on the scientists, and says that, far from being our saviours, they are ruining the world, and that any notion of progress is an illusion even as we move further and further away from the healthy, simple and balanced lives of the past. The *Discourse on Sciences* is a conscious salute to the kind of society advocated by **PLATO** two millennia earlier, and both a contrast with and a challenge to the prevailing orthodoxy of his times. Notwithstanding, or probably (in France) because of that, the essay was considered a great success, and earned Rousseau the Dijon prize.

In it, and in the later, more famous, *Discourse on Inequality* (1753), Rousseau argues that man in his natural state, far from being greedy or fearful, as described by Hobbes, is in fact in living in a peaceful, contented state, truly free. This is a freedom with three elements. The first is free will, the second is freedom from the rule of law (as there are no laws) and the third is personal freedom. It is this last that is the most important.

Rousseau says that the first people lived like animals. He says this not in any derogatory sense, merely in the sense that the original people sought only simple fulfilment of their physical needs. They would have had no need of speech, nor **CONCEPTS**, and certainly not property. Rousseau points out that much of the imagery in both Hobbes and Locke belongs to a property-owning society, not the supposed 'natural state' prior to the invention of property rights. By realising this, 'we are not obliged to make a man a philosopher before we can make him a man.' The first time people would have had a sense of property (he thinks) is when they settled in one location, when they built huts to live in. Even sexual union, Rousseau notes pragmatically, as well as reflecting on his own experience, is unlikely to have implied any exclusivity, being more likely to have been just a lustful episode no sooner experienced than forgotten, least of all in terms of the children. (Rousseau's view of women is at best romantic in an unenlightened sort of way. In *Emile* (1762), he confines the education of the fair sex to domestic science and recommends training from an early age in habits of docility and subservience.)

Since this primitive state is actually superior to those that followed it, Rousseau explains the change by the development of self-consciousness, and with it the desire for private property. According to Rousseau, at this point following Hobbes, society necessarily leads people to hate each other, in accordance with their different economic interests. But Hobbes' so-called 'Social Contract', is, in fact, made by the rich, as a way of doing down the poor. Actually, not even the rich benefit from it, as they warp themselves and become increasingly out of touch with nature's harmony, raised needlessly above their own proper state, just as the poor are pushed below theirs.

Rousseau offers instead just two laws, or principles, that could be said to be 'antecedent to reason'. The first is a powerful interest in self-preservation and our own well-being; the second is 'a natural aversion to seeing any other sentient being perish or suffer, especially if it is one of our own kind'. The only time 'natural man' would hurt another is when his own well-being requires it. In saying this, Rousseau is drawing a parallel for humankind with the animals who – unlike their masters – never harm each other out of malice alone.

Rousseau paints a mocking portrait of the rich man, seeking to protect his gains by pretending concern for his victims. 'Let us unite', says his rich man, 'to protect the weak from oppression, to ensure for each that which he owns, and create a system of justice and peace that all shall be bound to, without exception.' Rousseau thinks this explanation of civil law is more convincing than those offered by philosophers who suppose some sort of universal social contract, for, as he puts it, the poor have only one good – their freedom – and to voluntarily strip themselves of that without gaining anything in exchange would appear to be absolute folly. The rich, on the other hand, have much to gain.

The only way that the sovereign and the people can have a single and identical interest, so that all the movements of the civil machine tend to promote the common happiness, is for them to be one and the same. No one can be outside the law, for once they are, all the others are 'at their discretion'. Furthermore, there should be few laws, and new ones introduced only with the greatest circumspection, so that 'before the constitution could be disturbed, there would be time enough for everyone to reflect that it is above all the great antiquity of the laws that makes them sacred and inviolable'.

The details of institutions of government are not of much interest to Rousseau, although his later work, the *Social Contract* (1762), attempts to indicate a way to harmonise collective decision-making rule with individual freedoms, once their essentially malign character has been identified. He merely adds that if law and property are the first stage in human society, and the institutions of government are the second, then the third and last stage is the transformation of legitimate into arbitrary power. Human society leads people to hate each other in proportion 'to the extent that their interests conflict'. People pretend to do each other services while actually trying to exploit them and do them down. 'We must attribute to the institution of property, and hence to society, murders, poisonings, highway robbery and indeed, the punishments of those crimes.' That is at the individual level. On the national scale, 'Inequality, being almost non-

## ROUSSEAU'S LIFE

Jean-Jacques Rousseau was a thinker who wore many hats, not just the philosophical one. He reinvented himself too as an expert on music, and on education. He was one of the key figures in the Romantic movement in the arts, a standard bearer of the Romantic tradition. Yet, at the same time, he has to be judged as a posturing hypocrite, an unscrupulous and selfish man who, despite the fine words of his child-centred educational philosophy, packed his own five illegitimate children off to the harsh world of the local foundling home, and henceforth refused even to see them. Once, having wickedly accused a servant, a maid, of stealing something in fact he himself had taken, he admitted later, in his *Confessions*, that what he had done had actually been the cowardly product of his childish resentment at being rebuffed by her.

Although the *Discourse on Inequality* and the *Social Contract* are dedicated to his fellow free citizens of Geneva, and to the 'Magnificent and Most Honoured lords' who governed what was then a tiny, independent state, relations with the unappreciative burghers of Geneva were never particularly good. The *Social Contract* was publicly burnt in the City Square of Geneva in 1762, along with Rousseau's idealistic work on education, *Emile*. Rousseau became notoriously insecure, suspicious of everyone he met, and considering offers of help always to be trickery. He constantly complained of being 'misrepresented' and by the end of his life was almost certainly suffering from the madness of full-blown paranoia.

existent in the state of nature. . . becomes fixed and legitimate through the institution of property and laws'. When society has, as it inevitably will, degenerated into tyranny and all are slaves again, the circle is complete, for 'all individuals become equal again when they are nothing'. And all the time 'Civil man' torments himself constantly in search of ever more laborious occupations, working himself to death, 'renouncing life in order to achieve immortality'. Civil society is, in fact, a society of people 'who nearly all complain and several of whom indeed deprive themselves of their existence'. This is the logic of property ownership and capitalism.

Rousseau died in 1778, the same year as his critic, Voltaire, possibly by his own hand, and certainly in sad and lonely circumstances. But as Goethe commented: 'with Voltaire an age ended, with Rousseau, a new one began'.

Contributor: Martin Cohen

## RUSSELL, BERTRAND (1872–1970)

Bertrand Arthur William Russell, an Earl of somewhere or other, the son of a Victorian prime minister, and a professor of philosophy and mathematics at Trinity College, Cambridge, was also something of a social misfit and political radical. Indeed, he was expelled from his college in 1916 and jailed two years later for speaking out against the First Word War. Even in 1940, his views on God (not existing) prevented him obtaining a philosophy post in New York. So he went back to England and campaigned against nuclear weapons, obtaining in due course another spell in prison.

In *Principia Mathematica* (1910–13, co-written with Alfred North Whitehead) he argues that MATHEMATICS is simply a kind of LOGIC. Following this line of reasoning, he came upon a number of paradoxical features in logic, famously the so-called 'BARBER PARADOX' (or 'Russell's paradox'). Philosophical problems, he claimed, had to be stripped of their 'cannibal assumptions' (as he rather ethnocentrically put it) to reveal their logical essence. For example, to say that 'snow is frozen water' needs clarification as to what sense of 'is' is being employed. Is it 'is' as in 'equals'? Or as in describing a property of snow? Or just saying something about snow in an 'existential' sense? Anyway, these are the sorts of questions Russell raises. His most celebrated solution to a LINGUISTIC problem relates to treatment of phrases, where he suggests they need to be expressed as classes. For example, 'there are three dogs in the car' means something $x$ is a car and something $y$ is a dog and $x$ is not a dog and $x$ is not anything else either, nor is $y$ a car, nor is $y$ anything else but a dog. The reader should be warned at this point that Russell's philosophical logic is obscure and nowadays considered more as of historical interest.

But if Russell's reputation as a great logician is dubious, his contribution to the popularisation and, more, clarification, of philosophy, through works like *The Problems of Philosophy* (1911) and *History of Western Philosophy* (1946), has stood the test of time.

## RUSSIAN PHILOSOPHY

### Essentials of Russian philosophy

The characteristic of Russian philosophy has always been towards 'the future' and the 'new man', a concept bitterly fought over by the NIHILISTS, the SOCIALISTS and the ANARCHISTS. The tradition is both utopian and PRAGMATIC, as evidenced by MARX's words condemning the philosophers who 'merely seek to understand the world'.

### The truth is out there

Russian philosophy appears as an independent tradition towards the end of the nineteenth century. Before that time it largely reiterated foreign philosophy, drawn from the European tradition. It was not original; always attempting secondary applications of KANTIANISM, HEGELIANISM, NIETZSCHEANISM, and so on.

By the end of the nineteenth century, however, if there was no Russian original philosophy, there was a deep and rich tradition of Russian literature and criticism. It seems that Russian writers were having deeper and more original thoughts than the professional Russian philosophers.

So the history of its development defines the peculiarities of Russian philosophy. For instance, despite widespread borrowings from the West, philosophy in Russia was not an academic science. First, it was largely created by critics, publicists and writers (like Tolstoy and Dostoevsky), and not by natural scientists; and second, because the Russian 'enlightenment' continued through the first two decades of the twentieth century (LENIN's programme for the elimination of illiteracy is part of this enlightenment), philosophers actively aspired to write for general readers. Indeed, the first university courses specifically on philosophy did not appear until the end of the nineteenth century.

And so, philosophy books in Russia were written for common people and not for the researcher, in accord with Dostoevsky's famous words: 'All real Russian people are philosophers'. For this reason it has special interests in ETHICS and religious ideas (Solovyov's tradition), AESTHETICS and art criticism (Florensky, Losev, BAKHTIN) and, most especially, in social philosophy (notably the vast area of Russian MARXISM). There was little interest in ONTOLOGY, theory of mind, LOGIC and investigation of language. The truth, according to Russian thinkers, was not rational, but existential, therefore it should not be rationalised or 'cognized' – but lived. Pavel Florensky, in this way, traces back the derivation of the Russian word for 'truth' from the verb 'to be'. To be true means to exist, and to exist means to be true. In such a way, Florensky concludes that falsehood is just an illusion of a mind, it cannot truly exist. Other thinkers have continued to develop this idea and supposed that that objective world constructed by rationalism as epitomised by Kant's a priori forms of perception is also not true.

At the beginning of the twentieth century, the thought that 'truth is out here' was the distinctive slogan of religious Russian philosophy. Lev Shestov, writing in *The Conquest of the Self-Evident* (1921), believed that 'we may perhaps have to admit that certainty is not a predicate of truth, or, to express it better, that certainty has absolutely nothing in common with truth.' The Soviet philosopher, Merab Mamardashvili, writing in *How Do I Understand Philosophy?* (1990), offers an analogous non-acceptance of reality: 'I always had a distaste of all the surrounding order of life and there was none of the inner dependence on ideology and ideals that were created by that order.'

Above all, many Russian thinkers were fond of Dostoevsky's EXISTENTIALISM. It was the first serious and original philosophical resource for all further Russian philosophy. Of course, Dostoevsky himself was not a philosopher, but investigation of his ideas has been prolific ground for philosophical writing in the twentieth century. This fact alone shows that philosophy is always a commentary on the texts, or on the research of knowledge, rather than the producer of knowledge.

Philosophy, according to the Greek base, is not a wisdom, but a 'love of wisdom': Philosophers should not be wise, SOCRATES believed, but through a dialogue with other philosophers, assist in the birth of truth. In just such a Socratic way, Shestov forewarns the philosopher against knowledge, and the seduction of the call to become experts.

Russian philosophy also borrowed from Dostoevsky a criticism of Western RATIONALISM and its habit of searching for general laws of being, indifferent to the person, creating ALIENATION in objectification, research and work. This last problem was consonant with Marx's own appeal to workers to overcome the alienation of CAPITALISM. Paradoxically, Dostoevsky's religious ideas meshed together with Marx's ATHEISM; these doctrines were coherent as part of the whole, as the revolutionary project continues a religious moralisation. Many Russian philosophers seek to combine SOCIALISM with religious Orthodoxy, and some of them even read Marx as a religious thinker. For example, Bulgakhov supposed Marx to be on a religious mission.

Ultimately, because Russian philosophy has never been an academic discipline, it is difficult to separate Russian philosophers from the other thinkers: psychologists like Vygotsky, philologists, linguists, economists and lawyers. Russian writers remain great Russian philosophers too. Today, the most important Russian thinkers are Mikhail Bakhtin, Alexander KOJEVE and Jury Lotman.

Contributor: Dmitry Olshansky

## RYLE, GILBERT (1900–76)

Ryle was an English philosophy professor and advocate of what became known as 'logical behaviourism'. The idea, as set out in *The Concept of Mind* (1949), is that traditional notions of will, imagination, perception, thought, and so on, are all contaminated by Cartesianism, and we need to jettison this 'ghost in the machine' for a kind of behaviourist model of how the MIND works. It is, he explains, a kind of 'CATEGORY MISTAKE' to treat mental phenomena in the same way as we treat physical phenomena – actions are not made up of the two parts DESCARTES proposes, the mental idea and the physical action, but are just one part: 'behaviour'.

Ryle, like many of his contemporaries, saw himself as wielding the tools of logical analysis to solve and clarify all other philosophical questions, in the manner of Cambridge University's celebrated iconoclast, WITTGENSTEIN.

# S

## SANKARA (*C.* 700–750 CE)

Sankara was born at Kalati, Kerala in southern India. He became a philosopher-monk, teaching the Hindu *VEDANTA* philosophy, which emphasises the realisation of a supposed fundamental reality. Known as *Brahman*, this is best achieved through contemplating the *UPANISHADS*, considered as containing sacred knowledge that

### *ADVAITA* PHILOSOPHY

Sankara advocated the *Advaita* philosophy. In the then prevailing *Sankhya* system, God did not exist. Conversely, the *Advaita* system advocates that God is all.

- There is nothing but God, not the God of the theists, but *Nirguna Brahma* – all-prevailing reality devoid of attributes. The phenomenal world is a figment of your imagination. It is *Maya* – nothing but illusions. The Real is in you. It is yourself.

- You cannot be released from the Real, on the contrary, you grow into it through *Jnana* knowledge. *Jnana* is won by devoted study. By means of meditation you achieve unity with the Real. Such an adept is a *Jivan-Mukta*, living in the world but not part of it, working tirelessly for others until death, the final illusion.

- The *Advaita* system has an amoral intellectualism that links back to *Shiva* with his mix of erotic energy, asceticism and those above the moral mores of society. Seeking realisation rather than release set the *Advaita* system aside from the orthodox Hindu religions, Buddhism and Jainism, in being positive instead of pessimistic.

Contributor: Colin Kirk

describes and reveals human nature and the cosmos.

Sankara was greatly influenced by the *Bhagavad-Gita* and wrote a famous commentary on it, arguing against the existence of cause and effect, or indeed any other kind of relation or difference in the world, saying that these imply an infinite regress in other causes, effects and relationships. The world is nether real nor unreal, but merely a dream created out of ignorance. The 'transcendentally true' world is one of consciousness, and is indicated by cryptical statements such as 'You are that', or 'All is Brahman'. Methodologically backward-looking and authority-driven, his writings are essentially commentaries on past Vedanta texts, but his influence continues in HINDU culture today.

## SANTAYANA, GEORGE (1863–1952)

George Santayana was born in Spain but spent his life in the USA, where he wrote poetry and novels as well as philosophy. He became a professor at Harvard, before, in 1912, shocking his colleagues by resigning and returning to Europe, where he lived mostly in hotels.

In *The Sense of Beauty* (1896) he says that beauty is pleasure that is then attributed to the object being contemplated. Beauty becomes 'objectified pleasure'. The five volumes of *The Life of Reason; or The Phases of Human Progress* (1905–06) explore the relationships between various fields of human endeavour (thinking and conceptualising; social organisation and life; religions; arts and sciences) and the philosophical concept of 'reason'. This in due course became his 'PRAGMATIC' view of knowledge, that it is not certain in the traditional philosophical sense, but merely sufficiently reliable for practical purposes. He offers four 'realms' of knowledge: matter (the flux of the physical universe); spirit (the consciousness that is a by-product of animal brains interacting with the physical world); essence (which seems to be a bit like PLATO's 'World of Forms' or concepts) and 'truth' (whatever that is).

Santayana then went on to explore the essence of 'pure being' in the manner of the European EXISTENTIALISTS, but this part of his work is surely less original and less characteristic. Other writings surveyed ethics and psychology, often in his characteristically rich language. Of his spirituality Bertrand RUSSELL once quipped that Santayana believed there was no God, but that Mary was his mother.

## SAPIR-WHORF HYPOTHESIS

See Whorf.

## SARTRE, JEAN PAUL (1905–80)

Sartre was brought up in rural France, where he describes spending most of his childhood in his grandfather's library, and his adolescence in France's elite colleges, emerging into the bright light of the world only to become a school-teacher. At least, this being France, he was able to be a teacher of philosophy, but he still disliked the experience and, in particular, his surroundings, the port of Le Havre, which he would later deride, in his first novel, *Nausea* (1938), as Bouville.

When the Second World War arrived he became a meteorologist in the Army, and when the French surrendered to the victorious Nazis, he found himself a prisoner of war, albeit on a long leash which allowed him parole to organise his first play, and indeed to return to philosophy teaching (this time in sophisticated Paris) mid-war. He considered becoming active in the Resistance, but this, he explained later, would have involved subordinating himself to either the Communists or the Gaullists. The solution he arrived at instead was to concentrate on his writing, and finishing what would be his magnum opus, *Being and Nothingness* (1943).

When the war ended, the official history goes, he decided against life as a professor, instead choosing that of a writer and intellectual, together with campaigning for liberation movements, such as the cause of the Vietnamese

against the Americans, or of the Algerians against France itself. Meanwhile, his fiction writing was triumphantly received everywhere, and in 1964 he was offered the Nobel Prize for Literature, but chose not to accept it.

Sartre's philosophy emphasises the use of the imagination, which is the purest form of freedom available to us. In his *Critique of Dialectical Reason* (1960) he offers by way of an example, workers engaged in monotonous tasks who, he says, are prone to having sexual fantasies, thus demonstrating the power and counter-factual freedom of the imagination.

He emphasises what is not, over what is, the latter being a rather humdrum sort of affair consisting of the kind of facts that scientists examine, while the 'what is not' is really much more interesting. He sums up his view thus: 'The Nature of consciousness simultaneously is to be what is not and not to be what it is'. Hence we come back to our own natures, our own 'essences'. We exist, yes, but how do we 'define ourselves'?

This spotlight on 'consciousness' is what made Sartre's name.

*She Came to Stay* (also 1943), by Sartre's life-long intellectual confidant and companion, Simone DE BEAUVOIR, also describes various kinds of consciousness, in passages ranging from wandering through an empty theatre (the stage, the walls, the chairs, unable to come alive until there is an audience) to watching a woman in a restaurant ignore the fact that her male companion has begun stroking her arm – as well as describing the 'terrifying' reality of being perceived by other conscious beings: 'We get the impression of no longer being anything but a figment of someone else's mind.'

Sartre even records in his diary how de Beauvoir had to correct him several times for his clumsy misunderstanding of the 'EXISTEN-TIALIST' philosophy!

## SCEPTICISM AND THE SCEPTICS

Scepticism derives from the Greek word *skepsis* for 'consideration', but nowadays scepticism implies doubting various things. The evidence of the senses is suspect, given the (occasional) inability to distinguish between 'true' perception and 'false' perception, which led Greek Sceptics such as Arcesilaus of Pitane (*c.* 315–240 BCE) and Carneades of Cyrene (*c.* 210–130 BCE) to say that there was never any justification for claiming 'knowledge' about

Scepticism in antiquity divides into two traditions. The first is associated with Plato's Academy and so is known as Academic Scepticism. Its most famous figure is probably Carneades, who engaged in lengthy disputes with the Stoics (these reported by Cicero). The second tradition claims to trace itself back to the philosopher Pyrrho and so is known as Pyrrhonian Scepticism. The most important Pyrrhonian Sceptic is Sextus Empiricus, author of the *Outlines of Pyrrhonism*. According to a Pyrrhonian like Sextus, the Academic Sceptics are best characterised as negative dogmatists, confidently proclaiming that knowledge is impossible. In contrast, the Pyrrhonian Sceptics do not make any claims about the possibility of knowledge; they simply suspend judgement when faced with conflicting evidence or opposing but equally strong arguments, remaining open to the possibility of being convinced at some later date. Pyrrhonian Scepticism is not a philosophy of doubt; it is one of continuing enquiry. However, it does seem to make the assumption that the enquiry will never end, for one will always be able to find counter-arguments or opposing evidence to even the most convincing proposition.

Contributor: John Sellars

anything in the world, but only naïve and optimistic assertion.

The STOICS later insisted that there were ways of dividing knowledge and sense data up and distinguishing arrant nonsense from well-founded evidence, but this was never the view of the true Sceptics. In the Renaissance period the debate resurfaced with renewed interest in the writings of SEXTUS EMPIRICUS (c. 150–210 CE), who discusses the possible criterion for such Stoic distinctions. This debate is carried on today in philosophy, with the conventional position being that knowledge is 'justified true belief'.

DESCARTES offers a (useless) criterion in his writings of knowledge as anything that is perceived 'clearly and distinctly', this in turn resting on the claim that God would not play tricks, while the shrewder response of Bishop BERKELEY to sceptical claims about what we think we perceive was to say that what we think we perceive is exactly what we perceive, as there

is nothing 'higher' or more 'real' than the thoughts.

SEE ALSO

Knowledge

## SCHELLING, FRIEDRICH WILLIAM JOSEPH VON (1775–1854)

Schelling is seen as being the 'missing link' between the 'subjective' idealism of FICHTE, his predecessor at Jena as professor of philosophy, and the 'absolute' idealism of HEGEL. In *Naturophilosophie* (1797) Schelling tries to correct the tendency in Fichte to see the natural world as there only as a consequence of its perception by the 'I', saying NATURE is 'invisible mind' and MIND is 'invisible Nature'. In this way his philosophy was also an antidote to the prevailing materialism of the times, and indeed, he was appointed to the Chair of Philosophy in Berlin to shore up spiritual values. In his *System of Transcendental Idealism* (1800) he says that art is the 'organ of philosophy' and makes clear the identity of 'conscious productivity' that is the mind, and 'unconscious productivity' which is nature. In this he stresses too his view that the distinction between organic and inorganic nature is misleading, as everything is made up of mind, nature is not merely a 'machine'. Art is important as it reveals more at its creation than can be derived from consideration of the original conscious intentions. Indeed the highest values are not moral, but artistic ones, and the universe itself is best understood as God's work of art.

In 1804 Schelling became concerned about the transition of the 'manifest' to the 'ABSOLUTE', and the conflict between 'necessity' and 'freedom'. History is portrayed as great drama, in which the Absolute reveals Itself.

## SCHILLER, JOHANN CHRISTOPH FRIEDRICH (1759–1805)

Not to be confused the later Oxford humanist, Ferdinand Schiller (1864–1937), although there are similarities, both being German and both disputing various arguments of KANT's. Johann Schiller was a playwright as well as a historian and philosopher, who once argued, in an essay 'On Grace and Dignity' (1793), that Kant's moral theory was distorted by its emphasis on duty and 'dignity', as well as by opposing humanity's sensual nature and its rational aspirations. Morality comes rather, he explains in *Letters on the Aesthetic Education of Mankind* (1794–95), through an AESTHETIC sense of what is more harmonious, proper and right. The ethical life can be best sought through art.

## SCHLICK, MORITZ (1882–1936)

Schlick was born in Berlin but taught at the University of Vienna, where he was shot by a student while on the way to a lecture. At the time of his death he was at the forefront of the debate over the true purpose of philosophy and was the 'hub' of the famous VIENNA CIRCLE, which aimed to resolve this debate in favour of technical rationality. Schlick himself originated a principle of verifiability which splits all statements into kinds: those that are true by virtue of themselves (like 'now is frozen water'), and those which are either true or false depending on the outcome of empirical investigations (such as 'all wine is delicious', although, funnily enough, Schlick also argued that ETHICS was essentially an empirical study of what people in general thought about something). Philosophers have delighted in pointing out that the principle fails its own test.

### SEE ALSO

Logical positivism

## SCHOLASTICISM

'Scholasticism' was the dominant style in philosophy for most of the medieval period, that is from the fifth century to the middle of the seventeenth century, the name coming from 'the schools' or Christian universities in which it was taught and studied. The hallmarks of scholasticism are the study of ancient texts, notably those of ARISTOTLE, and the production of 'commentaries' on them. Its most characteristic figure was Thomas AQUINAS, but others include John DUNS SCOTUS and William OCKHAM. One important difference between scholasticism and traditional monastic learning was that the approach favoured debate, in particular the use of the technique known as 'disputations'. The aim of the study, however, was to show that the evidence of reason inevitably pointed the same way as the promptings of the Christian faith.

## SCHOPENHAUER, ARTHUR (1788–1860)

### The essential Schopenhauer

Schopenhauer was born in Danzig and worked all his life in Germany, building upon and adapting KANT's philosophy, with elements from Buddhism and Platonism too. His influence has been greatest outside the narrow range of philosophy, including Leo Tolstoy, Thomas Hardy, Thomas Mann, Richard Wagner and Sigmund FREUD. Unlike his contemporaries, he admired the English, noting approvingly, for example, their concern for animals, and even considered translating Kant's *Kritik der reinen Vernunft* into English. Within philosophy, his followers, to some extent, were NIETZSCHE, KIERKEGAARD and WITTGENSTEIN.

### Arthur Schopenhauer's landlady

Bertrand RUSSELL did not have a very high opinion of Arthur Schopenhauer, writing in *A History of Western Philosophy* that:

> Schopenhauer's gospel of resignation is not very consistent and not very sincere. . . He agreed that what commonly passes for knowledge belongs to the realm of *Maya*, but when we pierce the veil, we behold not God, but Satan, the wicked omnipotent will, perpetually busied in weaving a web of suffering for the torture of its creatures. Terrified by the Diabolic vision the sage replies 'Avaunt!' and seeks refuge in non-existence. *It is an insult to the mystics to claim them as believers in this mythology. . .*

But that is not the only thing Professor Russell has against him:

> Nor is the doctrine sincere, if we may judge by Schopenhauer's life. He habitually dined well, at a good restaurant: he had many trivial love-affairs, which were sensual but not passionate: he was exceedingly quarrelsome and usually avaricious.

It is as well that Schopenahuer was not around to write about Russell! But for whatever reason, Arthur (so-called by his parents to ease him into a career, they hoped, of business) Schopenhauer is not generally counted as one of the truly great philosophers – sometimes not even one of the great German philosophers. There is more interest in asking why he pushed his landlady down the stairs than in his other theories. He lurks in the shadow not only of his celebrated contemporaries, Professors HEGEL and Kant, but of MARX and Nietzsche too. In fact, he is sometimes only remembered for his lengthy and vitriolic attacks on academic philosophy, epitomised by the detested Hegel, who he described as a 'stupid and clumsy charlatan . . . paid to play "jiggery-pokery" in front of an 'audience of fools', thereby demonstrating a considerable talent for insult (which helps explain why this most original of thinkers has been largely confined to a bit part in the theatrical performance that is philosophy).

Yet Schopenhauer believed he had a message far more important than that of his contemporaries. He believed he was a kind of metaphysical cryptographer who had stumbled on to the key to understanding the universe – and the key was this: each individual – not just some supposed philosophical elite – is already in touch with the ultimate underlying reality. And not only tentatively, contemplatively in touch – we are all so many puppets twitching and dancing to its whim.

'Will', 'instinct', 'desire', is the basic force. Life is meaningless, since birth leads to death and the only purpose of activity between the two seems to be to produce offspring who can then repeat the cycle. There is nothing behind it – no strategy, no reason, no purpose. It is outside space and time, after all, it creates these regularities, these 'appearances'. It is primary, it sweeps perception before it, it dictates all actions. It even drives evolution, not the other way round as DARWIN would have it. Animals reflect their wills in their forms – the timid rabbit is determined by its large ears, always ready to detect the faintest whiff of threat. The hawk's cruel beak and talons reflects its permanent desire to rip other creatures apart. We are like so many mayflies, created one day, dead the next, leaving only our eggs. Nature has more use for species than for individuals, but species too must come and go as part of a larger cycle.

Will is also irrational, it can create reasons but is by no means bound by them. The will to live, the will to procreate are irrational: they obey no rules and accept no logic. To demonstrate this, Schopenhauer describes the grisly tale of the Australian ant, a nasty example of its kind, which, when decapitated, turns into two grotesque fighting machines – the head will try to bite the thorax, which will attempt to sting to death the other.

Schopenhauer does write, as Russell says, of the need to penetrate the 'veil of Maya' in order to see the common reality of 'will', which is

Maharakya or 'Great World', HINDU wisdom. (He is one of very few philosophers to relate his work equally to Eastern as to Western works). And pain is the norm and happiness the exception. From BUDDHISM, too, comes his solution: nothingness. Nothingness is exactly the best you can obtain. It is the consequence of 'NIRVANA'.

Contributor: Martin Cohen

## Further reading

Schopenhauer, A. (1818) *The World as Will and Representation*

## SCIENCE

Until late in the eighteenth century, what we now call 'science' was merely a branch of philosophy, the philosophy of 'nature', studied by such as COPERNICUS, Kepler, GALILEO, BACON and DESCARTES. Equally (if confusingly) what was then called 'science' was really philosophy, or 'knowledge of what is necessarily true'. Indeed, in many ways science only 'began' with Isaac NEWTON, who as well as making several excellent discoveries, drew up a new system of nomenclature, in its way as influential as ARISTOTLE's 2000 years earlier. After Newton, we had not only 'physiks', but science too.

The central assumption of science is that the world follows rules that can be investigated and identified. The most important of these is that of 'cause and effect'. The world is orderly and consistent, and it is assumed that identical conditions will produce identical outcomes.

## SEA-BATTLE PARADOX

Is a statement such as: 'There will be a sea battle off Beachy Head tomorrow' true when uttered – or only after the event has taken place? If it is true, then that implies a fatalistic universe. If it is false, the same thing. There cannot be a battle there tomorrow whatever we do. But if it is 'neither true nor false', then we have to rethink our general rules for KNOWLEDGE – which is what the Polish professor, Jan Lukasiewicz, attempted in the twentieth century, coming up with a new 'three-valued logic'.

Aristotle briefly discusses the problem in *Of Interpretations* (*de Interpretatione*, Chapter IX), apparently thinking that such statements about the future should be considered 'potentially' true or false, but not actually so.

## SELF

The Greek oracle advised that knowledge of yourself was the most important study of them all, but philosophers have still made little progress on the question of the essence of the 'self'. Sometimes the self is taken to be the EGO, the 'I'; sometimes it is hyphenated into 'self-consciousness'; sometimes it is reduced to being (in HUME's words) a 'bundle of perceptions'.

## SEMANTICS AND SEMIOTICS

Semantics is the study of linguistic 'signs', in particular the interpretation of sentences and worlds of languages. In *Foundations of the Theory of Signs* (1938), the American philosopher Charles Morris divided the general study of 'signs' into three parts: the study of the relation of signs to other signs, which is to do with syntax; 'communication' or the relation of signs to their users, which is PRAGMATICS; and the relation of signs to the things they represent. This last is 'semantics'.

Semiotics is the general theory concerned with 'signs', in this case distinguishing between icons, such as pictures that look like what they are supposed to represent (typical of traffic signs for falling rocks, and so on); 'natural signs' (such as grey clouds, signifying rain); and conventional signs (such as a four-leaf clover, signifying good fortune).

## SENECA (*C.* 4 BCE–65 CE)

Roman statesman and philosopher, born in Cordoba, Spain, Seneca is infamous for being tutor to the Emperor Nero. He is equally infamous for the hypocrisy of preaching the simple life while being fabulously wealthy. Both of these charges are somewhat unfair, however, and he was very much a critic rather than a follower of the decadent tendencies of his day. His philosophical works, all highly accessible, comprise a series of *Letters to Lucilius*, a collection of *Essays* on a range of broadly ethical topics, and a work of physical theory known as the *Natural Questions*. Many of these were composed in unfortunate circumstances, such as while he was in exile on Corsica, or during the period at the end of his life when he was awaiting the order from the Emperor to commit suicide. Alongside EPICTETUS, Seneca is one of the most important adherents of STOICISM whose works survive.

## SENGHOR, LÉOPOLD

See African philosophy.

## SENSE, SENSE DATA AND SENSATION

Philosophers generally invent new entities to explain old ones. So, sensory perception by the senses is explained by saying that we sense . . . sense data. This term became popular in the early twentieth century in English language philosophy, particularly through the writings of G.E. MOORE and Bertrand RUSSELL, but other (largely anglophone) philosophers had hinted at the need for such a new entity. LOCKE speaks of 'ideas of sense' and BERKELEY of 'sensible qualities', while HUME conjures with 'impressions'. William JAMES and others thought that psychology required such a distinction too. Many philosophers have argued since that it is only these sense data that we perceive, and hence that we perceive the sense data very well, and the 'real world' very badly. Berkeley, in particular, dismisses the idea that we feel, say, a warm stone, as it would ascribe a quality to an inanimate object that rightly does not belong there – the 'warmth' is simply a feeling we have in our minds. Similarly, Berkeley complains that when we approach a tree, it becomes bigger; which 'in reality' it does not, it merely appears to change. This change in appearance was roundly dismissed by the Scottish Presbyterian and very down-to-earth philosopher, Thomas Reid (1710–96), as exactly what we should expect – if we are looking at a real object, it should change as our position in relation to it changes.

## SENTIMENT

According to Frances HUTCHESON, David HUME and Adam SMITH (among others), sentiment is the basis of morality. Good actions please and bad actions offend. Sentiment is thus the engine of moral approval or disapproval. Hutcheson speaks of the 'moral sense', Hume of 'approbation' and Smith of 'sympathy'.

In the *Wealth of Nations,* Smith follows up his earlier theory, set out in the *Moral Sentiments,* that the central motivation of mankind is a desire for approval by others. 'Sympathy', or 'awareness of other's feelings' (we might say 'empathy'), explains morality; the division of labour explains economics. 'Sympathy' also creates a social bond. Human beings, Smith explains, have a spontaneous tendency to observe others. From this, we turn to judging ourselves. The moral identity of the individual develops, in this way, from social interaction. A human being growing up in isolation will have no sense of right and wrong – nor any need for the concept.

Were it possible that a human creature could grow up to manhood in a solitary place, without any communication with his own species, he could no more think of his own character, or the propriety or demerit of his own sentiments and conduct, of the beauty or deformity of his own mind, than the beauty or deformity of his own face. . . . Bring him into society and he is immediately provided with the mirror. . .

## SETS

A set is a collection of distinct entities, or 'things', if you prefer, all of which are distinguished by sharing a property or attribute that nothing outside the set has. The pioneer of 'set theory' was Georg CANTOR, who used it to demonstrate that there are different 'levels' of infinity, countable ones and uncountable ones, and it is indeed a powerful tool for mathematicians. However, for philosophers, it leads to PARADOXES.

## SEX

Philosophers do not like sex. It is, after all, highly irrational. PLATO even had SOCRATES ask his friend Glaucon, in his usual rhetorical manner, whether 'true love can have any contact with frenzy or excess of any kind?' The answer, Glaucon gives obligingly, is most certainly not, but Socrates, unusually, goes on to spell it out.

SOCRATES: True love can have no contact with this sexual pleasure, and lovers whose love is true must neither of them indulge in it.
GLAUCON: They certainly must not, Socrates.
SOCRATES: And so, I suppose you will lay down laws in the state we are founding [discussing] that will allow a lover to associate with his boy-friend and kiss him and touch him, if he permits it, as a father does his son, if his motives are good; but require that his association with anyone he's fond of must never give rise to the least

suspicion of anything beyond this, otherwise he will be thought a man of no taste or education.
GLAUCON: That is how I should legislate.

(*Republic*, Book III, 403)

But SCHOPENHAUER is surely right: the reproductive urge, be it simply the sexual one or the more respectable procreative one, is so strong, it is somehow fundamental, and really

### THE EROTIC

Plato is perhaps the first great philosophical thinker of the erotic, in dialogues such as the *Symposium* and the *Phaedrus*. Here, 'eros' is distinguished from the more basic sexual instincts and aligned with a kind of spiritual 'mania' which can put us in touch with the divine. In the medieval period, 'eros' is sublimated into the concept of 'agape', which is linked to love of God and viewed positively once it is kept within these confines. 'Agape' designates love as revealed in Jesus, seen as spiritual and self-less and a model for humanity and love that is spiritual, not sexual, in its nature. A consequent interpretation of 'eros' as overtly sexual desire prevails and is radicalised through its linkages in Augustine to the concept of 'original sin' and the female body. It is arguable that civilisation still has not recovered from this Christianisation of the concept. In more modern times, Nietzsche's emphasis on embodiment and Freud's psychological work on the erotic has led philosophers to reject the dualistic picture of mind vs body inherited from Christianity (and subsequently Cartesianism) and to concentrate on a more integrated picture. Feminism has argued quite convincingly that the suppression of the erotic in the history of philosophy was intrinsically linked to a latent misogyny. Interdisciplinary work between philosophy, psychology and sociology has led to a greater theoretical subtlety in the area of sexology, and the boundaries between sex and the erotic have become increasingly refined. Michel Foucault's monumental four-volume *History of Sexuality* is paradigmatic here (an interesting and formidable contrast might be Roger Scruton's *Sexual Desire*). There is also increasingly collaborative work between philosophy and the arts in this context.

philosophers are being a bit evasive if they continue to discuss the nature of human life without any reference at all to it. At least Plato did value a sort of filial love, the kind ever since called 'Platonic'. Unfortunately, the Christian Church (leaving aside other religious traditions) taught a rather extreme version of the doctrine for most of the millennia between Socrates and Schopenhauer, which culminated in the most bizarre and hypocritical attitudes towards sex (a point made by the contemporary French philosopher Michel FOUCAULT).

## SEXTUS EMPIRICUS (*C.* 200 CE)

Sextus Empiricus was a SCEPTIC who, in excellently entitled works such as *Against the Dogmatists* and *Against the Professors*, examined at length various claims made in the arts and sciences and suggested ways to undermine them. He is critical of all philosophers and all philosophical positions except one: that of PYRRHO, who was also a Sceptic. Despite this rather negative style, he claimed to be positively motivated to promote a more tranquil existence based on the futility of striving for knowledge. Whatever the truth of that, his writings have been an important historical source for subsequent thinkers.

## SIN, AND ORIGINAL SIN

### Essentials of sin

There are many bad things people do, but only some of them actually offend God. These are 'sins'. According to the Christian and early Hebrew Bible, Adam and Eve, while enjoying the Garden of Eden, disobeyed a divine command not to eat the fruit of the Tree of Knowledge. Thereafter they were thrown out of the Garden and their children inherited their wicked nature. This was made clear by Saint AUGUSTINE, who rails against the newborn babe suckling its mother's milk, for the infant's greed and selfishness. Only God, the Christian orthodox would have, can 'forgive us' this legacy of sinfulness, and that is why it is most unfortunate for a child to die unbaptised – for it has sinned already and now cannot be forgiven. If it seems strange that neither Jesus nor Mary inherited the sinfulness, perhaps that is because the doctrine needed Saint Paul to invent it first. Both John LOCKE and Immanuel KANT criticise the notion, but it caught on.

### The concept of sin

In more than 2500 years of philosophical speculation, the subject of ethics has been consistently at the forefront of human thinking. From PLATO's *Republic* to ARISTOTLE's *Ethics* and up to Kant's *Groundwork of Morals*, clarification of what constitutes a good life has been a primary concern. Simultaneous with this concern for doing the right thing has existed, by definition, a focus on its very opposite, not doing the right thing – doing wrong or sinning. Whether we refer to 'sin', 'evil' or 'vice', we are often referring to much the same thing. However, while sin involves, in strict definitional terms, an 'offence against God', evil and vice can be understood to mean a more 'general wrongdoing'. We can trace this distinction between respective theological and secular conceptions back to the transition from Greek to medieval philosophy. As early as HERACLITUS, philosophy was concerned with a notion of evil (*kakos*), as is evidenced in the fragment 'good and evil are one'.

This MONISTIC approach to the notion of wrongdoing, where the discrete distinctions of morality seem to be subsumed into the unified being of ONTOLOGY, was rejected by both Plato and Aristotle. For Plato, evil represents a privation, a lack, whereas goodness (*agathos*) represents a fullness of being. The task of the philosopher is to gain self-knowledge, and in attaining self-knowledge of one's own being, one achieves goodness. As SOCRATES often claims, 'virtue is knowledge'. Aristotle regarded this Platonic approach to ethics as naïve and idealistic. In his *Ethics*, he argues for a more nuanced concept of the 'weakness of the will', where even with self-knowledge the will can often falter and fail morally – do the wrong thing.

No Greek philosopher of the first period is concerned with the concept of sin and it is not until the birth of Christianity that philosophy begins to engage in discussion concerning the relevance of sin to human affairs. Two things can be noted here: first, that the earlier Greek idea of vice or evil is employed by both St Paul and Augustine most especially to provide a hermeneutics of the biblical conception of original sin. Second, that in this hermeneutic assimilation of pagan ideas, the notion of wrongdoing undergoes a significant transformation and radicalisation.

This can be seen especially in the work of Augustine. In early texts such as *The Confessions*, Augustine is already foregrounding the notion of sin as constitutive of human activity, although here he sees it as possible for humanity to turn away from sin and repent. His approach at this juncture is also tinged with humour: 'Lord make me chaste, but not yet'! By his final text, *The City of God*, Augustine's hermeneutics of sin has lost its lightheartedness. The human being is now a kind of divine plaything, riven and defined by the stains of original sin from birth, incapacitated by vice, predestined and apparently damned, whose only hope is the arbitrary will of a distant God. Significantly, the taint of sin is associated by Augustine most particularly with the body and with sexuality, especially female sexuality: 'We are born between faeces and urine.' By the later medieval period this radical view of human sin and depravity has been qualified by the influence of Aquinas' more Aristotelian approach to the possibilities and probabilities of human virtue and vice – 'grace perfects nature'. Nature is no longer depraved, but rather has contrary tendencies, which require some divine support and succour.

One might imagine that the modern period in philosophy simply developed Aquinas' philosophy in a more secular direction, but closer inspection reveals a more ambiguous situation. Certainly, the ethical systems of thinkers such as SPINOZA, Kant and even the moral scepticism of HUME can all be seen as, in different ways, arguing for a certain human autonomy and willing capacity in matters of ethics, thus siding, at least in principle, with Aquinas. However, particularly with regard to the religious philosophy of Protestantism (for example, Calvinism and Lutheranism), the more Augustinian conception of a depraved humanity, the over-preponderance of sin, and even the claim of predestination, can be seen to return to haunt the image of human self-sufficiency and self-worth. A similar emphasis can be traced through Jansenist thought.

The attempted de-theologisation of philosophy in the later aspects of modernity and the beginnings of postmodernity, through the NIETZSCHEAN figure of the Antichrist, can be seen as a pivotal effort to oust this residual medievalism. 'If God is dead,' Dostoevsky proclaimed, 'then everything is permitted.' In other words, sin is no longer a reality – we have killed it along with God and all the other idols, we have moved into a new philosophical space 'beyond good and evil'. However, it is arguable, despite these appearances, that the development into POSTMODERNIST thinking and philosophy has witnessed an actual intensification of the quasi-Augustinian interest in sin and depravity.

Early twentieth-century thinkers, such as Georges Bataille and Pierre Klossowski, cite the lure of evil and sin, their irreducibility and philosophical resilience. Julia Kristeva's concern with the concept of 'abjection' and Hannah ARENDT's focus on 'the banality of evil' can also be seen as related thematics. The historical example of the Holocaust has also been at the forefront of more recent analyses of the significance of evil and sin for thinking about ethics and virtue, in the work of thinkers such as DERRIDA, Lyotard and Baudrillard. It is also not coincidental that the resurgence of the concepts of sin and evil has been simultaneous to a 're-theologisation' of both ANGLO-AMERICAN and CONTINENTAL philosophy, through figures such as Taylor and MacIntyre, and Badiou and Marion respectively.

Contributor: Jones Irwin

## SLAVERY

The taking of slaves has a long history, be they slaves from birth, conquest or capture. ARISTOTLE and PLATO both produced justifications for slavery, centred on the lower abilities of slaves, seen as more akin to animals. Both Christianity and Islam have been apologists for the practice, despite Muhammad setting free his own slaves and instructing that all men should be brothers and treated as equals. (Well, that is half the human race freed, anyway.)

For 300 years, the infamous African slave trade was based on and facilitated by African customs of selling their neighbours. The peculiar contribution of the Europeans was to develop a theory of racial superiority to justify their own involvement. When the British undertook a census of India in 1841 they found *ten million* slaves (which they now wanted to set free). Today, there are still thought to be at least 200,000 child slaves sold by African nations alone. Some countries maintain this is a 'custom', in which children are given 'work experience' abroad. In 2001, the world's interest was briefly kindled when what appeared to be a modern-day slave ship, the *Etireno*, en route to Gabon, was accused of having thrown 250 children overboard (as surplus to orders).

**SLAVES**

In 2004, in Niger alone, there were officially 43,000 slaves. They were descendants of prisoners taken during wars, and were obliged to wear bracelets indicating themselves as such. As well as working for their masters for nothing, they were often castrated or told who they were to marry, and families were split up at the owners' whim. They ate only the 'left-overs'. Naturally, their children became slaves too.

This practice has been prevalent in sub-Saharan Africa since the seventh century, and continues today in Mauritania, Mali and Chad, for example. Happily, in Niger, since 2004, the practice has been declared 'incompatible with Islam' and is now illegal under heavy penalties.

Today, we find churches spearheading social change, calling for civil rights, the protection of unborn children, an end to human rights abuses in other countries, and so on. This has not always been the case. It has often been said that on issues such as women's rights and human slavery, religion has impeded social progress. The church of the past rarely considered slavery to be a moral evil. The Protestant churches of Virginia, South Carolina and other southern states actually passed resolutions in favour of the human slave traffic. Human slavery was called 'by Divine Appointment', 'a Divine institution', 'not immoral' but 'founded in right'. Typical of this was one Buckner H. Payne, styling himself 'Ariel', who wrote in 1867 that 'the tempter in the Garden of Eden . . . was a beast, a talking beast . . . the negro'.

Many New Testament verses call for obedience and subservience on the part of slaves (Colossians 3:22–25; Ephesians 6:5–9; I Peter 2:18–25; Titus 2:9–10; I Timothy 6:1–2) and were used to justify human slavery. Many of Jesus' parables refer to slaves, while Paul's infamous epistle to Philemon concerns a runaway slave who he unambiguously states should be returned to his master. Other than Deuteronomy, in the Old Testament, which says 'You shall not surrender to his master a slave who has taken refuge with you', the abolitionist had to find non-biblical sources to argue the immoral nature of slavery, a cautionary tale for those who take their lead from religion.

## 'SLIPPERY SLOPE' ARGUMENTS

A 'slippery slope' argument is one that warns against doing something because, it suggests, that step will inevitably lead to others, which in turn become disastrous. Thus, I might warn you against eating that cake as, I might say, 'if you eat one cake, you will then eat more and become obsessed with eating and become obese and . . . eventually explode!' The argument is not very convincing, but it serves to illustrate. It becomes more convincing, for example, if I say, 'if you eat chocolate cake for tea today, you will want chocolate cake for tea every day and then you will become overweight'. Thus, the similarity of the steps is important.

Another kind of argument is often seen in ETHICS and public policy, where the steps are not particularly similar, but a psychological motivation is supposed. For example, the government will say, 'if I let you smoke cannabis, you will want to smoke other drugs too, and soon you will be smoking opium. Therefore you cannot smoke cannabis.'

Although philosophers tend to sneer at 'slippery slope' arguments, they are actually part and parcel of political life and decision-making. For example, when Baroness Warnock, looking into the matter of the regulation of pregnancies for the UK government, decided that abortion was 'all right' up until the thirteenth week and not after, she was seeking to locate policy precisely halfway up the slippery slope between no terminations of unwanted babies and 'abortion on demand'. And as the slope is indeed slippery, such positions are hard to hold or justify.

SEE ALSO

Arguments and argument types

## SMITH, ADAM (1723–90)

### The essential Smith

The first edition of *An Inquiry into the Nature and Causes of the Wealth of Nations* cost 1 pound and 16 shillings, and sold out within 6 months. Smith's publisher, William Stahern, had just produced another bestseller: Gibbon's *Decline and Fall of the Roman Empire*. It was thought that *Wealth of Nations* was too technical for the popular readership of *Decline and Fall*, but Gibbon himself realised that there was a great strength to be found in Smith's book. It was there in 'the most profound ideas expressed in the most perspicuous language'.

And it was there because the *Wealth of Nations* is, despite the title, not merely concerned with economics. It is a much more comprehensive vision of society, and in its pages economics is merely a by-product, albeit a necessary one, of social life. So Smith is concerned not only with money, but with justice and equity. If his findings are nowadays adopted by those of a different disposition, that is not his fault.

## Smith's hidden sympathies

Adam Smith is a much more radical philosopher than he is usually given credit for. Where earlier philosophers, such as **PLATO** and John **LOCKE**, saw society as needing to be based on altruism, or at least the suppression of selfishness (as in Niccolo **MACHIAVELLI** and Thomas **HOBBES**), Smith allows society to be determined by an entirely greater, non-human force – economics. It is 'self-interest' that makes the world go round. As he famously explains in the *Wealth of Nations*, which became one of the best-selling books of all time, it is not out of the benevolence of the butcher or the baker that we can expect our supper, it is from their enlightened notion of their own self interest. Yet if this is the motive, it is not in itself to be scorned, for:

> . . . how destructive so ever this system may appear, it could never have imposed upon so great a number of persons, nor have occasioned so general an alarm among those who are the friends of better principles had it not in some respects bordered up on the truth.
>
> (*Moral Sentiments*, Book VII, part ii)

Alongside *Wealth of Nations*, published in the same year as the American Declaration of Independence (1766), and still a popular read with right-wing politicians, is another significant work, written rather earlier, *The Theory of the Moral Sentiments* (1759). Although a less popular work, this ties his colours firmly to the mast erected by his friend and fellow Scot, David

### SMITH AND THE MORAL SENTIMENTS

Like Freud, Smith sees moral behaviour as built up in the mind from the influence of parents, teachers, school fellows (peer group, we might say today) and society in general. The conscience acts as a kind of 'impartial spectator', watching and judging us. Where Freud would allow the 'unconscious' to still lead us astray, Smith makes his impartial spectator similar in role to that of the Freudian super ego, and quite capable of leading us towards the light.

> It is chiefly from this regard to the sentiments of mankind that we pursue riches and avoid poverty. For to what purpose is all the toil and bustle of the world? What is the end of avarice and ambition, of the pursuit of wealth, of power, or pre-eminence?. . . To be observed, to be attended to, to be taken notice of with sympathy, complacency, and approbation, are all the advantages which we can propose to derive from it. It is the vanity, not the ease or the pleasure, which interests us.
>
> (*Moral Sentiments*, I, iii, 2, 1)

There are four factors determining people's respect for others: personal qualities, age, fortune and birth. The first is open to debate, so age is a better yardstick. Fortune, or wealth, is, Smith notes, a surprising source of respect. Rich people are admired and benefit in terms of social esteem just by their wealth. Poor people lose in two ways. The 'conditions of human nature were peculiarly hard, if those affections, which by the very nature of our being, ought frequently to included our conduct, could upon no occasion appear virtuous, or deserve esteem and commendation from any body.' (*Moral Sentiments*, VII, ii, 3, 18)

Smith is aware of the possibility of self-deception, and curses it as the source of 'half of the disorders of human life'. If only, he wrote in the *Moral Sentiments*, we could see ourselves as others see us, 'a reformation would be unavoidable. We could not otherwise endure the sight.'

To judge your own behaviour requires you – at least for a moment – to divide into two people, and one be the spectator of the actions of the other. Nature had endowed each of us with a desire not only to be approved of, 'but with a desire of being what ought to be approved of' (which is rather harder). (*Moral Sentiments* III, ii, 7)

The law of unintended social outcomes becomes, through Smith's phrase, 'the invisible hand'.

Every individual necessarily labours to render the annual revenue of the society as great as he can. He generally, indeed, neither intends to promote the publick intent, nor knows how much he is promoting it . . . he intends only his own gain, and he is in this, as in many other cases, led by an invisible hand to promote an end which was no part of his intention.

HUME, of ethics as social convention. Smith declares that moral identity, indeed all moral behaviour, depends on social interaction and originates in the observation of others. Upholding 'Justice' becomes the key task of governments, even as economic forces are allowed to let rip.

Although Smith is synonymous with the economics of 'laissez-faire', where the business of running society is left to the 'hidden hand' of the market, this is not out of any lack of concern for the weakest in society, rather out of a conviction that this is simply the best possible arrangement for everyone. Smith himself lived very simply and gave most of his wealth to charity.

The wheels of the watch are all admirably adjusted to the end for which it was made, the pointing of the hour. All their various motions conspire in the nicest manner to produce this effect. If they were endowed with a desire and intention to produce it, they could not do it better. Yet we never ascribe any such intention or desire to them, but to the watchmaker, and we know that they are put into motion by a spring, which intends the effect it produces as little as they do.

Moral Sentiments (1759) VII, ii

Contributor: Martin Cohen

## Further reading

Smith, A. (1766) An Inquiry into the Nature and Causes of the Wealth of Nations

## SOCIAL DARWINISM

Perhaps the most influential form of social Darwinism appeared in the fields of economic life, where it was assumed that both the 'fittest' companies and the 'fittest' individuals would survive a free market, laissez-faire environment. Similarly, art and the production of policies themselves can be left to the forces of the market in the optimistic belief that bad things perish and good things thrive. In fact, in terms of human birthrates, the more educated, and indeed the more economically advanced, a society, the less its population growth rate, so that clearly, for a social Darwinist, the best arrangement is to have a lot of poor uneducated people. Truly, the poor shall inherit the earth.

SEE ALSO

Smith

## SOCIAL FACTS

According to DURKHEIM, social facts emerge from the scientific study of society, and can be considered to be objective and precise. Social facts are statistical generalisations like the fact that (as Durkheim found) religion acts as a social bond for members of a society, making them less inclined to commit suicide. He explained in The Rules of Sociological Method: (1895):

A social fact is every way of acting, fixed or not, capable of exercising on the individual an external constraint; or again, every way of acting which is general throughout a given society, while at the same time existing in its own right independent of its individual manifestations.

## SOCIALISM

The term 'socialism' was first used by critics of the emerging industrial societies in the nineteenth century, such as Robert Owen, Saint Simon and Pierre PROUDHON. They were concerned to prevent the excesses of CAPITALISM, for example in the unprecedentedly grim conditions of work in the factories, and to replace it instead with social production, organised often on a small scale by communities of workers. MARX derided such aspirations, as reforms incapable of addressing the fundamental problems of capitalism. Instead, he proposed to attain 'socialism' through COMMUNISM, which has a number of dogmatic elements set out in *The Communist Manifesto*, such as State ownership of the 'means of production'. Contrary to the 'reformists', that implies the 'State ownership' of the people too.

# SOCIAL SCIENCE AND SOCIOLOGY

## Essentials of socsci

The linkages between sociology and social science in general, on one side, and philosophy and ethics on the other side, are both numerous and complex. Although definitions vary, social science is usually taken as anthropology, political science, economics and sociology, along (sometimes) with psychology and interdisciplinary combinations like social psychology, social history, urban studies or sociology of law. Industrial relations, international relations and media studies also arise from the social sciences.

## The social construction of reality

Judging behaviours or giving advice is not the aim of social scientists, who focus rather on the roots and origins of opinions, representations and ideologies. Cultural studies focus on the way power relationships can model popular culture, and how elements of a specific popular culture can be appropriated by audiences and individuals into their own building of their identity. As ADORNO and Horkheimer explained in the USA in the mid-1940s, mass culture does not emerge from the masses; it is rather conceived for massive audiences, produced and distributed as any industrial process.

Sociology can be defined as the study of how groups and societies operate, as well as the interactions between individuals. The classical example of the sociological approach is Emile DURKHEIM's study on suicide, which demonstrates that suicide is not just an individual phenomenon, but a social phenomenon that changes according to the individual's religious beliefs and social position.

Philosophers such as Jean-Jacques ROUSSEAU, Alexis de Tocqueville and Karl MARX are all considered as precursors or founders of sociology, although the term was coined by Auguste COMTE (1798–1857). Max WEBER introduced various concepts of rationality as the way to understand people, and completed Marx's theory of class conflict by adding a symbolic element, the social status, which indicates the specific position everyone occupies in his own social group. Emile Durkheim and his nephew, Marcel Mauss, had also insisted on the importance of symbols in social life.

Thomas HOBBES, John LOCKE and Jean-Jacques Rousseau helped to conceptualise the social contract, which defines the implicit rules in a society. The individual trades a portion of liberty for the social protection from the State at every level, accepting the group's rules, conventions, norms and laws.

And political science cannot ignore the influence of ideologies and systems of beliefs. Anthropologists observe and analyse rituals, myths, magic and various forms of belief, seen as the 'primitive' thoughts that everyone has at some point, no matter where or how they live.

Since the 1920s, German philosophers of the so-called Frankfurt School (such as Theodor Adorno and Max Horkheimer, or later, Karl Mannheim and Jürgen HABERMAS) have questioned the processes of domination in industrialised societies, drawing on the writings of Marx and FREUD, forging so-called 'CRITICAL THEORY'. In France, Louis ALTHUSSER (also influenced by Marx) had a durable influence in political science and sociology, with his own theory about dominant ideologies and the 'State Apparatus', which implies that the dominant ideology in a State is maintained by all institutions in a society (industries, media, schools), no matter if these components are related or not with the government. Questioning practical issues related to ethics, French sociologists have investigated issues in MODERNITY, while US theoreticians have concentrated on the sociology of science, the sociology of knowledge and the 'social construction of reality'.

POSTMODERNISM has brought new inferences between philosophy and social science: postmodern authors such as Jean Baudrillard and Zygmunt Bauman, who have produced critiques of consumer culture, are also sociologists. Zygmunt Bauman redefined in the mid-1990s the new poor, not in terms of ownership or wages, but rather as the individual who cannot consume.

All these new problems and issues have also led to new trends in research, but also in education: we now have new interdisciplinary domains such as environmental education, citizenship education, media literacy and public understanding of science, that all include ethical and social dimensions.

Contributor: Yves Laberge

## Further reading

de Tocqueville, A. (1835–40) *Democracy in America* (2 vols).

Spencer, H. (1873) *The Classification of Sciences*

Mead, G.H. (1934) *Mind, Self and Society, from the Standpoint of a Social Behaviorist*

# SOCRATES (470–399 BCE)

## The essential Socrates

Socrates taught and discussed philosophy in Athens during the golden age of Greek philosophy, but wrote nothing himself (as far as we know). His views are relayed instead by Aristophanes in his play *The Clouds*, by Xenophon in his writings and, most of all, by his pupil, PLATO, in the *Dialogues*. In these, Socrates is always the star, employing the characteristic method of dialectical questioning that takes his name to elicit knowledge. Nonetheless, no one can be sure that it really is Socrates who is represented there – or Plato – or even just a philosophical position. Socrates remains an enigma.

## Socrates the sorcerer

There is little enough that is agreed on about Socrates, but there is perhaps one thing: that he is the most influential philosopher of them all. This despite the fact that no one is quite sure what he said. (Let alone thought . . .) There are scraps enough, to be sure, but the real Socrates remains an elusive figure. His footprints are everywhere, yet Socrates himself, like MacCavity the mystery cat, is nowhere to be found.

There are stories aplenty though: of the dogmatic Socrates instructing a young and naïve Plato to destroy his youthful attempts at poetry; of the fanatical Socrates standing for a day and a night rooted to the spot (wrestling with a thought), while others brought up mattresses to watch and take bets, and of course there is that death-wish scene described so eloquently in the *Apology*:

> For let me tell you, Gentlemen, that to be afraid of death is only another form of thinking that one is wise when one is not. It is to think that one knows what one does not know.

Historians consider DIOGENES LAERTIUS to be the most, indeed the only reliable source for facts about the 'historical Socrates'. Otherwise, all the accounts say more about their author's preferences than they do about Socrates. Xenophon, the shopkeeper, draws a picture of a dull, practical Socrates, holding forth in a harmless but insignificant way. HEGEL, the philosopher of 'historical determinism' and of the dialectic, sees Socrates as a pivotal figure in the tide of world history, a Janus god with two faces, one surveying the past and the other facing the future. And NIETZSCHE, writing in the *Gay Science*, describes Socrates as a 'mocking and enamoured monster', a kind of philosophical 'pied piper of Athens'.

But overshadowing them all, it is the Platonic picture that has created the Socratic philosophy. Plato, the idealist, offers up an idol, a master-figure for philosophy. A saint, a prophet of 'the Sun-Good', a teacher condemned for his teachings as a heretic. It is he who tells the most eloquent Socratic story. In the dialogue, the *Symposium*, for instance, Plato portrays an eccentric figure:

> Immersed in some problem at dawn, he stood in the same spot considering it, and when he found it a tough problem, he would not give it up but stood there trying to understand it. Time drew on until midday, and the men began to notice him, saying to one another in wonder: 'Socrates has been standing there in contemplation, since dawn!' The result was that in the evening, after they had eaten their suppers, this being summer, some of the Ionians brought out their rugs and mattresses and took their sleep in the cool: thus they waited to see if Socrates would go on standing all night too. He stood till dawn came and the sun rose, then walked way, after offering a prayer to the Sun.

Elsewhere in the same dialogue, the good and bad twins, Aristodemus and Alcibiades, offer two more, opposing, views, which Plato uses to paint a picture of a Socrates as 'Eros', the god of sexuality, and a figure beyond everyday categories. Socrates is neither ignorant nor wise, tragic nor comic, male nor female – but outside all such distinctions. He can walk barefoot on ice during winter, drink wine without becoming drunk (for all that he needs to perform such feats is the knowledge of the good). Even his supposed ugliness is counted as an advantage, for having eyes set towards the sides of his head is claimed to enable him to perceive a wider field of vision, while having a flat, distorted nose allows him to receive scents from all directions. And those disproportionately thick lips can now be seen as able to receive all the more kisses.

Contributor: Martin Cohen

## Further reading

Plato *Apology*

Plato *Symposium*

## SOPHISTS

The sophists originally were 'wise men' (from the Greek, *sophia*, for wisdom) and included great and respected philosophers such as PROTAGORAS. The sophists were experts in grammar, rhetoric and law (fitting with their later reputation), but were responsible for distinguishing between the two kinds of knowledge, that of nature and that of humanity, and thus inspiring SOCRATES and PLATO, even though in the dialogues, the sophists are the butt of many criticisms. Plato disliked the Sophist tradition of earning money for their rhetorical skills, and by the time of ARISTOTLE their reputation had sunk to the point that he wrote of them as those who took money for appearing wise, without actually being so. Karl POPPER and others have suggested that what Plato and other later philosophers, too, really had against the sophists was their egalitarian approach and challenging of elites, including philosophical ones.

## SOUL

The breath of life, the presence of which causes the body to be conscious and the absence of which leaves the body dead. Thus the soul enables thought to take place. PYTHAGORAS said that the soul was immortal and flowed between different parts of the world. A misreading of this led to the debate over 'individual souls', and thus individual identity and survival 'after death' that carries on to today.

PLATO divided the soul into three parts: the rational, the emotive and the 'appetitive' (the part with appetites), insisting that only human beings have the rational part. The distinction

lives on in psychology under different guises, and although many now seek to replace the term with 'mind', in turn replacing that with 'brains' and 'brain states', the soul remains *essential*.

## SPACE

### Essentials of space

Space, from the Latin *spatium*, meaning 'race-track', designates either an empty expanse among things (such as the gap between words or musical notes), or a boundless, all-encompassing entity – nowadays described as having a number of dimensions, of which the various magnitudes together specify locations within.

### A finite plenum

Ancient ATOMISM defined space as the infinite void in which atoms move, although it was generally verbalised not as an expanse that *contains* everything, but rather the nothingness *outside* all things. ARISTOTLE defined the cosmos as a finite plenum and reduced space to the sum of all places pertaining to physical things. This view prevailed until the fourteenth century. With the Renaissance, and later, the Copernican Revolution, the revitalisation of atomism and the advent of the modern scientific era saw space as once again infinite and homogeneous.

Philosophical controversy persisted though as to the precise nature of itself; whether such a thing can be 'empty'; whether it can exist independently of physical bodies; whether it is finite or infinite; and, of particular concern, whether it should be thought of as an independently existing *thing*, or as an abstraction from the spatial relations of physical bodies.

For Isaac NEWTON, the transparent, empty arena in which we are all immersed, in which all motion takes place, exists as a real, physical (immutable) entity, supplying invisible scaffolding that gives the cosmos shape and structure – an inert, universal, cosmic stage on which events play themselves out. In his *Principia Mathematica*, he called this 'absolute space'. (Although, conversely, in his posthumous *De gravitatione et aequipondio fluidorum*, Newton claimed that space is neither a substance nor an attribute of a substance, but has 'its own manner of existence' in which each point of space is individual only by virtue of its relations to the other points of space.)

However, for LEIBNIZ, space is not a real or

independent entity, merely the vocabulary of relations between where objects are – a way of encoding where things are in relation to one another. The debate between Leibnizian relationalists and Newtonian substantialists raged on until the success of Newtonian physics finally decided the debate.

Philosophers, like Newton, were interested in, among other things, how our perceptions of objects necessarily conform to the objects themselves. Immanuel KANT, however, considered rather how objects necessarily conform to our representations. That is, for Kant, bodies do not exist 'in space' as such. The source of spatial order is the mind: the bodies we perceive as existing 'in space' are in actual fact, mere appearances or phenomena, not the actual or underlying reality or 'noumena' world that gives rise to these phenomena.

For Newton, bodies exist 'in space'; for Leibniz, they merely exist, and space is our way of encoding where one is in relation to another. However, for Kant, space is a form of appearance or 'intuition'. It has no objective reality; it is not a substance, an attribute of a substance or a relation: it is a purely subjective condition imposed (and tacitly known, a priori) by the mind on sense impressions or phenomena that allow them to be ordered in a certain way and grasped as presentations of objects. That is, space does not exist outside of us; it is merely part of our perceptual apparatus, the way we apprehend the world. Whatever we see is first and foremost perceived as phenomena in time and space, which precede experience.

So, for Kant, space is neither a thing in itself (as it was for Newton) nor a relation of things in themselves (Leibniz), but rather a precondition of human knowledge, committing him to the truth of Euclidean geometry, seen as inherent in human spatial perception. Certainly, by the eighteenth century, a number of factors led to the identification of physical with geometrical space.

However, if geometry is to be a theory of physical space, then its axioms must be true of this space. But in 1829–30, Nikolai Lobachevski founded, and published a paper on, non-Euclidean geometry. This showed that Euclid's axioms are not known with certainty, a priori, but are hypotheses which may – or may not – correspond to physical space. And not only do we now possess examples of non-Euclidean geometry, but our modern conception of space, based on EINSTEIN's theory of general relativity, actually dispenses altogether with the truth of Euclidean geometry. Instead, it proposes that the geometry or 'curvature' of space (or, more precisely, space-time) is dependent on the bodies immersed in it.

Indeed, early on in the twentieth century, the question of the corporeality of space became outmoded: Einstein proposed that although space (or rather space-time, the embodiment of the gravitational field) is the raw material underlying reality, it is not independent and absolute, but flexible and dynamic, enmeshed with time and relative. We no longer tend to think of space as independent from time. Space and spatial relations are observer-dependent manifestations of space-time; space is relative, but space-time is an absolute entity: it is a *something*.

In our own era, we have come to envision space as suffused with quantum fields, and possibly diffused with a uniform energy called the cosmological constant – a modern echo of the old space-filling aether. Mature science may force us to rethink some of our philosophical questions. Indeed, new theories of 'quantum connections' are challenging the very basic assumption that we have of space as a medium by which one object is separated from another.

Contributor: Dean D'Souza

## SPECIES

DARWIN himself remarks, in *Origin of Species*:

> Many years ago, when comparing, and seeing others compare, the birds from the separate islands of the Galapagos Archipelago, both one with another, and with those from the American mainland, I was much struck how entirely vague and arbitrary is the distinction between species and varieties.

Species, he continues, are terms 'arbitrarily given for the sake of convenience' to what are in reality all unique creatures bearing more or less resemblance to each other. And, as Holmes Rolston, an environmental writer, has pointed out, our 'Duties to Endangered Species' depend on these rather arbitrary distinctions.

For example, *Betula lenta uber*, a kind of birch tree, is unusual in that the ends of its leaves are round. Originally, it attracted no significance, but in the 1960s a distinguished botanist announced it qualified as a distinct species. As

If in a city we had six vacant lots available to the youngsters of a certain neighbourhood for playing ball, it might be 'development' to build houses on the first, and the second, and the third, and the fourth, and even the fifth, but when we build houses on the last one, we forget what houses are for. The sixth house would not be development at all, but rather it would be mere short-sighted stupidity.

## SPINOZA, BENEDICT DE (1632–77)

Spinoza was the Dutch lens-grinder who turned down a chair in philosophy at Heidelberg to continue his polishing and grinding. He thought that everything was one thing – mind and body were two aspects of something else, which has many aspects, including that of being God. The heart of his ideas comes from the Eastern tradition, but the style of his writings, supposedly a series of proofs in the 'Euclidean' or mathematical style (and he was EINSTEIN's favourite philosopher), is heavily footnoted and pettifogging, and very much from the West.

Although influenced by DESCARTES, he disagreed with several key Cartesian ideas, such as the separation of mind and body – indeed, he did not count either as 'substance'; nor did he believe in free will. In his *Theological-Political Treatise* (1670) he makes an innovative examination of the Bible as a 'text' to be analysed, and analysed without necessarily assuming its 'truth'. He advances freedom of expression and other liberal values. The more famous *Ethics* appeared

there are only two known places where it grows, both in Virginia, USA, it was clearly an endangered one at that, and the proud Virginians dutifully put sturdy fences around both of them. Going the other way, the endangered 'Mexican duck' became rather less worrisome when it was recently 'de-listed' and became just another kind of common mallard. Holmes Rolston suggests we should understand the distinctions not so much as 'lines of latitude or longitude as like mountains and rivers, phenomena objectively there... [but] the edges of all these kinds will sometimes be fuzzy, to some extent discretionary'.

That said, as all around us habitat disappears, do we have a duty to provide a little space on earth for other species? Aldo Leopold wrote of development:

soon after his death and formalised his differences with Judaism, resulting in his condemnation as an **ATHEIST**. As the *Ethics,* like Descartes' *Meditations*, is concerned to provide a logical basis for believing in God, this might seem odd, but Spinoza's God is stripped of so many attributes (such as having wishes, ideas or preferences) that in everyday terms the accusation was just.

**SEE ALSO**

Zionism (box)

## SPORT

See James, C.L.R. (box)

## STATE, THE

The organisation of a geographically and usually also culturally defined group of people. To count as a 'State' the government is able to implement its policies, to 'regulate the behaviour' of its citizenry and, traditionally, the institutions within its boundaries too. Today, with the expansion of transnational trade and production, the 'globalisation' of shopping, media and leisure and international institutions such as banks, trade bodies and courts, this last part is barely true.

**SEE ALSO**

Plato, Hobbes, Anarchism

## STATE OF NATURE

See Hobbes.

## STOICISM

### Essentials of Stoicism

Stoicism, one of the **HELLENISTIC** schools of philosophy, was founded by **ZENO OF CITIUM** around 300 BCE. It proved especially popular with the Romans, and famous Stoics included **SENECA** and the Emperor Marcus **AURELIUS**. The Stoics were materialists, but also identified God with nature. They held only virtue to be properly good, but acknowledged that it is always better to be rich than poor, even though neither state should alter one's happiness. They argued that emotions are unhelpful, being based on mistaken judgements, and so, via an analysis of one's judgements, should be overcome. In their strict rationalism they followed

**SOCRATES**, and in fact some of the Stoics wished also to be called Socratics.

### The Breath of the Cosmos

Zeno of Citium used to meet with his pupils at the Painted Stoa on the northern side of the Agora in the centre of Athens. Initially, his pupils were known as Zenonians, but later were known as Stoics after the place where they met. After Zeno's death the school was headed by Cleanthes, and, after him, **CHRYSIPPUS**. Chrysippus was a prolific author and a gifted logician who did much to develop and systematise Stoicism. It was said in antiquity that if there had been no Chrysippus there would have been no Stoa. The school continued, and two later notable figures were Panaetius and Posidonius. These have sometimes been labelled middle Stoics in order to signify the fact that both drew upon philosophical ideas from other schools rather than maintaining a rigid orthodoxy. However, recent scholars have suggested that this was a feature of the so-called early Stoics as well.

The school in Athens does not appear to have survived beyond the first century BCE. But Stoicism as a philosophy proved popular among the Romans and continued to flourish. In the first century CE it attracted the Roman statesman and dramatist Seneca. At the same time, Musonius Rufus taught Stoicism in Rome and among his pupils was **EPICTETUS** – an ex-slave from Asia Minor who went on to found his own school in Nicopolis on the western coast of Greece. Epictetus wrote nothing himself (it is usually, although not universally, supposed) and the works that have come down to us under his name are traditionally attributed to his pupil, Arrian. In the following century Stoicism found perhaps its most high-profile adherent in the Emperor Marcus Aurelius (121–180 CE), author of the *Meditations*, a personal philosophical text that draws upon the central doctrines of Stoicism. Marcus founded four chairs in philosophy at Athens, one of which was in Stoic philosophy, and the polemics against Stoicism by Alexander of Aphrodisias, the holder of the peripatetic chair, suggest that Stoicism remained an important philosophy around 200 CE. However, its fortunes appear to have declined fairly quickly thereafter.

None of the works of the early or middle Stoics survive intact. We have to rely on quotations and reports from other, often hostile, authors. Important among these are CICERO, Plutarch, SEXTUS EMPIRICUS and DIOGENES LAERTIUS. The later Stoics have fared better, and we have *Essays* and *Letters* by Seneca, *Discourses* and a *Handbook* by Epictetus (or Arrian) and the *Meditations* of Marcus Aurelius. Some less well-known Stoic texts to survive include the *Heavens* by Cleomedes, the *Compendium of Theology* by Cornutus and the *Elements of Ethics* by Hierocles (all probably dating from the first two centuries CE).

In ONTOLOGY the Stoics are materialists; only bodies or corporeals exist. However, they do acknowledge the existence (or perhaps we should say subsistence) of four incorporeals: time, place, void and sayables. However, they reject the existence of universal concepts and so hold a form of nominalism.

They identify the cosmos with God. God is either nature, or the *pneuma* (breath) within nature, or the reason within nature. Everything that happens within the cosmos is determined by previous causes, yet at the same time, God providentially orders events. Periodically the whole cosmos is destroyed by fire and then reborn, creating an eternal cycle.

Just as God is the *pneuma* pervading the cosmos as a whole, so a human's soul is the *pneuma* pervading its body. This *pneuma* can be in varying degrees of tension. The *pneuma* in a physical object gives it its cohesion. The tenser *pneuma* in a plant gives it its life. Even tenser *pneuma* in animals gives them perception, and in humans higher levels of tension give consciousness and rationality. Thus the Stoics are able to give completely physical accounts of virtue, wisdom and reason, all of which are simply *pneuma* in the soul disposed in a certain state.

Stoic ethics begins with the idea that every animal desires its own self-preservation and strives always to preserve its own physical constitution. Consequently, an animal will always pursue whatever is good for it (or in accord with its own nature) and reject whatever is harmful. For an irrational animal these goods will be things such as food and shelter. For a rational animal, however, pursuing those things that preserve rationality will also become important; things such as wisdom and virtue.

For the Stoics, only virtue is (properly speaking) good and only vice is (properly speaking) bad. Virtue may be characterised as an excellent state of mind. Everything else, including wealth, health and other externals, is strictly speaking indifferent. While such material things may help one to exist merely as an animal, they get in the way of one existing as a perfected, rational animal. However, the Stoics acknowledge that while wealth may not have any intrinsic value, it is often better to be rich than poor. Thus they classify wealth as a preferred indifferent, and call poverty (along with illness and other nasty externals) a non-preferred indifferent. While there is nothing wrong with choosing wealth rather than poverty, it is not necessary in order to live well, and pursuing it should never get in the way of one's pursuit of virtue, which is sufficient on its own to secure happiness.

The Stoics are of course famous for their rejection of emotion. Emotional responses are the product of judgements that something bad has happened. But as external things have no intrinsic value, such judgements are a mistake. If a thief takes one's possessions then all one has lost are some preferred indifferents that are of no consequence. So long as one's virtue is intact, nothing bad has really happened, for only this has intrinsic value.

Stoic ideas influenced a number of the Church Fathers and remained in circulation during the Middle Ages, thanks to the readily accessible Latin works of Cicero and Seneca. The Renaissance led to increased interest in Stoicism as other sources came to light and Stoicism proved especially popular in the sixteenth and seventeenth centuries.

Contributor: John Sellars

# STRAW-MAN FALLACY

The tactic used in arguments to misrepresent the opponent's position – and then defeat it (the misrepresentation, that is). For example: all those who oppose drilling for oil in the Arctic would like to see cars abolished and the world returned to a feudal society. This is very silly. Therefore: drilling should be allowed as it is more in keeping with social reality.

**SEE ALSO**

Fallacies

# STRAWSON, PETER FREDERICK (1919–2006)

Sir Peter, the distinguished English philosopher who accused RUSSELL of confusing 'reference' with 'description', later produced what he dubbed a new 'descriptive metaphysics' as part of an effort to define individuals. This was set out in a book of that name, *Individuals*, in 1959. In his work on logic he returns to ARISTOTLE's assumption that to speak of a subject class, we can indeed assume it exists. In general, he attempts to remodel KANT's ideas in what he intends as a more logically rigorous manner.

## STREAM OF CONSCIOUSNESS

It was William JAMES who launched this metaphor on a sleeping world, at the end of the nineteenth century. The stream of consciousness is personal, seems to be forward in direction, continuous and always in a state of flux and change. The metaphor is there used to indicate that consciousness is just part of a wider 'sea' of ideas – this he dubs less memorably 'the fringe of consciousness'.

## STRUCTURALISM

Structuralism originated with the linguistic philosophy of Ferdinand de Saussure (1857–1913), whose work became fashionable in the second half of the twentieth century. Saussure's idea was that it is the structure of language, rather than the rules of logic, that explain how we think and speak. His notion of the 'sign' and of language as a system, called semiology, resurrected an older distinction between the structure of language, which he now called *langue*, and manifestations of *langue*, called *parole*. Chess can be used to illustrate this. The rules exist only in abstract, but their embodiment is a particular game. Language is a system of signs used to express ideas – comparable to writing, to sign language for deaf people, and to symbolic rituals. The sign, of course, is arbitrary. It is only the system that gives signs their meaning.

Claude LÉVI-STRAUSS rediscovered this structural linguistics and applied it to culture as a whole, as an anthropologist. He believed that since language was humanity's distinctive feature, it also defined cultural phenomena. If you speak of humanity you speak of language, and if you speak of language you speak of society. Structuralists looked below the surface of words to discover the hidden signifying system – the *langue*. All philosophical problems became problems of analysing systems of signs that structured the world. In this respect, the structuralists are harking back to the ancient Chinese 'School of Names' (*c*. 380 BC), a group of early logicians with an equally theoretical interest in the relationship of language and reality.

The structuralists offer an explanation of sorts for some of the PARADOXES mentioned in this book: what we know about the external world we apprehend through our senses. The phenomena we perceive have the characteristics we attribute to them because of the way our senses operate and the way the human brain is designed to order and interpret the stimuli that are fed into it. One very important feature of this ordering process is that we cut up the continua of space and time with which we are surrounded into segments so that we are predisposed to think of the environment as consisting of vast numbers of separate things belonging to named classes, and to think of the passage of time as consisting of sequences of separate events.

What started as a theoretical method for understanding language became an all-embracing philosophy. Everything, even the unconscious mind, was said to be structured like a language. Everything became predetermined and fixed. Later, the French philosopher, Michel FOUCAULT, developed a theory that power operates through complex social structures, which incorporated the view that far from knowledge and truth being fixed, they were constantly changing. He was in some respects the first post-structuralist.

Jacques DERRIDA attempted to pull down the entire structuralist edifice when he wrote that their creations were merely metaphysical imaginings. To look for a science of signs was as irrelevant, he said, as DESCARTES' suggestion that the body and soul ran together like two synchronised clocks. The way concepts have been used historically, and philosophy's claims to grapple with truth, are a pretence: the whole exercise is nothing but jiggery-pokery.

## SUBJECTIVITY

The poor handmaiden in philosophy to its much sought-after sister: objectivity. Søren KIERKEGAARD writes of the subjective truths of the heart, particularly those of passion, religious faith and 'unreasoning' commitment. Even the philosophies of DESCARTES, LOCKE, KANT and HEGEL, seeking 'objectivity', have all (reluctantly) admitted that their roots are in subjectivity. Recent CONTINENTAL PHILOSOPHERS, such as DERRIDA and FOUCAULT, have denied the existence of 'the subject', saying that what we imagine it to be is in fact a 'construction' – of politics and prejudices.

## SUFFICIENT REASON, PRINCIPLE OF

The principle can be traced back to MEDIEVAL PHILOSOPHY, but is best known in the form LEIBNIZ gave, namely: there can be found no fact that is true or existent, or any true proposition, without there being a sufficient reason for its being so, and not otherwise, although we cannot know the reason in most cases. Or, in sum: nothing is without a reason. Leibniz considered this to be one of the great principles of reasoning, along with the principle of 'non-contradiction'.

SCHOPENHAUER recognised the importance of the approach, saying that it requires us 'everywhere to search for the *why*'. And he gives four different kinds of acceptable explanation: the physical (changes explained by cause and effect); the logical (or analytic, where explanations consist of showing one thing 'entails' another); the mathematical (or geometrical); and the moral (where action is explained by referring to the motives lying behind it).

However, Schopenhauer criticised Leibniz for failing to distinguish in this way between 'reasons' and 'causes'.

## SUICIDE

Is there a right to take your own life, to decide when it should end? Or is there an obligation to others that overrides your personal preference? KANT accused would-be suicides of threatening the degradation of all humanity, by treating themselves in this way, specifically as things, rather than persons with their (he considered) inherent merits. But it is Thomas AQUINAS who gives the conventional arguments against suicide, explaining that suicide is 'altogether unlawful', as it is (a) unnatural (nature has designed animals to strive to live); (b) injurious to the community, and each individual is part of a community; and (c) as life is given by God, only God has the right to take it away. To do so oneself, he says warningly, is a sin.

HUME wrote an essay, 'On Suicide', challenging this, proclaiming suicide to be a right, and claiming in some circumstances suicide was a benefit to both the individual and the community – but he took care to leave the book unpublished until after his own death. Modern legal thinking tends to repeat these arguments to explain the decriminalisation of suicide.

## SYLLOGISM

See Logic (box), Arguments and argument types

## SYMPATHY

See Sentiment

## SYNTAX (AND SEMANTICS)

That part of the grammar of a language concerned with the correct arrangement, or structure, of words is called the syntax. It is opposed to the part concerned with the meaning of words or phrases, which is known as SEMANTICS. The phrase 'the beer what philosophers drink' is syntactically incorrect, although it may mean something, whereas the famous example (of Noam CHOMSKY) that 'colourless green ides sleep furiously' is syntactically correct, but is semantically deficient – it does not mean anything. . .

## SYNTHETIC JUDGEMENTS

Literally, synthetic means 'put together', which is why we use the word generally to mean 'artificial'. The task of finding the 'synthetic a priori' is created (along with the terms) in the introduction of KANT's *Critique of Pure Reason*. Here, a priori truths are defined as both independent of experience and absolutely certain and universal. The LOGICAL POSITIVISTS rightly complained that Kant was putting two terms together that were logically contradictory.

## *TABULA RASA*

From the Latin, meaning a 'blank slate'. 'Blank', for the STOICS and John LOCKE in particular, is the state of the human mind at birth. PLATO, however, thought there was information on the slate, waiting to be rediscovered as we grow older.

## TAGORE, RABINDRANATH (1861–1941)

The philosopher-poet-artist-critic-teacher *and* humanist aesthete who won a Nobel Prize for literature and refused a knighthood. Tagore's theme is that it is the 'universal I' enjoying the world that bestows on it beauty and value, and hence meaning. One who craves for the love of another remains 'unknown', but one who uses their powers of creativity becomes a king, able to communicate with the Cosmic Artist – which is God.

## TANTRA (SANSKRIT PHILOSOPHY)

Tantra are rituals and meditations. Tantra originated as part of the BUDDHIST development of YOGA, credited to NAGARJUNA in the second century CE. Tantric metaphysics aims to recreate the original primordial unity in the yogi's own body by ritual and meditation.

Tantric liturgy involves ritualistic practices with vestments, incense, chants, bells, symbols and construction of *mandala*. These are complex, mainly geometric drawings, often in vivid colours, portraying the cosmos. They are used both as instruction to the participants and inducement to the deities.

However, some sages feared that spiritual spontaneity and vigour had been lost; realisation was no longer possible for the masses, and the sources of spiritual life needed refreshment. Tara, the Earth Mother of ancient India, was reinvented as Sakti, the cosmic force. The eternal mystery of woman was explained by every woman being an incarnation of Sakti. Shiva, the third member of the Vedic triad, was recognised as present in every man as the passive principle of cosmic consciousness. Through repeated ritualised sexual union, realisation is achieved. All indulgences that build up erotic energy are beneficial in achieving this spiritual goal.

From the sixth century onwards, Tantra became a pan-Indian vogue throughout HINDU, Buddhist and JAIN society, by which time it had absorbed all the exotic and erotic connotations that made it irresistible. Currently, Tantra is more popular in the Far East than in India, where, since the eleventh century CE, Tantra has been tempered by VEDANTA.

## TAO AND TAOISM

The Tao is probably the central idea in CHINESE PHILOSOPHY, and its echoes are there in ancient Greek texts, too. Despite that, conventional Western philosophy refuses to acknowledge it as a serious historical theory. The ancient text of the *I Ching* (*c.* 900 BCE), or *Book of Changes*, is essentially an investigation of the Tao, and how to understand the world. Jung wrote of the *I Ching*, 'this is a book for lovers of wisdom', and so it is, but it is foremost a guide to action, a guide to achieving the best outcome in the circumstances. It has been used as a practical manual for action for the last 3000 years, consulted by farmers and generals as much as by emperors and sages. Chinese philosophies, in particular, regard thinking and acting as two aspects of one activity – two sides of the same coin. *T'ai Chi* – ultimate reality – is a combination of mind (*li*) and matter (*chi*), and the aim, ultimately, is to align yourself with the *Tao*. But what is the *Tao*? *Tao* is empty, LAO TZU wrote in the fourth chapter of the *Tao Te Ching* (350–250 BCE):

> . . . like a bowl, it may be used, but is never
> emptied, it is bottomless, the ancestor of all
> things, it blunts sharpness, it unties knots, it
> softens the light, it becomes one with the
> dusty world – deep and still, it exists for ever.

## TARSKI, ALFRED (1902–83)

The Polish logician who worked largely in the USA, where he eventually came up with the 'semantic theory of truth', exploring the nature of meaning. Presented in formal language, that is, in incomprehensible logical notation, it treats the particles 'is true' and 'is false' as part of a meta-language, that is, a language sitting above our normal language; all this intended as a way of avoiding the 'BARBER' (or Russell's) paradox.

## TAUTOLOGY

From the Greek, *tautos* (same) and *logos* (word), meaning 'same thing said'. In ordinary language, tautology is used as a technical term; in propositional logic, for compound expressions which take the truth-value True for all the different assignments of truth-values to its components. (As illustrated in an appropriate TRUTH-TABLE.)

In plainer language, tautologies are the saying of the same thing twice, only in different words. Sentences such as, 'It is either Saturday or Sunday or it is the weekend already', are tautologies, but so also are apparently meaningful ones such as 'snow is frozen water' or even the famous '2+2 = 4'. The ancient Greeks particularly liked geometrical truths, such as the reliable fact that the three angles of a triangle will add up to 180°, or that the square on th~

hypotenuse is equal to the sum of the squares on the other two sides. A lot of scientific 'knowledge' could be said to be tautologous too – water boils at 100°C (and 100 degrees centigrade is defined as the temperature that water boils at), while each molecule is made up of two hydrogen atoms and one oxygen atom.

WITTGENSTEIN identified tautologies as being particularly important for logic – in fact, he wrote that all truth in logic was tautology and that mathematical and logical proofs were just ways of identifying the tautology hidden in lots of essentially irrelevant subclauses.

## TELEOLOGY

The study of ends or final causes, hence the argument that suggests God exists as the world appears to have a purpose is sometimes called the 'teleological argument' (also known as the 'argument from design'). Much of ARISTOTLE's reasoning is based on seeking out the purpose or final 'end' of things, both abstract and mundane, and he was only following PLATO in spirit. The approach is opposed to the search for 'efficient' causes, or mechanisms.

## TERRORISM

Terrorism is a term freely used, for example to cover almost any activity, according to taste. The African National Congress, campaigning partly through violent action for majority rule by black South Africans, was denounced as 'terrorist' for years, up until the point when the South African government entered into negotiations to transfer power. Shortly afterwards, Nelson Mandela, the leader whom Margaret Thatcher, then UK Prime Minister, had firmly refused to countenance ever meeting, was given the Nobel Peace prize! And *mutatis mutandis*, the radical Jews behind the campaign to found Israel, whose policies specifically required creating terror among the resident Arab population, a terror achieved through indiscriminate bombings and assassinations, are now celebrated as the founding heroes of the nation which is determined to eliminate 'terrorists'.

Others might cite the 'terrorism' of China; Indonesia; Byelorussia; Uzbekistan; states of the Islamic world; or collapsing dictatorships in Africa. The list of governments and terrorist organisations guilty of serious violence and violation of human rights is long, and so the selection of the 'terrorists' becomes a political exercise.

But that is not to say that these are the only hypocrites: after all, the USA is the only country ever to be condemned by the UN for sponsoring terror, after its bloody 'covert' campaigns in South America in the 1970s and 1980s. The condemnation came not for any of the massacres carried out by its agents and proxies, nor for the killing of nuns or indeed Archbishop Romero in El Salvador (although that raised questions back home), but for the mining of the Nicaraguan harbours.

So in practice, 'terrorism' seems to be activities involving causing either harm or the apprehension of harm by any individual or group, with the exception of the kinds of harm caused by conventional State forces, such as the police, the secret police and the army. Terrorism is reduced to being political violence carried out by what have been termed 'sub-state groups'. Even if we accept that, though, since the term continues to be used to refer to 'deviant' States, it seems to be little more than a term of approbation, lacking any specific content.

Guerrilla armies who plant bombs in public places will generally be called terrorist, but if their intention is not to create fear in the 'enemy', but to disrupt, say, the economy of a government they wish to obtain a political concession from, then the creation of 'fear' is not necessary for their aims. However, if a State wishes to discourage a discontented minority from taking up sabotage and assassination activities in resistance against it, once the known 'terrorists' have been rounded up and imprisoned or executed, to create a fear of acting can become for some States the preferred tactic.

If we define terrorism to cover those actions intended not so much for their practical effect as for their calculated ability to create fear, and we add that this fear is to be instilled not in the minds of 'combatants' or governments, but in civilians or 'non-combatants', the term surely still has a purpose. And clearly, too, the greatest fears today are created by governments with their bombs and other weapons of mass destruction, or through their use of surveillance, torture and extrajudicial execution.

## Further reading

Gilbert, P. (2005) *New Terror, New Wars*

# THALES (OF MILETUS) (C. 625–545 BCE)

Thales has the honour of being counted as one of the Seven Wise Men of the Ancient World, credited with great mathematical and astronomical wisdom, which he was considered to put to good use. Among his achievements was predicting the eclipse of 585 BCE, which was almost total and took place during a battle. Another story, told by ARISTOTLE, recounts how he predicted a good season and so hired in advance all the olive presses in Miletus. When indeed there was a bumper crop he was able to hire them out at a considerable profit.

PLATO tells a different story in the *Theaetetus*, of a Thales so busy staring at the stars that he fell down a well, and was laughed at there by a passing Thracian serving girl.

Aristotle, however, credits Thales with pioneering the study of 'essences', the search for defining features of entities, over and above their unreliable surface attributes. Like Aristotle, Thales was prepared to do this by considering nature, rather than postulating theoretical entities. Thales concluded that the world was 'in essence' water, and that the human soul was a kind of magnet that had an invisible power to move the body.

# THOMISM

The system of philosophy and theology of St Thomas AQUINAS (1225–74) and his followers, which is essentially a Christian interpretation of ARISTOTLE's philosophy, part of SCHOLASTICISM. In spite of frequent assertions to the contrary, St Thomas is punctilious in differentiating between natural philosophy and theology, and his commentaries on Aristotle's texts are definitely works of philosophy. *De Anima* ends with the advice: 'Hence after the body's death the soul no longer knows anything in the same way as before. But how it does know anything then is not part of our present enquiry.' Eminent neo-Thomists of the twentieth century include Etienne Gilson (1884–1978), who, in addition to reinterpreting medieval philosophy for a modern readership, wrote on the interaction between philosophy and aesthetics; and Jacques Maritain (1882–1973), who promoted a renewal of Thomism with works such as *The Degrees of Knowledge* and *Redeeming the Time*.

# THOREAU, HENRY DAVID (1817–62)

Thoreau is counted, alongside Emerson, as one of the key figures of 'New England Transcendentalism', a view of the world in which nature is seen as offering absolute freedom and 'creative spontaneity', as opposed to human society, which is evil. Not surprisingly, he advocated CIVIL DISOBEDIENCE in many areas of political life, such as not paying taxes and disobeying unjust laws. This results in people going to prison, but also may act as the nucleus for a movement to create social change. His best known work, *Walden: or Life in the Woods* (1895), condemns most people for living superficially, pursuing wealth and following social customs, and advocates instead a kind of individualist ANARCHISM. He himself pursued a simple and self-reliant lifestyle, communing with nature on Brook Farm, an experimental alternative community.

# THOUGHT EXPERIMENTS

## The essential thought experiment

Thought experiments are theoretical hypotheses, intended to test out certain assumptions, through imagining a series of logically implied consequences, and to employ intuition to discover new information and create new relationships.

In a way, they are not all that different from 'real' experiments. They, too, test assumptions and rely on an intuitive stage in the design and origination of the experiments, although instead of 'thought' leading the scientist to a conclusion, events are observed and empirical measurements are made. The thought experimenter creates the apparatus out of words by describing the scenario and (like good scientists) outlining their assumptions. Their apparatus still needs to be set up, the ingredients still need to be supplied, even though the experiment ultimately proceeds courtesy of the power of imagination (guided by logic) when they begin to ask what will happen if. . .

## The laboratory of the mind

The ancient Greeks particularly liked to explore using the technique. HERACLITUS (*c.* 500 BCE) considered that as 'all is flux', it was only by the power of the mind, which can contemplate 'what is not', rather than by senses forever limited to examining merely what is, that the truly important things can be found.

For PLATO, as for Heraclitus, those wishing to understand phenomena in the natural world should recognise that experience of events was a poor guide. Plato's dialogues include Gyges with his magic ring exploring the nature of morality; the 'mad friend' hunting for his knife; and the (less well-known) 'breeding experiment' in which he advances the case for eugenics for the good of society; not to forget the metaphor, little agreed upon, of the prisoners in the CAVE, that seems to be telling us something about the nature of knowledge. Indeed, the entire process of the development of society outlined in the *Republic* is a carefully crafted thought experiment.

Even ARISTOTLE, who, like a certain kind of scientist, usually maintained the supremacy of observation, tried one or two thought experiments. In his *Metaphysics* (VII iii), for instance, he offers the experiment of two individuals, Plato and Socrates, having their 'nonessential' properties stripped away, leaving only their 'essence'. How many essences are there, he asks? One or two? The same sort of experiment has been repeated many times, in different guises, more recently by Bernard Williams and Derek Parfit.

Not all experiments stand the test of time equally well. PTOLEMY (87–150 CE), the inspiration of future mathematicians and geometers, as well as geographers and cosmologists, uses various arguments that sit somewhere between 'thought experiments' and real experiments. In particular, he argues that since all bodies fall to the centre of the universe, the Earth must be fixed there at the centre, otherwise falling objects would not be seen to drop towards the centre of the Earth; and that the Earth must be at the centre of the universe, completely motionless, as otherwise objects thrown vertically upwards would not fall back to the same place, but would fall back slightly to one side.

Ptolemy's record is not encouraging, but medieval philosophers enthusiastically employed thought experiments in their debating technique of 'challenges' or disputations. But it was the Renaissance that produced the richest crop of thought experiments, including those of GALILEO, DESCARTES, NEWTON, DARWIN, HUME and LEIBNIZ. These were thinkers whose interests lay in 'Natural Philosophy' and who considered that the best experiments work by making conscious and obvious what these assumed laws of nature really are. Descartes used the technique particularly enthusiastically, offering in his *Meditations* (1641) the original 'brain in a vat' scenario, along with a 'possible world' peopled by automata, another run by a malicious Demon (along with the general philosophical problem of whether we might all be dreaming) and, finally, the solitary introspection in the celebrated second *Meditation*, where he finds that he cannot even imagine thinking away thinking and so is led to the conclusion that the only certain thing is thought itself.

Galileo's ship argument, which simply asks us to imagine we are on a ship in a cabin observing goldfish that swim towards the front of their bowl and butterflies that continue their flight around the cabin entirely indifferent to the ship's motion, provided the foundations of relativity, and created a world in which dogmatic assertion began to weaken.

Sometimes (quite erroneously) the philosophical examination of thought experiments is only traced back to the Danish scientist, Hans Christian Oersted (1777–1851). Oersted saw them as not so much concerned with predictions or substituting for measurement, but as a tool for arriving at a better understanding of nature. For him, the value of the technique lay in first of all supposing some kind of 'law of nature' and then asking the experimenter to apply the law in a new – perplexing – setting.

Such is certainly the style of EINSTEIN's famous 'falling elevator' thought experiment. In this, Einstein imagines that a physicist has been drugged and wakes up in a box being pulled steadily upwards by a rope. Into this box a beam of light is projected. The 'elevator' as it became known, is designed to demonstrate the equivalence of constant acceleration and gravitational field effects, by showing that the light ray will appear to bend in both cases. In such musings lay the germ of the special theory of relativity. As he wrote later, 'from the very beginning it appeared to me intuitively clear that, judged from the standpoint of such an observer, everything would have to happen according to the same laws as for an observer who (relative to the earth) was at rest. For how, otherwise, should the first observer know, *i.e.* be able to determine, that he is in a state of fast uniform motion?'

Contributor: Martin Cohen

## Further reading

Cohen, M. (2004) *Wittgenstein's Beetle and Other Classic Thought Experiments*

# TIME
## Essentials of time

PLATO called time 'a moving image of eternity', which, although poetic, is not very helpful. ARISTOTLE discussed the nature of 'time' in more detail in his writings on 'Physics', saying that time is an effect of change in the material world. Since objects change in a smoothly continuous way, so, he deduced, must time be a continuum. Of course, as PLOTINUS pointed out shortly afterwards, this definition of time involves reference to the thing being discussed in the process, a feature of a bad definition. As Plotinus himself put it, 'Time is in every Soul of the order of the All-Soul, present in like form in all; for all the Souls are the one Soul'. This is why time has the character of encompassing everything, being one whole.

More recent philosophers have wondered about that strange quality of time whereby, in T.S. Eliot's phrase, it is a 'pattern of timeless moments'. Everything hinges on that infinitely brief moment of the present, the fountain where the river of time gushes out of nothingness, producing the bottomless lake of the past, and events, having swum into being and floated away, are eternally real, while the future does not exist at all.

## Contemporary issues in the philosophy of time

Attempts to characterise time seem to throw up paradox at every turn. Some of the most famous of the paradoxes are also the oldest – those due to Aristotle and ZENO, as described in Aristotle's *Physics*. For example, Zeno argued that in order to traverse any distance, one must always first traverse half that distance; but since this half is itself a distance to be traversed, one must in turn first traverse half of the half, and so on, ad infinitum. Since it is impossible to traverse an infinite number of distances in a finite time, all motion must be impossible – indeed, incoherent. A similar argument can be used to show that a line cannot be composed of a set of points, a problem which was only satisfactorily resolved with the development of the modern mathematics of infinity. A central question for the philosophy of time, then, becomes whether (and how) the mathematics of infinity applies to time.

Zeno was a student of PARMENIDES, and his paradoxes were designed to support the Parmenidean doctrine that reality itself is unchanging. Parmenides in turn had written largely in response to HERACLITUS, who had proposed that reality was permanently in flux. Contemporary issues in the philosophy of time have turned out to be continuous in many ways with this PRE-SOCRATIC concern with the reality of temporal change. The dispute can be framed in terms of where to locate the flow of time, metaphysically speaking – is it located in the world, or is it located in our experience of the world? We can refer to the former as the Heraclitean view of time and the latter the Parmenidean view of time.

A recent and influential Zeno-like argument in the Parmenidean tradition is due to John MCTAGGART. McTaggart began by distinguishing two ways in which times may be ordered. First, times may be ordered with respect to the present: one day ago, now, and one day from now, for example, into what McTaggart called the 'A-series'. Second, times may be ordered with respect to other times: one day before, simultaneous with, and one day later than, for example, into the 'B-series'. McTaggart argued that the 'A-series' is 'incoherent' – each time must at some point be each of past, present and future; and yet, these properties are incompatible with each other, since no time can be at once past, present and future. McTaggart further argued for a kind of error-theory about time: since notions of the present and of change are constitutive of our very concept of time, and since only the (incoherent) 'A-series' contains these notions, time itself does not exist.

A simpler argument against the Heraclitean view is that if time flows, it must flow at some particular rate. But this also seems 'incoherent' – rates are conventionally defined with respect to times, and it seems as unmotivated to say that time flows at one second per second as it does to say that space flows at one metre per metre. Alternatively, to appeal to some other dimension in which time flows, leads both to vicious regress and to questions of how this might be measured.

A different kind of challenge to the Heraclitean view of time is raised by the special theory of relativity in physics. According to that theory, simultaneity is defined relative to inertial reference frames, and moreover there seems no natural candidate for a privileged reference frame for the purposes of defining a unique global present. Relativity marks the first significant break between the scientific conception of time and our everyday experience of time, since without a uniquely defined notion of simultaneity we lose the objectivity of the present, and with it any objective distinction between the past and the future.

*Contributor: Brad Weslake*

## 'TO BE' (SPECIAL ROLE OF THE VERB)

How many ways can an 'is' be? RUSSELL declared it was a disgrace if you had more than one. Much better, he thought, to split up all the different ways of using the most important verb. There are then various different uses, which he tidily lists. Albeit his list is slightly different from that of ARISTOTLE, or AQUINAS, or DUNS SCOTUS. . .

## TOLERATION

There is a paradox of toleration, which is that you either tolerate the people who are themselves intolerant (aggressive, selfish, bigoted) or do not tolerate them, in order to stop them being intolerant. But then you yourself become a source of intolerance.

Politically, toleration became a key concept in the West during the European Wars of Religion, between Catholics and Protestants, where the price involved in imposing orthodoxy seemed to be less and less affordable, and the alternative of living in 'toleration' of religious differences became an acceptable political strategy. Today, religious toleration is still a key issue, with many Islamic authorities decreeing the death penalty for 'apostates' – Muslims who convert to Christianity. But in the Western 'democracies', religious toleration has become so obvious that it is unremarked (up to a point, of course), and the toleration debate has been extended to other areas in society instead, such as sexual mores and lifestyle. Philosophic advocates of tolerance include SPINOZA, LOCKE and, 'most tolerant of them all', John Stuart MILL.

## TORTURE

People have generally favoured the use of torture over the ages, interest in it confined merely to devising new and more horrible forms of it. Dungeons were part of the process too, ingeniously constructed to destroy the will of the prisoner. One in the Bastille in Paris was a downwards-pointing cone constructed so that it would be impossible to stand, let alone sit or lie down.

After confessions of misdeeds have been obtained through torture, a painful death is also the historical norm, with burning probably the most cruel and yet the most easily arranged. In 1252, the Church gave torture its seal of approval when Pope Innocent IV issued a papal bull authorising the setting up of the 'machinery for systematic persecution', the so-called Inquisition, as a way of obtaining confessions to heresy. Four years later, with licensed secular torturers struggling to keep up with demand, Pope Alexander IV authorised church officials to use torture too. For 12 generations the Inquisition did an imaginative job in providing an advance view of Hell for the people of Europe on earth too.

Even so, throughout the Middle Ages, there was one 'out-of-step' European country, England, which declined to adopt the use of torture as a judicial method – other than the 'pressing of prisoners' under heavy weights. Barbaro, a Venetian ambassador of the sixteenth century, observed that the English were concerned that torture of the innocent 'spoils the body and an innocent life', and strangely thought it better to 'release a criminal than punish an innocent man'!

Today, torture is alive and well in many countries. The British were found to be torturing suspects in Ulster. As part of the so-called 'War on Terror', memos (some now disowned) circulated in the US administration legitimising the use of torture as long as it did not (normally) cause major organ failure or death, and the US authorities allegedly fine-tuned methods such as sleep deprivation, beatings and sexual humiliation for use in special camps scattered around the world. Philosophically, the issue is one of UTILITARIAN arguments against rival approaches, notably those formulated in terms of HUMAN RIGHTS.

## TRANSCENDENTALISM

To 'transcend' something is to go beyond it and, in philosophy, transcendentalism is the search for and postulation of just such ambitious and obscure entities. God, the 'heavenly Forms' of PLATO, the HEGELIAN 'Absolute' are all 'transcendental'. Some philosophers, wishing to be tricky, have said that the material world is also transcendental, as we only know our 'sense data', and create the supposed world of objects, time, space, and so on, later. The New England Transcendentalists, like THOREAU, affirmed the essential goodness of humanity, and the perfect unity of the universe, nature and mankind, in contrast to the CALVINIST and other Christian views of man as flawed and sinful.

## TROTSKY, LEON (1879–1940)

Trotsky was actually called Lev Davidovich Bronstein, but like the best movie stars, he found a more memorable moniker. Second only to LENIN in the Russian Revolution, he should have succeeded him, had it not been for the alternative political philosophy of Josef Stalin, which involved dictatorial powers and eliminating all his opponents. (Stalin eventually had Trotsky killed in Mexico by an agent armed with an ice pick.) Had Trotsky been in charge, aficionados think he would have emphasised the need for global communist revolution and revolutionary violence, but also (perhaps in the spirit of 'the early' MAO) put a greater emphasis on creativity and education. Certainly, for a period, he defended the range of scientific enquiry against the Marxist orthodoxy of those who said it must proceed through a kind of dialectical progression.

## TRUTH

### Essentials of truth

'Truth' is always something of a problematic word in itself for philosophers, even if, in the *Republic*, PLATO cites truth as the virtue of the philosopher and the main aim of philosophy. For Plato, something was true if it describes things as they are (in the *Sophist* dialogue), a definition which has not been improved on, despite being entirely useless. This is also called the 'correspondence theory' of truth; whereas the 'coherence' theory says that something is true if it fits within a framework of other claims, for instance, as a 'true' mathematical statement does.

William JAMES offered as an alternative that something was true if it had useful consequences – the pragmatic theory – but even the most relativist among us have qualms about this approach. And that's not to mention truth values, of which there are normally two, being true or false, but some say there is also a third, 'undetermined' truth value (see SEA-BATTLE PARADOX).

### Frameworks for comprehending truth

Truth is a rather broad, bold and beautiful conception of reality in connection to humanity. As thinkers, knowers, believers and agents of their own actions, humans desire to know, to find, to will and to construct truths. There is truth in reality, name, number, logic, proposition and science. Various theories entail differing positions and perspectives on truth. First, for correspondence theory, truth is what is actually the case, and obtains in humanity, nature, objects and relations in the world. Under coherence theory, truth is human knowledge about the world, stemming from mental consciousness, linguistic abilities, skills and expertise. Such truth may refer to a complete, systematic vision of ultimate reality, based upon a divine being, or some basic, underlying substratum, or structure and ordering of reality. Alternatively, truth may be said to be nominal, 'ascribable' in name and in terminology only; or truth is logical and definitional in reference to the subject and object under investigation. Under common sense, consensus, pragmatic or willed theories, truth is a construction, a generalisation, a norm, an invention or a rule of thumb required to modify and guide practical, ethical and social behaviour.

These three frameworks for comprehending truth can be further divided into theoretical and practical branches. As is apparent from this short survey of options, the meaning, senses, value and utility of the question, theory and communication of truth engage all kinds of philosophies: metaphysics or ontology (theories of reality and being); epistemology (theories of knowledge and truth-conditions for knowledge); ethics; logic; aesthetics; politics.

One of the earliest Western philosophers, PARMENIDES of Elea (early fifth century BCE), conceived and worked out the meanings and reference of truth to reality in his long prose poem known as 'In the Way of Truth'. He proclaimed there that truth is 'what must be and cannot be otherwise'. That truth is the wholeness of being and reality he describes as the 'unshaken heart of well-rounded truth'. This whole – reality, being, truth – is the triad constituting the One eternal, unvarying and unwavering reality – the nature of all things.

Plato (427–347 BCE) transforms Western philosophy with his own triad of Truth, Beauty and the Good. As he describes it, truth acts like a shining light, revealing the world in goodness and beauty to humanity. Plato suggests that these three equally constitute and explain the complex unity of all being and reality. Truth, then, has often been intimately tied to other central ideas in the history of philosophy: necessity, goodness, beauty, utility and rightness.

Varieties of truth significantly manifest themselves also in imaginative, creative processes and symbolic forms, as in John Keats' insight in 'Ode to a Grecian Urn': 'Truth, Beauty, Beauty, Truth'. Other varieties are more human centred, as historical, temporal truths of the past, present and future, or as factual truths and truths of logic, definition, reasoning and scientific investigation. Human truths and truth-determination, truth-telling (and personal authenticity), seem intrinsically partial and limited in contrast to whole, enduring, unchanging, universal, religious or divine truths: truth, that is, from a God's-eye perspective.

Truth is subject to differing, even opposing, criteria and conditions for its determination, validation, justification and acceptance. David HUME (1711–76), in his empiricist philosophy of SCEPTICISM, denies that humans can know future truths with certainty, or produce necessary truth claims and true connections about ourselves and the external world, according to laws of science and nature, based upon past knowledge and experience.

Since NIETZSCHE at the end of the nineteenth century, the notion that all truth is 'perspectival' – that is, stemming from a subjective or contextual perspective – has been further developed in ways that are alternately restricted, sceptical or liberating. Truth is understood here as always an interpretation of the object in question, either contextual, that is, restricted and limited to the situation in which people find themselves when making claims about the way things are 'true' in context; or a 'consensual' point of view, as in contemporary CONTINENTAL PHILOSOPHY. And a third perspective, that truth is enlightenment, insight and wisdom, refers to objective truth, yielding correct assessment and reference to humanity, being itself, and the way things really are.

Closed concepts and conditions of truth are found in orthodoxy and dogma, in either religious or political systems, or similarly in systems of truth (biology, psychology) construed as the unchanging, ultimate, understanding of human thought and behaviour. God's truth is determinate, fixed, immutable and eternal. It regulates individuals as they live according to it by serving, administering and implementing truth by means of their life on earth. However, equally potent are those open theories of truth evident in history, science, language and culture, wherein truths change, and are subject to controversy, having other alternatives and options for behaviour, even conflicting ones. The weighing, balancing and compromising of one ethical truth, in terms of other truths, can lead to indifference or inherent doubt concerning whether there is any true determination about what is moral.

Given these disparate bases for discussing truth, its meanings and importance, ethical connections accompany the truth wherever it may be found, known and applied. Arguably, truth possesses coercive power. After all, the truth is claimed to be the real, proven, correct thing; hence, it cannot or should not be denied. As such, truth imposes itself on our being and knowing of reality. This rendition of the truth is not open to dispute, consent and agreement; rather it is imposed and enforced upon humans in order to act and to be in their world. Truth may thus be constricting and confining humanity inside both open and closed systems of analysis, government, culture and religion, given their conditions placed upon us in daily life and behaviour.

In a separate vein, personal or collective truths, under open or closed systems, may be sincerely held with enthusiasm; truths of the heart and soul, so to speak: loving, seeking, following, and enacting truth. As a result, humans may effectively implement their novel and visionary truths. Seeking and finding truth for oneself and others seems constitutive of human subjectivity and realities.

We may disagree about whether truth should or should not trump desirable values and worthwhile ideals, like goodness, utility, beauty, justice, love, peace, prosperity and happiness. Yet, even partial truths, and truth itself as a central ideal, can and do result in advancing other enduring values. This is testimony to the power of truth. Through personal and collective commitment and action to the truth (Joan of Arc; King Arthur; Emma Goldstein; Mohandas **GANDHI**; Martin Luther King), truth as a human-made, or divinely inspired construction, enters the world. Thought, will and behaviour process and achieve truth in our participatory human relationship with reality.

Contributor: Mary Lenzi

## TRUTH TABLES

A truth table is a way of setting out all the possibilities of a statement (or of several statements comprising an argument). For philosophers, it offers an alternative way to investigate whether an argument is 'valid' or not, but the technique has powerful applications for computer programming and 'the real world' too. Since no matter how complicated the logical argument is, each component part of it has only two possible values, that is, it is either true or it is false, it is possible, albeit rather time-consuming, to tabulate every single possibility. (So we will not do anything complicated here.)

The table below represents that most important philosophical concept of 'implication', if P then Q. If it is the day of the logic test, then the classroom will be half empty, for instance. On the left are the four possible arrangements of P and Q, when P is true and Q is true, when P is true but Q is false, and so on. On the right are the values P-> Q takes.

Clearly, if P is true, Q should have been true too. On the other hand, if 'P is false', we do not really know anything about the truth or otherwise of the statement 'if P then Q', so it counts

| P | Q | P ⇨ Q |
|---|---|---|
| T | T | T |
| T | F | F |
| F | T | T |
| F | F | T |

here as 'true'. If pigs can fly, then the moon is a balloon. In logic, the only time an implication is said to be false is when the first term, P, is true, and yet the second term, Q, is false. Put like that, it all sounds rather complicated, and that is why truth tables, unwieldy or not, have a certain intrinsic elegance and appeal.

## TURING MACHINE

Alan Turing (1912–54) was primarily a mathematician, but was enlisted in the Second World War into code-breaking as part of the British war effort. At Bletchley Park, the German Enigma Machine had been captured, but even so, to decode messages required the mechanical processing of tens of thousands of possible settings. Turing thus was in the forefront of computing. But in fact, the so-called 'Turing Machine' (also sometimes called the 'Universal Machine') was described before the war (while he was a lecturer at London University) in a paper in 1936 addressing a challenge by the German mathematician David **HILBERT**, as to whether it was possible to convert the procedures for solving mathematical questions into a series of simple instructions. The idea is not at all mechanical but simply logical. A machine with a read/write head like a computer is generally imagined, but more simply, it could equally well be a person with a very long (strictly, an infinitely long) notepad, and a perpetually writing pen. Turing demonstrated that if the person reads off a single symbol at a time, and (depending on what it is) either leaves it on the pad and turns the page to read the next symbol, or rubs it out and writes a new symbol down, or occasionally even backtracks one page and changes the symbol written there, then, it turns out, they can indeed solve mathematical problems. And long-windedness, of course, is no problem for computers. The usual choice of symbol is between a '0' and a '1', but this of course, like the design of a computer, is arbitrary. The key thing, though, is the rules they are following in deciding which course to take – to read another symbol, to write a different one down, to backtrack. Turing demonstrated that – given the right rules and this simple procedure – a lot could be done 'mechanically', but he also left open the question of how to decide the rules. On the face of it, it needs some creativity.

So, not surprisingly, Turing also explored how a machine could generate creative solutions, and described an early kind of 'neural network' using pieces of paper. Neural networks are used today to perform tasks like fingerprint recognition, or to spot counterfeit banknotes. Unlike conventional programs, which consist of a long list of 'rules' for various circumstances (like a Turing Machine), their characteristic is that they have only a handful of simple 'rules', but 'teach themselves' as a result of practical testing and feedback, thereby evolving apparently sophisticated criteria for decisions.

Turing, like many contemporary 'cognitive scientists', thought this was how the human brain worked too. We may have some rules 'biologically wired in', but the bulk of our ability to think is developed through interacting with the environment and getting feedback. The Turing Machine also shows a way for simple processes to become complex ones, in the manner of biological and chemical signals in the brain being part of something much more.

## 'TWIN EARTH' (PUTNAM'S THOUGHT EXPERIMENT OF)

A well-known thought experiment about a planet, 'Twin Earth', which is identical to ours except that the water on it has a different chemical composition. It is drinkable, looks like water and does everything else that water normally does. Is it water? The 'inventor' of the experiment, Hilary Putnam, says not, and the fact that the inhabitants of Twin Earth call it 'water' shows that being water is something more than what people think. Anyway, it is a 'thought', is it not?

**SEE ALSO**

Thought experiments

## TYPES (RUSSELL'S THEORY OF)

See Russell.

## UNAMUNO, MIGUEL DE (1865–1936)

Unamuno was a Spanish philosopher and poet who felt that life probably had no purpose, but that it was nonetheless important to behave as if

it did (like Don Quixote, or even Jesus, as he says). He wrote the *Tragic Sense of Life* (1913) on the eve of the First World War, and died as Hitler came to power in Germany to launch the Second.

## UNCERTAINTY PRINCIPLE (HEISENBERG'S)

The uncertainty principle is very popular with philosophers, seeming to offer a little hole in the edifice of science. Coined by the physicist, Werner HEISENBERG (1901–76), co-founder with Erwin Schrodinger of modern quantum physics, it puts a limit on the accuracy with which one can specify the position and momentum of subatomic particles. (Loosely speaking, of course.) He allows that you might be able to specify one precisely, but not the other. Heisenberg saw this as affecting our ability to predict the future behaviour of particles, and hence the future generally. The phenomena of atomic physics are still 'real', but the elementary particles themselves are shadows. They are merely potentialities and possibilities in a world of probabilities.

---

**UNCERTAINTY**

In the experiments of atomic physics we have to do with things and facts, with phenomena that are just as real as any phenomena in daily life, but the atoms or the elementary particles themselves are not as real; they form a world of potentialities or possibilities rather than one of things or facts.

(Werner Heisenberg (1958), *Physics and Philosophy*)

---

The principle is intended as a refinement to the 'semi-classical' model of Planck, EINSTEIN and Bohr.

## UNCONSCIOUS (AND SUBCONSCIOUS)

Although FREUD is generously credited with 'discovering' the unconscious mind, there are many allusions to it from classical times to the present. The slave boy, Meno, in PLATO's dialogue of the same name, is supposedly using his 'subconscious' to retrieve lost knowledge of geometry. But it is in the German philosophy of the nineteenth century that the notion is really explored. Freud says that the unconscious has desires of which we are unaware 'consciously', but which drive our behaviour. He disliked the term 'subconscious', which he felt confused things (as I have just done, subconsciously).

## UNDECIDABILITY

Undecidability, in maths and for DERRIDA, is a recognition that if two theories both work, it is arbitrary to choose one over the other.

## UNDISTRIBUTED MIDDLE

The 'middle' is a technical term in the theory of categorical SYLLOGISMS. It designates the one and only term that occurs once in each of the two premisses, as 'pretty' does here: All cats are pretty; this dog is pretty – *therefore!* – this dog is a cat.

SEE ALSO

Logic

## UNIVERSAL DECLARATION OF HUMAN RIGHTS

A '*Magna Carta* for mankind'. On 10 December 1948, with key roles played by such as Mahatma Gandhi and Eleanor Roosevelt, the United Nations approved in Paris a Universal Declaration of Human Rights stating that:

All human beings are born free and equal
in dignity and rights.

The Declaration is sometimes said to be both the most quoted and most ignored international document of modern times. (Eleanor Roosevelt called it 'a *Magna Carta* for mankind', referring to the document obtained by the English aristocrats from King John in 1215, which, by setting limits on the Crown's powers also set out certain 'rights' for the people.) The Declaration, much of which has been translated into national laws around the world, shuns discrimination, slavery, torture, arbitrary arrest or exile. Since its signing, millions of people have died in massacres such as those in Cambodia, Rwanda and Bosnia. In many countries, inhabitants are denied the most basic civil liberties, in spite of the fact that Article 25 states:

Everyone has the right to a standard of
living adequate for the health and well-
being of himself and his family . . .

Evidently, the world is still far from ready to move from rhetoric to action regarding the declaration's pronouncements on economic rights.

> **ELEANOR ROOSEVELT**
>
> Eleanor Roosevelt (1884–1962), who was the wife of President Franklin Delano Roosevelt, largely created the role in American politics of 'First Ladies', and was a champion of human rights (resigning, for example, from the *Daughters of the American Revolution* after the organisation barred black singer Marian Anderson from performing at Constitution Hall). At a time when extreme racism (for example, segregation and lynchings) was commonplace in the USA, she was a board member of the National Association for the Advancement of Colored People (NAACP).
>
> After her husband's death, she served as a UN delegate and became the first chair of the UN Commission on Human Rights. She, like the philosopher Jacques Maritain, played a key role in drafting the Universal Declaration of Human Rights and used her influence to help secure its adoption.

According to UN figures, at the turn of the millennium, 1.5 billion people subsisted on less than $1 a day.

As Mary Robinson, the Irish Human Rights Representative put it, add up '50 years of human rights mechanisms, 30 years of multibillion-dollar development programs and endless high-level rhetoric, and the global impact is quite underwhelming'. She also noted that the Declaration has up to now made little impact on the lives of millions of women in developing countries.

## UNIVERSALS

Universals are terms like 'golden' or 'warm'. SOCRATES is a universal too, if we want to use it as such; for example, we could say that Zenon Stavrinides, the contemporary philosopher, is the 'Socrates of the North'. The 'problem' about them is discussed by PLATO at length, for example in *Cratylus*, where it is suggested to Socrates that all such terms are a matter of convention arising from the chance choices of actual use. Socrates, of course, will have none of this, insisting that there is a 'real' 'gold' thing and a real 'warm' thing too, which is where the 'forms' come in, the entities that our approximate judgements relate to.

SEE ALSO

Plato (on 'the forms')

## *UPANISHADS*

Like the more ancient and sacred *Vedas*, the *Upanishads* originated as oral tradition, in the form of metrical aphorisms, or *Sutras*. The name comes from three words, meaning 'sit down and listen closely'.

The *Upanishads* are speculative works, full of ontological uncertainty:

Nobody knows the source of the cosmos
whether it is created or always was.
He who looks down from the highest heaven
only he knows, or maybe he doesn't.

Some of them are in the form of riddles, like the story of ten people, none of whom can ever find the tenth, because they forget to count themselves. Others are parables, like the tale of the son of a prostitute who always spoke the plain truth, and was thus promoted to the highest caste.

## UTILITARIANISM

The most 'useful' ethical principle for considering the consequence of actions is that of utilitarianism – although in a very real sense it is not an ethical principle at all.

It is usually ascribed to Jeremy BENTHAM in the eighteenth century, but in fact, in the Platonic dialogue the *Protagoras*, a suggestion is made that what is needed is the ability to weigh up the pleasures against the pains likely to result from an activity (or catalogue) – an early kind of 'hedonic calculus', in fact. (*Hedone* being Greek for pleasure – we have the word 'hedonist' still in common usage.)

Utilitarianism was formulated by Jeremy Bentham as saying that the right action is the one that brings about the greatest happiness of the greatest number: the general happiness is the best thing. John Stuart MILL (1806–73) adopted this theory and specifically rejected alternative moral theories, arguing that they represented the interests of the ruling class, and not justice at all. Those who taught the virtue of a life of sacrifice, Mill wrote, wanted others to sacrifice their lives to them. Mill and Bentham say that people desire to be happy, and that this is actually the only thing they desire. When various people's desires conflict, the utilitarian theory weighs up the consequences and decides which action produces the greater happiness.

However, the ancient Greeks could not agree on that. While some, like the astronomer Eudoxus, claimed that 'pleasure' was the sole good (all other things that we consider good are so only because in some way they increase the amount of pleasure), Speusippus, on the contrary, held that pleasure (and pain) were two sides of the same thing – and that thing was evil. Utilitarianism thus is a way of maximising the amount of evil in the world.

## VALIDITY

In LOGIC, an argument is 'valid' only when it is impossible for all its assumptions (premises) to be true, and the conclusion false. This gives the reassurance that if you are sure your assumptions are true, then the conclusion does indeed follow from the argument – unarguable, as it were. This is an attractive notion to everyday folk, and so the term 'valid' is often appealed to in the most inappropriate contexts, for example, individual points of view, and even mere factual claims (as opposed to chains of reasoning), are sometimes said to be 'valid'.

## VALUES

'Values' were at the heart of ancient Greek philosophy, with interest not only in ethical values, but also in the aesthetic values of form, the 'golden mean', the 'heavenly spheres' and the elegance generally of truth and mathematics. PLATO is unusual in that his investigation of ethical values, the search for the 'good', knowledge of which colours all other judgements, predominates. But there are also 'instrumental values', the usefulness of something as a 'means to an end' and 'intrinsic values' – that is 'as an end in itself'. G.E. MOORE thought that the intrinsic value of something, say a TV, would remain, even if everything else in the world disappeared.

## *VEDANTA* **AND THE** *VEDAS*

The *Vedanta* are philosophical speculations and practices based on the ancient Indian texts, the *Vedas*, which include the *UPANISHADS*. The term means 'the end of the *Vedas*', while *Vedas* itself comes from the Sanskrit *vid*: to know.

The *Vedas* are recognised as revealed wisdom

by **HINDUS**, **BUDDHISTS** and **JAINS**. Often called The Hymns of Divine Knowledge, the dates of the *Vedas* are not certain, but it is thought the oldest were composed between 1500 and 1000 BCE. The style of the *Vedas* records hymns that reveal nomads leading a pastoral lifestyle:

Indra, joy of ancestral voices,
like cool waters to parched dry throats,
send food to us who sing your praises,
take us to a safe place with flowing streams.

Nowadays, *Vedanta* is used to signify the prevailing system of **INDIAN PHILOSOPHY**, while in everyday Indian parlance *Vedanta* has come to mean philosophical discussion generally, and its adherents are known as *Vedantins*. Of the many schools of *Vedanta* philosophy, the most celebrated are the *Sankhya* system, which denies the existence of God; the **ADVAITA**, which maintains there is nothing but God; and the *Vishishta Advaita*, which is a qualified monotheism. Vedanta arises out of *Uttara Mimamsa*, a philosophical system using the collection of *Vedanta Sutras* put together in the fourth century CE by Bandarayana.

As *Vishishta Advaita* is the prevailing school of Indian Philosophy, it and *Vedanta* are commonly regarded as the same thing. Ramanuja, an eleventh-century sage from southern India, wrote the texts based on the *Vedanta Sutras*, which are the source books of *Vishishta Advaita*. For Ramanuja, God, soul and matter make up the universe and are interdependent. God is essential to all existence, but soul and matter have separate existence. The object of life is deliverance from the cycles of births and deaths, but the liberated soul retains its individuality, as in Christianity and Islam, but unlike Hinduism and Buddhism generally.

However, the practices are like the rest of Hinduism and Buddhism. Deliverance is achieved by *Karmayoga* (right activity) and *Jnanayoga* (knowledge), tempered by *Bhakti* – loving devotion to the personal and benevolent God, or better still by *Papapatti* – total surrender to God. *Vedanta* is a doctrine readily understood and accepted, providing a personal God to whom the devotee can pray and from whom forgiveness can be received.

*Vedanta*'s similarity to Christianity may arise from the penetration of Christianity into southern India, Ramanuja's homeland, at the time he was developing his ideas. Be that as it may, *Vedanta* provided India with a native philosophy comprehensible to those from Western Europe, who were later to rule India, and from whom India eventually wrested its independence under the leadership of **GANDHI**.

**SEE ALSO**

Indian philosophy

# VEGETARIANISM
## Essentials of vegetarianism

Vegetarianism (that range of human diets, from those who will eat only the seeds of plants, to those who allow honey, eggs, milk and cheese, and even fish and birds, but hesitate at mammals) is not an issue accorded much space in standard encyclopaedias of philosophy, even if it has come to be recognised as part of debates over 'animal rights'. Yet vegetarianism occupies a central position in early Eastern and Western philosophy, when it was often linked to the concept of **REINCARNATION**. However, vegetarianism was also advocated as the natural human diet.

**PLUTARCH**, however, was one of the few writers in the ancient world to advocate vegetarianism for other reasons, and his essay 'On Eating Flesh' is considered a literary, if not a philosophical, classic. Warning that meat eating corrupts morals, he challenges the 'flesh-eaters', who insist that nature has intended them to be predators, in that case to kill their meals for themselves – and eat the raw meat uncooked, with their bare hands.

'Oh, my fellow men!' exclaimed Pythagoras.
'Do not defile your bodies with sinful foods.
We have corn. We have apples bending
down the branches with their weight, and
grapes swelling on the vines. There are
sweet flavoured herbs and vegetables which
can be cooked and softened over the fire.
Nor are you denied milk or thyme-scented
honey. The earth affords you a lavish supply
of riches, of innocent foods, and offers you
banquets that involve no bloodshed or
slaughter.'

## A brief history of meat eating

Nowadays, we are all used to the idea of humans eating meat, but that is not to say the activity is in evolutionary terms a very old one. Baron Cuvier, who established the sciences of palaeontology and comparative anatomy, wrote:

The natural food of man, judging from his structure, appears to consist principally of fruits, roots and other succulent parts of vegetables. His hands afford every facility for gathering them; his short but moderately strong jaws on the other hand and his canines being equal only in length to the other teeth, together with his tuberculated molars would scarcely permit him either to masticate herbage, or to devour flesh, were these condiments not previously prepared for cooking.

Yet dentition and aeons of behaviour are no barrier to radical change of diet. Horses have been trained to eat meat and sheep have become so accustomed to it as to refuse grass.

Killing and eating animals is held to be the natural state of affairs for mankind by most of the world's religions. In Genesis, Yahweh gave man absolute rights over animals. This God, it seemed, favoured the slaughter, cooking and savouring of animals, especially lambs. The Temple at Jerusalem must have been a vast slaughter house that ran with blood and molten fat at Passover. The stench of barbecued flesh would have hung over the Temple permanently, pleasing both human and divine nostrils.

Zarathrustra was the most likely initiator of vegetarianism. His exact dates are unknown, but were early sixth century BCE. He spent his youth in Media but moved to Khorosan, where he was assassinated. He held that:

■ horticulture with the rearing and caring for animals are all that is noble in life,
■ for all time there are opposing spirits of Good and Evil, and that giving Life or condemning to Non-Life is the fundamental dualism, and that
■ air, water, fire and earth are pure elements never to be defiled.

On these principles Zarathrustra based a vegetarian, teetotal, pacifist lifestyle, using animals solely for transport and watering his sacred and wholly horticultural state in Eastern Iran, where he settled after being driven from his native Media.

The paradise gardens of Persia, full of edible ornamental fruit and vegetables, originated with this culture. Many edible plants were introduced from China, which Lauffer in 'Sino-Iranica' identifies from later documents and common derivation of names.

Zarathrusta's ideas spread east and west with travellers on the land trade route that Alexander later followed from the Hellespont across the Iranian Plateau to the Indus Valley. His influence in the Persian empire was disseminated from the teaching centre in Babylon.

Babylon was ruled, among others, by various of the Archaemenian great kings, early members of which dynasty had harboured Zarathrusta in Khorosan. The Hanging Gardens of Babylon, in Philo of Byzantium's late third-century account, were long established areas of cultivation, with workers ploughing fields and an abundance of fruit and vegetables. The Jews were taken to Babylon in 586 BCE and released by Cyrus in 537 BCE, when a minority chose to return to Jerusalem.

The Bible at Genesis 1:29 has God instruct:

'Kill neither men, nor beasts, nor yet your food which goes into your mouth. For if you eat living food, the same will quicken you, but if you kill your food, the dead food will kill you also. For life comes only from life, and death comes always from death. For everything which kills your food, kills your bodies also . . . And your bodies become what your foods are, even as your spirits, likewise, become what your thoughts are.'

Yet the God who said that was Ahura-Mazdah, the God of Zarathrustra, not Yahweh, the God of Abraham and Isaac.

In any case, of course, Adam and Eve are then ejected from their paradise garden a little later in the Bible, and the thinking in Genesis 1:29 quietly forgotten. In practice, Judaism, Christianity and Islam have all perpetuated the notion of meat-eating as the natural state for mankind. The Chinese shared with Semites and Aryans generally an acceptance of eating meat, but preferred to live more harmoniously with nature. Curiously enough, even **BUDDHISM**, which along with those parts of **HINDUISM** and **JAINISM** based upon it, is the only worldwide vegetarian religion, allows within it a strand – Tibetan Buddhism – which sanctions meat-eating as the 'practical' choice for the region.

**PYTHAGORAS** of Samos travelled too, first to the Greek teachers of his age, then to Egypt and after to Babylon, where he came into contact with Zoroastrianism. After staying briefly back home on Samos he went to Crotona, one of the richest of the Greek cities of Southern Italy, and set up his Academy there. Remembered now as a mathematician and music theorist as well as a philosopher, he then attracted large numbers of

## PLUTARCH ON EATING FLESH

Plutarch warms to his theme:

It all began the same way that tyrants began to slaughter men. At Athens the first man they put to death was the worst of their informers, who everyone said deserved it. The second was the same sort of man, and so was the third. But after that, the Athenians were accustomed to bloodshed and looked on passively when Niceratus, son of Nicias, and the general Thramenes, and Polemarchus the philosopher were executed. In the same way the first animal was killed and eaten was a wild and mischievous beast, and then a bird and a fish were caught. And murder, being thus tried and practised upon creatures like these, arrived at the labouring ox, and the sheep that clothes us, and the cock that guards our house. And little by little, our desires hardening, we proceeded to the slaughter of men, wars and massacres.

Can you really ask what reason Pythagoras had for abstaining from flesh? For my part I rather wonder both by what accident and in what state of soul or mind the first man did so, touched his mouth to gore and brought his lips to the flesh of a dead creature, he who set forth tables of dead, stale bodies and ventured to call food and nourishment the parts that had a little before bellowed and cried, moved and lived. How could his eyes endure the slaughter when throats were slit and hides flayed and limbs torn from limb? How could his nose endure the stench? How was it that the pollution did not turn away his taste, which made contact with the sores of others and sucked juices and serums from mortal wounds. . .

## THE ENVIRONMENTAL COST OF MEAT

Today's meat eaters, or more precisely meat producers, are the number one industrial polluters, contributing to half the water pollution in the USA, responsible for the poisoning of rivers all over the world and even the slow death of the seas as wetlands disappear and poisons accumulate. The water that goes into a thousand-pound steer could float a destroyer. It takes 25 gallons of water to produce a pound of wheat, but 2500 gallons to produce a pound of meat. Remarkably, the livestock population of the USA alone today consumes enough grain and soybeans to feed over five times the entire human population. American cows, pigs, chicken, sheep, and so on, eat up 90 per cent of the country's wheat, 80 per cent of the corn, and 95 per cent of the oats. Less than half of the harvested agricultural acreage in the USA is for human consumption. Most of it is used to grow livestock feed. How natural is that?

followers who adopted his vegetarian lifestyle as an integral part of his teaching.

**PLATO** is a source of information on Crotona, which he visited on his tour of the teaching centres of his age. Ovid's crucial reference in The Doctrines of Pythagoras – 'Those accustomed to abominate the slaughter of other animals think it more unjust to kill a man or to engage in war' – is evident in Plato's thinking in the *Republic.*

An economic link between flesh-eating and war can also be found in Plato's *Republic*. Plato records a dialogue between **SOCRATES** and Glaucon in which Socrates extols the peace and happiness that come to people eating a vegetarian diet. The citizens, Socrates says, will feast upon barley meal and wheat flour, making 'noble cakes', as well as salt, olives and cheese, 'for relish', all served on a mat of reeds. For dessert, some roasted myrtle berries or acorns, even boiled figs and roots. These are the foods of peace and good health: 'And with such a diet they may be expected to live in peace and health to a good old age, and bequeath a similar life to their children after them.'

Vegetarianism, however, was not favoured by Plato's pupil, **ARISTOTLE**, who held that animals exist to be useful to mankind. As Aristotle's thinking in many matters could be squared with that of the Bible and its derivative the Koran, his philosophy was the most influential on the development of first Islam and then Christianity during the Middle Ages.

Duality as a religious principle continued on in Roman times as the MANICHEAN faith and in Christendom as the Manichean heresy, taking vegetarian lifestyles with it. The Manichean heresy, called the Albigensian heresy in France, continued with the Cathars, who were ruthlessly exterminated by noble Norman knights sent by the Church to assist St Dominic with his missionary work. Vegetarianism was subsequently used by the inquisition to identify heretics.

It was left to Shelley to rediscover Plato and Ovid as guides to lifestyle and compassion for man and beast. He was avant-garde to the modern vegetarian and humanist movements.

Contributors: Colin Kirk and Martin Cohen

## VEIL OF IGNORANCE

See Rawls.

## VERIFICATION

To verify something is, strictly speaking, to establish it as being true. Verification as an approach is associated with the logical positivists, who held that the meaning of a statement is connected to what would count as evidence for it being true. The logical positivists noted that for some statements there was no conceivable way to 'verify' them, and hence they decided that these sorts of claim must be literally 'meaningless'.

SEE ALSO

Logical positivism

## VICE, GIAMBATTISTA (1668–1744)

In *Scienza Nuova* (*The New Science*, 1744) the Italian philosopher offers an alternative to the 'enlightenment' view of the nature of knowledge, as epitomised by René DESCARTES with his introspection for clear and distinct ideas. Vice says that truth and certainty are created by the actions we take in investigating them. Mathematics is certain because we have constructed the systems to be certain, and physical experiments produce findings as a result of the way the experiments are designed in the first place. But above all, human beings construct their own history, producing an apparently factual narrative out of a mythological past. Every nation follows a cycle of three stages: the divine, the heroic and the rational. Understanding this implies that the methods of human sciences are different from the methods of natural science.

Vice's views have been influential – particularly in the areas of history and SOCIAL SCIENCE.

## VIENNA CIRCLE

See Logical positivism.

## VIRTUES

Literally, a 'virtue' is a property, but one that is not so much actual as potential. Opium, famously, has the 'dormitive virtue'. And a good person has the virtue of being kind to animals in that when they see an animal, they are kind to them.

Not, of course, that everyone agrees on virtues, just as not everyone agrees on what is 'good' either. In the twelfth century, Moses MAIMONIDES, the Spanish-North African rabbi-philosopher (1155–1204), advised in his *Guide to the Perplexed* (*c.* 1190) that virtue is simply a means of becoming good at following the religious code.

And virtues like those ARISTOTLE would attach so much importance to, such as being 'balanced', honourable, magnificent, and so on, were for the STOICS only valuable inasmuch as they may assist someone to achieve harmony with the world as it is. Even the difference between 'virtue' and 'vice' is not very important. This is because both are intellectual states. Virtue is the result of the appliance of the science of the good, the activity of the wise. Vice is the result of allowing an excessive role of the passions, leading to errors of judgement.

But later on, the Christian virtues harked back to something not unlike the Socratic ones: justice, prudence, temperance, fortitude, faith, hope and charity. Crucially, virtue, for SOCRATES and for Christians, is truly its own reward. Yet even here, Aristotle comes to a different conclusion. His 'Magnanimous Man', sometimes called the 'great-souled' man, or the 'magnificent' man, who is virtuous in the sense of being excellent in all he does, is proud of it, too.

After all, '. . . greatness in every virtue would seem to be characteristic of a proud man. And it would be most unbecoming for a proud man to fly from danger, swinging his arms by his sides, or to wrong another; for to what end should he do disgraceful acts, he to whom nothing is great?', Aristotle explains in the *Nicomachean*

## Table of Virtues and Vices or 'The Goldilocks Table'

| Sphere of applicability | too much | too little | 'just right' |
| --- | --- | --- | --- |
| fear | rash | cowardly | courageous |
| pleasure | licentious | 'cold fish' | temperate |
| spending | prodigal | stingy | generous |
| honour | vain | pusillanimous | magnanimous |
| anger | irritable | lacking spirit | patient |
| expressiveness | boastful | humble | truthful |
| conversation | buffoonery | boorish | witty |
| social skills | flatterer | cantankerous | friendly |
| social conduct | shy | shameless | modest |
| view of others | envious | malicious | lofty and superior |

(as described in the *Nicomachean Ethics*, Book II 1107b 18–20)

*Ethics*, the key text often referred to these days in the elaboration of so-called 'Virtue Ethics' (seen as an alternative to the otherwise all-pervading UTILITARIAN ethics).

As the Greek word *arete* ('virtue') is a quality related to being good at doing things, and is not just about 'virtuous' intentions as we nowadays understand it (although there is still a shared emphasis on 'how to be' over 'what to do'), it is to be expected that any virtuous man would be tall, and handsome and strong too. We still respect this cultural value in our celebration of the Olympic champions.

Further, a slow step is thought proper to the proud man, a deep voice, and a level utterance; for the man who takes few things seriously is not likely to be hurried, nor the man who thinks nothing great to be excited, while a shrill voice and a rapid gait are the results of hurry and excitement.

For part of virtue for Aristotle is finding the 'golden mean' in (nearly) all things. Actually, the oriental philosophers put it more radically, saying that *nothing* is all bad, and *nothing* is all good, but Aristotle allows that some things (justice, for example) are always good. 'Magnanimous Man' is angry 'in the right way, at the right time', considers those who aim 'at being pleasant with no ulterior object' obse-quious; the others irreconcilably 'churlish and contentious'. The next best thing to being 'Magnanimous' is to be 'Mock-modest', to understate things and 'speak not for gain but to avoid parade'; disclaim reputation, 'as Socrates used to do'.

# VISUALISATION

## Essentials of visualisation

Visualisation, or 'realisation', is a way of looking at the world, perceiving its fundamental realities, that probably originates with the Buddha and generally inspires Eastern philosophy. The notion of visualisation (or 'seeing reality') was the life-work of Count Alfred Korzybski (not considered very highly in conventional philosophy circles, if acknowledged for his work on general semantics), who made the communication of the idea to the West his main, albeit rather unsuccessful, aim. Hence its alternative name, 'Korzybskian thinking'.

## Korzybskian thinking – the lifelong quest

So what is the theory? What is visualisation all about? Let me offer ten pointers.

1. When children learn words the joy of their childhood ends and the colours fade into a black and white world of words. Later many of them are bored, they want to get away on

holidays, to be entertained, and so on. Yet there is a wonderland all around them.

2. Words throw out senses; thus our senses, which are in touch with reality, are replaced by words that have nothing to do with reality. Korzybski called words a primitive language, not even having the same structure as reality; only mathematics has the same structure as reality.

3. Visualisation is the language of reality for it mirrors reality; its pictures are of real things. Its written language is higher mathematics. It unmasks abstractions: words that are not about reality.

However, even 'mathematics' is not wholly accurate. Albert **EINSTEIN** once said: 'As far as the Laws of mathematics refer to reality, they are uncertain; and as far as they are certain, they do not refer to reality'. Korzybski thinks, as he puts it, that 'visualisation represents the most beneficial and efficient form of human "thought"'.

4. Visualisation is the most beautiful language. One of the greatest mystics, Kabir, said we must '. . . make our body a house of pictures'. We can make it what we will – a garden more magnificent than any physical garden, or a hell. He visualised an Ocean of Pearls and made it his real home: his homeland. Visualisation is the light of the mind.

5. The Indian Guru, Rajneesh, wrote that senses are the doors of the body into the infinite. If we do not use them the body is a dungeon; moreover, without visualisation it is a dungeon without light. Examples of people using the senses are artists, poets and creative people who all sense and do not recognise or see similarities with other things. Artists teaching at an art school were always saying to students 'look at the model'. Students had their own idea in their minds of an arm, leading to grotesque arms; they were not seeing reality – not seeing real arms.

6. Korzybskian thinking is not just useful for the arts but for all life, including the everyday, practical matters, because by using it we force ourselves to see reality.

7. Love and its fading is caused by a change from an emotional and sense relationship to a verbal and intellectual one, whereas animals never lose their owners' affection because it is a sensing friendship, not an intellectual one. This is a knowledge that can give a large benefit in human relations. Words act like a barrier, but it is sensing and emotions, including visualisation, that lead to rapport.

8. Nothing is more rare than a truly original or first-hand idea. We are taught things, we read things, we see things on the internet, we recognise things, we see resemblances between things. All this is second-hand. What is original and first-hand? You can go out into the first-hand universe and see or sense something in a new way, like an artist. That is original.

9. Senses have been neglected. For instance, in a survey of American men and women, it seems 80 per cent of men and 70 per cent of women could not tell the difference between the four primary tastes: sweet, sour, salty, musty. It is as Aldous Huxley once wrote in the *Doors of Perception*: 'only drugs will induce a wonderful view of reality'. Yet we do not have to take drugs; we can instead just cultivate the senses and sense reality. Reality truly is wonderful – a wonderland.

10. Finally, remember that Korzybski studied the way Einstein thought. Creativity follows from Korzybskian thinking. H.D. **THOREAU** made his whole life a creative art. Every day he went out to look for beautiful ideas. He called his life his Elysium.

Korzybskian thinking is mainly about using the senses; this does not mean recognition or knowing, but perception, which leads to regaining use of the senses. (It is words that usurp the functions of senses. Perception, visualisation and the unspeakable are keys to the infinite that end human isolation.) Before words, children live in a technicolour and sense world until words replace their senses, joy ends and the colours fade into a black and white world of words. They change from 'the Quest' to 'knowing'.

Senses are like subtle threads that bind us to reality, whereas words that replace them do not. There is a double illusion (from poorly sensed or merely recognised pictures outside to noise/words inside). The second illusion is that we immediately translate what we see into words, whereas reality outside is of shape, texture, and soon, so it reaches us in the form of streams of light particles: we see pictures made of light. Only seeing a picture of a thing in the mind (visualisation) is accurate because it is a mirror image of it. These two illusions condemn us to an artificial existence. We are alienated from the real physical world and our fellow human beings, for our relationships are part of the same illusions. As with senses, visualisation gives the mind direct contact with reality, which is structural, therefore visualisable; visualisation creates images and also mirrors reality so its pictures are of real things. Korzybski wrote: 'Visualisation represents the most beneficial and efficient form of human "Thought".' Moreover, its loss is worse than blindness for it is the eyes and light of the mind. This is illustrated by the 'structural differential'.

Korzybski's discussion of 'Invention and Creativity' in *Science and Sanity* claims that invention starts with sensing; that is to say, with intuition, feeling, hunches, and so on. This is the basis of creative science. Only afterwards do these feelings and visualisations become hypotheses and, later, theories. For architects they would become bridges, buildings; for artists, paintings, or whatever.

The structural differential explains how to think. Korzybski considered it to be effectively the only way to master this method of thinking.

Most people recognise objects, they do not 'sense' them, thus their thinking is done below the line at the verbal level: the non-real and non-creative. The first label is the name (soldier); the second is an abstraction (e.g. regimental); the third is a higher abstraction (such as military), and so on. Words are translations from reality. The words are the shadows that the prisoners of Plato's CAVE believed were reality.

The unspeakable (the Quest part) is a springboard into the Infinite: above the line is creativity, poetry and invention, as well as sensing. Just as with nature, we sense it, allowing it to speak – we do not impose our truly limited knowledge upon it. human beings must be treated in the same way: listen, be friendly and courteous. As A.J. Arberry's Discourses say of Rumi:

To think and speak well of others is to sow round your house flowers and aromatic herbs. Whenever you look out you see flowers and a flower garden and are always in paradise. But if you speak badly of them it is as if when you think of them an enemy appears: a snake or a scorpion. Love all people and you will always dwell among flowers!

Visualisation and creativity are almost inseparable: from them come the greatest joys. They add to our Quest of Life, a quest for beauty. Their intuitions, visions, and so on, are crystallised into coloured pictures, which are real and become real things: great theories such as Einstein's; awe-inspiring architecture; sublime poetry and paintings. Even as we visualise, the mind fills with lovely images, we furnish and adorn it. Kabir ordered us: 'Make your body a house of pictures.' This picture-house of the mind is our most precious possession and a joy lifelong: even in old age and when bedridden, like a film or kaleidoscope, these pictures never cease.

Perhaps as important as the way of science and art is the sheer seeing and sensing of reality. This is called realisation that gives liberation from the verbal illusion that traps nearly all people of the world in a prison from which they never escape.

In *Gulliver's Travels*, Jonathan Swift wrote of the most afflicted of humanity: intellectual verbalisers. The Intelligentsia of the Laputans had minders like seeing-eye dogs to prompt them when to speak and to warn them of pits and obstacles, so wrapped up were they in their cogitations. Our prison is very subtle, else there would be few verbalisers. We pass our lives knowing nothing of it: yet it is a prison of which we are both the jailers and the prisoners. This illusion has been called a veil of words that is between us and reality. For Korzybski, there are only two remedies: one is to become realised and see and understand the illusion; the other is to visualise (and sense). Realisation ends the illusion: visualisation shows us by mirror images what real things are – we think in reality.

Contributor: Ted Falconar

# VIVES, JUAN LUIS (1492–1540)

One of the most cited writers of the sixteenth and seventeenth centuries, the humanist writer Vives' works are little known. He himself foresaw it when denouncing the scholastic trend of categorising thinkers according to their place of birth, 'as if wise men were to be judged by the soil or region that produces them – as we do with fruits and wines'.

The son of a Jewish-converted merchant family, Vives lived in Spain until he was 17, when he travelled to study in Paris. In 1519 he was appointed professor of humanities at Louvain, where he wrote *De Subventione Pauperum*, the first ever appeal for public assistance to the

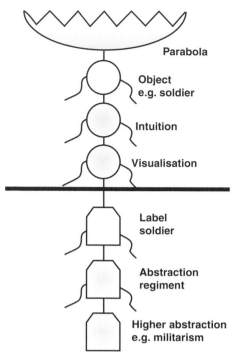

Parabola

Object
e.g. soldier

Intuition

Visualisation

Label
soldier

Abstraction
regiment

Higher abstraction
e.g. militarism

The structural differential

## THE STRUCTURAL DIFFERENTIAL

The first figure, the parabola (e.g. soldier) has a jagged top (cut off) to show its characteristics are infinite. The three circles are: the object (actual soldier), then sensing, seeing, feeling, intuiting, and finally, visualising. These are turned into words: the Unspeakable; the Real; the Creative. The line between the upper and lower level is like Alice's looking-glass into Wonderland, the Infinite.

## EARNEST CONTEMPLATION

The Buddhist way of explaining the idea of contemplation familiar to those in the West, comes via the Zen philosophy of Japan, which itself came out of *Chan* (the same word) in China and *Dhyan*, the original Indian version. The method of Zen is to confront students with riddles called *koans*. The first was said to come from the Buddha. When asked what reality was he simply held a rose over his head and smiled. This meant that the rose has to be sensed, it is beyond words, it can only be known through the senses.

Most *koans* are nonsensical, with the purpose of making students understand the limitation and unreality of words. One such of these paradoxical *koans* is called the 'Sound of the One Hand'. 'In clapping the hands a sound is heard: What is the sound of the One Hand?'

Alas, the results from this way of explanation are very poor, hardly any students have become 'realised'.

The Tibetan method of teaching realisation is more rational and entails actual meditation in various states: *Dharani*, *Samath* and finally *Samadhi* – respectively: absorption, tranquilisation and what D.T. Suzuki, author of *Essays in Zen Buddhism*, called 'earnest contemplation'. This last comes near to being realisation.

critique of the scholastic methods of study.

Historians of philosophy have granted the patronising epithet of 'disciple of Erasmus' to Vives. Although his first work – a commentary on Saint Augustine's *Civitas Dei*, was indeed written under the guidance of Erasmus in Paris, both humanists developed a different approach to philosophy; as Carlos Noreña put it, in the history of philosophy: 'Erasmus deserves a place only because the philosophical assumptions of the "Philosophia Christi" were highly symptomatic of the intellectual crises out of which the modern mind was born . . . [whereas] Vives belongs to the history of European philosophy because he was, on his own merit, a pioneer of new trends of thought.'

Vives could also be praised on account of his reappraisal of **ARISTOTLE**'s works – an accomplishment that prompted one scholar to describe *De tradendis disciplinis* as a more significant work than **BACON**'s *Novum Organon*. In

poor. Deeply affected by the religious intolerance of his native country – half his family was prosecuted and burnt by the Spanish Inquisition – he rejected a lecturing chair at the University of Salamanca. In 1522, under the protection of Queen Catherine of Aragon, he moved to Oxford, where he became a Corpus Christi College fellow. During the royal divorce affair Vives sided with the Queen, a decision that cost him his post. After having endured a six-week solitary confinement he moved back to the Netherlands, where he lived a precarious existence until his early death. In 1531 he published *De tradendis disciplinis* (1531), the first systematic the same vein, it has been pointed out that Vives' works are more often plundered than quoted. In some respects, Vives is the forerunner of both Telesio and SPINOZA, underlying his approach to the study of man from a psychological standpoint, free of metaphysical presumptions.

An exile for almost his entire life, Vives displayed his classical erudition with a cosmopolitan sensitivity. In a clime of religious intolerance he serenely wrote that pagans 'may attain the glory of a Christian by keeping the two abstracts of all the Law and the Prophets, perfect love of God and his neighbours'. His epistemology is not based in the formulation of a stable truth – which he called 'the daughter of time' – but on the premise that wisdom without virtue is vain, for, like SOCRATES, he grasped ethics as the worthiest pursuit of philosophy.

## VOLTAIRE (1694–1778)

François-Marie Arouet Voltaire went through several stages in his philosophical life. At one point he followed Isaac NEWTON's lead and supposed that the world just might be divinely ordered to be the 'best of all possible worlds', as Dr Pangloss would put it. 'It is not inequality that is the real evil, but dependence', he wrote, reflecting the same view as his contemporary, Adam SMITH. But as an older man, Voltaire became more pessimistic and instead reworked Newton's view of the universe as a kind of giant machine to mean that we are all doomed – a view sometimes known as 'pessimistic fatalism'. (Which it is.)

Happily, this was a temporary phase, and towards the end of his life Voltaire discovered a chink of light, in that it might be possible for us to take certain small, positive actions, even in the face of a hostile and godless universe.

His influence through his plays, novels and *Lettres philosophiques* (1734) was profound, a HUMANIST campaigning for freedom of religion and (among other things) animal rights.

## WANG, HAO (1921–)

Wang Hao was born and educated in China, but worked in the USA. Here he aided Willard van QUINE with some axioms for his theory of set membership, but what is more interesting is that he wrote an early working computer program (in 1959) that briskly proved all the first-order theorems that Whitehead and RUSSELL had sweated over to so little effect just half a century before.

## WAR

Where does warfare fit in to human life? Is it just large-scale wicked violence, or an essential part of the cycle of creation – the destructive part?

In one of PLATO's dialogues, SOCRATES convinces Cephalus that it is impossible that harming other people can also be the act of the 'just'. But Socrates was not typical. Most of the ancients thought that – at the very least – wars provided the forum for developing manly virtues, such as 'courage'. Erasmus, however, wrote sceptically of that and of the warriors themselves as 'military idiots, thick-headed lords . . . not even human except in appearance'. As to the ethics of those who dispatch the armies, war merely served rulers as a mask behind which they could carry out actions that would otherwise be unthinkable, not only to the enemy, but to their own people. But much later, HEGEL was back favouring war in itself as providing timely reminders of the 'transitory nature' of human existence.

HUMANISTS have a high opinion of human beings, whatever else that term may or may not imply. In *Perpetual Peace* (1795) KANT opines that the 'sanction of the citizens is necessary to decide whether there shall be a war or not', and that if they were consulted, 'nothing is more natural than that they would think long before beginning such a terrible game'.

Even so, Kant, like Thomas HOBBES with his famous 'Warre of all on all', saw the natural state of humankind as one of either active or threatened conflict. But eternal peace was undoubtedly the goal; indeed this quest was 'the entire end and purpose of a theory of rights within the limits of pure reason'.

Jeremy BENTHAM busied himself in his study for a while before emerging with a *Plan for Universal and Perpetual Peace* (1789), essentially relying on a supranational 'eye' to police the world – not by force, of course, but by the free exchange of information, shaming any transgressor nations into line.

'Globalisation' was another route identified by philosophers for reaching Kant's dream. Adam

SMITH thought the profit motive was the antidote to this warrior impulse: 'If commerce were permitted to act to the universal extent it is capable, it would extirpate the system of war and produce a revolution in the uncivilised state of governments.' Similarly, in 1848, John Stuart MILL wrote in the *Principles of Political Economy* that:

> It is commerce which is rapidly rendering war obsolete, by strengthening and multiplying the personal interests which act in natural opposition to it. And it may be said without exaggeration that the great extent and rapid increase of international trade, in being the principle guarantee of the peace of the world, is the great permanent security for the uninterrupted progress of the ideas, the institutions, and the character of the human race.

Unfortunately, as global trade increased in the nineteenth century, so did global wars. Nonetheless, even with the clouds of the First World War gathering, this was still the story favoured by the middle classes. H.G. Wells offered the only remaining rationale, predicting that this would be 'the war that will end war'.

In any case, at the Yalta Conference, towards the end of the Second World War, rather than pledge to not have any more wars, the Allies promised to set up a 'United Nations' organisation prepared to 'take effective collective measures for the prevention and removal of threats to the peace and for the suppression of acts of aggression or other breaches of the peace'. The United Nations would wage 'just' wars, for example to stop acts of genocide.

Perhaps the error was the reliance on human nature being essentially peace-loving. George Bernard Shaw wrote in contrast that 'all classes in proportion to their lack of travel and familiarity with foreign literature are bellicose, prejudiced against foreigners, fond of fighting as cruel sport – in short, dog-like in their notions of foreign policy'.

## WEBER, MAX (1864–1920)

Weber's career was largely spent in several professorial positions in respectable German universities, churning out his heavy-handed theories, although he was actually, for a period, a bureaucrat himself (as a hospital administrator during the First World War). He defines 'sociology' (in typically heavy style) as the science of the analysis of the social causes of social effects. As a science, it must be 'value-free': a notion that was important for Weber and led to an intense and prolonged academic debate within Germany. Of course, Weber realised, values are often present in individual perceptions, and his investigation of the relationship of Christianity, in its Protestant form, and capitalism, exemplifies the central role values play in social life.

At the same time, it seems Weber's approach is value-laden in itself, as he insists, almost as an axiom of his theories, that rationality is good. Any activity without conscious intent is mere 'behaviour'. It is not enough to explain activity in terms of causes and mechanisms – there must be a purpose, and bureaucracies, Weber thinks, naturally promote a 'rationalist' way of life, just as rationality itself is inclined to prefer government according to rules, rather than mere authority. The best form of rationality is when the choice of means and ends either:

- ◼ 'accord with the canons of logic, the procedures of science or of successful economic behaviour',

or

- ◼ 'constitute a way of achieving certain ends, when the means chosen to achieve them accord with factual and theoretical knowledge'.

Otherwise, if the ends are motivated (contaminated) by values – religious, moral or aesthetic – or if values influence or determine the means employed, then the behaviour is 'value-rational' (which is not as good).

Sometimes the ends may be decided by tradition, which is a kind of value, but one which, he thinks, hinders economic progress. Then again, sometimes behaviour is affected by emotions and passions, this is 'affectual action', and that, too, is opposed to rational behaviour.

It is *zweckrational*, or goal-rational, behaviour that is most logical, similar perhaps also to the more simple-minded models of market economists or UTILITARIANS. For example, if someone wishes to buy a gold watch, they may start doing overtime at work to save money for the purchase. Capitalism depends on rationality in two ways: for the movement of free and property-less workers in response to the demands of the free market; and for the freedom of those with capital to invest – such as entrepreneurs – to choose where, based on maximising profit, to do so.

Weber's particular insight, set out in his best-known work, *The Protestant Ethic and the Spirit of Capitalism* (1905, first published in English in 1930), was that the Industrial Revolution in Europe was linked to a rejection of traditional and elaborate Catholic religious practice, for a Protestant ideology which emphasised the virtue of a lifetime spent working hard, with no greater aim than serving God. The second stage of this realisation was a view of material goods, which held them to be only important in that they reflected God's approval of one's efforts. For the new breed of capitalist, Weber thought, this made the success of the entrepreneur something worth striving for. It also, conveniently, justified reducing the workers to the absolute bare minimum required for successful production.

In particular, Weber argued that the development of capitalism occurred in Holland and England because they were Protestant powers, and that the economic discoveries associated with the time flowed from this pre-existing fact, rather than vice versa, a view that harmonises with DURKHEIM's approach, by putting the social before the economic.

Not that Weber is in favour of this. In *The Origin of Modern Capitalism*, Weber argues that '. . . in the east it was essentially ritualistic considerations, including caste and clan organisations, which prevented the development of a deliberate economic policy' and thus, that capitalism could only develop once the political administration – the bureaucracy – was created, as in the British parliamentary system.

Weber also makes the individual's perception of the world the key to understanding society. His study of attitudes to work, *The Protestant Ethic and the Spirit of Capitalism*, published in the early years of the twentieth century, attempts to show how individual perceptions are tied up with economic practice. Weber's work in the early years of the twentieth century on SOCIAL SCIENCE in general, such as the *Methodology of Social Sciences*, and the uncompleted *Wirtschaft und Gesellschaft* (part one eventually translated as *Social and Economic Organisation*), contain three new ideas which became highly influential.

## Further reading

Weber, M. (1920) *The Origin of Modern Capitalism*

Weber, M. (1922) *Social Psychology of World Religions*

## WEIL, SIMONE (1909–43)

From a comfortable middle-class Parisian background, Simone Weil became a left-wing radical who took leave from her university teaching to work in a factory. In 1938 she reported a mystical experience and became something of an evangelical Christian, and most of her writings reflect this evangelism. She saw her political past differently too, describing the revolutionary mindset as a 'cult' worshipping 'productive' labour and revolutionary action for itself. At the same time, like others, she warned about the 'dehumanising' and socially destructive implications of market forces and capitalism, particularly in conjunction with the uncritical introduction of technology. She saw a kind of MARXIST *anomie* or alienation in capitalism, but also in any technocratic society, and argued that human beings need such things as hierarchy and property, as well as freedom and equality.

## Further reading

Weil, S. (1955) *Oppression et Liberté* (Oppression and Liberty).

## WHORF, BENJAMIN LEE (1897–1941)

Whorf is not taken very seriously these days – not as an anthropologist, not as a linguist, not *even* as a philosopher. In fact, he is not taken very much at all. His groundbreaking work on the language patterns of the Hopi Indians of North America is nowadays dismissed by populists like Stephen Pinker as 'unintentionally comic'. Within his own discipline, Noam CHOMSKY has described his work as 'entirely premature', not based on enough evidence and 'lacking in precision', while in mainstream philosophy, Robert Kirk, a professor in the UK, (completely differently) says it consists of little more than truisms.

Perhaps this academic disapproval of Whorf is because he preferred to work outside academia for the whole of his short life as (wait for it) an insurance investigator. Then again, perhaps it has something to do with the fact that his arguments are unwelcome to many. For some, they appear to elevate irrational thinking over rational, the ways of the American Indian over the ways of the American academic – a scandalous supposition made much worse by being couched in scientific language. Whorf is 'notorious' for advancing what is clearly labelled as *the principle of linguistic relativity* – but which subsequent academics, for their own reasons, have insisted on renaming as *the Sapir-Whorf Hypothesis*. In essence, it is the theory that:

We dissect nature along lines laid down by our native languages. The categories and types that we isolate from the world of phenomena we do not find there because they stare every observer in the face; on the contrary, the world is presented in a kaleidoscopic flux of impressions which has to be organised by our minds – and this means largely by the linguistic systems in our minds. We cut nature up, organise it into concepts, and ascribe significances as we do, largely because we are parties to an agreement that holds throughout our speech community and is codified in the patterns of our language. The agreement is, of course, an implicit and unstated one, but its terms are absolutely obligatory; we cannot talk at all except by subscribing to the organisation and classification of data which the agreement decrees.

Benjamin Lee Whorf was born in Winthrop, Massachusetts on 24 April 1897. As a child, he was fascinated by ciphers and puzzles, and read widely on botany, astrology, Mexican history, Mayan archaeology and photography. He came to anthropology via the unusual route of physics, JUNGIAN synchronicity, systems theory, GESTALT PSYCHOLOGY (with its foregrounding and backgrounding) and, above all, linguistics – all of which he was able to pursue only in his spare hours and on business trips.

His day-job was surprisingly mundane – Investigator and Engineer for the Hartford Fire Insurance Company. Yet the time was by no means wasted. Within his work he came across many examples that he would later see as language influencing thought patterns, and his linguistic theory appeared in several influential articles set around the topic of fire prevention. People, he observed in the first of these, tended to be careless around 'empty drums' of gasoline, drums 'empty' of petrol, but equally 'full' of vapours more explosive than the liquid. He noticed how people were complacent towards industrial 'waste water' and 'spun limestone', both, again, flammable and dangerous despite the innocuousness that the words

'water' and 'stone' convey.

In the 1920s, while still working full-time, he entered into correspondence with the leading US scholars of the day in anthropology, archaeology and linguistics. From 1931 onwards he studied linguistics (part-time) under the supervision of Edward Sapir, one of the key figures in the new discipline of sociolinguistics. Under Sapir's guidance, he made his in-depth and highly original study of the language structures of the Hopi Indians. A stream of detailed yet almost poetic papers established his name and he became a research fellow and occasional lecturer at Yale.

Linguistic relativity is in itself not new; indeed it is rather older than the physics variety, going back at least to the nineteenth century and Baron Wilhelm von Humboldt, the founder of linguistics. The Baron himself viewed thought as being entirely impossible without language, saying that language completely determined thought, which is not Whorf's position at all. But von Humboldt's theory took on new life after EINSTEIN's demonstration of the 'relativity' of space and time, Einstein himself citing it in a radio programme. Whorf, with a scientific background in chemistry, was not claiming to have invented anything; rather, he wanted to unite the new thinking in 'hard science' with the older philosophical theory.

## Further reading

Whorf, Benjamin (1956) *Language, Thought and Reality – Selected Writings* (A collection of Whorf's papers and essays edited by John Carroll and published by the MIT Press)

# WISDOM

## Essentials of wisdom

Wisdom is one of the four 'cardinal virtues' and what philosophy is meant to be the love of, but it is often the poor handmaiden to the Aristotelian interests of cataloguing and analysing, instead.

## Being wise

Is there a difference between being wise and being clever? It is easy to see why this question is important, for wisdom is something people need for sound decision-making, not only in the public world of politics, but also in personal life. Wisdom involves accepting the stabilising constraints of reason and rationality, but it is a richer concept than these, involving feeling as well as intellectual judgement.

There are wisdom traditions in the world's great cultures and religions. Ancient Egyptian teachings have been found from as early as 2500 BCE. Later, Chinese CONFUCIANISM, BUDDHISM, HINDUISM and the Hebrew sages of the Old Testament all offered maxims and counsels for the conduct of life. Past philosophers in the Western tradition, too, had something to say about these matters; indeed, 'philosophy' is the ancient word for the love of wisdom, and it was philosophers who set up the first 'academy' or university in Athens in the fifth century BCE. Philosophy today, though, is often more concerned with slickness and skill in argument than with answering the question 'how to live'.

This can be explained partly by the fact that both philosophers and educators in the liberal democracies rightly take pride in the freedom they enjoy to approach subjects of study in an open and critical way and so try to avoid any appearance of dogmatism. But criticism is not a value in itself. If it is to generate wisdom, it has to be accompanied by humility and a recognition of your own limitations. Some parts of the world have different learning traditions, in which classical authors and texts are studied for the insights they can offer, rather than for any errors they may have made, and this contrasts with the Western tendency to criticise and attack the writers and thinkers central to its traditions. But in education, this may not do as much to encourage freedom of thought as it appears. For the critical approach often trades in what are no more than standard criticisms which must themselves be learned, while genuine originality continues to earn *nul points*.

True wisdom comes from something deeper and more intuitive than any of this. It involves, too, a kind of empathy, not only with other people, but with the natural world in which we find ourselves. Wisdom can be linked to the perennial search for meaning in life, summed up in the question, 'What is it all for?' As such, it is the quest for order, plan, purpose and method in the face of the arbitrary contingency of the world and of events. For the STOIC Roman emperor, Marcus AURELIUS, as later for SPINOZA, the seventeenth-century Dutch philosopher, this quest is best met by accepting the inevitability of things, not wasting time

resenting or fearing the course of events, but recognising that all that happens is bound into a web of causes and consequences. For the Stoics, this meant learning to live free from emotional attachments, but perhaps a braver conclusion from such a philosophical view would be to engage with the world, while accepting the inevitable disappointments that will bring.

So, wisdom need not be understood as an exclusively metaphysical concept. On the contrary, it is better understood as in some way connecting with the choices people make in their personal lives – choices such as those of lifestyle, partner, place or career that form the stuff and substance of an individual life. For it is in close personal relationships – whether between adults or between parents and children – that many people find meaning for their lives. But wise private choices do in the end make for wise public and community life, while large-scale carelessness in the personal life of individuals can lead to the disintegration or unravelling of the social fabric.

Contributor: Brenda Almond

# WITTGENSTEIN, LUDWIG (1889–1951)

Ludwig Wittgenstein was the peculiar maths teacher-soldier-engineer and, eventually – reluctantly – philosopher. His reputation rests on just two philosophy books. The first, written in 1922, in which he numbered each sentence as he went along, in a self-conscious attempt at indicating the importance of his insights, is the *Tractatus Logico-Philosophicus*. This says that all philosophy problems have been solved, and is straightforwardly in opposition to everyone else.

Wittgenstein's thinking was at this time distinctly LOGICAL POSITIVIST in flavour, considering words to be directly linked to reality; what anthropologists call the 'Bow wow wow' theory of language, 'picturing facts', in the way that a police model of an accident resembles the accident. Where this simple notion fell down, as it does in most of ethics, metaphysics and, indeed, traditional philosophy, he followed the logical positivists as dismissing the talk as empty grunting and nonsense. And indeed, he says, not once but twice, in the *Tractatus*, 'whereof one cannot speak, one must remain silent'. This has contributed to the often repeated view that he was a 'leading light' or even the ' inspiration' of the movement. Yet it seems unlikely, as

Wittgenstein was himself inclined to mysticism, and simply meant that philosophical analysis is useless as a vehicle to attaining these supposed 'higher truths'. Logic itself could never provide any new insights, as it is merely tautologies. Not for nothing did he mark the occasion of his only attendance at the Circle by reading out a poem to them with his back turned the whole time.

However, in his later, posthumously published book, *Philosophical Investigations* (1953), he reversed many of his earlier findings, and compared words and sentences to the tools in a toolbox, or to the controls of a locomotive, saying that meaning is use. He also tried to incorporate elements of FREUDIAN psychology, making 'man the measure' again of all things.

These days, he is very highly regarded by academic philosophers, who erroneously credit him with insights, such as the theory of 'family resemblances', for explaining how terms come about, that can be found in the work of earlier, much clearer, philosophers, for example, John LOCKE and René DESCARTES.

## Further reading

Wittgenstein, L. (1953) *Philosophical Investigations*

## WOLLSTONECRAFT, MARY (1759–97)

One of the first overtly 'feminist' philosophers, Wollstonecraft argued that the relations between men and women are corrupted by artificial notions of gender, just as relations between men and other men can be by notions of rank, or wealth, or heredity. Virtue, she says, including political virtue, is gender-blind. Writing in England, where she lived with the anarchist philosopher William GODWIN, Wollstonecraft offered a radical personal narrative endorsing the aims of the French Revolution, even as many of her immediate circle were being led to the scaffold.

Influences from ROUSSEAU's style of 'philosophical anthropology' (drawing in diverse elements from religion and psychology) and from LOCKE are apparent, with Thomas PAINE, the main conduit of Locke's ideas to America, one of Wollstonecraft's contemporaries. Writing, as it were, in parallel with Paine, she produced an anonymous *Vindication of the Rights of Man* days before Paine's work was published. Another work, *A Vindication of the Rights of Women* (1792), pushed forward Locke's liberal hypothesis on women's political importance, with a wide-ranging denunciation of 'male' rationality' and power, criticising Rousseau in particular. For this, Wollstonecraft earned the dislike of many prominent male intellectuals of the time, and the sobriquet of being a 'hyena in petticoats' from Horace Walpole.

## XENOCRATES (396–314 BCE)

Xenocrates was the third head of the ACADEMY, PLATO being the first and Speusippus the second. He set out a 'formal' system for interpreting Plato, in which he tended to divide things into three all the time, rather than the more usual binary oppositions. Souls were defined as a kind of number, that 'moves toward itself', and Xenocrates gives a key role to daemons in the universe.

## XENOPHANES (*C.* 570–470 BCE)

Xenophanes was born in Colophon in Ionia more than two and half thousand years ago, and spent the greater part of the sixth century BCE as a wandering poet, singing drinking-songs and retelling tales of Zeus and the other Greek gods. Eventually, however, he settled in Elea, southern Italy, and it was there that he founded one of the first schools of philosophy, the ELEATIC school.

In a long philosophical poem known as *On Nature*, Xenophanes challenged many of the central assumptions of contemporary Greek religion, substituting for the wide range of deities one single and eternal God (preferably sphere-shaped), and introducing a new style of argument, the method of comparison. He challenges 'anthropomorphic' views of the Gods (ones that treat Gods as sharing the same ways of thinking and behaving as people), writing famously that if cows or horses or lions had gods, they would imagine them to be cows or horses or lions respectively too.

Xenophanes is also remembered for having observed fossil fish and shells, and concluding that the land where they were found must have been underwater at some time. From this he suggested that the world might have formed from the condensation of water and 'primordial mud'. (But then his background lay with the Milesian school of Ionia, founded by THALES, who considered that everything, but *everything*, was made originally from water.) He further surmised from the existence of fossils that the world evolved from a mixture of earth and water, and that the Earth will gradually be re-dissolved. He believed that the Earth had already gone through this cycle several times.

On other occasions, he observed the Earth's shadow on the moon during eclipses, and concluded that the Earth must have the same shape as its shadow – namely that it must be a perfect circle. Therefore, the Earth is not flat (as EMPEDOCLES and Anaximenes thought); nor drum-shaped (as believed by LEUCIPPUS); nor bowl-shaped (as HERACLITUS); nor hollow (as DEMOCRITUS); nor cylindrical (as Anaximander); nor even does it extend infinitely downward (as Xenophon taught); but it must be a perfect sphere.

In another fragment, Xenophanes dismisses the rainbows in which others saw the workings of the goddess Isis as but 'simply a cloud that appears crimson, red and yellowish green'. Elsewhere, he states that 'men can have no certain knowledge, only opinion', and that although by searching, people can improve their understanding, this 'will always fall short of knowledge.'

## XUNZI (*C.* 330–230 BCE)

Xunzi is sometimes called the 'Chinese Aristotle', and is highly respected within CHINESE PHILOSOPHY as an interpreter of CONFUCIUS. His particular interest was in the relationship between morality and human nature and the strategies necessary for leading the 'ethical life'. To this end he produced a series of rules of proper conduct, *li*, and argues that other philosophers have neglected the holism of *dao* by concentrating on particular aspects of life and philosophy.

## YIN AND YANG

At the same time as HERACLITUS was outlining his theory of perpetual, cyclical change, the Chinese sage LAO TZU expounded the cyclical nature of the Tao, manifested in the famous interplay of yin and yang: yin, the negative and passive force; yang the positive and active force. But the two opposites are united by change: they change into each other. And change is the fundamental reality of the universe. The highest, 'divine' perspective sees all the opposites: 'day and night, winter and summer, war and peace, plenty and famine', are the same, as Heraclitus puts it. With the divine perspective, even good and evil are the same.

## YOGA

Yoga is the practical system of INDIAN PHILOSOPHY used to achieve liberation or realisation. The *Yoga Sutras* of Patanjali, fifth century CE, are accepted as authoritative by all Indian religions. The Sanskrit root *yuj*, means 'to bind together' and is the source of the French *joug*: a yoke.

A serious Indian student will go to Benares or Haridwar, seek out a guru and practise yoga through to liberation. Practice first involves being acceptable and only then will training begin with *asanas* (postures), *pranayama* (breath control), *pratyahara* (withdrawal) and *dharana*, *dhyana* and *samadhi* (increasing forms of concentration). During the last of these, practice eventually leads to NIRVANA.

In physiological terms, the early stages of yoga involve positive effects on the nervous system, and later, on the non-dominant hemisphere of the cortex. In therapeutic terms, yoga is akin to psychotherapy but with more beneficial and lasting results.

# Z

## ZENO OF CITIUM (335–263 BCE)

The founder of STOICISM, Zeno attended the lectures of Polemon the Academic and Diodorus the Megarian, before becoming a pupil of Crates the CYNIC. He eventually broke away to teach in his own name at the Painted Stoa on the northern edge of the Agora in Athens. His most famous work is his *Republic*, a utopian work of political philosophy, reportedly written against PLATO and under the influence of Crates. Only fragments survive. In this work Zeno appears to have advocated the abolition of traditional education, marriage and currency, proposing a future in which all humankind would live as one political body sharing the same way of life, like a herd grazing together on a common pasture.

## ZENO OF ELEA (FIFTH CENTURY BCE)

Zeno predates PLATO, although he may have just known SOCRATES. He is even older than Euclid, whose fabulous geometrical systems,

### ZENO'S FOUR PARADOXES OF MOTION

The 'Racecourse' states that one cannot ever reach the finishing line, because first one must arrive at a point halfway along the course, then a point halfway along the second half of the course . . . and so on. . .

In the more famous race between 'Achilles and the tortoise', Achilles finds that, having generously given the animal a head start, he is unable to overtake the tortoise as he must first reach the point where it was, and no matter how slowly the tortoise goes, it will always move a little bit further on in the meantime.

In the 'Arrow' paradox, Zeno worries that the arrow must at any given moment be at a certain position, and that being at a certain position implies being at rest, so that the arrow should fall stunned, as it were, to the ground.

Finally, the two rows of moving bodies in the 'Stadium' paradox offer apparently contradictory conclusions about relative motion.

developed from those of the North Africans, so impressed the philosophers. But nonetheless, much of Zeno is about geometry and the nature of numbers – particularly the strange quantities infinity and zero.

He is best remembered for his four paradoxes of motion.

The reasoning behind Zeno's paradoxes is described ostensibly by the man himself in Plato's dialogue *Parmenides*. There, unusually, Socrates is taken to task himself by Zeno, specifically over the matter of whether it makes any difference to say the universe is 'all one' or 'definitely not many'. But then, Socrates was still very young!

In the dialogue, Zeno is reading his book to Socrates and Parmenides. (Unfortunately, Zeno's book got lost somewhere down the millennia. )

SOCRATES: Parmenides, I understand that Zeno wants to be on intimate terms with you not only in friendship but in his book. He has, in a way, written the same thing as you, only changing it around so as to fool us into thinking he has said something different. You say in your poem that all is one, and you give splendid and elegant proofs for that; and he, for his part, says that everything is 'not many', and gives a vast array of excellent proofs for that of his own. So with one of you saying 'one' and the other saying 'not many', and with each of you speaking in a way that sounds as if you are not saying the same thing – even though you mean practically the same thing – what you say seems to be said over the top of heads of the rest of us!

ZENO: Yes, Socrates, but you still haven't discerned the main point about my book, although you have chased its arguments and followed their scents with the enthusiasm of a young Spartan hound. First of all, you have missed this point: the book doesn't at all preen itself on having been written with the secret intention you describe, whilst disguising its purpose from people, as if that were some great accomplishment. You have mentioned something that happened accidentally. The truth is that the book comes to the defence of Parmenides' argument against those who say that if everything is one, it leads to absurdities and self-contradictions. Accordingly, my book pays them back in kind, with something for good measure, since it aims to show that their approach, that the universe is many, would, if someone examined the matter thoroughly, result in consequences even more absurd than those suffered by it being one.

I wrote a book, then, in that competitive spirit, when I was a young man. Someone made a copy without consulting me, so I didn't even have a chance to decide whether it should see the light.

# ZIONISM

## Essential Zionism

Zionism began as a political movement in the late nineteenth century. Its aim was the creation of a Jewish state, preferably in Palestine. Historically it has come in many guises – political, practical, cultural, territorialist, socialist and revisionist, to name but a few. But there is one idea common to all: that only the creation of a Jewish State would solve what was known as the 'Jewish Question', and preserve both Jewish identity and values. However, by being constructed as a reaction to 'anti-Semitism', it was destined to radically change that identity.

Zionism is an appropriate note on which to end this book, as it combines both a practical social and political philosophy with a religious creed – and by elevating one group's interests over another's challenges secular ethical standards.

## A thoroughly modern political movement

Like many nationalist movements, Zionism sought to rewrite the present in terms of the past. For centuries there had been nothing stopping Jews 'returning' to Palestine, apart from the poverty that awaited them, and some very religious Jews did indeed go there to study and die. Yet now it was said, the Jewish people, having spent 2000 years in 'exile', longed only to 'return' to Palestine to escape persecution and become a 'normal' people once again.

However, Zionism is a thoroughly modern political movement. It was no coincidence that

the First Zionist Congress was held in Basle in 1897 (after the Jewish residents of Munich had objected to it being held there) rather than in 1497. This was the era of colonialism and the white man's burden. Opening up new territories to European settlement was a good thing, and the views of the natives were of no account. Indeed they were invisible, mere ghosts. In Australia the policy followed was one of 'terra nullius' – an empty land. In Palestine, the Zionists' slogan was that they were settling a 'Land Without a People for a People Without a Land'.

Two political factors prevented the movement from sinking without trace, as it might easily have done, becoming just another utopian and messianic movement. One was the immense strategic value that Palestine acquired with the opening of the Suez Canal in the 1880s, as a route to India for the British Empire. The other was a series of pogroms against Jews in Russia, deliberately encouraged by the Tsarist regime.

The idea of a 'return of the Jews' to Palestine gradually caught the imagination of a layer of romantic imperialists and evangelical Christians, from George Eliot's fictional character Daniel Deronda, to Lord Shaftesbury, the noted reformer, and Ernest Laharanne, Secretary to Napoleon III. The idea of what Sir Ronald Storrs, Military Governor of Jerusalem, called 'a little loyal Jewish Ulster' in a sea of potentially hostile Arabism, gradually took root.

In Russia, following the assassination of Alexander II, in 1881, there had been a wave of pogroms against the Jews. Odessa, which suffered five days of anti-Jewish rioting, was the centre of the Haskalah, the Hebrew Enlightenment, which was the East European version of the Reform movement in Judaism. The events had a profound effect on a layer of Jewish intellectuals and Hebraists such as Peretz Smolenskin and Moshe Lillienbaum, who now despaired of the Jews ever finding a place in non-Jewish society. In their view, anti-Semitism was inevitable, and any social progress both irrelevant and unobtainable. As Eastern Europe struggled to emerge from feudalism, the Jews were thrown out of their previous economic positions, yet capitalism was unable to absorb them. They were wedged, in Abram Leon's words, 'between the anvil of decaying feudalism and the hammer of rotting capitalism'.

Zionism was a reaction to anti-Semitism, but it

was unique in that it accepted the basic tenets of anti-Semitism, namely that the Jews were strangers, a foreign body in non-Jewish society. Jewish life in *Galut* (exile) was, according to Jacob Klatzkin, a leading figure in the early World Zionist Organisation, 'not worthy of survival'. *Galut* could only 'drag out the disgrace of our people and sustain the existence of a people disfigured in both body and soul – in a word of a horror'.

Accordingly, it was useless and futile to combat or fight anti-Semitism. However, it took Theodore Herzl, an Austrian Jewish journalist and the founding father of modern political Zionism, to take this to its logical conclusion. If the rebirth of the Jewish nation required a Jewish State, then those who 'encouraged' the Jews to leave their homelands were actually helping Zionism along the way. As he wrote in his diaries, 'the anti-Semites will become our most dependable friends, the anti-Semitic countries our allies'. Writing shortly after the Dreyfuss Affair, which had split France and brought forth Émile Zola's *J'Accuse*, Herzl wrote that: 'In Paris, I achieved a free attitude towards anti-Semitism, which I now began to understand historically and to pardon'. His response to anti-Semitism was to try and use it to achieve his aims, in much the same way as a railway engine uses the power of steam.

Herzl shocked his Jewish (and non-Jewish) critics even further when, almost immediately after the Kishinev pogroms of Easter 1903, he journeyed to Moscow to visit the Tsar's ministers, including the author of the pogroms, his Interior Minister, Count Von Plehve. In return for support for the Zionist organisation in Russia, including lifting the ban on the sale of shares of the Jewish Colonial Bank, Herzl undertook to silence Jewish revolutionaries. For Herzl, Zionism was an 'antidote to socialist doctrines'.

Zionism, in its rejection of the place of Jews in non-Jewish society, also rejected the emancipation of European Jewry brought about by the French Revolution. By the 1860s, the remaining legal impediments to Jewish participation in Britain, Germany, Austria-Hungary and Italy had been removed. To the Zionist movement, as well as the Orthodox Rabbis, the removal of the ghetto walls also meant the removal of the barriers to the Jews assimilating with the non-Jewish population. Indeed, but for the reappearance of anti-Semitism in Eastern Europe, and with it the

## ZION, ALIENS AND THE BALFOUR DECLARATION

Zionism consciously sought an alliance with one or other imperial powers. Herzl himself travelled the length and breadth of Europe, meeting with the Pope, the Ottoman Sultan, the German Kaiser (in Palestine), the British Foreign Secretary, the Tsar's Ministers and assorted Grand Dukes and other anti-Semites. However, Herzl was a man before his time. It would not be until more than a decade after his death that the 'Eastern Question' would become pressing with the dissolution of the Ottoman Empire as a result of the First World War.

The idea of a Zionist colony in Britain's newly conquered Palestinian territories greatly appealed to Britain's imperial leaders. No greater supporter of the Zionist cause was there than Arthur J. Balfour, holder of the three great offices of state. In 1906 Balfour had introduced the Aliens Act, intended to keep out of Britain those Jews fleeing the pogroms in Russia. But it was Balfour who lent his name to the Balfour Declaration, the letter to Lord Rothschild which symbolised the agreement between the British Empire and the Zionist Movement.

For the next 30 years, Britain consciously bolstered and supported, by force of arms where necessary, the fledgling Zionist state, and, when the Arabs of Palestine revolted between 1936 and 1939, used the most brutal of methods to repress the uprising and strike. It was only under the pressure of imminent world war that Britain finally curtailed Jewish immigration into Palestine and it was this that led to the breach between Zionism and the British Empire, culminating in armed resistance post-1945.

mass migration of the *Ostjuden* to Western Europe and the USA, the Jews of Western Europe might have disappeared as a distinctive element in society.

Moses Hess, an erstwhile associate of Karl MARX, and the first Zionist ideologue, who had written over 30 years previously that 'should it prove true that the emancipation of the Jews is incompatible with Jewish nationalism, then the Jew must sacrifice emancipation', explained anti-Semitism not in religious but racial terms.

## PHILOSOPHY OF JUDAISM

'Jewish philosophy' is an attempt to understand the world as seen through a lens of a people's experience; in this case, seen as a series of historical vicissitudes and disasters. Many of these are recalled only through historically suspect religious texts such as those in the Hebrew Bible, perhaps describing the destruction of the first and second temples in Jerusalem, or the expulsion of the Jewish people from Israel, and the promised 'return'. To this is added many more recent and bitterly real disasters, not least the Holocaust.

Among the best-known Jewish philosophers are Philo of Alexandria, (15 BCE–50 CE), who attempted to combine the teachings of Moses with the philosophy of Plato and the ethics of the Stoics; Maimonides (1138–1204), the physician who lived in Egypt and wrote the celebrated *Guide to the Perplexed*, and Spinoza (1632–77), whose rationalistic approach to ethical questions, notably in *Ethics Demonstrated in a Geometrical Manner*, published only posthumously, was profoundly at odds with the historicist norms of Judaism. Spinoza, sometimes described as 'Judaism's greatest philosopher', despite being this strict rationalist, was indeed eventually 'excommunicated' from his synagogue, worked as a lens grinder and died of consumption aged only 45.

Contributor: Martin Cohen

Reform, conversion, education and emancipation – none of these open the gates of society to the German Jew; hence his desire to deny his racial origin – the tendency of some Jews to deny their racial descent is equally foredoomed to failure. Jewish noses cannot be reformed, and the black and wavy hair of the Jews will not be changed into blond by conversion or straightened out by constant combing. . .

If anti-Semitism, especially of the modern kind, could not be explained by social or religious antagonism or economic competition and causes, then race was the key. The 'Jewish Question' was a question of race and biology, and nothing could be done to change that immutable fact. Only emigration and the formation of a Jewish State might.

The concept of race lies at the heart of Zionist ideology and does much to explain the nature of the Israeli State today and its obsession with Jewish demography and the ethnic purity of the State. Even at its height, the Zionist movement never took issue with Nazism or European anti-Semitism on the grounds of its racism.

This attitude of the Zionist movement, to make use of anti-Semitism and the 'futility' of opposing it, carried through to its dealings with the Nazis. Alone among Jewish groups, the Zionist organisation was legal and its newspaper, *Judische Rundschau*, was allowed. As one of its leaders, Rabbi Dr Joachim Prinz, noted: 'the majority of the German Jews considered the Zionists to be men of evil who agreed with the Nazis. . .' It was morally disturbing to seem to be considered as the favoured children of the Nazi Government, particularly when it dissolved the anti-Zionist youth groups, and seemed in other ways to prefer the Zionists. The Nazis asked for a 'more Zionist behaviour'.

Indeed the Zionist leadership were bitterly opposed to either the USA, Britain or indeed Australia lowering their immigration barriers to Jewish refugees. Zionism was not a refugee movement, they explained. If Jews could escape to America, what use was there for a Jewish national home in Palestine? After the war, the Zionist leaders were equally hostile to the idea of those living in the Displaced Persons Camps of Europe coming to the West.

It was this belief in the theory of race that led to the expulsion of over 80 per cent of the Palestinian population in 1947–48 from the newly founded Israeli 'Jewish' state.

From its inception, those most bitterly opposed to Zionism were Jewish people themselves, seeing in it the victory of anti-Semitism. Indeed, when the Argentinean Junta of the early 1980s began persecuting Jewish radicals, to the extent that 10 per cent of those who 'disappeared' or died under torture were Jewish, it was widely felt that Israel turned its back on them. It seemed now that these 'left-wingers' were not the 'right type' of Jew. For those who had fought to become accepted in non-Jewish society, it was a bitter pill to swallow for Zionists to say that it was all futile.

Yet Zionism created a Jewish State that would be Jewish only in terms of its racial demographics. Zionism created a state that is unique in the world, in that there is no such thing as an Israeli nationality – there is a Jewish nationality and a

Muslim, Druze and other various nationalities: a state where the number of 'Jewish' as opposed to 'non-Jewish' potatoes and tomatoes are listed in agricultural statistics; where land is reserved for settlement or 'redemption' by Jews and barred to non-Jews; an armed surrogate of the USA standing in stark opposition to the universal Jewish values espoused by SPINOZA, Marx and Mendlessohn.

Contributor: Tony Greenstein

## Further reading

An intelligent 'pro-Zionist' book and two Marxist histories are:

Lucas, N. (1975) *The Modern History of Israel*

Weinstock, N. (1979) *Zionism: False Messiah*

Leon, A. (1974) *The Jewish Question – A Marxist Interpretation*